W9-CBK-549

BUSINESS DATA PROCESSING AND COMPUTER PROGRAMMING

MIKE MURACH

SCIENCE RESEARCH ASSOCIATES, INC.
Chicago, Palo Alto, Toronto, Henley-on-Thames, Sydney, Paris
A Subsidiary of IBM

Library of Congress Catalog Card Number: 72-94032

ISBN 0-574-17960-7

We gratefully acknowledge the following for their permission to reprint or adapt the materials listed.

Reprinted by permission of International Business Machines Corporation: figures 1-3, 1-5, 3-1, 3-3, 3-6, 3-8, 3-11, 3-16, 4-13, 5-1, 5-2, 5-5, 5-6, 5-7, 5-8, 5-9, 6-2, 6-5, 6-6, 6-16, 7-2, 7-6, 7-9, 8-2, 8-10, 10-1, 10-5, 10-7, 10-9, 10-10, 11-1, 11-9, 11-10, 11-11, 11-13, 11-16, 11-17, 11-20, 12-6, 18-9, E-1, E-2, and E-3; the list of COBOL reserved words in Appendix C; the 5081 card; and forms GX24-6599, GX20-1776; GX20-1702, GX20-8021, and GX28-7327.

From PRINCIPLES OF BUSINESS DATA PROCESSING by Mike Murach. © 1970, Science Research Associates, Inc. Reprinted by permission: figures 7-3, 7-4, 8-1, 8-4, 8-5, 9-4, 9-8, 9-9, 12-2, 12-4, 12-8, 13-1, 13-2, 13-3, 13-5, 13-6, 13-7, 14-1, and 14-2.

Courtesy of the Univac Division of Sperry Rand Corporation: figures 1-1 and 2-14.

Courtesy of The National Cash Register Company: figures 1-4, 8-8, 9-7, and 11-7.

Courtesy of Control Data Corporation: figures 6-4 and 11-14.

Courtesy of The Burroughs Corporation: figures 7-8, 8-9, and 11-8.

Courtesy of Teletype Corporation: figure 8-3.

Courtesy of Singer Business Machines: figures 11-2 and 11-21.

Courtesy of Mohawk Data Sciences Corporation: figure 11-3.

Courtesy of United California Bank: figure 11-15.

Courtesy of Digitronics Division of Iomec Inc.: figure 11-18.

Business Data Processing and Computer Programming is designed for a one-semester (or one-quarter) introductory course in business data processing. Since there are sections on COBOL and FORTRAN, either of these languages can be taught as part of the course. In fact, this book covers the content of the Introduction to Computing course that is recommended by the Association for Computing Machinery's "Curriculum 68" (course B1). In addition, there is a strong systems and applications emphasis, thus making the book particularly applicable to business curriculum.

One of the features of this book is its design. After reading the first four chapters (section I), the student can proceed with any of the other sections. In particular, the book is organized as follows:

Section		Prerequisite Section	Development
I	Introductory Concepts	—	Sequential
II	Basic Computer Systems	I	Sequential
III	Auxiliary Subjects	I	Random
IV	COBOL	I	Chapter 17 is core content; either chapter 18 or 19 can be assigned next.
V	FORTRAN	I	Sequential

This means that the chapters in sections II and V should be studied in sequence, that the chapters in section III can be studied in any sequence, and that in section IV either chapter 18 or 19 can be studied immediately after chapter 17. Within these limitations, you are free to determine the sequence of instruction and to emphasize what you think is best for your course. Although you will probably not have time to cover all twenty-one chapters, you will be able to select those that are most appropriate for your class.

A second feature of this book is its content. If I may be critical for a moment, much of the content in other introductory data-processing textbooks is irrelevant: the abacus and Pascal's adding machine, how the print chain of a 1403 works, how the sense wire in core memory works, flip-flop circuits, complement arithmetic, binary addition and subtraction, hexadecimal multiplication—all of these are irrelevant to the needs of the programmer, system analyst, or businessman. They are doubly irrelevant for the introductory student.

In contrast, the content of this book has been selected on the basis of relevancy. If it isn't of significance to a programmer, system analyst, or businessman, it hasn't been included. As a result, you won't find much of the traditional introductory content in this book, but you will find a considerable amount of new material.

A third feature of the book is that the relationships between equipment, application, system design, and programming are continually shown. Two just criticisms of previous books are that (1) they are equipment-oriented and (2) they don't show these relationships. In this book, however, equipment, applications, system design, and programming are introduced in the first four chapters. Thereafter, all subjects are described in their proper context. Equipment is never described without relating it to applications, system design, and programming. Similarly, system design techniques are never discussed without relating them to applications and equipment. To paraphrase Jacques Barzun in *The American University* — technique without purpose never introduced anybody to anything but boredom.

A fourth feature worth noting is the organization within the individual chapters. As a chapter progresses, it becomes more detailed and more rigorous. Thus, you, as the instructor, can adjust the text to the capabilities of the class by making assignments that cover less than a complete chapter. For example, chapter 6 is divided into three topics:

Topic 1   Tape Characteristics
Topic 2   Tape System Design
Topic 3   Programming and System Considerations

Topic 1 includes everything the traditional textbook normally covers in regard to magnetic tape; in topic 2, the equipment is related to applications and system design; then, the programming and system complications that are peculiar to tape systems are discussed in topic 3. Depending on the capabilities of the class and the emphasis of the course, you can assign only topic 1, topics 1 and 2, or the entire chapter.

A final feature of this book is that the student begins learning about computers right from the start. This may seem to be a trivial point, but there is no better way to kill the enthusiasm of an introductory data-processing class than to begin with a subject other than computers (as most textbooks do). To a student, it seems, business data processing means computers (and I'm inclined to agree with them). Later in the semester, you can assign chapter 9, Manual and Mechanical Methods of Processing Data, and chapter 10, Punched-Card Systems, to give some perspective.

Available with this text are a Student Workbook and an Instructor's Guide, which includes a set of 94 masters for preparing overhead-projector foils (OPFs). The workbook is a no-nonsense, no-busywork (no multiple-choice, no true/false, no matching) soft-cover book that consists of behavioral objectives, practice problems and case situations, solutions and explanations for immediate feedback, and problems for classroom or laboratory solution. A complete description and explanation of its contents is given in the Instructor's Guide.

The Instructor's Guide includes behavioral objectives for each chapter, progress tests based on the objectives, model test answers, lists of test data for the COBOL and FORTRAN lab problems, and solutions to the unanswered workbook problems. The last section contains the OPF master set, which consists of many of the text illustrations, plus supporting materials.

ACKNOWLEDGMENT

The following information is reprinted from *COBOL Edition 1965*, published by the Conference on Data Systems Languages (CODASYL) and printed by the U.S. Government Printing Office.

Any organization interested in reproducing the COBOL report and specifications in whole or in part, using ideas taken from this report as the basis for an instruction manual or for any other purpose, is free to do so. However, all such organizations are requested to reproduce this section as part of the introduction to the document. Those using a short passage, as in a book review, are requested to mention "COBOL" in acknowledgment of the source, but need not quote this entire section.

COBOL is an industry language and is not the property of any company or group of companies, or of any organization or group of organizations.

No warranty, expressed or implied, is made by any contributor or by the COBOL Committee as to the accuracy and functioning of the programming system and language. Moreover, no responsibility is assumed by any contributor, or by the committee, in connection therewith.

Procedures have been established for the maintenance of COBOL. Inquiries concerning the procedures for proposing changes should be directed to the Executive Committee of the Conference on Data Systems Languages.

The authors and copyright holders of the copyrighted materials used herein

> FLOW-MATIC (Trademark of Sperry Rand Corporation), Programming for the Univac (R) I and II, Data Automation Systems copyrighted 1958, 1959, by Sperry Rand Corporation; IBM Commercial Translator Form No. F28-8013, copyrighted 1959 by IBM; FACT, DSI 27A5260-2760, copyrighted 1960 by Minneapolis-Honeywell

have specifically authorized the use of this material in whole or in part, in the COBOL specifications. Such authorization extends to the reproduction and use of COBOL specifications in programming manuals of similar publications.

CONTENTS

As you read this book, you will of course learn what data processing means and what it involves. As a preliminary definition, though, you should know that *data processing* refers to a sequence of operations, often mathematical, that are performed on facts and figures. *Business data processing* refers to the processing of business facts and figures. This processing can be accomplished by clerks using pencil and paper, by clerks using mechanical devices such as adding machines and typewriters, or by electronic machines such as computers. In a small business, data processing is likely to be handled by one or more clerks with the aid of some simple mechanical devices. A large business is likely to use many methods of processing data, ranging from pencil and paper to a large computer. A *data-processing*, or *DP*, *system* is made up of the people, equipment, and procedures that process data.

Business data processing is an important subject because it greatly affects a company's operations. Consider, for example, that one out of six persons in industry today performs clerical work. This means that data processing, or paperwork, is one of the major overhead costs of running a business. Thus, reducing this expense can have a significant effect on profits. Furthermore, opportunities for cost reduction are often greater in the clerical field than in any other part of a business. Cost reductions of 10 percent and more in selected data-processing areas are not in the least unrealistic. This does not imply a move toward automation; it only means eliminating or improving inefficient clerical procedures that too often develop as an institution grows.

One chemical company, for example, decided to study its business forms as a possible area for cost reduction. The company was using over 15,000 different forms. Many of these duplicated functions, were difficult to use, or were obsolete. By consolidating, eliminating, and redesigning forms, the total number was reduced to 11,000 and the resultant cost savings was over $250,000 per year. One expert in the control of business forms estimates that a company that has never conducted a program for forms control can cut printing costs by a minimum of 20 percent, to say nothing of reduced clerical costs.

Other companies have had similar successes as a result of improving data-processing procedures. One company reduced its order-processing personnel from 275 to 145 in one year's time without affecting the quality of service. Another company reduced paperwork by 70 percent and clerical costs by $40,000 per year when its management reporting system was redesigned. And a large manufacturer eliminated 400 expediters and 200 clerks by installing an automated production-control system.

But costs are only part of the story. Data processing can be the cause of many common business problems. Late or incomplete shipments of merchandise, overbilling customers, excessive accounts receivables, idle assembly lines—all of these may result from a faulty data-processing system. At its worst, an ineffective DP system can burden sales and technical personnel with paperwork, lose sales through poor customer service, and destroy employee morale.

Management expects a data-processing system to provide them with information. This aspect has been emphasized so much lately that data processing is now also being referred to as *information processing*, and data-processing systems as *information systems*. By providing current information, a data-processing system can assist a manager in making decisions such as whether or not to market a new product, in what areas advertising funds should be used, and to what extent a company can reasonably increase its indebtedness. If the information helps management make better decisions, the increased revenue and decreased expenses resulting from these decisions can well be the most important benefit of a company's data-processing system.

Although business data processing doesn't require the use of computers, this book is about data-processing systems that use computers. Such systems, called *computer systems*, or *electronic data-processing (EDP) systems*, already dominate DP activities in companies with over 500 employees, and it seems certain that they will also dominate in smaller companies. With recent announcements of computers that cost less than $1000 a month, any company with over 100 employees is a likely prospect for a computer system. And since companies with 20 to 100 employees can either share a computer or rent a computer service, computer processing is an important consideration for additional thousands of companies.

THE DESIGN OF THIS BOOK

Before you can really understand computer systems, you must be familiar with four somewhat independent areas of knowledge. You must understand the capabilities of the computing *equipment*. You must understand how *programs* are used to direct the operation of a computer and what the processing limitations of a program are. You should be familiar with data-processing *applications*—the uses to which a computer is put. And, finally, you need to know how the equipment and programs are coordinated through a system of procedures; this is commonly referred to as *system design*, or *system analysis*.

Section I of this book covers these four areas of knowledge. Chapter 1 introduces you to computer equipment; chapter 2 describes the common DP applications; chapter 3 illustrates a simple computer system and its related system design; and chapter 4 presents basic programming concepts. By the end of the first section, then, the mystery surrounding computer systems should be gone. You will know how a computer can do the work of 100,000 mathematicians, how a computer can do the work of an inventory-control clerk, and, on the negative side, how a computer system can make mistakes — such as causing checks totaling $67,694 to be sent to welfare recipients no longer eligible for payments.

After section I, you can proceed with any other section in the book. In section II, computer systems of progressively greater complexity are described and system design and equipment are emphasized. Two of the most widely used programming languages, COBOL and FORTRAN, are presented in Sections IV and V, which thus have a programming emphasis. The chapters in section III can be read in any order; they cover a variety of subjects from manual and mechanical methods of processing data to some complex programming considerations. I suggest that you read these chapters in the order that they become of interest to you. If you study all five sections of this book, you should be able to write programs in two languages, have a solid understanding of computer systems, and be well prepared for further study in programming, system design, or the control of business systems from the business management point of view.

FOR REVIEW

data processing
business data processing
data-processing system
DP system
information processing

information system
computer system
electronic data-processing
   system
EDP system

I

INTRODUCTORY CONCEPTS

CHAPTER ONE

Before you begin the study of computer applications, system design, or programming, you should become familiar with some of the terms associated with various types of computer systems. This chapter, then, provides that base of terminology.

To begin with, a *computer* is a machine that accepts input data, processes it, and gives output data. For example, a computer can read sales data from punched cards, process this data, and provide output in the form of a printed sales report. A computer can also accept many other forms of input, such as magnetic tapes or checks recorded in magnetic ink, and give many other forms of output, such as data on magnetic disks or displays on television-like devices. Because a computer's processing depends on the sequence of instructions (the program) that it is given prior to doing a job, a computer can process data in an almost endless variety of ways.

In general, a computer, also known as a *computer system*, consists of one or more input devices, one or more output devices, and a *central processing unit (CPU)*. A small system consists of a CPU and only a few *input/output (I/O) devices*, while a large system consists of a CPU and dozens of I/O devices. Theoretically, at least, the components of a computer system are chosen to fulfill the needs of the user: the system should be large enough to do all the jobs required by the user but not so large that processing capacity goes to waste.

The smallest computer systems usually consist of four components: a card reader for input, a card punch and a printer for output, and a CPU for processing. These components are shown in figure 1-1. Because the punched card is its only input, a system like this is commonly

AN INTRODUCTION TO COMPUTERS

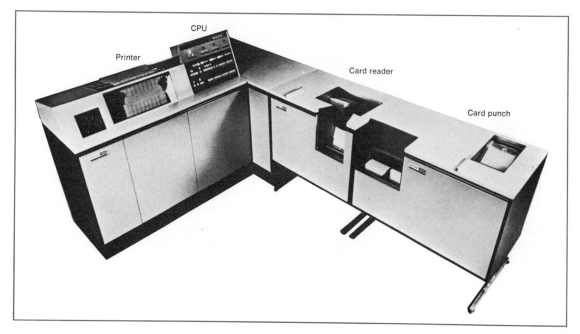

FIGURE 1-1   A card computer system

called a *card system*. The standard punched card, which can hold up to eighty characters of data, is described in detail in chapter 3.

Although the four components shown in figure 1-1 are physically separate, they are connected electronically by cables that are usually placed under a raised floor. During operation, the four components work together. When punched-card data is read by the card reader, it is transferred to the storage of the CPU, where it can be processed. When data is printed on the printer or punched into cards by the card punch, the data is transferred from the storage of the CPU to the output device. All operations—input, processing, and output—take place under control of instructions stored in the CPU.

The *card reader* of a computer system usually has one input hopper and one or more output stackers, depending on the model of the device. As the cards are read, one at a time, they pass from the input hopper to one of the stackers. Although some card readers can read over 2000 cards per minute, a card reader in a card system is more likely to read from 200 to 600 cards per minute.

A *card punch*, which looks very much like a card reader, also has one input hopper and one or more output stackers. Although both the punch and the reader may be separate physical units, as they are in figure 1-1, they are often combined into one unit. In most cases, however, even when combined into one unit, they continue to operate separately. As a rule, card punches operate somewhat slower than card readers—typically, in the range of 100 to 300 cards per minute.

Printer speeds for card systems commonly vary from 300 to 600 lines per minute. So that a printer can operate at such high speeds, it prints on continuous, rather than cut, forms. *Continuous forms* are attached to each other in a continuous band of paper, as illustrated in figure 1-2. They are fed through the printer by a mechanism that fits into the tiny holes on both sides of the forms. After the forms are printed, the sides can be removed and the forms themselves separated, usually at perforations. Because a printer can be adjusted to forms of many widths and lengths, it can be used to print very small forms such as mailing labels as well as sixteen-inch wide management reports.

A printer also has the capability of skipping to appropriate lines before printing. For example, in preparing the monthly statement

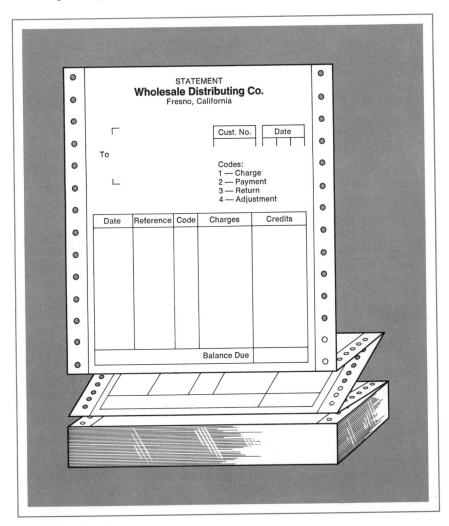

FIGURE 1-2   A continuous-form statement

illustrated in figure 1-2, the printer skips to the top of the form before printing the customer's name and address, to the body of the form before printing detailed information about the amounts billed and payments received, and to the total line of the form before printing the balance owed. This capability, commonly called *forms control*, is described in detail in chapter 3. By using forms control, a computer system can meet the printing requirements of almost all business forms.

The CPU of a computer system is usually a large rectangular unit with a panel of lights, dials, and operational keys on the front. This panel, called the *console* of the system, is used by the computer operator. On many systems, a typewriter-like device, called the *console typewriter*, is located on or near the console. This typewriter can be used as an output device (functioning as a slow-speed printer because it prints one character at a time) or, when data is keyed on its keyboard, as an input device.

When an institution outgrows a card system, it normally moves up to a *tape system or a direct-access system*. A tape system uses magnetic tape as its primary input and output. The magnetic tape is a long strip of plastic tape that is wound on a reel like a motion-picture film. When the reel of tape is mounted on a tape I/O device, data can be read from or written on the tape at speeds much faster than those of card or printing operations. Although a large number of tapes can be used on a single

FIGURE 1-3   A tape system

computer system, a typical tape system, as shown in figure 1-3, consists of a CPU, a card reader, a card punch, a printer, and four tape units called *tape drives*.

Direct-access systems use direct-access devices as the primary input and output of the system. The most widely used direct-access device, the *magnetic disk*, consists of several platters (disks) stacked on a central spindle. The unique characteristic of a direct-access device is that any one of the records stored on the device can be accessed without reading the other records. For example, one model disk can store approximately 44,000 100-character records; yet, any one of these records can be accessed and read in an average of about 88/1000 second. Contrast this with magnetic tape, in which the first 5999 records on a tape must be read before the six-thousandth record can be read. Although a direct-access system can have many direct-access devices attached to it, a small system such as the one in figure 1-4 consists of a CPU, a card reader, a printer, and two disk units called *disk drives*.

FIGURE 1-4 A disk system

When a computer system has both tape and direct-access devices, it is commonly called a direct-access system.

The term *data communication* refers to the electronic transmission of data from one location to another. Thus, a *data-communication system* can receive data from and send data to locations that are removed from the computer itself. For instance, many airlines have data-communication systems to handle passenger reservations. In each reservation office there is a device that is similar to a console typewriter; it is linked to a central computer by means of telephone or telegraph lines. This I/O device is called a *terminal* since it is at the end of a communication line. When a customer requests a reservation, the airline clerk uses the terminal to type the flight number and number of seats requested. This data is sent to the computer, which checks a reservation file stored on a direct-access device to determine whether seats are available. The computer then sends a response to the terminal, confirming or denying the reservation. Because data travels over communication lines at approximately the speed of light, the entire process takes but a few seconds. Even if the terminal and the computer are located thousands of miles apart, the effect is as though they were in the same room.

As you might guess, however, there are many different kinds of data-communication systems; the airline reservation system is only one example—and a sophisticated one at that. In contrast, a simple data-communication system transmits data from one terminal to another rather than directly to a computer. For example, punched-card data may be read in a branch office by a card-reader terminal. This data is transmitted over telegraph lines to a card-punch terminal in the data-processing center, where cards identical to those in the branch are punched. These cards can then be used as input to the computer system.

Between a simple data-communication system and a sophisticated one, there are many other levels. Some systems transmit batches of data directly to the computer in a one-way communication, while others transmit batches of data both to and from the computer. Some use general-purpose terminals such as the teletypewriter, while others use specialized terminals such as a banking terminal that can print on savings-account passbooks. Regardless of the degree of sophistication, however, the identifying characteristic of a data-communication system is the ability to transmit data electronically.

To identify a specific computer system, it is common to give the manufacturer's name and the model number of the CPU. For example, one computer is referred to as a Burroughs B3500 or just B3500, where Burroughs Corporation is the manufacturer and B3500 is the model number. Another computer is referred to as an IBM System/360 Model 25, where IBM (International Business Machines) is the manufacturer and System/360 Model 25 specifies the model. The computer in figure 1-1 is a Univac 9200 (Univac is the computer division of Sperry Rand); the computer in figure 1-3 is an IBM System/360 Model 40; and figure

1-4 shows an NCR (National Cash Register Company) Century 100 computer.

To more specifically identify a computer, the type of system and the major I/O components are commonly stated. For example, you might hear a programmer describe his company's system as an "HIS (Honeywell Information Systems) 115 disk system." Or you might hear a system designer describe a system as a "Model 135 System/370 with eight tape drives, five disk drives, a drum, and data-communication capabilities."

Incidentally, some people make a distinction between a computer and a computer system; that is, the CPU is the computer and the CPU plus the attached I/O devices is the computer system. However, this distinction is becoming less and less common, particularly in conversational usage. In this book, either term is used to mean the CPU and all connected devices.

DISCUSSION

It should be clear by now that computer systems vary tremendously as to the components that make them up, their capabilities . . . and their price. A small card system may rent for as little as $1000 per month, while a large direct-access system may cost well over $100,000 per month. Purchase prices for computer systems vary accordingly; generally, they are about forty-five times as much as the monthly rental price. (In most cases, the computer user has the option of either renting or buying a computer system.)

Before a computer can be used to process data, it must be given a detailed sequence of instructions called a *program*. In other words, the equipment (or *hardware*) must be combined with programs (or *software*). A separate program is required for each job that a computer does; thus, a typical computer installation has hundreds of different programs. Because of the time required to write programs, about as much money is spent for programming as is spent for computer rental.

Before a program can be *executed* by a computer system, it must be *loaded* into the CPU. From an operator's point of view, this process of loading and executing a program is generally quite simple. For example, to load and execute a program on a card system such as the System/360 Model 20, the operator follows these steps:

1. He places a deck of punched cards, called the *object deck*, into the card reader. This deck contains the machine-language instructions of the program.

2. He then places the deck of cards to be processed, called the *data deck*, on top of the object deck in the card reader.

3. He pushes the START button on the card reader.

4. If the card punch is going to be used, he puts blank cards in it and pushes the START button.

5. If the printer is going to be used, he inserts the appropriate continuous form and pushes the START button.

6. He then pushes the LOAD button on the console of the CPU. This causes the instructions in the object deck to be read by the card reader, loaded into the CPU, and executed.

To illustrate the procedures for loading and executing a program on a card system, assume that the computer system is to read payroll cards for the employees of a company, process the cards, print the week's payroll checks, and punch one output card per check to be used for check reconciliation. The operator starts by placing the object deck for the check-writing program in the card reader. He then places the data deck (the employee payroll cards) on top of the object deck in the card reader. Next, he adjusts the continuous-form payroll checks in the printer and puts blank cards in the card punch. When the operator pushes the START buttons on the card reader, the card punch, and the printer, and the LOAD button on the CPU, the computer system loads and executes the payroll program. This procedure is illustrated in figure 1-5.

On a tape or a direct-access system, the programs to be executed are normally stored on magnetic tapes or direct-access devices. To load a

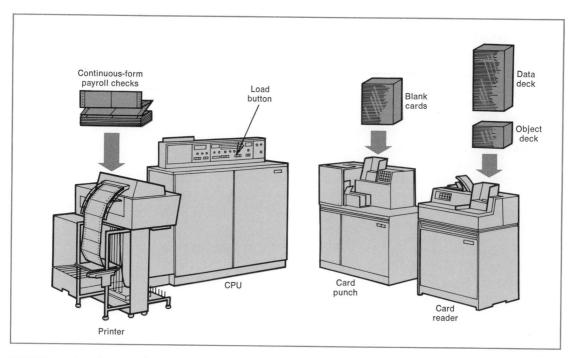

FIGURE 1-5   Loading and executing a program

program, the operator makes ready the I/O devices that are going to be used; he then puts one or more *job-control cards* in the card reader to indicate which program is to be loaded. After the computer system reads the job-control cards, it finds the desired program on the program tape or direct-access device, loads the program into the CPU, and executes it. If punched cards are used as input to the program, the data deck is placed on top of the job-control cards in the card reader.

Two striking features of even the simplest computer system are the speed and the accuracy with which it can process data. The speed can be broken down into I/O speed and CPU speed. In the check-writing program just described, for example, suppose that there are 2400 cards in the input deck (2 cards for each of 1200 employees), that 3 lines are printed on each payroll check (a total of 3600 lines), and that 1200 check-reconciliation cards are punched. At a card-reading speed of 600 cards per minute, a printing speed of 600 lines per minute, and a punching speed of 200 cards per minute, reading would take 4 minutes, printing 6 minutes, and punching 6 minutes. And, if the payroll records were stored on tape or disk rather than in cards, input speeds would be cut considerably. On a typical tape drive, for example, 2400 80-character records can be read in less than 1 minute.

CPU speeds, on the other hand, are commonly measured in micro-seconds (millionths of a second) and even nanoseconds (billionths of a second). One medium-sized computer, for instance, can do 100,000 additions in a second. That's one every 10 microseconds. If the CPU of a card system requires an average of 100 microseconds per instruction and 200 instructions per employee, that's only 1/50 second per employee, or 24 seconds of processing time for all 1200 employees.

As for a computer's accuracy, electronic checking circuitry is built into all I/O devices as well as the CPU to make sure that all errors are caught. A card reader, for example, doesn't simply read a card. If it did, a faulty reading mechanism might cause inaccurate data to be read into the CPU. Instead, most card readers read data twice, at two different reading stations. The data that is read at the first reading station is compared with the data read at the second station. If the two readings aren't the same, an error is detected and the computer system stops. Similarly, electronic checking circuitry is built into the CPU, printer, card punch, and all other I/O units that may be attached to a system. As a result, computer errors that go undetected by a modern computer system are extremely rare. Upon investigation, errors that are blamed on the computer can be traced to errors in system design, programming, or operating procedure.

CONCLUSION

You have now been introduced to some of the terminology associated with computer systems. Don't worry if some of these terms are still hazy;

all of the concepts will be covered in depth as you progress through this book. For example, there is a chapter on card systems, a chapter on tape systems, a chapter on direct-access systems, a chapter on data-communication systems, several chapters on programming, and so on.

On the other hand, even if you have mastered the terminology, you really haven't learned much about computers. You still don't know what computers are used for, or why; or how errors can occur within a computerized data-processing system; or what the logical and arithmetical limits of a computer program are. In other words, though you've learned some terms, you still need to know the underlying concepts of computer processing. That is what the remaining chapters of this section are dedicated to teaching.

SUMMARY

1. A computer, or a computer system, is made up of a CPU and at least one input and one output device. A typical card computer system consists of a CPU, a card reader, a card punch, and a printer. A computer system also has a console and will often have a console typewriter.

2. The three basic types of computer systems are card, tape, and direct-access; they are identified by the primary form of I/O devices used. A data-communication system is a system that has the ability to electronically transmit data from one location to another.

3. To load and execute a program on a card system, an object deck and a data deck are placed in the card reader. First, the object deck is read by the card reader, thus loading the program's instructions into the CPU. Then, the program is executed, thus processing the data deck.

4. Because checking circuitry is built into all of the components of a computer system, an undetected computer error is extremely rare. For all practical purposes, a computer processes data with 100 percent accuracy.

FOR REVIEW

computer
computer system
central processing unit
CPU
input/output device
I/O device
card system
card reader
card punch
printer

continuous form
forms control
console
console typewriter
tape system
tape drive
direct-access system
magnetic disk
disk drive
data communication

data-communication system
terminal
program
executing a program

loading a program
object deck
data deck
job-control cards

CHAPTER TWO

This chapter is divided into two topics. The first topic, called Basic Business Applications, describes computer applications that are common to most businesses. These applications are used as examples throughout this book. The second topic, called Advanced Applications, describes the full range of computer uses, including some of the more sophisticated applications.

A *computer application* is a problem or operation to which a computer system can be applied. Since billing is a business operation that can be carried out by a computer system, billing is a computer application. Similarly, sales reporting and inventory control are computer applications.

Although applications vary depending on the type of business involved, there are eight that are common to most businesses. When a business installs its first computer system, it is likely to start with one or more of these basic applications. Each of these basic applications, then, is described in some detail in this topic.

One of the goals of this topic is to show that each basic application, no matter how trivial it may seem at first, can have a significant effect on the profitability of a business. As you read about each application, you should (1) become familiar with the input and output documents used, and (2) note how the application can affect profits. (In business terminology, *document* refers to any form or report. Thus, a payroll check, a bill, a profit-and-loss statement, and a routing slip are all documents.)

COMPUTER APPLICATIONS

ORDER WRITING

When a customer places an order with a company, he can do it in several ways. He can telephone the order to the company; he can give the order to a salesman; he can mail in his own purchase order; or he can send the order in by telegram. This original order, known as the *customer order* (or *sales order*) is the input document of the *order-writing* application. An example of a customer order is given in figure 2-1.

Customer Order

Wholesale Distributing Co.
Fresno, California

Sold To _ALLWORTHY EQUIPMENT_
2446 SIMPSON STREET
TURLOCK, CA. 95380

Order No.
22109

New customer
Credit OK

Date	Cust. order No.	Salesman No.	Cust. No.
10-2-73	Q 29 H273	16	1257

Quantity	Item Number	Description	Unit Price
15	11141	½ INCH ADJ. WRENCH	2.75
3	12303	ECONOMY ¼ INCH DRILL	11.29
5	21214	6 PC. OPEN END SET	10.49

Shipping instructions	Order taker
VIA TRUCK	gm

FIGURE 2-1   A customer order

The output document of the order-writing application is a *shipping order* such as the one illustrated in figure 2-2. In preparing the shipping order, customer codes, names, and addresses are usually checked against customer master files; item codes, descriptions, and prices are usually checked against item master files; and, in some cases, particularly for a new account, a customer's credit may be checked. If a company has many items in its product line, they may be rearranged on the shipping order into a sequence that corresponds to the sequence of items in the shipping department; the warehouse locations of the items may also be printed on the shipping order. Such aids to the order picker increase his efficiency by as much as 20 to 30 percent.

The shipping order is normally prepared in several copies, one of

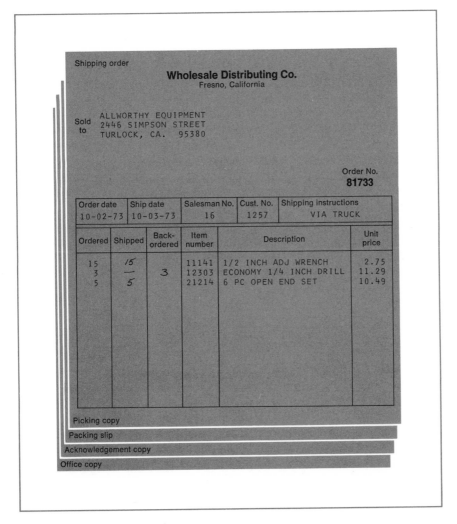

FIGURE 2-2   A shipping order

which is called the picking copy and is sent to the shipping department to be used for picking the order. A second copy may be sent to the customer as an acknowledgment that the order has been received; another copy may be enclosed with the shipment as a packing slip. A fourth copy may be retained in the data-processing department as an office copy.

As an order is filled, the order picker indicates in the back-ordered column of the picking copy which items are not in stock and therefore can't be delivered. These items, called back-ordered items, or back orders, will be shipped to the customer when they become available. In figure 2-2, the order picker has back-ordered 3 Economy 1/4-Inch Drills, thus indicating that they aren't in stock. When the order picker has finished, the picking copy is returned to the data-processing department so that the customer's bill can be prepared.

The objective of the order-writing application is simply to prepare the shipping order as accurately and rapidly as is practical since both accuracy and speed can affect profits. An inaccurate shipping order, for example, can mean that the wrong items or quantities are shipped to a customer or that the order is delivered to the wrong address. Since all of these conditions affect customer satisfaction, inaccurate shipping orders can eventually mean lost sales.

Because the speed of an order-writing application determines to a certain extent how fast orders are shipped, it too can affect customer satisfaction. If it takes two weeks from receipt of a customer order until a shipping order reaches the warehouse, one-week deliveries are of course impossible. Since the sales in many industries are dependent on fast deliveries—as in the toy industry during the Christmas season—order-writing speed can be critical to a company's sales. On the other hand, in some mail-order businesses where fast deliveries aren't expected, an order-writing delay of a day or two has no effect on sales.

BILLING

After the shipping order is returned to the data-processing department, the customer's bill, or invoice, must be prepared. The input document of the billing application is the shipping order; the output document is the bill. The goal of the application is to quickly and accurately prepare the bills.

If you compare the bill in figure 2-3 with the shipping order in figure 2-2, you can see that the primary difference between the two documents is that the line items on the bill are extended. The term line item refers to each of the lines that describes a type of item sold; the bill illustrated has three line items. To get the extension of each line item, the quantity shipped is multiplied by the unit price. Thus, the extension of the first line item is $41.25, of the third line item, $52.45.

At least two copies of an invoice are normally prepared: the original

Invoice — Customer copy

Wholesale Distributing Co.
Fresno, California

Sold to: ALLWORTHY EQUIPMENT
2446 SIMPSON STREET
TURLOCK, CA. 95380

PAGE 01

Invoice No.
55423

Invoice No.	Invoice date	Salesman No.	Customer No.	Terms
55423	10-05-73	16	1257	2% /10 — NET/30

Shipped	Back-ordered	Item number	Description	Unit price	Amount
15		11141	1/2 INCH ADJ WRENCH	2.75	41.25
	3	12303	ECONOMY 1/4 INCH DRILL	11.29	
5		21214	6 PC OPEN END SET	10.49	52.45

BACK-ORDERED PORTION OF THIS ORDER
TO BE SHIPPED WITHIN 21 DAYS.

Invoice total: 93.70

FIGURE 2-3 An invoice

for the customer and the copy for the office file. Other copies may be prepared for use in keeping track of back orders, salesman commissions, or amounts owed to the company.

As with most applications, both speed and accuracy are critical in billing. An inaccurate bill can result in overcharging or undercharging a customer. An incorrect address can mean delays in getting the bill to the customer.

Speed in billing is important because it affects the amount of money owed to a company. To appreciate this, suppose that a company ships an average of $20,000 of merchandise per day and bills the customers for the merchandise 10 days after shipping. If the customers pay their bills an average of 30 days after receiving them, approximately $800,000 will be owed to the company at any one time. (10 days plus 30 days equals 40 days; 40 times $20,000 equals $800,000.)

Now suppose the company reduces the delay in billing from 10 days to 2. Then, approximately $640,000 will be owed at any one time, a difference of $160,000. At 5 percent interest, this difference in uncollected debts would mean $8,000 in increased company profits. Even more than the interest, though, it would mean $160,000 is available for expansion: developing new products or markets, buying new equipment, or financing new buildings.

Depending on the company, billing may or may not be an important application. If, for example, a company writes only a few invoices a day with only a few line items per invoice, billing can be done easily with a typewriter and a calculator. On the other hand, a company that does many thousands of line items of billing per day would very likely profit by an automated billing system.

Customer

ALLWORTHY EQUIPMENT
2446 SIMPSON STREET
TURLOCK, CA.   95380

Cust. No. 1257	Salesman CURRIER		Credit limit $3,000.00	
Date	Reference	Charges	Credits	Balance
			Balance forward	212.00
6-06-73	46141	186.02		398.02
6-15-73	47733	711.94		1109.96
6-27-73	48120	945.95		2055.91
6-28-73	11480		212.00	1843.91
7-05-73	48777	77.40		1921.31
7-24-73	50200	388.67		2309.98
7-31-73	12733		1843.91	466.07
8-15-73	51101	568.65		1034.72
9-05-73	51772	106.63		1221.35
9-07-73	51933	363.20		1584.55
9-13-73	52022	676.89		2261.44
9-19-73	53788	475.64		2737.08
9-26-73	14498		568.65	2168.43
10-05-73	55423	93.70		2262.13

FIGURE 2-4   An accounts receivable ledger card

ACCOUNTS RECEIVABLE

Accounts receivable refers to the amounts owed to a company by its customers (accounts). The accounts receivable application is concerned with keeping records of the amounts owed and providing information that will help a company control the amounts owed.

The input documents for the accounts receivable application are invoices, payment vouchers (records of payment), and credit and debit memos (records of adjustments to a customer's account). The output documents are (1) individual customer records, such as the one in figure 2-4, showing at least the present balance owed and, often, the individual charges and credits; (2) monthly statements, such as the one in figure 1-2, reminding the customer of his debts; and (3) management reports such as the aged trial balance and delinquent-account list in figure 2-5. If an account is delinquent, a reminder is usually sent to the customer. If the delinquency continues, the customer is then contacted personally.

```
                        DELINQUENT-ACCOUNT LIST

   10-31-73                                                    PAGE 0001

   CUST.      CUSTOMER          --------- LAST 12 MOS. ---------   AMOUNT
    NO.         NAME            TIMES OVER 30 ---- TIMES OVER 60   OVER 60

   1153   ALFIE'S GARDEN SHOP          12                1          70.90
   1257   ALLWORTHY EQUIPMENT           2                1         466.07
   1755   CONSOLIDATED HARDWARE         1                1         102.50
   2501   J. W. MOORE CO.               6                4        1024.12
   2753   LAS VEGAS NURSERY             2                2         108.50

                        AGED TRIAL BALANCE

   10-31-73                                                    PAGE 0001

   CUST.      CUSTOMER          TOTAL     CURRENT    OVER    OVER    OVER
    NO.         NAME            BALANCE                30      60      90

   1057   A & A EQUIPMENT SUPPLY   815.25   815.25
   1153   ALFIE'S GARDEN SHOP    1109.66   742.00   296.76            70.90
   1257   ALLWORTHY EQUIPMENT    2262.13    93.70  1702.36  466.07
   1351   ARNOLD'S BARGAIN BARN   552.93   552.93
   1453   BENGSTON'S SEED STORE   129.00   129.00
   1653   CAMPUS GARDEN SHOP      781.71   781.71
   1755   CONSOLIDATED HARDWARE   915.13   812.63           102.50
   1855   DOWNTOWN HARDWARE CO.  1299.00  1299.00
   2257   GENERAL EQUIPMENT CO.    49.50    49.50
   2501   J. W. MOORE CO.        1737.44   543.00   170.32 1024.12
   2753   LAS VEGAS NURSERY       427.76   319.26                    108.50
   3007   MC CORD'S LUMBER CO.     53.00    53.00
```

FIGURE 2-5 Accounts receivable reports

The accounts receivable record illustrated in figure 2-4 is called a *ledger card*; it is typical of the records used in a noncomputerized system. The entire file of ledger cards, one per customer, represents the total amount owed to the company. As records of charges and credits are received, they are recorded on the appropriate ledger card and the new balance owed is calculated. This is referred to as *posting accounts receivable.* In contrast, the records of a computerized system, though they contain similar information, are in the form of punched cards, magnetic-tape records, or direct-access records.

To control the amounts owed to a company, management needs information similar to that given in the reports in figure 2-5. The first report, the *aged trial balance*, indicates the amounts owed by each customer and the length of time the amounts have been owed. Thus, there is a column for current debts (owed for less than thirty days), plus columns for debts owed over thirty, sixty, and ninety days. The second report, the delinquent-accounts list, shows only those customers with debts older than sixty days. A report such as this can be used for contacting all the delinquent customers.

One of the major differences in accounts receivable systems is whether a customer's payment is applied to specific unpaid invoices or to the balance owed. In general, manufacturers and wholesale distributors are paid by the invoice (called an *open-item system*); retail stores receive payments that are applied to the balance owed (called a *balance-forward* system). The difference between an open-item system and a balance-forward system will become evident in chapter 5, where computerized procedures for an open-item system are described.

Since accounts receivable records represent money owed to a company, the importance of accuracy within the application is obvious. Besides causing revenue to be lost outright, inaccurate records or statements can be an annoyance to a customer. Similarly, processing delays can lead to customer dissatisfaction. If a statement dated April 30 doesn't show payments received on April 29, confusion can result. And if delinquent reminders dated May 15 are sent to customers who paid outstanding balances on May 10, ill will can arise.

On the other hand, an accounts receivable system that is both fast and accurate while providing up-to-date management information can be a significant help in reducing the accounts receivable total. One oil and gasoline company, for example, reports that its accounts receivable total was reduced by $400,000 when a better system was installed. The new system not only shortens statement-preparation time from nine days to two, but also provides information that helps to quickly spot and terminate bad credit risks. Under the old system, it would take as long as forty-five days to spot a bad risk—even an intentional offender—but with the new system, it takes less than a week.

INVENTORY CONTROL

An _inventory-control_ system has two basic goals. The first is to keep the amount of money invested in inventory as low as possible. This goal is critical to the success of many companies because of the high cost of carrying inventory. For every $100 of inventory carried throughout the year, as much as $30 may be spent on carrying costs such as inventory taxes, insurance, storage, handling, physical deterioration, and the cost of the money invested. Although the rate used for estimating carrying costs varies from company to company, one commonly used figure is 25 percent of the average inventory investment.

To appreciate the significance of this first inventory goal, suppose a company has gross sales of $10 million and an average inventory of $2 million. At a carrying-cost rate of 25 percent, the company spends $500,000 per year to maintain its inventory, or 5 percent of its gross sales. If the average inventory could be reduced by 20 percent ($400,000), profits could be increased by $100,000.

The second goal of an inventory-control system is to improve customer service by avoiding stockouts. One measure of customer service, called the _service level_, is calculated by dividing the value of orders placed into the value of orders filled:

$$\left[\text{Service level} = \frac{\$ \text{ Orders filled}}{\$ \text{ Orders placed}} \right]$$

If, for example, a company receives orders for $100,000 worth of merchandise but can fill only $80,000 worth because of stockouts, the service level is 80 percent. A service level of 100 percent indicates that all orders were filled from the available stock.

To appreciate the significance of this second goal, suppose a retail grocery chain has a service level of 80 percent. In this particular business, stockouts usually mean lost sales because a buyer normally can find the item in another store. So if a store does an annual business of $8 million at a service level of 80 percent, it would gross $8.5 million at an increased service level of 85 percent. With an average markup of 35 percent, this would result in increased profits of about $175,000 (35 percent of $500,000).

Unfortunately, the two goals of the inventory-control system are contradictory. The one sure way of avoiding stockouts is to keep large inventories. But, if inventories are reduced to keep the money invested as low as possible, stockouts are more likely. The problem of the inventory-control application, then, is to help a company reach the most profitable balance between the two goals — to let the company keep inventories as low as possible while still maintaining an adequate service level.

The input documents of the inventory-control application are records of items sold, returned, received, destroyed, and lost. These records include shipping orders or invoices, return notices, receiving reports, scrap notices, and adjustment slips. The output documents are (1) inventory records, such as the ledger-card record in figure 2-6, and (2) management reports, as illustrated in figure 2-7, that provide control information. These reports should answer questions such as: What items should be reordered? What amounts should be reordered? What items have had unusual increases or decreases in demand? What items are becoming obsolete? What items have a poor service level?

In a typical business, particularly a small business, reducing inven-

Item No. 21214	Description 6 PC OPEN END SET			Unit cost 8.99	Unit price 10.49	Reorder point 160
Date	Reference	Issues	Receipts	On hand	On order
6-15-73	47731	3		212	
6-20-73	48111	55		157	
6-27-73	5543			157	250
7-05-73	48770	3		154	250
7-06-73	48805	20		134	250
7-11-73	49001	20		114	250
7-11-73	49002	5		109	250
7-13-73	49150	15		94	250
7-17-73	49244	5		89	250
7-18-73	77265		250	339	
7-26-73	50499	7		332	
7-27-73	50505	10		322	
8-02-73	50737	5		317	
8-03-73	50800	35		282	
8-08-73	50811	2		280	
8-13-73	50941	10		270	
8-14-73	51009	8		262	
8-15-73	51101	5		257	
8-24-73	51443	20		237	
8-31-73	51667	5		232	
9-04-73	51699	3		229	
9-05-73	51773	10		219	
9-10-73	52001	5		214	
9-11-73	52005	3		211	
9-18-73	53733	2		209	
9-18-73	53737	25		184	
9-20-73	53888	15		169	
9-21-73	53911	4		165	
9-26-73	54299	3		162	
10-05-73	55423	5		157	

FIGURE 2-6 An inventory ledger card

SERVICE-LEVEL REPORT FOR MONTH ENDING 10-31-73

ITEM NO.	DESCRIPTION	THIS MONTH VALUE ORDERED	THIS MONTH BACK ORDERED	THIS MONTH SERVICE LEVEL	YTD SERVICE LEVEL
12122	8 AMP BELT SANDER	3,230.50		100.0%	94.4%
12210	JET SCREWDRIVER	428.35	65.90	84.6%	89.2%
12301	1/4 INCH VAR SPEED DRILL	413.25		100.0%	91.0%
12303	ECONOMY 1/4 INCH DRILL	282.25	112.90	60.0%	70.9%
12401	7 INCH POWER SAW	1,523.88		100.0%	98.5%

MONTHLY SALES BY ITEM

MONTH ENDING 10-31-73   PAGE 003

ITEM NO.	DESCRIPTION	MONTHLY SALES THIS YEAR	MONTHLY SALES LAST YEAR	PERCENT INC/DEC	YEAR-TO-DATE SALES THIS YTD	YEAR-TO-DATE SALES LAST YTD	PERCENT INC/DEC
21114	11 PC SOCKET SET	402.35	439.49	8.4CR	4,363.95	3,744.95	16.5
21116	19 PC SOCKET/WRENCH SET	125.00	62.50	100.0	625.00	750.00	16.7CR
21210	12 PC BOX END SET	192.50			2,117.50		
21212	6 PC COMBINATION SET	2,783.80	1,355.98	105.3	22,450.00	15,472.54	45.0
21214	6 PC OPEN END SET	734.30	713.32	2.9	8,392.00	8,288.00	1.3
21310	MITER BOX AND SAW	647.40	1,079.00	39.9CR	3,776.50	10,843.95	65.2CR

DAILY REORDER LISTING--10/05/73

ITEM NO.	DESCRIPTION	ON HAND	ON ORDER	REORDER POINT
11143	3/4 INCH ADJ WRENCH	55		60
11222	CAMPER AXE	107		125
11510	6 VIAL LEVEL	12	60	75
12110	2 AMP ORBITAL SANDER	21		28
12303	ECONOMY 1/4 INCH DRILL		125	150
21114	11 PC SOCKET SET	38		50
21214	6 PC OPEN END SET	157		160
21410	24 PC TAP AND DIE SET	24	30	60
31140	RD POINT DIRT SHOVEL	85		100

FIGURE 2-7 Inventory reports

tory by 20 percent without decreasing the service level is not in the least unrealistic. Why? Because most businesses do not use modern inventory-management techniques.

To illustrate, consider what takes place in a typical ledger-card system for inventory control. For each item in the product line, a ledger card such as the one in figure 2-6 is kept. As transactions occur, they are posted to the ledger cards and the on-hand balances are brought up to date. This posting to inventory records can be done either manually or by a posting machine, the method usually determined by the number of items in the product line and the number of daily transactions.

Periodically, perhaps once a week, a clerk or manager in the inventory-control department reviews the ledger cards to determine which items should be reordered. If the on-hand balance is below the reorder point, the ledger card is put in the reorder pile. Of course, if an order has already been placed, the item doesn't need to be reordered unless on hand plus on order is below the reorder point. A variation of this system is to compare on hand with the reorder point during the posting operation and, if necessary, to place the ledger cards in a reorder pile. Since the ledger card in figure 2-6 shows that on hand is below the reorder point and that a new order hasn't been placed, this item should be reordered.

To determine the reorder point, an inventory-control manager first considers two factors: (1) the clerical time required for posting and reviewing the ledger cards and (2) the *lead time*—the amount of time it takes to receive an order after it has been placed. Suppose, for example, that it takes three working days from the time shipments are made until the issues are actually posted to the ledger cards. Suppose also that it takes three days after posting before the ledger cards are reviewed and new orders are placed. Once the order is placed, the supplier takes three weeks for delivery. In this case, if the average weekly sales for the item is 20, the reorder point must be at least four weeks' usage, or about 80. Thus, the actual on-hand balance will reach zero just as the new order is received.

However, if the sales are above average because of normal fluctuations in demand, a stockout will occur. As a result, some amount of *safety stock* is added to the reorder point. For example, if a one-month supply of the item is used as safety stock (80 units), the reorder point is 160 (80 + 80). Then, the average demand will have to double before a stockout will occur. (Incidentally, a typical rule to follow when setting reorder points is to use a one-month supply as safety stock for all inventory items.)

The amount that is reordered in a typical system (the order quantity) is also based on a fixed usage, such as a two- or three-month supply. For example, a typical company may have a rule of reordering a three-month supply whenever an order is placed. In figure 2-6, since usage for the last three months has been about 250, 250 units will be reordered. By using a three-month rule for determining order quantity, each item in inventory will have to be ordered about four times per year.

Although a ledger-card system may very well be the most profitable system for a company, there are many ways in which the system just described can be improved. Perhaps the simplest way is to cut the processing and review time so that all transactions are processed and all records are reviewed on a daily basis. By reducing the clerical time, reorder points can be lowered, thus reducing inventory levels without any change in the service level. For example, if the clerical time is reduced by five days (one work week), the reorder point can be reduced by about one week's usage and, thus, the average inventory investment can also be reduced.

Beyond this simple measure, modern management techniques can be used to determine reorder point and order quantity. To determine order quantity, for example, an arbitrary rule such as the three-month usage rule is rarely the most profitable method. Instead, the carrying costs of inventory should be balanced against the costs of placing an order. For example, if it costs $10 each time an order is placed, the annual usage of an item is 1000 units, the unit cost is $8, the carrying cost is 25 percent of the average inventory investment, and the average monthly usage is 80, then the best order quantity is 100—not 250 as derived by the three-month rule. To prove that an order quantity of 100 maximizes profits, you can calculate costs using order quantities both above and below 100, as in the following table:

Order Quantity	Orders per Year	Annual Ordering Cost	Average Inventory Investment	Annual Carrying Cost	Total Yearly Cost
50	20	$200	$200	$50	$250
100	10	100	400	100	200
125	8	80	500	125	205
250	4	40	1000	250	290

In this case, the difference in yearly costs for the three-month rule method and for the best order quantity is $90. If an inventory consists of thousands of items, the effect on profits of scientifically determining the order quantity can be tremendous.

The best or most profitable order quantity, called the economic order quantity (EOQ), is determined by using the following formula:

$$EOQ = \sqrt{\frac{2 \text{ (Annual usage) (Cost of placing one order)}}{\text{(Unit cost of item) (Carrying cost as a decimal fraction)}}}$$

You might guess why all companies don't use economic order quantities. To determine them, a considerable amount of computation is required.

In addition, because the EOQ is based on annual usage and annual usage is continually changing, EOQs must be continually readjusted. So it is not a one-time calculation; it must be redone whenever demand changes. With a computer system, of course, the EOQ calculation is relatively routine and can be done in a fraction of a second; thus, the computational difficulties aren't a problem.

Similarly, there is a better way to determine safety stock and therefore reorder point than by using an arbitrary rule such as the one-month usage rule. To establish safety stock, both the average monthly usage and the amount of deviation from this average must be calculated. For example, suppose an item has an average monthly demand of 50, with a variation in usage from 40 to 60. If lead time is one month, a safety stock of one month's usage (50) is much too high—a safety stock of only 10 will provide a service level of 100 percent. Similarly, if an item's usage varies from 10 to 1000 with an average of 250, the one-month usage rule for safety stock will certainly lead to stockouts.

To determine the optimum safety stock and hence the reorder point, some rather extensive computations are required. This involves forecasting the demand and then keeping track of the average deviation from this forecast. Once the average deviation is known, however, the amount of safety stock required to maintain a given service level can be predicted with great accuracy. Because about half of a typical inventory consists of safety stock, making a more exact determination of safety stock can considerably improve the effectiveness of an inventory-control system. Once again, however, the difficulty of the record keeping and the computation required makes optimum determination of safety stock impractical on all but computerized systems.

Whether or not a company uses scientific techniques for determining reorder point and order quantity, one message should be clear: It takes information to determine a profitable balance between the conflicting goals of inventory management. To this end, reports such as those in figure 2-7 are helpful. The first report, the daily reorder listing, lists those items that need to be reordered—on hand plus on order is below the reorder point. The second report, called a monthly sales-by-item report, indicates items that are increasing or decreasing in demand. This information will help inventory personnel to pinpoint the items that require a change in reorder point or order quantity. Similarly, the third report, a monthly service-level report, indicates items for which a larger or smaller safety stock should be considered.

In summary, the inventory-control application can be complex, but it can also be the source of the greatest increase in company profits resulting from a changeover to a computerized system. Many computer systems, in fact, have been justified by this application alone. Although the documented success stories are many, one auto and machine parts distributor typifies what can be accomplished. By using modern management techniques for 30 percent of its 13,000 items (the ones with the largest investments), the company was able to decrease its average inventory investment on those items by 26 percent. At the same time, the service level for those items increased from 94 to 96 percent.

SALES ANALYSIS

The purpose of the *sales-analysis* application is to provide information for management. The input documents are the records of shipments and returns, the invoices, and the return notices. The output documents are sales reports designed to answer questions such as: Who are our most profitable salesmen? Should we drop a product from the product line? Should a new product be developed? Where should our advertising dollars be spent?

Figure 2-8 illustrates two typical sales reports. The first shows total sales and gross profit for each salesman. The fact that the biggest selling

MONTHLY SALES BY CUSTOMER

MONTH ENDING 10-31-73   PAGE 001

CUST. NAME	CUST. NO.	SALES THIS MONTH	THIS YEAR	LAST YEAR	INC/DEC
A & A EQUIPMENT SUPPLY	1057	8,752.98	81,825.44	76,655.62	5,169.82
ALFIE'S GARDEN SHOP	1153	336.29	2,106.90	1,265.99	840.91
ALLWORTHY EQUIPMENT	1257	735.57	8,490.34	9,473.00	982.66CR
ARNOLD'S BARGAIN BARN	1351	3,333.90	44,947.05	25,280.00	19,667.05
BENGSTON'S SEED STORE	1453	415.35	11,458.58	38,857.50	27,398.92CR
CALLEY HARDWARE CO.	1555	16,408.81	90,511.33	86,645.12	3,866.21

MONTHLY SALES BY SALESMAN

MONTH ENDING 10-31-73   PAGE 001

SALESMAN NAME	SALESMAN NO.	NET SALES	COST OF SALES	GROSS PROFIT
CRAMER	10	25,280.29	19,405.79	5,874.50
CRAWFORD	13	3,547.25	2,930.83	616.42
CURRIER	16	18,062.34	14,823.54	3,238.80
GRAHAM	19	19,746.37	15,839.97	3,906.40
HEMPHILL	22	35,165.43	29,923.90	5,241.53
HENNIS	25	32,261.85	25,343.79	6,918.06
MCDONALD	28	23,726.26	18,793.96	4,932.30
MASTERS	32	18,777.50	14,990.05	3,787.45

FIGURE 2-8   Sales-analysis reports

salesman is not the one that brings the largest gross profit to the company indicates that perhaps a different incentive system should be considered. The second report gives the sales for each customer and compares year-to-date sales with the previous year-to-date sales. By studying unusual decreases, a manager can determine sales losses as they develop and take action to recover the lost business.

In some companies, of course, sales analysis is not an important application. For example, if a company has a limited number of products, salesmen, and customers, sales analysis may be a relatively insignificant application. On the other hand, if a company has thousands of items and products, a large sales staff, and several sales offices, sales analysis is likely to be critical. Without adequate information, management can't make effective decisions.

PAYROLL

The primary goal of the _payroll_ application is to prepare accurate payroll checks and to get them into the hands of the employees on payday. The input documents are attendance and time records in the form of time cards, time sheets, and job tickets indicating the amount of time an employee spends on a particular job. The output is the _payroll check and earnings statement._ The earnings statement, which is required by law, must show the amounts of federal tax and social security tax withheld. It also shows other deductions such as union dues, insurance premiums, and state and local taxes.

A payroll system must also provide several other types of output. First, up-to-date records of wages paid and deductions retained for each employee must be kept. In a small company, this information is often kept on ledger cards, one for each employee. Second, quarterly and annual reports to the government and to the employees indicating wages paid, taxes withheld, and unemployment tax contributions must be prepared. The W-2 form sent to each employee on or before January 31 of each year is an example of a form required by the government. Third, the system should provide management with information that will help to control labor costs. This information should answer questions such as: What departments have excessive absenteeism or labor turnover? What is the amount of overtime for each department? Is labor performing above or below efficiency standards?

Within a company there may be several different types of payrolls. For example, a manufacturer may have a monthly salaried payroll for office employees and a weekly incentive payroll for factory workers. The incentive wages are dependent on the employee's performance as compared to established standards. In addition, a company may have a sales staff that is paid on a commission or bonus basis.

Because of the amount of computation required for payroll, particularly in an incentive payroll plan, computers have long been used for this application. In fact, when a company first installs a computer system, payroll is commonly the first computer application. Because of its computational speeds, a computer can very often reduce the costs of the payroll application.

ACCOUNTS PAYABLE

Since accounts payable refers to the amounts owed to other companies, the *accounts payable* application involves keeping track of amounts owed and writing checks payable to suppliers (*vendors*). The input documents are purchase orders, receiving records, and vendor invoices. The purchase order, normally issued by the purchasing department, indicates what was ordered; the receiving report indicates what has been received. By comparing purchase order, receiving report, and vendor invoice, a company can determine whether it has been billed correctly. If so, the bill is authorized for payment.

The primary outputs on an accounts payable system are (1) accounts payable records indicating charges and payments, and (2) *payables checks* and *remittance statements* as shown in figure 2-9. In a small company, as you might guess by now, accounts payable records are often kept on ledger cards. Because vendors are normally paid on an open-item basis, the remittance statement issued with the check indicates which invoices are being paid. Although it is primarily concerned with making payments to outside vendors, the accounts payable application also keeps records of and writes checks for internal expenses such as petty cash and salesman expense accounts.

To encourage early payment of bills, vendors often offer a cash discount for early payment—for example, a 2 percent discount if the bill is paid within ten days. This is usually indicated on the invoice in an abbreviated form such as 2%/10–NET/30. (NET/30 means the full amount should be paid within thirty days if the discount isn't taken.) Because 2 percent is a substantial discount, one of the objectives of the accounts payable application is to pay all checks on the last day of the discount period. That way the company's cash is retained for as long as possible, but all discounts are received.

The third output of an accounts payable system is management information. Because the accounts payable application keeps track of all payments other than paychecks, it controls a vast amount of cost data. By having this data organized into various types of reports, management can use it to control costs more effectively. The travel and expense report in figure 2-9, for example, breaks down selling expenses by salesman. Other reports may answer questions such as who the largest suppliers are, which vendors have the most goods returned to them, what cash discounts have been lost, and what the daily cash requirements are.

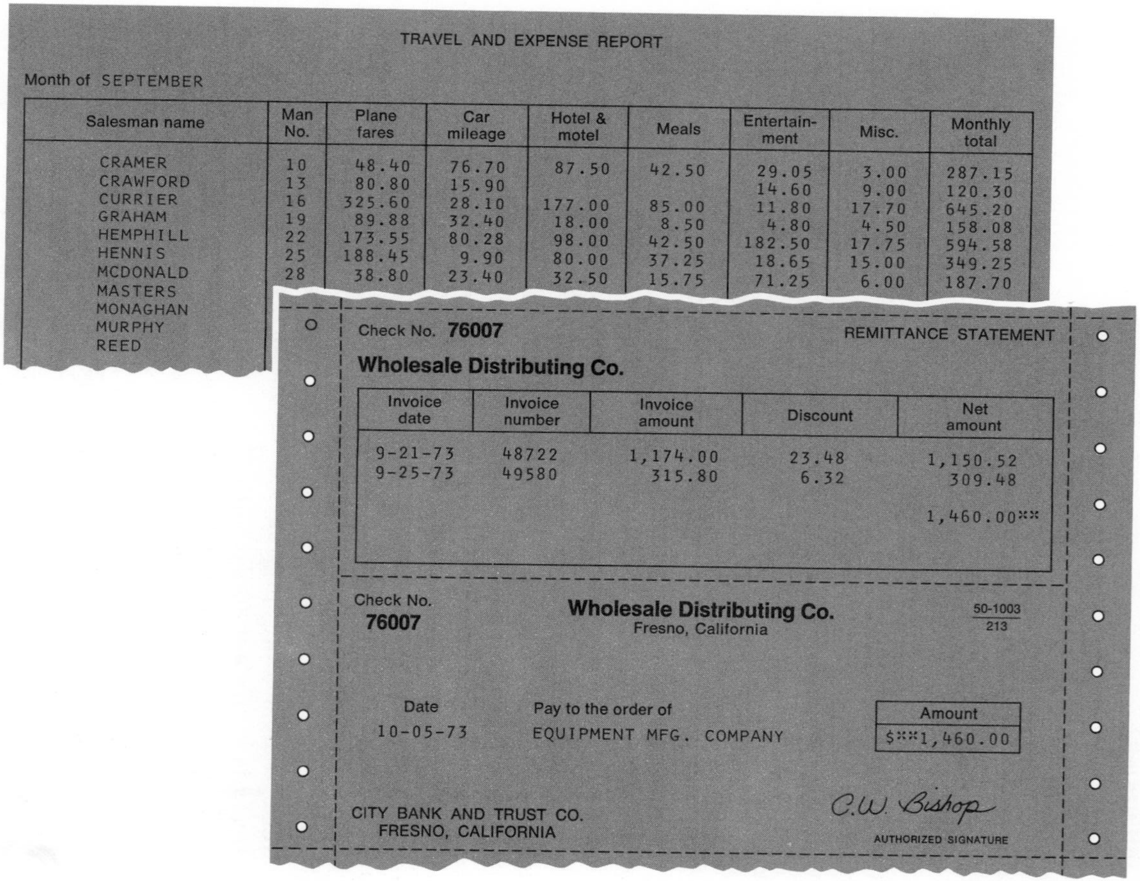

TRAVEL AND EXPENSE REPORT

Month of SEPTEMBER

Salesman name	Man No.	Plane fares	Car mileage	Hotel & motel	Meals	Entertainment	Misc.	Monthly total
CRAMER	10	48.40	76.70	87.50	42.50	29.05	3.00	287.15
CRAWFORD	13	80.80	15.90			14.60	9.00	120.30
CURRIER	16	325.60	28.10	177.00	85.00	11.80	17.70	645.20
GRAHAM	19	89.88	32.40	18.00	8.50	4.80	4.50	158.08
HEMPHILL	22	173.55	80.28	98.00	42.50	182.50	17.75	594.58
HENNIS	25	188.45	9.90	80.00	37.25	18.65	15.00	349.25
MCDONALD	28	38.80	23.40	32.50	15.75	71.25	6.00	187.70
MASTERS								
MONAGHAN								
MURPHY								
REED								

Check No. 76007

Wholesale Distributing Co.

REMITTANCE STATEMENT

Invoice date	Invoice number	Invoice amount	Discount	Net amount
9-21-73	48722	1,174.00	23.48	1,150.52
9-25-73	49580	315.80	6.32	309.48
				1,460.00**

Wholesale Distributing Co.
Fresno, California

Check No. 76007

50-1003
213

Date 10-05-73

Pay to the order of EQUIPMENT MFG. COMPANY

Amount
$***1,460.00

C.W. Bishop
AUTHORIZED SIGNATURE

CITY BANK AND TRUST CO.
FRESNO, CALIFORNIA

FIGURE 2-9   Accounts payable documents

GENERAL LEDGER

The term *general ledger*, as any accounting student knows, refers to the records of a company's revenues and expenses, assets and liabilities. The individual records within the general ledger are referred to as *accounts*. Accounts receivable and accounts payable, for example, are two of the general-ledger accounts. Other typical accounts are gross sales, merchandise purchases, and salaries and wages. Although a small company may keep account records in a single general-ledger book, these records are likely to be kept in punched cards, on magnetic tapes, or on direct-access devices when an automated general-ledger system is used.

The input documents for a general-ledger system are primarily records from the accounts receivable, inventory, accounts payable, payroll, and sales-analysis applications. In addition, some other accounting records are needed, such as those that give the present value of land, buildings, and equipment owned by the company.

The major output documents of a general-ledger system are the *balance sheet* and the *income statement* (also known as the *operating statement* or the *profit-and-loss statement*). These documents are illustrated in simplified form in figure 2-10. The balance sheet indicates a company's assets, liabilities, and net worth as of a certain date. Note that it does not show changes in assets, liabilities, or net worth; for this information it must be compared with the balance sheet for a previous period. While totals for some of the accounts on the balance sheet are derived from the basic applications such as the accounts receivable, inventory, and accounts payable applications, totals for accounts such as cash, land, and buildings must be obtained from other accounting records. Note that total assets must equal total liabilities plus net worth; otherwise, there is an error in one or more of the general-ledger accounts.

The income statement shows the revenues and expenses of a company over a certain period of time, such as a month, a quarter, or a year. Most of the data for this report can be derived from the sales-analysis, accounts payable, and payroll applications. Quite simply, all expenses are subtracted from total revenue to derive the profit or the loss for a particular accounting period. The profit is carried over to the balance sheet as retained earnings.

Because financial data is critical to the management of a company, the general-ledger system should provide financial information beyond that given in the balance sheet and the income statement. Depending on the preferences of a company's financial officers, then, a general-ledger system may also provide reports similar to those in figure 2-11. The first report compares the present balance sheet with that of the previous period; the second shows the ratios of expenses to revenue. Other reports may break down expenses and revenues by branch offices

INCOME STATEMENT
YEAR ENDING DEC. 31, 1972

```
REVENUES
  SALES                                    5,460,000
  LESS RETURNS                                 4,300
         NET SALES                                       5,455,700 *

COST OF GOODS SOLD                                       3,990,000 *

GROSS PROFIT                                             1,465,700 * *

SELLING EXPENSES
  SALESMEN SALARIES                          205,800
  SALESMEN COMMISSIONS                       109,200
  SALES OFFICE SALARIES                       36,000
  SALES OFFICE MAINTENANCE                    16,000
  MAINT. OF DELIVERY EQUIP.                   26,000
  DEPRECIATION OF DEL. EQUIP.                  7,200
         TOTAL SELLING EXPENSES                            400,200 *

GEN. AND ADM. EXPENSES
  OFFICERS' SALARIES                         360,000
  GEN. OFFICE SALARIES                       144,000
  PROPERTY TAX                                12,500
  INSURANCE                                    8,400
  RENT                                        36,000
         TOTAL G & A EXPENSES                              560,900 *

TOTAL OPERATING EXPENSES                                  961,100 *

NET OPERATING INCOME                                     504,600 * *

OTHER EXPENSES
  INTEREST PAID                               42,400
  CASH DISCOUNTS ALLOWED                      22,700
         TOTAL OTHER EXPENSES                              65,100 *

NET INCOME BEFORE TAXES                                  439,500 * *

INCOME TAXES                                             202,000 *

PROFIT OR LOSS                                           237,500 * *
```

BALANCE SHEET--DEC. 31, 1972

ASSETS

```
CURRENT ASSETS
  CASH                                        19,200
  ACCOUNTS RECEIVABLE                        225,800
  MERCHANDISE INVENTORY                      850,500
         TOTAL CURRENT ASSETS                          1,095,500

FIXED ASSETS
  LAND                                        90,000
  BUILDINGS AND FIXTURES                     737,800
  EQUIPMENT                                  148,000
         TOTAL FIXED ASSETS                              975,800 *

TOTAL ASSETS                                          $2,071,300 * *
```

LIABILITIES AND NET WORTH

```
CURRENT LIABILITIES
  ACCOUNTS PAYABLE                           122,800
  INCOME TAXES PAYABLE                        51,000
         TOTAL CURRENT LIABILITIES                       173,800 *

LONG-TERM LIABILITIES
  BONDS PAYABLE                              500,000
  CONTRACTS PAYABLE                           30,000
         TOTAL LONG-TERM LIABILITIES                     530,000 *

NET WORTH
  CAPITAL STOCK AND PAID-IN SURPLUS        1,130,000
  RETAINED EARNINGS                          237,500
         TOTAL NET WORTH                               1,367,500 *

TOTAL LIABILITIES AND NET WORTH                       $2,071,300 * *
```

FIGURE 2-10 General-ledger documents

```
                    COMPARATIVE  BALANCE  SHEET

                                 THIS      LAST     OVER (+) OR
            DESCRIPTION          YEAR      YEAR     UNDER (-)

    CASH                        19,200    27,500     8,300 -
    ACCOUNTS  RECEIVABLE       225,800   175,220    50,580 +
    MERCHANDISE  INVENTORY     850,500   705,000   145,500 +

    LAND                        90,000    90,000
    BUILDINGS  AND  FIXTURES   737,800   558,500   179,300 +
    EQUIPMENT                  148,000   163,500    15,500 -

    ACCOUNTS  PAYABLE
```

EXPENSE-TO-REVENUE STATEMENT		
DESCRIPTION	AMOUNT	% OF NET SALES
NET SALES	5,455,700	100.0
COST OF GOODS SOLD	3,990,000	73.1
GROSS PROFIT	1,465,700	26.9
SELLING EXPENSE	400,200	7.3
GEN. AND ADM. EXPENSES	560,900	10.3
NET OPERATING INCOME	504,600	9.3
OTHER EXPENSES	65,100	1.2
NET INCOME BEFORE TAXES	439,500	8.1

FIGURE 2-11 General-ledger reports

or by departments, compare one branch office's income statement with those of other branches, or compare expenses with budgeted expenses. A general-ledger system should also be able to provide a detailed breakdown of expenses, thereby helping management to analyze those operations in which expenses are unusual or unexpected.

DISCUSSION

Although I have described the major documents and characteristics of the basic applications, these descriptions are brief and simplified. As you go from industry to industry and from company to company, there are significant variations in the way that applications are handled. To illustrate, consider the differences in the order-writing, billing, and accounts receivable applications as you go from a wholesale to a retail distributor. First, the retail distributor normally doesn't write an order while the wholesale distributor does. The retail customer selects his merchandise and brings it to a checkout counter. Second, a retail store often doesn't prepare a bill if the sale is a cash payment (although some stores do). If the sale is a charge, a bill is written and one copy is handed to the customer. In contrast, the wholesale distributor prepares a bill for each shipment of merchandise. Third, the wholesale distributor keeps accounts receivable records on an open-item basis, the retail distributor on a balance-forward basis. Retail payments are applied to the balance owed, not to individual invoices.

Beyond these variations, there are many others. The formats of the various documents differ from company to company. In some industries, customers will not accept back-ordered items—the sale is simply lost. And many companies combine the order-writing and billing applications so that the shipping order is actually a copy of the bill. To do this, inventory records are checked before preparing the shipping order and bill to determine in advance if an item is available in stock.

Regardless of the procedural variations, these eight basic applications provide you with a good base of knowledge since they are common to most businesses or other institutions. Manufacturers and wholesale distributors, for example, perform all eight applications. Service businesses also perform all eight applications; although they don't have merchandise, they write service orders and bill for the services. And, although they don't keep an inventory of merchandise, they do keep inventories of service parts and maintenance supplies. Retail distributors may not write orders, but they do perform the other basic applications. Similarly, banks, insurance companies, hospitals, and even government agencies perform most of these basic applications, even though the applications may appear significantly different. A hospital may keep inventory records of available beds; the insurance company's bill is a premium notice; social security checks are part of a government accounts payable application.

Besides the basic applications, industries such as banking, insurance, and education have specialized applications. Demand-deposit accounting, for example, is the banking application that keeps track of checking-account balances. Similarly, claims handling and grade reporting are applications common to insurance companies and schools. Because 65 percent of a manufacturing company's budget may go into production costs, production control is likely to be a major application for a manufacturer.

Although the basic applications are described separately in this chapter, it is important to realize that groups of applications are often closely related. For example, the output of the order-writing application, the shipping order, is the input to the billing application. Similarly, the bill is an input document for the accounts receivable, inventory, and sales-analysis applications. Because these five applications are related in this way, they are often referred to as a family of applications — specifically, the *distribution family of applications.*

Accounts payable and payroll are related because they form the basis of a cost-accounting system. For example, if material and labor costs are combined, the true product costs can be determined. Similarly, the costs of labor and supplies by department are needed for comparison with budgeted costs.

Finally, the records of the accounts receivable, inventory, sales-analysis, payroll, and accounts payable applications are brought together in the general-ledger application. By combining these records with other accounting records, the balance sheet and the income statement can be prepared.

The interrelationship of the applications is an important concept because it helps explain why computer processing of data is economical. Once data is recorded in a machine-readable document such as the punched card, the card can be processed by the computer to prepare a variety of outputs. As you will see in chapter 3, the punched card that represents one line item on a shipping order can be used to prepare invoices, update inventory records, and print sales reports. By using the same input cards in several applications, the cost of preparing the output documents is reduced.

Because of the many ways in which any one application can affect the profits of a company, it is often difficult to decide which of two systems is best for an application. Four factors to consider are (1) the data-processing cost of the application, (2) the speed of processing in terms of how fast the output documents are prepared, (3) the accuracy of the output documents, and (4) the value of the management information provided by the system. Although all four factors — cost, speed, accuracy, and information — are likely to affect profits, it may be difficult to place a numerical value on any of the factors other than cost.

To illustrate, suppose a wholesale distributor is considering a new system for the billing and accounts receivable applications. The present system — call it system A — costs approximately $1200 per month for personnel and equipment. Bills are sent out an average of five days after shipments and, in the opinion of the office manager, are rarely inaccurate. The accounts receivable records are updated an average of two days after billing; monthly statements are sent out the first Friday of every month; and for management information, an aged trial balance is printed within seven days from the month's end. The credit manager discovers occasional errors in accounts receivable documents but not to such an extent that he feels a change is necessary.

Based on present volumes, the proposed system, system B, will cost about $1500 per month for personnel and equipment. However, invoices will be prepared and accounts receivable records updated the day after shipment. Monthly statements will be sent on the first day of each month and near perfect accuracy is expected throughout the system. An aged trial balance will be printed weekly, along with lists of accounts that have been delinquent for over sixty days.

Which system, then, is most profitable for the company? Although it seems best to keep system A since it costs $3600 per year less than system B, a system analyst must attempt to evaluate the speed, accuracy, and information of both the systems. For example, if the daily billing volume is $20,000, an analyst might predict a reduction in accounts receivable of $80,000 by using system B. At a return of 5 percent, this value alone might justify the installation of system B. The value of other qualities such as improved accuracy or better management information must likewise be determined. One of the present challenges of system design is to develop better methods for measuring intangible factors such as speed, accuracy, and management information.

When evaluating management information, the concept of _exception reporting, or management-by-exception_, should be considered. The theory is that information is more valuable if it reports only the exceptional conditions to management—those conditions that require attention. For example, the delinquent-account list in figure 2-5 and the reorder listing in figure 2-7 are exception reports. The first report lists customers to be contacted; the second lists items to be reordered. In contrast, the aged trial balance (figure 2-5) and the sales-by-item report (figure 2-7) are not exception reports—they list all customers and all inventory items. Because a computer has the logical capability to determine which information items are exceptional, it can easily be used for exception reporting. However, the concept of exception reporting is valuable regardless of the type of data-processing equipment used.

In conclusion, the study of computer applications can easily be a subject in itself, for the study of applications is the study of business. Although this chapter is about computer applications, I do not mean to imply that a computer is the best processing method for any particular application. The choice of equipment depends on the size of the company, the volumes of data to be processed, and the type of industry, in addition to many other factors.

SUMMARY

1. The eight applications common to most businesses are order writing, billing, accounts receivable, inventory control, sales analysis, payroll, accounts payable, and general ledger. The speed, accuracy, and information of each application can significantly affect the profits of a company.

2. In general, groups of applications within a business are related. For example, the output of one application is likely to be the input to

another. This fact helps to explain why automatic data-processing methods can be justified economically.

3. To determine which of two systems is best for a particular application, a system analyst must evaluate the cost, speed, accuracy, and information of each system. One of the challenges of system analysis is to assign meaningful values to intangible factors.

4. Management-by-exception means reporting only exceptional conditions to management. This relieves management from studying routine data and thus improves management's effectiveness.

computer application
document
customer order
sales order
order writing
shipping order
back-ordered item
back order
bill
invoice
billing
line item
extension
accounts receivable
ledger card
posting accounts receivable
aged trial balance
open-item accounts receivable
balance-forward accounts
   receivable
inventory control
service level

lead time
safety stock
economic order quantity
EOQ
sales analysis
payroll
payroll check
earnings statement
accounts payable
vendor
payables check
remittance statement
general ledger
account
balance sheet
income statement
operating statement
profit-and-loss statement
distribution family of
   applications
exception reporting
management-by-exception

TOPIC TWO
ADVANCED APPLICATIONS

Although the applications described in topic 1 are basic to most businesses, they make up only a small fraction of all computer applications. In fact, several thousand different computer applications have been identified and more are being discovered every day. If you pick up a newspaper, you are likely to read about a computer controlling an oil refinery, predicting the outcome of an election, or designing a highway.

To give you some perspective on computer uses, six types of computer applications are described in this topic. Included are (1) accounting, (2) operational control, (3) management-information systems, (4) management science, (5) process control, and (6) scientific and engineering. These classifications do not necessarily encompass all computer applications, and, as you will see, the distinction between two classifications isn't always clear-cut. Nevertheless, they do illustrate the major computer activities.

ACCOUNTING

Accounting applications are concerned with recording and reporting costs and revenues (sales) within an organization. Thus, accounts receivable, accounts payable, payroll, sales analysis, and general ledger are accounting applications. Because order writing, billing, and inventory control deal with basic accounting data, they too are commonly considered to be accounting applications. Thus, all of the basic applications described in topic 1 can be called accounting applications.

Depending on the industry, there are many other types of accounting applications; for example, demand-deposit accounting and mortgage-loan accounting in banking, income tax and appropriation accounting in government, and premium and claim-payment accounting in insurance. As a class, accounting applications are likely to be the first applications computerized by an institution.

Because the computer has enabled accounting systems to more accurately represent the actual costs within an activity, some unexpected facts are often uncovered as a result of computerizing the accounting systems. For instance, supermarkets traditionally have not considered the cost of shelf space when determining the profits made by each product. Although the store costs, and therefore shelf costs, have been considered, actual shelf costs per product were too difficult to assign. When at last some stores calculated the shelf space and shelf cost for each product and combined this with product, packaging, and handling costs, there were some surprising results. One store, for example, discovered that it wasn't making a profit on beef and flour!

OPERATIONAL CONTROL

During the last several years, many companies have discovered that a computer can be of more value when used to help control an operation than when used simply to account for an operation. In a typical manufacturing company, for example, improving production efficiency is likely to have a far greater effect on profits than improving the accounting system.

When a computer is used for *operational control*, it does more than merely record or report operations after they have occurred. In controlling operations, the computer is used to plan, schedule, and monitor the operations as they take place. In production control, for example, the computer can be used in all three phases. First, it can be used to forecast the demand for finished products and to plan material requirements based on these forecasts. Second, it can schedule machine operations, taking into consideration time requirements and machine capacities. Finally, it can monitor shop-floor operations as they occur and alert management to any deviations from the production schedule. As in a typical cost-accounting system, the computer can then be used to account for the material costs and labor involved in each product.

When computers are applied to production control, the improvements are often well worth the cost of the computer system. One company, for example, reduced the production time for its products from 8.2 weeks to 6.3 weeks while it increased production capacity by 36 percent. Another company reports production times dropped from 15 weeks down to 5 weeks and the service level of finished parts increased from 88 percent to a new level of 98 percent.

Operational-control systems can, of course, be applied to many operational areas within a business. Thus, there are systems for warehousing that determine the most efficient locations for items and the order in which items should be picked. There are customer-service systems in insurance companies that store all policyholder information on direct-access devices and retrieve the desired information upon request. When an inventory-control system forecasts demands, determines order quantities and reorder points, and prints purchase orders, it too becomes an operational-control system.

MANAGEMENT-INFORMATION SYSTEMS

In topic 1, management information was shown to be an important aspect of many applications: accounts receivable, inventory control, sales analysis, payroll, accounts payable, and, of course, general ledger. A *management-information system (MIS)*, however, implies more than just the traditional information. It is a system that (quite ambitiously) tries to provide all the information required by the managers of a company when they need it. As a result, even though the information is derived mainly from the files used in accounting and operational-control applications, an MIS is often treated as an application in itself.

An MIS is difficult to design because it must provide information at different levels. Within any company, for instance, there are several levels of management: top management; one or more levels of middle management; and operational, or lower, management. Because the information requirements differ for each level, the system must be able to arrange the same data into varying levels of information. Figure 2-12, for example, shows budget analysis reports for three levels of management. At the top level, the report indicates that selling expenses are over budget. At the next level, the four sales offices that are over budget are listed. At the third level, the over-budget selling expenses of the Denver sales office are indicated. Needless to say, there can be levels below those shown, such as traveling and telephone expenses by salesman.

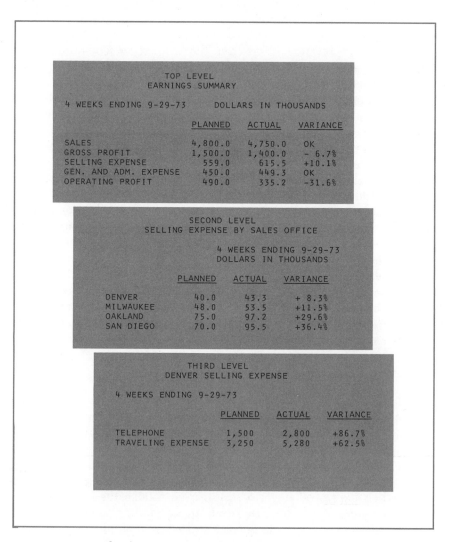

FIGURE 2-12   Levels of management information

One of the basic concepts of an MIS is management-by-exception. In designing a system, acceptable variances from standards are determined so that exceptional conditions can be indicated on all reports. Thus, the first level in figure 2-12 indicates items that have exceeded budget by more than 3 percent or items that are below budget by more than 5 percent—the others are labeled OK. At the second level, only the exceptional sales offices are listed; at the third level, only the exceptional budget items are listed.

Since a major goal of an MIS is to provide information when it is needed, data communications are normally involved. By keying an inquiry into a terminal, a manager can request the information he desires. The information is assembled by the computer and printed or displayed on the manager's terminal. If a manager requests successively lower levels of information—for example, the president may request both the first and second levels shown in figure 2-12—the system should be able to provide them.

Although there are many pros and cons, the concept of an MIS has great sales appeal. As a result, many MIS systems are being either developed or planned. One of the primary questions raised by objectors to MIS systems is whether the expense of such a system is justified by improved management. Here again, it is a problem of comparing a measurable quantity—cost—with an intangible quality—the value of management information.

MANAGEMENT SCIENCE

Management science refers to statistical and mathematical techniques and theories as they are applied to business problems. Although these techniques can be used in manual computation, the computer is often used for management-science applications because of its computational speeds. For example, a computation that takes twelve hours for a person working with pencil and paper can be done in less than a minute by a computer.

A typical management-science problem is to determine the shipping routes that will lead to the lowest total shipping costs. For example, suppose a company has five production plants and fifty warehouses located throughout the country. The sales of each warehouse are known and the production capacity of each plant is known. Also, the shipping cost between each plant and each warehouse is known. The problem is: Which warehouses should be supplied from which plants to minimize shipping costs? It is not just a matter of supplying each warehouse from the nearest plant because the requirements of the East Coast warehouses exceed the capacities of the East Coast plants.

By using mathematical techniques, the best solution can be determined. And by using a computer, the solution can be determined in a very short time and redetermined whenever the requirements of the warehouses change. To appreciate the complexity of the problem, consider that if there were only four plants and five warehouses, there would be 1024 possible solutions, with only one being lowest in cost.

Two techniques that are commonly used within the field of management science are *linear programming* and *simulation*. Linear programming is a mathematical technique that can be used to find an optimum solution when the relationships between the factors involved can be expressed in a series of linear equations. Thus, it is used to allocate resources in order to achieve the best (most profitable or lowest cost) balance between conflicting demands. For example, cattle companies use linear programming to determine the lowest-cost mix of grains that will meet certain nutritional requirements. The cost and nutritional makeup of the grains available for mixing and the nutritional requirements of the final product, the cattle feed, are the input data. The output is the best feed formula.

Simulation involves representing aspects of a business in terms of numbers or symbols that can be manipulated by a computer. By trying various alternatives on the simulation model, results in the real world can be more accurately predicted. For example, if a simulation model for investment practices has been developed, various investment strategies can be tried to determine which has the greatest likelihood of success.

In addition to linear programming and simulation, there are many other management-science techniques, all of which try to apply the techniques of science and mathematics to management problems. Although there have been many success stories so far, this area of applications is still in its infancy. Because of the expense of developing managment-science solutions, most companies have yet to try them. Nevertheless, some management-science people claim that the best solution derived by management-science techniques is from 5 to 15 percent better than a typical manual solution. If so, many businesses could profit by more extensive use of management science.

PROCESS CONTROL

Process control refers to computer control of a production process. For example, paper production is a typical process-control application. As wood pulp is moved through a long series of operations, the computer receives test and measurement data such as rate of flow, temperature, pressure, and humidity. The computer processes this data and makes the appropriate adjustments to valves and other actuators that control the process. Thus, the process-control computer actually takes the place of the operator or operators who conventionally control the process.

The advantages of process control can be significant. Guaranteed uniformity, greater productivity, lower costs, reduced waste and scrap, better quality—all have been claimed in one process-control application or another. The overall claim of experts is that the best performance otherwise attainable (and then, only occasionally) is the average for a process-control system.

Because of its advantages, all leading companies in the processing industries use computers to control one or more processes. Some typical applications are oil refining, steel milling, and bakery blending. In all, more than 2500 different process-control applications have been installed or are being installed. In simple systems, input may come from a few or several dozen input sensors; in complex systems, the computer may monitor hundreds of input measurements and make appropriate adjustments.

To illustrate a simple process-control system, consider an application in the food-processing industry called *net-weight monitoring*. In accordance with government regulations, a food processor must print the net weight (product weight) on the outside of the container and fill it with at least as much product—such as processed cheese—as is specified. Because there are penalties for underweight packages, a food processor is likely to overfill rather than underfill. In a typical operation, the containers are weighed automatically after being filled by the machine. If they are underfilled or overfilled, they are pushed to the side. When too much product is being diverted from the filling line, the operator who watches this process makes an adjustment to the filling machine. Note, however, that the system measures gross weight—container weight plus product weight—so variations in container weight are not taken into consideration. Also, there is apt to be considerable delay in the adjustment process and much chance for error.

As an alternative, consider the system illustrated in figure 2-13. Here, a computer constantly monitors the process. Each container is automatically weighed both before and after it is filled. These measurements are input to the computer, which calculates the exact net weight (gross weight minus container weight) and, if necessary, makes immediate adjustments to the filling machine. If the density of the product changes during the process, the system will detect it, adjust the filling machine, and continue to fill the correct net weight.

The advantages of this second system should be obvious. Less product is given away because of overfills, and there is absolute assurance against underfills. Costs are usually reduced since filling-machine operators aren't needed and one computer can monitor several filling lines.

SCIENTIFIC AND ENGINEERING

Some of the first uses of computers were to solve scientific and engineering problems. By using the computer and its fantastic computational speeds, scientists and engineers were able to relieve themselves from the

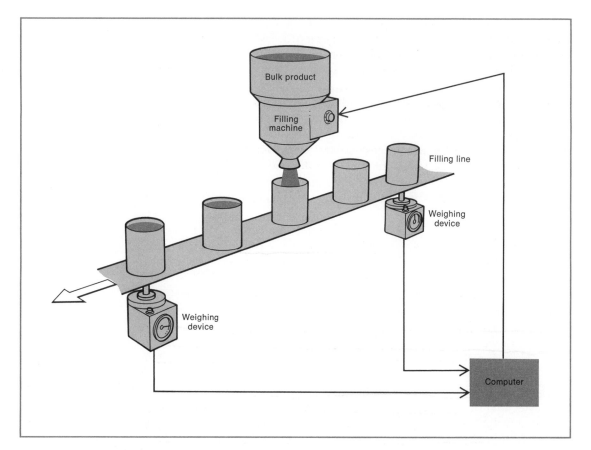

FIGURE 2-13   Net-weight monitoring—process control

details of computation and spend more time on the problems themselves. Because the human mind is able to conceive solutions that it
cannot carry out in a lifetime of manual calculations, the computer has
actually solved problems that never would have been solved using other
methods. With the development of the computer, man has only to state
the steps required in a solution—he does not have to actually perform
the computation.

To help the scientist and engineer communicate with the computer,
a number of programming languages have been developed to allow problems to be expressed in mathematical or engineering notation. One of
the oldest of these languages, FORTRAN, is designed to make it possible
to express any mathematical computation in a type of mathematical
notation. Similarly, there are languages to express various types of engineering problems, such as calculating the area of a triangular plot of
ground when the lengths of two sides and the size of one angle are known.
Thus, the scientist or engineer doesn't have to learn the computer's language but only a modification of a language with which he is familiar.

FIGURE 2-14   Using a light pen and a visual-display
terminal for engineering applications

So that a number of engineers can make efficient use of a single computer, data-communication systems are often found in engineering departments. For example, if twelve typewriter terminals are located in
an engineering department, twelve engineers can work on twelve different problems at one time. Because the computer works at speeds far
beyond those of man, each engineer feels that only he is working with
the computer, even though the computer may be skipping from terminal
to terminal many times a second. A system such as this, which may have
dozens of terminals connected to a single computer, is referred to as a
time-sharing system.

Besides doing computation, computers can assist engineers by storing
and retrieving engineering designs. Using a visual-display terminal such
as the one in figure 2-14, an engineer can request a certain design and
have it displayed before him. He can then make modifications to the

design with a light pen. The light pen is input to the computer, and upon request, the computer stores these modifications. The engineer can thus experiment without making an extensive series of drawings. Because of the speed with which a computer can perform these visual-display operations, time sharing is also normally used for systems such as this.

Of course, to truly understand scientific and engineering applications, you have to be a scientist or an engineer. As a result, other than this superficial introduction, this book will not go into these applications.

DISCUSSION

As I said at the start of this topic, these six classifications of computer applications are not all-inclusive or clear-cut. For example, inventory control can be both an accounting and an operational-control application. Similarly, management-science techniques and theories are often used in operational-control applications—the economic-order-quantity formula, for instance, is an outgrowth of management science. Nevertheless, most computer activities fall into these classifications.

One distinction that is somewhat clear-cut, however, is that between *scientific and business applications*. The first is concerned with computation and problem solving; the second with the repetitive processing of business data. The computing requirements are so distinct, in fact, that computers were often designed for either scientific or business applications. In general, the scientific computer has rapid internal speeds; the business computer has rapid I/O speeds. But even this distinction is becoming less clear-cut. As scientific methods were applied to more and more business problems, computers that could handle both scientific and business applications were developed. Today, both scientific and business applications are often run on the same computer.

Within any one company, all six types of applications might be found. For example, a company might have one computer that is used by the engineering and the research and development departments on a time-sharing basis. A second computer might be used to control a process on the factory floor. A third computer, located in the data-processing department, might be used for accounting, operational-control, management-information, and management-science applications. Although the trend is toward greater application in the process-control, management-information, and management-science areas, an overwhelming amount of the work done by computers can still be attributed to the accounting and operational-control applications.

SUMMARY

There are six major types of computer applications, which are referred to as accounting, operational-control, management-information systems, management science, process control, and scientific and engineering. The major emphasis of this book is on the accounting applications.

**FOR
REVIEW**

accounting application
operational-control
  application
management-information
  system
MIS
management science

linear programming
simulation
process control
net-weight monitoring
time-sharing system
scientific application
business application

CHAPTER THREE

Before you can appreciate how a card computer system is used in a business application, you need to learn about the punched card and the punched-card machines that are used with a computer. Thus, the punched card and punched-card coding are explained in topic 1 of this chapter, while some commonly used punched-card machines are described in topic 2. Then, in topic 3, you are shown how the punched-card machines and the computer are coordinated in a data-processing system.

At one time or another, you have probably come into contact with a standard punched card—perhaps in the form of a payroll check, a utility bill, or a student registration card. The question is: Can you decode the data that is punched in a card?

Figure 3-1 presents the basic characteristics of a standard punched card. The card has eighty vertical columns, numbered from left to right. A hole can be punched in twelve different positions in each card column. For the purpose of illustration, each of these punching positions is punched in column 2 of the card. From bottom to top, these punches are called the 9-punch, 8-, 7-, 6-, 5-, 4-, 3-, 2-, 1-, 0- (zero), 11-, and 12-punch. Because an 11-punch is often used to distinguish one type of card from another, it is also referred to as an X-punch. (For example, an 11-punch in column 1 of a card may indicate that it is a payroll card.) As you can see at the right edge of the card, the 0- through 9-punches are called digit punches; and the 12-, 11- and 0-punches are called zone punches. The 0-punch, therefore, can be either a zone or a digit punch.

COMPUTER SYSTEM DESIGN

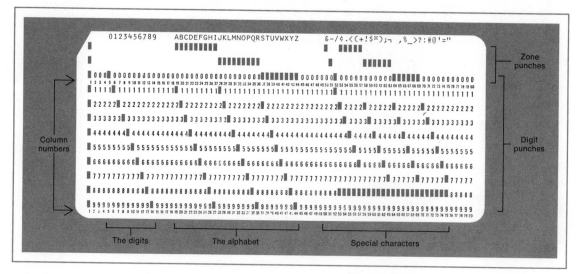

FIGURE 3-1   The standard punched card

It is a digit punch when no other punch is recorded in the column; but it is a zone punch if a digit punch is recorded below it.

Each column of a punched card can contain one character of data; namely, a number (0 through 9), a letter (A through Z), or a *special character* (such as an asterisk, a dollar sign, or a decimal point). In the illustration, the numbers are punched in columns 5 through 14, the letters in columns 19 through 44, and twenty-seven special characters in columns 50 through 76. The character punched in each column is printed at the top of the card directly over the column.

The combinations of punches used to represent characters in a punched card make up a code called Hollerith code, named after Herman Hollerith, inventor of the punched card. As you can see in the illustration, the numbers 0 through 9 are represented by the corresponding digit punch; and the letters by the combination of a zone and a digit punch. The special characters are represented by one, two, or three punches in a single card column. For example, a decimal point consists of a 12-, 3-, and 8-punch, while a hyphen (-) consists of an 11-punch only.

When a punched card is used to represent business data, groups of adjacent columns, called fields, represent specific data items. For instance, columns 21–40 (21 through 40) may be used for the description of a product, while columns 76–80 are used for the number of the customer that bought the product. In the card in figure 3-2, there are ten fields in columns 1–60. From left to right, they are the card-code field, the salesman-number field, the customer-number field, the order-number field, the transaction-date field, and so on. If an item is back-ordered, column 61 is supposed to contain an X-punch. Because a card like this contains information relating to a single business record—in this case, one line item of billing—punched cards are sometimes referred to as *unit-record cards*.

If you study the fields in figure 3-2, you can see that they are punched differently, depending on whether they are numeric or *alphanumeric*. (An alphanumeric field may contain letters, numbers, or special characters.) For an alphanumeric field, the data begins in the leftmost column of the field and continues to the right. When there are no more characters to be punched, the remainder of the field is left blank. Thus, the item-description field contains 1/2 INCH ADJ WRENCH in columns 32–50 and blanks in columns 51–55.

In contrast, numeric fields are punched to correspond with an assumed decimal point—the decimal point itself isn't punched. For example, the unit-price field in figure 3-2 assumes two decimal places, as indicated by the dotted line. Thus, the unit price of $2.75 is punched as the number 275 in columns 58–60. Since all columns of a numeric field should be punched with a digit, zeros are punched in columns 56 and 57 to fill the unit-price field.

In some cases, a numeric field in a card may contain a negative number. This is normally indicated by an X-punch in the rightmost column of the field. For example, a customer may have a credit balance of $12.85 in his accounts receivable record with a company. If the balance field is in columns 51–56, the field would contain 00128N. Since N is the combination of an X-punch and a 5-punch and two decimal places are assumed, it would indicate a negative 12.85.

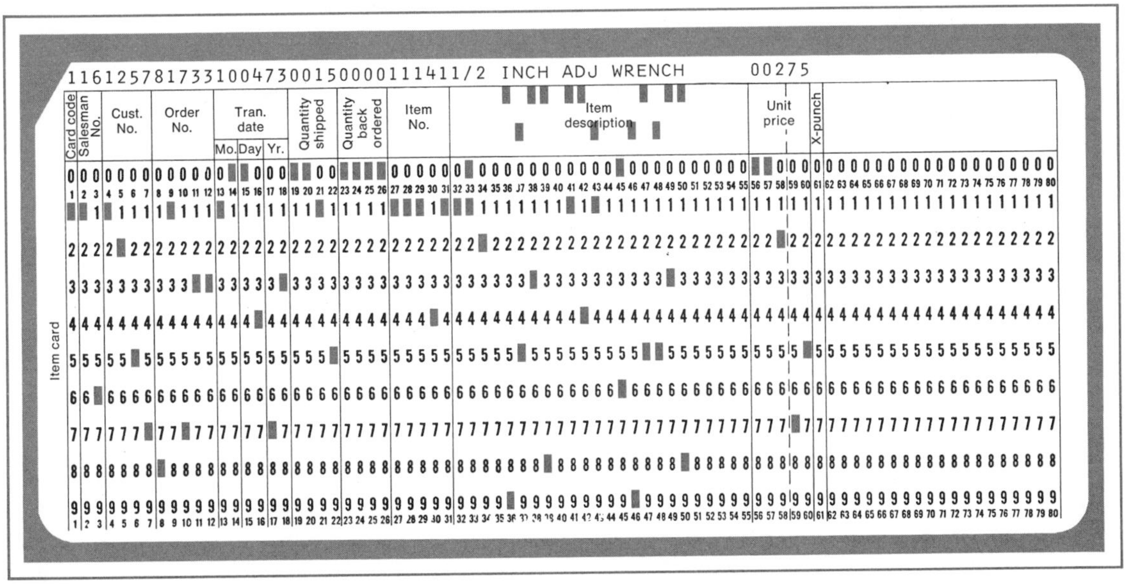

FIGURE 3-2   A unit-record card

Incidentally, although the punched card is a standard size, it can be printed or colored in any way. Thus, a typical computer installation will have cards of several different colors. For example, green cards may be used in the payroll application, while yellow cards may represent the line items in a billing application. Similarly, punched cards can be printed to indicate the location of fields (as in figure 3-2) or to represent a check or a utility bill. Since machines read only the holes punched in the card, both color coding and printing are for the convenience of those working with the punched cards.

A corner cut, as illustrated in figure 3-2, is used to be sure that all cards in a deck are facing the same way. For example, if a card is turned upside down in a deck with right corner cuts, that card will stick out at the right corner. The corner cut can be on either the left or the right, but all corner cuts should be on the same side for any one deck of cards.

Although the eighty-column card is by far the most common, there is nothing unique about the number eighty. For many years, Sperry Rand Corporation (Univac) manufactured machinery for use with ninety-column cards. In the last few years, a ninety-six-column card for use with IBM's System/3 has become popular. This card is described in chapter 5. Regardless of the number of columns or the code used, however, the principles are the same.

SUMMARY

The standard punched card is an eighty-column card that can store up to eighty characters of data, one character per column. By assigning groups of adjacent card columns to various items of data, a card is divided into fields.

FOR REVIEW

column
X-punch
digit punch
zone punch
special character
Hollerith code
field
unit-record card
alphanumeric

Before a card computer system can process data, the data must be punched into cards and the resulting card decks must be sorted into acceptable sequences. To do this, a number of punched-card machines must be used with a card system. The keypunch, for example, is used to punch the data into cards; the sorter is used to sort the decks of cards. In this topic, five punched-card machines are described: the keypunch (also known as the card punch), the verifier, the sorter, the collator, and the interpreter.

Unlike the computer system, which was first marketed in 1951, the punched-card machines date back to the late 1800s. At that time, Dr. Herman Hollerith developed the punched card and a number of punched-card machines. Since the punched card is also referred to as a unit-record card, punched-card machines are often called unit-record machines. Prior to the development of computer systems, these machines were used in punched-card, or unit-record, systems. These systems consisted of only punched-card machines, with two of them—the calculator and the accounting machine—doing the required calculating and document printing. These punched-card systems, which are described in more detail in chapter 10, are still in use in hundreds of companies too small for computers. For now, though, concentrate on the five machines described in this topic and their use in computer systems.

KEYPUNCH

The keypunch, shown in figure 3-3, is used to record data in punched cards. The keypunch operator places blank cards in the input hopper of the machine and sits at the typewriter-like keyboard. To the left of the operator are printed documents, called source documents, from which data is to be keypunched. As the operator's fingers strike the keys, the corresponding Hollerith codes are punched into the columns of the cards, one column per keystroke. At the end of the job, the newly punched cards are in the stacker on the left of the machine.

During the keypunching operation, some functions take place automatically—for example, feeding cards, skipping over fields that aren't going to be punched, and duplicating data from one card into the following card. This increases the speed at which an operator can keypunch data. Since the automatic functions can be changed quite easily at the beginning of each job, the keypunch can be used to punch cards in any format. One major difference between keypunches is that some print the data being punched over the column in which it is punched; others do not print the data.

Figure 3-4 illustrates a typical source document, a shipping order, and the transaction cards that were punched from it. The data printed at the top of each field represents the data that is punched in the field. As you can see, the data in columns 2–18 of each card is found in the heading of the shipping order, while the data in columns 19–60 comes from

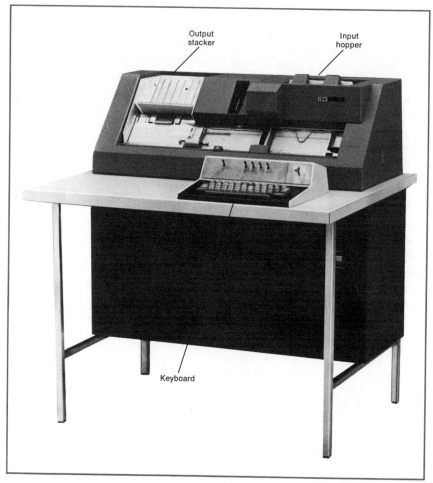

FIGURE 3-3   The keypunch

the line items of the order. In column 61 of the second card, the operator has keyed an X-punch, which prints as a hyphen (-), to indicate a back-ordered item. Because the first eighteen columns of the cards contain identical data, these columns can be duplicated automatically from the first card to the second, and from the second to the third, thus saving keypunch time. In other keypunching operations, the source documents may be time cards, receiving reports, purchase orders, or any other data-processing documents.

VERIFIER

To insure that the data punched in cards is accurate, the keypunch operation is usually followed by a verifying operation. The *verifier* looks much like the keypunch, and the verifying operation closely

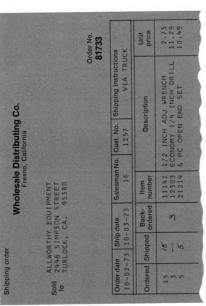

FIGURE 3-4 A source document and punched cards

parallels the keypunching operation. The verifier operator uses the same source documents that were used during keypunching. He places the keypunched cards in the input hopper of the verifier, and then types data on the keyboard of the verifier exactly as if he were operating the keypunch. The difference is that the verifier, instead of punching, checks to see that the holes in a card column correspond to the key that the operator strikes. If all of the characters of data that the operator keys for a card agree with the characters already punched in the card, a *correct-card notch* is cut on the right side of the card, indicating that its data has been verified.

Suppose, however, that the verifier operator keys the digit 3 for column 12 of a card, but the card column contains the digit 2. In this case, the keyboard locks and an error light turns on. The operator checks the source document to be sure that the digit 3 is correct, pushes a button to release the keyboard, and strikes the digit 3 again. If the character in the card and the character keyed do not agree this time, the keyboard locks again and the error light turns on. The operator then repeats the process one more time to be absolutely sure that the correct character is 3, and, if so, keys it again. If the verifier still detects an error, an *error notch* is cut over the card column, and the verifier moves on to the next column. Figure 3-5 shows a punched card with two error notches and a card with a correct-card notch.

SORTER

Once data has been keypunched and verified, it is ready to be proc-essed by the computer system — provided the punched-card decks are in an acceptable sequence for processing. The *sorter* is used to arrange card decks into these sequences.

The sorter, as shown in figure 3-6, has one input hopper and thirteen output pockets. From left to right, these pockets are called the 9-, 8-, 7-, 6-, 5-, 4-, 3-, 2-, 1-, 0-, 11-, 12-, and R- (reject) pockets. On the right side of the machine is the input hopper and a reading mechanism, which is a metal reading brush that can be set over any of the eighty card columns but can read only one column at a time. As the cards pass through the sorter, they are directed to the pocket corresponding to the data punched in the card column that is being read. If a column contains more than one punch, the card is sent to the pocket corresponding to the first punch that is read, starting with the 9-edge of the card.

The most common use of the sorter is to sort a deck of cards based on the data in a numeric field — for example, customer number. To do this, the sorter operator passes the cards through the sorter once for each column in the field, from the righthand column to the left. If the customer is punched in columns 61–65, the operator sets the sorting brush on column 65, places the deck in the input hopper, and starts the machine.

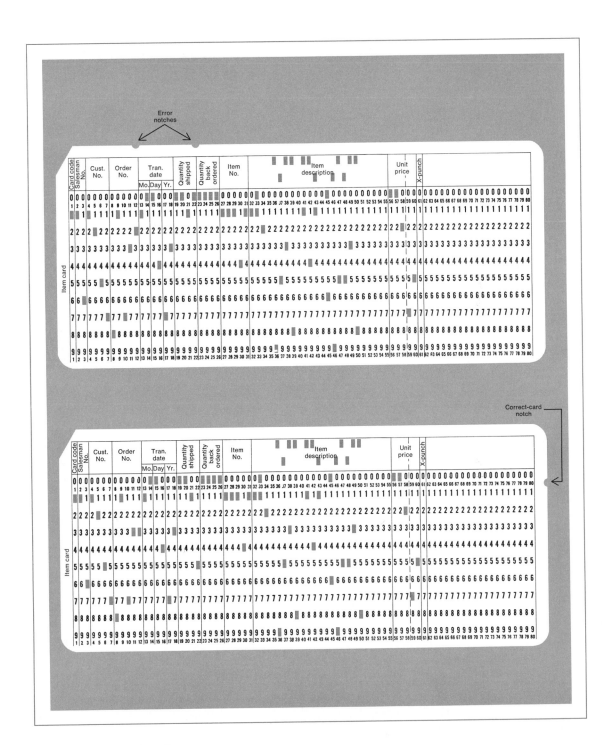

FIGURE 3-5 Verified cards

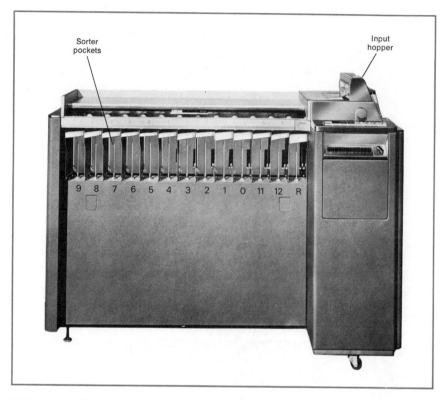

FIGURE 3-6   The sorter

After the cards have passed through the machine—at perhaps 1000 cards per minute—he collects the cards from the pockets, places the deck in the input hopper, sets the sorting brush to the next column in the field (column 64), and starts the machine again. He continues in this way until the deck is sorted by the leftmost column of the field, column 61. At this time, the deck is in customer-number order.

Figure 3-7 schematically illustrates the sorting of a two-column numeric field. The numbers on each card represent the contents of the field that is being sorted. In the first pass, the cards are sorted on the rightmost column of the field; in the second pass, on the leftmost. Although this is a simplified example, requiring only four sorter pockets, it does illustrate numeric sorting.

By adjusting its switches, a sorter can also be used to sort a deck on an alphabetic field. The procedure is basically the same—sorting proceeds from the righthand column of the field to the left—but two passes are required for each column. The operator adjusts the switches so that each column is first sorted by digit punch and then by zone punch. Because of the extra time required for sorting on alphabetic fields—two passes for each column instead of one—it is avoided whenever possible.

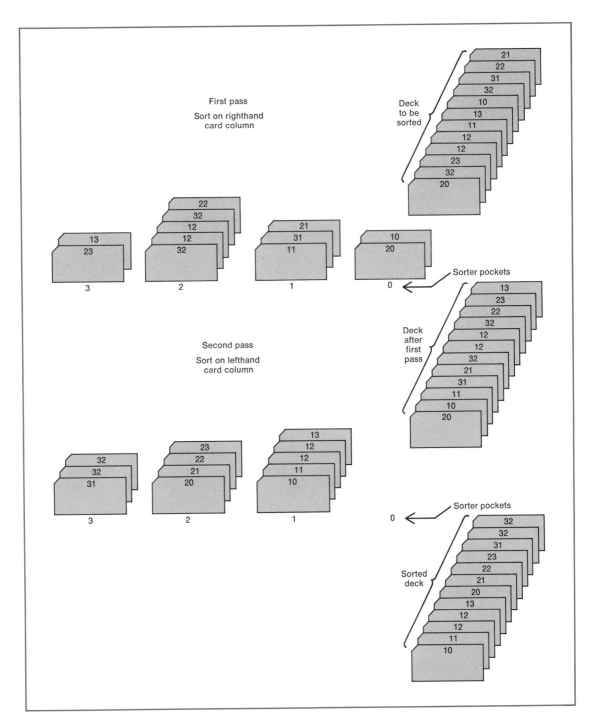

FIGURE 3-7   Sorting cards on a two-column numeric field

COLLATOR

The *collator* is another machine used to arrange a card deck into a sequence suitable for processing. A typical collator, such as the one illustrated in figure 3-8, has two input hoppers and five output stackers. One input hopper is called the *primary feed*; the other, the *secondary feed.* The functions of the collator are controlled by a wired control panel that is inserted into the control-panel housing at the start of each job. There is one control panel for each job that is run. Although a collator can perform several different functions, only two of its most useful ones—*merging* and *match-merging*—are described in this topic.

To merge two decks of cards means to bring them together in alphabetic or numeric sequence. The field on which the merging is based is

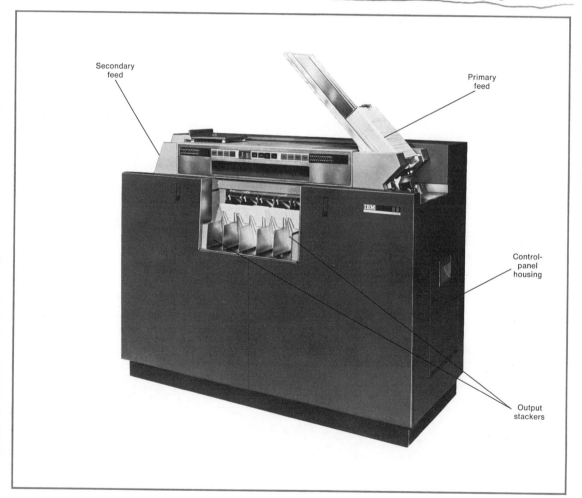

FIGURE 3-8 The collator

called the _control field_. For example, if two decks are going to be merged by customer number, the customer-number field is the control field. To illustrate merging, suppose two decks of cards are sorted into sequence by customer number. They can then be merged, using customer number as the control field, by following these steps: (1) the operator puts one of the decks into the primary hopper of the collator; (2) he puts the other deck in the secondary hopper; (3) he inserts the appropriate control panel and pushes the start button; (4) the collator reads the primary and secondary cards, merges them, and stacks the merged deck in one of the output stackers. Once started, the collator operates without further attention from the operator.

The merging process is illustrated in figure 3-9. The number on each card represents the customer number punched in the card. As you can see, when both primary and secondary cards have the same customer number, the primary card is stacked before the secondary card. For example, the primary card number 1351 comes before the three secondary cards with the same control-field number. The result is a merged deck in customer-number sequence.

A match-merging operation using the same input decks is illustrated in figure 3-10. Here, unmatched primary cards—cards that do not have secondary cards with the same customer number—are stacked in stacker 2. Unmatched secondary cards—cards with no matching primary cards—are stacked in stacker 4. The merged deck, consisting of matched primary and secondary cards, is stacked in stacker 3. In some cases, it is desirable to leave unmatched primary cards in the merged deck, and thus only the unmatched secondary cards will be stacked in a separate stacker. This, of course, depends on the control-panel wiring and the requirements of the job.

Incidentally, merging can also be done on a sorter. If two decks are to be merged by customer number, the operator puts the primary deck in the hopper of the sorter and puts the secondary deck on top of it. The machine then sorts by customer number. Because the primary cards will be stacked ahead of the secondary cards with the same control number, the merged deck will be the same as that in figure 3-9. To merge with a sorter, however, the control field for both the primary and the secondary cards must be in the same card columns—for example, columns 8–11 of both decks. In contrast, when the collator is used, the control field can be in different locations—say columns 68–71 of the primary cards and columns 12–15 of the secondary cards.

INTERPRETER

Interpreting, in data-processing terminology, means printing the data punched in a card on the card itself. Thus, the card in figure 3-2 has been interpreted by the keypunch.

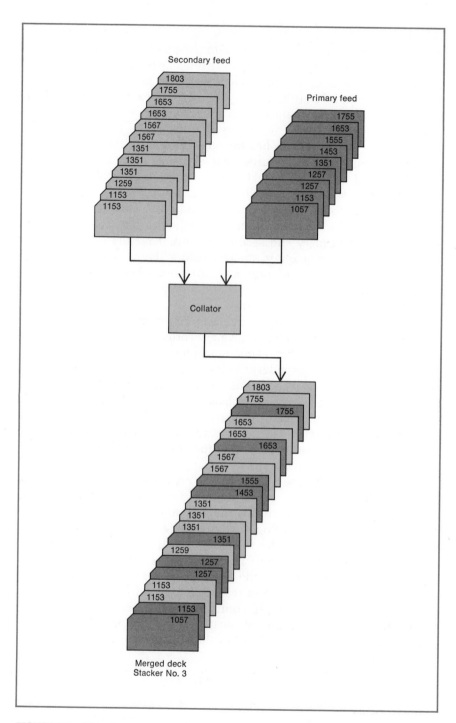

FIGURE 3-9 Merging

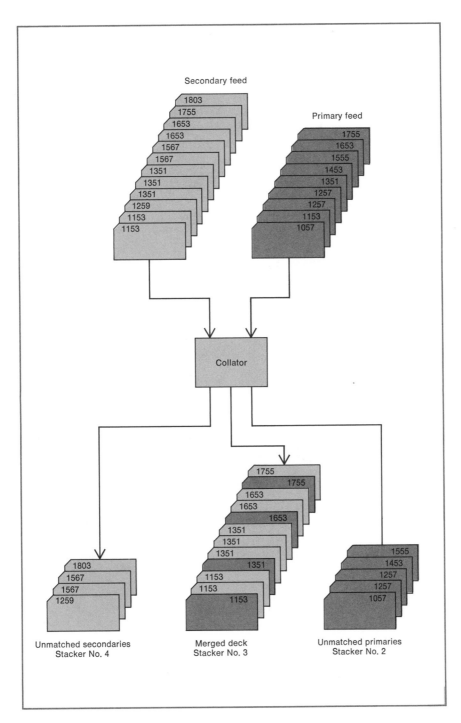

FIGURE 3-10 Match-merging

The *interpreter*, shown in figure 3-11, has one input hopper and one output stacker. As cards pass through the machine from the input hopper, the interpreter prints the punched data on the cards. The interpreter can print sixty characters per line of printing, and, depending on the model, can print from two to twenty-five lines on one side of the card. The model shown can print two lines at the top of the card.

Unlike the keypunch, the interpreter can print data anywhere on the card—it does not have to print directly over the card columns that contain the data being interpreted. Furthermore, only selected fields need be printed. The columns to be interpreted and the location of the printing

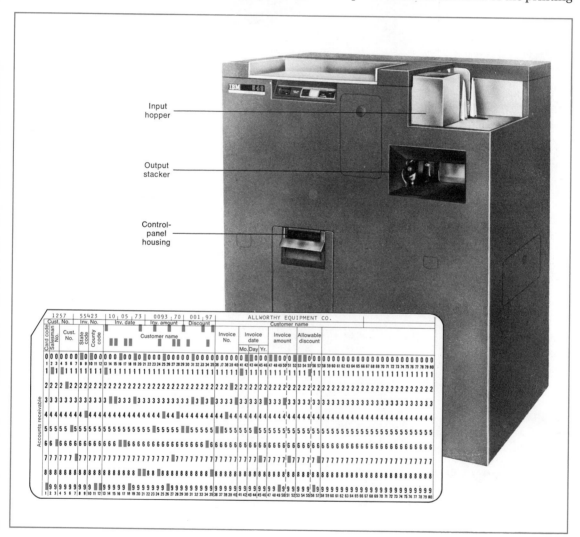

FIGURE 3-11   The interpreter

depends on the wiring of the control panel placed in the machine at the beginning of the job. As you can see on the interpreted card in figure 3-11, only customer number, customer name, invoice number, date, amount, and discount have been interpreted. And, a field such as invoice number, in columns 36–40, has been printed over columns 7–12 of the card.

SUMMARY

1. One or more punched-card machines are commonly used in conjunction with a computer system in order to process data.

2. The keypunch is used to punch data from source documents into punched cards. For each key struck by the keypunch operator, one column of data is punched.

3. The verifying operation is similar to the keypunch operation. For each key struck, one column is checked to be sure that the data it contains is the same as the data keyed. If a column has been punched incorrectly, an error notch is cut over the column; if all of the columns of a card have been punched correctly, a correct-card notch is cut.

4. The sorter is used to arrange card decks into sequences suitable for processing by a computer. Although a deck can be sorted on either an alphabetic or a numeric field, numeric sorting is much more common.

5. The collator is used to arrange two input decks into one or more output decks. Two of its common operations are merging and match-merging.

6. The interpreter is used to print punched-card data on the face of the card.

FOR REVIEW

punched-card machine
unit-record machine
punched-card system
unit-record system
keypunch
source document
verifier
correct-card notch
error notch

sorter
collator
primary feed
secondary feed
merging
match-merging
control field
interpreting
interpreter

TOPIC THREE

AN
INTRODUCTION
TO SYSTEM
DESIGN

Now that you are familiar with the punched card and some punched-card machines, you are ready to learn what takes place within a data-processing system. In this topic, a card computer system for the billing application is first illustrated, followed by a card system for sales analysis. Finally, the speed, accuracy, information, and cost of the computerized billing and sales-analysis systems are analyzed.

THE BILLING APPLICATION

Suppose that a data-processing installation is to be used for billing. For this application, the input document, as shown in figure 2-2, is the shipping order after it has been returned from the shipping department; the output document is the invoice, as illustrated in figure 2-3. The following equipment is available within the installation: two keypunches, one verifier, one sorter, one collator, and a card computer system consisting of a CPU, a card reader, a card punch, and a printer. The question is: Using the shipping order as the source document, what steps must be followed in order to print the invoices?

To describe a system such as this, a system designer commonly uses a _system flowchart_, as illustrated in figure 3-12. This flowchart symbolically represents the steps that must be followed to derive the required output documents from the available input. Although the system flowchart may look somewhat imposing at first, once familiar with it, you will find that studying a system flowchart is the easiest way to learn what is happening within a system—far easier than reading a written description.

The symbols used in the system flowcharts for card systems are summarized in figure 3-13. Thus, a trapezoid represents a manual operation; a rectangle represents a processing run on the computer. Other symbols represent documents, punched cards, punched-card files, and various functions performed on punched-card machines. The annotation symbol can be used anywhere in a flowchart for comments or explanation. While the punched-card symbol can be used to represent one card or an entire deck of cards, the symbol for the punched-card file represents a group of related cards that make up a file. For example, the file symbol would be used to represent a file of name-and-address cards, one per customer, containing name, address, city, and state. In the flowchart in figure 3-12, there are six processing steps, indicated by a number to the upper right of the symbol. Thus, the first step is keypunching, the second is verifying, and so on.

To read a system flowchart, you begin in the upper lefthand corner and follow the flowlines that connect the symbols. As you read, follow the flowlines down and to the right except when arrowheads indicate movement to the left or up. Thus, the billing flowchart begins with the shipping order and continues with the keypunch operation, item cards, verifying operation, sorting operation, and so on.

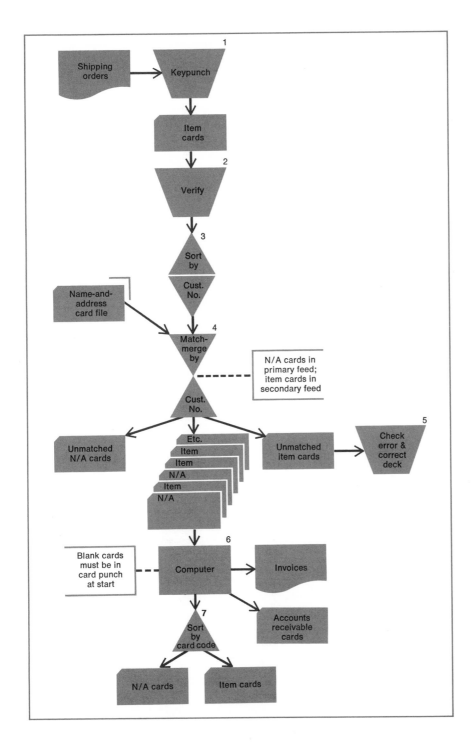

FIGURE 3-12   System flowchart for billing

SYMBOL	SYMBOL NAME	MEANING
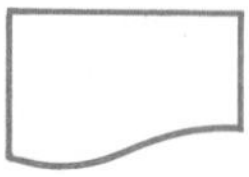	Document	One or more input or output documents
	Punched card	One or more input or output punched cards
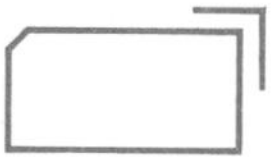	File of cards	A collection of related punched-card records
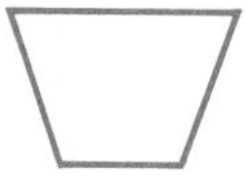	Manual operation	An operation done by a person, including keying operations such as keypunching and verifying
	Sort	Arranging a deck of cards into a particular sequence
	Merge	Combining two or more decks of cards into one
	Extract	Removing one or more types of cards from a merged deck
	Collate	Match-merging: combining two or more decks of cards into one, but also removing (extracting) selected card types — for example, unmatched secondaries — from the deck
	Auxiliary operation	An operation performed on equipment not under control of the computer; for example, interpreting
	Process	A processing step done by the computer system
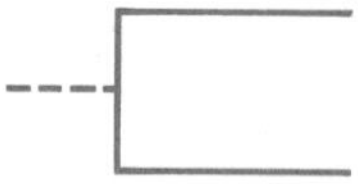	Annotation	Descriptive comments or explanatory notes

FIGURE 3-13   System flowchart symbols

Another document used by the system designer in explaining a system such as this is the *multiple-card layout form,* as illustrated in figure 3-14. This form gives the formats of the different cards used within the system. Up to six card formats can be shown on one multiple-card layout form; however, as shown in the illustration, the billing application requires only four different card types. The four cards used are called the item cards, the name-and-address (N/A) cards, the accounts receivable cards, and the date card. By studying this form, you should be able to see that the item-number field of the item card is in columns 27–31, that the customer-number field of the N/A card is in columns 4–7, that the invoice-amount field of the accounts receivable card is in columns 47–52, and that the date field of the date card is in columns 2–7.

When referring to types of cards within a system, the terms *master card* and *transaction card* are often used. In general, a master card contains semipermanent information such as a customer's name and address. In contrast, a transaction card such as the item card in figure 3-14 contains daily transaction data. A transaction card, also known as a *detail card*, may represent transactions such as sales in a billing application, hours worked in a payroll application, or amount billed in an accounts payable application. Because the accounts receivable cards in figure 3-14 represent individual amounts billed, they can be considered transaction or detail cards.

By using the system flowchart and multiple-card layout form, you should be able to determine what takes place within a system. For example, in the first step of the system illustrated in figure 3-12, item cards are keypunched using the shipping order as the source document. A typical shipping order and the resulting transaction cards are illustrated in figure 3-4. If there are 400 shipping orders with an average of five line items per order, the item-card deck will consist of 2000 cards when this step is completed.

In the second step, the item cards are verified. Although all sixty-one columns of the card could be verified, it is common to verify only numeric data and thus reduce verifying time. This is based on the theory that an error in an alphanumeric field generally isn't serious.

The third step is a sorting step. The item cards are sorted by customer number. Since customer number is in columns 4–7, the operator sorts the deck starting with column 7 and ending with column 4.

The fourth step is a match-merge operation on the collator. There are two input decks—the master file of name-and-address cards and the deck of sorted item cards. Since the name-and-address file is kept in customer-number order, the decks can be match-merged using customer number as the control field. There are three flowlines leaving the collate symbol, thus indicating three output decks. The unmatched name-and-address cards are stacked in one stacker, the unmatched item cards in another, and the merged deck in a third. The series of card images

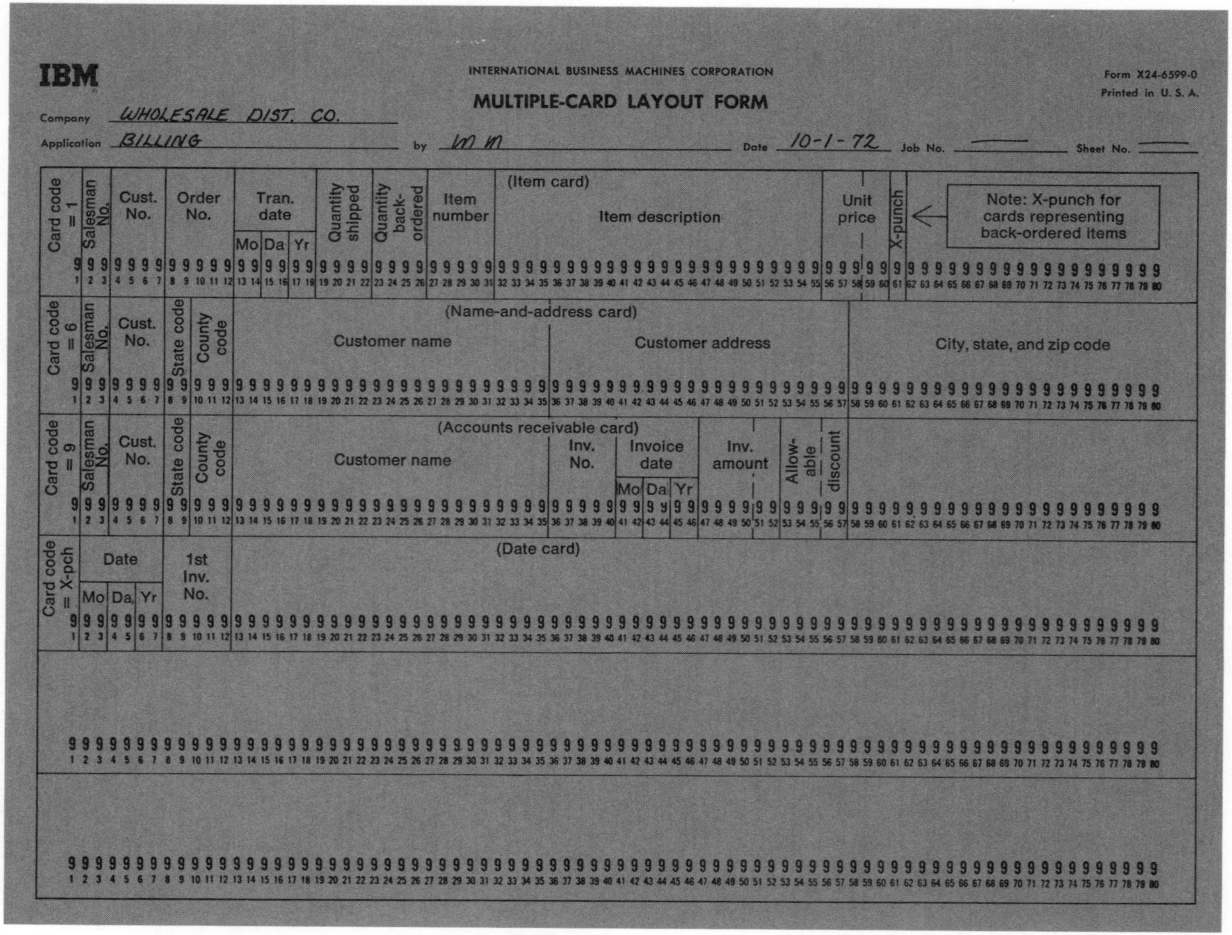

FIGURE 3-14 Card formats for billing

representing the merged deck on the flowchart shows that name-and-address cards precede item cards with the same customer number. Thus, as indicated by the explanatory note, the name-and-address cards must be in the primary feed of the collator and the item cards in the secondary feed at the beginning of the step.

Step 5 is a manual step. Because all item cards should be matched, unmatched item cards represent an error condition. Either a name-and-address card is missing or the customer number in the unmatched item card is incorrect. The operator must therefore determine the cause of the unmatched item cards and, if necessary, make adjustments to the merged deck.

At this stage, the merged deck of name-and-address and item cards is ready for processing by the computer (step 6). There is one name-and-address card for each invoice to be printed, followed by one item card for each line item on the invoice. After loading the invoicing program, the operator puts the continuous-form invoices in the printer and blank cards in the card punch. Before putting the merged deck in the card reader, he places a date card at the start of the deck. This card contains the invoicing date and the invoice number of the first invoice to be printed. Although this isn't shown on the flowchart, the use of a date card is a standard operating procedure on card systems.

When the invoicing program is executed, the invoices are printed and accounts receivable cards are punched. Because the accounts receivable cards summarize the data for one invoice, a punching procedure such as this is often referred to as summary punching. The accounts receivable cards are then held for use in an accounts receivable or sales-analysis application.

The invoicing run is illustrated schematically in figure 3-15. The cards used to prepare an invoice and the resulting invoice and accounts receivable card are shown. By analysis, you can see that the computer prints four lines from the name-and-address card—the three address lines, plus a miscellaneous line showing invoice number, invoice date, customer number, and salesman number. The customer number and salesman number are taken from the name-and-address card; the invoice number and date come from the date card read at the start of the program. The computer then skips to the body of the invoice, calculates the extensions, and prints one line item for each item card. When all item cards for a customer have been processed, the computer skips to the total line of the form, prints the accumulated invoice total, and summary-punches the accounts receivable card. After the total is printed, the form is skipped to the heading line of the next invoice.

To skip to the various parts of the invoicing form before printing, the computer uses the forms-control capability of the printer. This is accomplished on most printers by using a forms-control tape, which is a loop of paper tape punched with holes that correspond to the printing

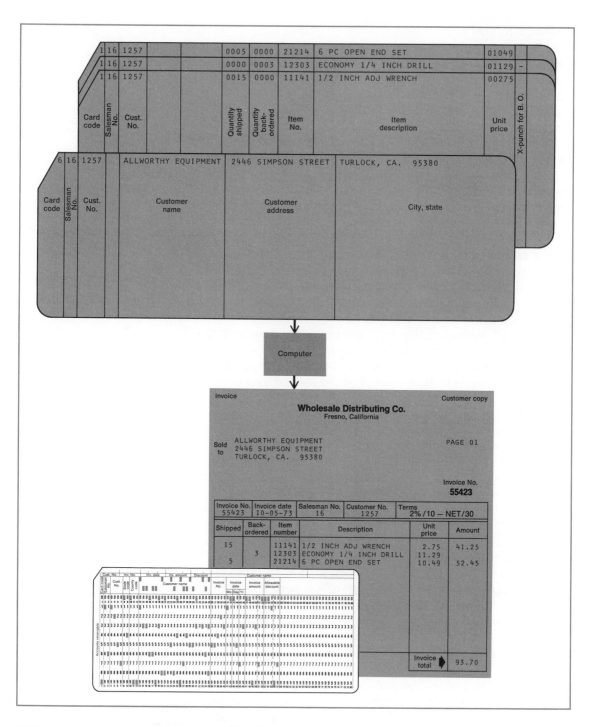

FIGURE 3-15 Schematic illustration of the billing run

lines of a form. Figure 3-16, for example, shows the forms-control tape used to print the invoices. A 1-punch in the forms-control tape corresponds to the heading line, a 2-punch corresponds to the miscellaneous line, a 3-punch to the first line item, and a 5-punch to the total line. As you can see, there are twelve punching positions in the forms-control tape, all of which can be used if necessary. Although the 1-punch is commonly used to represent the first printing line of a form, the use of forms-control punches 2 through 11 is determined by the system designer or programmer.

After the forms-control tape is planned, the required holes are punched in the tape with a hand punch. Then, the tape is cut to the length of the form and the ends are pasted together to form a loop. When this loop is placed in the forms-control mechanism of the printer, the control tape moves in conjunction with the continuous form. As a result, if the printer is instructed to skip to a 1-punch in the control tape, the continuous form is skipped to the first heading line of the invoice. If the printer skips to the 2-punch in the control tape, the continuous form is skipped to the miscellaneous line. Although it is difficult to visualize the operation of a forms-control tape when reading about it, it is quite easy to understand when you actually see it work.

The 12-punch in a forms-control tape has a special purpose. It is used to indicate where the last printing line (other than the total line) should appear on a form. As you can see in figure 3-16, the 12-punch corresponds to the line before the total line. The printer can be programmed to skip to any one of the other eleven punches whenever a 12-punch is sensed by the forms-control mechanism. In the billing run, the computer would probably be programmed to skip to the heading line of the next invoice when a 12-punch is sensed. The computer would then print the customer's name, skip to the miscellaneous line and reprint this data, and then continue with the next line item of billing. This skipping from one form to another is commonly referred to as forms overflow.

After the invoicing run on the computer, the billing application is largely completed. However, the various cards still need to be returned to their files. In step 7, therefore, the merged deck is separated using the sorter. Since the name-and-address cards have a 6-punch in column 1 while the item cards have a 1-punch, sorting on column 1 will separate the cards. All name-and-address cards will end up in pocket 6 of the sorter; all item cards will end up in pocket 1. The cards can then be returned to file or held for further processing. Although it isn't shown in figure 3-12, to restore the name-and-address file to its original form, the unmatched name-and-address cards resulting from step 4 would have to be merged with the name-and-address cards extracted in step 7.

In summary, there are generally four phases that take place within a card application such as billing. First, the cards to be used must be created (keypunching and verifying). These cards must be designed so

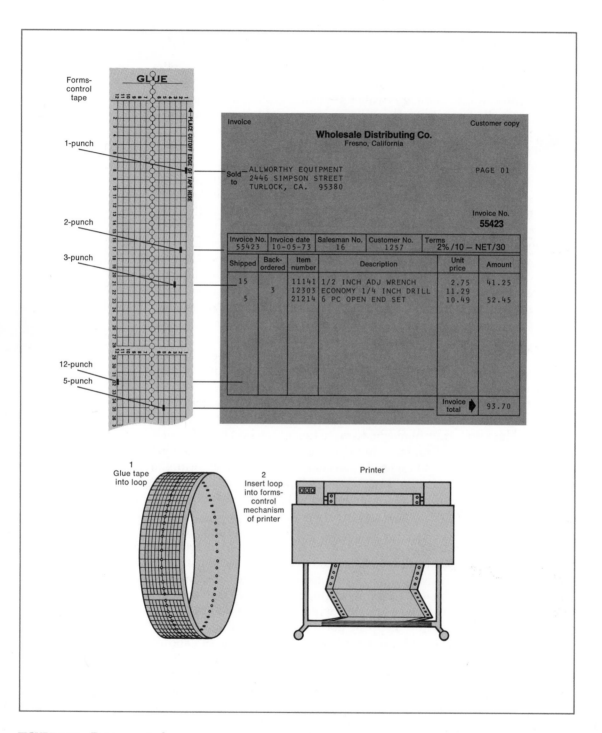

FIGURE 3-16   Forms control

that the computer can derive all of the required output data from the input data. In other words, if the date card isn't read at the start of the invoicing run, the computer can't print the invoice date and number on each invoice. By reading the date card, the computer can store the date and the first invoice number. Then, whenever an invoice is printed, one is added to the invoice number so that it is kept up to date.

Second, before processing by the computer, the card decks must be in acceptable sequences. The sorter and collator are used for this purpose. In general, the input cards must be in the same sequence as the data that is to be printed. Match-merging is valuable because it allows error conditions such as unmatched item cards to be detected before processing.

In the third phase, the computer processes the input decks. The output can be printed documents, punched cards, or both. If the application requires printing on several different parts of a form, the forms-control ability of the computer is used. You might notice that loading a program is not shown on a system flowchart. It is simply understood that before each computer run the appropriate program must be loaded.

In the last phase, the various cards used in the application are returned to their files. To separate cards in a merged deck, the sorter is used. By sorting on a column that has a distinctive punch for each type of card in the merged deck, all cards can be separated in a single pass through the sorter. Then, the collator is used to merge parts of a file back together.

THE SALES-ANALYSIS APPLICATION

Because the billing application is somewhat complicated, you may be a bit confused at this stage of your learning. A second, somewhat simpler, application may help to clarify things. Suppose, for example, that the item cards created in the billing application are used as the basis for a sales-analysis application. The item cards are accumulated until the end of the month; as shown in the flowchart in figure 3-17, they are then used to print monthly sales reports. If an average of 2000 item cards are created each day and there are twenty-two working days in the month, the monthly item-card deck will consist of 44,000 cards. By sorting this deck into various sequences, such as item-number and customer-number sequence, reports such as sales-by-item and sales-by-customer can be prepared by the computer. The card formats used in this system are given in figure 3-18.

As shown by the flowchart, two reports are prepared by this sales-analysis system. The first, called a sales-by-item report, requires two steps. First, the item cards are sorted into item-number sequence (columns 27–31). Second, as shown schematically in figure 3-19, the sorted deck is processed by the computer system. The computer cal-

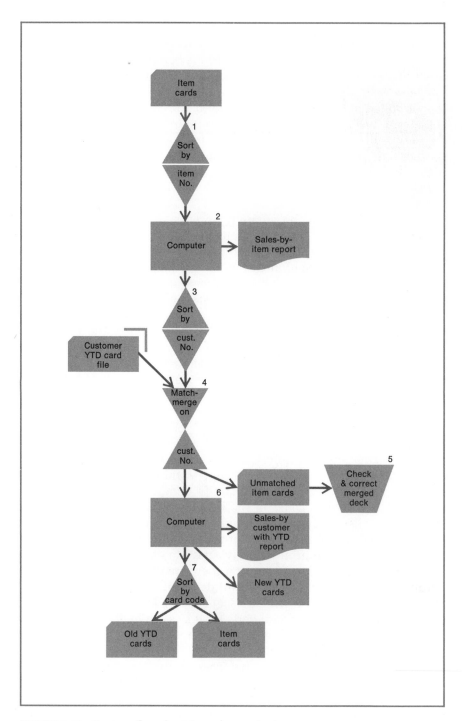

FIGURE 3-17 System flowchart for sales analysis

IBM

Company **WHOLESALE DIST. CO.**

Application **SALES ANALYSIS** by **m m** Date **10/05/72** Job No. _____ Sheet No. _____

INTERNATIONAL BUSINESS MACHINES CORPORATION

MULTIPLE-CARD LAYOUT FORM

Form X24-6599-0
Printed in U.S.A.

Card code = 1	Salesman No.	Cust. No.	Order No.	Tran. date	Quantity shipped	Quantity back-ordered	Item No.	(Item card) Item description	Unit price	X-punch	
				Mo Da Yr							

| Card code = K | Mo. No. | Cust. No. | | | Customer name | | (Customer year-to-date card) YTD sales amount | | | | |

FIGURE 3-18   Card formats for sales analysis

culates the extension for each item card, and accumulates the amounts for each item number. Whenever the item number changes, the computer prints the accumulated monthly sales, one line for each item number. At the end of the report, the computer prints the total sales for the month.

Incidentally, there are two types of reports commonly printed by a computer system. In the first type, called a _listing_ or _detail-printed report_, one line is printed for each input record. Interspersed among the detail lines, there may be summary lines giving accumulated totals for a group of records. In the second type of report, called a _group-printed report_, one line is printed for each group of cards. Since the report in figure 3-19 shows only one line for each item-number group, it is a group-printed report.

The second report prepared by the system illustrated in figure 3-17 is a sales-by-customer report with year-to-date totals. It requires four steps and two different card types. First, the item cards are sorted into customer-number sequence. Second, the year-to-date (YTD) cards are match-merged with the item cards. Third, the cause of the unmatched item cards, an error condition, is investigated and the merged deck adjusted accordingly. Fourth, as illustrated schematically in figure 3-20, the merged deck is processed by the computer. For each line printed, customer name is taken from the YTD card, sales this month is accumulated from the extensions of the item cards, and year-to-date sales is the sum of the YTD field of the YTD card plus the accumulated this-month-sales total. For each customer number, a new YTD card is summary-punched with the up-to-date yearly sales total. This card will be used to

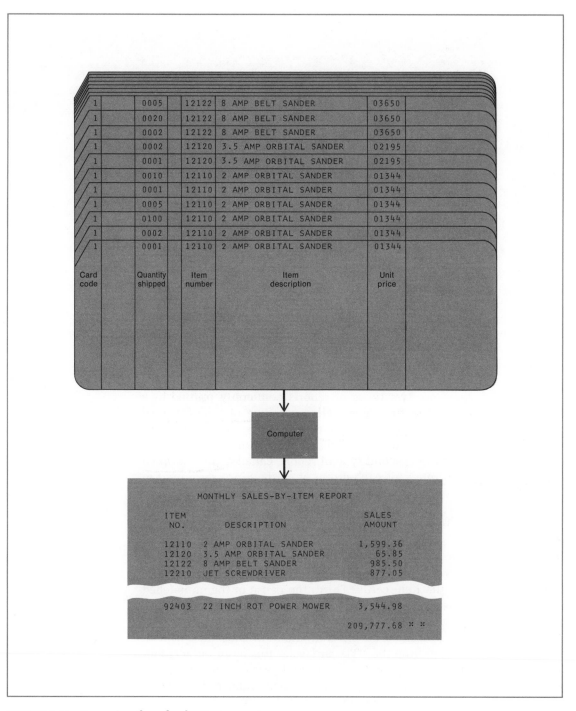

FIGURE 3-19   Preparing the sales-by-item report

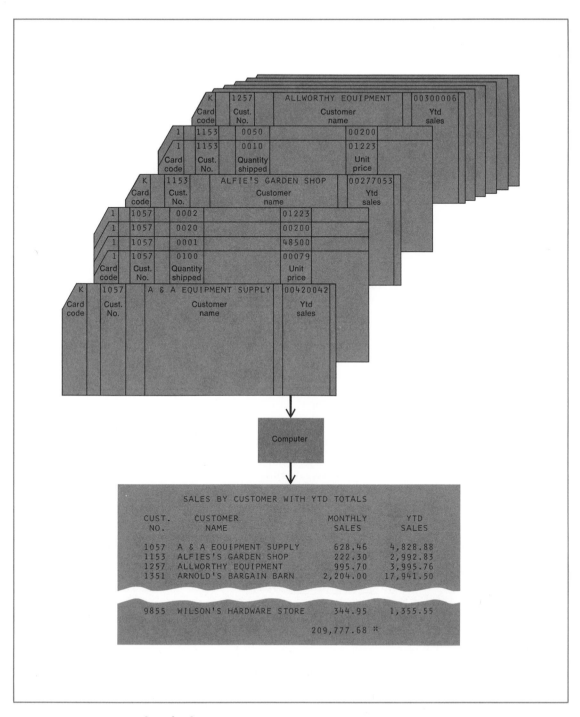

FIGURE 3-20   Preparing the sales-by-customer report

prepare next month's report. Because the sales-by-customer report shows one line for each customer group, it is a group-printed report.

After these two reports are prepared, the item and year-to-date cards can be returned to file. The cards are separated by sorting on column 1 of the cards (step 7). The old YTD cards, which have the character K in column 1, will be stacked in the 2-pocket (since K is the combination of an 11-punch and a 2-punch); the item cards will be in the 1-pocket.

You might notice that in this simple system, the report dates aren't printed. In actual practice, however, a date card would be read at the start of each program and the report dates would be printed. The headings themselves—such as the words MONTHLY SALES-BY-ITEM REPORT—are loaded into storage as part of the object program and are later printed from storage.

DISCUSSION

The billing and sales-analysis applications just described are, of course, simplified. In actual practice, billing procedures must provide for freight charges, multiple shipping addresses, sales taxes, and so on. Similarly, sales reports are likely to include much more information than shown in either figure 3-19 or 3-20. Nevertheless, these simple applications do provide a basis for considering the speed, accuracy, information, and cost of an EDP system.

Speed

To appreciate the speed of an EDP system, you must calculate the approximate times for each step within the system. To illustrate, suppose that the billing system just described prints approximately 400 invoices per day with an average of 5 line items per invoice, a total of 2000 line items of billing per day. The company has 2000 customers and 800 items in the product line. Figure 3-21, then, summarizes the times for each step in the billing and sales-analysis systems, assuming typical machine speeds for each step in the system.

In the billing system, keypunching takes about 13.5 hours. Because each item card requires 54 keystrokes (card code and transaction date do not require keystrokes because they are automatically duplicated from card to card), a total of 108,000 keystrokes are required per day. Using a rate of 8000 keystrokes per hour—a reasonable speed for a keypunch operator—a total of 13.5 hours is derived.

Similarly, verifying takes about 7.5 hours per day. This assumes only 30 keystrokes per card since item description need not be verified.

The assumed speed for the sorter is 1000 cards per minute (cpm) per column sorted; the assumed speed for the collator is 250 cpm for both the primary and secondary feeds. Thus, step 3 in the billing system takes about 8 minutes (2 minutes per column and 4 columns in the sort field). Step 4 takes 16 minutes, with 2000 name-and-address cards in the primary feed and 2000 item cards in the secondary feed. (Although a collator actually feeds cards from both hoppers at the same time when merging, calculating the time required for each hopper and adding them together is a reasonable approximation of the total time required.)

In step 6, the billing run on the computer, assume a computer system with a 500-cpm card reader, a 200-cpm card punch, and a 400-line-per-minute (lpm) printer. By calculating reading, punching, and printing times separately and adding them together, a total time of just under

		DAILY BILLING APPLICATION		
Assumptions:	2000 N/A cards in file 400 Invoices per day 2000 Line items per day			
Step	Machine	Machine/operator speed	Volume	Job time
1	Keypunch	8000 keystrokes/hr.	2000 cards 54 columns/card	13.5 hr.
2	Verifier	8000 keystrokes/hr.	2000 cards 30 columns/card	7.5 hr.
3	Sorter	1000 cpm/column	2000 cards 4-column field	8.0 min.
4	Collator	250 cpm/feed	2000 N/A cards 2000 item cards	16.0 min.
5	——	Clerical speed	Should be none	——
6	Computer	500-cpm card reader 400-lpm printer 200-cpm card punch	Read: 2400 cards Print: 3600 lines Punch: 400 cards	15.8 min.
7	Sorter	1000 cpm/column	2400 cards 1-column field	2.4 min.
		MONTHLY SALES ANALYSIS APPLICATION		
Assumptions:	44,000 Item cards at month's end 2,000 Customer YTD cards 800 Items in product line			
Step	Machine	Machine/operator speed	Volume	Job time
1	Sorter	1000 cpm/column	44,000 cards 5-column field	3.67 hr.
2	Computer	500-cpm card reader 400-lpm printer	Read: 44,000 cards Print: 800 lines	1.50 hr.
3	Sorter	1000 cpm/column	44,000 cards 4-column field	2.93 hr.
4	Collator	250 cpm/feed	2000 YTD cards 44,000 item cards	3.07 hr.
5	——	Clerical speed	Should be none	——
6	Computer	500-cpm card reader 400-lpm printer 200-cpm card punch	Read: 46,000 cards Print: 2,000 lines Punch: 2,000 cards	1.78 hr.
7	Sorter	1000 cpm/column	46,000 cards 1 column	46.00 min.

FIGURE 3-21   Timing summary

16 minutes is derived. Although modern computer systems generally overlap input, output, and processing, adding the individual times together at least gives an approximation of the maximum amount of time the run will take. (The CPU time required for the computer runs is disregarded since it is generally insignificant in comparison to input and output times.)

In the sales-analysis system, the same assumptions and similar calculations are made. Because the card volumes are considerably higher (consisting of an accumulation of item cards for an entire month), machine runs in this system take as long as several hours each.

One factor not considered in the summary of times is card handling. In a sort operation, for example, card handling may increase the total machine time by 10 percent or more. Nevertheless, the approximations shown in the summary are typical and do allow us to draw several conclusions, which apply to more advanced computer systems as well as to card systems.

The first conclusion is that converting source data into punched cards consumes a major portion of the time in any card system. In the billing application, approximately 18.5 hours of machine time is spent on keypunching and verifying, while only minutes are required to print the invoices. This disparity makes it desirable to keep the amount of keypunching required in an application as low as possible. Since tape and direct-access systems commonly use punched cards as a form of computer input, the keypunch problem applies to most systems. In chapter 11, The Keypunch Bottleneck, some alternatives to keypunching are described.

Second, it is certainly possible for a computer system to be slower than the system it replaces. For example, using the system illustrated in figure 3-12, if the previous day's shipping orders are brought to the data-processing department each morning at nine, it could easily take two days before the invoices are prepared. Assuming both of the company's keypunches are used for keypunching item cards and only one verifier is available, the approximate machine times for the billing application are as follows:

Keypunching	6.25 hours
Verifying	7.50 hours
Steps 3–7	42.2 minutes

Assuming an 8-hour working day, the invoices would not be printed until late the second day. In contrast, one operator using a billing machine—a type of calculating typewriter—can do approximately 1000 line items of billing per day. Thus, two billing machines and two operators can do the same amount of billing as the EDP system in less time.

Third, the scheduling of operations can greatly affect the speed of an application. If significant delays take place between the steps in a system—suppose several hours elapse between keypunching and verifying—it may take three or more days to prepare the bills. This is not in the least unrealistic. A recent survey of computerized billing systems in the retail industry showed billing delays of three and four weeks to be common. Considering the speed of computer runs, this can only be explained by delays between operations.

On the other hand, *overlapping operations* can reduce the time required for an application below the total of the machine times. For example, there is no reason that all of the item cards must be keypunched before verifying begins. If the shipping orders are separated into batches of twenty, verifying can begin after the first batch has been keypunched. By overlapping verifying and keypunching, it is possible that the item cards be punched and verified in an 8-hour day.

Similarly, merging and sorting operations can often be overlapped. In step 3 of the sales-analysis system, for example, if the lefthand column of the item-number field is sorted first, the item deck would be separated into ten parts: item numbers 00000–09999, item numbers 10000–19999, and so on. Then, by sorting each of the ten groups separately starting with item numbers 00000–09999, collating could begin after the first of the ten groups was sorted. By overlapping operations in this way, the total time required for steps 3 and 4 could be reduced to perhaps just over 4 hours.

The final conclusion to be drawn is that system design can have a significant effect on speed. In the billing system, for example, there is probably a more efficient way of creating the source cards than by keypunching all sixty-one columns. One alternative, for instance, is to use tub files of partially punched item cards—say column 1 and columns 27–60 are prepunched. Clerks could then pull the item cards for each order from the tub files and only columns 2–26 and column 61 for back orders would have to be keypunched. This method would cut keypunching time in half and cut verifying by ten columns per card, a reduction of one-third.

Similarly, there are a number of system alternatives in the sales-analysis system. One is to prepare the sales-by-customer report by using the accounts receivable cards for the month together with the year-to-date cards. This would cut card volumes by about one-fifth. Another alternative is to process the item cards on a weekly basis and prepare summary cards by item and by customer. These *summary cards* could then be used to prepare the monthly reports, again reducing card volumes considerably.

In summary, the speed of a computer system is somewhat relative. Because of the keypunch bottleneck, it is possible that a computerized application be slower than some other semiautomated method of processing. This is certainly true if poor operational procedures or system design techniques are used. On the other hand, once data is converted to a machine-readable form, a computer can process it at great speeds— consider summarizing 44,000 line items of data in a few hours.

Accuracy

Because of electronic checking circuitry within the components of the computer system itself, computer processing is, for all practical purposes, 100 percent accurate. However, this does not mean that the EDP system for any given application is 100 percent accurate.

The primary cause of errors in a computer system is input preparation. If the source documents themselves are inaccurate—say a shipping clerk has marked an item as back-ordered instead of shipped—the billing system illustrated in figure 3-12 will never catch the error. Similarly, it is possible that both the keypunch and verifier operators misread a slightly illegible character on the source document in the same way—say a 3 when it should have been an 8—with a resulting error in the punched card. If source documents are lost or misplaced before being keypunched or if punched cards are lost or misplaced after being keypunched, this too means inaccurate input and, thus, inaccurate output.

A second source of errors is in programming. Although all programs are tested before they are actually used, a programming error is always possible. In fact, some classic blunders have resulted from programming errors. When one state's computer sent $67,000 to welfare recipients no longer eligible for benefits, it was due to a programming error. The program failed to test correctly for the last date on which recipients were eligible for benefits.

A third source of errors involves operations. A punched-card machine operator who picks up the cards wrong during the sorting operation, a computer operator who puts the wrong data deck in the card reader—these are operational errors. In addition, because they are mechanical rather then electronic, punched-card machines malfunction once in awhile. For instance, a sorter will occasionally sort a card into the wrong pocket.

In general, operational errors are obvious and easy to catch. Since a program normally checks to be sure that the input deck is in the right sequence, an out-of-sequence card would cause the computer to print an error message and halt. The cards can then be returned to the sorter and sorted correctly. Similarly, a data deck with the wrong format usually results in gibberish being printed by the computer or in an automatic halt due to incorrect format. Input and programming errors, however, are not so easy to catch.

Fortunately, there is one technique that will help to assure the accuracy of an EDP system. It is called *balancing to controls, or control balancing.* The idea is simple: totals accumulated during computer processing runs are compared with control totals accumulated by other processing methods. To illustrate, suppose that the shipping department of a company keeps two daily control totals: (1) the number of shipments made and (2) the total number of items shipped. After the day's item cards are keypunched and verified, they are sorted into customer-number sequence and processed by the computer, which also accumulates these control totals. If the computer totals and the shipping department's totals agree, there is assurance that no source documents have been lost and that the quantity-shipped field in all item cards is correct. If they do not balance, an error is indicated and steps can be taken to correct the source data. This control procedure is shown in the flowchart in figure 3-22. After the balancing-to-controls step, the billing system can proceed as in steps 4 through 7 of figure 3-12.

To further assure the accuracy of the billing system, other control totals can be kept. For example, the item numbers and unit prices of each line item can be added prior to keypunching. If these totals — called *hash totals* since they have no particular meaning — balance with computer totals, there is assurance that the data within the item-number and unit-price fields of each item card is correct.

Control balancing is so critical to the accuracy of a system that it should be done after most computer runs. After each sales report is printed in the sales-analysis system, a grand total of the monthly sales should be balanced to a control sheet that has accumulated the monthly sales total from daily amounts. If they balance, it is reasonable to assume that the data within the body of the report is also correct. Although there are many other techniques of system design, programming, and operations that can improve the accuracy of an EDP system, control balancing is the most essential.

Information

The reports in the sales-analysis system shown in figure 3-17 are simplified. With little extra complexity, a system can prepare reports that compare last year's totals with this year's, give percentage increases and decreases, and so on. Nevertheless, this simple system illustrates that once data has been punched and verified, it can be processed to provide management information at relatively high speed with relatively high accuracy. If the monthly sales totals are balanced to controls, the sales reports should be completely accurate; and, if operations are efficiently handled, both reports should be prepared within a day or two of the month's end. In contrast, using manual methods to extract information such as this can be very slow indeed; there is also a high likelihood of error (even though control balancing should eventually detect the errors).

Information is perhaps the highlight of an EDP system. If a system is used to prepare routine documents such as invoices, accounts receivable records, and payroll checks, information is a relatively inexpensive by-product. A wide variety of reports can be prepared rapidly and accurately, and, if exception reporting is desired, the logical ability of the

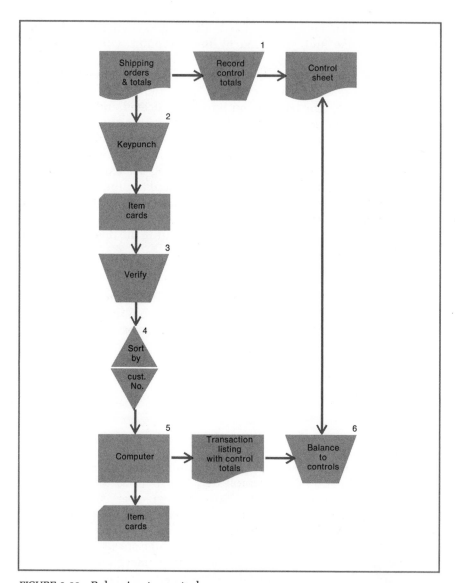

FIGURE 3-22 Balancing to controls

computer can be used to meet most requirements. As a general rule, then, a computer system is clearly superior to any other type of system when it comes to providing information.

Cost

Although the speed, accuracy, and information of a system greatly affect the profitability of a company, the primary factor on which a computer system is likely to be judged is cost (since it's the easiest to measure). For a typical card system, the monthly rental will probably be in the neighborhood of $1500 per month. In addition, however, the cost of supplies, punched-card machines, keypunch and verifier operators, punched-card equipment operators, computer operators, programmers, system designers, and the room or building that houses the computer and data-processing department must be considered. Generally, for every $1 spent for the computer, another $2 is spent for auxiliary equipment, supplies, and personnel. The total system may therefore cost between $3000 and $4500 per month.

In contrast, two billing machines and two operators can handle the same amount of billing for about $1500 to $2000 per month, including supplies, machines, and operators. This second system doesn't provide the two sales reports, but, are these reports really worth $100 or more per month?

The point being made here is that you don't use a computer system for one or two applications. In fact, you don't normally use punched cards to prepare a single document. Because of the time and cost of keypunching and verifying, there is probably another method that is faster, as accurate, and lower in cost. It is a curiosity of business, however, that data from one batch of source documents can be used to prepare documents for many different purposes and departments. Thus, the item cards prepared in the billing application can be used to print the shipping orders, to update inventory records, and to prepare additional sales reports. The accounts receivable cards can be used as the basis for an accounts receivable application and to prepare monthly statements, the aged trial balance, and other accounts receivable reports. The name-and-address cards from the billing application can be used to prepare mailing labels whenever promotional material is to be sent to a company's customers. By using the computer system for these additional applications, the cost of keypunching and verifying the source cards and the cost of the system itself is spread over several applications. Then, the cost of a computer system compares favorably with any other processing method.

Conclusion

I hope by now one message is clear: A computer system by itself is neither good nor bad. Some of the classic blunders in installing systems have perhaps originated with the notion that a computer can cure a company's data-processing problems. However, without efficient system design, adequate programming, and well-managed operations, a computer system can represent a lot of wasted potential. In fact, one study of computer operations indicates that two out of three computer installations aren't making money on their computer investment. Another study says: "From a profit standpoint, computer efforts in all but a few exceptional companies are in real, if often unacknowledged, trouble."

On the other hand, if properly selected, designed, installed, and operated, the computer system can improve all aspects of a company's data-processing operations—speed, accuracy, information, and cost.

SUMMARY

1. The system flowchart and the card layout form are two of the system designer's tools. The card layout form gives the format of the various card types within an application. The system flowchart is a method of symbolically illustrating what takes place within a system.

2. Forms control refers to the capability of a printer to skip to predetermined lines of an output form. This is accomplished on most printers by using a forms-control tape, which is punched, pasted into a loop, and inserted into the printer.

3. Four phases commonly take place within a card system: (1) the source data is recorded in punched cards; (2) the punched cards are arranged into sequences acceptable by the computer; (3) the computer reads the input cards, processes them, and gives output; and (4) the cards are returned to their various files.

4. Primarily because of the input bottleneck, there can be considerable delays in the processing done by a computer system. Two factors that can significantly affect the speed of a system are (1) overlapping operations and (2) system design.

5. Errors can occur in an EDP system because of input, operational, or programming problems. One technique that assures the accuracy of a system is called balancing to controls.

6. One of the more important aspects of an EDP system is likely to be information that is current and complete while pinpointing exceptional conditions.

7. Because the cost of an EDP system will probably be high in comparison to alternative processing methods, an EDP system must be used for several applications, thus reducing the cost per document prepared.

**FOR
REVIEW**

system flowchart
multiple-card layout form
master card
transaction card
detail card
summary punching
forms control
forms-control tape
forms overflow

listing
detail-printed report
group-printed report
overlapping operations
summary cards
balancing to controls
control balancing
hash total

CHAPTER FOUR

This chapter is divided into three topics. The first is intended to give you an understanding of what a computer program is and what it can do. The second topic presents several programming languages that can be used to create programs, while the third topic describes the activities of a programmer.

One of the questions most baffling to the computer novice is: What exactly can a computer do? To understand this, though, you must understand the nature of a stored program. This topic is designed to give that conceptual understanding.

STORAGE

When a program is loaded into a computer, it is placed in the storage of the CPU. That's why a computer program is often referred to as a stored program. That's also why the length and complexity of a program depend to a certain extent on the storage capacity of a computer. Small computers may have only a limited amount of storage — say 4000 storage positions — while some of the largest computers have over 1 million storage positions. Because the word kilo indicates 1000, K is often used to refer to 1000 storage positions: a 16K computer has approximately 16,000 storage positions. (I say approximately because one K is actually 1024 storage positions, so 16K is 16,384 storage positions. In normal conversation, however, the excess storage positions are dropped.)

Associated with each of the storage positions of a computer is a num-

PROGRAMMING CONCEPTS

ber that identifies it, called the _address_ of the storage position. A computer with 8000 storage positions, for instance, has addresses ranging from 0000 to 7999. You can therefore talk about the contents of the storage position with address 0180 or the contents of storage position 482.

In a typical computer, data can be stored in two or more different forms. To keep this explanation simple, however, let's consider only the form in which one character is stored in each storage position. To illustrate, suppose the following boxes represent the twenty storage positions from 0480 to 0499:

Contents: | G | E | O | R | G | E | 3 | 4 | 3 | 9 | 9 | 8 | 2 | | * | 1 | 1 | 2 | 1 | 4 |

Addresses: 48_0 48_5 49_0 49_5

You can then say that storage position 480 contains the letter G, storage position 487 contains the number 4, position 494 contains an asterisk, and position 493 contains a blank. Or you can say that there is a 2 at address 497 and the number 343 is stored in positions 486 through 488. This is simply the way data-processing people talk about storage and its contents.

Of course, a storage position of a computer isn't really a small box with a character of data in it. Instead, each storage position of most computers consists of a number of tiny doughnut-shaped components called _magnetic cores_. These cores can be turned "on" or "off" by wires running through their centers. Thus, a string of cores can be used to represent a character of data by using a different combination of "on" and "off" cores for each character. On the IBM System/360, for example, each storage position is made up of a string of eight cores. In figure 4-1, which represents twenty-four cores making up three storage positions, the codes for the characters B29 are shown (the colored cores are on; the white ones are off). Other eight-core combinations are used to represent the other letters, numbers, and special characters. Because the storage of most computers is made up of magnetic cores, you will often hear storage referred to as _core storage_.

Although the number of cores at each storage position and the codes used vary from one type of computer to another, the idea of using off-on combinations to represent data is used by all computers. Chapter 12, CPU Concepts, describes some of the codes used in storing data, as well as some of the other forms of data representation. In System/360, for example, there are four different forms in which numeric data can be stored, three of which are described in chapter 12.

INSTRUCTIONS

While a program is being executed, both the instructions of the program and the data being processed are contained in storage. The instruc-

FIGURE 4-1   Core storage

tions, in coded form, indicate the operations to be performed and give
the addresses of the storage positions that hold the data to be operated
upon. The number of storage positions required to store an instruction
varies from computer to computer and from instruction to instruction.
In System/360, instructions are two, four, or six storage positions in
length, depending on the function of the instruction.

Although a program may consist of thousands of instructions, there
are basically only four types of instructions that a computer can execute,
plus some miscellaneous instructions. As a result, a program with
6000 instructions consists of the same types of instructions being executed over and over again. These basic types are (1) input and output
(I/O), (2) data-movement, (3) arithmetic, and (4) logic instructions.

I/O Instructions

An I/O instruction specifies the type of input or output operation to be performed and the storage positions to be used in performing the operation. For example, an input instruction such as the card read instruction might specify that a card is to be read and its data is to be stored in the eighty storage positions beginning with address 501. In this case, storage positions 501–580 (read as 501 through 580) are called the *card input area*, or just the *input area*, of storage. When the read instruction is executed, the data that is read from a card replaces the data that the card input area originally contained. The data from card column 1 is stored in storage position 501, the data from card column 2 is stored in storage position 502, and so on, until the data from card column 80 is stored in storage position 580.

Similarly, an output instruction such as the print instruction specifies the storage positions from which the output line is to be printed (called the *printer output area*, or just *output area*, of storage). If a print instruction specifies that a line should be printed from locations 601–700, the contents of storage position 601 is printed in print position 1 on the printer (the far left of the form), the contents of storage position 602 is printed in print position 2, and so on. Since a typical printer may have up to 144 print positions between the left and right margins, the printer output area may require up to 144 storage positions.

Depending on the computer, the print instruction may also contain a code for spacing or skipping the continuous form. For example, one print instruction may indicate one space after printing; another print instruction may indicate a skip to a 5-punch in the forms-control tape after printing; a third may indicate two spaces after printing. On some computers, spacing and skipping may be controlled by I/O instructions separate from the print instruction.

Other I/O instructions enable a computer to make use of the other I/O capabilities of the system. For example, a read instruction for the card reader may cause a card to be stacked in an alternative output stacker. Instructions for card punches can cause cards to be punched from output areas, while instructions for tape units can cause tape records to be read into input areas or written from output areas.

Data-Movement Instructions

Data-movement instructions allow a computer to move data from one group of storage positions (called a *storage field*) to another group of storage positions. The basic data-movement instruction, commonly called the move instruction, causes the data from one field to be moved unchanged to another field. If, for example, a move instruction specifies that the contents of storage positions 541–545 should be moved to storage positions 701–705, the execution of the instruction can be shown as follows:

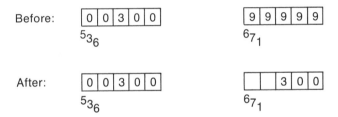

The effect is that the data in the first field is duplicated in the second field.

Another basic move instruction is the move with zero suppression. This is like a move instruction except that the insignificant zeros are changed to blanks. (Insignificant zeros are those to the left of a number, such as the italicized zeros in 00140.) If the contents of positions 536–540 are moved with zero suppression to positions 671–675, the execution takes place as follows:

Before:

0	0	3	0	0

536

9	9	9	9	9

671

After:

0	0	3	0	0

536

		3	0	0

671

The main purpose of this instruction is to move data into a printer output area in a form that will be more readable when printed. For instance, it is easier to read 300 than 00300.

Other data-movement instructions may further refine data for printing or convert data from one storage form to another. When a computer uses several different forms of data representation, a significant portion of a program may consist of data-conversion instructions.

Arithmetic Instructions

In general, there are two different ways in which arithmetic instructions operate within a computer. In one, the instruction specifies the arithmetic operations and the two fields to be operated upon. The result of the arithmetic operation replaces the second field specified, while the first field remains unchanged. This type of instruction is illustrated here.

Typical arithmetic instructions are the add, subtract, multiply, and divide instructions. To illustrate the add, suppose the contents of storage positions 546–550 are to be added to the contents of storage positions 701–705. Then, the execution takes place as follows:

Before:

0	0	0	7	5

54_6

0	0	1	5	0

70_1

After:

0	0	0	7	5

54_6

0	0	2	2	5

70_1

In actuality, another form of data representation is normally used for data involved in arithmetic operations, but conceptually, this is what happens.

Because the result of a multiplication or addition may be larger than either field operated upon—555 plus 500 equals 1055—the second field is usually moved to a larger field before the calculation takes place. Similarly, because the result of a division has a remainder, the number that is divided must be placed in a larger field, part of which becomes the quotient and part of which becomes the remainder.

Logic Instructions

The basic logic instruction and the basis of logic in the computer is the branch instruction. When a program is initially loaded into storage, the object deck specifies in which storage positions the instructions are to be stored and at which storage position the computer is to begin executing the program. When the computer finishes executing one instruction, it continues with the next instruction in storage. After executing the instruction in positions 1000–1005, for example, the computer executes the instruction starting with address 1006. The only exception to this sequence results from the use of the branch instruction. When the branch instruction is executed, it can cause the computer to break the sequence and jump to the instruction beginning at the address specified in the branch instruction.

For instance, one type of branch instruction tells the computer to branch whenever it is executed. This is called an *unconditional branch*. Suppose then that an unconditional branch instruction, stored in positions 4032–4035, specifies a branch to address 801. When it is executed, the computer will continue with the instruction starting in storage position 801.

Conditional branch instructions cause branching only when specified conditions are met. For example, one type of conditional branch instruction specifies a branch if the result of an arithmetic instruction is negative. Suppose this instruction occupies storage positions 2044–2047 and specifies that the computer should branch to address 1000 if the result of the preceding arithmetic instruction is negative. If the result is zero or positive, the computer continues with the instruction starting at address 2048, the next instruction in storage. If the result is negative, however, the computer branches to and executes the instruction starting at address 1000.

Other branch instructions specify that a branch should take place when the result of an arithmetic calculation is zero, when the result of an arithmetic calculation is larger than the result field, or when an I/O device isn't working. Perhaps the most used branch instruction, however, specifies a branch based on the results of a comparison between two fields in storage. This branch instruction is used in conjunction with the other type of logic instruction, the compare instruction.

The compare instruction specifies that two fields are to be compared. When it is executed, the computer determines the relationship between the two fields: Are they equal? Is the first field greater in value than the second? Is the first field less than the second? The branch instruction then specifies a branch based on any of these three conditions. If, for example, the compare instruction compares two fields representing ages, the branch instruction can specify a branch if the first age is less than the second.

A compare instruction can operate on alphanumeric as well as numeric fields. For example, if two fields containing alphabetic names are compared, the branch instruction can specify a branch when the second name is higher in alphabetic sequence than the first name. Or, if a one-position alphanumeric code is compared with a storage position containing the code M, the branch instruction can specify a branch when the codes are equal.

Miscellaneous Instructions

Besides these four types of instructions, a computer may have a number of miscellaneous instructions. Perhaps the most important of these is the halt instruction, which, when executed, causes the computer to stop. It can be used to stop the computer at the end of a program or when a processing error is detected.

PROGRAM EXECUTION

Are these four types of instructions more limited than you expected? Although individually their functions may seem limited, in combination they are capable of instructing a computer to do complex arithmetic and logic operations. To appreciate this, consider a simple program that allows a computer to do the work of an inventory-control clerk.

One of the jobs of an inventory-control clerk is to determine which items of inventory should be reordered. The clerk usually does this by going through the inventory records and making a list of those items that have less on-hand stock than has previously been determined to be necessary (the reorder point). For example, if the inventory manager has determined that the reorder point for drive shafts is 300, the clerk will list drive shafts if the on-hand balance is less than 300. Of course, if additional stock has already been ordered, he will list drive shafts only if the amount on order plus the on-hand balance is less than the reorder point. If the on-hand stock is 200 but 300 are on order, drive shafts need not be reordered.

The computer can perform this same job if the status of the inventory items is punched into cards such as the balance card in figure 4-2. In this case, the balance cards, one for each inventory item, are the input to an inventory-control program. The output of the program is a listing of the items to be reordered. The logic of the program is simply this: if on hand plus on order is less than the reorder point, list the item.

Figure 4-3 schematically represents the operation of the reorder-listing program on five input cards. The data printed at the top of the five cards represents the data punched in the fields of the cards. As you can see, of the five items represented by the input cards, only drive shafts and generators need to be reordered. Therefore, only two lines are printed on the inventory report.

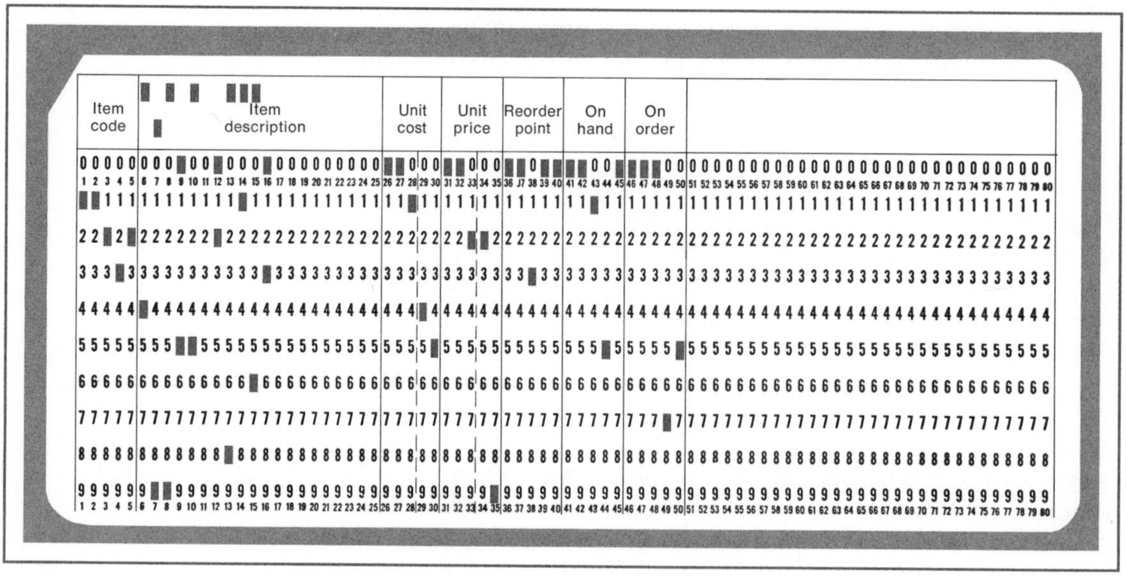

FIGURE 4-2   An inventory balance card

The steps that must be followed in the reorder-listing program can be symbolically represented by a *program flowchart* as shown in figure 4-4. In this flowchart, the following symbols are used:

Symbol	Name	Meaning
	Terminal	Start or end of a sequence of operations
	Input/output	I/O operation
	Process	Any kind of processing function
	Decision	A logical or branching operation

The reorder-listing program therefore follows these steps:

Step 1: Read a card.

Step 2: Add on hand to on order, deriving available.

Step 3: If available is not less than the reorder point, branch to the first instruction.

Step 4: If available is less than the reorder point, move the appropriate data to the output area of storage and print a line.

Step 5: Branch to the first instruction.

By "looping" back to the first instruction whenever a card has been processed, the program will continue to process cards until there are no more cards in the input deck.

The actual program used to accomplish this processing would require a sequence of instructions something like those in figure 4-5. Here, the instructions are loaded into storage positions 801–878, the card input area is in positions 501–580, the printer output area is in positions 601–700, and positions 701–705 are used for the field named "available." Although the instructions are written in long form in the illustration, remember that when they are loaded into the computer they are in a short, coded machine language, requiring but a few storage positions per instruction.

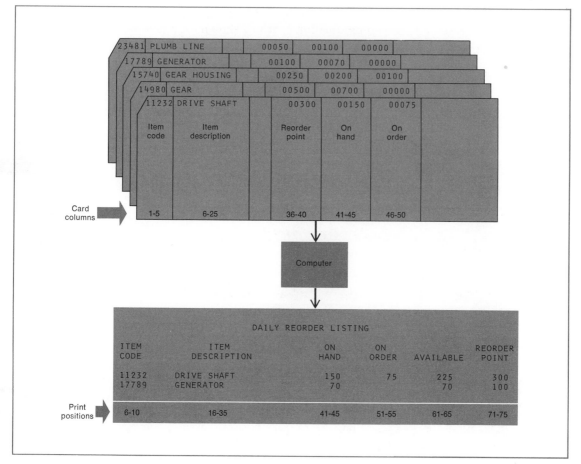

FIGURE 4-3   Schematic of the reorder-listing program

By going through the instructions of the program in figure 4-5 and using the data of the first two input cards shown in figure 4-3, you will begin to appreciate the nature of the stored program. You will see how the compare instruction is used to determine whether "available" is less than the reorder point and how the branch instructions alter processing based on this comparison. If a reorder line is supposed to be printed, the program moves the output data fields into the printer output area, with the arrangement of data in the output area corresponding to the arrangement of data in the output line. After a line is printed, the program branches unconditionally to the start of the program. You can use figure 4-6 as a check on your understanding of the program; it represents storage positions 501–709 after the first fourteen instructions of the program have been executed.

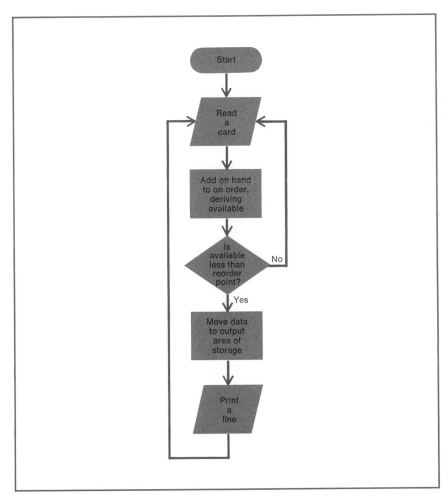

FIGURE 4-4   Program flowchart for the reorder-listing program

PRINTING HEADINGS AND THE LAST-CARD TEST

Although this program gives the essential steps of a reorder-listing program, it is simplified. In actual practice, a program such as this would print headings at the top of the report before reading any of the input cards. A routine for testing whether the last card has been read would also be included. When the last card is read, a program branches to instructions that perhaps print a message such as END OF JOB on the printer; the program then halts the computer.

To print headings, the heading data is loaded into storage along with the instructions of the program. Thus, a program usually consists of data, called *constants*, as well as instructions. (Constants are simply

Instruction number	Instruction location	Instruction
1	801—806	Read card into 501—580.
2	807—812	Move 541—545 to 701—705.
3	813—818	Add 546—550 to 701—705.
4	819—824	Compare 701—705 with 536—540.
5	825—828	Branch to 801 if 701—705 is greater than 536—540.
6	829—832	Branch to 801 if 701—705 is equal to 536—540.
7	833—838	Move 501—505 to 606—610.
8	839—844	Move 506—525 to 616—635.
9	845—850	Move and zero-suppress 541—545 to 641—645.
10	851—856	Move and zero-suppress 546—550 to 651—655.
11	857—862	Move and zero-suppress 701—705 to 661—665.
12	863—868	Move and zero-suppress 536—540 to 671—675.
13	869—874	Print 601—700, space one line after.
14	875—878	Branch to 801.

FIGURE 4-5   Machine language for the reorder-listing program

data fields that normally do not change during the execution of a program.) For example, if the heading DAILY REORDER LISTING is to be printed, the words DAILY, REORDER, and LISTING are constants that are loaded into storage along with the instructions. At the start of the program, then, the instructions move the constants into the printer output area and print the heading line.

Although there are several ways to determine when the last card in an input deck has been read, one is to check for a card containing /* in columns 1 and 2 (slash in column 1, asterisk in column 2). When a /* card is read, there are no more cards to be processed. The program can then branch to a sequence of instructions that perform any final processing functions before halting the program.

The flowchart in figure 4-7 represents the basic reorder-listing program with a few refinements. In the first step, blanks are moved to the printer output area. This is a typical procedure performed at the start of a program to insure that no data from a previous program occupies the storage positions used for the output area. If the output area did contain foreign data, it would print when the print instruction is executed.

The second, third, and fourth blocks of the flowchart represent the printing of one heading line. First, the heading data is moved to the output area; then, it is printed; finally, blanks are once again moved to

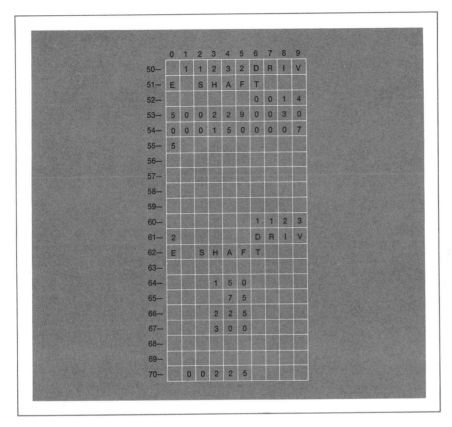

FIGURE 4-6   Storage grid for the reorder-listing program

the output area. This clears the area so that heading data will not be printed in any of the other lines of the report.

The last-card test and the associated processing is shown in blocks 6, 11, 12, and 13. After a card is read, a test is made to see if columns 1 and 2 contain /*. If so, blanks are moved to the output area to clear it, the constant END OF JOB is moved to the output area, the final line is printed, and the program is halted. If the card doesn't contain /*, the program processes the balance card as usual.

Figure 4-8 represents the instructions for the refined reorder-listing program. Here, the instructions are loaded into storage positions 801–932, and constants are loaded into positions 933–1065. For example, a constant consisting of 100 blanks is loaded into storage positions 933–1032, and a constant consisting of /* is loaded into storage positions 1054 and 1055. (Remember that in data-processing terminology the blank is considered to be a character.) By going through this program, you will have a better idea of how constants are used.

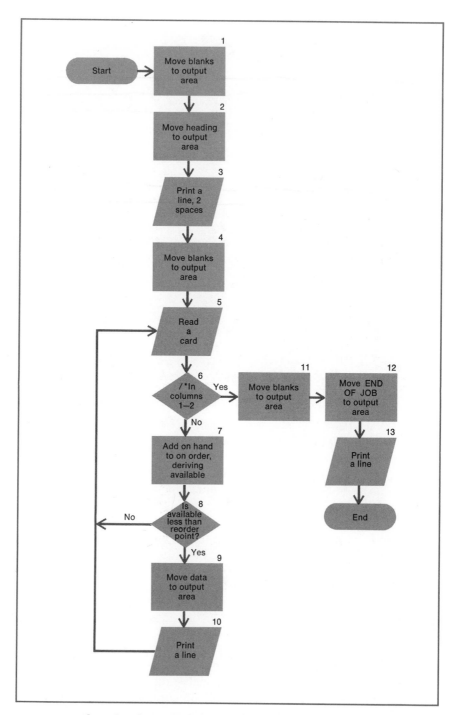

FIGURE 4-7 The refined reorder-listing program

Instruction number	Instruction location	Instruction or constant
1	801—806	Move 933—1032 to 601—700.
2	807—812	Move 1033—1053 to 630—650.
3	813—818	Print 601—700, space two lines after.
4	819—824	Move 933—1032 to 601—700.
5	825—830	Read card into 501—580.
6	831—836	Compare 1054—1055 with 501—502.
7	837—840	Branch to 913 if 501—502 is equal to 1054—1055.
8	841—846	Move 541—545 to 701—705.
9	847—852	Add 546—550 to 701—705.
10	853—858	Compare 701—705 with 536—540.
11	859—862	Branch to 825 if 701—705 is greater than 536—540.
12	863—866	Branch to 825 if 701—705 is equal to 536—540.
13	867—872	Move 501—505 to 606—610.
14	873—878	Move 506—525 to 616—635.
15	879—884	Move and zero-suppress 541—545 to 641—645.
16	885—890	Move and zero-suppress 546—550 to 651—655.
17	891—896	Move and zero-suppress 701—705 to 661—665.
18	897—902	Move and zero-suppress 536—540 to 671—675.
19	903—908	Print 601—700, space one line after.
20	909—912	Branch to 825.
21	913—918	Move 933—1032 to 601—700.
22	919—924	Move 1056—1065 to 601—610.
23	925—930	Print 601—700, space one line after.
24	931—932	Halt.
Constant	933—1032	A constant consisting of 100 blanks.
Constant	1033—1053	The constant: DAILY REORDER LISTING
Constant	1054—1055	The constant: /*
Constant	1056—1065	The constant: END OF JOB

FIGURE 4-8   Instructions for the refined reorder-listing program

DISCUSSION

One purpose in presenting all of this is to establish once and for all that a computer is a machine. It processes data by executing a sequence of precisely coded instructions. If one minute detail of one instruction is not correct, the instruction—and therefore the program—will not perform as intended. As for the much-talked-about logic ability of the computer, it is simply the ability to branch from one sequence of instructions to another. This is accomplished by a branch instruction or by the combination of a compare and a branch instruction.

Although this has been a simplified explanation of how the instructions of a computer operate, it is a good analogy of the actual operation of a computer. There are two concepts that you should now understand. The first concerns input/output areas in storage. Quite simply, when an input record is read from a card reader, tape drive, or direct-access device, it is read into an input area. Similarly, before a record is written out on a printer, tape, or direct-access device, it must be arranged properly in the output area for that device. Although this is a simple idea, it is referenced in other chapters in this book and has application in several different programming languages.

The second concept is that a program flowchart can quite adequately represent the instructions of a program. The I/O symbol represents I/O instructions, the decision symbol represents logic instructions, and the process symbol represents data-movement and arithmetic instructions. Because a flowchart is much easier to follow than a sequence of written instructions, program flowcharts will be used from this point on to represent the sequence of processing within a program.

With this introduction as background, you can now reflect upon two types of computer programs. The first type performs the same sequence of operations for each input record or set of input records. The reorder-listing program, for example, will process as many balance cards as the input deck contains and will list all the items that should be reordered. Because a program like this can be used over and over again, several times a day if necessary, it relieves man of many routine and monotonous duties.

The second type of program repeatedly performs a series of calculations in an effort to derive an answer to a problem or to derive a result that is a reasonably close approximation to an answer. To illustrate this type of program, consider a somewhat trivial problem. In 1627, Manhattan Island was purchased from the Indians for $24. If the Indians had put the $24 in a savings account at 4½ percent interest compounded annually, how much would they have in their savings account today?

The flowchart in figure 4-9 represents a program that could be used for solving this problem. Briefly, the interest is calculated each year and added to the principal; then 1 is added to the year field, which started at 1627. This sequence of instructions is repeated until the year field is equal to the present year. Then, the total in the principal field is printed.

Although the method of solving this problem is simple, it would take a human many hours to perform the series of calculations, even with a calculator. If you don't think so, consider that in 1973 the answer is $98,752,090.11. When this program is executed by a computer, however, the result is calculated in a matter of seconds.

This type of program illustrates how the computer can extend the capabilities of man. No longer does he have to actually solve a problem. With the computer, he needs only to conceive the series of steps that will

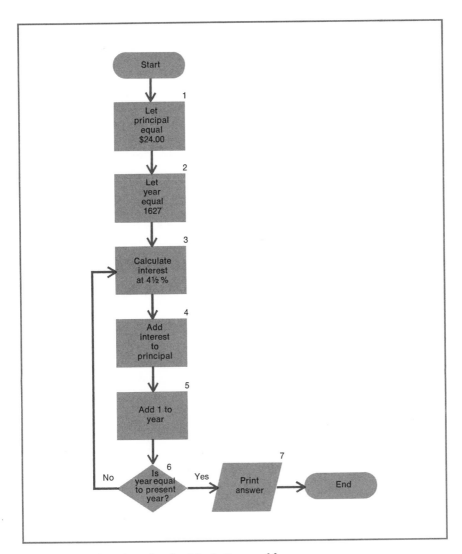

FIGURE 4-9   Flowchart for the Manhattan problem

lead to a solution. Because the computer's electronic circuits operate several million times faster than human nerve cells. the computer can perform in minutes calculations that would take man a lifetime to perform. It is in this respect that the computer has been credited with solving problems that were considered unsolvable. It is also in this respect that the computer has been advertised as capable of doing the work of 100,000 mathematicians.

Although there are many variations of these two types of programs— the two techniques are often used within the same program—they do typify the power of the computer. On the one hand, the computer can relieve man of the tedious aspects of his occupation; on the other hand, the computer can extend man's problem-solving capabilities.

SUMMARY

1. The storage of a computer is made up of a number of storage positions—usually 4000 (4K) or more—each having a unique storage address. In one common form of data representation, one character is stored in each storage position. However, there are several other storage forms, which are described later in this book.

2. In general, there are four types of instructions that can be executed by a computer: I/O, data movement, arithmetic, and logic. Though these may seem limited, they are capable of directing extensive processing sequences when they are combined in a program.

3. Input areas are areas in storage into which data records are read. Output areas are areas from which output records are written.

4. The program flowchart is a means of symbolically representing the operation of a program.

5. The power of a computer becomes evident when you consider the two types of programs it performs. In the first, the same sequence of instructions is repeated for many different sets of input data. In the second, generally involving mathematical procedures, a sequence of instructions is repeated many times for a single set of input data.

FOR REVIEW

storage position
K
storage address
core storage
card input area
input area
printer output area
output area
storage field
zero suppression
unconditional branch
conditional branch
program flowchart
constant

There are many different languages in which a programmer can write a program. On the lowest level, a programmer can code instructions and constants using the same codes and addresses that are used by the computer. That is, he can write a program in <u>machine language.</u> These machine-language instructions and constants can then be keypunched into an object deck that can be loaded and executed by the computer.

In actual practice, however, nobody writes a program in machine language because it is an extremely tedious job. The machine-language programmer would have to know the machine codes for all of the instructions that can be executed by a computer (often over 100) and would have to keep track of the actual machine addresses used for all storage fields of the program. In addition, he would need detailed knowledge of what takes place when each type of instruction is executed. To compound the difficulty, the codes and addresses of machine language usually are not represented by our regular alphabet and decimal number system. Instead, some other system of representation, such as the hexadecimal number system, is used. As a result, a simple System/360 instruction that moves data from one storage field to another might be written as

D204F080F068

Because of the difficulties in using machine language, various programming languages were developed. The first of these was a symbolic language called *assembler language*. By using easily remembered symbols for instruction codes and storage addresses, the programmer was relieved of much of the detail required by machine language. For example, a move instruction in System/360 assembler language might be

MVC FIELD2,FIELD1

Here, MVC stands for Move Characters, FIELD2 is the symbolic name for the receiving field, and FIELD1 is the symbolic name of the field being moved.

After a programmer has completed an assembler-language program, the symbolic code must be converted to the machine language of an object program. This is done by the computer itself under control of a translator program called an <u>assembler.</u>

The translation process, called an *assembly*, is illustrated in figure 4-10. It takes place in three steps:

1. The assembler-language program is keypunched into a deck of cards, one card per coding line. The resulting card deck is called the <u>source deck</u>.

2. The translator program, the assembler, is loaded into the computer from cards, tape, or a direct-access device. (In figure 4-10, an assembler stored on magnetic tape is indicated.)

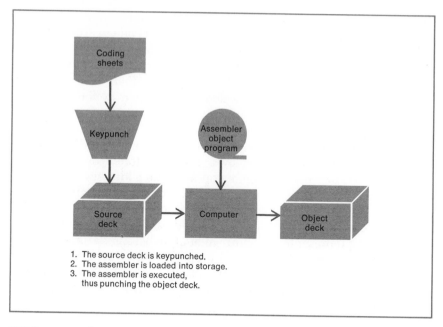

FIGURE 4-10   The assembly

3. The computer executes the assembler, thus processing the source deck and punching an object deck. This newly created object deck can be loaded into the computer and executed.

Traditionally, the distinguishing feature of an assembler language has been that one machine-language instruction is assembled for each symbolic instruction. As assembler languages developed, however, macro instructions were added. When a macro instruction is executed, more than one machine-language instruction is assembled. In fact, in some cases, dozens of machine-language instructions are assembled from a single macro instruction. This means less coding for the programmer. Nevertheless, an assembler language is still primarily translated on a one-for-one basis: one machine-language instruction for each symbolic instruction.

Although an assembler language, in comparison to machine language, greatly reduces the time required for preparing programs, it has limitations. Perhaps most limiting is the fact that an assembler-language programmer still must write detailed instructions that correspond to the instructions of the computer itself. Thus, he still must have detailed knowledge of the way a computer's instructions are executed. How much better it would be if a programmer could write a program in terms of the type of problem he is trying to solve!

In contrast to assembler language, which is machine-oriented, high-level languages are often referred to as *problem-oriented* or *procedure-*

oriented languages. This implies that they are designed to express various types of programming problems or procedures. For instance, COBOL, which stands for COmmon Business Oriented Language, was designed for business programs. FORTRAN, which stands for FORmula TRANslator, was designed to simplify expressing any mathematical computation. And RPG, which stands for Report Program Generator, was initially designed to make it easy to create programs that print reports. In addition, there are a number of other high-level languages, such as PL/I, APL, and BASIC.

When writing a program in a high-level language, the source language is keypunched into a source deck that, in turn, is translated into machine language by the computer system. This translation process is called a *compilation.* In contrast to an assembler language, one high-level language statement is usually translated into more than one machine-language instruction; in some cases, one symbolic statement may generate dozens of machine-language instructions. As a result, high-level languages are sometimes referred to as macro languages.

From an operator's point of view, a compilation is very similar to an assembly. First, the program that does the translating, the compiler, is loaded into the computer. For example, there is a compiler for COBOL, and there is a compiler for FORTRAN. Second, the compiler is executed, thus converting the source program to machine language and punching an object deck. The object deck can then be loaded into the computer and executed.

So that you can appreciate more fully the characteristics of a problem-oriented language, consider two of the oldest and most commonly used languages, COBOL and FORTRAN. COBOL, which was introduced in 1959, is one of the most widely used languages for business problems. In recent years, standard COBOL compilers have been developed for most business computers, so COBOL programs can be transferred from one computer to another with relative ease.

One of the objectives of the designers of the COBOL language was to make it easy to read and to understand. As a result, COBOL approximates English perhaps more closely than any of the other programming language. For example, the following COBOL statements correspond to blocks 5 through 8 of the flowchart in figure 4-7:

```
READ BAL-FWD-FILE AT END GO TO END OF JOB.
ADD ON-HAND, ON-ORDER GIVING AVAILABLE.
IF AVAILABLE IS LESS THAN REORDER-POINT,
    GO TO PRINT-LINE.
GO TO BEGIN.
```

Of course, in writing these COBOL statements, the programmer had to follow the precise rules of the COBOL language.

FORTRAN, on the other hand, is designed to express any problem involving numerical computation. Thus, its language corresponds to mathematical notation. For example, the equation

$$X = \frac{(A + B) \, (A - C)}{(B + D)}$$

can be expressed in FORTRAN as

$$X = (A + B) * (A - C) / (B + D)$$

Here, * represents multiplication and / represents division. Because of its mathematical orientation, FORTRAN is easily learned by scientists, engineers, and mathematicians.

DISCUSSION

In general, there is an assembler language for each type of business computer. For example, the Univac 9200 has an assembler language and the IBM 1130 has an assembler language. Because they correspond to machine capabilities, assembler languages for two different types of computers are not the same and indeed may be very dissimilar.

In addition to its assembler language, each type of computer may have one or more problem-oriented languages, depending on whether the appropriate compiler has been developed for that machine. For example, COBOL and FORTRAN are available with the NCR Century 100; COBOL, FORTRAN, and a Report Program Generator language are available with the Burroughs B2500.

One question you might raise is why several languages are needed for one computer. Or, to put it another way, why shouldn't one company write all of its programs in the same language? Each language has its advantages and its limitations. Because of the nature of the RPG language, for example, programs with relatively simple logic requirements can be prepared faster in RPG than in COBOL or FORTRAN. On the other hand, RPG has definite limitations when performing certain types of logical operations and cannot be used with some I/O devices and for certain I/O operations on direct-access devices. In addition, the resulting object program is likely to require more storage positions and take longer to execute than if the same program were written in assembler language or COBOL. When deciding whether to use RPG, then, programming time must be balanced against execution time.

Other languages have similar advantages and limitations. COBOL is easy to use and can be used on most computers, but it cannot be used for all I/O devices nor for all types of I/O operations on direct-access devices. FORTRAN makes the coding of mathematical problems relatively easy, but coding certain alphanumeric operations is difficult; FORTRAN cannot be used at all for many types of I/O operations and devices. Because it is a symbolic machine language, assembler language can be used to express all of a computer's capabilities, and when used

by a good programmer, it will result in a compact, efficient object program. However, assembler language requires more programming time
than any of the other high-level languages.

Because of the conflicting features of the various languages, choosing
the best one for a particular program can be difficult. If a good choice
is made, the program likely will be written in a reasonable amount of
time, and the resulting object program will use a reasonable amount of
storage and execute at a reasonable speed. If a poor choice is made,
programming time, storage use, and execution speed might all be
excessive. Although a programming manager is often forced to choose
between programming speed and execution speed, the trend is toward
greater use of the high-level languages. In general, these languages
allow greater speed in programming at the cost of somewhat diminished
execution speeds.

SUMMARY

1. Assembler language is symbolic machine language. Thus, it can be
used to represent all of a computer's functions, but its use requires
detailed knowledge of a computer's instructions.

2. The high-level programming languages are designed to express
programming problems in the language of the problem itself. Thus,
these languages are called problem-oriented languages. Two of the
oldest are COBOL and FORTRAN.

3. Several languages are likely to be available with a computer system
because each language has its own advantages and limitations. When
several languages are available, a programming manager must choose
the best language for each programming problem.

**FOR
REVIEW**

machine language
assembler language
assembler
assembly
source deck
macro instruction

problem-oriented language
procedure-oriented language
COBOL
FORTRAN
compilation
compiler

TOPIC THREE

WRITING
A PROGRAM

Regardless of what language a programmer uses, he goes through five phases when writing a program: (1) he defines the problem to be programmed; (2) he plans a solution to the problem; (3) he codes the solution in whatever language he is using; (4) he tests his program to be sure that it performs as intended; and (5) he documents the tested program. These five steps are explained in this topic.

DEFINING THE PROBLEM

Defining the problem is simply making sure that you know what the program you are going to write is supposed to do. You must understand what the input is going to be, what the output of the program must be, and what calculations or other procedures must be followed in deriving the output from the input. Two documents that are often used for defining card input and printer output are the *card layout form* and the *print chart*.

Card layout forms have many different formats. Some show the layout of several different types of input cards; some give the layout of only one card. You have already seen one type of layout form, the multiple-card layout form, in figures 3-14 and 3-18 of chapter 3. Up to six different card layouts can be shown on this form.

A print chart, such as the one in figure 4-11, shows the layout of a printed report or other document. It indicates the print positions to be used for each item of data on the report and the headings to be printed. It also shows where totals at the end of a report should be printed. On the left of the chart is a representation of a forms-control tape; it indicates which forms-control punches should be used for the various lines on the output document.

As indicated by the print chart in figure 4-11, the heading is supposed to start on the second line of the page; a 1-punch in the control tape is to be used for skipping to this second line of each page. The printed data lines (as opposed to heading lines) are to be printed with item code in print positions 6–10, item description in print positions 16–35, and so on. After fifty data lines are printed on one page, the program is to skip to the next page. At the end of the report, a total of the amount invested is to be printed after skipping two lines; this total is indicated by two asterisks printed in positions 51 and 53. Although figure 4-11 indicates only 60 print positions from left to right, a complete print chart usually has 144 or more—at least as many as available on the printer being used.

In actual practice, a programmer usually questions the person who assigns the program to him since certain aspects of the problem are likely to be indefinite. For instance, suppose you are asked to write a program that prepares a report like the one in figure 4-11 from a deck of input cards with the format shown in figure 4-2. What additional in-

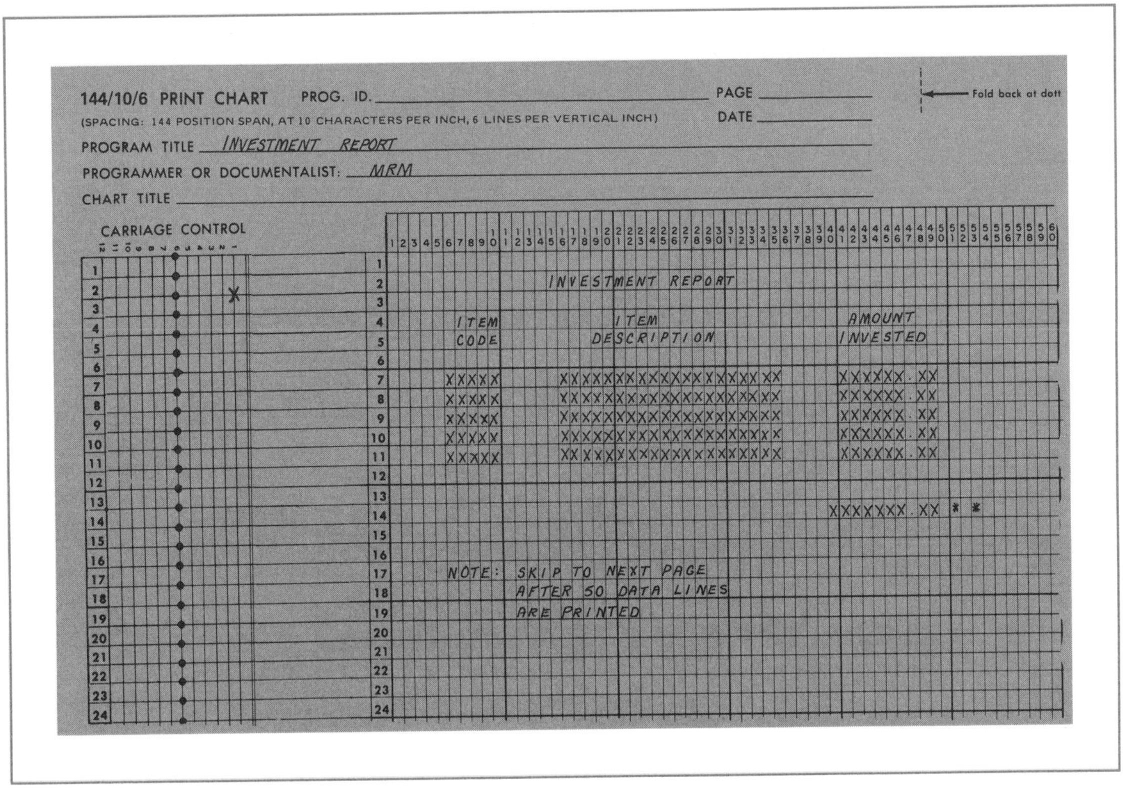

FIGURE 4-11 A print chart

formation would you need from the person who assigned the problem to you? Here are some ideas:

1. How is the amount invested calculated? Is it the on-hand balance multiplied by unit cost, or is it on-hand balance multiplied by unit price?

2. Should the input deck be checked to be sure it is in numerical sequence? (This is a common programming practice.)

3. Is one line supposed to be printed for each card in the input deck or would it be better to print a line for only certain items—say those items with an inventory investment of over $10,000?

The point is that you must know exactly what the program is supposed to do before you can write the program.

PLANNING THE SOLUTION

Planning the solution to a programming problem means deciding what must be done to solve the problem. This commonly concerns itself with the sequences of instructions to be used and the logic required to derive the output from the input. When planning a program in most languages, the programmer draws a program flowchart of the planned solution—something like the flowchart in figure 4-12. The flowchart can then be used as an aid in coding the program.

Basically, there are two levels of program flowcharts that may be drawn: general and detailed. A *general flowchart (or block diagram)* gives the gross logic of the program. When coding, several instructions or statements may be required for each of its blocks. The *detailed flowchart*, on the other hand, closely corresponds to the coding of the programming language to be used: one line of coding is usually written for each block of the flowchart.

Whether both general and detailed flowcharts are used depends on the language. Although both are normally used when programming in assembler-language, there is some question as to the value of detailed flowcharts when programming in compiler languages such as COBOL and FORTRAN. As a result, many companies that use high-level languages require only general flowcharts. In an extensive program, if the general flowchart doesn't provide enough detail to facilitate coding, portions of the flowchart might be redrawn at a semidetailed level. In this book, general and semidetailed flowcharts are used.

Figure 4-12 is a general flowchart for an inventory program that prepares a listing of the amount invested in each inventory item from a deck of balance cards. The symbols used here, and throughout this book, conform to the flowcharting standards approved by the American National Standards Institute. Since you have already been introduced to the terminal, I/O, process, and decision symbols (in topic 1), only the small circle, called the connector symbol, is new to you. Two connector symbols containing the same code, such as the digit 2, indicates that the flow passes from one connector circle to the next.

Can you follow the flowchart in figure 4-12? As a general rule, you start at the top and read down and to the right unless arrows indicate otherwise. When you come to a connector circle with a number in it, you continue at a connector circle containing the same number. For example, after printing a data line, the flowchart reaches a connector circle containing a 2 if fifty lines have been printed. This means that the flow of the program continues at the connector circle leading into the PRINT HEADINGS symbol.

When drawing general flowcharts, the main concern is that all processing and all branches required by the program are indicated. In this respect, if the words used in the symbols clearly indicate what operations are taking place, they serve their purpose. When programming in a language such as COBOL or FORTRAN, though, the programmer normally uses words and symbols that correspond to the programming language—this makes it easier to code the program later.

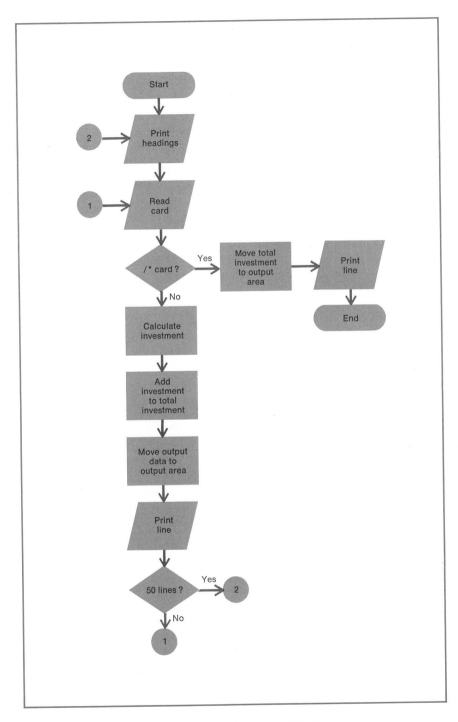

FIGURE 4-12 Program flowchart for an investment listing

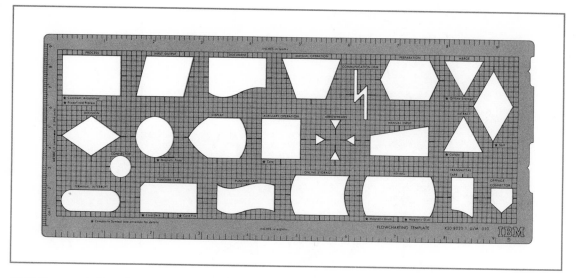

FIGURE 4-13   A flowcharting template

As an aid in drawing the symbols, a programmer uses a plastic flow-charting template such as the one shown in figure 4-13. By placing a pencil or pen in the symbol to be drawn, the programmer is able to draw a more exact symbol than can be done freehand. Because using the template is somewhat slower than drawing freehand, a programmer is likely to make one or more freehand sketches of a flowchart before using the template to draw the final version.

CODING

Coding a program varies depending on the programming language used. For most languages, special coding sheets are used, and, when the program is finished, one card is keypunched for each coding line on the coding sheets. The resulting deck of cards is the source deck.

Since the source deck may contain keypunching or programming errors, the programmer _desk-checks_ the source deck after it has been keypunched. This is done by either studying the printing at the top of the source cards (done by the keypunch) or studying a listing of the contents of the source cards. Figure 4-14 illustrates these two alternatives. If the programmer finds any errors, he makes the appropriate corrections to the source deck. When he is sure that the source deck is as accurate as he can make it, it is then ready to be assembled or compiled into an object program.

After assembly or compilation, the newly created object program can be loaded into the computer and executed—provided the source deck doesn't contain any clerical errors or violations of the rules of the language used. Unfortunately, such errors normally exist and are caught by the computer during assembly or compilation. These errors are printed out at the end of the compilation in a *diagnostic* listing. Each line on the listing, called a *diagnostic*, calls attention to one programming error.

If there are diagnostics, the programmer makes the necessary corrections to the source deck and the deck is then reassembled or recompiled. This process is repeated until there are no more errors in the diagnostic listing. At this stage, the object program is ready to be tested.

TESTING

To test a program, the programmer runs his object program using *test data.* This test data is intended to simulate all of the conditions that may occur when the program is actually used. On a card system, the

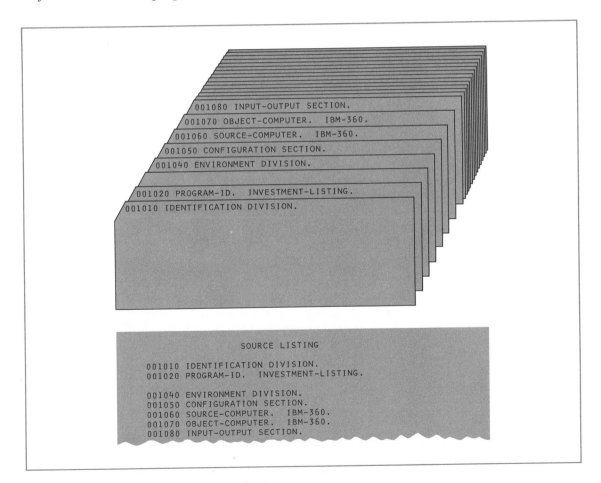

FIGURE 4-14   Source cards and a source listing

test data is punched into cards, but on other systems, the test data may include card decks, tapes, disks, and any other form of input used by the system. After the program is executed, the programmer compares the actual output with the expected output. If they agree, he can assume that the program functioned as intended.

More likely, however, the actual output and the intended output will not agree. The programmer must then *debug* the program. He must find the errors (bugs), make the necessary corrections to the source deck, reassemble or recompile the source program, and make another *test run*. This process is repeated until the program executes as intended.

Although debugging techniques vary depending on the language used, testing is often the most difficult phase of programming. In a program consisting of thousands of instructions, the original deck may have dozens of bugs, require dozens of reassemblies or recompilations, and take months to debug.

In actual practice, a series of test runs are made using different sets of test data. The data for the first test run is usually low in volume and may be designed to test only the main processing functions. After the program is debugged using this data, it may be tested with data that tries all conditions that may possibly occur during execution of the program. This set of test data is usually much greater in volume than the first set. When the program executes correctly with this data, a test run may be made using actual data. Then, an entire group of programs may be tested together to be sure that the output from one program is valid input to the next program. A program is considered ready for use only after it has proved itself under conditions that are as close as possible to being real.

DOCUMENTATION

In data-processing terminology, *documentation* refers to the collection of records that specifies what is being done and what is going to be done within a data-processing system. For each program in an installation, there is a collection of records referred to as *program documentation*. One of the jobs of a programmer is to provide this documentation.

Why is programming documentation necessary? Data-processing requirements change. For example, consider tax laws: in 1970 the social security tax was 4.8 percent of gross income; in 1972, 5.2 percent; in 1975, 5.65 percent; and so on. Company policies also change. Discounts may vary from year to year, production departments may use new forecasting techniques, and accounting practices may change. For each change, all affected programs must be modified.

Change is so common, in fact, that large companies have special maintenance programmers to modify existing programs. This frees other programmers to work on new programs without interruption. Without adequate documentation, however, maintenance programmers could not make changes within a reasonable amount of time. Even when a programmer modifies his own programs, documentation is valuable. Three months after writing a program, you can barely recognize it.

Some of the more important documents likely to be required by a company's documentation standards are the following:

1. Specifications that give the detailed requirements of the program.
2. Layouts of all input and output records on special layout forms.
3. A general flowchart of the entire program.
4. Semidetailed flowcharts of difficult routines within the general flowchart.
5. The source listing created during compilation.
6. Listings of the input data used for testing and listings of the output results.

Most of these documents, of course, are prepared and used as the program is developed. The flowchart, for instance, is both an aid for coding the program and a record of the complete program. Nevertheless, a programmer normally spends considerable time refining and finishing documentation when he completes a program. As a result, a company usually tries to reach a balance between too much and too little documentation.

CONCLUSION

Figure 4-15 represents the proportion of time a programmer might spend on each of the five phases of programming. These estimates vary somewhat depending on the language used. For example, if a high-level language is used, a smaller percentage of time is likely to be spent on flowcharting and debugging. The one point to note is that as much time is likely to be given to problem definition and debugging as is given to coding.

SUMMARY

1. There are five phases that a programmer must carry out to prepare a finished object program. He must define the problem, plan and code the solution, and test and document the program.

2. In the planning stage, a programmer normally flowcharts the planned solution, using standard flowcharting symbols. The flowchart should be detailed enough to indicate all processing requirements of the program.

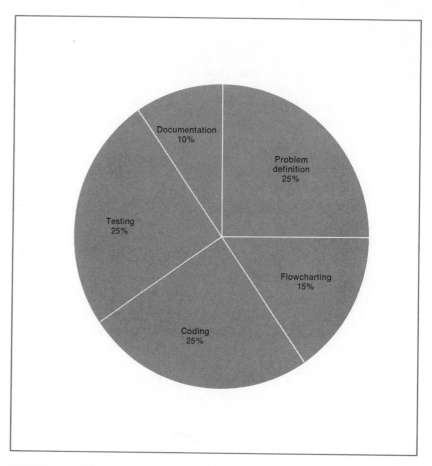

FIGURE 4-15   How a programmer's time is spent

FOR REVIEW

card layout form
print chart
general flowchart
block diagram
detailed flowchart
desk checking
diagnostic listing
diagnostic
test data
debug
test run
documentation
program documentation

II

BASIC
COMPUTER
SYSTEMS

CHAPTER FIVE

In chapter 3, you were introduced to a billing and sales-analysis system that centered around a traditional card computer. In this chapter, which consists of two topics, some variations in card computers are first presented. Then, in topic 2, a system for order writing, billing, accounts receivable, and inventory control is described. This system makes use of some of the hardware variations described in topic 1.

The traditional card computer system is made up of a CPU, a printer, a card reader, and a card punch. To supplement the system, a number of punched-card machines such as the keypunch, verifier, sorter, and collator are required. Before each computer run, the punched-card machines are used to create the cards to be processed and to arrange these cards into acceptable sequences for processing. One of the limitations of a system such as this is the amount of card handling required. For each computer run, there may be several sorting and collating steps.

THE MULTIFUNCTION CARD MACHINE

To reduce card handling, the *multifunction card machine (MFCM)* was developed for the IBM System/360 Model 20. The MFCM, shown in figure 5-1, has two input hoppers and five output stackers. As cards pass through the machine from either hopper, they can be read, punched, or both read and punched, and they can be stacked in any of the five stackers. An optional feature allows the MFCM to print on cards from

CARD SYSTEMS

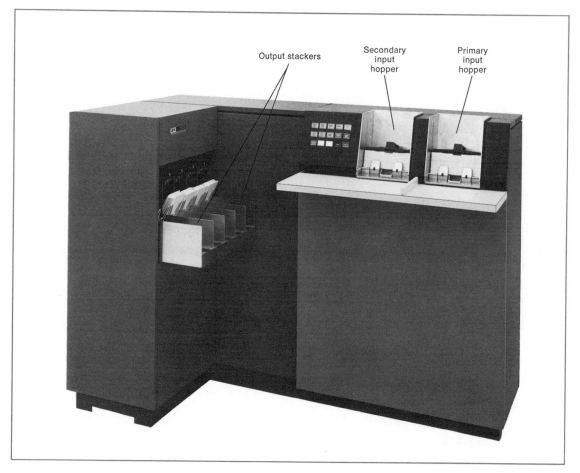

Output stackers   Secondary input hopper   Primary input hopper

FIGURE 5-1   The multifunction card machine

either hopper as they pass through the machine. In figure 5-2, the schematic drawing of the card path of the MFCM shows that cards from either hopper pass through read, punch, and print stations. Hopper 1 of the MFCM is usually referred to as the *primary hopper* and hopper 2 as the *secondary hopper*.

The advantage of the MFCM is that it can reduce the number of steps required to do a job on a computer system. To illustrate, compare a Model 20 card system that has a card reader and a card punch with a Model 20 system that has an MFCM. Figure 5-3, then, presents two system flowcharts showing how a sales-by-customer report can be prepared from customer master cards and daily transaction cards.

System A of figure 5-3 represents the preparation of the sales report with a card reader. In the first step, the customer master cards and the transaction cards, both in customer-number sequence, are merged using

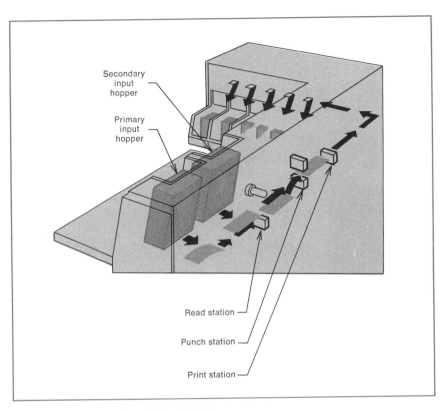

FIGURE 5-2 Card paths of the MFCM

the collator. The merged deck is then placed in the input hopper of the card reader, and the computer system prepares the sales report (step 2). In the third step, the merged deck is separated by sorting the cards again. Normally, the master cards are distinguished from the transaction cards by some control punch so that in one pass of the cards through the sorter, all master cards are stacked in one pocket and all transaction cards in another.

In contrast to system A, system B, which uses the MFCM, requires only one step. The master cards are placed in hopper 1 of the MFCM, the transaction cards are placed in hopper 2, and the program is executed. As the cards pass through the MFCM, they are stacked in separate stackers.

Figure 5-4 gives another example of how an MFCM can improve the efficiency of a card system. Invoices are prepared from name-and-address (N/A) and item cards. As the invoices are printed, accounts receivable (A/R) cards are to be punched, and customer number and name and invoice number, date, amount and allowable discount are to be printed on the face of the cards.

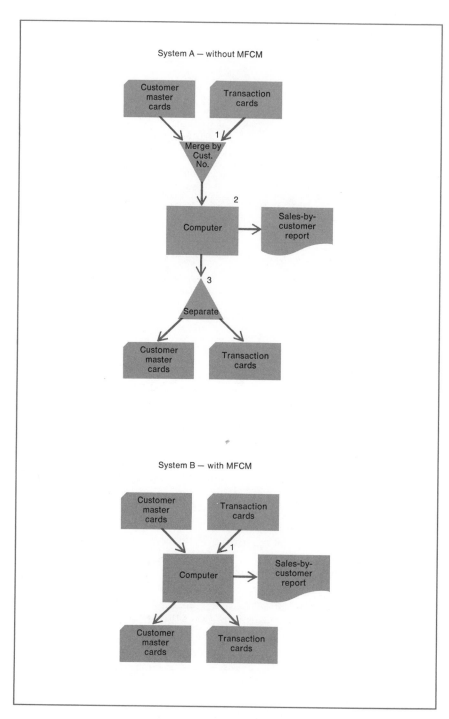

FIGURE 5-3 Comparing two card systems—example 1

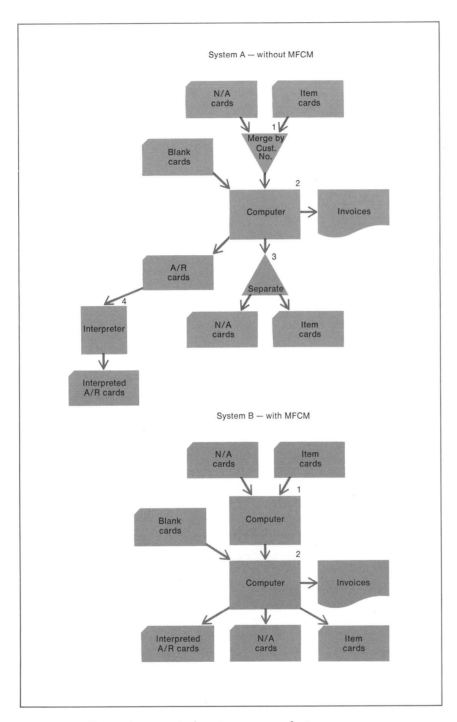

FIGURE 5-4   Comparing two card systems—example 2

System A, with the card reader and card punch, requires four steps. First, the name-and-address and item cards are merged by customer number using the collator. Second, as the merged deck is read by the card reader, the computer system prints the invoices and summary-punches accounts receivable cards. Third, the name-and-address cards and item cards are separated by the sorter. Fourth, the data in the accounts receivable cards is printed on the cards by the interpreter.

Using an MFCM as in system B, only two steps are required. First, the name-and-address and item cards are merged on the computer system itself. The name-and-address cards are placed in the primary hopper, the item cards in the secondary hopper, and the merged deck is stacked in one of the output stackers. (This merge step assumes that both decks are in customer-number order before merging.) In the second step, the merged deck is placed in the primary hopper of the MFCM and blank cards in the secondary hopper. As the program is executed, the invoices are printed, the accounts receivable cards are punched and printed, and the accounts receivable, name-and-address, and item cards are stacked in separate stackers.

As you can see, then, the MFCM can considerably reduce the amount of card handling required by a card system. It can also reduce the amount of punched-card equipment used. Because the MFCM can perform the functions of a collator and an interpreter, these machines aren't needed.

Although a typical MFCM system will consist of a CPU, a printer, and an MFCM, other card readers and card punches can be added to further reduce card handling. For example, if a system consists of a CPU, a printer, a card reader, and an MFCM, the invoices and accounts receivable cards prepared by the systems in figure 5-4 can be prepared in one step. The name-and-address cards are placed in the card reader, the item cards in hopper 1 of the MFCM, and blank cards in hopper 2, This eliminates the need to merge the name-and-address and item cards before processing.

One particular advantage of the card-printing feature of the MFCM is its ability to prepare a punched-card bill, statement, or check. Because the MFCM can print in sixty-four printing positions on twenty-five different lines on the face of a card, it can be used to prepare a document such as the monthly statement in figure 5-5. Notice that starting in column 1, customer number, statement date, and balance owed are also punched in the card. If the card is returned with the payment of $33.15, the statement itself can be used as a transaction card when updating the customer's accounts receivable balance. This, of course, eliminates the need for keypunching a transaction card. A card like this, which is both output from a computer system (the statement) and input to a computer system (the transaction card), is often referred to as a *turnaround document.*

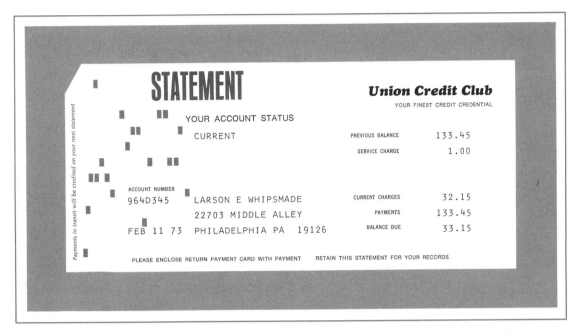

FIGURE 5-5   A turnaround document printed by the MFCM

THE SYSTEM/3 CARD SYSTEM

In 1969 IBM announced a new card computer system, called the System/3, that was designed for small companies who until then had not been able to afford a computer system. The unique feature of the System/3 is that it does not use the standard eighty-column punched card. Instead, it uses a ninety-six-column card that is less than half the size of the standard card. Because the card is smaller, the card-handling components of the system are also reduced in size, thus cutting the manufacturing costs of the components. And, because each card can store ninety-six characters of data, fewer cards are likely to be needed for any one application. Since the introduction of this new card, ninety-six-column card-reading devices have also been developed for use with the System/360-370 and the Burroughs B1700 series of computers.

The ninety-six-column card is illustrated in figure 5-6. As you can see, ninety-six columns are stacked in three *tiers*, each consisting of thirty-two columns of data. The first tier contains columns 1–32, the second tier columns 33–64, the third tier columns 65–96. At the top of the card, there is space for four lines, or 128 characters, of printing. The keypunch can print in the first three rows of the card; the multi-function card unit used by the System/3 can print in all four printing rows. In the illustration, the digits 1–9 and 0 are punched and printed in

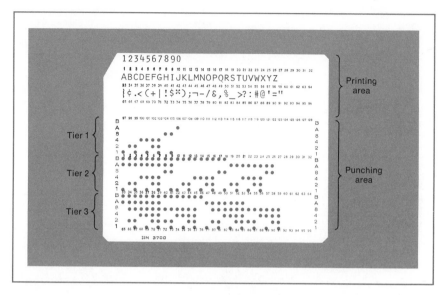

FIGURE 5-6   The ninety-six-column card

columns 1–10, the letters in columns 33–58, and twenty-seven special characters in columns 65–91.

For each card column, there are six punching positions referred to, from top to bottom, as the B-, A-, 8-, 4-, 2-, and 1-positions. These punching positions correspond to standard punched-card code in that the B- and A-punches are *zone punches*, the 8-, 4-, 2-, and 1-punches are *digit punches*. With one exception, a digit is represented by one or more digit punches, a letter by a combination of zone and digit punches, and special characters by digit punches, zone punches, or both zone and digit punches.

The codes for the digits 0–9 are as follows:

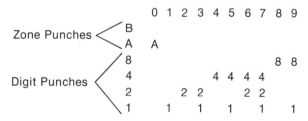

The zero consists of an A-punch only, while the digits 1-9 are made up of one or more digit punches. To convert the code to the digit, you add the values of the digit punches. Thus, a 1- and a 2-punch represent the digit 3 $(1 + 2 = 3)$; a 4-, 2-, and 1-punch represent the digit 7.

By referring to figure 5-6 again, you can see that both the A- and B-punches are used for the letters A–I, the B-punch for the letters J–R,

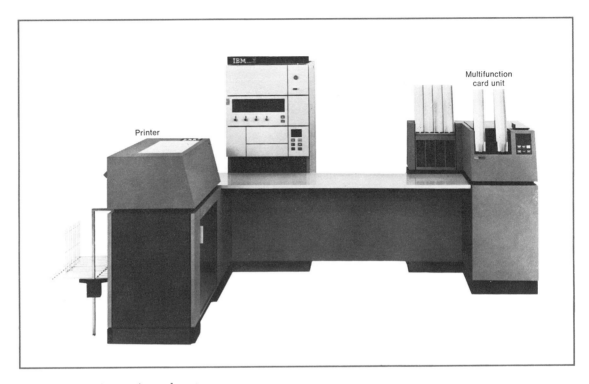

Printer

Multifunction
card unit

FIGURE 5-7   A System/3 card system

and the A-punch for the letters S–Z. These zone punches are combined with digit punches in order to represent all twenty-six letters.

As shown in figure 5-7, the basic components of a System/3 card system are a CPU, a printer, and a *multifunction card unit (MFCU)*. Unlike most IBM printers, the System/3 printer does not use a forms-control tape for controlling form movement. Instead, the form is controlled entirely by programming. In contrast to the MFCM, the MFCU has only four output stackers and can print on only four lines at the top of the card. Otherwise, it functions much the same as an MFCM. As cards pass through the MFCU from either of the two hoppers, they can be read, punched, and printed, and then stacked in any of the four output stackers.

Two other components used with the System/3 are the 5496 data recorder, which is used to keypunch and verify, and the 5486 card sorter. Although these devices operate in much the same way as the traditional keypunch, verifier, and sorter, they do have some additional features worth mentioning.

The data recorder, shown in figure 5-8, is unique in that no punching takes place until all ninety-six columns have been keyed. Thus, an operator can correct mistakes without completely repunching a card.

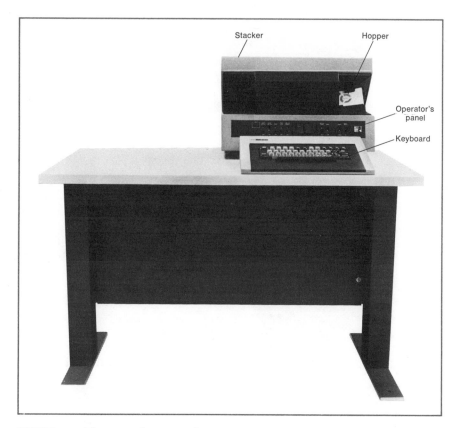

FIGURE 5-8   The 5496 data recorder

She simply backspaces and erases the incorrect columns, and then keys the correct data. The data that has been keyed is held in a ninety-six-column storage area, called a *buffer*, until the next card in the input hopper is ready to be keyed; then, the data in the buffer is punched.

When the data recorder is used for verifying, the operator proceeds much the same as when using a traditional verifier. However, when all ninety-six columns have been verified and one or more columns have proven to be incorrect, the correct data is stored in the buffer storage area of the device. Then, when the operator inserts a blank card in the input hopper, the correct data from the buffer is punched into it. This eliminates the need to rekeypunch all incorrect cards after the verifying procedure. If a card is correct, a correct-card notch is cut on the right side of the third tier.

The card sorter, shown in figure 5-9, has only six pockets. Thus, sorting a deck of cards on a numeric field requires two phases for each card column in the sort field. To illustrate, suppose a deck of cards is

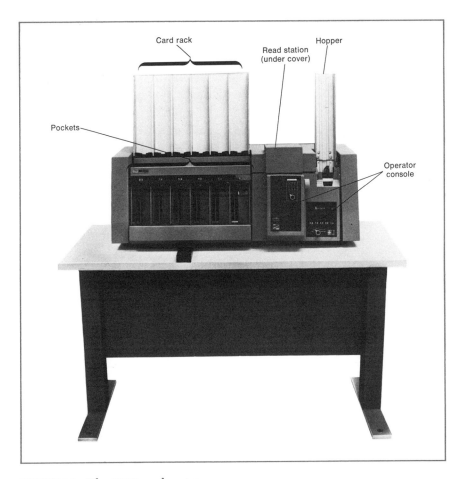

FIGURE 5-9   The 5486 card sorter

being sorted into numeric sequence based on columns 21 and 22. This procedure is illustrated in figure 5-10.

Because sorting proceeds from right to left, the column selector is first set to column 22. In the first phase for this column, the cards containing even digits are stacked in their respective pockets, while cards containing odd digits are stacked in the reject pocket. For example, a column containing the code for the digit 4 is stacked in the 4-pocket; a card containing the code for a 7 is stacked in the reject pocket. In the second phase, the cards are taken from the reject pocket and sorted again. This time the odd-digit cards are stacked on top of the even-digit cards. When the cards are removed from the sorter pockets from right to left, the deck is in sequence based on column 22. By repeating this procedure for column 21, the deck will be arranged in the desired sequence.

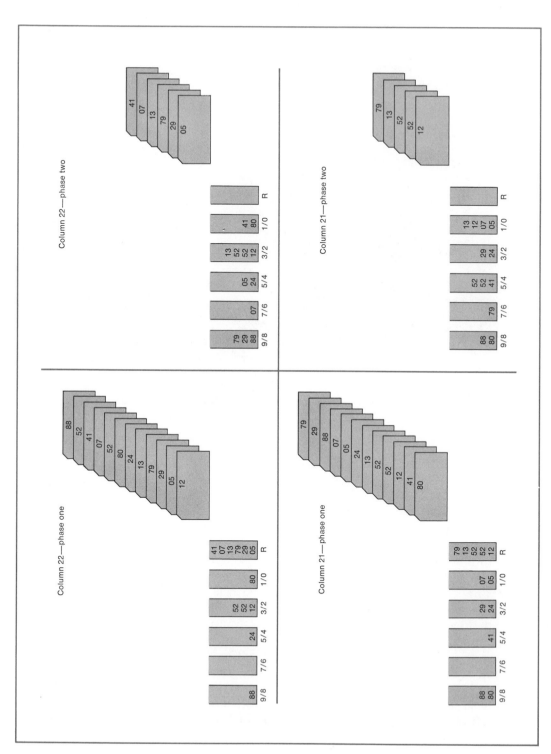

FIGURE 5-10 Sorting with the 5486 card sorter (columns 21 and 22)

To sort a deck on an alphabetic field, three phases are required for each card column. After the digit sort (phases 1 and 2) for each card column, a third phase, which sorts by zone punches, is required. Because of the extra time required, alphabetic sorting is generally avoided when designing a system.

In summary, the components of the System/3 differ in several ways from the components of a traditional card system. However, these differences generally affect operator procedures rather than system design. For instance, although sorting is done quite differently on the 5486 card sorter than on a traditional thirteen-pocket sorter, the end result, a sorted deck, is still the same. Similarly, although keypunching and verifying procedures vary considerably from traditional methods, the end result, a verified card deck, is the same. In short, a system flowchart for a System/3 card application is likely to be identical to a system flowchart for a System/360 Model 20 with an MFCM.

CONCLUSION

The MFCM and the System/3 represent some major hardware variations in card computer systems. In addition, however, there are many minor variations. For example, some card computers use a combined card reader and punch consisting of one hopper and two stackers. As the cards pass through this device, they can be read, punched, or both read and punched; and they can be stacked in either stacker. Needless to say, a device such as this can significantly affect the design of a system.

Some hardware variations that aren't so apparent concern the ways in which cards are read or documents are printed. For example, the reading mechanism of some card readers consists of metal brushes that pass through the holes in the cards. Other readers use light and photoelectric cells to determine whether a hole is punched. Some card readers read the cards column by column; others read row by row. Some printers use print drums; some use a print chain. Since these types of variations generally affect only the speed of the device and not its function, they are not normally mentioned in this book.

1. The MFCM is a device that can read, punch, or print on cards fed from either of its two input hoppers. It can also stack cards from either hopper in any of its five stackers. As a result, it significantly reduces the card handling required by a card system.

2. The System/3 card system, which processes ninety-six-column cards, consists of an MFCU, a printer, and a CPU. Auxiliary equipment includes a six-pocket sorter and a data recorder that can both keypunch and verify. Although the techniques used for System/3 opera-

SUMMARY

tions vary considerably from those for traditional operations, the principles of system design are much the same.

3. The ninety-six-column card is made up of three tiers of thirty-two columns. Each column consists of six punching positions—two zone punches and four digit punches.

4. To sort cards on one column using the six-pocket sorter, the cards with even-numbered digits are sorted first and the odd-digit cards are stacked in the reject pocket. Then, the odd-digit cards from the reject pocket are sorted and stacked on top of the even-digit cards.

**FOR
REVIEW**

multifunction card machine
MFCM
primary hopper
secondary hopper
turnaround document
tier
zone punch
digit punch
multifunction card unit
MFCU
buffer

In chapter 3, you were introduced to system flowcharts and the design of card systems. To keep the explanation manageable, the system described was simplified in several ways. In this topic, then, a more complete system is presented — one that will illustrate more fully the complexity of even a small system.

The card layouts in figures 5-11 and 5-14 and the flowcharts in figures 5-12, 5-15, 5-18, and 5-19 represent the input documents and major procedures of an order-writing, billing, inventory, and accounts receivable system. The computer used is a card system consisting of a CPU, a printer, and an MFCM. Auxiliary equipment includes key-punches, verifiers, and sorters.

A system with an MFCM is used in this example since the majority of all card systems probably have an MFCM or an MFCU. This does not imply, however, that a system with an MFCM is best for any given user. On the contrary, a system with a card punch and a card reader may be best. Thus, a prospective user should consider several alternative systems and choose the one that can perform the required functions for the lowest cost.

PROCEDURES

Flowcharts 1, 2, and 3 represent daily procedures, while flowchart 4 represents month-end procedures. On a daily basis, then, inventory records are updated (flowchart 1), shipping orders and invoices are printed on a combined form and the accounts receivable file is updated (flowchart 2), and cash receipts are posted to the accounts receivable file (flowchart 3). At the end of the month, an aged trial balance and monthly statements are printed (flowchart 4).

To give some perspective on the procedures involved in these flowcharts, consider first the billing run in flowchart 2 (step 5). Here, the shipping order and the invoice for each customer are actually two different copies of the same form. One copy is sent to the shipping department as the shipping order; and one is sent to the customer as the invoice. Because inventory records are checked in flowchart 1 — before invoices are printed — back-ordered items have already been determined and are printed on the shipping-order and invoice form. This is in contrast to the system illustrated in chapter 3, which prepares invoices after the shipping orders are returned from the shipping department and back orders are noted by the order picker.

A billing system that prepares invoices before actually shipping the items is a *prebilling system*. A system that prepares invoices after items are shipped and shipping orders are returned from the shipping department is a *postbilling system*. Since a postbilling system prepares two documents instead of one, it will probably be more expensive than a prebilling system. Thus, advanced systems are more likely to use prebilling than postbilling. When prebilling is used, however, it is important to keep absolutely accurate inventory records. Otherwise, items may be listed as back-ordered when they are available and listed as shipped when they are out of stock.

Whenever a company has back orders (some industries will not accept back orders), the data-processing system must have procedures to keep track of the back-ordered items. When an inventory of a back-ordered item becomes available, the system must select the back orders that can be shipped and prepare a shipping order and invoice for them. In flowchart 2, then, step 11 merges the back-ordered items from the billing run into the back-order card file. This file is checked every day during the inventory-update procedures (step 6 of flowchart 1) to determine whether any back orders can be filled.

Flowchart 1

With this background, you should be better able to understand the inventory procedures in flowchart 1 (figure 5-12). Five types of cards, illustrated in figure 5-11, are used in this procedure. The balance-forward cards represent the current stock status of an inventory item, while the item, receipt, return, and adjustment cards represent transactions affecting inventory balances. If an item is back-ordered, the item card receives an X-punch in column 79 (X79). An X-punch in column 80 (X80) indicates that the back order is filled, and an X-punch in column 78 (X78) indicates a partial shipment of the total amount ordered.

In steps 1–5 of flowchart 1, the item cards are created using a customer order (such as the one in figure 2-1) as the source document. To reduce keypunching, only columns 1–30 and 35–39 are keypunched; columns 31–34 are punched by the computer in step 14, and columns 40–73 are punched by the computer in step 11. In step 4, the cards are listed in a document called an order *register* (figure 5-13), and in step 5 the totals are balanced to control totals taken before keypunching. A register is simply a listing of data punched in transaction cards. Because a register can be used to locate a missing card or an erroneous transaction, it is common to print a register immediately after punched cards are created. In the applications in this topic, several different registers are prepared.

In step 6, the back-order file is processed against receipt, return, and adjustment cards. If a receipt, a return, or a merchandise adjustment allows a back order to be filled, the card receives an X-punch in column 80 and is merged into the transaction deck. Unfilled back-order cards remain in the back-order file. Although it is not shown, the receipt, return, and adjustment cards are created in procedures similar to those for creating item cards. They are keypunched and verified, and registers are printed and balanced to controls.

In steps 8–13, the item and balance-forward cards are merged into

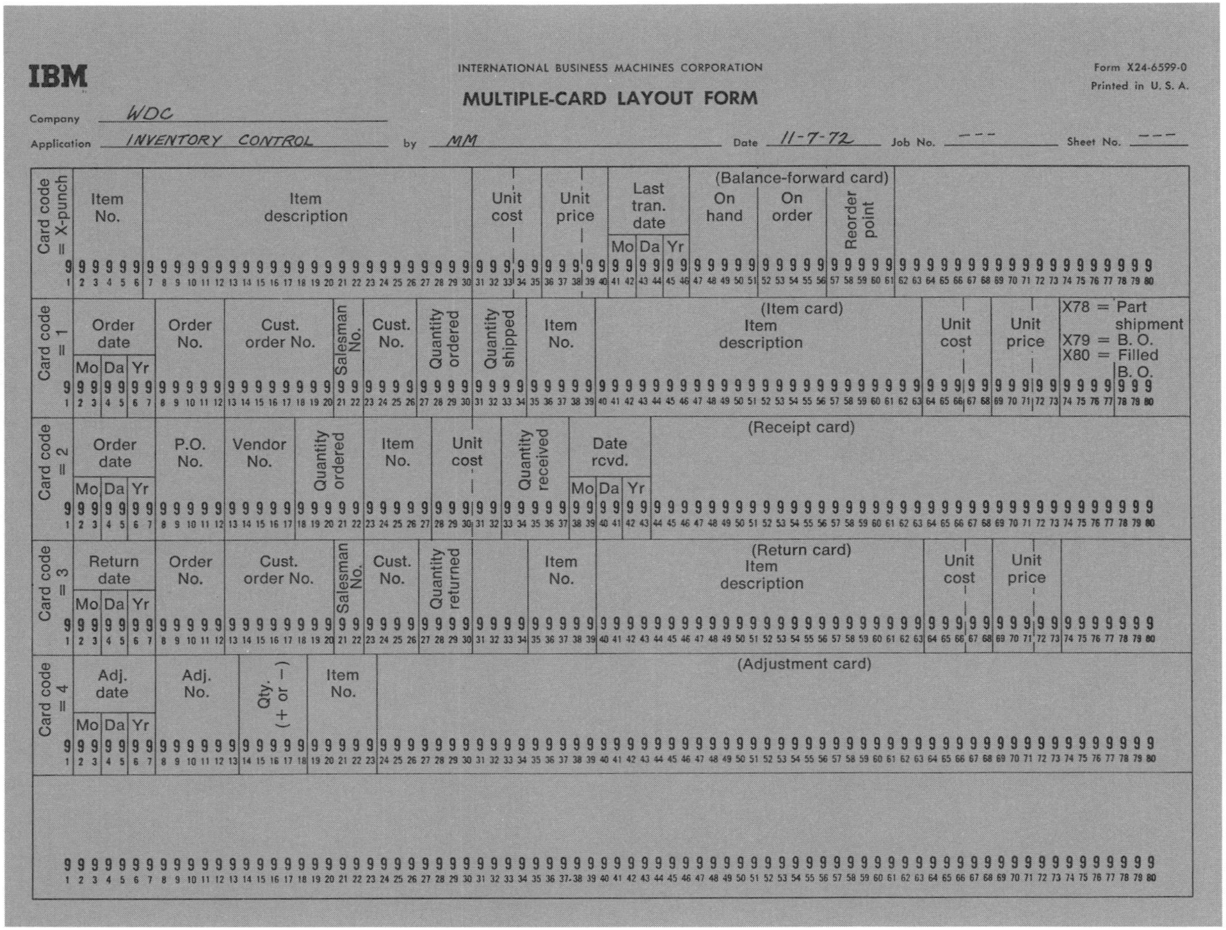

IBM

INTERNATIONAL BUSINESS MACHINES CORPORATION

MULTIPLE-CARD LAYOUT FORM

Company __WDC__

Application __INVENTORY CONTROL__ by __MM__ Date __11-7-72__ Job No. _____ Sheet No. _____

Form X24-6599-0
Printed in U.S.A.

Card code = X-punch — (Item card)
Item No. | Order date (Mo Da Yr) | Order No. | Cust. order No. | Salesman No. | Cust. No. | Quantity ordered | Quantity shipped | Unit cost | Unit price | Last tran. date (Mo Da Yr) | On hand | On order | Reorder point (Balance-forward card) | Item description | Unit cost | Unit price

X78 = Part shipment
X79 = B.O. Filled
X80 = B.O.

Card code = 1 — (Receipt card)
Item No. | Order date (Mo Da Yr) | P.O. No. | Vendor No. | Salesman No. | Item No. | Quantity ordered | Quantity received | Unit cost | Item No. | Date rcvd. (Mo Da Yr) | Item description | Unit cost | Unit price

Card code = 2 — (Return card)
Item No. | Return date (Mo Da Yr) | Order No. | Cust. order No. | Cust. No. | Quantity returned | Item No. | Item description | Unit cost | Unit price

Card code = 3 — (Adjustment card)
Item No. | Adj. date (Mo Da Yr) | Adj. No. | Item No. | Qty. (+ or −)

Card code = 4

FIGURE 5-11 Card formats for inventory control

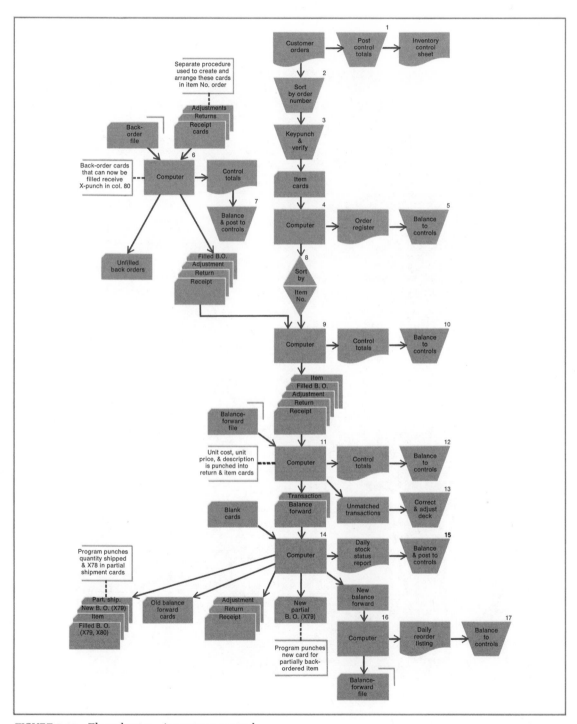

FIGURE 5-12 Flowchart 1 — inventory control

```
                       ORDER REGISTER

    DATE 10-03-73                                      PAGE 01


    ORDER      CUST.       ORDER      CUST.  SLSMN  QUANTITY    ITEM
    NO.     ORDER NO.      DATE       NO.     NO.   ORDERED     NO.

    22109   029 H273    10-02-73     1257      16       15     11141
                                                         3     12303
                                                         5     21214

    22110   500749      10-03-73     2257      28       10     11123
                                                        15     11212
                                                        12     11410
                                                         5     21410

    22111   P241        10-02-73     1351      19      100     11310
                                                         3     21210
                                                         5     21410
                                                        25     31210
                                                         2     32201
                                                         2     32403
```

FIGURE 5-13   An order register

one deck, along with the receipt, return, adjustment, and filled back-order cards. After each merging step on the computer system, computer totals are compared with the control sheet to make sure that all transaction cards are still present. In step 11, item description, unit price, and unit cost are read from the balance-forward cards and punched into the item cards. After this step, unmatched transaction cards are checked by the computer operator and adjustments are made to the merged deck.

Step 14 is the inventory-update step. Here, transactions are processed against the balance-forward file and new balance-forward cards are punched. The two equations used are

1. NEW ON HAND = OLD ON HAND + RECEIPTS + RETURNS
   ± ADJUSTMENTS − ITEMS TO BE SHIPPED
   − FILLED BACK ORDERS
2. NEW ON ORDER = OLD ON ORDER − RECEIPTS

During processing, the computer determines whether there is sufficient stock of an item to fill an order. If there is no stock left (on hand equals zero), an X-punch is punched in column 79 of the item card and the item is completely back-ordered. If enough stock is left for a partial shipment, an X-punch is punched in column 78 of the item card, and the amount actually available to be shipped is punched in the quantity-shipped field (columns 31–34). Then, a partial back-order card is punched, identical in format to an item card, with an X-punch in column 79 and the amount yet to be shipped in the quantity-ordered field. During this run, various types of cards are selected to various stackers, with the cards to be used in the billing procedure—the item, new back-order, filled back-order, and partial shipment cards—stacked together. As the inventory records are updated, a stock status report is printed, showing the current on hand, on order, and reorder point for each item. This report can be used to check the current stock status of an inventory item.

In step 16, a daily reorder listing is printed from the new balance-forward file—one line is printed for each item for which on hand plus on order is less than the reorder point. Control totals accumulated during this run are compared (in step 17) with prior totals to make sure that all balance-forward cards are present in the balance-forward file. The daily inventory procedures are then completed.

Flowchart 2

After the daily inventory procedures, the item, new back-order (X79), filled back-order (X79, X80), and partial shipment (X78) cards are used in the billing procedure diagrammed in flowchart 2 (figure 5-15). Other cards required in this procedure—the name-and-address and accounts receivable cards—are shown in figure 5-14, along with the item card. In step 1, then, the transaction cards are sorted by customer number. Since the filled back orders are to be printed last on each invoice, the cards with an X-punch in column 80 are first separated from the other cards and placed last in the deck to be sorted. Then, when the deck is sorted, the filled back-order cards follow the other transaction cards for each customer number.

In step 2, the name-and-address cards are merged with the transaction cards in preparation for the billing run. In step 3, control totals are balanced, and in step 4, unmatched transactions are reconciled and the merged deck is adjusted. Then, in step 5, the shipping orders and invoices are printed as illustrated in the schematic in figure 5-16. As you can see, one or more lines are printed in the body of the invoice for each transaction card. To determine whether an item card represents a shipment, partial shipment, new back order, or filled back order, the computer tests columns 78, 79, and 80 for X-punches. For a partial-shipment card, the quantity actually shipped is printed in the quantity-shipped field, and the quantity ordered minus quantity shipped is printed in the back-ordered field. Before filled back orders are printed, one space is skipped and the heading, FILLED BACK ORDERS, is printed. After each filled back-order line, the original customer order number is

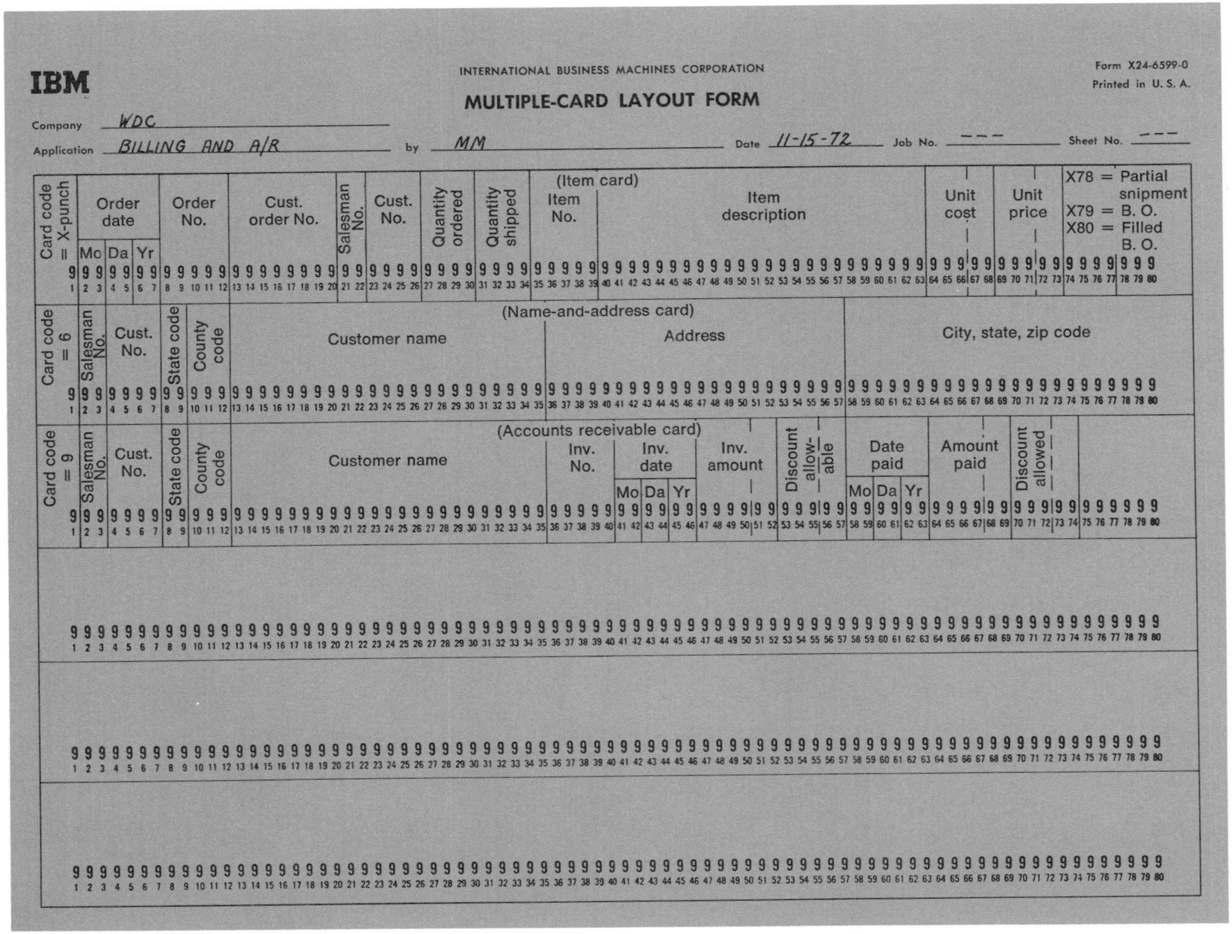

IBM

INTERNATIONAL BUSINESS MACHINES CORPORATION

MULTIPLE-CARD LAYOUT FORM

Form X24-6599-0
Printed in U.S.A.

Company _WDC_ by _MM_ Date _11-15-72_ Job No. _ _ _ Sheet No. _ _ _ _

Application _BILLING AND A/R_

Card code = X-punch

X78 = Partial shipment
X79 = B. O.
X80 = Filled B. O.

(Item card)

Order date — Mo Da Yr
Order No.
Cust. order No.
Salesman No.
Cust. No.
Quantity ordered
Quantity shipped
Item No.
Item description
Unit cost
Unit price

Card code = 9

(Name-and-address card)

Cust. No.
Salesman No.
State code
County code
Customer name
Address
City, state, zip code

Card code = 9

(Accounts receivable card)

Cust. No.
Salesman No.
State code
County code
Customer name
Inv. No.
Inv. date — Mo Da Yr
Inv. amount
Discount allowable
Date paid — Mo Da Yr
Amount paid
Discount allowed

FIGURE 5-14   Card formats for billing and accounts receivable

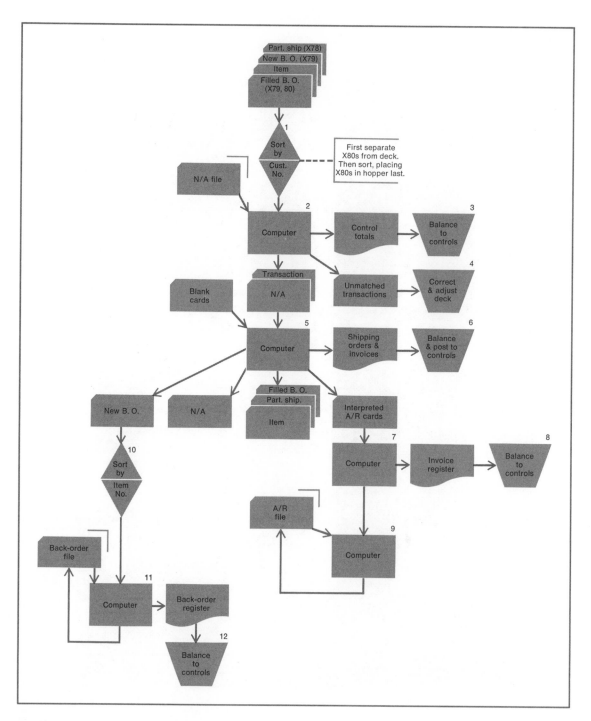

FIGURE 5-15   Flowchart 2—billing and accounts receivable

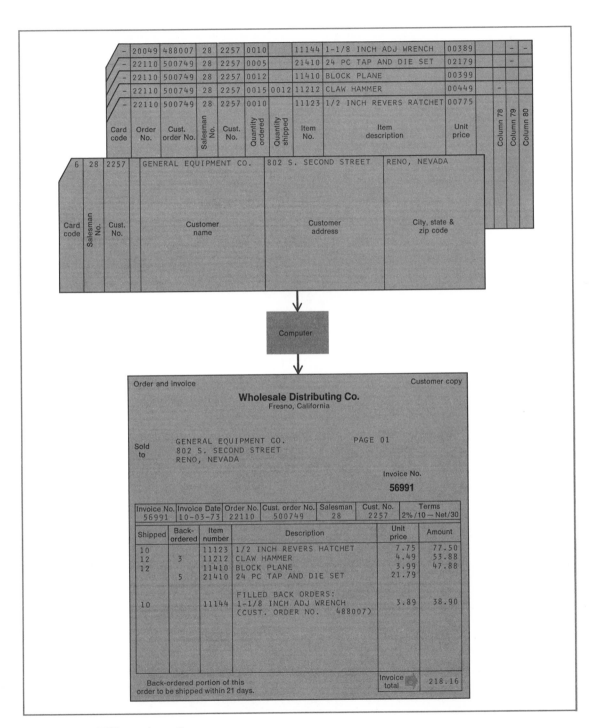

Card code	Order No.	Cust. order No.	Salesman No.	Cust. No.	Quantity ordered	Quantity shipped	Item No.	Item description	Unit price	Column 78	Column 79	Column 80
-	20049	488007	28	2257	0010		11144	1-1/8 INCH ADJ WRENCH	00389		-	-
-	22110	500749	28	2257	0005		21410	24 PC TAP AND DIE SET	02179			-
-	22110	500749	28	2257	0012		11410	BLOCK PLANE	00399			
-	22110	500749	28	2257	0015	0012	11212	CLAW HAMMER	00449		-	
-	22110	500749	28	2257	0010		11123	1/2 INCH REVERS RATCHET	00775			

Card code	Salesman No.	Cust. No.	Customer name	Customer address	City, state & zip code
6	28	2257	GENERAL EQUIPMENT CO.	802 S. SECOND STREET	RENO, NEVADA

Computer

Order and invoice   Customer copy

Wholesale Distributing Co.
Fresno, California

Sold
to
GENERAL EQUIPMENT CO.   PAGE 01
802 S. SECOND STREET
RENO, NEVADA

Invoice No.
56991

Invoice No. 56991	Invoice Date 10-03-73	Order No. 22110	Cust. order No. 500749	Salesman 28	Cust. No. 2257	Terms 2%/10 — Net/30	

Shipped	Back-ordered	Item number	Description	Unit price	Amount
10		11123	1/2 INCH REVERS HATCHET	7.75	77.50
12	3	11212	CLAW HAMMER	4.49	53.88
12		11410	BLOCK PLANE	3.99	47.88
	5	21410	24 PC TAP AND DIE SET	21.79	
10		11144	FILLED BACK ORDERS: 1-1/8 INCH ADJ WRENCH (CUST. ORDER NO. 488007)	3.89	38.90

Back-ordered portion of this
order to be shipped within 21 days.

Invoice total   218.16

FIGURE 5-16   Billing schematic

printed. For each invoice, one accounts receivable card is punched and interpreted.

In steps 7 and 8, the accounts receivable cards are registered and balanced to controls. Then, in step 9, they are merged into the accounts receivable card file, which is kept in sequence by invoice number within customer number. As a result, the new accounts receivable card will be the last one for each customer number. Since this file consists of one card for each invoice amount owed to the company, it is the basis of an open-item accounts receivable system. To determine the total amount owed to the company, the file need only be processed by the computer. A typical accounts receivable file and accounts receivable card is illustrated in figure 5-17.

In steps 10–12, the new back-order cards are sorted by item number and merged into the back-order file. This file is processed in step 6 of

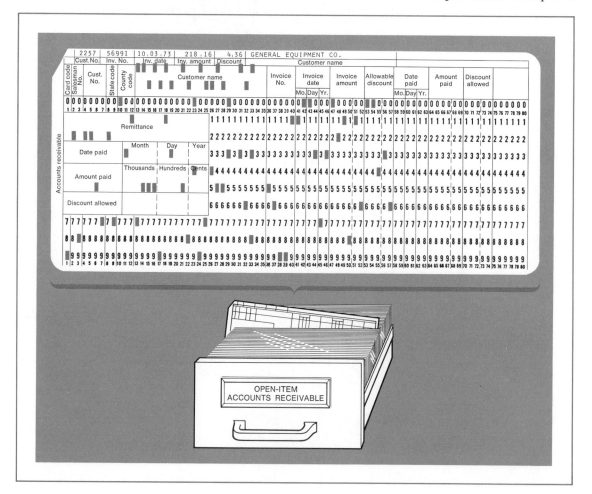

FIGURE 5-17   An open-item accounts receivable file

the inventory procedures (flowchart 1). As items are added to inventory, the back-ordered items are shipped and billed.

Flowchart 3

Flowchart 3 (figure 5-18) represents the daily procedures for posting cash payments to the accounts receivable file. The basic idea is to remove accounts receivable cards from the file as they are paid by the customer. Then the file will always represent only those amounts still owed. Although an actual cash-receipts procedure would have to provide for partial payments, the procedure illustrated assumes that all payments cover one or more complete invoices.

In steps 1–3, the checks and remittance advices from customers are sorted into alphabetic sequence (which is also customer-number sequence), and the check amount is recorded on the remittance advice. Then, a bank deposit is made, and totals are taken and posted to control sheets.

In step 4, clerks pull from the invoice file the accounts receivable cards that have been paid. On the face of each card (see figure 5-17), the clerk writes the amount actually paid, the date paid, and the discount allowed. Then, in step 5, these fields are keypunched into the cards and then verified. In this case, the keypunch and verifier operators read the source data from the face of the card as it passes through the machines.

In step 6, the payment cards are sorted into sequence by invoice number within customer number. This means that the cards are first sorted by invoice number, and then by customer number. After being listed in a cash-receipts register in step 7 and balanced to controls in step 8, the cards are filed in a paid file, to be used later for preparing accounts receivable reports.

Flowchart 4

Flowcharts 1, 2, and 3 represent daily procedures for order writing, billing, accounts receivable, and inventory control. As by-products of these procedures, card files are created and maintained that can be used for preparing a wide variety of inventory, accounts receivable, and sales-analysis reports. To illustrate the ease of preparing these documents, consider flowchart 4 (figure 5-19), which illustrates the preparation of an aged trial balance and monthly statements from the accounts receivable file.

To prepare an aged trial balance, the accounts receivable file is processed by the computer (step 1). Since each accounts receivable card contains the date and amount owed, the computer can determine whether the charge is current, over thirty, over sixty, or over ninety days, provided the present date is read into storage from a date card at the start of the program. Since the accounts receivable file is updated daily (flowcharts 2 and 3), the aged trial balance can be prepared at any time.

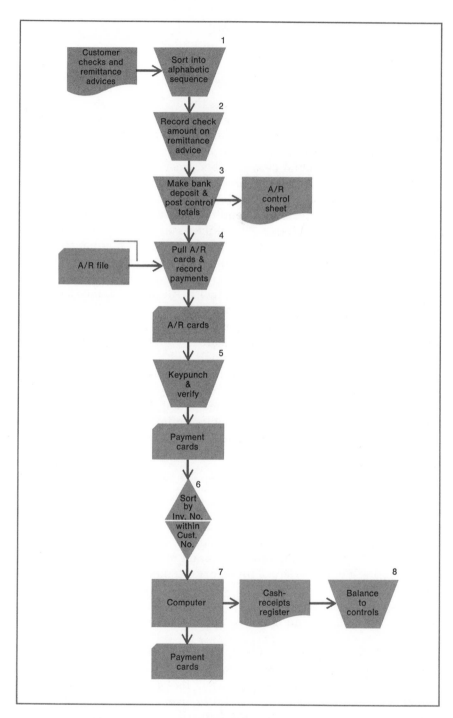

FIGURE 5-18   Flowchart 3 – posting cash receipts

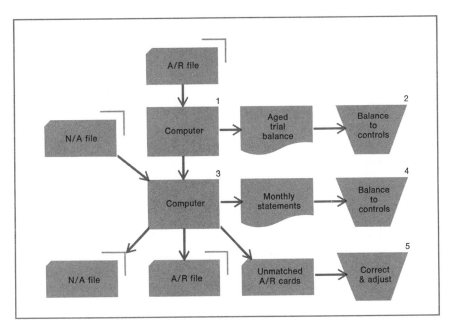

FIGURE 5-19   Flowchart 4—monthly accounts receivable procedures

To prepare monthly statements, the name-and-address cards are placed in one hopper of the MFCM and the accounts receivable file is placed in the other. For each customer, the name and address, the amounts owed, and the total owed is printed on the statement. If desired, aging can also be shown on the statement.

CONTROLS

Control posting and balancing steps are shown throughout flowcharts 1 through 4. *Posting* refers to initially recording a control total; balancing refers to comparing a control total accumulated by the computer with a posted control total. Control balancing is important because it is the only means of assuring the accuracy of a system.

To more fully illustrate the use of controls, consider the accounts receivable control sheet in figure 5-20. The basic idea is that the balance shown in column 8 should always be equal to the sum of the invoice amounts stored in the accounts receivable card file. If they are equal, you can assume that accounts receivable operations have proceeded correctly.

To keep the accounts receivable balance on the control sheet up to date, columns 1–7 are posted each work day. Invoices billed is posted in step 6 of flowchart 2, while invoices paid, cash received, and discounts allowed are posted in step 8 of flowchart 3. Returns and miscellaneous adjustments are posted during other procedures. After the first

ACCOUNTS RECEIVABLE CONTROL SHEET

Date	Invoices billed Debit A/R	Invoices paid Credit A/R	Cash received	Discounts allowed	Returns Credit A/R	Miscellaneous Exp.	Miscellaneous DB A/R	Miscellaneous CR A/R	Balance owed
Last month									170 492 25
10-1	11 422 30	10 027 61	9 843 21	184 40					171 886 94
10-2	9 800 35	11 594 25	11 381 45	212 80	67 50				170 025 54
10-3	12 398 87	8 181 75	8 043 98	137 77	12 75				174 229 91
10-4									
10-5									
10-8									
10-9									
10-10									
10-11									
10-12									
10-15									
10-16									
10-17									
10-18									
10-19									
10-22									
10-23									
10-24									
10-25									
10-26									
10-29									
10-30									
10-31									

FIGURE 5-20   An accounts receivable control sheet

seven columns are posted, the new accounts receivable balance is derived by using the following equation:

$$\text{NEW A/R BALANCE} = \text{OLD BALANCE} + \text{INVOICES BILLED}$$
$$- \text{INVOICES PAID} - \text{RETURNS}$$
$$\pm \text{MISCELLANEOUS}$$

To make sure that columns 3, 4, and 5 have been posted correctly, the control clerk checks to be sure that

$$\text{INVOICES PAID} = \text{CASH RECEIVED} + \text{DISCOUNTS ALLOWED}$$

After the daily postings are made to the control sheet, other control steps are balanced to it. For example, the accounts receivable balance would be accumulated by the computer when the aged trial balance and monthly statements are prepared in flowchart 4. Then, in steps 2 and 4, these totals are compared to the control-sheet total. If equal, the aged trial balance and monthly statements are assumed to be correct.

What happens, though, if controls don't balance? Suppose, for example, that an accounts receivable card has been lost because of a clerical error. Then, the accounts receivable total accumulated during step 1 of flowchart 4 will be less than the control-sheet total. How is this error corrected?

Because daily registers are prepared for invoices billed, cash receipts, returns, and miscellaneous, any transaction can be recreated and any error corrected. In this case, the paid file and the accounts receivable file can be processed as follows:

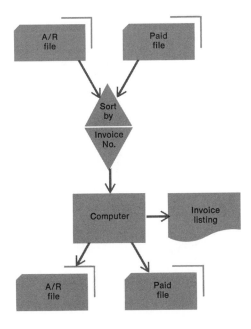

The invoice listing can then be scanned to determine which invoice numbers are missing. By finding the missing invoice number on the daily invoice registers, the lost card can be recreated and returned to the accounts receivable file.

Similar procedures are used in other applications. Figure 5-21, for instance, illustrates two control sheets that can be used in the inventory application—one for the inventory file and one for the back-order file. Instead of dollar amounts, these sheets show quantities. As daily control totals such as quantities ordered, back-ordered, received, and returned are accumulated, they are posted to the control sheets. The new on-hand balance is then derived by using the following formula:

$$\text{NEW ON HAND} = \text{OLD ON HAND} - \text{ORDERED} + \text{NEW B.O.}$$
$$- \text{FILLED B.O.} + \text{RECEIPTS} + \text{RETURNS}$$
$$\pm \text{ADJUSTMENTS}$$

The new back-order balance is derived using

$$\text{NEW BACK-ORDER BALANCE} = \text{OLD BALANCE} - \text{FILLED B.O.}$$
$$+ \text{NEW B.O.}$$

BACK-ORDER FILE CONTROL SHEET

Date	Starting B.O.	B.O. Filled	New B.O.	Ending B.O. bal.	Cross-foot?	Initials
10-1	1 430	180	43	1 293	YES	AM
10-2	1 293	202	—	1 091	YES	AM
10-3	1 091	—	35	1 126	YES	AM

INVENTORY MASTER FILE CONTROL SHEET

Date	Ordered (−)	New B.O. (+)	Filled B.O. (−)	Receipt (+)	Returns (+)	Adj. (±)	Total on hand
Last month							180 444
10-1	1 807	43	180	433	12		178 945
10-2	1 980		202	2 600		− 305	179 058
10-3	2 422	35		1 580			178 251

FIGURE 5-21   Inventory control sheets

Once the transaction totals are posted and the file balances are derived, subsequent processing runs are balanced to these totals. Thus, step 10 of flowchart 1 might balance quantities ordered, received, returned, and adjusted and back orders filled to the control sheet; step 17 of flowchart 1 would balance the on-hand total to the control sheet; step 12 of flowchart 2 would balance the back-ordered total to the control sheet. If totals are not in balance, other procedures are used to locate the error. If data must be recreated, the daily transaction registers are used.

In summary, control procedures are an important part of any system. They must be elaborate enough to locate all errors, but not so elaborate that they impair the efficiency of a system. Registers must be prepared when records are created, and procedures must be designed to help locate an error and then to recreate the lost record from the registers.

FILE MAINTENANCE

One procedure that is common to all data-processing systems is *file maintenance*, which means adding, deleting, changing, and updating records in a file. On a card system, updating a file is accomplished by processing transaction records against balance-forward records, as done in step 14 of flowchart 1. When the data for the new balance-forward card has been calculated by the computer, it is summary-punched into a blank card.

Adding, deleting, or changing a record in a card file is normally a manual operation. To change the address in a name-and-address card, for example, a new card is keypunched with the new address, the old card is removed from the master file, and the new card is added to the file. If the number of additions or changes is large, a computer or collator can be used to merge the new cards into a file and to remove the old cards from the file. Because the accuracy of a file is critical to the processing of a system, controls must be carefully planned for file-maintenance procedures.

CONCLUSION

In this topic, the major procedures of an order-writing, billing, inventory, and accounts receivable system have been presented. Although the procedures are typical, by no means do they cover all of the requirements of the applications. For example, additional flowcharts would be required for creating and merging the receipt, return, and adjustment cards prior to step 6 of flowchart 1. Similarly, procedures would have to be developed for crediting returns to accounts receivable and for file maintenance. Before actually implementing a system, procedures must be developed for every situation that is likely to occur.

Because system design is new to you, you probably have many un-answered questions about the procedures described. However, by searching for the answers to these questions, you are likely to learn far more about card-system design than you would if every detail of each procedure was described for you. If a question arises about alternative methods of achieving the same results, remember that there are many different ways of designing a system. In actual practice, a system designer considers all of the reasonable alternatives and chooses the one that he thinks provides the best combination of speed and accuracy.

SUMMARY

1. A prebilling system prepares bills before the inventory items are actually shipped. Thus, this type of system depends heavily on the accuracy of inventory records.

2. A large part of any system concerns itself with maintaining and updating files. The procedures described in this topic, for example, use inventory balance-forward, back-order, name-and-address, and accounts receivable files. When files are kept accurate and up to date, documents such as the daily reorder listing and the aged trial balance can be prepared from them at any time.

3. Because control balancing is the only way to insure the accuracy of a system, controls are always included in a system. In addition to posting and balancing control totals, control procedures must provide for determining and correcting the cause of an imbalance.

FOR REVIEW

prebilling system
postbilling system
register
posting
file maintenance

CHAPTER SIX

This chapter is divided into three topics. In the first, the characteristics of the magnetic tape and its associated I/O devices, the tape drives, are described. In the second topic, the use of magnetic tape within a data-processing system is discussed. Then, the programming and system complications peculiar to systems that use tape are covered in the last topic.

A magnetic tape is a continuous strip of plastic wound on a reel, as shown in figure 6-1. Although a typical tape is 2400 feet long and 1/2 inch wide, there are other widths and lengths, in particular, 1200-, 600-, and 250-foot reels. Data is recorded on the surface of the tape as patterns of magnetized spots on a magnetic surface coating. Between the individual data records on the tape are spaces—usually 0.6 or 0.75 inch—with no data recorded on them. These spaces are called *interrecord gaps*, or *IRGs*. Although there are some limitations, for most uses a data record can be as short or as long as necessary.

Figure 6-2 illustrates one type of coding used on tape. In this code, there are nine vertical positions in which a magnetized spot, called a *bit*, may or may not be recorded. The letters, numbers, and special characters are represented by combinations of these "on" or "off" bits. In figure 6-2, the on-bits are indicated by a line in a bit position, the off-bits by a space. Because the human eye is unable to see the bits recorded on a tape, there is no point in describing the actual codes used. You only need to know that each letter, number, or special character is represented by a unique combination of bits.

TAPE SYSTEMS

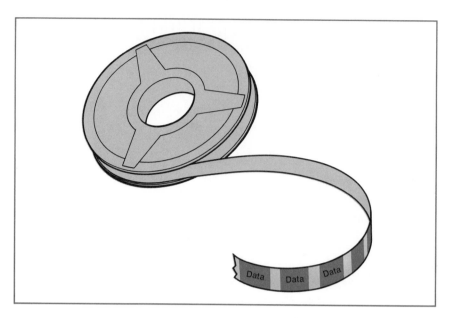

FIGURE 6-1   A magnetic tape

Because each of the nine vertical bit positions in figure 6-2 forms a horizontal track, a tape such as this is called a nine-track tape. Although these tapes are the most common right now, seven-track tapes are still used by many companies.

Actually, only eight of the nine bit positions are used in the code for each character. The ninth bit, called a *check bit*, or *parity bit*, is used as a check on the accuracy of tape operations. The idea is to make the number of on-bits in the individual codes either all odd or all even. Because the parity bits are adjusted accordingly, all of the codes in figure 6-2 contain an odd number of on-bits—the letter A has three, the letter B has three, the letter C has five, and so on. Then, if a character is read that consists of an even number of on-bits, the computer system has detected an input error.

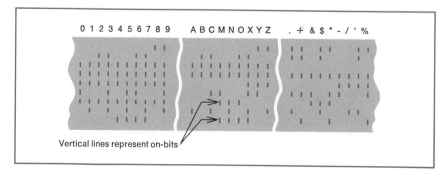

FIGURE 6-2   Coding on tape

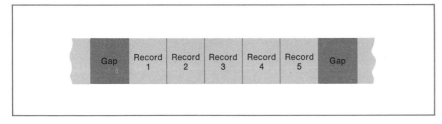

FIGURE 6-3   Blocked records

Parity checking of the code for a single character—which may be called *vertical parity checking*—is only one of the checks done in tape operations. At the end of each tape record is a *longitudinal check character*—the last character before the interrecord gap. This character consists of off-on bits that make the sum of the on-bits in each horizontal track either odd or even, depending on the computer. Then, if a computer that uses even parity finds an odd number of bits in a track, it has detected an input error. With the combination of vertical and *horizontal parity checking*, most tape input errors can be caught. Incidentally, from the point of view of programming or system design, it isn't necessary to understand parity checking. You should, however, realize that all input and output operations on tape are checked.

In many cases, more than one data record is recorded between two interrecord gaps. This is called *blocking* records, and the group of records between gaps is called a *block* of records. The *blocking factor* of a file of records is the number of records stored in one block. In figure 6-3, for example, the blocking factor is 5—five records are stored between the gaps. Because blocking is such a common practice when using tape files, the IRG is often referred to as the *interblock gap*, or *IBG*. The advantage of blocking is that it increases the storage capacity of a reel of tape as well as the speed at which the records on the tape can be read or written.

THE TAPE DRIVE

The *tape drive*, shown in figure 6-4, is used to write records on tape and read records from tape. To mount a tape on the tape drive, the computer operator threads the tape through a read/write mechanism in the center of the unit and then onto an empty take-up reel, as shown in figure 6-5. This process is similar to mounting a tape on a tape recorder.

Once the tape is mounted, the operator pushes the start button; the tape drive locates the first record on the file by searching for a *load-point marker*, which is a reflective spot on the surface of the tape. Tape records can then be read or written under control of a stored program. When data is read from a tape, the data on the tape remains unaltered; thus, it can be read many times. When data is written on a tape, it re-

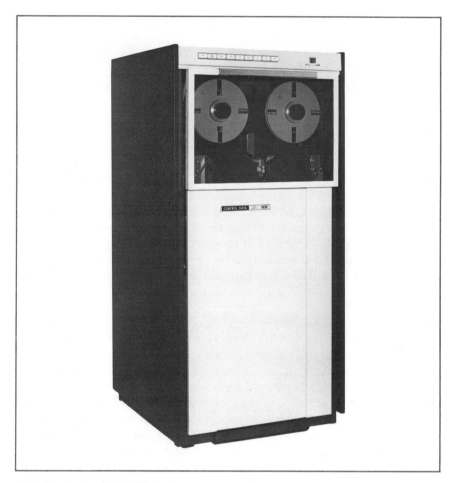

FIGURE 6-4   The tape drive

places (and thus destroys) the data that was on the tape. Before removing a tape from the tape drive, the tape is rewound onto the original reel, ready to be read or written again.

Although the basic programmable functions of a tape drive are reading and writing records, there are a number of others. For example, most tape drives can be programmed to rewind a tape, to backspace a tape one block of records, and to skip over faulty sections of tape. In addition, some tape drives can be programmed to read tapes backwards, which in some applications can increase the speed of tape operations.

During reading operations, input records are checked for vertical and horizontal parity. In writing operations, output records can be checked immediately after being written since the reading mechanism is located just after the writing mechanism. As soon as a character or block of records is written, it is checked for vertical and horizontal parity by the reading mechanism.

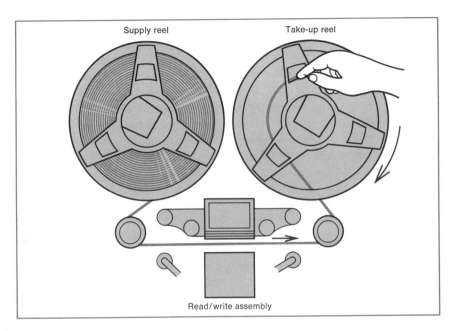

Supply reel   Take-up reel

Read/write assembly

FIGURE 6-5   Mounting a tape

A computer system may have one or many tape drives attached to it. A medium-sized direct-access system, for example, may consist of a card reader, a card punch, a printer, a CPU, four disk units, and two tape drives. A tape system, however, usually consists of a card reader, a card punch, a printer, a CPU, and four or more tape drives.

TAPE SPEED AND CAPACITY

One measure of the speed of tape operations is the *transfer rate*, or *transfer speed*, of a tape drive. It is measured in characters or *bytes* per second and measures how long it takes to transfer data from the tape drive to storage, or vice versa. For example, one common tape drive has a transfer rate of 60,000 bytes per second. (Chapter 12, CPU Concepts explains the nature of the byte, but for now think of it as the equivalent of a character—most of the time, it is.) Other tape drives have speeds that range from about 5000 bytes per second all the way up to 400,000 bytes per second. To appreciate tape speeds, consider that a transfer rate of 80,000 bytes per second is the equivalent of reading 1000 eighty-column cards per second, or 60,000 cards—a stack thirty-five feet high—in a minute.

Transfer rate is misleading because a tape drive actually stops and starts every time that it comes to an IBG—yet transfer rate does not reflect this *start/stop time*. To appreciate this, suppose that a file of 6000 records, each consisting of 100 bytes of data, were stored on a tape with a blocking factor of 1. At 60,000 bytes per second, it would take 10 seconds (600,000 bytes divided by 60,000) to read the data in the file. However, the tape would also have to stop and start 6000 times. Since the start/stop time of a typical tape drive is 8/1000 second (8 milliseconds), the time required for stopping and starting would be 48 seconds (0.008 times 6000). In other words, the tape drive spends 10 seconds reading data and 48 seconds starting and stopping. The effective transfer rate, therefore, is much less than 60,000 bytes per second.

Now suppose the records are blocked with a blocking factor of 10. Ten seconds are still required for reading the 600,000 bytes of data, but only 4.8 seconds are required for starting and stopping. Since the total time for reading the file is reduced from 58 seconds to 14.8 seconds, you can see the effect of blocking in the speed of tape operations.

The capacity of a reel of tape depends on the length of the tape, the length of the IBGs, and the *density* of the tape. Density measures the number of characters or bytes of data that can be recorded on an inch of tape. For example, one model tape drive records data at a density of 800 bytes per inch and has an IBG that is 0.6 inch. Common densities are 200, 556, 800, and 1600 bytes per inch; common IBG lengths are 0.6 and 0.75 inch.

To appreciate the effect of blocking on the capacity of a tape, consider how much tape is required to store 8000 records, 100 bytes each, with a blocking factor of 1. Here, the data requires 1000 inches of tape (800,000 bytes divided by 800), and the IBGs require 4800 inches of tape (8000 times 0.6 inch). If the blocking factor is increased to 10, however, only 480 inches of tape are required for IBGs and the entire file is reduced from 5800 to 1480 inches.

How large can a blocking factor be? It depends on the storage capacity of the computer. When a block of records is read, all of the data between the two IBGs is transferred into storage. As a result, if a block of records consists of 4000 bytes of data, the input area of storage must be 4000 storage positions. The blocking factor of a tape file is usually set by a system designer after considering all of the programs for which the file will be input or output. The block length can be only as large as the input or output area of the longest program that uses the tape.

To illustrate, suppose a tape file is going to be used by three programs and 16,000 storage positions are available for the programs. Not including the input area for the tape file, program A requires 12,000 storage positions, program B 7,500 storage positions, and program C 14,500 storage positions. The maximum block length is therefore 1500 bytes. This concept is illustrated in figure 6-6.

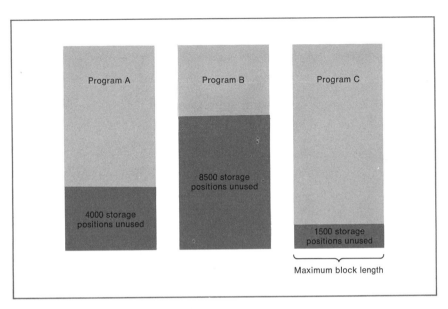

FIGURE 6-6   Determining the blocking factor

SUMMARY

1. The magnetic tape is a compact storage medium that can be read or written at high speed by I/O units called tape drives.

2. To increase the storage capacity of a reel of tape and to increase the speed at which the reel can be read or written, tape records are normally blocked. The blocking factor is made as large as possible without exceeding the core storage available during the execution of any of the programs using the tape.

FOR REVIEW

interrecord gap	blocking factor
IRG	interblock gap
bit	IBG
check bit	tape drive
parity bit	load-point marker
vertical parity checking	transfer rate
longitudinal check character	transfer speed
horizontal parity checking	byte
blocking records	start/stop time
block of records	density

TOPIC TWO

TAPE SYSTEM DESIGN

In any data-processing installation, much of the processing time is devoted to maintaining files. For example, inventory records, accounts receivable records, sales-analysis records, and payroll records must be continually updated. Periodically, reports and other documents are printed from these files.

Figure 6-7 shows a system flowchart that represents the four steps usually involved in updating a file on a tape system. This flowchart uses the following symbol to represent a tape file:

The first step is keypunching and verifying data. The procedure is much the same as that for a card system; for example, the keypunch operator punches the data from source documents. Depending on the file being updated, the transactions may represent orders, inventory receipts, hours worked, and so on.

The second step, called a *card-to-tape run*, converts the card data into tape records. This requires a relatively simple program that reads a card, processes it, and writes a tape record. However, the program should also *edit* the input data. *Editing* refers to programmed testing for valid input data. Editing routines may include tests to make sure that alphabetic fields contain alphabetic data, that numeric fields contain numeric data, that numeric fields do not contain blanks, that transaction codes are valid, and that the contents of a field are within reasonable limits. As output, an editing run provides a printed listing of all invalid transactions in order that they may be corrected. These invalid transactions are not included on the output tape file so that processing can continue without them.

The third step is to sort the transaction records on tape into the sequence of the master file that is going to be updated. For example, if an inventory master file is in item-number order, the inventory transaction records should be sorted into item-number order.

When records are sorted on a tape system, three or more tape drives are used—even though the system flowchart shows only one input tape and one output tape. During execution, each of the tapes used will be read and written several times. A *sort program* is a very complex program that is usually written and supplied by the computer manufacturer. To use the program, a computer user need only supply the sort specifications—such as the location of the field on which the records are going to be sorted. Since sorting may account for a large percentage of

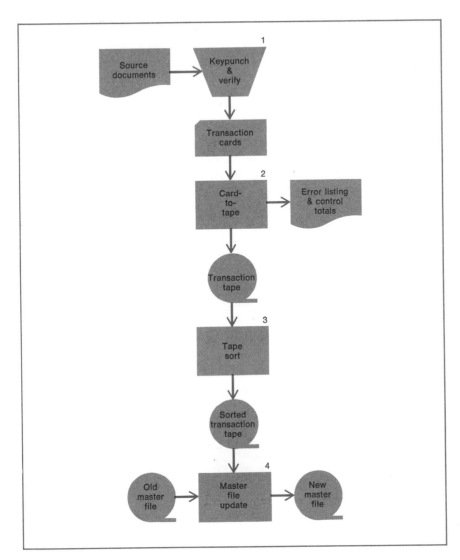

FIGURE 6-7   System flowchart for updating a master file

the processing done on a tape system, the efficiency of a sort program can significantly affect the efficiency of the tape system.

The fourth step is the *update run*. In an update program, the master records and the transaction records are read into storage. If one or more transaction records apply to a master record, the affected fields in the master record are changed accordingly. If a master record has no transactions that apply to it, the master record remains unchanged. The output tape—the updated or new master tape—consists of all the master records, both those that were changed and those that were not changed.

To illustrate, consider the example shown schematically in figure 6-8. Suppose the first ten master records of an inventory file have these item numbers: 01, 03, 04, 06, 09, 12, 13, 17, 18, and 19. The first three transaction records have these item numbers: 09, 17, and 17. The update program starts by reading one master record and one transaction record. Since the first transaction—item number 09—doesn't match the first master record—item number 01—the master record is written unchanged on the new master tape. Then, the next master record—03—is read. Since it too is unmatched, it is written unchanged. The same is true for master records 04 and 06.

The first master record to be matched is item number 09. The transaction for this item number is processed against the master, the master is updated, and another transaction is read. Since the next transaction record applies to master record 17, master record 09 is written on the new tape and another master is read. After master records 12 and 13 are written unchanged, the two transaction records for master 17 are processed. The program continues in this way until all of the master and

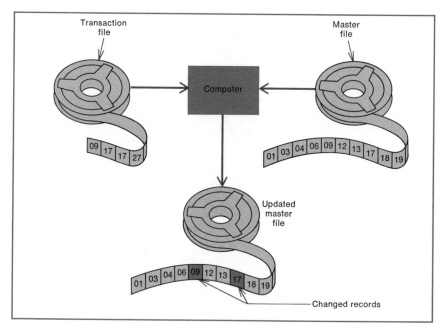

FIGURE 6-8   Schematic of the master file update

transaction records have been read. If there are 5000 master records in the file, 5000 master records will be written—regardless of the number that are actually affected by transactions.

Of course, a report may also be printed during an update program. For example, during an inventory update, a listing of items to be reordered could be printed. This is shown on a system flowchart as follows:

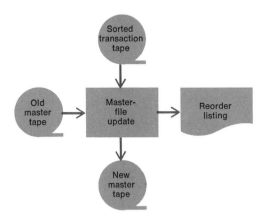

Otherwise, reports can be printed at any time from master files, using *tape-to-printer programs*. For example, a sales report could be printed from a sales master file, as follows:

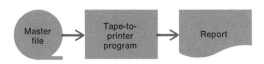

A tape-to-printer program is a relatively simple program that reads a tape record, converts the data to a readable form, and prints the data.

To delete, change, or add records to a master file, a procedure such as the one in figure 6-9 is normally followed. First, the deletion, change, and addition cards are keypunched and verified. Second, using a card sorter, the cards are sorted into master-file sequence. Third, a file-maintenance program is run, with the old master file as input and an updated master file as output. To insure accuracy, a list of all changes to the master file is printed along with control totals. Regardless of the number of changes, all the records must be read from the old master file and written on the new one.

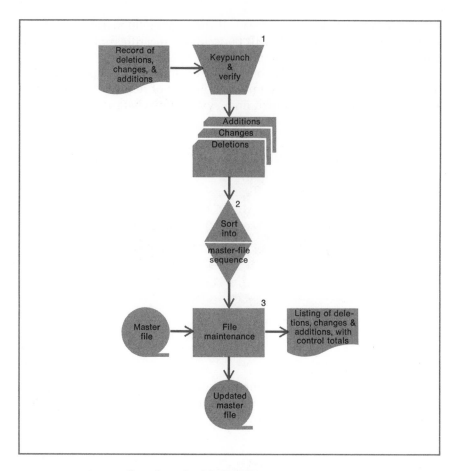

FIGURE 6-9   System flowchart for file maintenance

TAPE APPLICATIONS

With this background, you are ready for a description of a group of applications. Figure 6-10 shows a system flowchart of the daily procedures for the order-writing, billing, inventory, and accounts receivable applications. In the eleven steps shown, inventory records and accounts receivable records are updated, and shipping orders and invoices are printed. Since this application allows back orders, procedures are included for maintaining a back-order file and for filling back orders when inventory items are received. Because invoices are printed before items are shipped, this is a prebilling system. Although control posting and balancing steps would normally be shown on a flowchart such as this, they are omitted here in order to emphasize processing.

Figure 6-11 is a record layout form that shows the layouts of the card and tape records used in the system. Eight record formats are given—the

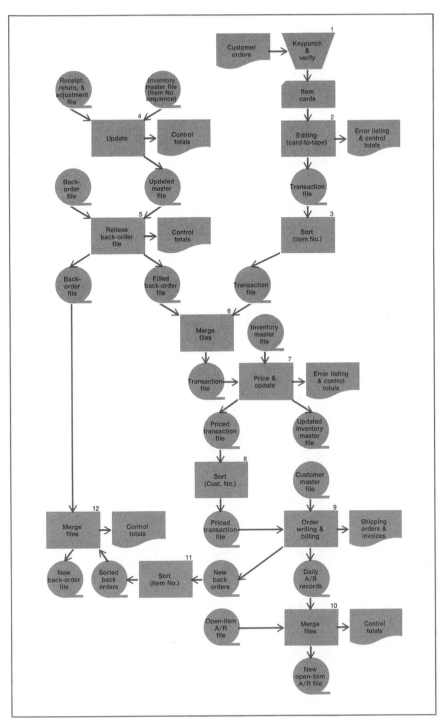

FIGURE 6-10 System flowchart for order writing, billing, inventory, and accounts receivable

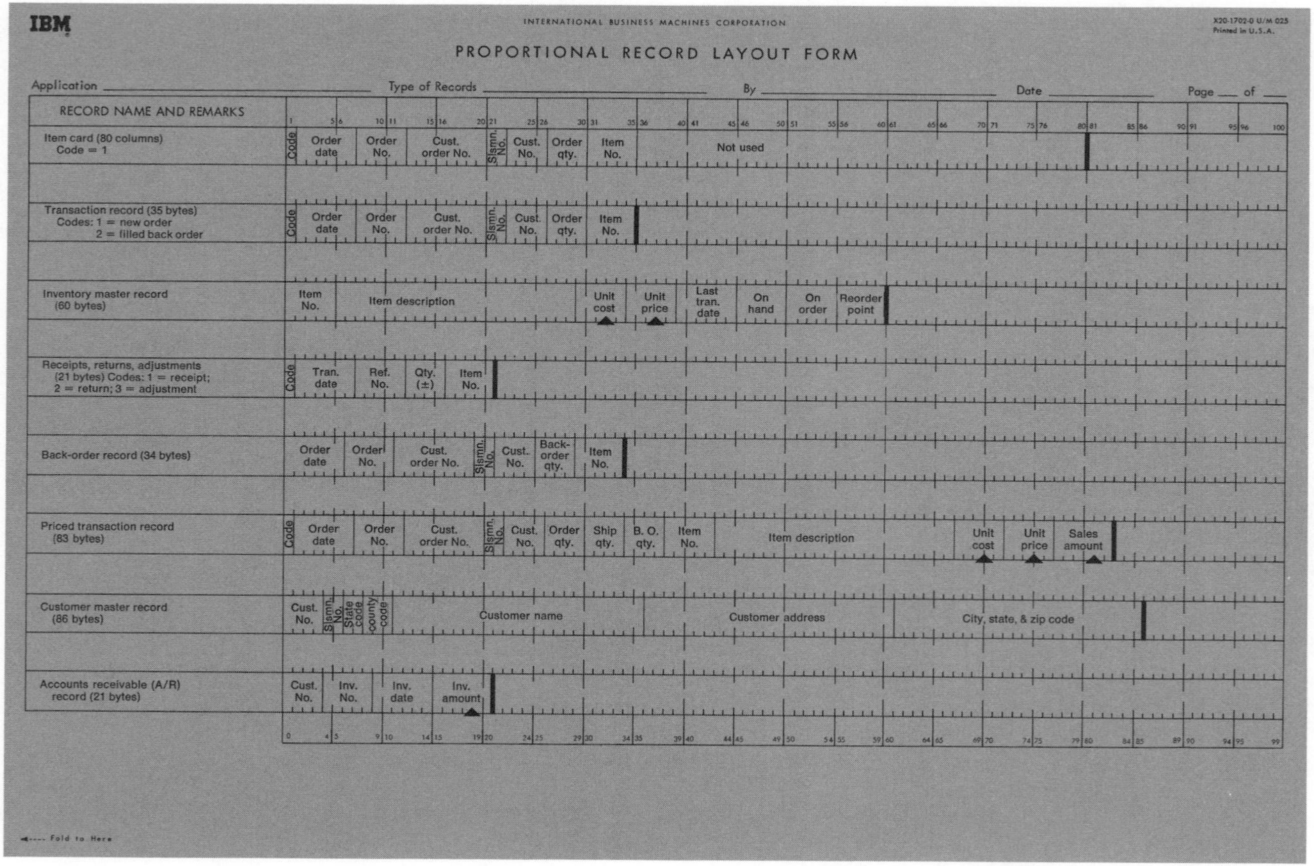

FIGURE 6-11   Formats for the tape applications

first is for the item card, the other seven for tape records. Since 100 positions can be laid out on each line of the form, a tape record of over 100 positions requires more than one line. In this example, all records are less than 100 positions long. The small black triangles, called carets, indicate the location of a decimal point in a field.

The system used in this application consists of a CPU, a combined card reader and punch, a printer, and four tape drives. Auxiliary equipment required consists of keypunches and verifiers. If additional tape drives were available on the system, the procedures would be much the same, although in some cases two steps could be combined into one.

In steps 1–3, item cards are keypunched and verified, converted to tape records, and sorted into item-number sequence in preparation for an inventory-update run. During step 2, editing routines are performed and a listing of invalid cards is printed. As you can see from the record layouts for the item card and the transaction record on tape, none of the data fields are changed during the conversion from card to tape, although the record size is reduced from eighty to thirty-five characters. The blocking factor for the transaction file and all other files indicated in this flowchart would be as large as the available core storage would permit.

In step 4, daily receipts, returns, and adjustments are processed against the inventory master file, thus providing an updated master file. The back-order file and the inventory master file are then processed together to determine if any back orders can now be filled. If so, those back orders that can be filled are written on a separate tape to be used in subsequent processing steps. The still unfilled back orders are written on another tape to represent the new back-order file.

In step 6, the filled back-order tape and the transaction tape are merged in preparation for an inventory-update run and for order writing and billing. The output tape consists of new orders and filled back orders in item-number sequence.

Step 7 is an inventory-update run. In addition, a priced transaction tape is created during this step. As you can see from the record layout in figure 6-11, the priced transaction records have the same fields as the transaction records, plus some additional ones. By comparing quantity ordered with the on-hand balance of the inventory master record, quantity shipped and quantity back-ordered are derived. Item description, unit cost, and unit price are taken from the inventory master record. Sales amount is calculated by multiplying quantity shipped by unit price. The priced transaction records are thus ready to be used to print the line items on an invoice or to prepare sales reports.

In steps 8 and 9, the priced transaction records are sorted into customer-number sequence, and the shipping orders and invoices are printed. Two additional tapes are created during the billing run. One consists of new back-order records; the other consists of accounts receivable records, one record for each invoice.

In step 10, the new accounts receivable records are merged into the open-item file of accounts receivable records. This file represents the unpaid invoices for all customers. It can be used to prepare monthly statements or an aged trial balance at the end of the month.

In step 11, the new back orders are sorted into item-number sequence, and in step 12, they are merged with the old back orders to create an up-to-date back-order file. This file is checked daily (step 5) to determine if any of the back orders can be filled.

In summary, although these procedures are typical, they are intended to show only the processing that takes place within the order-writing, billing, inventory, and accounts receivable applications. Thus, they do not necessarily demonstrate the full processing capabilities of a tape system. For example, the inventory master records could be expanded to include fields for monthly and year-to-date sales. During the update run, step 7, these fields could be updated. At the end of the month, then, an up-to-date sales report could be printed from the inventory master file in a tape-to-printer run. By using techniques such as this, the number of steps required to prepare sales, inventory, or accounts receivable reports can be reduced.

DISCUSSION

When you compare card and tape systems, you will find several advantages in tape systems. First, because of the difference between card and tape I/O speeds, a tape system can handle much larger volumes of data than a card system. Second, a tape system generally requires fewer steps for comparable processing results. For example, compare the tape flowchart in figure 6-10 with the card flowcharts in figures 5-12 and 5-15. Disregarding the control posting and balancing steps, which are not shown for the tape system, you will find that the card system requires several extra steps—and that's a card system with an MFCM. When you compare a tape system with a traditional card system, the difference is even more pronounced.

Third, because data on tape is easier to handle than data in cards, a tape system is likely to spend more time executing programs and less time waiting for an operator to get the system ready to load and execute a program. For instance, imagine the difference between stacking 10,000 cards in a card reader and mounting one tape on a tape drive. A good operator can mount a tape in less than fifteen seconds. In addition, programs in a tape system are loaded from an object tape. This is considerably more efficient than using an object deck for each program.

Finally, there is little chance of a record being lost when tapes are used. Thus, in control procedures, less emphasis can be placed on determining if all records in a file have been processed. In fact, as you will see in the next topic, control totals of the number of records in a file can be kept on the tape itself, and when reading a file, the computer can check to be sure that all records have been processed. If not, the computer prints a message on the console typewriter to alert the computer operator in regard to the error.

On the negative side, tape systems—as you would expect—cost more than card systems. For example, a typical card system might rent for $2000 per month, whereas a small tape system using the same CPU and four tape drives might cost $3000 per month. The idea, of course, is that the increased processing capabilities of the tape system more than make up the difference in cost.

Regardless of its features, a tape system comes out far less favorably when compared with a direct-access system. Because a direct-access device can read any record in a file without reading the preceding records, it can perform file-maintenance routines in ways that are impossible on a tape system. As a result, the concept of direct-access processing has pervaded the computer industry to such a degree that today there are relatively few pure tape systems. Instead, tape devices are normally used in conjunction with direct-access systems. For example, a small direct-access system is likely to consist of a CPU, a card reader and punch, a printer, four disk drives, and two tape drives.

Tape is valuable on a direct-access system for two reasons. First, it is much less expensive to store data on a tape than on a direct-access storage device. For example, a magnetic tape costs about $30, while a comparable amount of storage on a direct-access storage device is likely to cost over $500. When you consider that a company such as American Telephone and Telegraph has over 30,000 tapes in its storage files, you can appreciate the tremendous difference in costs.

Second, tape is the most efficient way of transferring data from one computer system to another. Although direct-access devices often cannot be transferred from one type of computer system to another, tapes are somewhat standard. As a general rule, tape from one computer system can be read on a comparable system, even that of another manufacturer.

In summary, the place of tape in the computer industry is changing. Where once a computer user moved from a card system to a tape system when his processing volumes grew, today he is likely to move to a direct-access system. As a result, the use of magnetic tape is still growing but at a slower rate than the rest of the computer industry. Nevertheless, magnetic tape will continue to play an important role, first as a storage medium and second as a medium for transferring data from system to system.

SUMMARY

1. One of the basic procedures in a tape system is updating a master file. After transactions are converted into tape records, they are sorted into master-file sequence and processed against the master file. The result is a new (updated) master file.

2. A tape system has several advantages over a card system, including faster I/O speeds, fewer procedural steps, ease in handling data and programs, and greater accuracy due to less chance of losing records.

3. Because of the merits of direct-access devices, the use of tape is growing more slowly than the rest of the computer industry. Nevertheless, tape continues to be important (1) as an inexpensive storage medium and (2) as a medium for transferring data between systems.

FOR
REVIEW

card-to-tape run
editing
sort program
update run
tape-to-printer program

When a computer user moves from one system to a larger or more sophisticated system, he usually encounters increased programming and system complexity. This topic presents some of the considerations peculiar to tape-system users.

PROGRAMMING CONSIDERATIONS

As much as 40 percent of an object program using tape input and output may be taken up by input and output routines. Some of the most important of these are error-recovery, blocking and deblocking, and label-checking routines. Although a programmer today doesn't actually have to write these routines, he must understand what they do and be able to state related specifications.

Error-Recovery Routines

When an error is detected during a card-reading operation, the program has no alternative but to ignore the card or halt processing. When a tape-reading error is detected, however, the error may often be recovered. If, for example, a piece of dust or dirt on the surface of the tape caused an error, it may be brushed off as the tape passes through the reading mechanism. If the tape is backspaced and the record is reread, the data can then be transferred to storage without error. In a typical tape routine, such as the one represented by the program flowchart in figure 6-12, a tape is backspaced and reread ninety-nine times before the program stops trying to recover the error. If the error still exists, a message is printed on the console typewriter and the system is temporarily halted.

The same type of programming routine is used for a writing operation. If a writing error is detected, a program backspaces and tries again. After a number of attempts, the program may skip a certain amount of tape — the equivalent of a long IRG — and try again. If errors still persist, the programming routine ends the job.

Blocking and Deblocking Routines

When a tape drive is given a read command, it reads an entire block of records into storage. However, a program usually processes only one record of a block at a time. As a result, *deblocking routines* are needed to keep track of which record in storage is being processed and which record is to be processed next. When writing a block of records, *blocking routines* must move the individual records into the output area of storage before the entire block is written.

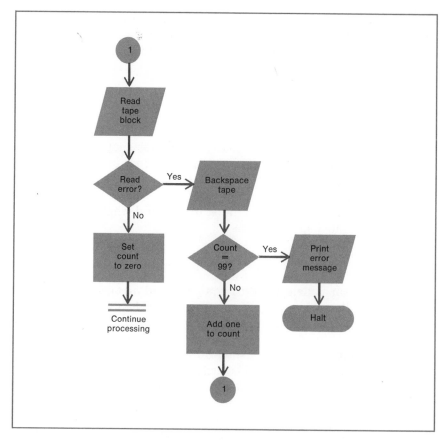

FIGURE 6-12   Program flowchart for an error-recovery routine

Label-Checking Routines

The instructions given to a computer operator for running a job tell
him which reel of tape to mount on which tape drive. The reels of tape
are identified by external labels on the outside of the reels. Suppose,
however, that the operator makes a mistake. He mounts a tape containing current accounts receivable records on a tape drive that is going
to write a file of updated inventory records. If this mistake isn't caught,
the accounts receivable records will be replaced by inventory records.

To prevent this type of error, *internal labels*—labels that are actually
records on the tape itself—are used. For example, a typical tape file
consists of the three label records shown in figure 6-13. (IBGs aren't
shown in this illustration.) The *volume label*, which is immediately
after the load-point marker, identifies the reel of tape. The *header label*,
which contains information such as the file name, the date the file was
created, and the date after which it can be destroyed, identifies the file.
The *trailer label*, found after the data records of the file, contains the

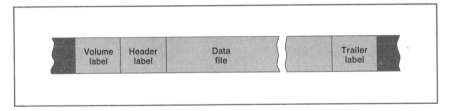

FIGURE 6-13   Labels for a tape file

same data as the header label, plus a block count indicating the number of blocks of data the file contains.

On a typical system, these labels are processed by comparing the data that the labels contain with data supplied by *job-control cards* at the time the object program is run. The job-control cards indicate which program should be loaded and executed, as well as which file should be mounted on which tape drive and what the volume and header labels should contain. Chapter 14, Operating Systems and Job-Control Language, goes into greater depth on the contents and format of labels and job-control cards.

To appreciate the value of label checking, consider how a typical program checks header labels before writing an output file. After the operator mounts a tape on a tape drive, the reading mechanism is positioned just before the volume and header labels. The first thing the program does is to read these labels and analyze the volume number of the volume label and the expiration date in the header label. If the volume number agrees with the volume number given in the job-control cards and if the expiration date has passed (that is, the file can be destroyed), the program backspaces the tape, writes a header label for the output file, and then begins processing. Otherwise, a message to the operator is printed, indicating that he has mounted the wrong file; thus, a costly error is avoided.

For input files, the header labels are checked to make sure that the identifying information agrees with the information given in the job-control cards. At the end of the file, the block count given in the trailer label is compared with a block count accumulated by the program. This is a type of automatic balancing to controls. If the block count in the trailer label and the block count accumulated during program execution are the same, all blocks on the tape have been read. If they aren't the same, the computer prints a message on the console typewriter to alert the operator to the error.

In many cases, a file of records will require more than one reel (volume) of tape. This is referred to as a *multivolume file* and requires additional label-checking routines. When writing a multivolume file, the tape drive must check for a reflective spot near the end of each tape—known as the *end-of-reel marker*. When it is encountered, the label-

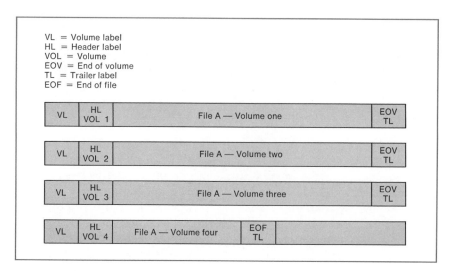

FIGURE 6-14   A multivolume file

checking routines write a trailer label, called an *end-of-volume label*, that includes the block count for that reel of tape. The routines then check the labels on the next reel of tape. If the next reel is accepted for processing, a header label is written, containing a volume sequence number that indicates the order in which the reels of tape should be read. On the last reel of the multivolume file, the program writes a file trailer label, called an *end-of-file label*, again containing the block count for the reel. This switching from one reel of tape to another is called *tape switching*. A four-volume multivolume file and the associated labels are illustrated in figure 6-14.

For multivolume input files, the label-checking routines check the header label of each reel to be sure that the correct file is being processed and that the reels are being processed in sequence. Thus, the first reel in the file must have a volume sequence number 1, the second must have sequence number 2, and so on. If the wrong file has been mounted, a message is printed and the program halted. At the end of each reel, prior to tape switching, the program checks the block count in the trailer label against a block count accumulated by the program to determine if all blocks have been read.

One final aspect of label-checking routines concerns *multifile volumes (multifile reels)*. These are reels of tape that have more than one file stored on them—for example, an inventory file, a billing file, and a sales-reporting file. In this case, as shown in figure 6-15, each file is preceded by a header label and followed by a trailer label. When reading a file from a multifile volume, the label-checking routines must be able to scan the tape until the correct label is located. When writing a file in any but the first position of a multifile volume, the label-checking

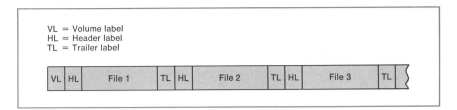

VL = Volume label
HL = Header label
TL = Trailer label

| VL | HL | File 1 | TL | HL | File 2 | TL | HL | File 3 | TL |

FIGURE 6-15   A multifile volume

routines must provide for locating the correct position for the output file.

What the Programmer Must Know

If the programmer had to write these I/O routines for each program, programming for tape systems would be an extremely tedious and repetitive job. Fortunately, however, most programming languages automatically assemble or compile the coding for tape I/O routines. The programmer need only know how to specify characteristics such as the record length, block length, and location of a multifile reel. Once these specifications are given, the programmer uses simple macro instructions that cause the appropriate I/O routines to be executed.

SYSTEM CONSIDERATIONS

Even with label-checking procedures, it is possible to destroy a current file of records by writing other records on the same tape. One way that this can happen is to disregard the error message printed by the computer, indicating an unexpired file. For example, if the computer operator keys a code on the console that indicates it is okay to write on the unexpired file, the file can be destroyed.

To decrease the likelihood of this type of error, *file-protection rings* must be mounted with a tape before a tape drive can write on the tape. The file-protection ring, illustrated in figure 6-16, pushes in a pin that is part of the tape drive, thus allowing writing operations to take place. The operator's instructions for a computer run indicate which tapes are to be mounted on which drives and which tapes should be mounted with file-protection rings. If the ring is not present, the file cannot be written on, and thus destroyed, no matter what other errors take place.

Even with the precautions of label-checking and file-protection rings, however, a system designer must provide for *backup*. Backup refers to the ability of a system to recreate tape files should they become lost or destroyed. For example, if the surface of a portion of a tape becomes damaged, the system must be able to recreate the lost records. Similarly, in case of fire or theft, the system must provide for backup.

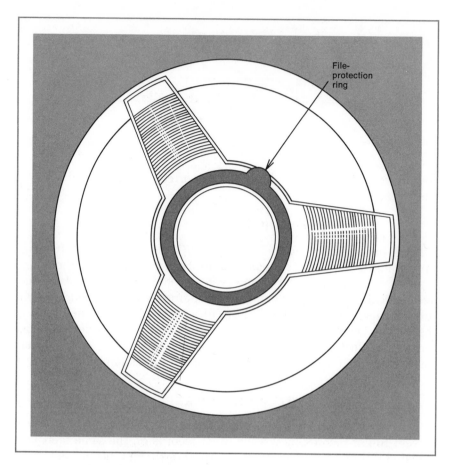

File-
protection
ring

FIGURE 6-16   The file-protection ring

On a tape system, backup is provided by saving the old master file and the transaction tape whenever a file is updated. Then, if the new master file is destroyed, it can be recreated by repeating the processing of the transactions against the old master file. In case both new and old master file are destroyed, the master file from which the old master was created is also saved, along with the transactions used to update it. This method of backup is referred to as the *grandfather-father-son method* since, for every current file (the son), two previous files (the grandfather and father) are kept. To insure that all three generations of tapes aren't destroyed by some disaster, the backup master files and transaction tapes are kept either in a separate building or in a fireproof vault.

SUMMARY

1. I/O routines for tape files must provide for error recovery, blocking and deblocking, label checking, tape switching for multivolume files, and tape searching for multifile volumes. Fortunately, modern programming languages provide these routines automatically when specifications are given by the programmer.

2. Even with label checking and file-protection rings, the system designer must provide for backup on a tape system. Normally, the grandfather-father-son method is used.

FOR REVIEW

error-recovery routine
deblocking routine
blocking routine
label-checking routine
internal label
volume label
header label
trailer label
job-control card
multivolume file

end-of-reel marker
end-of-volume label
end-of-file label
tape switching
multifile volume
multifile reel
file-protection ring
backup
grandfather-father-son method

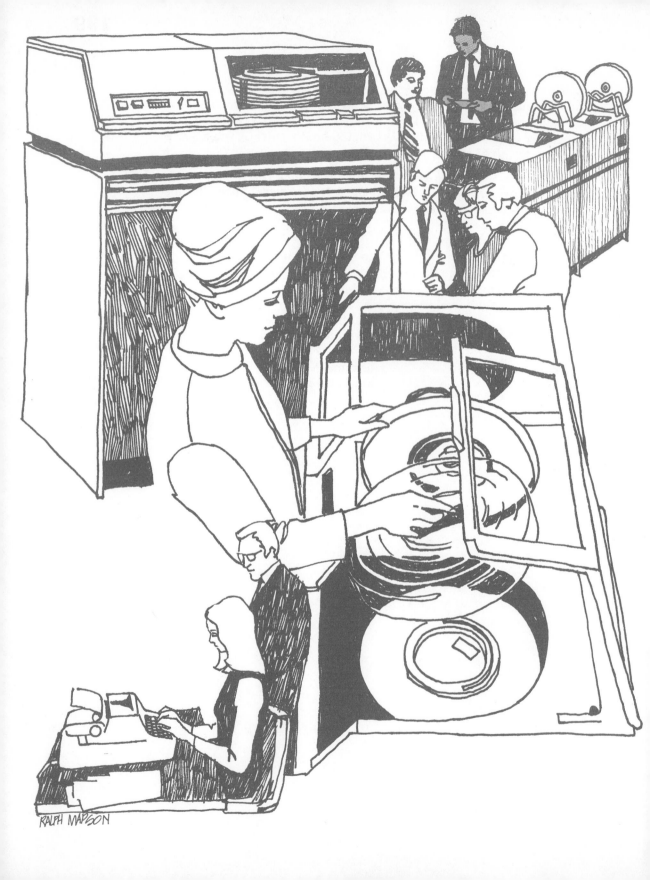

CHAPTER SEVEN

This chapter is divided into four topics. The hardware characteristics of some typical direct-access devices are described in the first topic, while several ways in which records can be stored on and accessed from direct-access devices are discussed in the second topic. After topic 3 covers the use of direct-access devices in a data-processing system—in particular, in an order-writing, billing, inventory, and accounts receivable system—topic 4 presents some programming and system considerations peculiar to direct-access systems.

Unlike tape devices, direct-access devices vary considerably in physical characteristics. For example, *disks* record data on platters that are somewhat analogous to phonograph records in a stack; *drums* record data on the outside of cylindrical (drum-like) surfaces; and *data cells* record data on plastic strips that are kept in bins. For each type of device, there are further variations depending on manufacturer and model. For instance, some disks have eight, some ten, and some twenty recording surfaces. Because of the variations, it is impractical to describe all of the direct-access devices in detail.

One of the most widely used direct-access devices is the disk—in particular, the IBM 2314 disk that is used on the System/360-370. With regard to system design and programming, the 2314 disk is also one of the most complex of the direct-access devices. By learning the concepts that apply to it, you will learn not only most of the concepts that apply to other disk models, but also most of those that apply to all direct-access devices.

TOPIC ONE
DIRECT-ACCESS DEVICES

DIRECT-ACCESS SYSTEMS

After the 2314 disk is described, the Burroughs B9372 disk is covered. This device illustrates many of the direct-access concepts not illustrated by the 2314. On the theory that it is better to learn about one or two devices in depth than to learn about many devices superficially, the 2314 and the B9372 are the only direct-access devices described in detail in this book.

THE IBM 2314 DISK DRIVE AND DISK PACK

The *disk pack* is the device on which data is recorded; the *disk drive* is the input/output unit that writes data on and reads data from a disk pack. The disk pack used with the 2314 disk drive, called the 2316 pack, is schematically illustrated in figure 7-1. It consists of eleven metal disks—fourteen inches in diameter—permanently stacked on a central spindle. When the disk pack is mounted on the 2314 disk drive, it rotates at a constant speed of forty revolutions per second while data is read from or written on it. When the disk pack is removed from the disk drive, a protective plastic cover is placed over it for storage.

Except for the top surface of the top disk and the bottom surface of the bottom disk, data can be recorded on both sides of the eleven disks that make up the 2316 pack; this is similar to sound being recorded on both sides of a phonograph record. Thus, this disk pack has a total of

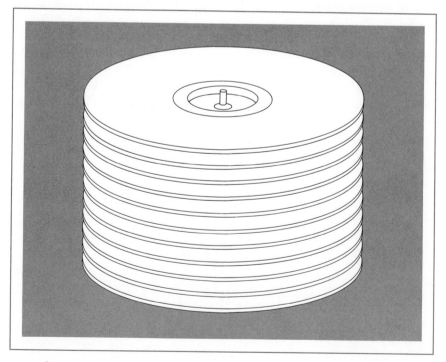

FIGURE 7-1   The disk pack

twenty recording surfaces, each of which has a magnetic surface coating on which data can be recorded.

On each of the twenty recording surfaces are 200 concentric circles called *tracks*, as illustrated in figure 7-2. These tracks are numbered from 000 through 199. Since there are twenty surfaces and 200 tracks per surface, the 2316 pack has a total of 4000 tracks on which data can be recorded. Although these tracks get smaller toward the center of the disk, each of the tracks can hold the same amount of data, a maximum of 7294 characters, or *bytes*.

Data is recorded on a track in the form of magnetized spots, called *bits*. These bits, which can be either "on" or "off," are strung together on a track so that eight bits make up one byte of data. To illustrate, suppose that figure 7-3 represents a portion of one track on one recording surface. If 0 represents an off-bit and 1 represents an on-bit, this portion of track contains three bytes of data. In System/360 code, the first byte, 11000001, represents the letter A; the second byte, 11110010,

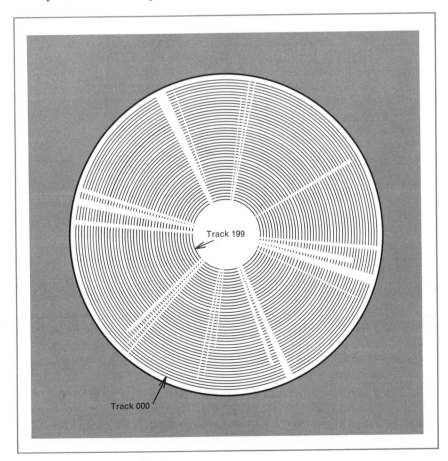

FIGURE 7-2   Tracks on a disk surface

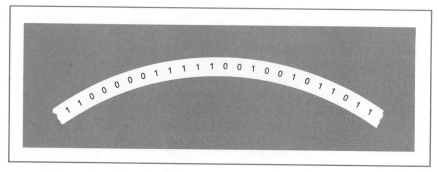

FIGURE 7-3   Coding on one section of a track

represents the digit 2; and the third byte, 01011011, represents the special character $. Other bit combinations are used to represent the remaining letters, numbers, and special characters.

The actual number of records on any track of a disk pack for the 2314 varies depending on the size of the records being stored. For example, one track can hold one 7294-byte record, two 3520-byte records, or three 2298-byte records. You can see that the capacity of a track decreases as the number of records on the track increases. If records are stored one per track, the track capacity is 7294 bytes; if two per track, the capacity is 7040 bytes (2 times 3520); if three per track, the capacity is 6894 bytes; and so on. By the time you get to records that are 100 bytes long, the track capacity is only thirty-six records, or 3600 bytes.

When records are stored on a disk pack, they can be stored in either of two track formats. The first, called the *count-data format*, is illustrated in figure 7-4. In this format, each record (*data area*) on a track is preceded by a *count area*. Since the illustration, which represents only one track, has four data areas, there are four count areas on the track. Each count area contains the *disk address* of the record following it. Just as a storage address identifies one and only one storage position, a disk address identifies one and only one data area on a disk pack. By using the count area, each of the records on a disk pack can be directly accessed and read.

In addition to count areas and data areas, each track in the count-data format has a *home address*. The home address, which is located immediately before the first count area on a track, uniquely identifies each of the tracks on a disk pack. On the 2316 disk pack, there are 4000 different home addresses, one for each of the 4000 tracks.

The second track format that can be used is called the *count-key-data format*. As in the count-data format, there is a home address at the start of each track. However, unlike the count-data format, there is a key area between each count and data area, as shown in figure 7-5. This *key area*, which can be from 1 through 255 bytes in length, contains control data that uniquely identifies a record in a file. For example,

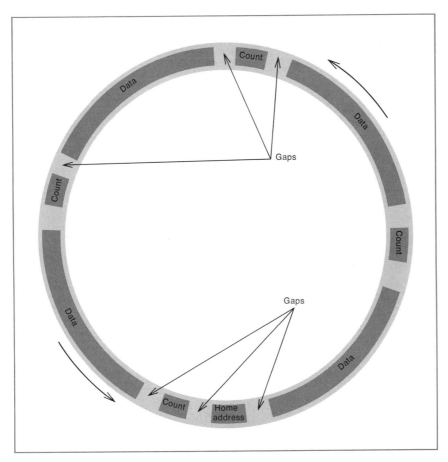

FIGURE 7-4   The count-data format

in a file of inventory master records, the part number would logically be recorded in the key area. In a file of master payroll records, the employee number would be recorded in the key area. The difference, then, between count and key areas is that the count area contains a disk address that uniquely identifies a record location on the disk pack, and the key area contains a control field that uniquely identifies a record in a file. As you will see later, both count and key areas can be used to locate records when directly addressing them.

Because the count-key-data format has gaps separating the key from the count and data areas, the track capacity of this format is less than that of the count-data format. For example, with one record per track (one home address, one count, one key, and one data area), the track capacity for the count-key-data format is 7249 bytes. This includes both key and data areas—say a 10-byte key and a 7239-byte data area. In contrast, the capacity of the track in count-data format is 7294 bytes. Similarly, with a 5-byte key and a 95-byte data area (a total of 100

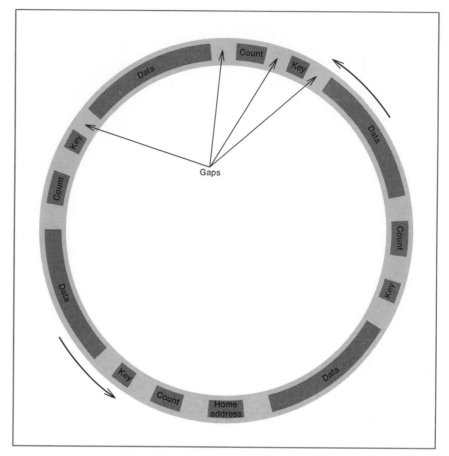

FIGURE 7-5   The count-key-data format

bytes of data), only twenty-nine records can be recorded per track in contrast to thirty-six records with the count-data format.

The Disk Drive

The IBM 2314 Direct-Access Storage Facility contains from one to nine independent disk drives. In figure 7-6, for example, a facility with five disk drives is shown. To mount a disk pack on one of the five drives, the operator pulls out the selected disk drive, places the disk pack on the drive's spindle, and pushes the compartment back into the facility. In a multidrive device such as this, a drive is often referred to as a *spindle*. Thus, the device in figure 7-6 can be called a 2314 with five spindles.

When the operator pushes the start button of the unit, the disk pack begins rotating until it reaches a speed of forty revolutions per minute. At this speed, the drive can read data from or write data on the recording

FIGURE 7-6 The 2314 direct-access storage facility

surfaces. When it reads data, the data on the disk pack remains unchanged; when it writes data, the data that is written replaces the data that was previously in that location on the disk.

The *access mechanism*, which is illustrated in side view in figure 7-7, is used to read and write data on the 2314. It consists of twenty *read/write heads*, one for each of the twenty recording surfaces. These heads are numbered from 0 through 19. Only one of the twenty heads can be turned on at any one time; thus, only one track can be operated upon at a time. Each of the heads can both read and write data but can do only one operation at a time.

In order to operate on all 200 tracks of each recording surface, the access mechanism moves to the track that is to be operated upon. When the access mechanism moves, all twenty heads move in unison so that 20 tracks can be operated upon in any one setting of the access mechanism. These 20 tracks are said to make up one *cylinder* of data. In other words, if the access mechanism is positioned at the seventy-fifth cylinder, the seventy-fifth track on each recording surface can be read or written. Since there are 200 tracks on each surface of the 2316 pack, there are 200 different settings of the access mechanism—and 200 cylinders. In figure 7-7, the access mechanism is positioned at approximately the sixty-fifth cylinder.

When directly accessing and reading a record on a disk, there are four phases that the disk drive goes through. During the first phase, called *access-mechanism movement*, the access mechanism moves to the cylinder that is going to be operated upon. The time required for this

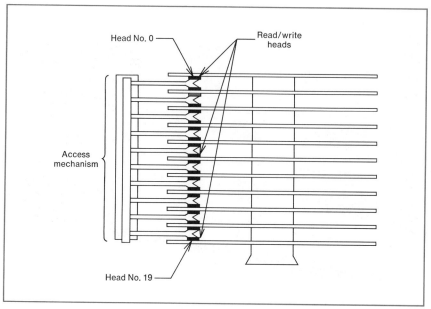

FIGURE 7-7   Side view of the access mechanism

movement depends on the number of cylinders moved. If it is just one cylinder — for instance, a move from the twenty-fifth to the twenty-sixth cylinder — it takes 25 milliseconds (25/1000 second). On the other hand, if the movement is 180 cylinders — say from the tenth to the one-hundred-ninetieth cylinder — the time required is 115 to 120 milliseconds, depending on the model used. In any event, the more cylinders moved, the more time required for access-mechanism movement. The average access-mechanism movement when processing a file that uses all 200 cylinders of the disk pack is 75 milliseconds on one model of the 2314, 60 milliseconds on another.

Once the heads are moved to the correct cylinder, the appropriate head must be turned on. This is called *head switching*. If the track on the third recording surface is supposed to be read, head number 2 is turned on. In figure 7-7, head number 2, which is on, is colored while the others are black. Since head switching takes place at electronic speeds, it has a negligible effect on the total amount of time required to read or write a record.

After the head is turned on, there is a delay while the appropriate record rotates around to the head. This phase is called *rotational delay* (or *latency*). Since one complete rotation on the 2314 takes 25 milliseconds, the maximum time that rotational delay could be is 25 milliseconds. On the other hand, the appropriate record might just be reaching the head as the head is switched on. In this case, rotational delay would be 0 milliseconds. Since rotational delay will vary between 0 and 25 milliseconds, the average delay is about 12.5 milliseconds.

The last phase in the process of accessing and reading a record is called *data transfer*. Here, data is transferred from the disk to storage in the CPU. On the 2314, data transfer takes place at a rate of 312,000 bytes per second. At this speed, a 312-byte record requires 1 millisecond for data transfer.

When accessing and writing a record, the same four phases are completed. First, the access mechanism is moved; second, the appropriate head is turned on; third, rotational delay takes place; and, fourth, the data is transferred from storage to the disk. In either a reading or a writing operation, access-mechanism movement and rotational delay are by far the most time-consuming phases.

Like other I/O devices on a computer system, the disk drive checks to make sure that reading and writing take place without error. Although I didn't mention it before, there are actually two *cyclic check characters* at the end of each count, key, and data area that are used as a check on accuracy. During a writing operation, these characters are calculated based on the combinations of bits used in the count, key, or data area. Then, when a record is read, the cyclic check characters are recalculated and compared with those that are read. If they don't agree, an input error is indicated.

A writing operation may be checked by using the Write-Verify instruction. When this instruction is executed following a Write instruction, the data that has just been written is read and the cyclic check characters are checked as in a read operation. If there is a discrepancy, it indicates that the writing operation did not take place correctly. The Write-Verify, however, is time consuming since the disk must make one complete rotation before the record that has been written can be read. Nevertheless, Write-Verification is commonly used when recording permanent files.

The actual *commands* (I/O instructions on System/360 are called commands) that a 2314 disk drive can be programmed to execute are many. These commands can be broken down into five types: Seek, Search, Read, Write, and Write-Verify.

The Seek command causes the access mechanism to be moved to the specified cylinder and the specified head to be turned on. A typical Search command searches a track until it finds a count or key equal to the one specified in the command. Rotational delay takes place during a Search. If the specified key or count isn't found, the search may be continued on successive tracks in the cylinder.

Once the Seek and Search have been executed, a Read or Write can take place. This is the data-transfer phase of the operation. In a typical business program, data only or data plus key is transferred during a Read or Write command. Following the Write command, a Write-Verify can be executed.

To illustrate the use of the commands, suppose that the fifth record on the seventh track of the one-hundred-twentieth cylinder must be accessed and read. The Seek command would specify that the access mechanism be moved to the one-hundred-twentieth cylinder and the seventh head (head number 6) be turned on. Next, a Search command would compare the counts on the track with the count specified in the command. Since the count for a record indicates the cylinder number, head number, and record number on the track, the count for this record would indicate that it is the fifth record on the track. When the count in the command and the count on the track are equal, the Read command would be issued, thus causing the data area following the count to be read.

When using the count-key-data format, a slightly different set of instructions can be used. First, the Seek finds the selected cylinder and turns on the selected head. Second, the Search looks for a key on the track that is equal to the one specified in the command. When they match, a Read command is issued, thus transferring the data area following the selected key into storage.

THE BURROUGHS B9372 DISK DRIVE

The Burroughs B9372 Disk File consists of one to five disk drives. Instead of a removable pack, each drive consists of nonremovable disks that are referred to as a disk module. Each module has four disk platters and eight surfaces on which data can be recorded. Disk files with two modules are shown in figure 7-8. There are several models of the B9372; the description that follows applies to the Model 1 unit.

Like the 2316 pack, there are circular tracks on each recording surface of the B9372. Data is recorded on these tracks as strings of bits, eight of which make up one character or byte of data. Unlike the format of the 2316 disk pack, however, each track of the B9372 consists of fixed-length 100-byte *segments*. Since 12,500 segments can be recorded on each surface, the storage capacity of each storage module is 10 million bytes (8 surfaces $\times$ 12,500 segments $\times$ 100 bytes).

One of the outstanding features of the B9372 drive is that there is one read/write head for each track of the storage module. As a result, there is no access mechanism and no access-mechanism movement. To access a record, the appropriate read/write head is switched on, the selected record rotates to the head (rotational delay), and the data is transferred. Since one rotation of the disk takes 40 milliseconds, the average rotational delay is 20 milliseconds. Because the time for head switching is negligible and there is no access-mechanism movement the total access time for each record averages 20 milliseconds.

One of the other features of the B9372 is the way in which records are addressed. Since there is no access mechanism, the concept of cylinders does not apply to this type of disk storage. Instead, the 100,000 segments in each storage module are numbered consecutively, starting with zero. The first module contains segments 0000000 to 0099999, the

FIGURE 7-8   The Burroughs B9372 disk file

second module (if there is one) contains segments 0100000 to 0199999, and so on. You can therefore think of storage on the B9372 as consecutively addressed 100-byte storage areas. Unlike the 2314, each record can be accessed in approximately the same amount of time (20 milliseconds), no matter where it is located on the disk.

Besides these major variations, the 2314 and B9372 differ in some other ways. The B9372 has a transfer rate of 208,000 bytes per second, as compared to 312,000 bytes per second for the 2314. However, the B9372 doesn't require a Seek command because it doesn't have access-mechanism movement. In contrast to the 2314, which uses cyclic check characters for checking the accuracy of input operations, the B9372 uses vertical and longitudinal parity checking, much like a tape drive does.

OTHER DIRECT-ACCESS DEVICES

Besides the 2314 and the B9372, there are many other disk models made up of various combinations of the characteristics illustrated thus far. Disk models vary as to number of recording surfaces, number of tracks, byte capacity per track, rotation speed, and so on. This results in a choice of devices with varying storage capacities, transfer rates, and access speeds.

Although the disk is by far the most common direct-access device, two

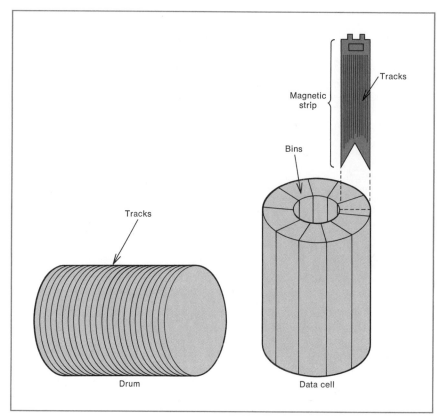

FIGURE 7-9   The drum and the data cell

others that you might come in contact with are the drum and the data cell; these are illustrated in figure 7-9. The drum is a cylindrical device with data recorded in tracks on the outside of the device. Because there is one read/write head for each track, the average access time is equal to the rotational delay, often less than 10 milliseconds per record. The two outstanding features of this device are (1) access speed and (2) transfer speed. One model drum, for example, has a transfer speed of over 1 million bytes per second—more than three times as fast as the 2314.

The data cell is a device that reads data from tracks recorded on magnetic strips, which are kept in bins. Before a record can be read or written, the selected bin must be rotated to a fixed read/write mechanism. Then, the selected strip is lifted from the bin, wrapped around a drum within the read/write mechanism, read or written, and returned to the bin. Because of the mechanical method of accessing a strip, a data cell has a relatively slow access speed—as much as 3/4 second per record, depending on how far the selected bin has to be rotated before reaching the read/write mechanism. The advantages of the data cell are its large capacity and relatively low cost. In contrast to the 2314, which has a capacity of 29 million bytes, one data cell can store 400 million bytes of data. With eight data cells attached to a computer system, 3.2 billion bytes can be directly accessed by a single computer system.

Regardless of the device, there are two basic record formats — variable format as with the 2314 and fixed format as with the B9372. When a device has a fixed format each addressable portion of a track is called a segment or *sector*, depending on the terminology used by the manufacturer. While many devices follow the idea of cylinder, track, and record or sector when addressing a record, other devices consecutively number the sectors and address them by sector number.

SUMMARY

1. The 2314 is a disk device consisting of one to nine spindles. It uses removable disk packs that have a variable track format. To read or write a record on the 2314 requires four phases: access-mechanism movement, head switching, rotational delay, and data transfer.

2. The B9372 consists of one to five modules with nonremovable disks and features one read/write head per track. It has a fixed track format — 100 bytes per segment — and addresses records by segment number. To read or write a record on the B9372 requires three phases: head switching, rotational delay, and data transfer.

3. There are many other types of disk devices, plus the drum and the data cell. The drum is noted for fast access and transfer speeds; the data cell for large storage capacities.

FOR
REVIEW

disk
drum
data cell
disk pack
disk drive
track
byte
bit
count-data format
data area
count area
disk address
home address
count-key-data format

key area
spindle
access mechanism
read/write head
cylinder
access-mechanism movement
head switching
rotational delay
latency
data transfer
cyclic check character
command
segment
sector

TOPIC TWO

FILE ORGANIZATION

For a device such as a tape drive or a card reader, the records in the file may be organized in only one way: sequentially. On a direct-access device, however, there are a number of possible file organizations. Three of the most common are: (1) sequential, (2) direct, and (3) indexed sequential.

SEQUENTIAL FILE ORGANIZATION

Although direct-access devices were designed for directly accessing records, they may also store and process records sequentially. In fact, sequential organization is the most efficient method for some files. When writing records sequentially on a 2314 disk device, the first record of the file is stored in the first record position on the first track of the first cylinder of the file, the second record is stored in the second record position on the first track of the first cylinder of the file, and so on. Sequential records on the B9372 are stored in consecutively numbered segments.

When reading the records in a sequential file, they are read beginning with the first physical location of the file and continuing consecutively until an end-of-file record is reached. Because the records in a sequential file are almost always processed sequentially, keys aren't needed on the 2314 and the count-data format is used.

To make efficient use of direct-access storage, the records in a sequentially organized file are usually *blocked*. This means that more than one record is read or written in a single Read or Write command. To illustrate, suppose a block consists of five 120-byte records. On the 2314, there will be 600 bytes in the data area following each count and five records will be read by one Read command. On the B9372, six segments containing five records will be read or written by a single I/O command.

Blocking is important because it reduces the time required to read or write a sequential file. With unblocked records, one Search and, therefore, one rotational delay is required for each record that is accessed. If the records are blocked, however, only one Search (rotational delay) is required for each block of records. When one Read command is executed, an entire block of records is read into storage. By eliminating rotational delay, blocking can significantly reduce the time required to read the records in a sequential file.

Blocking also affects the storage capacity of a direct-access device. On the 2314, for example, 7200 100-byte records will take 200 tracks, or ten cylinders, if the records are unblocked. If they are blocked nine to a block, however, seven such blocks may be recorded on each track—a total of 63 records per track. Then, the entire file requires only 115 tracks, or less than six cylinders.

On a device with segments or sectors, blocking helps to make full use of storage by eliminating wasted bytes within a sector. If 120-byte records are to be stored on the B9372, for example, each unblocked record will require two segments since a Read or Write command can only operate on complete segments. Thus, 80 bytes of storage are wasted for each record stored. If the records are blocked with a blocking factor of 5, however, no storage space is wasted. Then, five records are stored in six segments.

DIRECT FILE ORGANIZATION

In direct file organization, the records on the direct-access device are in no particular sequence. When a program is ready to read or write a record using this organization, it must supply the information required to locate the record on the device. On the B9372, for example, the program must supply the segment number of the desired record before the Search can be executed. On the 2314, the program must supply the cylinder and head number of the desired record before the Seek can be executed. And before the Search can be executed, either the record location on the track or the key of the desired record must be supplied. The trick in processing records in direct file organization, then, is determining the direct-access address for each record that is to be processed. This information is normally developed in a programming routine called a *randomizing routine*.

To illustrate the use of randomizing routines, suppose that 9600 inventory master records are to be stored on a 2314. These records are going to be in the count-key-data format with a key length of 7 bytes and a data area of 149 bytes. As you would guess, the key area for each record will contain the part number of the master inventory item.

Since twenty-four 149-byte records with 7-byte keys can be stored on one 2314 track, this file requires 400 tracks (9600 ÷ 24), or twenty cylinders. However, because of the difficulty of assigning these records to a specific track and because additional master records may be added to the file later, twenty-five cylinders, or 500 tracks, are allotted for the file. These cylinders are numbered from 060 through 084.

For this file, the problem of the randomizing routine is to convert a record's part number, which may range from 100,000 through 9,000,000, to a specific cylinder and head number somewhere within cylinders 060–084. This data will be used in the Seek command when accessing a record. After the access mechanism has been moved to the selected cylinder and the selected head is turned on, the Search command will locate the record on the track by searching for a key equal to the record's part number.

One common method used in randomizing routines is called the *division/remainder method*. In this method, the part number is first divided by the prime number closest to and less than the number of tracks allotted to the file. (A prime number can be divided evenly by only 1 and itself; for example, 1, 2, 3, 7, 11, and so forth.) Since there are 500 tracks assigned to the file, the prime number is 499. If the part number is 254932, then, the quotient is 510 with a remainder of 442. In the division/remainder method, though, only the remainder of this first division is significant. This number, 442, gives the relative location of the track on which the record should be stored. Because the divisor is always 499 for this file, the remainder will always be from 000 through 498.

Once the relative track location is determined, the randomizing routine must convert it to a cylinder and head number. In the example, if the relative track, 442, is divided by 20 (the number of tracks in a cylinder), the remainder is a head number between 0 and 19. Then, if 60 is added to the quotient, the result is a cylinder number between 060 and 084. For the part number 254932, the cylinder number becomes 82 ($442 \div 20 = 22$; $22 + 60 = 82$) and the head number becomes 2 ($442 \div 20 = 22$ with a remainder of 2). Figure 7-10 summarizes the characteristics of the file and the randomizing routine used in this example.

A DIRECT-ACCESS FILE ON THE 2314

Characteristics of the file:
1. A file of 9600 inventory records is to be stored in cylinders 060 through 084.
2. Each track can hold a total of 24 inventory records, which consist of 149-byte data areas and 7-byte keys.
3. The part numbers, which are the keys, range from 100,000 to 9,000,000.

Problem of randomizing routine:
To convert the part numbers of the 9600 master records to cylinder and head numbers that are within the 25 cylinders assigned to the file.

The division/remainder method:
1. Divide part number by 499 — the remainder is the relative track, which will always be between 0 and 498.
2. Divide the remainder by 20 — the remainder is the head number.
3. Add 60 to the quotient of the second division to obtain the cylinder number.

Examples of randomizing:

Part No.	Cylinder No.	Head No.
100,000	70	0
254,932	82	2
794,210	75	1
1,048,342	82	2
9,000,000	61	16

Loading the records on the 2314:
1. Convert the part number to cylinder and head number.
2. Seek cylinder and head number.
3. Search for next available location on the track.
4. Write the record in the first available location.
(If entire track is filled, the record must be written in successive tracks of the cylinder or in an overflow area of the disk.)

FIGURE 7-10   Direct file organization

When initially loading the inventory records on the 2314, each master part number is converted to a cylinder and head number as described. Then, the record is written in the first available location on the track indicated. If the track is filled (it already has twenty-four records), additional programming routines are required. Two of the most widely used alternatives are (1) to write the record on the next track in the cylinder, assuming that it has an available record location, or (2) to write the record in an *overflow area* somewhere else on the disk.

An overflow area is simply an area that is used for records that cannot be stored in the locations assigned to them by the randomizing routine. In the example of the inventory file, cylinder 085 could be used as an overflow area. Then, if there is no room for record number 254932 on cylinder 82, head 2, the record could be written in the first available location in cylinder 085.

When accessing and reading an inventory record from a 2314 file, the part number of the desired record is first converted to cylinder and head number by the randomizing routine. Then, after the Seek locates the selected cylinder and head, the Search looks for a record with a key equal to the part number of the desired record. If it finds the selected key, the record is read into storage. If it does not find the key, programming routines are required that correspond to the routines used in loading the file. For example, if an overflow area is used, the program must seek the overflow cylinder and search for the selected record there.

Although the randomizing routine summarized in figure 7-10 creates a valid cylinder and head number for each record in the master file, it may not be the best randomizing method available. One major problem is that 17,835 other part numbers between 100,000 and 9,000,000 will randomize to the same cylinder and track as part number 254932—but only 24 records can be stored per track and only 480 per cylinder. As a result, some other randomizing method may be more suitable for the file—the division/remainder method is only used as an example. In actual practice, a programmer or a system designer considers several different randomizing methods and sometimes actually tries one or more of the methods before making a final decision.

On the B9372, or any device that addresses records by sector number, the randomizing routine must convert the control number in a record to a segment or sector number. To illustrate, suppose 800 customer master records, 100 bytes long, are to be stored on the B9372. To give the randomizing routine some leeway, 1000 segments are assigned to the file—segments 8000–8999. The customer numbers are five-digit numbers ranging from 10000–99999.

Using the division/remainder method, the customer number is divided first by the prime number nearest but less than the total number of segments assigned to the file—in this case, 997 is used. The remainder of this division gives the relative segment number within the file. For example, if the customer number is 34405, the relative segment number is 507. Then, by adding 8000 to this number, a segment number between 8000 and 8999 is derived.

When initially loading a file on the disk, a problem arises when two or more records randomize to the same segment. When a record is already stored in a segment, the other records assigned to that address—called *synonyms*—must be assigned to unfilled segments. Customer number 34405, for example, has eighty-nine possible synonyms—eighty-nine other customer numbers that randomize to segment 8507. As a result, additional programming routines must be available to store synonyms in other segments.

There are several methods for handling synonyms on a fixed segment or sector device; one of these is to write the synonyms in the next available direct-access location. For example, if customer number 38393 randomizes to segment 8507 but record number 34405 is already stored in this segment, the randomizing routine tries to write record number 38393 in segment 8508. If this segment already contains a master record, segment 8509 is tried, and so on.

To help locate a synonym when accessing a record, a *chaining* technique is commonly used. This means that each record stored in the file contains a field, called a *chaining field*, that gives the segment or sector number of the first synonym that was not stored at its randomized address. This process is illustrated in figure 7-11. If you go through the sequence of records to be stored you will find that the first synonym is record number 41383, which randomizes to segment 8506. Since record number 11473 is already stored in this segment, record 41383—the synonym—is stored in the next available segment, segment 8508. As a result, segment number 8508 is stored in the chaining field of the record located in segment 8506.

To access a record when chaining is used, a program first determines the direct-access address by a randomizing routine. It then reads the record at this address and checks to see if the control field is the desired one. If not, it reads the segment address given by the chaining field. If this segment does not contain the correct record, the next segment in the chain is read. The program continues in this way until the desired record is found or no further chaining address is given. In the latter case, the program assumes that the record is not stored on the file.

When records in a direct file are blocked, additional programming routines are required. When loading a file, the records have to be randomized to a block of records rather than to an individual storage location. Overflow records for each block can be stored in the next available block or in overflow areas; and a chaining technique, with one chaining field for each block of records, may be used. Blocking is likely to improve the use of the available disk storage, but it will probably decrease the speed at which records are accessed and read. Thus, the use of blocking

A DIRECT-ACCESS FILE ON THE B9372

Characteristics of the file:
1. A file of 800 customer records is to be stored in segments 8000—8999 of a B9372.
2. The customer numbers range from 10000 to 99999.

Problem of randomizing routine:
To convert the customer numbers of the 800 master records to segment numbers from 8000 through 8999.

The division/remainder method:
1. Divide the customer number by 997 — the remainder is the relative segment number.
2. Add 8000 to the relative segment number.

Order of records to be stored:

Customer No.	Segment No.
34405	8507
11473	8506
21448	8511
41383	8506
34406	8508
61327	8510
24439	8514
60326	8506
30421	8514

Segments, records, and chaining fields:

Segment No.	Cust. No.		Chaining Field
8506	11473	DATA	8508
8507	34405	DATA	XXXX
8508	41383	DATA	8509
8509	34406	DATA	8512
8510	61327	DATA	XXXX
8511	21448	DATA	XXXX
8512	60326	DATA	XXXX
8513	XXXXX	DATA	XXXX
8514	24439	DATA	8515
8515	30421	DATA	XXXX

FIGURE 7-11   Direct file organization using segments

depends on considerations such as the addressing characteristics of the device used, the access speeds required, and the available storage capacity.

INDEXED SEQUENTIAL FILE ORGANIZATION

Although sequential and direct file organizations have their advantages, they also have their limitations. For example, while a blocked sequential file may make maximum use of the storage capacity of a direct-access device, it has many of the limitations of a tape file. To update a sequential file, all of the records in the file are read instead of just those affected by transactions, and the entire file has to be rewritten in order to add a record to the file. On the other hand, while direct file organization allows a record to be accessed rapidly, it wastes storage capacity. (Remember the example where twenty-five cylinders are assigned to a file consisting of twenty cylinders of data.) In addition, a direct file must usually be sorted into sequential order before a sequential report can be prepared from it.

Indexed sequential file organization is designed to allow both sequential and direct (or *random*) processing. (Random means that records are not processed in any particular sequence.) Using indexed sequential organization, the records of a file are stored on the direct-access device so that they can be read sequentially, but *indexes* are kept so that any record can be read randomly by looking up its location in the indexes. If records are added to the file, an additional file area called an overflow area is used, thus making it unnecessary to rewrite the entire file as done in sequential organization. When a record is stored in the overflow area, the indexes are changed so that the records can still be processed in sequence.

In a typical indexed sequential file on a 2314, two indexes are kept: a *cylinder index* and a *track index*. The cylinder index is used to find the cylinder in which a record is located. To illustrate, suppose a file of master customer records is stored in cylinders 11–15 of a disk pack and the cylinder index is kept on the first track of cylinder 16. Since five cylinders are used in the file, there will be five records in the cylinder index, always in the count-key-data format. The key in each index record contains the highest customer number stored in each cylinder of the file and the data area indicates in which cylinder the records are located. For example, the cylinder index might contain the following data:

Key	Data
1949	C11
3241	C12
5972	C13
7566	C14
9840	C15

By searching this index, a program can determine that the record for customer 6500 is stored in cylinder 14. (C is used to indicate that the number in the data area is a cylinder number.)

The same idea is used when searching track indexes. These indexes, which are found on the first track of each cylinder in the file, indicate the key of the highest customer number on each track of the cylinder.

For example, the track index for the fourteenth cylinder might contain
the following data:

Key	Data	Key	Data
6198	T2	6893	T11
6258	T3	6979	T12
6322	T4	7053	T13
6398	T5	7119	T14
6449	T6	7200	T15
6570	T7	7303	T16
6609	T8	7471	T17
6701	T9	7566	T18
6813	T10		

By searching this index, a program can determine that record 6500 is on
the seventh track of the cylinder. (T is used to indicate that the number
in the data area is a track number.)

Once the program has determined the track number, it can find a record by searching for a key equal to the control number in the record—
in this case, customer number 6500. Because the search is always for
key rather than count, indexed sequential files must always be in the
count-key-data format.

If you wonder why the track index in the above example indicates
only seventeen tracks (tracks 2–18), remember that the first track is
used for records that make up the track index. If there is space left over
on this first track, it can be used for storing data records, in which case,
there will be an index for track number 1 also. In the example, it is
assumed that the index uses the entire first track.

The nineteenth and twentieth tracks of the cylinder are used when
records are added to the file. These tracks make up the *cylinder overflow area*. They contrast tracks 2–18, which make up the *prime data
area* of the cylinder. The number of tracks assigned to the overflow area
is based on the number of records likely to be added to a cylinder.

When an indexed sequential file is created, the records are written in
sequence in the prime data area. As the records are written, the cylinder
and track indexes are created so the records in the file can be directly
accessed. When all of the records are stored on the file, an end-of-file
record is written just as if the file had sequential organization. After
the file is loaded, track 1 of each cylinder contains the track index
records, tracks 2–18 contain the records of the file in sequence, and
tracks 19–20, the cylinder overflow area, contain no data at all.

When a record is added to an indexed sequential file, it is placed in
its sequential location in the prime data area. All records on the track
with higher keys are moved up one record location and the record that
is moved off the track is placed in the cylinder overflow area. To allow

records in this overflow area to be processed sequentially as well as directly, overflow index records are kept in the track index along with the normal index records. When a record is placed in the overflow area, the overflow index is changed so that it locates the next record in sequence following the records on the normal track in the prime data area. If more than one record is moved from one normal track to the cylinder overflow area, a chaining field in each overflow record is used to point to the direct-access address of the next record in sequence. Thus, a chain of sequential records is maintained.

To illustrate the use of a cylinder overflow area, overflow index records, and chaining, consider the example in figure 7-12. It illustrates the normal and overflow index records in the track index of one cylinder, cylinder 11, as well as nine overflow records in the overflow area, cylinders 19 and 20. C, T, and R are used to indicate cylinder, track, and record numbers. Since the keys in the normal and overflow index records for track 2 are the same, it means that there are no overflow records for this track. The same is true with track 3. For track 4, however, the key of the normal index entry is 322, whereas the key of the overflow index record is 339. This means that there are one or more overflow records from this track. Both the normal and overflow records can be read sequentially, however, in this manner:

1. Read the records on the normal track in sequence. (These records are always in sequence.)

2. Read the overflow record indicated in the overflow index; namely, record 4 on track 19. This is the next record in sequence.

3. Read the record indicated in the chaining field of the overflow record. Since this field points to the second record on track 20, that record is next in sequence.

4. Continue reading the chain of records until the chaining field indicates record number 255; then continue with the first record on the next normal track—in this case, track 5.

The same logic holds for processing the other overflow records in sequence. As a result, the next records in sequence would be those from track 5, then those from track 6, then record 3 on track 20, then record 3 on track 19, then the records from track 7, and so forth. If you wonder why the records in the overflow area aren't in sequence, it is because the records are placed there in the order in which additions are made to the file. The only sequential linkage between these records comes from the chaining fields.

To directly access records when there are overflow records, a somewhat different logic is used. First, the track indexes are searched as usual—the order of these indexes is track 1 normal index, track 1 overflow index, track 2 normal index, track 2 overflow index, and so

TRACK 1   TRACK INDEX RECORDS

NORMAL		OVERFLOW	
Key	Data	Key	Data
187	T2	187	T2
284	T3	284	T3
322	T4	339	T19, R4
397	T5	397	T5
513	T6	580	T20, R3
641	T7	641	T7
787	T8	787	T8
940	T9	949	T20, R1
991	T10	991	T10
1205	T11	1205	T11
1297	T12	1297	T12
1391	T13	1404	T19, R2
1522	T14	1522	T14
1639	T15	1639	T15
1740	T16	1742	T19, R5
1833	T17	1833	T17
1949	T18	1949	T18

TRACKS 2–18   THE PRIME DATA AREA

Track	Keys on Track					
2	012	041	049	094	101	187
3	188	210	218	247	250	284
4	287	291	294	301	307	322
5	341	348	354	363	370	397
6	410	415	420	434	470	513
7	585	592	601	615	621	641
8	660	680	685	710	740	787
9	812	819	901	914	927	940
10	951	957	967	984	985	991
11	1032	1105	1117	1121	1187	1205
12	1207	1208	1231	1239	1250	1297
13	1330	1337	1341	1355	1366	1391
14	1410	1415	1423	1480	1481	1522
15	1523	1530	1537	1539	1599	1639
16	1641	1645	1691	1701	1703	1740
17	1748	1780	1788	1790	1805	1833
18	1838	1847	1897	1901	1930	1949

TRACKS 19–20   THE CYLINDER OVERFLOW AREA

Count	Key	Chaining Field	Data Record
C11, T19, R1	339	R255	DATA
C11, T19, R2	1397	T19, R6	DATA
C11, T19, R3	580	R255	DATA
C11, T19, R4	331	T20, R2	DATA
C11, T19, R5	1742	R255	DATA
C11, T19, R6	1404	R255	DATA
C11, T20, R1	949	R255	DATA
C11, T20, R2	333	T19, R1	DATA
C11, T20, R3	555	T19, R3	DATA

FIGURE 7-12   Indexed sequential file organization

on. If the desired record is in the prime data area, the track is searched for the selected key as if there were no overflow records. If the desired key falls in the overflow area, however, the record indicated by the overflow index is searched for and read. If this isn't the desired record, the record indicated in the chaining field is searched and read. This search is continued until the desired record is found or the end of the chain is reached.

To illustrate, consider a search for record number 555 in figure 7-12. Since 555 is greater than 513 but less than 580, the track indexes indicate that the record is in the cylinder overflow area. As a result, the search begins with the record indicated in the overflow index record, record 3 of track 20. Since this record is the desired record, the search ends. However, if it were not record 555, the search would continue with the record indicated in the chaining field. Because of the extra searching (rotational delay) required for records in the overflow area, indexed sequential files should be reorganized periodically so that all records are returned to the prime data area.

On a device such as the B9372, the concept of indexed sequential is similar, although the details are different. Rather than loading the file sequentially, the file can be loaded in any order; chaining fields are used in all records so that the file can be accessed sequentially. Since the B9372 doesn't have cylinders, the terms cylinder index and track index don't apply. Instead, a *coarse index* and a *fine index* are used. The coarse index gives the location of the fine index to be used; the fine index gives the location of individual records to be accessed. Thus, the coarse index may indicate that the location of record number 73349 can be determined from the fine index starting in segment 10025. Then the fine index may indicate that the record is located in segment 12104. When records are added to a file, a chaining technique is used so that the records in the overflow area can be accessed in both sequential and random order.

In addition to the concepts described, there may be many other variations in the organization and handling of indexed sequential files. Nevertheless, any indexed sequential file can be processed in sequential or random order with relative ease—the major feature of this method of file organization. When processing sequentially, however, an indexed sequential file is likely to be slower than a sequential file. (Consider the extra searches for records in the overflow areas.) Similarly, when processed randomly, an indexed sequential file is likely to be slower than a direct file. (Consider the seeks and searches required for finding a record in the indexes used.) Because each type of file organization has its advantages and limitations, you can only decide which type of organization to use after considering a file's characteristics as well as all of the uses to which a file will be put.

1. Sequential files on direct-access devices are comparable to tape files. They can be read only in the sequence in which the records are located on the direct-access device. To maximize I/O speed and storage use, sequential files are normally blocked.

2. In direct files, the records are loaded based on a randomizing routine. The control number in the record to be stored must be converted to a direct-access address such as cylinder and track number or sector number. Additional routines must be available to handle overflow records or synonyms.

3. Indexed sequential file organization is designed to allow records to be processed on either a sequential or a random basis. Two or more indexes are kept to locate records on a random basis, and overflow areas are used for additions to the file. So that records in the overflow area can be processed in sequence, chaining is used.

SUMMARY

sequential file organization
blocking
direct file organization
randomizing routine
division/remainder method
overflow area
synonym
chaining
chaining field

indexed sequential file organization
random
index
cylinder index
track index
cylinder overflow area
prime data area
coarse index
fine index

**FOR
REVIEW**

TOPIC THREE

SYSTEM DESIGN

In a system flowchart for a direct-access system, the following symbols are used:

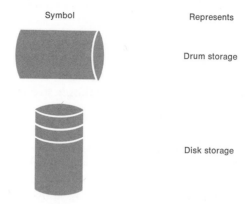

Symbol	Represents
	Drum storage
	Disk storage

Since disk is by far the most common direct-access device, this book uses only the disk symbol. Remember, however, that the steps required within a system are much the same, regardless of the type of direct-access device used.

One of the basic procedures in any system is the procedure for updating a master file. For example, inventory records, accounts receivable records, sales records, and payroll records must be continually updated. In figure 7-13, a system flowchart for one method of updating direct-access files is illustrated.

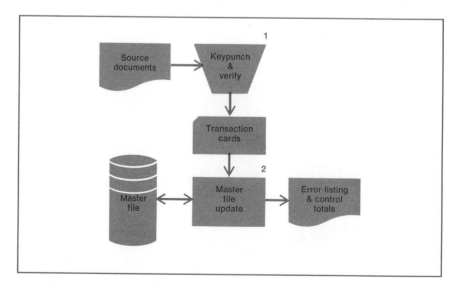

FIGURE 7-13   System flowchart for a master-file update

In step 1, transaction data from source documents is keypunched and verified. This is similar to the first step when processing data on a card or tape system.

The second and last step in the system is the *update run* on the computer. To illustrate what takes place here, assume that a master file of inventory records is stored with indexed sequential or direct file organization and that it is processed on a random basis. The first four transactions to be processed have item numbers 217, 109, 217, and 540. When the update program reads the first transaction, item number 217, it searches for master record 217, processes the record, and writes the updated master record in the same location from which it was read. When the program reads the second transaction, it searches for master record 109, updates the record, and writes it on the disk in its original location. The program continues in this way with records 217 and 540. During the program, various checks on the validity of input data may be performed and a list of error transactions may be printed. Invalid transactions are ignored, so they do not affect the master file.

Although transaction records for random updates do not have to be in sequential order, it is often more efficient if they are. In the previous example, because the transactions weren't in order, master record 217 had to be read and written twice, once for each transaction. In contrast, if the input records had been in sequence — 109, 217, 217, and 540 — master record 217 would have been read and written only once. For this reason, transaction records are often sorted before processing, even though they are processed on a random basis.

Unlike tape processing, there is no old master file when a direct-access file is updated. Because the updated record replaces the old record, the old record is destroyed. As a result, it is extremely important that no mistakes are made during an update program. Consequently, an editing program for transaction data is usually run before the update actually takes place. This program checks to be sure that all fields in the transaction records contain valid data by testing that numeric fields contain numeric data, that transaction codes are valid, that the contents of a field are within acceptable limits, and so on.

Figure 7-14, then, presents another procedure for updating a master file. In step 1, the transactions are keypunched and verified. In step 2, the card transactions are edited and converted into a sequential disk file by a *card-to-disk program* that includes editing routines.

Step 3 is a sort step in which the sequential transaction file is sorted into master-file order. Although a *sort program* will use several different areas of the disk or several different disks, only one input and one output file is shown on a flowchart. A disk sort program is complex and usually supplied by the computer manufacturer. To use the program, the user supplies only the specifications of the sort to be run; the sort program

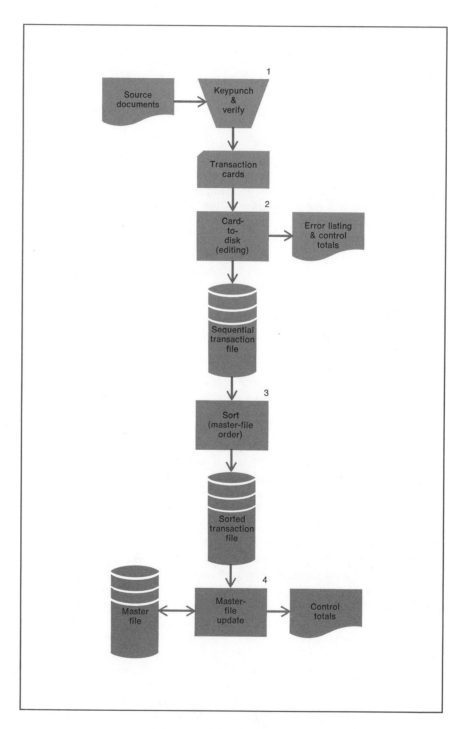

FIGURE 7-14 System flowchart for the refined master-file update

does the rest. Because of the unique capabilities of a direct-access device, a disk sort program is likely to take considerably less time to execute than a comparable tape sort program.

In step 4, the update program is executed as previously described. Because the transactions are in master-file order, however, each affected master record is read and written only once.

If you compare the flowchart in figure 7-14 with the flowchart for a tape update (figure 6-7), you will find them very similar. In fact, if the master file in figure 7-14 has sequential or indexed sequential organization, it could be processed sequentially. The update would then be the same as tape processing with these exceptions: (1) the updated master record is written in its original location on a direct-access device, and (2) it is not necessary to rewrite a master record on the device if it has not been affected by transactions.

The decision as to whether sequential or random processing is used depends on how many of the records in a master file are affected during a typical day's processing. If 80 percent of the records are affected, sequential processing will likely be more efficient. If only 10 percent of the records are affected, random processing will probably be more efficient. The important feature of a direct-access device is that it allows the computer user to choose whichever method is better.

To add, change, or delete records on a master file, a procedure such as the one in figure 7-13 is likely to be used. Records that are added to an indexed sequential file make use of the overflow area of the file; records that are added to a direct file are stored using the logic of the file-creation program. Normally, deleted records are not removed from the file. Instead, a code is placed in the deleted record indicating that it is no longer active. For example, an asterisk in the first byte of a record can indicate that it has been deleted. Because additions, changes, and deletions are commonly handled on a random basis, only the affected master records are read or written.

If records are processed on a random basis, more than one master file can be updated by the same set of transactions during the same update run. For example, both inventory and salesman records can be updated by transaction records that indicate which items have been sold to which customers by which salesman. The multiple update can be shown as follows:

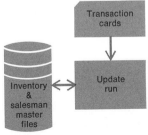

Here, the files could be on the same or separate disk drives. For each transaction card, two master records—the inventory and salesman records—are updated.

Using *disk-to-printer programs*, reports may be printed at any time from up-to-date master files. For example, a sales-by-salesman report could be printed from a file of salesman master records as follows:

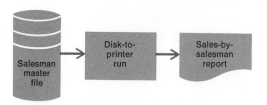

A disk-to-printer program normally processes records in sequential order; it simply reads a record, converts the data to a readable form, and prints the data. If the file is stored in direct organization, the records are sorted into sequential order by a sort program before the disk-to-printer program is executed.

DISK APPLICATIONS

Because of the direct-access capabilities of a disk, a disk system can eliminate many of the steps common to sequential systems. Sorting and merging can be eliminated and more than one file can be updated by a single program. In a simple billing, inventory, and accounts receivable application, for example, two files can be updated and invoices can be printed in just a few steps. This is illustrated in the flowchart in figure 7-15. Because invoices are printed after the items are shipped, this is a postbilling system. In step 1, the transaction records are keypunched and verified. In step 2, the input data is edited and converted to disk. In step 3, the invoices are printed, and the inventory and accounts receivable files are updated.

The processing within the update program follows steps such as these:

1. Read a transaction record.
2. Read the customer, accounts receivable, and inventory master records indicated by the transaction record.
3. Print the heading of the invoice from the data in the customer master and transaction records.
4. Print a line item on the invoice, taking item description and unit price from the inventory master record and calculating the extension.
5. Update the inventory master record by subtracting quantity shipped from the on-hand balance. Then write the updated record in its original location on the disk.

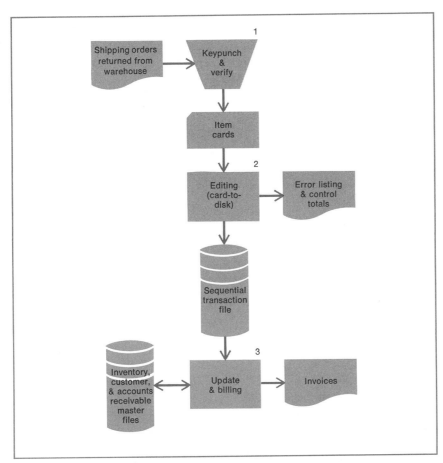

FIGURE 7-15 Flowchart for a billing, inventory,
and accounts receivable system

6. Read another transaction record. If the customer number is the
same as for the previous transaction record, read the indicated
inventory master record and repeat steps 4–6. If the customer number has changed, print the invoice total, update the accounts receivable record, and write the accounts receivable record in its
original location on the disk. Then continue with step 2.

As you can see, one or more master records are read and written on a
random basis each time a transaction record is read.

This procedure of course does not provide for the handling of back
orders or the processing of receipt, return, and adjustment records
against the inventory file. Figure 7-16, then, presents a more complete
system. In the eight steps shown, inventory, accounts receivable, and
back-order files are updated; back orders are relieved; and shipping
orders and invoices are printed. Since invoices are printed before items
are actually shipped, this is a prebilling system. Although control post-

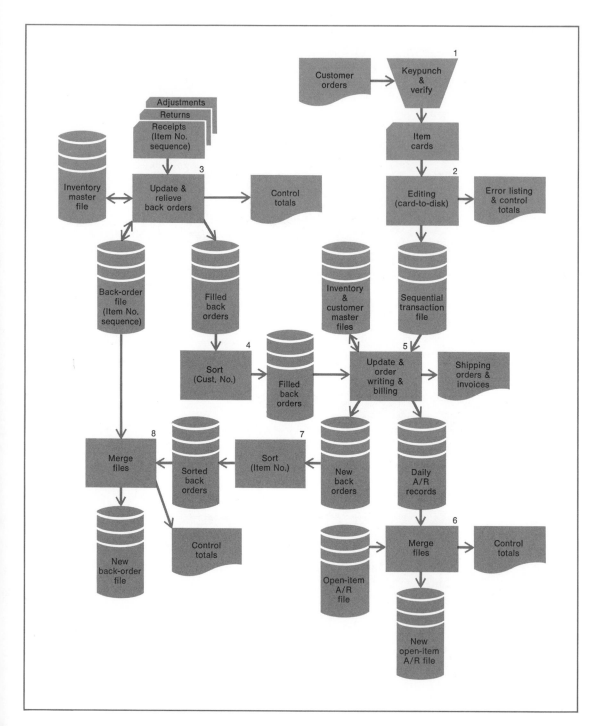

FIGURE 7-16 Direct-access applications

ing and balancing steps would normally be shown, they are omitted here to emphasize processing.

Figure 7-17 is a record layout form that gives the layouts of the card and disk records used in this system. Seven record formats are shown—the first two for the item and receipt, return, and adjustment cards, the other five for disk records. Notice that the inventory and customer master records have indexed sequential file organization so they can be processed on either a sequential or random basis. The back-order and accounts receivable files are kept in sequential organization. The system used consists of a CPU, a combined card reader and punch, a printer, and a direct-access device with four spindles. Auxiliary equipment consists of keypunches and verifiers.

In steps 1 and 2, the item records are keypunched and verified, edited, and converted into a sequential disk file. This file is then ready to be processed in the order-writing and invoicing run (step 5).

In step 3, receipts, returns, and adjustments in item-number order are processed to update the inventory master file. At the same time, the back-order file, also in item-number order, is processed to determine whether any of the back orders can now be filled. If so, the filled back-order record is written on a new disk file, the filled back-order file. To delete filled back orders from the back-order master file, an asterisk is placed in the first byte of the deleted record. Remember that although three separate disk symbols are shown on the flowchart, all three disk files could be stored in separate areas of the same disk drive.

In step 4, the filled back-order file is sorted into customer-number order in preparation for the billing run of step 5. Here again, several areas of one or more disk drives are used during the sort, although they are not shown on the flowchart.

In step 5, inventory master records are updated and the shipping orders and invoices are printed. For each new customer number, the corresponding customer master record is read and used to print the heading of the invoice. Then, as each transaction record or filled back-order record is read, the corresponding inventory master record is read to determine whether the item ordered can be filled. If so, item description and unit price are taken from the master record to print the line item on the invoice. If the item can't be filled, a back-order record is written on the new back-order file. After all transactions and filled back orders for one customer have been processed, the total line of the invoice is printed and an accounts receivable record is written on the daily accounts receivable file.

In steps 6, 7, and 8, the open-item accounts receivable file and the back-order file, both with sequential organization, are updated by merging the new records into the files. This is comparable to what takes place on a tape system. Two input files are merged together, resulting in one output file.

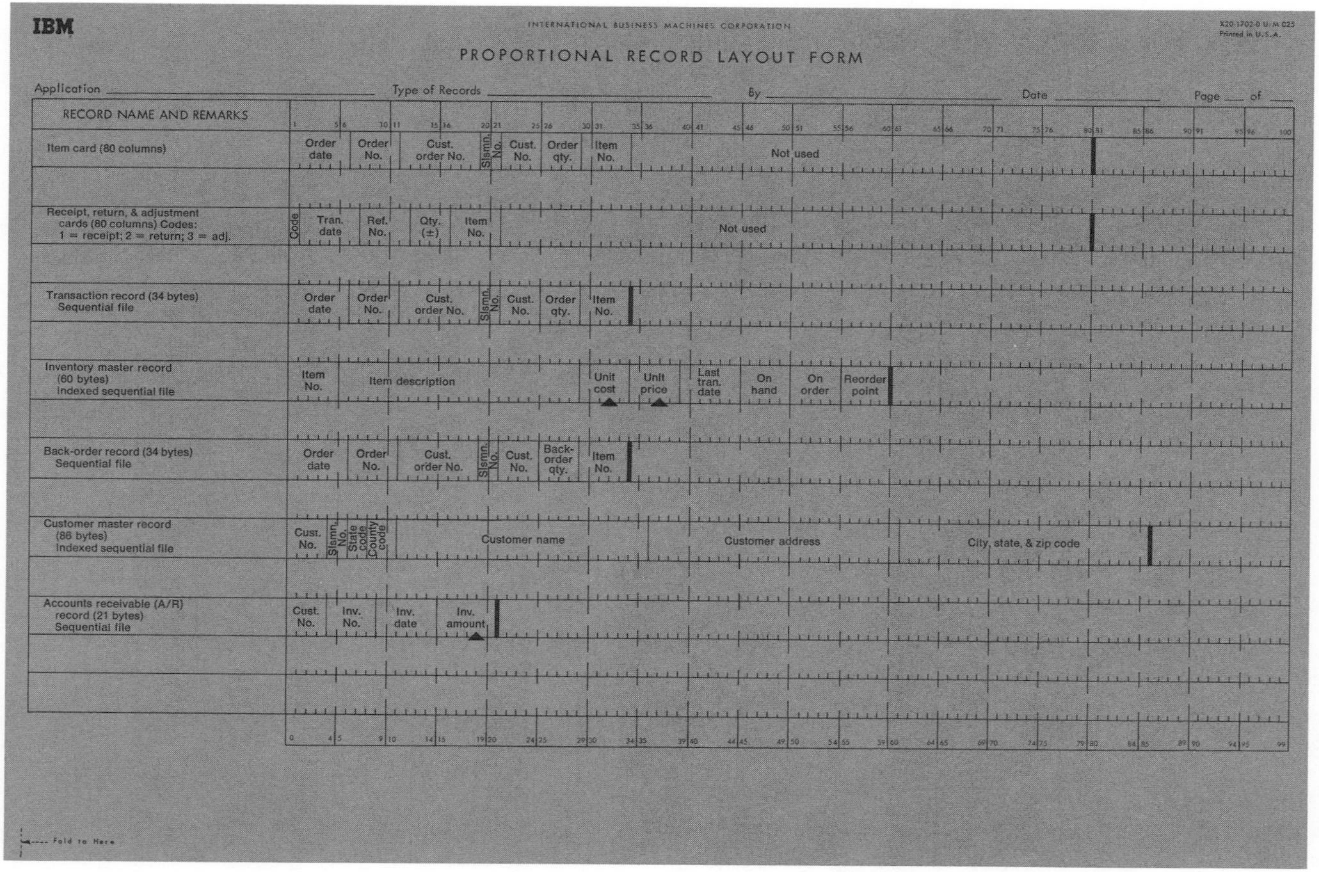

IBM

INTERNATIONAL BUSINESS MACHINES CORPORATION

X20-1702-0 U/M 025
Printed in U.S.A.

PROPORTIONAL RECORD LAYOUT FORM

Application ______ Type of Records ______ By ______ Date ______ Page ___ of ___

RECORD NAME AND REMARKS	Fields
Item card (80 columns)	Order date · Order No. · Cust. order No. · Slsmn. No. · Cust. No. · Order qty. · Item No. · Not used
Receipt, return, & adjustment cards (80 columns) Codes: 1 = receipt; 2 = return; 3 = adj.	Code · Tran. date · Ref. No. · Qty. (±) · Item No. · Not used
Transaction record (34 bytes) Sequential file	Order date · Order No. · Cust. order No. · Slsmn. No. · Cust. No. · Order qty. · Item No.
Inventory master record (60 bytes) Indexed sequential file	Item No. · Item description · Unit cost · Unit price · Last tran. date · On hand · On order · Reorder point
Back-order record (34 bytes) Sequential file	Order date · Order No. · Cust. order No. · Slsmn. No. · Cust. No. · Back-order qty. · Item No.
Customer master record (86 bytes) Indexed sequential file	Cust. No. · Slsmn. No. · State code · County code · Customer name · Customer address · City, state, & zip code
Accounts receivable (A/R) record (21 bytes) Sequential file	Cust. No. · Inv. No. · Inv. date · Inv. amount

Fold to Here

FIGURE 7-17 Formats for the direct-access applications

In summary, both sequential and random processing techniques can be used, and are likely to be used, within the procedures of a direct-access system. The system designer must consider both possibilities and choose the one that leads to the most efficient system.

DISCUSSION

In comparison to a tape system, a disk system has several advantages. The primary one is that a disk system generally requires fewer steps than a tape system. For example, the tape system in figure 6-10 requires twelve steps, while the comparable disk system in figure 7-16 requires only eight. As a result, the disk system should take less time for processing even if individual runs take longer than comparable tape runs. By eliminating a step, operator setup time is eliminated as well as the time required to load and execute the program.

A second advantage is that file-maintenance programs are likely to be executed faster on disk than on tape — particularly, if the percent of affected master records is low. To illustrate, suppose a file of 5000 master records is being maintained, but only 50 master records are affected. On a tape system, all 5000 records will be read and written during the file-maintenance run. In contrast, if the records are stored on a disk and processed on a random basis, only 50 master records will be processed.

A third advantage is that programs stored on disk can be accessed and loaded faster than programs on tape. Rather than searching sequentially for the selected program, the computer directly accesses the program, which is then loaded into storage at the relatively high transfer rate of disk.

One final advantage of a disk system is its inquiry capability. Because records on disk can be accessed in milliseconds, it is practical for a clerk or manager to inquire into the contents of a disk record. For example, an inventory-control clerk can inquire into the contents of an inventory master record by keying the item number on a typewriter-like device attached to the computer. This device can be in the same room as the computer or many miles away, attached via telephone lines. Under program control, the selected record is accessed, read, and printed on the typewriter device. Because a master inventory tape would have to be searched sequentially, this type of inquiry is time consuming, and thus impractical, on a tape system. Although the inquiry capability is not used on many direct-access systems, it is this capability that makes possible many types of data-communication systems, as described in the next chapter.

Regardless of the advantages of direct-access devices, tape drives are likely to be found on direct-access systems. For example, a typical direct-access system might consist of a CPU, a printer, a card reader and punch, a five-drive 2314, and two tape drives. Because tape storage is far less expensive than disk storage, the use of tape can reduce storage costs considerably.

On a disk system with nonremovable disks, tape drives are essential. To provide for backup, a disk file is copied onto tape by a disk-to-tape program. The tape can then be used to recreate the master file if it is destroyed or becomes unreadable. If the capacity of a fixed-disk system isn't large enough to store all of the files at once, tape must also be used as temporary storage of master files. For example, after updating a disk file, the file would be copied onto tape. The disk can then be used for some other file. Prior to the next update run, the tape is copied back onto the disk and the update program is executed.

Because of the features of direct-access processing, the future of direct-access devices seems certain. Although these systems already dominate, they continue to account for much of the growth in the computer industry. At present, the growth rate for direct-access devices is 25 percent in contrast to a rate of 6 or 7 percent for tape devices.

SUMMARY

1. A direct-access master file can be updated on a sequential or a random basis. The choice depends on the characteristics of the file and the device used. In a random update, only the affected master records are read and written. In a sequential update, all master records are read, but only the affected records are written.

2. The primary advantage of a disk system is that it allows a job to be done in fewer steps than a sequential system. In addition, a disk system makes it possible (1) to process only the affected records in a file-maintenance program, (2) to rapidly access and load object programs stored on disk, and (3) to inquire into master files on a random basis.

FOR REVIEW

update run
card-to-disk program
sort program
disk-to-printer program

When a computer user moves from a card or tape system to a disk system, he normally increases his processing capabilities considerably. However, he also increases the complexity of his system. In comparison to a sequential system, a disk system generally demands much more from operators, programmers, and system designers. Some of the programming and system complications common to direct-access systems are described in this topic.

TOPIC FOUR
PROGRAMMING AND SYSTEM CONSIDER- ATIONS

PROGRAMMING CONSIDERATIONS

In a direct-access program, 40 percent or more of the object code may be taken up by input and output routines. One immediate complication is that a program can't just read or write a record on a direct-access device. Instead, the program must use the proper combination of Seeks, Searches, Reads, and Writes. Beyond this, direct-access programs always require error-recovery and label-checking routines, and, depending on file organization, may require blocking, deblocking, and file-handling routines.

Error-Recovery Routines

When a record on a direct-access device is read, parity or the cyclic check characters are checked to be sure that the read operation has taken place without error. If an error is detected, however, it may be recovered. Sometimes, for example, a piece of dust that caused an error can be brushed off as the recording surface passes under the read/write head. If the program rereads the record by waiting one complete revolution while the record rotates under the read/write head again, the record may be read without error. In a typical error-recovery routine for a sequentially organized file, the record is reread ten times. If the error still exists, a message is printed on the console typewriter and the system is halted.

If an error is detected during a writing operation, it too may be corrected. In a typical routine, the record is written on an alternate track, and, if this attempt to write the record takes place without error, the program continues. A direct-access device commonly has several cylinders or tracks that can be used for alternate tracks in the event of writing errors. For example, the 2314 actually has 203 cylinders—the first 200 are used for normal processing and the last 3 are used for alternate tracks.

Label-Checking Routines

When using direct-access files, one danger is the possibility of destroying current records by mistakenly writing other records over them.

For example, suppose that an operator mounts a disk pack containing current accounts receivable records on a disk drive that is going to be used for writing payroll records. If the mistake isn't caught, the accounts receivable records will be destroyed when the payroll records are written.

Records can also be destroyed by programming error. If one disk pack contains two or more files—say accounts receivable records in cylinders 2–50 and inventory records in cylinders 51–200—a Seek to the wrong cylinder could mean disaster. If the inventory program mistakenly writes records in cylinders 2–50, the accounts receivable records would be destroyed.

To prevent this type of error, internal labels are used for each file that is stored on a direct-access device. These labels are actually records on the device itself. For example, all standard files on a 2314 have one or more *file labels* that are normally found beginning with the fourth record on the first track of the first cylinder. These labels indicate the name of the file, the expiration date of the file (the date after which the file may be destroyed), and the tracks that are used for the file. If a file is located in more than one area of the disk—say cylinders 11–20 and cylinders 41–49—this is indicated too. In addition, each disk pack has a *volume label*, which is the third record of the first track of the first cylinder. This label identifies the pack itself.

In System/360, labels are processed by comparing the data in the labels with data supplied in *job-control cards* at the time the program is executed. These job-control cards indicate which program should be run, as well as which pack should be mounted on which disk drive and what information the volume and file labels should contain. They also indicate the *extents* of each file that is going to be processed. The extents indicate which cylinders and tracks are assigned to each area of each file used by the program. (Chapter 14 goes into greater detail on the content and format of the job-control cards.)

To appreciate the value of label checking, consider how System/360 programs check labels before writing an output file on a 2314. After the operator mounts the disk pack and starts the drive, the program reads the volume label and compares it with information in the job-control cards. If the correct disk pack (volume) has been mounted on the correct drive, the program checks each label in the label section of the disk pack to make sure that the output file that is going to be written will not overlap the extents of any other file on the device. In other words, if the job-control cards indicate the output file will be written in cylinders 31–50, the label-checking routines make sure that all files in those cylinders have reached their expiration date. If cylinders 31–50 are clear or contain only expired files, the program continues by writing the file label of the output file in the label area and then executing the program. Otherwise, a message is printed to the operator and processing is stopped, thus avoiding a costly error.

For input files, the file labels are checked to be sure that the identifying data agrees with that given in the job-control cards. Also, the extents given in the file label are checked against the extents given in the job-control cards. If any discrepancy is detected, the operator is alerted.

When a direct-access file is stored on more than one device, the labels for all the devices are checked and processed. For a sequentially organized file, this processing takes place when the end of the first disk pack is reached. Thus, the label-checking routines provide for switching from one disk pack to the next. For an indexed sequential or direct file, the labels on all disk packs used for the file are checked at the start of the program.

Although System/360 label information is given in job-control cards at the time a program is executed, some manufacturers provide for certain label information to be supplied as part of the program itself. Thus, the programmer specifies in his program the name of the file and its expiration date.

Blocking and Deblocking Routines

If blocked records are used, all of the records in the block are read or written when a Read or a Write command is executed. As a result, when a program reads a block of five records, five records are placed in the input area of storage. *Deblocking routines* must then be used to keep track of which record in the block is being processed and which record is next to be processed. Similarly, before a block can be written, *blocking routines* must assemble the individual records in the output area of storage.

File-Handling Routines

Both direct and indexed sequential files require certain file-handling routines that aren't required by sequential files. For example, randomizing routines are needed for direct files. For indexed sequential files, special routines are needed to keep indexes up to date, to locate records by using the indexes, to add records to the overflow areas, and to search the chain of records in the overflow area. Such routines may require dozens of machine-language instructions.

What the Programmer Must Know

Because of the many I/O routines needed for direct-access files, it is fortunate that programming languages automatically assemble or compile the required routines. In general, a programmer need never worry about error-recovery, label-checking, blocking, or deblocking routines.

Also, he need not think about the individual Seek, Search, Read, Write, or Write-Verify commands or about the file-handling routines for indexed sequential files.

What then must the programmer know? He must be able to specify the blocking characteristics of the file—what the length of each record is and how many records are in each block. He must know which track format is being used, and, if keys are used, what the key length is. He must be able to specify the exact file organization being used, including such details as how overflow records or synonyms are to be handled; and he must know whether the records are to be processed in sequential or random order. Once these specifications are given, the programmer uses simple macro instructions that automatically generate the required I/O routines. When writing programs for direct files, however, the programmer is completely responsible for the logic of the randomizing routine.

SYSTEM CONSIDERATIONS

With regard to system design, a direct-access system is considerably more complicated than a tape system. Because of the flexibility of direct-access devices, there are many different ways that a system can be designed and still provide the desired results. Before deciding on a system, the designer must consider all of the alternatives; he then chooses the one that meets the requirements of speed and accuracy, but still minimizes cost. Because the difference between a well-designed and a poorly designed system is significant, the design will in large part determine whether or not a system is effective. Two problems of particular significance to the design of a direct-access system are (1) file organization and (2) backup.

File Organization

The choice of file organization is of course closely tied in with the system flow. If a random file update is planned, the master file must have direct or indexed sequential file organization. If a sequential update is planned, the file must have sequential or indexed sequential organization. Remember, however, that a direct file can be converted into a sequential file by sorting prior to processing.

To illustrate the problem of determining file organization, consider the three flowcharts in figure 7-18. Although they are different, all three accomplish the same things—updating a master file and printing a sequential exception report from the master file. The first system, using a sequential file, prints the exception report when the master file is being updated. The second system, using an indexed sequential file, updates the master file on a random basis, then prints the sequential

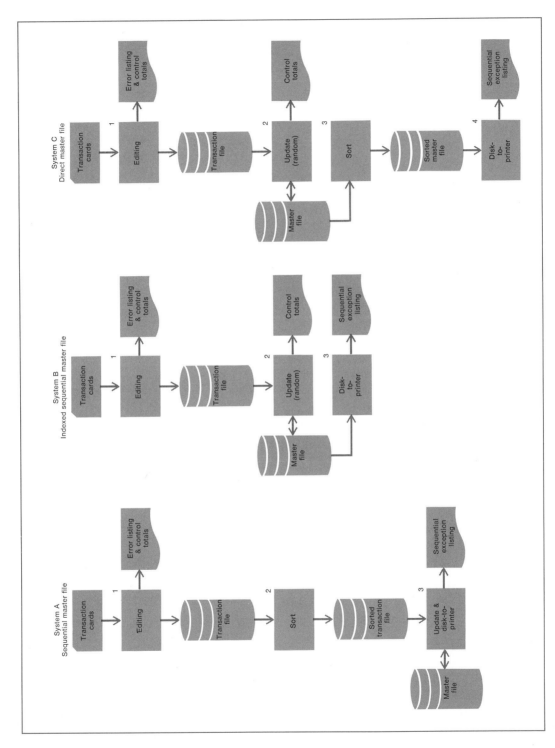

FIGURE 7-18 Determining file organization

exception report. The third system, using a direct file, updates on a random basis, sorts the master file into sequence, and then prints the sequential exception report.

The question is: Which of these systems is most efficient? To decide, the system designer must estimate the time required for all the steps within each system in order to determine which system requires the least time. Because each estimate depends on factors such as the number of records in the file, the exact characteristics of the method of file organization, and the percent of master records affected during an update, the decision depends on a complicated, time-consuming analysis. In actual practice, a master file is used in several (rather than only two) different processing runs, plus file-maintenance runs; thus, the decision is all the more complicated.

Once a general plan for file organization is chosen, there are many questions on a more detailed level yet to be answered. For an indexed sequential file, how many tracks per cylinder should be assigned for file additions; how often should the file be reorganized so all records are returned to the prime data area; should an independent overflow area be assigned in case a cylinder overflow area becomes filled? For a direct file, how many extra tracks should be assigned to the file to reduce synonyms; what randomizing technique should be used; how should synonyms be handled? In making decisions such as these, the system designer tries to keep the number of Seeks and Searches required to read or write a file as low as possible, thus reducing the processing times.

Although these questions are often very technical, they can have a significant effect on the run times for all programs that involve the file. For example, one company reports that it reduced run times 55 percent by changing a master file from one type of indexed sequential organization to another. In other words, a master-file update program that took two hours was reduced to less than an hour.

Backup

Although label-checking routines greatly reduce the chance that a direct-access file can be destroyed accidentially, they are not foolproof. In addition, there is a chance that direct-access records can be damaged by mechanical failure or destroyed by fire or theft. As a result, the designer of a direct-access system must provide for *backup*. Because the old master record is normally replaced by the new record in a direct-access update run, the grandfather-father-son method of backup cannot be used. However, there are several different methods of backup used on direct-access systems, all of which require extra computer time.

With removable disk packs, one method of providing backup is to copy the old master file onto a second disk pack after each update run;

this is done by using a disk-to-disk program. Then, if the master file is destroyed, a backup file is available. This, of course, is comparable to the grandfather-father-son method of backup on tape. If tape is available on the direct-access system, a master file can be copied onto tape after each update run by using a disk-to-tape program. Since a reel of tape is considerably less expensive than a disk pack, this is a less costly way of providing backup.

Because copying a file after an update run requires that all the records in the file be read and written, much of the advantage of a random update is negated. As a result, system designers have developed less time-consuming methods of providing backup. For example, instead of copying the entire master file after each update run, the entire file can be copied only once a week. Then, during the daily update runs, only the updated records are copied onto tape. If a master file has to be recreated, the weekly tape, the daily tapes, and the transactions that have occurred since the last daily tape was written are processed to recreate the current master file. This significantly reduces the amount of time required for copying master records even though it makes reconstruction of a master file more difficult.

SUMMARY

1. Programming considerations for direct-access systems include error-recovery, label-checking, blocking, deblocking, and file-handling routines. Although a programmer doesn't have to write these routines, he must be able to give specifications relating to them.

2. The choice of file organization is one of the critical decisions in designing a direct-access system. File organization is closely tied to system flow and, on a detailed level, affects the run times of individual programs.

3. Backup on a direct-access system involves copying master files onto disk packs or tapes. Since this requires computer time, an attempt is made to keep copying for backup to a minimum; otherwise, many of the advantages of direct access are lost.

**FOR
REVIEW**

file label
volume label
job-control cards
extents
blocking routine
deblocking routine
backup

CHAPTER EIGHT

This chapter is divided into two topics. In the first, the major types of data-communication systems and applications are described. Some of the considerations involved in determining whether a real-time system —one type of data-communication system—is justifiable are discussed in topic 2.

In the last twenty years, there have been many developments that have increased the processing speed of computer systems. The speeds of CPUs and I/O devices have been increased tremendously by technological developments, direct-access devices have been developed and improved, and techniques have been developed for overlapping I/O operations with CPU operations. When you consider the entire data-processing cycle, however, you will see that source data must be *collected* before it can be processed, and processed data must be *distributed* before it can be used. Thus, even if processing time is reduced to minutes, there can still be significant delays in a system.

To illustrate, suppose a wholesale distributing company consists of a home office, five branch sales offices, and a warehouse, all located in different cities. Customer orders, which are received in the branch offices, are collected in batches and mailed to the home office where they are processed. After the shipping orders are printed by the home-office computer, they are mailed to the warehouse for shipment. In this case, even if orders are processed immediately upon receipt in the home office, there is a delay of one or two days in collecting the orders and

DATA-COMMUNICATION SYSTEMS

a delay of one or two days in distributing the shipping orders to the warehouse.

Data-communication systems are designed to reduce the delays in collecting and distributing data. The term *data communication* refers to the electronic transmission of data from one location to another, usually over *communication lines* such as telephone or telegraph wires. Although there are many forms of data-communication systems, they can be broken down into four classifications: offline, online batch-processing, online real-time, and time-sharing systems.

Offline Systems

Offline means that the transmission of data is not directly to or from the computer. An example of offline communications is illustrated in figure 8-1. Here, transaction cards are keypunched in the branch offices. When a batch of cards has accumulated, they are read by a card reader in the branch office and the data in the cards is transmitted over communication lines to the home office. The card reader is called a *terminal* since it is at one end of the communication line. The receiving device, or terminal, in the home office is a card punch, which punches cards identical to those in the branch. After the transaction cards from each branch are transmitted and punched, they can be processed by the computer.

Offline data communication, then, is simply a means of eliminating the delays in sending data between two geographical points. In addition to card readers and punches, other devices such as tape drives and printers can be used as terminals. For example, if large volumes of data are to be transmitted, a tape drive in a branch can transmit to a tape drive

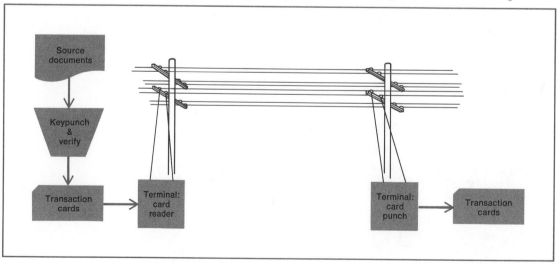

FIGURE 8-1   Offline data communication

in the home office. If a report is to be printed for branch-office management, data can be read by a tape drive in the home office and printed on a printer in the branch office.

One of the most widely used mediums for offline data communications has been the punched *paper tape*, which is illustrated in figure 8-2. Various coding schemes can be used, but the idea is that different combinations of punched holes represent different characters of information. When a reel of punched paper tape is mounted on a paper-tape reader, as illustrated in figure 8-3, it can be read and its data can be transmitted over communication lines. Similarly, a paper-tape punch, such as the one shown in figure 8-3, can be used as a receiving unit for offline transmission of data. Thus, there are data transmissions that convert data from paper tape to cards, card to tape, tape to printer, and so on.

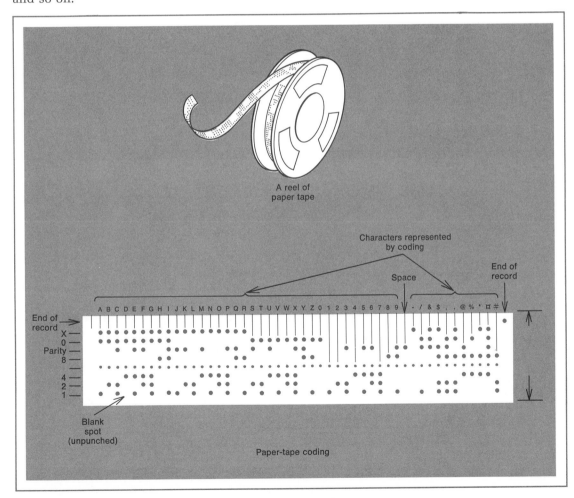

FIGURE 8-2   Paper tape

FIGURE 8-3   Paper-tape reading and punching terminals

Paper-tape readers can be used as input devices on computer systems; however, they are slow input devices, generally, somewhat slower than punched-card readers. Because the records on paper tape can't be sorted, paper tape is limited in use when compared with punched cards.

Paper tape is a popular data-communication medium because it can be prepared as a by-product of other office operations. A paper-tape punch is often part of a typewriter-like device. As the operator types on the keyboard, a paper tape is punched containing selected portions of the data that was typed. For example, while an operator is typing invoices, data pertaining to each line item can be punched into a paper tape for use in a sales-analysis application. This paper tape can then be used to transmit the data via communication lines.

Online Batch-Processing Systems

Online means that data is transmitted directly to the computer. Batch refers to the accumulation of transactions into groups or batches

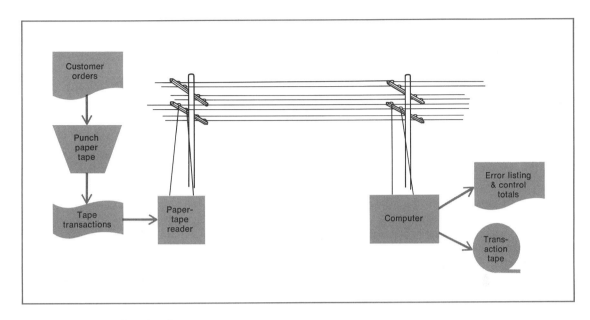

FIGURE 8-4   An online batch-processing system

before transmission. An online batch-processing system is illustrated in figure 8-4. Here, a punched paper tape is prepared from customer orders, and then used as input to the computer system via phone lines. In the home office, the computer performs an editing run while writing the transactions on magnetic tape. After the transactions from all the branches are edited and written, the tapes can be merged and processed.

Of course, there are many other forms of online batch processing. For example, the orders could be processed rather than just edited, and shipping orders could be printed based on the input data received. Data can also be transmitted from the computer to the branch office or warehouse. For example, after the paper tape containing order data is read and processed, the computer could send the data required to prepare shipping orders to the warehouse, where the orders would be printed on a printer terminal. Finally, terminals such as card readers or magnetic-tape drives can also be used as sending terminals in the branches.

Online Real-Time Systems

Real-time systems are online communication systems that provide a two-way communication between terminal and computer. The term *real time* means that the computer gives responses to inquiries from a terminal so fast that these responses can be used to answer a customer's questions, control an operation, or modify a process.

To illustrate, suppose a customer calls a branch office to ask whether a certain replacement part for a lawn mower is available for immediate delivery. Since the inventory records are kept in the home office, the branch office normally would call the home office to see if the part was available and then call the customer back. In a real-time system, however, the branch office communicates directly with the computer in the home office. With the customer still on the phone, the sales clerk types an inquiry on a typewriter-like terminal commonly called a *teletypewriter*. The inquiry might consist of a code indicating a request for inventory information, the part number of the item needed, and the quantity needed. This data is then transmitted to the computer, which searches a direct-access file for the selected inventory record, determines if the on-hand quantity is sufficient to fill the order, and then returns a response of yes or no to the teletypewriter; if no, it indicates when the part is expected to be in stock. Because of the high computing and transmission speeds of a data-communication system, this entire communication would take only a few seconds. Thus, the clerk can answer the customer's question after only a short pause.

If the part is available, the customer might then ask for immediate shipment. In a traditional system, this too would require a special call to the home office. In the real-time system, however, the order can be entered in much the same way that the inquiry was made. The clerk keys a code to indicate an order to be shipped, and then keys the customer number, the item number, and the quantity to be shipped. The computer processes the transaction data, updates the inventory records, and prepares a shipping order. If the warehouse has a printer terminal, the computer can transmit the data to the terminal so that the shipping order is printed in the warehouse within seconds from the time the customer placed the order. Think of the improvement in customer service!

An order-processing system is schematically shown in figure 8-5. Here, a typewriter terminal is located in every branch office, and a printer and typewriter terminal are located in the warehouse. As the transactions from the branch offices are processed, the inventory records are updated, the shipping orders are printed in the warehouse, accounts receivable records are updated, and a file of invoicing records is written. When shipments are received in the warehouse, the transactions are entered on the typewriter terminal, thus keeping inventory records constantly up to date. At the end of the day, the invoicing file is used to print invoices to be sent to the customers.

In actual practice, a real-time system often links many more than five terminals in a data-communication network. For example, Westinghouse Corporation has a real-time system that links more than 350 offices, factories, and warehouses. Within three seconds from the time that 90 percent of its 2000 daily orders are received, shipping instructions are printed on a terminal in the warehouse nearest the customer. As orders are processed, the system determines whether an inventory item

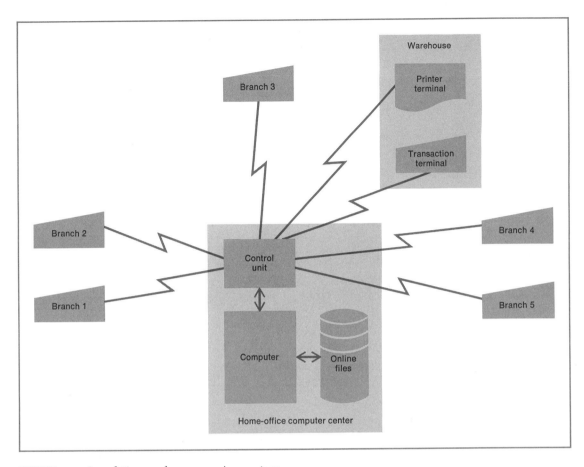

FIGURE 8-5   A real-time order-processing system

should be manufactured or reordered. If it should be, a purchase order
or production order is automatically prepared.

Time-Sharing Systems

A *time-sharing system* is an online real-time system in which many
users with different processing needs share one central computer. In a
university, for example, a half dozen or more typewriter terminals may
be linked to a computer, as illustrated in figure 8-6. These terminals
may be available to the engineering, math, and business departments. At
any one time, a student in the engineering department may be writing
a FORTRAN program, a student in the math department may be executing a program that solves systems of linear equations, and a student
in the business department may be developing a programming model
that projects profit and loss when any revenue or expense is varied.
Because the central computer moves from one terminal to another at

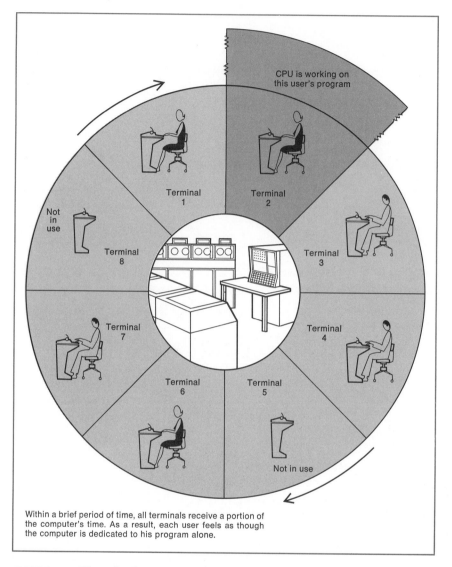

Within a brief period of time, all terminals receive a portion of the computer's time. As a result, each user feels as though the computer is dedicated to his program alone.

FIGURE 8-6   Time sharing

fantastic speeds, each person has the feeling that he alone is using the central computer, even though the computer works on only one user's program at a time.

To give you a better appreciation of the difference between human and computer speeds, consider that a typist working at 60 words per minute is typing 5 characters per second. In contrast, a typical time-sharing CPU is able to accept into storage over 1 million characters of data per second. Thus, a computer could accept the data from 200,000 typists working at 60 words per minute. In a time-sharing system, therefore, a computer is able to accept input, process it, and return a response to a terminal so fast that many such terminals can be handled by a single computer.

Although many companies and institutions own and operate their own time-sharing systems (known as *inhouse systems*), it is also possible to rent a time-sharing service. For example, if a company needs only one terminal for the engineering department, it can rent this service from an outside source, usually known as a time-sharing service bureau. In this case, the terminal user pays a monthly rent for the terminal, plus a rate based on the amount of time the terminal is connected to the computer and the amount of time the CPU is actually used by the terminal. In a typical commercial system, the service bureau rents to many companies throughout the country.

To illustrate the use of a time-sharing service, suppose a printing company rents one terminal from a service bureau to calculate printing costs. Since this is a complicated calculation based on factors such as page size, type of paper used, and number of copies to be printed, the printing company figures that the cost of the time-sharing service is justified by increased accuracy and reduced clerical costs.

To calculate a printing cost, the costing clerk dials the computer's number on a phone located next to the typewriter terminal. When the computer answers with a beeping noise, the clerk places the phone in a coupler attached to the terminal, thus connecting the terminal to the computer. A conversation, as shown in figure 8-7, then begins between the computer and the clerk. In the illustration, the lines printed by the computer are in black, and the lines typed by the clerk are in color. (In actual practice, of course, all of the lines would be in black.)

After giving the date and time, the computer asks for the identification (ID?) of the user. Since the user code given in response is valid, MM044, the computer types READY. When the clerk replies RUN COSTING, which indicates that the costing program should be executed, the computer loads the program named COSTING, prints OUTPUT, and executes the program. It begins with a series of questions relating to the cost calculation. When all of the questions have been asked and answered, the cost summary is calculated and printed. The computer then types END OF OUTPUT and READY to indicate that it is ready for another job. Because the user does not have a second job, he types LOGOFF. The computer then prints the time and the amount of CPU time the user will be charged for; and the terminal and computer are disconnected.

Remember that as the costing program is being executed, other terminals in the system are being used for other purposes. This, in fact, is what distinguishes a time-sharing system from other real-time systems. In a time-sharing system, the terminals in the system can be used for many different purposes. Thus, one terminal may be used for calculating printing costs, another terminal for making cash-flow pro-

```
          DATE 02/17/73  TIME 12.73  ID? MM044
          READY  RUN COSTING
          OUTPUT

                      PRINTING BID

          NUMBER OF PAGES?
          384

          PAGE SIZE?
          7.125, 10.125

          CODE FOR PAPER USED IN TEXT?
          50CM

          CODE FOR END SHEETS?
          80I
          INVALID CODE--TRY AGAIN.
          80K

          CODE FOR COVER?
          BL

          NUMBER OF COLORS--TEXT?
          2

          NUMBER OF COLORS--COVER?
          4

          BINDING CODE?
          C12

          QUANTITY TO BE PRINTED?
          10000

                COSTS

          PREP        1,424.00
          PLATES        858.00
          PRESS       6,309.00
          STOCK       5,924.00
          BINDING     9,038.00

          TOTAL... $23,553.00

          END OF OUTPUT
          READY  LOGOFF
          TIME 12.91  CPU TIME 1.9 SECONDS
```

FIGURE 8-7   A time-sharing example

jections, another for making an engineering calculation. In other real-time
systems, all terminals are used as part of one integrated system, such
as the order-processing system described earlier.

REAL-TIME APPLICATIONS

Although real-time systems can be used for basic business applications such as order writing, inventory, and payroll, they are more

likely to be used for specialized applications in industries such as insurance, banking, air transportation, manufacturing, and retail distribution. In the insurance industry, for example, handling customer inquiries can be a major problem for the customer-service department. To illustrate, suppose a health insurance company with several million policyholders has a home office in Chicago and branch offices in twenty-one cities throughout the country. To minimize duplication of records, all policy records are kept in the home office. When a policyholder calls the Kansas City branch to find out details of his coverage, the customer-service department must request the policy from the home office and then call the customer when the policy arrives. Because of mailing delays, the entire process is likely to take two or more days.

As an alternative, consider a real-time system in which all policy information is stored on direct-access devices in the home office and all branch offices are connected to the home office in a communication network. The terminals used in the branches are visual-display terminals as illustrated in figure 8-8. To make an inquiry, a clerk uses the keyboard of the terminal. When data is received, it is displayed on the screen. Thus, when a customer calls a branch for information, the clerk types the request for information on the keyboard, giving proper codes and policy numbers. This inquiry is transmitted to the computer in the home

FIGURE 8-8 A visual-display terminal

office, where the appropriate records are accessed from direct-access files. The requested information is then displayed on the visual-display terminal. Since the entire process takes only a few seconds, the clerk is able to give a reply to the customer after only a short pause.

A typical real-time application in banking is savings-account processing. In this type of system, teller terminals such as the one in figure 8-9 are connected to a central computer. These special-purpose terminals

FIGURE 8-9   A teller terminal

can accept data via the keyboard; they can also print data on a continuous form and on passbooks inserted into the slot on the right side of the device. The terminals can be located in the same building as the computer or in distant branch offices. When a customer wishes to withdraw money from his account, the teller places the passbook in the terminal and keys data such as transaction code, teller code, account number, and amount of withdrawal. Besides being printed on a continuous-form register within the terminal, this transaction data is transmitted to the computer, which accesses the master record, updates the record, and prints the transaction data and new balance in the passbook. At the end of the day, control totals accumulated by the computer for each teller are available to assist in balancing cash. If control totals don't balance, the transaction register in the terminal is available to help locate errors.

One of the first real-time business applications was the airline reservation system. In this application, an inventory of the available seats for every flight in the country is kept by one central computer. When a customer requests a reservation on a flight, the clerk keys the request on a terminal designed specifically for this purpose. Upon receiving the request, the computer checks the direct-access record for the flight to determine if space is available. If so, the reservation is confirmed, the number of available seats is reduced, and a confirmation message is printed on the terminal. If space isn't available, the customer can be advised immediately to seek another flight.

Just as important as making a reservation in an airline system is processing a cancellation. Here again, the transaction can be processed and the master record updated in a few seconds, thus making the cancelled seats available to any other terminal in the country. Since there was no way of keeping records current in earlier nonmechanized systems, flights that were supposedly filled took off filled to only 80 percent of capacity.

In manufacturing, real-time systems are used to control shop-floor production. For example, a shop-floor terminal such as the one in figure 8-10 can be used by factory workers to punch on and off a job. When a worker punches on a job, the input device reads an employee badge showing employee number and a punched card containing the number and description of the job he is to work on. The computer, which has a master production schedule available to it via direct-access files, can then compare the sequence of jobs done by a worker with the sequence of jobs scheduled for him. If a worker punches onto the wrong job, the computer responds with an immediate instruction on a printer terminal, indicating the job that should be done next. Thus, any deviation from the master schedule can be corrected before a problem is created.

When a worker punches off a job, he inserts his badge and the punched card giving the job description, and then, using the slides at the top

FIGURE 8-10   A shop-floor terminal

of the terminal, keys the number of pieces produced. The computer then updates production records so the current status of every job in the shop is always available. If a manager desires information about a particular job, the master record can be accessed and displayed on a visual-display or typewriter terminal. This contrasts a traditional system in which an expediter may spend several hours tracking down the location and status of a job.

One of the problems of a retail department store is authorizing credit transactions at the point of sale. If it takes too long, a customer may become dissatisfied. On the other hand, if authorization procedures become lax, profits can be lessened because of bad debts. One alternative is a real-time system using ordinary touch telephones for input and audio response through the phones (the human voice) for output. As the salesclerk fills out the sales slip for a credit transaction, he picks up the phone and keys the number of the computer. When the computer answers with a beeping tone, the clerk keys the account number and the amount of the sale. The computer then accesses the customer's record and determines if the transaction is okay. If so, a prerecorded reply such as "Transaction is okay" is given over the phone. If the transaction is not okay, the computer can reply with the name of the manager for the customer to contact for further information. Because the inquiry is made and answered in seconds, more credit authorizations can be made with less customer dissatisfaction.

Although this sampling of applications barely touches on the diversity and significance of real-time applications, it should be clear that real-time systems make possible new dimensions in customer service and management control. Using real-time technology, it is possible to answer customer inquiries without making return calls. It is possible to check a customer's credit without delaying him. It is possible to provide management information within seconds from the time that exceptional conditions occur.

THE USE OF MULTIPROGRAMMING

One common characteristic of real-time systems is the use of *multiprogramming*. Multiprogramming means that two or more programs are executed by a computer in the same period of time. Since a computer (or its CPU) can execute only one instruction at a time, this means that two or more programs are loaded into storage and the CPU switches back and forth between the programs. To make this possible, the computer must be equipped with certain hardware features, and a *supervisor program* (or just *supervisor*) must be available to handle the switching between programs.

To illustrate the need for multiprogramming, suppose a company uses a real-time system for processing orders. Since orders can come in from any of the branches throughout the day, the order-processing program must always be available in storage to handle transactions. On the other hand, there may be very few orders at certain periods of the day—for example, the lunch hour—so the system is likely to be idle much of the time. If multiprogramming is used, however, the idle time is used for other applications such as payroll, sales analysis, or financial reporting.

Suppose, then, that a second program—such as a payroll check-writing program—is loaded into storage along with the order-processing program and the supervisor program. This is illustrated in figure 8-11. Now, whenever the order-processing program is idle, the computer branches to the supervisor program, which in turn branches to the next instruction to be executed in the payroll program. Similarly, whenever a transaction is received from one of the branch offices, the payroll program is automatically interrupted and the location of the next instruction to be executed is stored for use by the supervisor. The computer then automatically branches to the supervisor, which branches to the proper instruction for handling the transaction in the order-process-

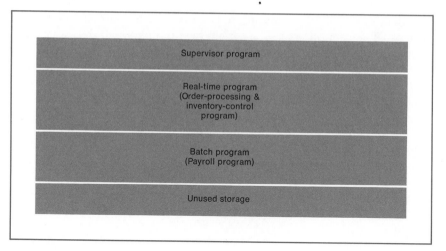

FIGURE 8-11   Core storage during multiprogramming

ing program. By using multiprogramming, the real-time program is always available for handling transactions, and batch programs are executed whenever the real-time program is not in use. The result is a more productive computer system.

The supervisor program, which is critical to the operation of multiprogramming, is available from the computer manufacturer or from companies that supply software (called software houses). Because the supervisor handles the switching from one program to another, the programmers who write the batch or real-time programs need not be concerned with multiprogramming. They write their programs as if they were going to be executed independent of all other programs. Although the use of multiprogramming requires some special hardware features in addition to the supervisor program, the increased costs are more than offset by increased system productivity.

Although multiprogramming is common for real-time systems, I do not mean to imply that all real-time systems use it. On the contrary, there seems to be a trend toward somewhat smaller computer systems that deal with a single real-time application. These systems are referred to as *dedicated systems* since no attempt is made to run batch-processing programs while the real-time system is in operation. If batch programs are to be run, they are executed when the real-time system is not being used, such as during the second or third shifts.

CONCLUSION

As you can now see, the term *data-communication system* covers a lot of ground. It can refer to an offline, online batch-processing, or online real-time system. It can refer to a system that uses offline terminals such as paper-tape readers or card readers; to a real-time system that uses general-purpose terminals such as teletypewriters, visual-display units, or telephones; or to a real-time system that uses special-purpose terminals such as teller terminals in banking or shop-floor terminals for production control. On the one hand, a data-communication system might involve only a simple offline connection between two branches of a company; on the other hand, it might involve 1600 terminals connected to an enormous computer system.

As the emphasis of this chapter might indicate, online real-time systems are the fascination of the computer industry. But even so, there is tremendous variation in systems. A real-time system might be a dedicated single-purpose system such as a reservation or order-processing system. Or, it might be a multipurpose system in which all of a company's major files are online and updated in real time.

SUMMARY

1. Data-communication systems are intended to reduce the time spent in collecting and distributing data within a system. There is wide variation in the types of systems, which include offline, online batch-processing, online real-time, and time-sharing systems.

2. Although real-time systems can be used for basic applications such as order processing, they are more likely to be found in specialized applications in industries such as banking, insurance, and manufacturing. A wide range of general- and special-purpose terminals is available to make these applications possible.

3. Multiprogramming is common on real-time systems so that batch programs can be run whenever the real-time program is idle. The increased productivity of the multiprogramming system offsets the cost of the added hardware features and the supervisor program required for multiprogramming.

**FOR
REVIEW**

collecting data	real-time system
distributing data	real time
data-communication system	teletypewriter
data communication	time-sharing system
communication line	inhouse system
offline	multiprogramming
terminal	supervisor program
paper tape	supervisor
online	dedicated system

TOPIC TWO

JUSTIFYING THE REAL-TIME SYSTEM

To determine whether a real-time system is advantageous for a company to install, the cost of the proposed system must be balanced against the expected benefits. When you compare the costs of a real-time system with the costs of a traditional system, however, you normally find a significant cost increase. Real-time systems involve hardware, programming and system-design costs that have no counterpart in batch systems. These costs must therefore be offset by some unusual benefits.

Hardware Costs

Some of the obvious hardware costs of a real-time system are terminals, communication lines, and large-capacity, fast-access, direct-access devices. In addition, a real-time system requires some special components that make possible the transmission of data between terminals and a computer. Between each terminal and its communication line, for example, there is a *modem* (*modulator/demodulator*) that converts data from EDP code to communication-line code, and vice versa. Similarly, between the computer and the communication lines, there is usually a device that controls the order in which data is sent and received by each of the online terminals. In addition, the CPU itself must be equipped with certain features that facilitate real-time processing and multiprogramming. Because of these hardware requirements, a real-time system is likely to cost considerably more than a batch-processing system.

Programming Costs

Just as a real-time system requires more complicated hardware, it requires more complicated programming. As a result, a real-time system normally requires more programming hours than a comparable batch system, as well as higher paid (better-trained) programmers. The net result is significantly higher programming budgets for real-time systems.

To illustrate the programming demands of a real-time system, consider that the real-time program must be able to handle any condition that comes up when a transaction is being handled. In making an airline reservation, for example, there are over eighty different operations that might be involved. Thus, the program must be able to handle all eighty operations in any combination. In contrast, many of the exceptional conditions in a batch-processing system can be handled through clerical procedures rather than programming routines.

In addition to the routines that are required by the application itself, though, a real-time system requires many hundreds of instructions that make possible the sending and receiving of data. For example, the controlling routines must be able to handle questions such as: Which terminal is next in line to send data? Did the transmission of data take place without error? Did the transaction contain a valid terminal address? If an incoming transmission contains an error, has the sending terminal been notified and the error corrected?

Because of the application and control routines required, real-time programs are likely to be exceptionally long and require several man-years of programming time. The real-time program for one company's airline reservation system, for example, consists of over 600,000 instructions. In practice, then, several programmers usually work together developing the routines for a single real-time program. This makes it possible to complete the program within a reasonable period of time, but it also increases the difficulties involved in testing and debugging the program.

System-Design Costs

The design costs for a real-time system are commonly several times more than those for a batch system. The problems of real-time design are such that they demand the best people in the computer industry, and thousands of man-hours of labor are required for the design of a typical system. In fact, real-time system design is becoming a study in itself. Many books have been written about the problems of real-time system design; these problems range from statistically projecting the volume of transactions to be handled by a system, to determining the best methods of file organization for the online files, to developing the most efficient operating procedures for the terminal operators. To give you some idea of the complexity and significance of real-time design problems, let me briefly describe just a few.

One of the major problems is determining the hardware requirements of a system. How many terminals are needed to handle the present volume of transactions and the volume expected in one, two, three, or more years? What type of communication lines should be used—telephone, telegraph, leased or purchased? If communication lines are to be purchased, which network of lines will keep costs to a minimum but still handle peak loads? Which direct-access devices are large enough and fast enough for the online files?

To complicate the problem, a computer user normally deals with three or more vendors when purchasing a real-time system—one for the computer, one for the communication lines, and one for the terminals. Thus, he must coordinate information from several sources. As an indication of how difficult this problem of determining hardware requirements can be, there have been some overwhelming mistakes made in the past. One airline company, for example, installed a system that required 50 percent more terminals and cost more than twice as much as originally expected. Unfortunately, because hardware planning is often done several years before a real-time system is actually installed, such gross errors are not uncommon.

A second problem is that of establishing accounting controls. In a system where all transactions are processed as they occur, how can you be sure at the end of the day that all transactions have been processed by the computer? And if processed, how can you be sure they've been processed correctly? Even more difficult, if the central computer fails (suppose a direct-access device isn't operating properly), how do you know which transactions have been processed correctly and which transactions need to be resubmitted?

This leads to another problem—that of backup. Since a real-time system is critical to a company's operations, alternative procedures must be available immediately if the main system should fail. In a small system, this may mean a return to manual procedures until the computer is repaired. Then, when the computer system is operating again, all transactions that have been processed manually can be processed by the computer system to update the files. In a large system such as an airline reservation system, however, a system failure would be a disaster. As a result, these systems are commonly made up of two or more complete computer systems (*duplexed computers*). Then, when one fails, the second system automatically takes over so that the real-time system never stops operating. In either case, however, there are many related problems to consider. How can you be sure that the switchover from one system to the next took place with no lost or incompletely processed transactions? How can each branch be notified as to which transaction was last to be processed and which transactions should be resubmitted when the system begins operating again?

In summary, the design of real-time systems is one of the most demanding problems in the computer industry today. In fact, it is fair to say that the lack of competent design personnel has been a major limitation in the development of real-time systems. Because of the cost of an experienced real-time system-design group, even deciding whether a real-time system is a practical consideration can be a significant expense.

The Benefits of Real-Time Systems

To determine whether a real-time system is economically justifiable, the benefits of the proposed system must, of course, be balanced against the cost of the system. All too often, however, the benefits are intangible or difficult to measure—such as improved customer service or increased control of operations or more timely management information. As a result, the system analyst must justify the system by balancing some hard-to-measure benefits against some very real hardware, programming, and system-design costs.

To illustrate, consider the real-time order-processing and inventory-control system described in topic 1. To justify the increased cost of the system, the analyst must evaluate characteristics such as improved customer service and its effect on sales, faster inventory updating and its effect on inventory levels, and greater order-handling efficiency and its effect on morale, absenteeism, and the employee turnover rate. In short, it is difficult, and at times impossible, to correctly estimate the effect on profits that a real-time system will have. Although this is also true for batch-processing systems, the problems are compounded when evaluating real-time systems.

This same type of reasoning applies to justifying time-sharing systems. In general, the cost of the system or service is compared with the increased productivity or morale of the persons using the service. For example, if an engineer making $1500 per month could increase his productivity 50 percent by using a time-sharing service that costs $300 per month, the service would be justified. Here again, though, the problem is in measuring something that is difficult to measure—in this case, increased productivity. Thus, there is still much debate as to the extent to which time-sharing services are justifiable.

In some cases, however, the benefits of a real-time or a time-sharing system seem to more than justify the costs. For example, today no major airline could afford to be without an airline reservation system. Such a system not only affects customer service but, more important, enables airlines to maintain higher loading rates than is otherwise possible. By keeping a more accurate and current inventory of available seats, airlines have been able to increase the average percentage of seats filled for each flight. Because this has a direct effect on profits, this benefit alone justifies a reservation system. One major airline, for instance, is reported to have increased revenues by over $1 million per year when it improved its load-planning capabilities. In addition, the airline claims that the reservation system has enabled its clerks to increase their productivity by 30 percent, even though the cost of the entire system is only 1.5 percent of total operating expenses.

To give another example, consider a hospital that is in the process of installing a real-time accounting system. Thirty-eight terminals throughout the hospital will be online to a central computer so that charges can be entered into a patient's account as the charges are actually incurred. Because many of the separate charges are normally lost through the inefficiency of the old manual system, the hospital estimates an increase of $625,000 each year in patient billings, not to mention the reduction in paperwork for the hospital's 400 nurses. If these estimates hold true, the increased billings alone will more than pay for the real-time system.

DISCUSSION

Although real-time systems have tremendous fascination from both a technical and a management point of view, two critical questions have been raised in recent years as to their practicality and contribution to profits. For one thing, as I mentioned before, some overwhelming errors have been made in the design and implementation of real-time systems: actual system costs have far exceeded the anticipated costs, and programming and system-design projects have fallen months and even years behind the original installation schedules. As a result, many companies question whether a real-time system can, in fact, be installed at a reasonable cost given the present hardware and communication-line costs and the present level of competency of design and programming personnel. Furthermore, many companies are questioning whether the actual benefits of real-time processing are as significant as they initially appeared to be.

The second question is whether or not several small single-purpose systems aren't better than one large multipurpose system. The reasoning here is that large systems using multiprogramming and real-time updating of several online files tend to make extraordinary demands on programmers and system designers. They also tend to reduce the overall productivity of the computer systems themselves. (There are technical reasons for this that we don't need to get into.) As a result, hardware, programming, and system-design costs tend to increase at a rate that is out of proportion to the benefits of the system. In contrast, some analysts say that several small systems, each concerning itself with a single application or family of applications, is a more profitable alternative.

A third question that must be answered in the years ahead concerns a particular type of real-time system—the *total information system*, or the *management-information system (MIS)*. The idea of a total system or MIS became popular in the mid-1960s and continues to interest executives throughout the country. The theory behind the management-information system is that one of management's traditional problems has been getting information that is current. However, if the major files—such as inventory, accounts receivable, and general ledger—could be stored on direct-access devices and updated on a real-time basis, it would be possible to provide management the information it needs within minutes from the time of the request. For example, if the vice-president in charge of sales requests the year-to-date sales totals for each branch office, this sales report could be printed or displayed on a terminal in his office within minutes from the time that he keyed the request. If a credit manager keys a request for the credit history of an account, this information could likewise be printed or displayed within seconds. Thus, by solving the problem of providing current information, the managers throughout a company will supposedly become more efficient and make business decisions that are more profitable. And this, of course, should give a company an advantage over its competitors.

The question concerning the management-information system is whether or not managers need real-time information at all. John Dearden, professor of Business Administration at the Harvard Business School, states this criticism in an article entitled "Myth of Real-time Management Information," *Harvard Business Review*, (May–June 1966): "It is my personal opinion that, of all the ridiculous things that have been foisted on the long-suffering executive in the name of science and progress, the real-time management-information system is the silliest." He then describes what he considers to be the major duties of top management and shows why these duties do not require real-time information. If his analysis is correct (needless to say, there is much disagreement on the issue), the millions of dollars that have been spent on developing MIS systems are certainly cause for concern.

I mention these issues to point out that the application of real-time systems to business problems is a developing art that is barely out of its infancy. That's why these rather basic issues are still unsettled. In the next few years, hardware costs are certain to drop, and the level of programming and system-design expertise is sure to rise. However, it will be years before all the profitable real-time applications are discovered, and all the unprofitable applications have been tried and abandoned. Similarly, it will be years before standard operating procedures for design and implementation are developed. Until then, this area of the computer industry will continue to be one of the most challenging and dynamic in the entire world of business.

SUMMARY

1. **Some extraordinary hardware, programming, and system-design costs put the burden of justifying the real-time system on correctly estimating the benefits of the system. In the past, some classic blunders have been made, both in estimating costs and benefits.**

2. **The fact that several major questions concerning the usefulness of real-time systems are still unsettled attests to the newness of real-time technology. These issues will continue to be debated until the technology and the programming and system-design expertise are more fully developed.**

**FOR
REVIEW**

modem
duplexed system
total information system
management-information system
MIS

III

AUXILIARY SUBJECTS

CHAPTER NINE

There are at least two reasons for learning about manual and mechanical methods of processing data. First, it gives you some perspective. To appreciate the speed, accuracy, and information capabilities of a computer system, you must learn what noncomputerized systems can provide. To appreciate why many people prefer noncomputerized billing to computerized billing, you must understand the nature of the noncomputerized system.

The second reason for studying noncomputerized methods is that they are common to all business systems, including EDP systems. No company can do all of its processing on computers alone. In fact, large companies are likely to have hundreds of office workers outside of the EDP department. Furthermore, the procedures used by these workers are likely to be critical to the efficiency of the EDP system.

To aid in the study and analysis of manual and mechanical procedures, *procedure charts* are used. These charts symbolically represent the operations within a system. The procedure chart in figure 9-1, for example, represents the operations within a manual order-writing and billing system. The symbols used are shown on the following page.

The purpose of the procedure chart is to show all operations that take place and to show the origin, flow, and final disposition of all documents used within a procedure. All the documents on the chart are

MANUAL AND MECHANICAL METHODS OF PROCESSING DATA

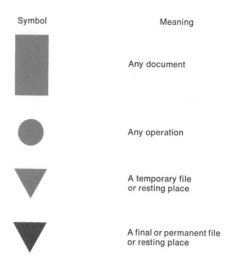

Symbol	Meaning
	Any document
	Any operation
	A temporary file or resting place
	A final or permanent file or resting place

numbered, and a document number placed on a flowline indicates the flow of the document. Thus,

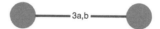

indicates that copies a and b of document number 3 are being moved from one operation to another. Arrowheads aren't necessary on a procedure chart since the direction of flow should be obvious.

The degree of detail shown in a procedure chart depends on the use of the chart. For an overall analysis of the flow of documents within a system, only the major processing operations need be shown. On the other hand, each step within an operation may be charted if the purpose of the chart is to determine ways of simplifying a procedure. In figure 9-2, for example, additional detail is given for steps 11 and 12 of figure 9-1.

In this book, procedure charts are used to illustrate the characteristics of a system using manual and mechanical methods of processing data. By analyzing the accuracy, speed, and information capabilities of these systems, you are better prepared to evaluate the advantages and disadvantages of computer systems.

Accuracy

Have you ever added columns of thirty numbers or more, filed 250 folders into a filing cabinet, or typed a twelve-page sales summary? If you have, you know that manual procedures are prone to error. It is relatively easy to misfile, miscalculate, or hit the wrong typewriter key. And if you do these jobs for several hours at a time, boredom and fatigue increase the likelihood of error. When analyzing a manual

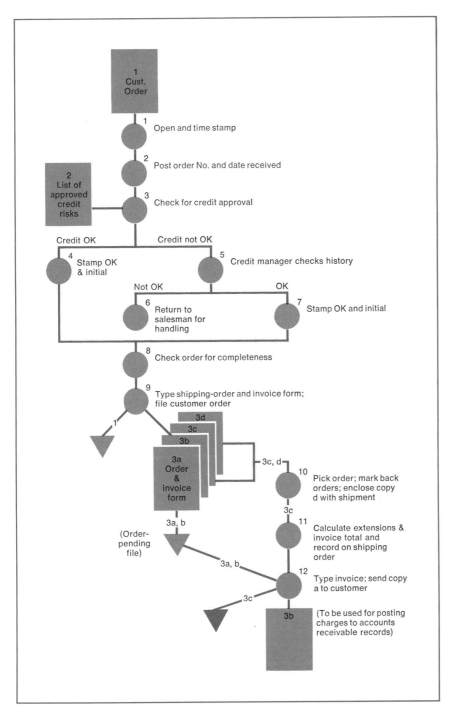

FIGURE 9-1   The order-writing and billing procedure

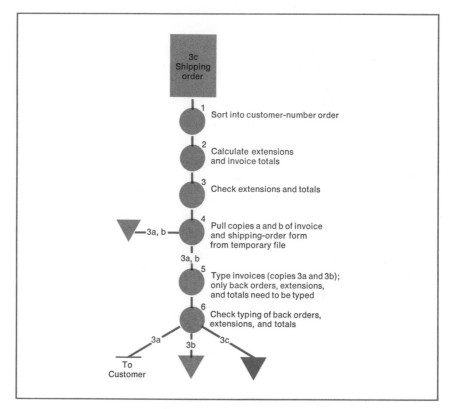

FIGURE 9-2   The billing procedure

procedure, the system analyst must remember that errors can occur in every operation in the procedure.

To increase the accuracy of manual procedures, checking operations normally follow arithmetic or recording operations. In the invoicing procedure in figure 9-2, for example, step 3 checks the calculations of step 2; step 6 checks the typing of step 5. It is common, in fact, for as much as 35 percent of a typical paperwork procedure to consist of checking operations. Because checking increases the cost as well as the accuracy of a procedure, a balance must be reached between the two. At some point, the cost of inaccuracy becomes less than the cost of increased checking.

Balancing to controls can also be used in a paperwork procedure. To illustrate, consider the procedure shown in figure 9-3. Here, invoice amounts are added to accounts receivable ledger cards and monthly statements, and new accounts receivable balances are calculated. As illustrated in figure 9-4, when the clerk records the charge on the monthly statement, it is also recorded on the ledger card and accounts receivable *journal*. By using carbon-backed documents, a single re-

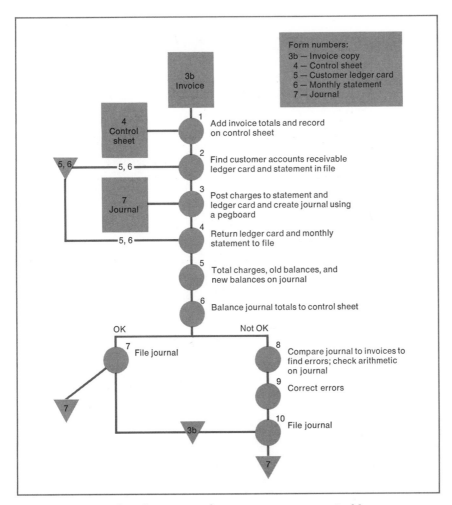

Form numbers:
3b — Invoice copy
4 — Control sheet
5 — Customer ledger card
6 — Monthly statement
7 — Journal

FIGURE 9-3   Procedure for posting charges to accounts receivable

cording by the clerk updates all three documents. The board that is used, called a *pegboard* or *writing board*, has pegs on the left side that are used to align the documents placed on the board.

After all charges have been posted to the accounts receivable records, the journal becomes a record of transactions for the day. It can thus be used for balancing to controls. In step 5, the charges, old balances, and new balances are added and recorded on the journal. In step 6, these totals are compared with totals on the accounts receivable control sheet. If the totals agree, you can assume that the individual transactions have been posted correctly; if they don't agree, the errors must be found.

Note here the difficulty of correcting an error if the totals don't balance.

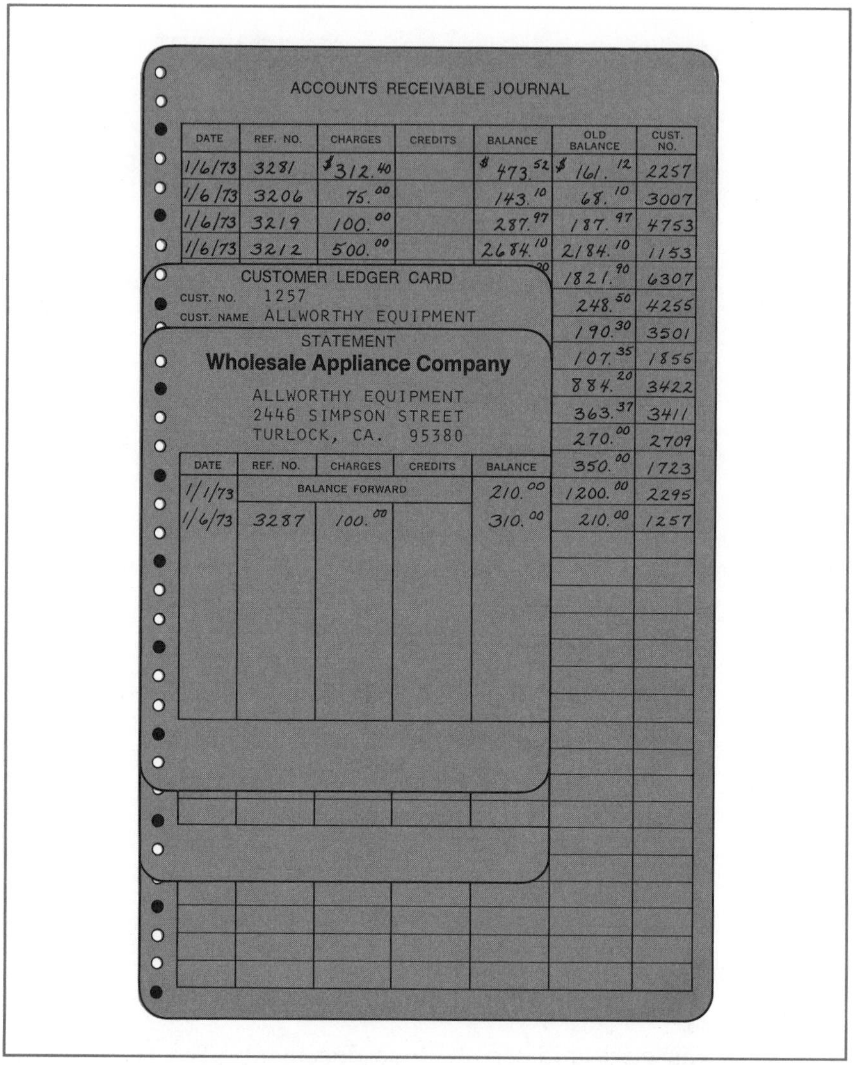

FIGURE 9-4   A pegboard application

If the charge total on the control sheet and the charge total on the journal are different, the charges may have been added incorrectly in either step 1 or step 5 of figure 9-3. If this addition proves correct, the clerk must compare the invoice amounts with the charge amounts on the journal. If there are many invoices, this can be a laborious job.

If the charges and old balances on the control sheet and journal are the same but the new balances differ, the addition on the control sheet and journal must be checked. If this is correct, an error was made in calculating the new balance on one or more individual records; thus, Old Balance + Charge = New Balance must be recalculated for each line on the journal until the error is found.

In conclusion, it is possible to achieve a high degree of accuracy in a manual system when checking and control balancing are used. On the other hand, when only checking is used, the likelihood of error is relatively high. In some cases, the error rate for clerical procedures has been as high as 5 percent, even when checking all operations. For those procedures that do not use control balancing or have limited checking, the error rate can be overwhelming.

Speed

The speed of a manual procedure is largely dependent on the delays within the procedure. For example, in the order-writing and billing procedure of figure 9-1, a delay is likely to take place after every operation as documents are moved from one clerk, desk, or department to another. Because a clerk normally performs several different operations a day, each clerk is likely to be working on one batch of documents when another batch for another operation is delivered. This second batch must wait to be processed until the clerk is finished with the first batch. If a clerk or department falls behind in work, several batches of documents may be waiting for a single clerk; thus, the delay between operations can extend to hours and even days.

Once a clerk or department falls behind in work, it is difficult to catch up. Unless the workload lightens or overtime hours are worked or additional people are hired, the group stays behind schedule and all documents involved continue to be delayed. In unexpected peak periods, a clerk or department may be overwhelmed by the volume of work. As incredible as it may sound, I have seen entire departments so overloaded with paperwork that incoming mail hadn't been opened for over three weeks.

Of course, top priority operations can always be handled separately. For instance, a rush order can be processed by having a single clerk handle the order in steps 1–9 of figure 9-1, and then deliver the order to the shipping department. Special handling is expensive, however, because it does not make use of the efficiencies of batch processing. Whenever batch processing is interrupted in favor of a special job, all other jobs are delayed.

Although a manual system can be bogged down by the delays between operations, it is also possible to have a perfectly efficient manual system. If the workload is predictable, if batches are kept small, and if operations are carefully planned and scheduled, a manual procedure can provide all the speed that is required of it.

Information

One of the features of an EDP system is its ability to provide management information. Once data has been recorded in a machine-readable form, it can be repeatedly processed to provide a wide variety of reports. Because the cost of the EDP system is spread over several applications and many documents, the cost of any one report is relatively low.

In contrast, the manual system normally requires a separate procedure for each report that is prepared — reports are not by-products of other procedures. For instance, the procedure in figure 9-5, which prepares

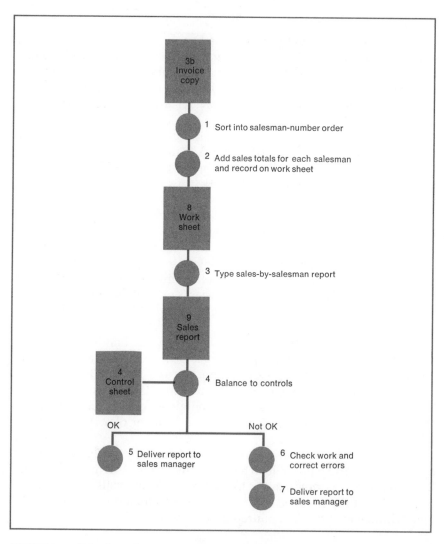

FIGURE 9-5   Sales-by-salesman report preparation

a monthly sales-by-salesman report, does not do any of the work needed to prepare a sales-by-customer or sales-by-item report. These reports would likely be prepared from accounts receivable and inventory ledger cards. Because of this characteristic of a manual system, information is relatively expensive to obtain.

You might also consider the speed and error-correction cost of a procedure such as the one in figure 9-5. If the volume of documents to be processed for the month is large—say more than a thousand—preparing the sales-by-salesman report can be a very time-consuming procedure. In addition, the chance of error and the chance that the control sheet and sales total won't balance is increased as the number of invoices increases. To find an error, a clerk must check the typing, and, if this doesn't reveal the error, must redo the calculations. In short, the amount of work required to correct an error (or the cost of error correction) is almost as great as the amount of work (or cost) required to create the report. Thus, with a large number of invoices, it is probably better to summarize them on a daily or weekly, rather than a monthly, basis. This reduces the amount of time required to prepare the report at the end of the month, but the cost of error correction is still relatively high.

Because of the nature of manual operations, reports that involve great detail or extensive calculations become impractical to prepare on a manual system. For example, an aged trial balance, which is a routine report in an EDP system, becomes a very expensive report when using a manual system. As a result, a small business is likely to prepare an aged trial balance only once or twice a year, rather than monthly. Similarly, inventory reports, such as a sales-by-item report showing this-year-to-date and last-year-to-date totals, and financial reports, such as a budget analysis showing the percent of actual costs over or under budget, are too expensive to prepare regularly when using manual procedures.

OFFICE EQUIPMENT

To increase the speed and accuracy and to decrease the cost of manual procedures, many varieties of office equipment have been developed. The adding machine and calculator, for example, are designed to improve arithmetic operations. In general, these machines can add, subtract, multiply, and even divide. The adding machine normally prints the results on a paper adding-machine tape, while calculators either print the results on a paper tape or display them in windows at the top of the machine. By using an adding machine or calculator, the speed and accuracy of operations such as totaling invoice charges and extending line items during billing can be improved.

To improve the efficiency of filing operations, many varieties of filing devices are available. *Tub files* have no tops, giving the effect of open file drawers at a height designed for filing efficiency. By eliminating the opening and closing of file drawers, records can be accessed more quickly. *Visible-record files,* such as the one in figure 9-6, are files in which the identifying information of records in a group is visible to the file clerk without any manual manipulation. After the clerk pulls out the appropriate group of records, she scans the visible portion of the records to find the required record, flips open the record, and reads or writes on it without removing it from the file. Since the record is never removed, there is no possibility of misfiling. In addition to tub and visible-record files, there are many varieties of mechanized files in which a selected group of records is rotated to the clerk after she presses the appropriate control buttons.

Writing boards such as the one shown in figure 9-4 make use of the fact that the same business data is recorded on several different forms. By using carbon-backed paper or chemically treated transfer paper, a single recording by a clerk is transferred to two or more different documents. Thus, an accounts receivable charge is recorded on the monthly statement, the customer ledger, and the journal in a single operation; an employee's earnings and deduction data are recorded on his paycheck, the employee ledger, and the payroll journal in a single operation. By reducing the number of times a clerk records data, both speed and accuracy are increased.

Two office machines you will likely come in contact with since they are so widely used are the posting machine and the billing machine. The *posting machine,* one model of which is illustrated in figure 9-7,

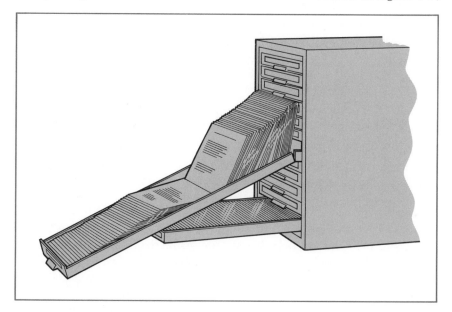

FIGURE 9-6   A visible-record file

combines the principles of the writing board, adding machine, and typewriter. Two or more documents can be overlaid in the machine at any one time, adding and subtracting are done automatically using the numeric keyboard, and the typewriter keyboard can be used to type data on the documents. The posting machine has the ability to store a limited amount of information in storage units commonly called *counters*, so some information—the date, for example—can be keyed into storage at the start of a job and can be printed automatically on all documents that are prepared. These counters can also be used to accumulate totals throughout an operation; thus, control totals can be printed automatically at the end of a job.

To illustrate the use of a posting machine, consider a typical posting operation—posting charges to accounts receivable records. At the start of the job, the operator inserts the accounts receivable journal into the machine, where it remains throughout the job. The day's date is then keyed into one of the machine's counters. After this preparation,

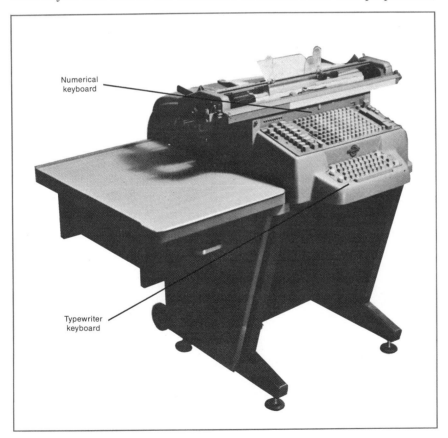

Numerical
keyboard

Typewriter
keyboard

FIGURE 9-7   A posting machine

the operator goes through the following steps for each invoice amount to be posted:

1. The operator pulls the customer ledger card and monthly statement for the invoice to be posted from a file, usually some sort of tub file.

2. The operator inserts the ledger and the statement into the posting machine so that they overlay the journal as in figure 9-8. The posting machine normally has an adjustable chute, making it relatively easy to insert the documents. Since the documents are carbon-backed, any data recorded on the statement is also recorded on the ledger and the journal.

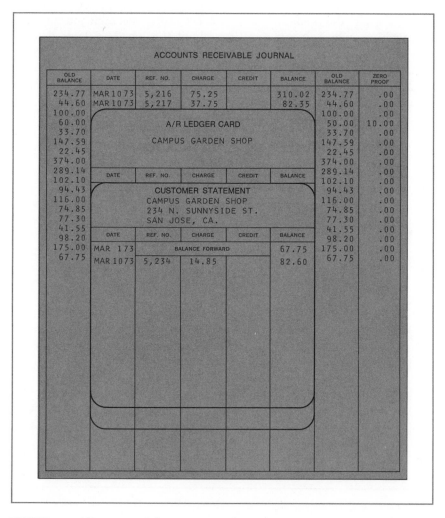

FIGURE 9-8   Alignment of documents in the posting machine

3. The operator keys the old balance read from the customer statement onto the numeric keyboard, thus entering it into one of the machine's counters and printing it in the lefthand column of the journal. Then, the machine automatically skips to the date column, prints the date, and skips to the reference-number column.

4. The operator keys the invoice number, which prints in the reference-number column.

5. The operator then keys the invoice amount, which prints in the charge column and is entered into one of the machine's counters. This amount is automatically added to the daily total of charges in one of the counters and is automatically added to the old balance to derive the new balance. The machine then skips to the balance column and prints the new balance.

6. The operator keys the old balance again as a check on accuracy. The machine prints this amount in the second old-balance column, subtracts the second old balance from the first old balance to derive an amount called the zero proof, and prints the zero proof in the zero-proof column. If the operator has keyed the old balance the same both times, the zero proof will be zero, thus indicating that the old balance has been keyed correctly.

7. The operator removes the ledger and the statement from the machine and returns them to the file.

The operator continues in this way until all of the charges for the day have been posted. Then, the operator aligns the machine at the charge column and presses a key that causes the final total of charges to print. At this time, the journal is used for balancing to controls. If the total charges balance to the total charges on the control sheet, all the amounts have been recorded correctly. If all zero proofs are zero, all old balances have been recorded correctly, so the new balances must be correct also.

A posting machine can also be used for other operations such as posting vendor charges to accounts payable or posting daily sales to salesman ledger cards. In addition, a posting machine can be used for summarizing expense or sales data. The document in figure 9-9, for example, is used to distribute sales into various categories. One line is recorded on the document for each invoice. Each of the amounts recorded in item classes 1 through 7 represents one line item of billing. Because a separate counter is used to total each column, the posting machine automatically prints the final total for each class at the bottom of the document. Because the number of counters available on a posting machine is limited, the number of classifications that can be used for summarizing data is also limited.

The automatic operations that a posting machine does—such as skipping, adding, and subtracting—are controlled in several different ways, depending on the machine model used. Two of the most common

SALES SUMMARY

REF. NO.	TOTAL BILLED	ITEM CLASS 1	ITEM CLASS 2	ITEM CLASS 3	ITEM CLASS 4	ITEM CLASS 5	ITEM CLASS 6	ITEM CLASS 7
5,445	39.95	24.00		10.00				5.95
5,446	110.00					106.90	3.10	
5,447	40.00		40.00					
5,448	82.12		59.00		3.12		20.00	
5,449	31.00							31.00
5,450	173.90	112.00		2.90		40.00		19.00
5,451	12.00		12.00					
5,452	64.00			14.00	50.00			
TOTALS	552.97	136.00	111.00	26.90	53.12	146.90	23.10	55.95

Note: All totals are accumulated and printed out automatically.

FIGURE 9-9   Sales summary prepared by a posting machine

control mechanisms are the control bar and the control panel. These mechanisms are set up by the manufacturer's representative for each job the posting-machine user intends to do. Before each job, the operator inserts the appropriate bar or panel for the job to be done. Regardless of the mechanism used, transition from one job to another is accomplished in a short period of time, usually less than a minute.

The *billing machine*, which looks and operates much like a posting machine, can multiply and sometimes divide. When used in a billing operation, the operator uses the typewriter keyboard to type the heading of the invoice. Some heading data, such as the date and invoice number, can be made to print automatically from the storage units of the machine. For each line item, the operator keys the quantity and unit price on the numeric keyboard, thus storing the data in counters. For item description and item number, the operator uses the typewriter keyboard. At the end of each line item, the machine automatically calculates the extension, prints it, and adds it to the invoice total. When all line items have been printed, the operator positions the machine at the total line, pushes a control button, and the invoice total is printed. Because one counter is used to accumulate the invoice totals, the billing total for the day can be printed at the end of the job. If desired, hash totals of quantities and item numbers can also be accumulated during the operation and printed at the end of the job.

Because of its calculating ability, the billing machine is also used for operations such as writing paychecks and calculating commission amounts. In addition, it can be used for many of the jobs done by a posting machine. Some billing machines are equipped with features that allow them to do billing and posting to accounts receivable in a single operation. After the invoice total is printed, the machine skips to the statement, ledger, and journal, and prints the date, invoice number, and charge amount automatically. This eliminates a second keying of these data items during the posting operation. Posting then proceeds as if a posting machine were being used.

Posting and billing machines are continually being improved; they are being made quieter, with more efficient keyboards, with more electronic and fewer mechanical parts, and with more automatic operations, thus allowing more operations to be combined. Nevertheless, the speed and accuracy of these machines depend to a large extent on the operator, who can still misfile ledgers, key amounts incorrectly, and type addresses wrong. And one operator is still able to do 35 percent more work on her billing machine than another operator is able to do on hers. As a result, much of what has been said so far about the accuracy, speed, and information of manual procedures remains true as mechanical devices are incorporated into a system. In particular, checking and control balancing are an important part of any manual or mechanical procedure; the cost of error correction is likely to be relatively high; and the preparation of management information is likely to be time consuming and expensive.

DISCUSSION

Although some of the limitations of manual and mechanical procedures have been pointed out in this chapter, it does not mean that computer systems are right for all businesses. On the contrary, because of cost, manual and mechanical procedures are right for many thousands of small companies and for many operations within the largest of companies. Furthermore, it is very likely that these procedures can be improved without moving from manual procedures to a computer system. Thus, a business that is large enough to have significant data-processing problems should consider revising existing procedures at the same time that they consider installing a computer. It may well be that a procedure revision is a more profitable alternative than installing a computer system.

In general, there are four ways of improving the efficiency of paperwork procedures. After charting the procedures so that they can be analyzed, each of the following changes should be considered:

1. Eliminating a step.
2. Combining two or more steps.
3. Changing the sequence of two or more steps.
4. Installing office equipment to help improve the efficiency of one or more steps.

For example, steps 3 and 4 of figure 9-2 could perhaps be combined for greater efficiency. Or steps 2 through 5 of figure 9-3 could be replaced by a posting-machine operation. Because most office procedures have evolved, rather than being carefully planned, it is common during analysis to discover documents that are no longer being used, steps that can be eliminated, and operations that long ago should have been combined. As a result, it is not unreasonable to expect a significant improvement in paperwork procedures by a careful analysis and revision of existing procedures.

In discussing manual procedures, one question worth considering is why consumers have become so critical of computerized billing. In view of the likelihood of errors and delays in noncomputerized systems, it seems unfair. The major criticism, however, seems to be that it is more difficult to get an error corrected on a computer-printed bill. In a 1971 survey, for example, 24 percent of the people interviewed said that they had had trouble getting computerized billing errors corrected. The question is why?

With this chapter as background, it is easy to see how noncomputerized errors can be corrected. For instance, if a company uses a posting machine for accounts receivable, a customer-service clerk can check the invoice in question, verify or deny the error by checking the source documents involved, and fill out the appropriate error-adjustment form. Then, the next time transactions are posted to accounts receivable records, the adjustment is posted and the error is corrected.

But why can't this be done on a computer system as well? Source documents and invoice copies are kept in computer systems just as they are in other systems. In addition, cash-receipt and invoice registers are available to help trace an error. Thus, it should be easy to determine whether an error has occurred. And if so, after the adjustment form is completed, the correction data can be keypunched and processed, and the error should be corrected.

Apparently, though, many correction procedures in computerized billing systems are poorly designed and controlled. As a result, it often takes two (or more) letters or calls to get a computer error corrected. In extreme cases, the correspondence between consumer and company has gone on for months. Although the final blame, it seems, has always fallen on the computer system, it is of course the computer system design that should be blamed.

If the ledger-card system has an advantage over the computer system, it is the fact that all of a customer's past transactions are recorded on a single document, the ledger card. When a company moves to a computer system, this document is no longer prepared. Although the information recorded on the ledger card can be found on other documents prepared by the computer system — such as various registers and reports — the one-time ledger-card user often feels that he has lost a valuable source of information. "The information that I used to be able to find out in five minutes now takes two weeks." Although this typical complaint is unfounded since the information can actually be found in a reasonably short period of time, the complaint should not be dismissed lightly. At the least, it indicates the resistance to new methods and the need for the retraining of personnel. Furthermore, there is no question that for some types of information searches, it is easier to consult one ledger card than to search through a series of documents. From a profit-making point of view, however, the speed, accuracy, and information capabilities of the computer system should more than offset the disadvantages resulting from the lost ledger card.

1. Although speed and accuracy can be achieved using manual procedures, delays, errors, and costly error corrections are likely if procedures aren't well-planned and controlled. The major limitation of manual procedures, however, is the limited information capability.

2. There are many varieties of office equipment and machines to help improve the speed and accuracy of manual procedures. Two office machines in common use are the posting machine and the billing machine.

3. Because office procedures have probably been developed without overall planning, it is reasonable to expect a significant improvement in performance as a result of procedure analysis and revision. Four possibilities to consider are (1) eliminating a step, (2) combining steps, (3) resequencing steps, and (4) installing office equipment.

SUMMARY

procedure chart
journal
pegboard
writing board
tub file

visible-record file
posting machine
counter
zero proof
billing machine

**FOR
REVIEW**

CHAPTER
TEN

As mentioned in chapter 3, *punched-card systems* date back to the late 1800s when Dr. Herman Hollerith invented the punched card and a number of punched-card machines. Until the computer was commercially marketed in the 1950s, punched-card systems were used in thousands of businesses—both large and small. It was commonplace, in fact, for a large company to use dozens and even hundreds of punched-card machines in a punched-card system—for example, forty-five keypunches, twenty-six verifiers, eight sorters, three collators, and so on.

Today, the punched-card system has been replaced by the computer in all but the very small companies. In addition, the price of small computers continues to drop so the number of punched-card systems in use should continue to drop. Thus, this chapter is primarily of historical interest. It may be many years before the punched-card system disappears altogether—it is still in use in thousands of businesses—but there is no question that the punched-card system will become obsolete. Consequently, this chapter is but a brief introduction to the nature of the punched-card system.

PUNCHED-CARD MACHINES

In chapter 3, you were introduced to several of the punched-card machines—in particular, the keypunch, verifier, sorter, collator, and interpreter. To complete the punched-card system, three other machines—the reproducer, calculator, and accounting machine—are needed. All three machines are controlled by wired control panels that are inserted into the control-panel housing before a job is run.

PUNCHED-CARD
SYSTEMS

The Reproducer

The *reproducer*, one model of which is shown in figure 10-1, punches data from one card into another card. The *read feed*, which is on the left side of the machine and consists of one hopper and one stacker, is used to read cards; the *punch feed*, which is in the middle of the machine and also consists of one hopper and one stacker, is used to punch or both read and punch cards. For some functions, both read and punch feeds are used; for others, only the punch feed. Although the machine can perform several different operations, only its major functions—reproducing, gangpunching, and interspersed gangpunching—are covered in this chapter.

Reproducing refers to punching data from one deck of cards into

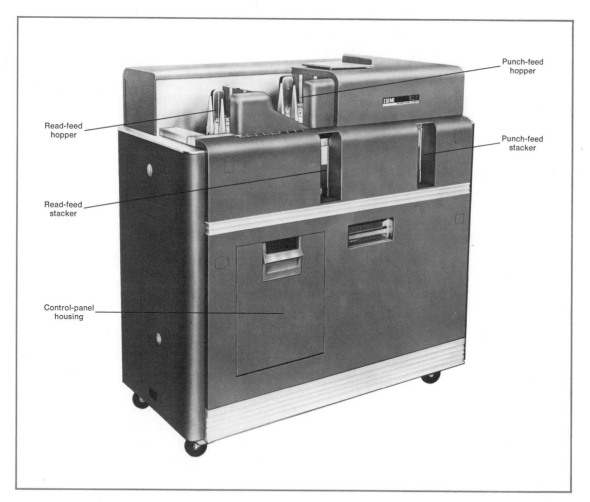

FIGURE 10-1   The reproducer

another deck of cards, as illustrated schematically in figure 10-2. The deck to be reproduced is placed in the read-feed hopper, the blank cards in the punch-feed hopper, and the control panel in the control-panel housing. After the operator pushes the start button, reproducing takes place without further operator intervention. At the end of the job, the original punched deck is in the read-feed stacker, and the newly punched deck is in the punch-feed stacker. As indicated by figure 10-2, the fields may be punched in card columns other than those in the original deck and not all fields have to be reproduced. In addition, the punch-feed deck does not have to be completely blank before reproducing—in some cases, it would be partially punched.

Gangpunching refers to punching data from one card into many other cards, as illustrated in figure 10-3. In this example, the first card, which contains the number 957 in one of its leftmost fields, is placed in the punch-feed hopper ahead of several partially punched cards. After the operator inserts the proper control panel and starts the machine, the data from the first card is punched (gangpunched) in all cards that

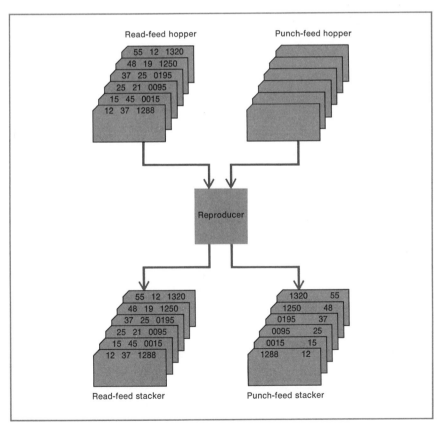

FIGURE 10-2   Reproducing

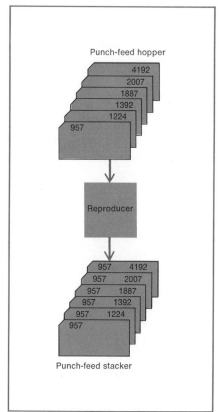

FIGURE 10-3 Gangpunching

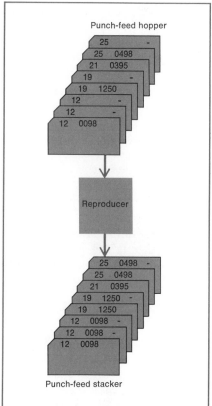

FIGURE 10-4 Interspersed
gangpunching

follow. Although only selected fields need be punched, a field is normally gangpunched into the same card columns as in the original card.

Interspersed gangpunching is illustrated in figure 10-4. Here, the input deck is placed in the punch-feed hopper and data is punched from master cards into the cards that follow (called *detail cards*). To distinguish master from detail cards, an X-punch is normally used. Thus, detail cards in figure 10-4 have X-punches in one of the rightmost columns (indicated by the hyphen), while master cards do not. When interspersed gangpunching takes place, selected fields from the master card are punched into the detail cards. When the next master card is read, punching is suspended so that the master cards are unchanged by the operation.

The Calculator

The *calculator*, shown in figure 10-5, has one hopper and one stacker. This machine can add, subtract, multiply, and sometimes divide; and

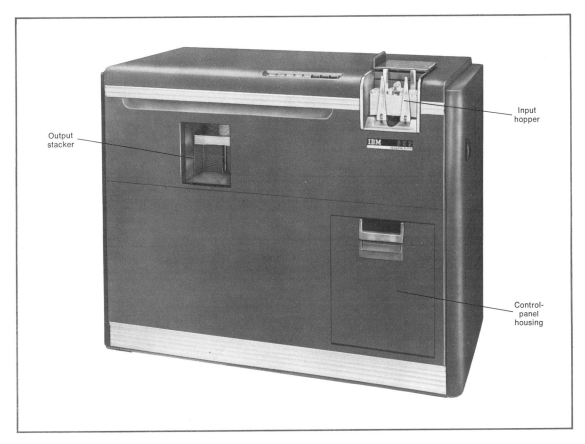

FIGURE 10-5   The calculator

it can perform a series of these calculations on a deck of cards in a single pass through the machine. Calculations are performed on the input fields of one or more cards, and the results are punched into other fields of the same cards or other cards.

Although it is difficult to describe the exact capabilities of a calculator without getting into a lengthy explanation, a typical operation is illustrated in figure 10-6. Here, the calculator is used to extend costs and prices in a billing application. In a single pass of the cards through the machine, the calculator does the following:

1. Multiplies unit price by quantity, giving total price.
2. Multiplies unit cost by quantity, giving total cost.
3. Subtracts total cost from total price, giving gross profit.

The result fields—total cost, total price, and gross profit—are punched in the same card from which quantity, unit cost, and unit price were read.

Because of its ability to do a series of calculations in a single opera-

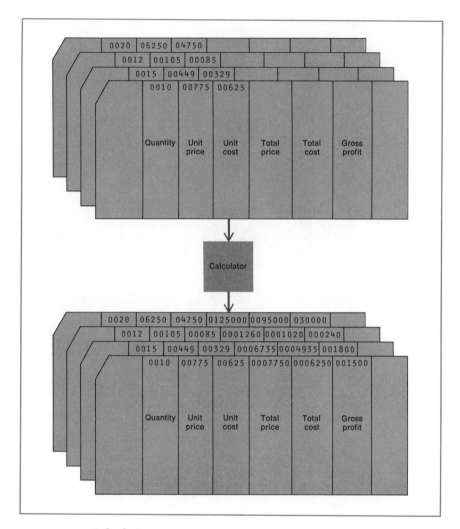

FIGURE 10-6   Calculating

tion, the calculator is very useful in a payroll application. In a typical
system, employee earnings and year-to-date cards are passed through
the calculator several times to derive gross pay, federal tax, social security tax, state tax (if any), and net pay. Note, however, that the calculator cannot print results; it can only punch them so that they can be
printed by the accounting machine.

The Accounting Machine

The *accounting machine*, shown in figure 10-7, reads an input deck
and prints on continuous-form output documents. By using a forms-

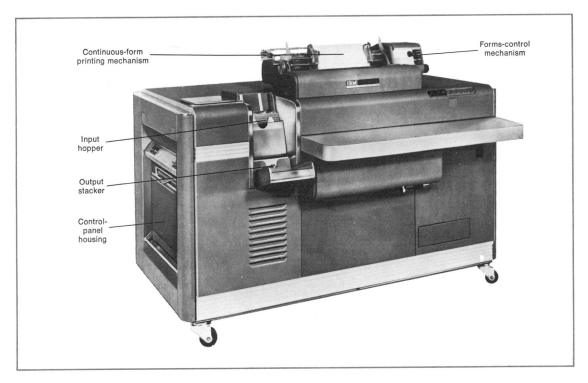

FIGURE 10-7   The accounting machine

control tape similar to that used on printers of computer systems, the accounting machine is able to skip to appropriate parts of a form before printing a line. However, because the accounting machine is normally limited to printing one line per card, it by no means has the printing flexibility of a computer system. In addition, some models of the accounting machine can print only numeric data in positions after print position 44; some models cannot print decimal points or commas so, as shown in figure 10-8, a vertical line must be used to indicate the location of the decimal point.

Unlike the computer system, the accounting machine has limited arithmetic capabilities—it can only add or subtract—and it must process data in a rigidly prescribed way. In general, there are two types of documents that can be printed by the accounting machine, examples of which are given in figure 10-8. The first type of document, called a *detail-printed report* or *document*, consists of one output line for each input card. In addition, totals can be accumulated for selected fields of the input cards, and then printed when the number in the control field changes or after the last card has been processed. In contrast, the second type of document, called a *group-printed report* or *document*, consists of one summary line for each group of related input cards.

	SALES BY ITEM		
SHEET 2 OF 4		MONTH OF AUGUST	
ITEM NO.	ITEM DESCRIPTION	SALES	
11202	SQ SHANK SWIVEL	1349	20
11202	SQ SHANK SWIVEL	101	88
11202	SQ SHANK SWIVEL	250	00
11202	SQ SHANK SWIVEL	378	90
11202	SQ SHANK SWIVEL	2345	00
11202	SQ SHANK SWIVEL	221	25
11202	SQ SHANK SWIVEL	270	90
		4917	23 ※
15102	CUSTOM BUILT	488	75
15102	CUSTOM BUILT	690	50
15102	CUSTOM BUILT	2890	00
15102	CUSTOM BUILT	2	80
		4072	05 ※
16115	SQ SOCKET RIGID	112	50

DETAIL-PRINTED REPORT

	SALES BY ITEM		
SHEET 2 OF 2		MONTH OF AUGUST	
ITEM NO.	ITEM DESCRIPTION	SALES	
11202	SQ SHANK SWIVEL	4917	23
15102	CUSTOM BUILT	4072	05
16115	SQ SOCKET RIGID	4981	42
17203	EXT SHANK WITH BRK	32	90
21103	SQ SHANK RIGID	6235	70
23302	EXTENSION SHANK	325	90
23702	ADJ ADAPTER SQUARE	4610	20
26104	HEX SOCKET RIGID	3995	76
26302	SQ SOCKET SWIVEL	4376	30
33202	FLAT TOP SWIVEL	563	70
33205	ROUND TOP SWIVEL	401	66
35105	HEX SHANK RIGID	3	81

GROUP-PRINTED REPORT

FIGURE 10-8   Detail- and group-printed reports

Like the detail-printed document, this type of document may or may not have totals at the end of the report.

When the reproducer is connected by cable to the accounting machine, as shown in figure 10-9, totals accumulated in the accounting machine can be *summary-punched* into blank cards in the punch feed of the reproducer. Thus, an accounts receivable card, one per invoice, can be summary-punched during a billing operation. Or a salesman year-to-date card can be summary-punched during the preparation of a sales-by-salesman report. Unlike summary punching on a computer system, only numeric data can be punched when the accounting machine and reproducer are used.

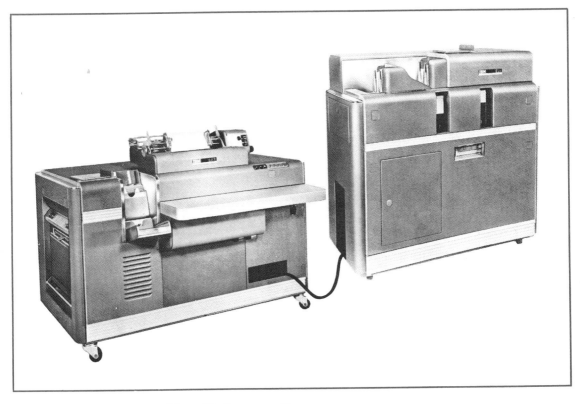

FIGURE 10-9   Summary punching with the accounting
machine and the reproducer

The Wired Control Panel

A wired control panel for an accounting machine is shown in figure 10-10. As you can see, the panel consists of dozens of little holes into which control wires are plugged. Because hundreds of wires are likely to be used for a simple accounting machine job, panel wiring can be a tedious and time-consuming job. For example, it may take two or three days to wire and test a panel for a billing job. Although control panels for other machines are smaller, wiring can still be time consuming. Once wired and tested, of course, the panels are stored in panel racks, ready for use.

THE PUNCHED-CARD SYSTEM

Punched-card systems can be made up of a few machines or many machines. The simplest punched-card system, for example, consists of a keypunch, a sorter, and an accounting machine. A system such as

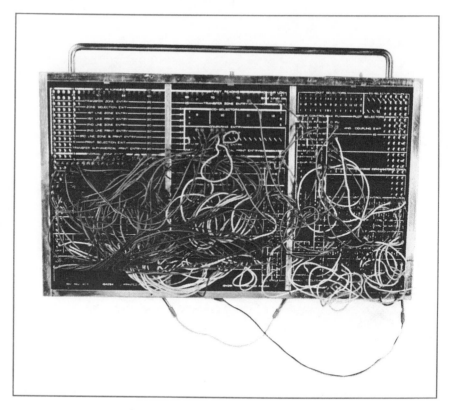

FIGURE 10-10   A wired control panel

this will rent for about $400 per month and must be supported by various manual procedures such as sight-checking keypunched cards and merging card files. On the other hand, a punched-card system might consist of several keypunches and verifiers, a sorter, a collator, a reproducer, a calculator, an accounting machine, and an interpreter. The cost of a system such as this is about the same as the cost of a small computer system; thus, the larger punched-card systems continue to be replaced by computer systems.

To illustrate the design of a punched-card system, suppose a system consisting of a keypunch, a verifier, a sorter, a calculator, and an accounting machine is going to be used in a billing application. The flowchart in figure 10-11, then, represents the steps required to prepare invoices from shipping orders after they have been returned from the shipping department. The required card layouts are given in figure 10-12.

After control totals are accumulated and recorded in step 1, miscellaneous and item cards are keypunched and verified. The miscellaneous cards contain the data relating to the individual orders; the item cards

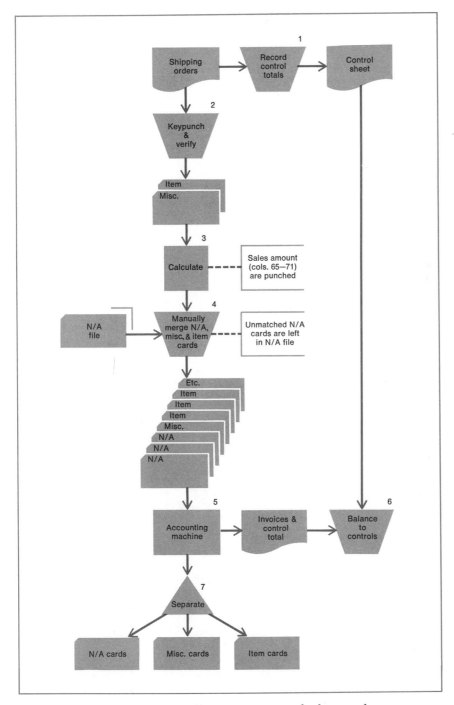

FIGURE 10-11 Flowchart for a billing system using the keypunch, verifier, calculator, and accounting machine

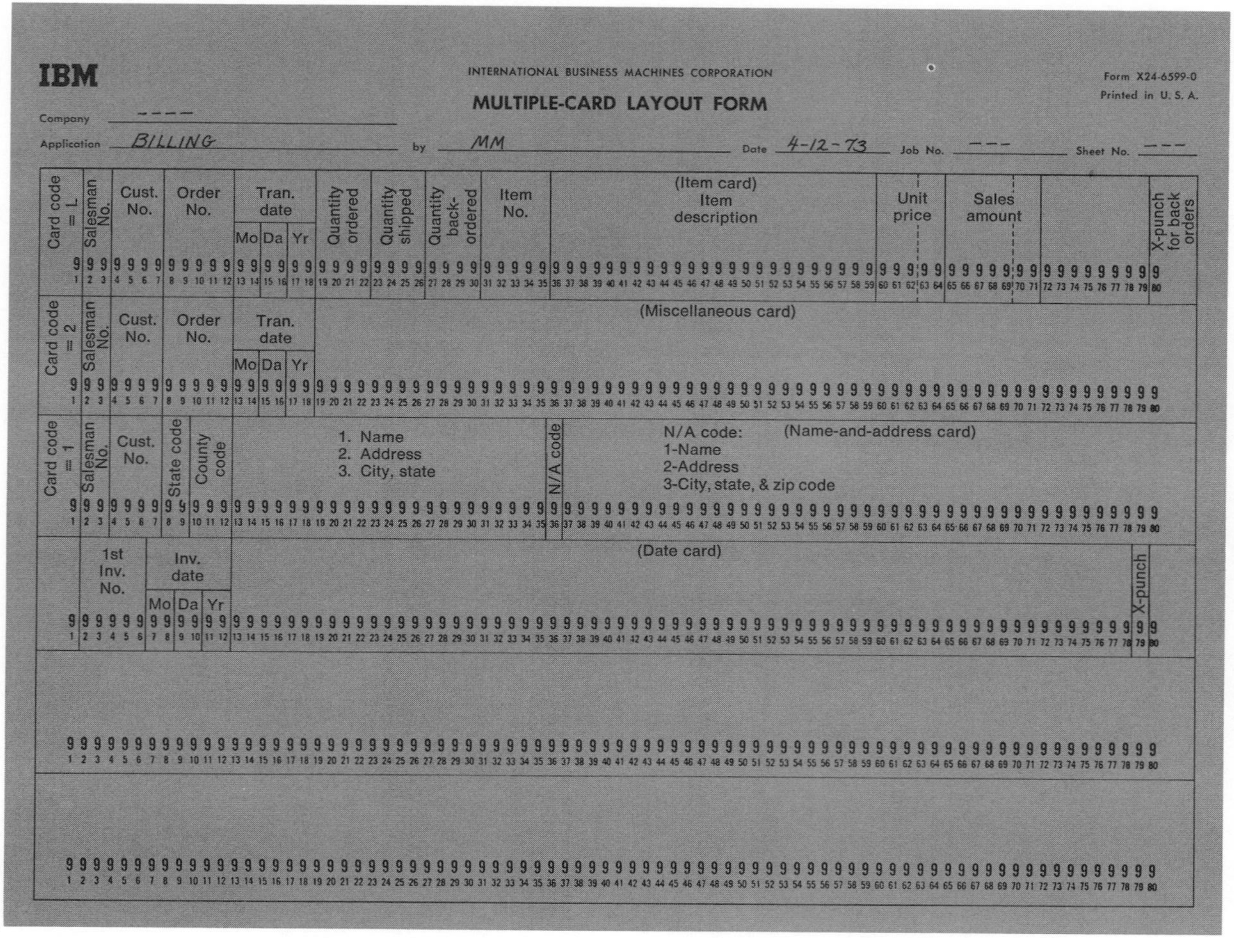

FIGURE 10-12 Card layouts for the billing application

contain the data pertinent to each line item of billing. Columns 1–64 are keypunched, and column 30 receives an X-punch whenever a line item is back-ordered.

In step 3, the calculator extends the line items and punches the extensions in the sales-amount fields. Because the miscellaneous cards do not have an X-punch in column 1 but the item cards do (an L is the combination of an X-punch and a 3-punch), the calculator can be wired to ignore the miscellaneous cards. This makes it unnecessary to remove the miscellaneous cards from the deck before the calculating run.

In step 4, a clerk inserts the proper name-and-address (N/A) cards before the miscellaneous and item cards for each invoice. If a collator were available, of course, this could be done by machine rather than manually. This step cannot be done on a sorter, however, since unmatched N/A cards must be removed from the deck prior to the invoicing run. Unlike the computer, the accounting machine cannot be wired to ignore unmatched master cards in a deck.

In step 5, the invoices are prepared as illustrated schematically in figure 10-13. Before putting the invoicing deck in the hopper of the accounting machine, a date card must be placed at the front of the deck so that the date and invoice number can be stored in counters and printed on each invoice. As each invoice is printed, the accounting machine will increase the invoice number by one. Note that, with the exception of the total line, there is one input card for each line that is printed on the invoice. Note also that decimal points and commas are not printed by the accounting machine. The only mathematical operation performed by the accounting machine is the addition required in deriving the invoice total and the control total of invoiced amounts for the day. If hash totals are used, these can also be accumulated by the accounting machine and printed at the end of the job. After billing, control totals are balanced, the cards are separated, and the cards are returned to files.

To illustrate a more advanced punched-card system, suppose a system consisting of a keypunch, a verifier, a sorter, a collator, a reproducer, a calculator, an interpreter, and an accounting machine is used in a billing and accounts receivable application. This system is flowcharted in figure 10-14. The primary cards used in this system have the same formats as those given in figure 10-12.

In steps 1–6 of this system, the data is punched into the miscellaneous and item cards. To keep keypunching to a minimum, only columns 1–35 of the item cards are keypunched. Then, in steps 2–5, the item cards are sorted, merged with item master cards, and the data in columns 36–64 of the master cards is interspersed gangpunched into the item cards. Figure 10-15 gives the formats of the item master cards and other cards used in this system. In step 6, the item masters are separated from the item cards and returned to file.

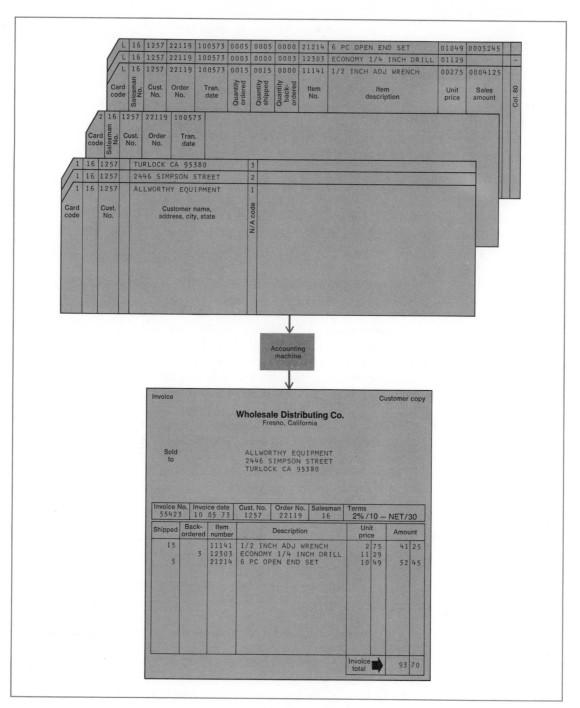

FIGURE 10-13   A billing operation on the accounting machine

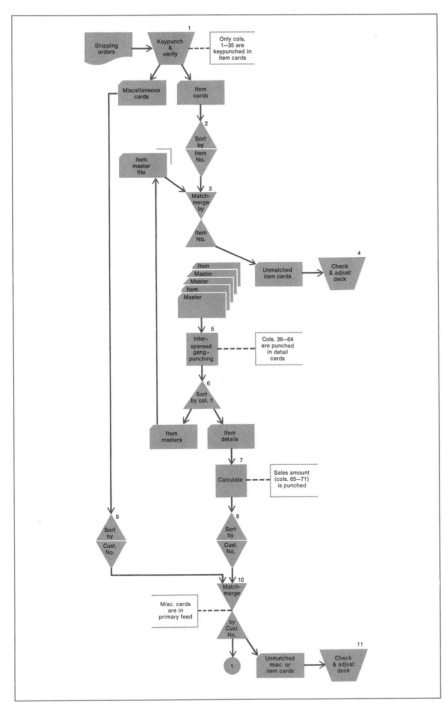

FIGURE 10-14   Flowchart for a billing and accounts receivable system
(Part 1 of 2)

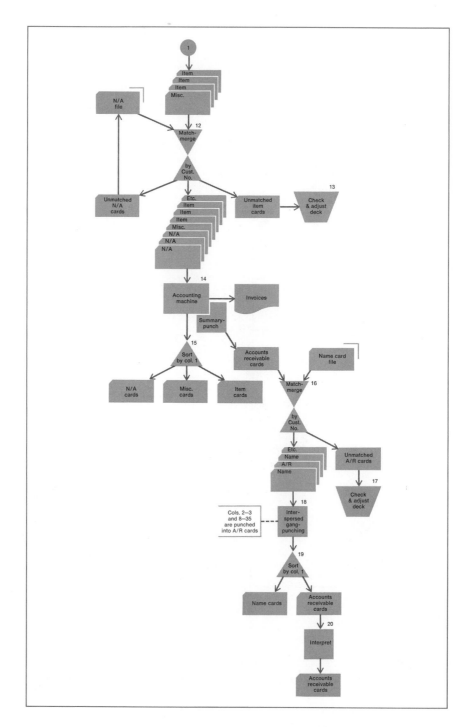

FIGURE 10-14 (Part 2 of 2)

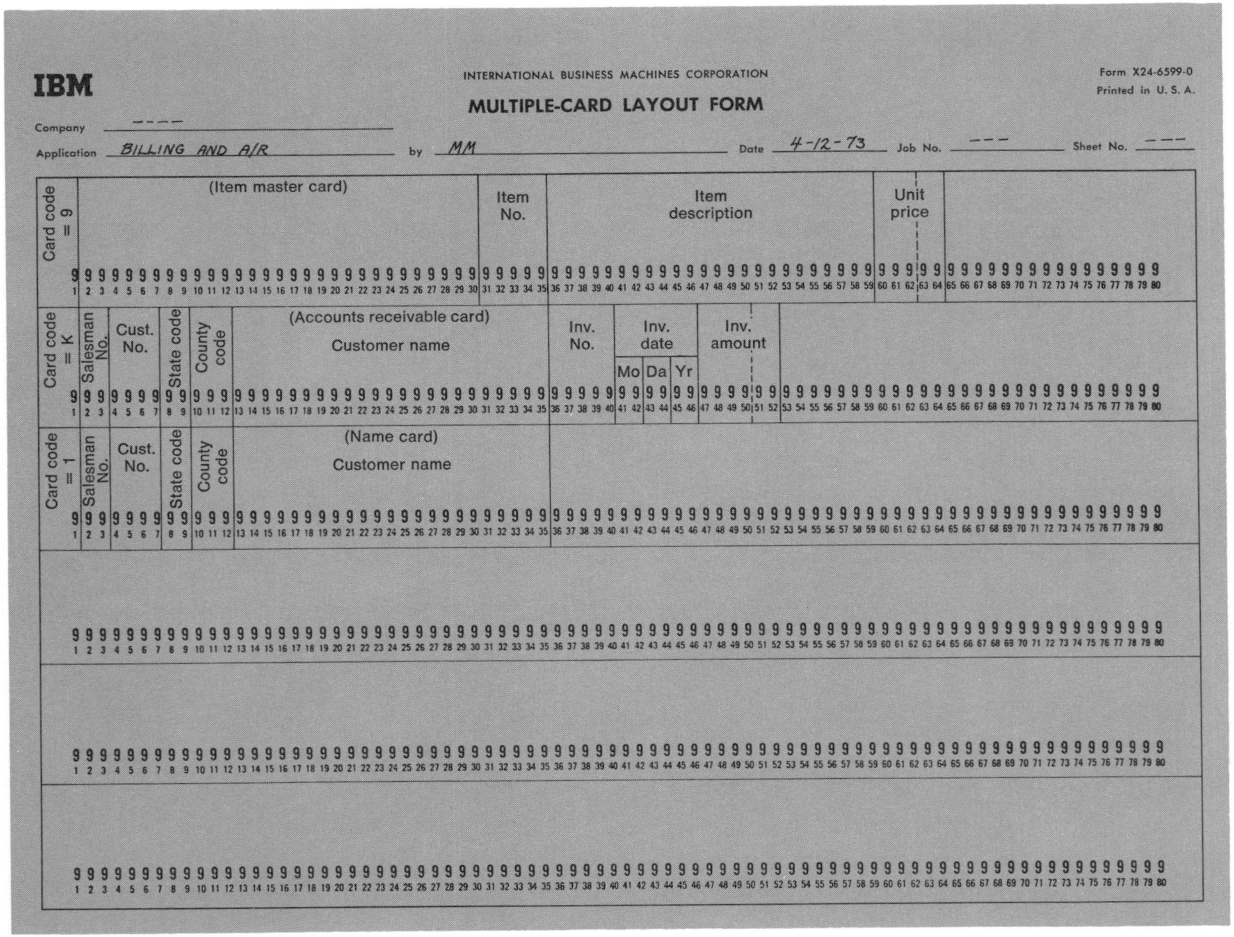

FIGURE 10-15 Additional card formats used in the billing and accounts receivable system

In steps 7–14, the item cards are passed through the calculator, thus punching sales amount; the item cards are merged with miscellaneous and N/A cards; and the invoices are printed. Because the accounting machine is connected to the reproducer, accounts receivable cards are summary-punched in step 14 for use in an accounts receivable application.

Since the accounting machine can summary-punch only numeric data, steps 16–19 are required to punch additional data into the accounts receivable cards. In step 16, the accounts receivable cards are merged with master name cards (see the card format in figure 10-15). Then data from the master cards is interspersed gangpunched into the accounts receivable cards (step 18). After being separated from the master cards, the accounts receivable cards are interpreted (step 20) so that they are ready for use in an open-item accounts receivable file.

Although this has been only a brief introduction, you should be able to see the basic characteristics of the punched-card system. First, the required data is punched into cards using a keypunch, reproducer, or calculator. Second, the decks are arranged in proper sequences by using the sorter and collator. Finally, the accounting machine is used to print the documents required by the system.

DISCUSSION

To appreciate why punched-card systems are replaced by computer systems, you need to consider the speed, accuracy, and information capability for the punched-card system relative to the computer system. On the other hand, many small businesses have replaced manual or mechanical procedures with small punched-card systems. To appreciate why, you must again consider speed, accuracy, and information.

The speed of an accounting machine is normally between 50 and 150 cards per minute, depending on the model. Other punched-card machines—in particular, the calculator—may run even slower. For example, a calculator doing a state tax calculation may operate at a speed of 25 cards per minute or less. In comparison to small computer systems that print at 350 lines per minute and do calculations in milliseconds, this is of course quite slow. In addition, because of the many different steps required by a punched-card system, card handling by the machine operator is likely to slow down processing. And one major error—such as gangpunching data into the wrong fields of partially punched transaction cards—can require significant amounts of machine time to correct.

For two reasons, a punched-card system is likely to be less accurate than a computer system. First, because of the large amount of card handling required by the punched-card system, the chance of operator error—for example, leaving one transaction card in a collator—is increased. Second, because punched-card machines are mechanical, it is possible for a machine malfunction to cause an error on an output document. For instance, a faulty punch die on a reproducer could mean a punching error; a faulty counter on a calculator could mean an error in addition; a faulty printing mechanism on an accounting machine could mean a printing error. Although both of these types of errors are likely to be caught by various operating techniques, by document inspection, or by balancing to controls, some errors will slip through the system, and, at the least, the error-correction procedures will slow down the system.

As for information, you must consider the arithmetic and logic limitations of a punched-card system in comparison to those of a computer system. The calculations that can be done by an accounting machine or a calculator are decidedly limited. An accounting machine can only add and subtract, and a calculator is limited, at most, to a few dozen operations in sequence. As a result, calculating the economic order quantity for an inventory item or the standard deviation of its demand is beyond the capabilities of a punched-card system. And simpler calculations such as determining the efficiency percentage of a factory worker or the percent of actual to budgeted costs for a financial report, though possible to perform, often require enough additional machine time to be impractical. In contrast, a computer can do a lengthy series of calculations in a few milliseconds.

Similarly, the logic capabilities of a punched-card system are limited. Unlike a computer, the accounting machine cannot operate on different input records in totally different ways. Instead, all input records are processed using the same sequence of operations. Although the accounting machine can vary calculations and printing based on control punches in input cards and on the results of calculations (plus, minus, or zero), the variations are limited. In general, the options are to print a field in one group of print positions or another group; to not print the field; to add a field to, or subtract it from, one counter or another; or to not add or subtract it. One result of this fixed sequence of processing operations is that the accounting machine has only two options with regard to report format—group printing and detail printing. Because of these arithmetic and logic limitations, many forms of reports are difficult or impossible to prepare on a punched-card system.

In summary, the punched-card system is relatively slow, inaccurate, and has limited information capabilities when compared to a computer system. But, bear in mind that it's all relative. While 50 lines per minute may seem slow to the computer user, it is extremely fast compared to a typist. So, if an accounting machine turns out 3000 line items of billing in two hours, the users of the system will probably be well-pleased.

Similarly, the punched-card system is likely to be extremely accurate in comparison to manual or mechanical procedures. Because verified data is processed by machines rather than people and because control totals are automatically accumulated and printed, there is relatively little opportunity for error. In fact, it has often been the case that the installation of a punched-card system uncovered a large number of errors that went undetected by the paperwork procedures previously used.

As for information preparation, the punched-card system has a clear advantage over paperwork procedures. Like the computer system, information is an automatic by-product of other punched-card procedures. Once punched and verified, transaction data can be repeatedly processed by the punched-card machines to prepare a wide variety of management reports. The accounting machine, in fact, is designed to summarize data into reports. While these reports may seem unsophisticated to the computer user, they are quite elaborate to the user of a non-automated system.

SUMMARY

1. The reproducer, calculator, and accounting machine are used along with the keypunch, verifier, sorter, collator, and interpreter in a typical punched-card system. The reproducer punches data from one group of cards into another. The calculator performs calculations on input fields and punches the results in cards. The accounting machine accumulates totals and prints the output documents of a system.

2. A punched-card system can consist of either a few machines or dozens of machines. In general, the keypunch, reproducer, and calculator are used to punch data into cards. The sorter and collator are used to arrange decks into desired sequences for processing by the reproducer, calculator, or accounting machine.

3. Although the punched card system may seem limited in comparison to the modern computer system, its previous importance should not be forgotten. For many years, the punched-card system was the most sophisticated method of processing data. The speed, accuracy, and information that the punched-card system provided surpassed that of any alternative method of processing.

FOR REVIEW

punched-card system
reproducer
read feed
punch feed
reproducing
gangpunching
interspersed gangpunching

detail card
calculator
accounting machine
detail-printed report
group-printed report
summary punching

CHAPTER ELEVEN

Because keypunching and verifying are manual operations, it is common for input preparation to take considerably longer than processing in an EDP system. For example, it may take three days to prepare employee job cards, but only three hours to process them and prepare payroll checks. Similarly, it may take several hours longer to prepare customer-order cards than it does to process them and print shipping orders and invoices. Because they are a primary source of delay within a system, keypunching and verifying are often referred to as the "keypunch bottleneck."

Input preparation can also be a significant cost in an EDP installation. A large computer user, for example, may have 150 or more keypunches and operators. At $600 or more per month per keypunch station (keypunch and operator), the keypunching budget may be well over $100,000 per year.

Because of its effect on the speed and cost of an EDP system, system designers have looked for alternatives to keypunching for many years. One of the traditional approaches has been to use *turnaround documents* such as the one in figure 11-1. This document is a premium notice issued by an insurance company, but when it is returned with the exact payment, it becomes input to the computer system as a record of payment. If you decode the holes punched in the card, you will see that customer number, payment period, due date, and amount due are punched in the card as well as printed on it; thus, the data can be processed by a computer if the customer pays the full amount. If a partial payment is made or if the notice isn't returned with the payment, auxiliary procedures must be used.

THE KEYPUNCH BOTTLENECK

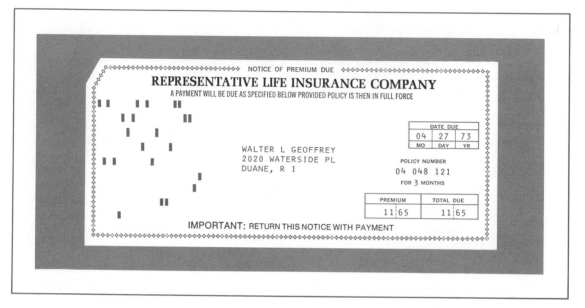

FIGURE 11-1 A turnaround premium notice

A turnaround document can be prepared in several ways. First, the cards can be punched by the computer system in one step and printed by an interpreter in a subsequent step. Second, the cards can be punched and printed in a single step by using a computer system with a multi-function card machine as described in chapter 5. Third, the cards can be punched by the computer system in one step and printed by the computer system in another step. For this purpose, there are printers that print on punched cards as well as continuous-form documents. These printers also have the ability to read the data punched in the cards; thus, the program can check that the data is being printed on the correct cards.

Another traditional approach to reducing keypunching is the preparation of a punched paper tape as a by-product of some manual operation. For instance, the device in figure 11-2 can be used to punch a paper tape while shipping orders are being typed on the typewriter keyboard. The punched paper tape, which contains order data in coded form, can be used as input to a computer system that has a paper-tape reader as an input device. In addition to typewriter devices, paper-tape punches can be attached to adding machines and cash registers.

These traditional approaches are of course limited to certain restricted applications. To use a turnaround premium notice, for example, a company must have a high percentage of the premium notices returned with payment; otherwise, the technique loses its value. Similarly, if nothing is gained by typing shipping orders (such as a gain in order-writing speed), the user might be better off keypunching cards and having the

FIGURE 11-2   A document writer with paper-tape output

computer system print the shipping orders. Obviously, then, other alternatives to keypunching are needed.

In the last several years, considerable emphasis has been placed on developing these alternatives. (Before 1965 or 1966, it seems system designers and manufacturers were too busy with other problems to worry about the keypunch problem.) The three alternatives that have been given the most attention are (1) replacing keypunches and verifiers with other key-operated devices such as key-to-tape devices, (2) the use of machine-readable source documents, and (3) source-data automation.

KEYPUNCH REPLACEMENT

In 1965 Mohawk Data Sciences Corporation introduced a device, called a *data recorder*, that is a replacement for the keypunch and verifier. This device is shown in figure 11-3. When the operator keys data on the keyboard, it is recorded on a magnetic tape. To correct an error, the operator backspaces the tape and keys the correct data, which then replaces the incorrect data. Similarly, when the data recorder is used for verifying, errors are corrected when the correct data is keyed over the incorrect data.

The data recorder can improve operations in two ways. First, because tape can be read by a computer system at a speed many times faster than card reading, less computer time is required for reading the input data.

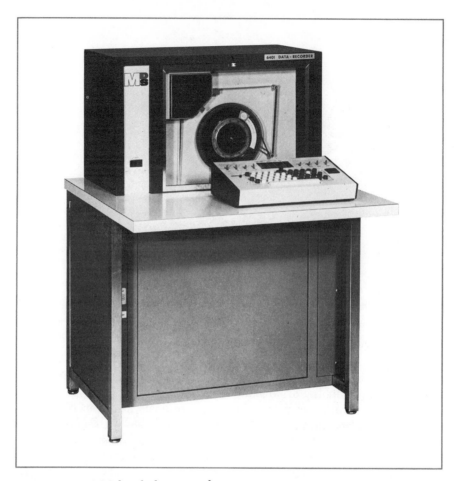

FIGURE 11-3   A Mohawk data recorder

Second, because card handling and card movement through the machine are eliminated and because of the ease of error correction, operator efficiency is improved. The disadvantage of using data recorders is that in many cases several tapes with a small amount of data on each—one tape for each operator—must be merged by the computer system into a single tape before the records can be sorted or edited.

Since the introduction of the Mohawk data recorder, other manufacturers have developed many varieties of key-to-tape devices and systems. Figure 11-4, for example, schematically illustrates one of the more recent developments, a key-to-tape (or key-to-disk) system. Here, eight keyboards are connected to a small computer that has both magnetic-disk and magnetic-tape input and output. During operation, all eight operators can be working on the same job or different jobs. As data is keyed, it is read into the computer, which performs certain editing oper-

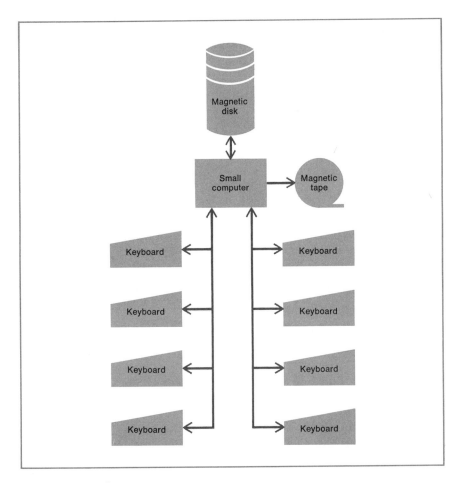

FIGURE 11-4   A key-to-tape system

ations to determine whether the data is valid. If invalid data is detected, the operator is notified immediately so that it can be corrected at once. If the data is valid, it is stored on the disk. At various times during the day, data recorded on the disk by one or more operators is written onto one tape by executing a disk-to-tape program. The tape can then be processed by the main computer system.

There are several advantages of a key-to-tape system such as this. First, because editing routines are executed when the keying takes place, many types of invalid fields can be corrected immediately. In contrast, when editing is done independent of the keying operations, error correction can be a time-consuming and costly job. Second, because card handling and card movement are eliminated and error correction is simplified, operator speed is increased by 25 percent or more as compared to a keypunching and verifying operation. Finally, in contrast to data-recorder operations, several tapes do not have to be merged into one tape by the main computer system. Instead, records keyed by several different operators are consolidated by a disk-to-tape run executed by the key-to-tape system.

The disadvantage of a key-to-tape system is downtime. If the computer that is central to the system fails, all operators that are using the system— as many as sixty-four—will be idle. In actual practice, however, these systems have proven to be highly reliable. As a result, it is a rare occurrence when a system is down for more than an hour.

MACHINE-READABLE SOURCE DOCUMENTS

Although replacement of the keypunch can improve operations, the basic bottleneck remains. A more complete solution consists of eliminating keying operations altogether by using source documents that can be read by a computer system. Four types of data that are readable by both humans and computers are (1) magnetic-ink characters, (2) optical marks, (3) optical characters, and (4) handwritten characters.

Magnetic-Ink Characters

Magnetic-ink character recognition (MICR) refers to the reading of characters (sometimes called *MICR characters*) that are printed in magnetic ink. These characters are used in the banking industry for processing the checks used in checking accounts. When a customer opens an account, he is issued checks similar to those in figure 11-5 (part A). Printed near the bottom of the checks are the customer's name, bank number, and other routing data. Because the data is printed in ink that contains magnetic particles, it can be read by a MICR reader that is connected to a computer system. Figure 11-6 shows the fourteen MICR characters that can be used in magnetic-ink character recognition—the ten decimal digits plus four control characters.

When a person writes a check and it is deposited in a bank, the amount must be recorded on the check in MICR characters as shown in figure 11-5 (part B). This is done using a MICR inscriber such as the one shown in figure 11-7. As data is keyed on the keyboard, MICR characters are printed on the check, ready for reading by a computer system. You might note, then, that keying operations are not eliminated entirely by the use of MICR characters—the amount must still be keyed.

To read and process MICR characters, a reader/sorter such as the one in figure 11-8 is used. This device, which has sixteen pockets, is used to sort the checks by bank number so they can be returned to the issuing bank. When it is used for sorting, the reader/sorter can be independent of the computer system. This is referred to as offline operation. Then, when the checks are processed by the issuing bank, the reader/sorter is *online* to the computer system. As the checks are read, the data can be

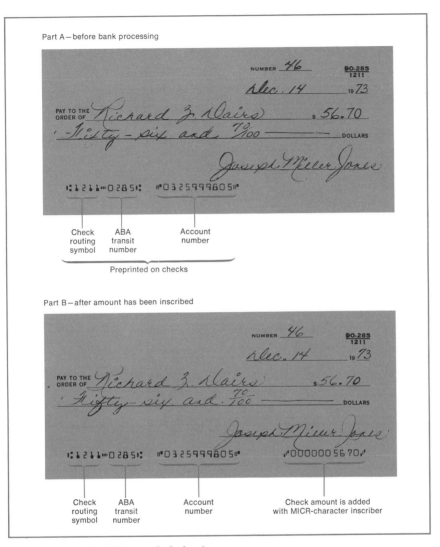

FIGURE 11-5   A MICR-encoded check

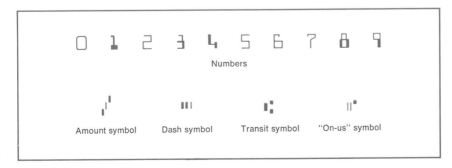

FIGURE 11-6   MICR characters

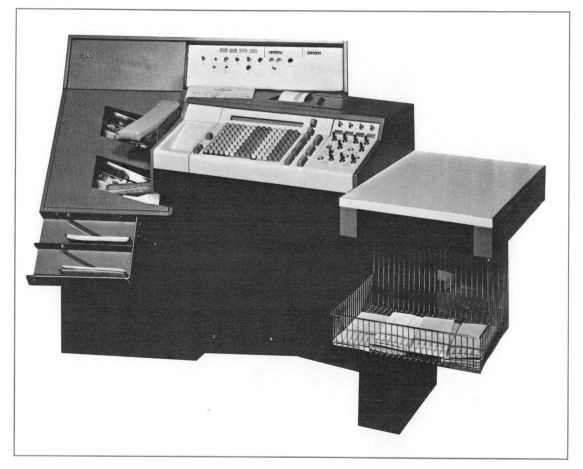

FIGURE 11-7   A MICR inscriber

processed immediately or written on magnetic tapes for later processing. In the issuing bank, checks are sorted into account-number sequence so they can be returned to the customer with the monthly statement.

The use of MICR characters began in the late 1950s. Then, in 1960 the American Banking Association (ABA) agreed on a standard shape for the MICR characters to be used throughout the industry. The use of MICR characters was so effective that in 1967 the Federal Reserve Banks announced that checks without magnetic-ink encoding would not be processed through the normal collection channels and might be subject to a service charge.

Optical Marks

A common use of *optical marks* is illustrated by the document in figure 11-9. This of course is a test scoring sheet on which a student

FIGURE 11-8   A MICR reader/sorter

makes marks indicating his answers. To read this type of document, an optical-mark page reader such as the one in figure 11-10 is used. When connected to a computer system, this reader reads the data directly into storage, thus eliminating keypunching entirely.

Although test scoring is a primary use of optical marks, they can also be used for many other applications in many different types of businesses. For example, the document in figure 11-11 can be used as an order form. When completed by a salesman or clerk, this source document becomes direct computer input. Similarly, optical-mark documents can be used for attendance reporting in schools, as insurance-policy applications, for marketing-research forms, for specifying inventory reorder amounts, and so on. In addition to full pages, optical marks can be recorded on and read from punched-card documents.

The main limitation of optical marks has been the increased possibil-

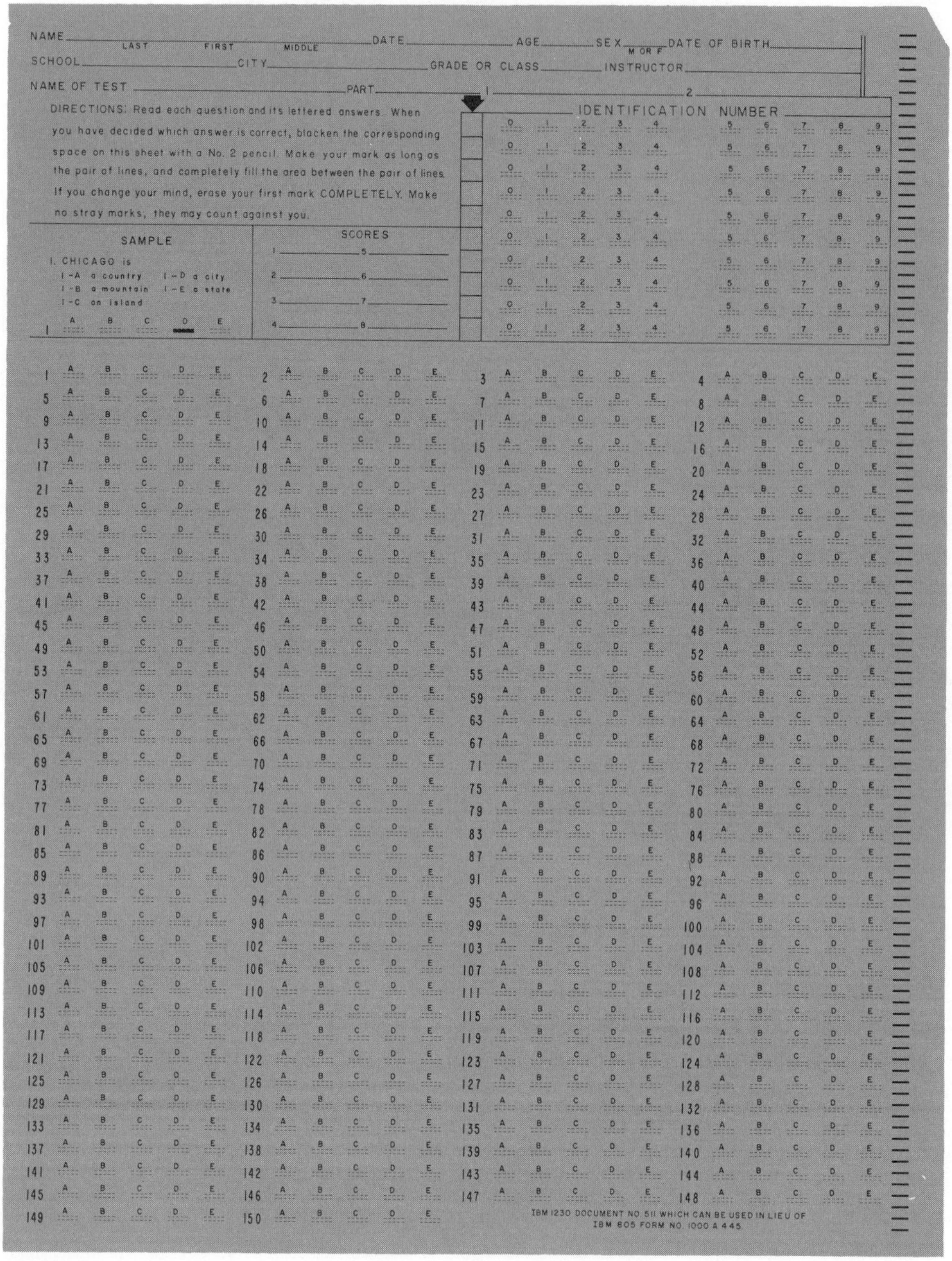

FIGURE 11-9 A test-scoring sheet

FIGURE 11-10   An optical-mark page reader

ity of error when recording the source data. Because accuracy depends on the location of the mark rather than the mark itself, errors are more common when using optical marks than when using traditional characters to record data. This is particularly true if the form is complex and many different items of data must be recorded. Furthermore, clerical workers often object to using optical marks, thus compounding the problems.

Nevertheless, optical marks have been used to great advantage by many companies. One company, for example, claims a saving of $32,000 a year in input preparation costs. This company uses optical marks for preparing the equivalent of 125,000 job cards per month in a payroll application.

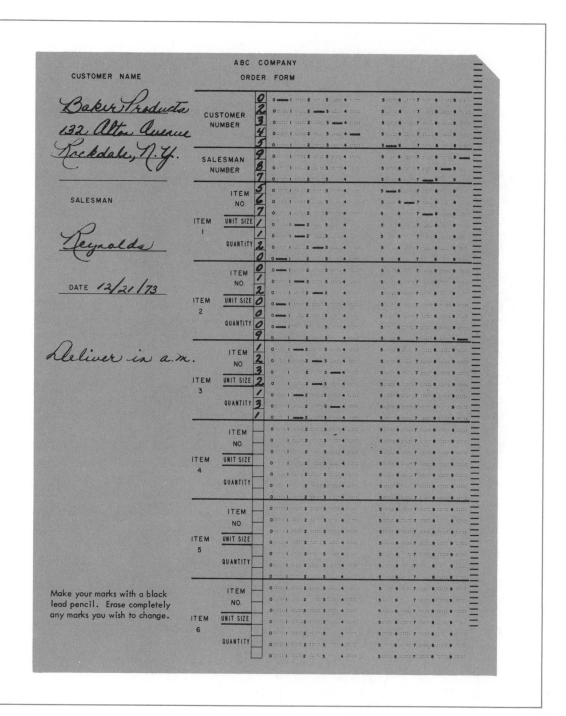

FIGURE 11-11   An order-writing form

FIGURE 11-12   OCR characters (Type OCR-A)

Optical Characters

Optical-character recognition (OCR) refers to equipment that can read optical characters (or *OCR characters*) such as those in figure 11-12. OCR equipment reads these characters by using a mechanism that shines a bright light on the characters to be read and, with photocells, senses the reflected pattern of the characters. The same type of mechanism is used for reading optical marks. There are several different typefaces (fonts) that can be used for OCR characters, two of the most widely used being OCR-A and OCR-B. OCR-A characters, which are those shown in figure 11-12, have distinctive characteristics so they can be interpreted more easily by OCR equipment. In contrast, OCR-B characters are easier for people to read but more difficult for machines to interpret.

OCR documents can be printed by computer printers, typewriters, cash registers, and time clocks. These documents can be full sheets of paper (8½ inches by 11 inches), cut forms of various sizes, cash-register rolls, or time cards. The document in figure 11-13, for example, is a cut-form utility bill. When this bill, which was printed by a computer printer, is returned by the customer, it becomes input to the computer system. It can be read by an OCR reader such as the one in figure 11-14. If a partial payment is made, optical marks can be entered on the left side of the form and read by the same OCR reader. It is common, in fact, for an OCR reader to be able to read optical marks as well as optical characters.

OCR characters can be used in a wide variety of applications. For example, if an item code is printed by a cash register along with the

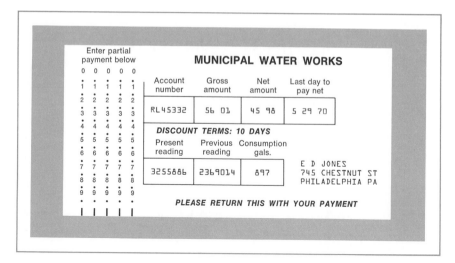

FIGURE 11-13   An OCR utility bill

charge amount, the cash-register roll can be input to an inventory or sales-analysis application. On the other hand, documents such as the one in figure 11-15 can be used to record information about new checking and savings accounts in the banking industry. After the data is typed on the form, the form becomes direct input to the computer system. Note that keypunching has been entirely eliminated in all cases.

FIGURE 11-14   An OCR reader

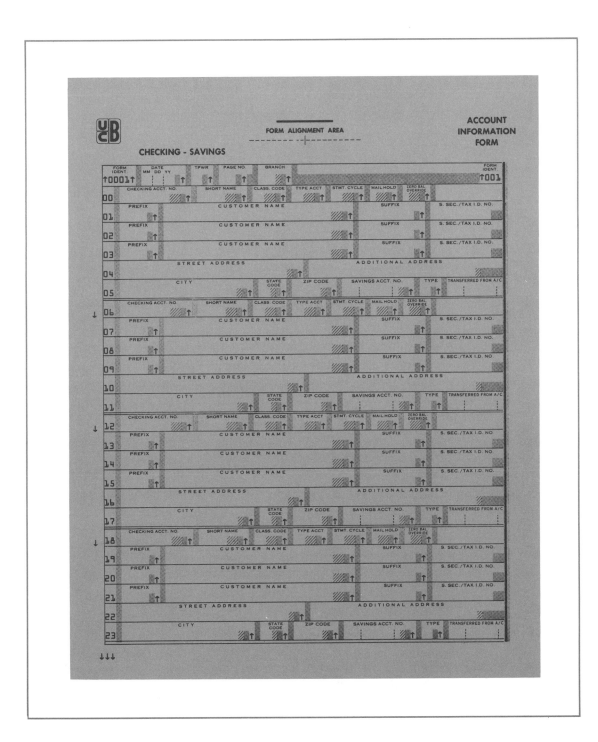

FIGURE 11-15 An OCR form for the banking industry

One of the primary problems with optical-character recognition is the reject rate. In most cases, when an OCR reader cannot interpret an OCR character, the document is stacked in a reject pocket. As an alternative, some readers stop with the unreadable character displayed in a window on the device. If the operator can recognize the character, he keys the correct character on the keyboard of the device and reading continues. In either case, if the reject rate is high—say as much as 5 percent—the value of optical-character recognition is reduced considerably.

One of the primary causes of rejects is the quality of printing on the source documents. The paper, the ink, the precision of the device used for printing—all can affect the reject rate. If the print quality is high, the reject rate should be low—perhaps less than 1 percent.

Although the potential of optical-character recognition seems to be high, it has yet to be adopted by a large percentage of the computer users. One of the major reasons for this is the cost of an OCR reader. A typical monthly rental, for example, is about $4000. At this price, a company has to displace about twelve keypunch operators in order to justify the device based on cost. As a result, optical-character recognition is not yet economical for the small computer user.

Regardless of its limitations and price, there are many success stories that support the use of OCR equipment. One company claims replacement of thirty keypunch operators by using an OCR reader. In a controlled test, another company discovered that documents that had required twelve hours of keypunching and verifying could be read by an OCR reader in thirteen minutes.

Handwritten Characters

Handwritten characters can also be read by some models of OCR readers, though this capability was developed somewhat later than the ability to read machine-printed documents. Thus far, only handwritten numbers and a few control letters can be read, but it is expected that equipment that can read the entire alphabet will soon be available. When handwritten numbers are used, they must be carefully written, as indicated by the examples in figure 11-16.

Figure 11-17 illustrates a handwritten sales slip that could be used in a retail store. The boxes on the form indicate exactly where the data must be printed. After the form is filled out, it is read by a device such as the one in figure 11-14. Because an OCR reader that can read handwritten characters can also read machine-printed characters, both types of characters can be combined on one form.

As with machine-printed characters, the problem with handwritten characters is the reject rate. In addition, an OCR reader will sometimes misread a handwritten character, and thus an incorrect character is read into storage. This is referred to as a *substitution*—an incorrect

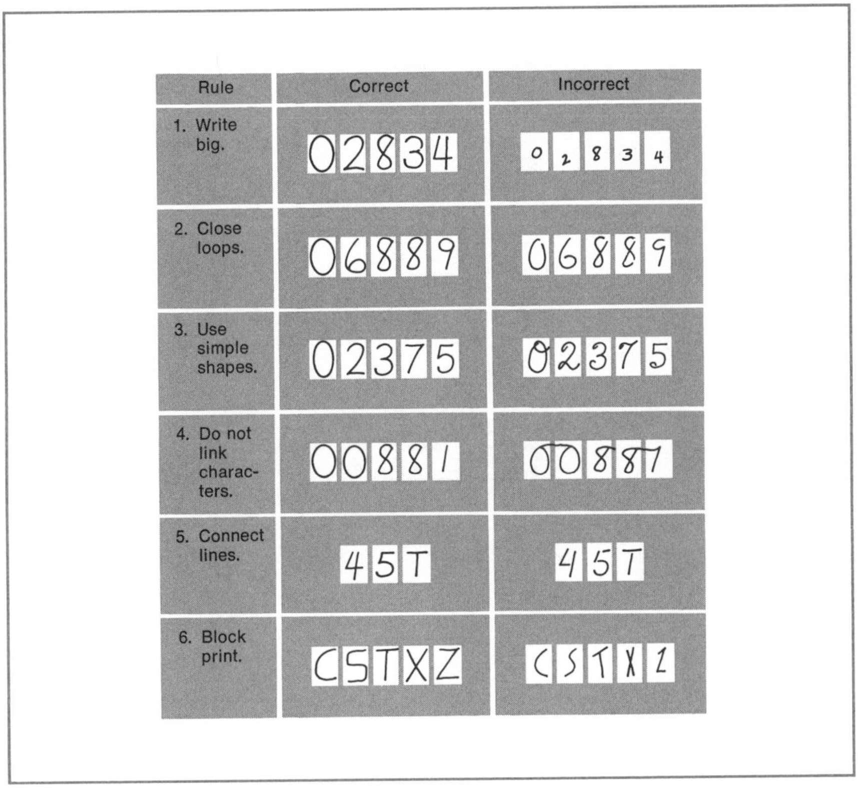

Rule	Correct	Incorrect
1. Write big.	02834	0 2 8 3 4
2. Close loops.	06889	06889
3. Use simple shapes.	02375	02375
4. Do not link characters.	00881	00881
5. Connect lines.	45T	45T
6. Block print.	CSTXZ	CSTXZ

FIGURE 11-16   Handwritten characters

character is substituted for the correct character. Needless to say, the reject rate and substitution rate is critical to the success of the system.

Here again, the major cause of rejections and substitutions is the printing itself. Some clerks, for example, will record data with low substitution and rejection rates, while others will record data with relatively high rejection and substitution rates. To cope with this problem requires adequate training of clerks, constant control of the handwriting quality, and retraining when necessary.

Because of the cost of OCR equipment and the human factors involved in quality control, handwritten characters are not used for computer input in a large number of businesses. Before handwritten characters will be widely accepted, two factors must change. First, equipment must be developed with larger tolerances for variations in the printed characters, thus reducing the reject and substitution rate. Second, the cost of the devices must be lowered. Nevertheless, the possibilities for handwritten input seem endless. If technological developments continue as they have in the past, handwritten characters could become a major input form.

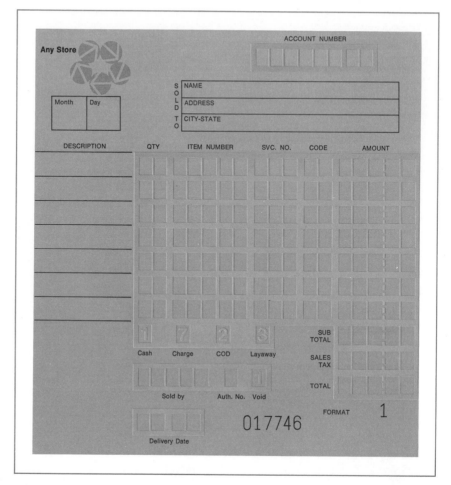

FIGURE 11-17   A handwritten sales document

SOURCE-DATA AUTOMATION

Source-data automation is another approach to eliminating the key-punch bottleneck. This term refers to the use of automated devices at the point where source data originates; it refers to devices that operate independently of the computer system as well as to devices that are connected to the computer and interact with it.

Figure 11-18 illustrates a device used for recording order information in an inventory application in a retail store. As the clerk walks down the aisle, he enters the item code of the items to be reordered on the adding machine keyboard of the self-powered device. The data is then recorded on a magnetic-tape cassette stored within a unit attached to the adding machine. At the end of the day or at various times during the day, the cassette can be transferred to a transmitting device that is connected to

FIGURE 11-18   A reorder-entry device

a telephone line so the data can be transmitted to the company's computer and inventory reorders can be processed.

In the factory, source-data automation is used to collect data concerning production operations. These systems, commonly called *data-collection systems,* can be either offline or online to the computer system. In an offline system, the data-entry device (called a *terminal*) is normally connected to a card punch, as schematically illustrated in figure 11-19. As data is entered at the terminals located throughout the factory, cards are punched for use as input to the computer system.

The basic data entered into a data-collection system are employee number, job number, operation number, and quantity of pieces produced. This data is entered into a terminal such as the one shown in figure

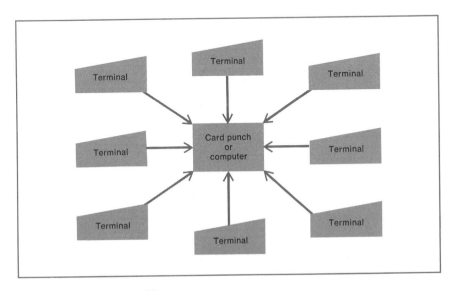

FIGURE 11-19   A data-collection system

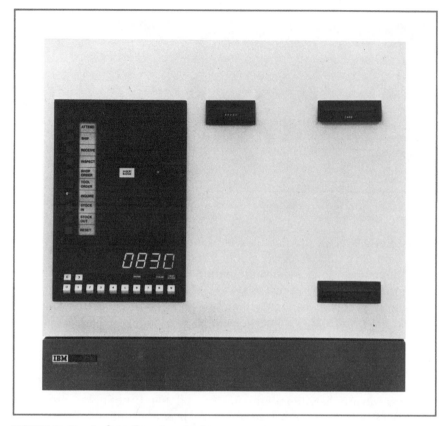

FIGURE 11-20   A shop-floor terminal

11-20 by inserting an employee badge for employee number, by inserting a punched card giving job number and operation number, and by keying or using manual slides for entering quantity produced.

In a more sophisticated data-collection system, the terminals are connected (online) to the computer system so that data is entered directly into the system. This eliminates the punching of cards and allows production records to be updated shortly after operations are completed on the factory floor. In this case, there is one-way transmittal of data—from terminal to computer.

The next level of sophistication is a two-way communication between terminals and computer. The terminals are online to the computer, and output from the computer system can be printed or displayed on the terminals. In this case, the computer can take over some of the functions of a foreman or supervisor. For example, if an employee enters data that indicates he is starting to work on the wrong job, the computer can indicate the job he should be doing. If an employee enters a quantity that is less than the required number of pieces for the job, the computer can indicate that more pieces must be completed. In other words, by checking the master production schedule stored on direct-access devices, the computer can monitor production. Because a system such as this gives a response in time to correct an operation that otherwise would be done in error, it is called a *real-time system*. (Real-time systems are explained in chapter 8, Data-Communication Systems.)

In retail operations, source-data automation is used to capture data at the point of sale. Such systems are called point-of-sale (or POS) systems and can vary in sophistication in much the same way that data-collection systems vary. In a typical *POS system*, terminals such as the one in figure 11-21 are used. Inventory and sales data is entered on the keyboard and then transmitted over communication lines at the end of the day to the home-office computer. In advanced systems, a POS terminal can be used in a real-time system. For example, a terminal can be used to check a customer's credit rating when a credit transaction is being processed. Because the response from the computer is given in seconds, the customer may never be aware that the credit check has taken place. Similarly, the computer can automatically calculate and print sales taxes and give responses to clerks that indicate when invalid item codes have been entered.

Although these examples only begin to illustrate the range of applica-

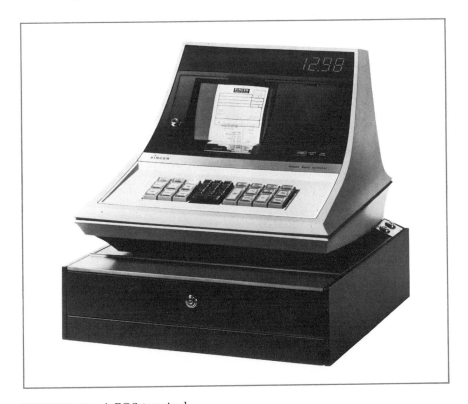

FIGURE 11-21   A POS terminal

tions for source-data automation, they do illustrate its potential. By entering data at its point of origin, the keypunch bottleneck is eliminated entirely. If speed is critical, the online or real-time system makes it possible to update files within seconds from the time a transaction takes place, and exception information can be printed or displayed on a manager's terminal seconds after that.

On the other hand, there are many problems pertinent to source-data automation systems—in particular, online systems. First, the cost of an online system is likely to be two or three times greater than that of a traditional system. This cost must therefore be justified by increased sales, reduced operating costs, or other benefits—a difficult justification to make. Second, if the equipment breaks down, backup procedures must be available. In an online retail operation, for instance, it would be a disaster if the computer broke down for even a few minutes and some method of backup weren't available. These backup costs can be extensive, thus making it still harder to justify the system. Finally, source-data automation is generally used in what system analysts call a "hostile environment." Fear of computers, resistance to new methods, grease smudges on punched cards that are inserted into factory terminals, factory dust settling into terminals—all of these make it difficult to install a successful system. As a result, many systems that looked good on paper have failed upon installation.

DISCUSSION

Each of the three solutions to the keypunch problem described in this chapter has advantages and limitations. Although keypunch replacement is the most flexible of the solutions (since it can be used for any type of source data), it is only a partial solution. Instead of the keypunch bottleneck, the user takes on the key-tape bottleneck. On the other hand, though optical-character recognition and source-data automation can eliminate the bottleneck, they are expensive and limited in application. Optical-character recognition may have the greatest potential of the three as far as cost reduction is concerned, but source-data automation can provide immediate entry of source data into a system.

Because of these advantages and limitations, it is not unusual for a company to use all three solutions in solving the keypunch problem. For instance, a company may use optical-character recognition for order entry, an online data-collection system for production control, and a key-to-tape system for all other input. Since most of the solutions for the input preparation problem are in an early stage of development, it remains to be seen as to which solutions will prove most profitable after technology and system expertise are more fully developed.

SUMMARY

1. Keypunching and verifying are a major source of cost and delay within an EDP system. Traditional solutions to this problem include the use of turnaround documents and punched paper tape that is a by-product of a paperwork procedure.

2. Key-to-tape devices and systems are one alternative to keypunching. Although they increase the speed of keying operations and reduce the input time on the computer, the basic problem of input preparation remains.

3. MICR characters, optical marks, OCR characters, and some hand-written characters can be read by a computer system, thus eliminating keypunching. Because of their limitations, however, they are not used in most businesses.

4. Source-data automation refers to automating the original recording of source data. Thus, source data is stored in tape cassettes, punched into cards, or transmitted directly to the computer system.

**FOR
REVIEW**

turnaround document
data recorder
MICR character
offline
online
optical mark
OCR character

substitution
source-data automation
data-collection system
terminal
real-time system
POS system

CHAPTER TWELVE

There is certainly a question as to how much a programmer should be taught about the internal operation of a computer—particularly, in an introductory course. Theoretically, if a programmer is using a high-level language such as COBOL or FORTRAN, he doesn't need to know anything about internal computer operations. However, a basic understanding of the hardware characteristics of a computer will probably help in writing and debugging high-level language programs more efficiently.

This same question applies to system designers and businessmen: How much should they be taught about internal computer operations? Although many get by with little knowledge of the CPU, familiarity with some basic concepts can be a help.

This chapter presents some of the basic concepts and terminology that you will likely encounter as programmer, system designer, or businessman. The first topic includes an explanation of how data is stored within a typical computer and presents some typical instructions used by a computer. The difficulty of drawing conclusions based on comparisons of hardware characteristics is considered in the second topic.

TOPIC ONE
STORAGE ORGANIZATION AND INSTRUCTION SETS

Each storage position in a computer is made up of a number of electronic components called *binary components* because they can be switched to either of two conditions. The two conditions are commonly referred to as "on" and "off."

The most commonly used storage component is the *magnetic core*. These tiny, doughnut-shaped components can be magnetized in either

CPU CONCEPTS

of two directions: clockwise and counterclockwise. When magnetized in one direction, a core is said to be *on*; when magnetized in the other direction, a core is said to be *off*. A string of cores makes up one storage position in a computer and thousands of cores in planes make up a computer's storage. Because most storage consists of magnetic cores, you will often hear it referred to as *core storage*.

In order to represent data, the individual cores at a storage position are turned on or off in selected combinations by wires that run through the center of the cores. Each combination of on and off cores represents a digit or digits, a letter, or a special character. Figure 12-1, for example, might represent three storage positions of eight cores each. By decoding the combination at each storage position, it might be determined that

FIGURE 12-1   Core storage

the characters B, 2, and 9 are represented. (The colored cores are on, and the white cores are off.)

Because the codes of a computer are represented by binary components, the *binary digits* 0 and 1 can be used to represent a binary code. If 1 is used to represent an on-core and 0 is used to represent an off-core, 11000010 represents the first string of cores in figure 12-1. Since a binary digit is referred to as a *bit* (a contraction of binary digit), magnetic cores are often called bits.

There are several computer codes commonly in use, and any one computer may use one or more of these codes. Perhaps the three most common codes used today are 4-bit BCD (Binary Coded Decimal), EBCDIC (Extended Binary Coded Decimal Interchange Code), and true binary.

4-Bit BCD

In 4-bit BCD, one decimal digit is represented by four bits, or cores. For example, the decimal 0 is represented by the binary 0000; the decimal 9 is represented by the binary 1001. Because binary codes are used to represent the decimal digits, this code is called Binary Coded Decimal, or BCD.

To convert a 4-bit BCD code to its decimal equivalent, each of the digits in the code is given a place value. From right to left, these values are 1, 2, 4, and 8. Therefore, the rightmost bit can be called the 1-bit, the second bit from the right the 2-bit, the next the 4-bit, and the leftmost the 8-bit. When the place values of the on-bits are added, the result is the decimal equivalent. In the binary 0101, for example, the 1-bit and the 4-bit are on. Thus, the decimal equivalent is 1 plus 4, or 5. Figure 12-2 shows the place values and the ten binary combinations used in 4-bit BCD.

Decimal equivalent	4-bit BCD code Place values			
	8	4	2	1
0	0	0	0	0
1	0	0	0	1
2	0	0	1	0
3	0	0	1	1
4	0	1	0	0
5	0	1	0	1
6	0	1	1	0
7	0	1	1	1
8	1	0	0	0
9	1	0	0	1

FIGURE 12-2   4-bit BCD code

To represent a decimal number of more than one digit, more than one group of four bits is used. Thus, 100100010010 represents the decimal number 912. When the binary number is separated into groups of four bits—as 1001 0001 0010—conversion to decimal is easy.

EBCDIC

EBCDIC (pronounced ee′-bee-dick or ib′-si-dick) is an 8-bit code. Because eight bits can be arranged in 256 different combinations, 256 characters could be coded in EBCDIC. Thus, EBCDIC can be used to represent the letters of the alphabet (both upper- and lower-case), the decimal digits, and many special characters. However, not all of the 256 combinations are used.

To help in decoding, the eight bits of an EBCDIC code can be divided into two groups of four bits each. The left group makes up the *zone bits* of each code, while the right group makes up the *digit bits*. These zone and digit bits correspond to the zone and digit punches of punched-card code. For letters and numbers, the zone bits 1100 correspond to a 12-punch, the bits 1101 to an 11-punch, 1110 to a 0-punch, and 1111 to no zone punch. The digit bits, on the other hand, are used as they are in 4-bit BCD. Thus, 0000 corresponds to a 0-punch, 0001 to a 1-punch, and so on. Figure 12-3, which gives the EBCDIC coding for the letters and numbers, shows the correspondence between EBCDIC and punched-card code. Each group of eight bits is separated to indicate the zone and digit bits.

For special characters, other zone-bit combinations are used. Thus, 01011011 is used for the dollar sign ($) and 01001101 for the left parenthesis. Although it is sometimes helpful for a programmer to know the EBCDIC codes for numbers, decoding EBCDIC letters and special characters is usually unnecessary. However, if it is required, the codes can be easily found in reference tables.

True Binary

A true binary number can be used to represent numeric data only. Although a true binary number can be composed of any number of bits, any one computer uses a fixed number of bits for its true binary numbers. For example, the System/360 uses binary numbers composed of sixteen, thirty-two, or sixty-four bits.

To decode a true binary number, the place values of the on-bits are added just as they are to decode 4-bit BCD. The place values start at the rightmost bit position with a value of 1 and double for each position to the left. Thus, the place values of a 32-bit true binary number are 1, 2, 4, 8, 16, 32, 64, and so on, until the next to the leftmost bit, the thirty-first

Character	EBCDIC		Punched-card code	Hexadecimal code
	Zone bits	Digit bits		
A	1100	0001	12-1	C1
B	1100	0010	12-2	C2
C	1100	0011	12-3	C3
D	1100	0100	12-4	C4
E	1100	0101	12-5	C5
F	1100	0110	12-6	C6
G	1100	0111	12-7	C7
H	1100	1000	12-8	C8
I	1100	1001	12-9	C9
J	1101	0001	11-1	D1
K	1101	0010	11-2	D2
L	1101	0011	11-3	D3
M	1101	0100	11-4	D4
N	1101	0101	11-5	D5
O	1101	0110	11-6	D6
P	1101	0111	11-7	D7
Q	1101	1000	11-8	D8
R	1101	1001	11-9	D9
S	1110	0010	0-2	E2
T	1110	0011	0-3	E3
U	1110	0100	0-4	E4
V	1110	0101	0-5	E5
W	1110	0110	0-6	E6
X	1110	0111	0-7	E7
Y	1110	1000	0-8	E8
Z	1110	1001	0-9	E9
0	1111	0000	0	F0
1	1111	0001	1	F1
2	1111	0010	2	F2
3	1111	0011	3	F3
4	1111	0100	4	F4
5	1111	0101	5	F5
6	1111	0110	6	F6
7	1111	0111	7	F7
8	1111	1000	8	F8
9	1111	1001	9	F9

FIGURE 12-3   EBCDIC

bit, which has a place value of 1,073,741,824. The leftmost bit is used to indicate the sign of the number—if 0, the number is positive; if 1, the number is negative. In a 16-bit binary number, fifteen bits are used for the number, while the leftmost bit indicates the sign of the number.

To illustrate true binary coding consider the following binary number: 0010010000011011. Since the leftmost bit is 0, the number is positive. By adding the place values of the on-bits, you can determine that the

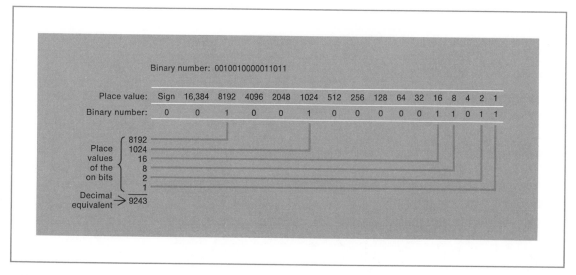

FIGURE 12-4   True binary coding

decimal equivalent is 9243. The decoding process is illustrated in figure 12-4. The maximum value of a 16-bit binary number is a positive 32,767; the maximum value of a 32-bit number is a positve 2,147,483,647.

STORAGE ORGANIZATION

To appreciate how the storage of computers can vary, let's consider first the storage organization of the System/360. Since this computer illustrates the use of three different codes, it will then be easy to understand the organization of other computers.

To begin with, each storage position in the System/360 is called a *byte* of data. This byte, and thus the storage position itself, is made up of eight data bits, plus one *parity bit*. The parity bit is used as a check on operations that take place within the CPU. Each time that a byte of data is moved into or out of storage during the execution of a program, the byte is *parity checked*. That is, the number of on-bits in the byte is checked to make sure that it is an odd number. If the number of on-bits is even, as in the code 011110011, an error is indicated and the system stops executing the program.

The parity bit at a storage position of System/360 is used to make the on-bits for each bit combination odd in number. As a result, the complete EBCDIC code for the letter A is 011000001, where the leftmost (or ninth) bit is the parity bit. Similarly, the complete code for the letter C is 111000011; for the number 9, it is 111111001.

Data is stored in the System/360 in one of three forms: EBCDIC, *packed decimal*, or binary. Regardless of the form of the data, the parity bit is used in each byte of storage; however, it is generally ignored when

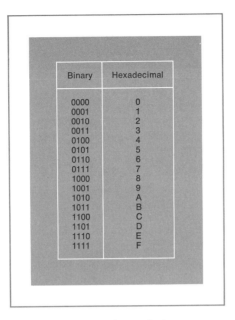

Binary	Hexadecimal
0000	0
0001	1
0010	2
0011	3
0100	4
0101	5
0110	6
0111	7
1000	8
1001	9
1010	A
1011	B
1100	C
1101	D
1110	E
1111	F

FIGURE 12-5   Hexadecimal chart

discussing codes. For instance, the System/360 is usually said to have an 8-bit, rather than a 9-bit, byte. Consequently, no further mention of parity checking will be made in this book. After all, parity checking is simply an electronic check on the accuracy of internal operations.

Because it is difficult and awkward for a person to work with binary numbers, *hexadecimal notation* is commonly used to represent the forms of System/360 storage. As a method of shorthand, the intent is to replace a group of four binary digits with one hexadecimal character. Figure 12-5 shows the relationship between binary and hexadecimal notation. Thus, the binary 1111 0010 is written as F2 in hexadecimal (or *hex*) notation; the binary 1001 0110 is written as 96 in hex. The hexadecimal for the EBCDIC letters and numbers is given in figure 12-3.

EBCDIC

To store letters or special characters in System/360, EBCDIC coding is used. One character of data is stored in each byte. The name SAM, stored in three bytes, can be represented in hexadecimal as follows:

| E2 | C1 | D4 |

EBCDIC can also be used for storing numbers, in which case one number is stored in each byte. To show the sign of a number, the zone portion of the rightmost byte of a numeric field is used. If the zone portion of this byte is 1111 (hex F) or 1100 (hex C), the nunber is positive; if the zone portion is 1101 (hex D), the number is negative. Thus, a positive 1234 in four storage positions can be shown as:

| F1 | F2 | F3 | F4 |

A negative 1234 can be shown as:

| F1 | F2 | F3 | D4 |

This form of representing numbers is often referred to as *zoned decimal*.

Packed Decimal

Packed decimal is a form of System/360 data representation that relates to 4-bit BCD. Except for the rightmost byte of a field, two 4-bit decimal digits are stored in each 8-bit byte. The rightmost byte of a field contains a decimal digit in its zone portion and the sign of the field in its digit portion. Using hex notation, a positive 12345 is stored in three storage positions as follows:

| 12 | 34 | 5C |

(Remember that either C or F is a valid sign for a positive field.) If a number is a negative 12345, it is stored like this:

| 12 | 34 | 5D |

Binary

Binary representation, of course, corresponds to true binary coding. In System/360, two, four, or eight consecutive bytes are used for a binary field. Since the decimal number 9243 is a binary 0010 0100 0001 1011, it can be stored in two bytes of storage; using hex, it can be shown like this:

| 24 | 1B |

If 9243 is stored as a four-byte binary number, it can be shown as:

| 00 | 00 | 24 | 1B |

In System/360, a two-byte binary field is referred to as a *halfword*, a four-byte binary field as a *fullword*, and an eight-byte binary field as a *doubleword*. These fields must have the proper *boundary alignment* before they can be operated upon by System/360 instructions. A halfword, for example, must start at a storage address that is a multiple of

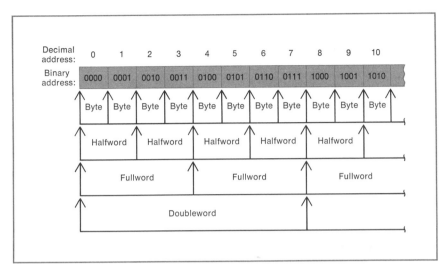

FIGURE 12-6   Storage boundaries

two (such as location 2, 4, 6, 8, or 10). This is called a *halfword bound-ary*. Similarly, a fullword must start at a *fullword boundary*, a storage address that is a multiple of four, and a doubleword must start at a *doubleword boundary*, a storage address that is a multiple of eight. Figure 12-6 summarizes this terminology as applied to the first ten positions of storage.

In System/360, the number of storage positions required for a numeric field is determined by the number of digits in the field and the type of data representation used. For example, if a field contains the number +205,597,474, it requires nine bytes of storage using zoned decimal, five bytes using packed decimal, and a fullword (four bytes) using binary. If a field consists of only one decimal digit such as the number +7, one byte of storage is required using zoned decimal, one byte using packed decimal, and a halfword (two bytes) using binary. Figure 12-7 summarizes these examples.

With this background, you can appreciate the storage organization of other computers. Each storage position of the Burroughs B6500, for example, is made up of forty-eight bits and one parity bit. Thus, six EBCDIC characters or one 48-bit binary number can be stored in a single storage position. In contrast, each storage position of the IBM 1130 consists of sixteen data bits and one parity bit, so one 16-bit binary number or two EBCDIC characters can be stored in one storage position.

INSTRUCTION SETS

The term *instruction set* applies to the collection of machine instructions that a specific computer can execute. The NCR Century 100,

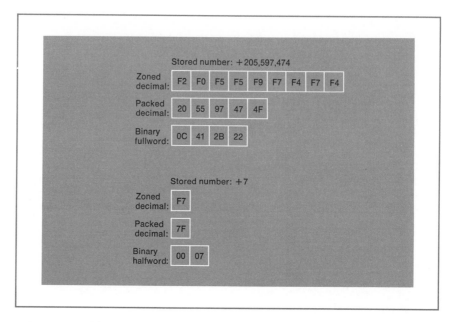

FIGURE 12-7   Storage use

for example, has 19 instructions in its instruction set. In contrast, the instruction set of the Control Data 3100 contains 164 different instructions.

To give you some appreciation of the instructions within a typical instruction set, consider some examples from the System/360 instruction set, which consists of 139 different operation codes. Because these instructions operate on data in three different formats—EBCDIC, packed decimal, and binary—the principles they illustrate apply to most computers.

A System/360 instruction is two, four, or six bytes in length. To understand the parts of a typical instruction, consider one of the several MOVE instructions. It is six bytes in length, with this format:

Op Code	Length Factor	Address-1	Address-2
0 7	8 15	16 31	32 47

The first byte of the instruction (bits 0–7) is the operation code. There is a unique code for each one of the 139 instructions. For the basic MOVE, the code is 11010010, or hex D2. The second byte of the instruction (bits 8–15) is the length factor, an 8-bit binary number from 0 through 255 that indicates how many storage positions should be moved. The last four bytes represent two addresses that specify the starting locations of the fields involved in the instruction. If the length factor is a binary 9 (indicating that ten bytes should be moved), the ten bytes of data starting at the location specified as address-2 are moved to the ten bytes of storage starting at the location specified as address-1.

An address in a System/360 instruction is actually made up of two parts: four bits that specify a *base register* and twelve bits that represent a *displacement factor*. The base register can be any one of the sixteen *general-purpose registers* that are components of the System/360 CPU. These general-purpose registers consist of thirty-two bit positions plus a sign bit. In the base register, twenty-four of the bit positions are used to represent a *base address*. To get the actual address, the base address is added to the displacement factor specified in the instruction.

To be more specific, then, the format of the MOVE instruction just described is this:

D2		L	B_1	D_1		B_2	D_2	
0	7	8	15 16 19	20	31	32 35	36	47

Here, D2 is the actual operation code in hex, L is the length factor, B_1 and B_2 are 4-bit binary numbers that specify one of the sixteen registers (numbered 0 through 15), and D_1 and D_2 are 12-bit binary numbers that represent displacement factors. If B_1 has a decimal equivalent of 5, D_1 has a decimal equivalent of 1000, and the contents of register 5 has a decimal equivalent of 4000, the data will be moved to the field beginning at address 5000.

Frankly, this is much more than a programmer or system analyst needs to know about machine language. There is, however, a good reason for going into this much detail: it points out the need for symbolic languages in general and high-level languages in particular. Unlike some earlier computers, the System/360 machine language can't even be expressed using familiar notation. Instead, hexadecimal notation is used. Thus, a MOVE instruction with the format just described might appear in a listing of the contents of storage as

D2043038A098

By breaking this down, you can determine that the operation code is D2, the length factor is 5 (hex 4), address-1 consists of a base address in register 3 plus a displacement of decimal 56 (hex 038), and address-2 consists of a base address in register 10 (hex A) plus a displacement of decimal 152 (hex 098). In short, programming in System/360 machine language would be a nightmare.

With 139 instructions, though, even assembler language can be extremely detailed. Just knowing the function of all the instructions is a demand not made by a high-level language. In contrast, a COBOL or FORTRAN programmer is able to write programs using only a few dozen statements.

Data-Movement Instructions

Besides the basic MOVE instruction just described, the System/360 has move instructions that move only the zone or digit portions of one field to another. There is also an EDIT instruction that can be used to zero-suppress insignificant zeros in a number and, at the same time, insert editing characters such as commas and the decimal point. For example, the packed-decimal number 0112389 can be edited as follows:

	Sending Field				Receiving Field									
Before:	01	12	38	9C		40	20	20	6B	20	20	21	4B	20	20
After:	01	12	38	9C		40	40	F1	6B	F1	F2	F3	4B	F8	F9

Because the hex characters 40, 6B, and 4B are the blank, comma, and decimal point, the resulting field is equivalent to 1,123.89. Notice that the receiving field must contain certain editing characters before the EDIT instruction can be executed and that the sending field must be in packed-decimal format.

Other data-movement instructions convert numeric fields from one form to another. For example, the PACK instruction moves and converts data from an EBCDIC field into a packed-decimal field, as shown here:

	Sending Field					Receiving Field		
Before:	F1	F2	F3	F4	F5	??	??	??
After:	F1	F2	F3	F4	F5	12	34	5F

In contrast, the UNPACK instruction moves data from a sending field in packed-decimal format to a receiving field in EBCDIC format.

To convert a numeric field to and from binary format, the Convert-to-Binary and Convert-to-Decimal instructions are used. As shown in the following example, the Convert-to-Binary instruction moves data from a sending field in packed-decimal format to one of the sixteen general-purpose registers in binary format. The sending field must be eight bytes in length (a doubleword).

	Sending Field								Receiving Register			
Before:	00	00	00	00	00	00	53	8C	??	??	??	??
After:	00	00	00	00	00	00	53	8C	00	00	02	1A

If desired, the contents of a register can be moved to storage by using a STORE instruction.

	Register	Receiving Field
Before:	00 00 02 1A	?? ?? ?? ??
After:	00 00 02 1A	00 00 02 1A

The LOAD and Convert-to-Decimal instructions can be used to convert a field from binary to packed-decimal format. First, by using a LOAD instruction, a binary fullword is loaded into a general register. Second, the contents of the register are moved to a receiving field that is a doubleword and are converted to packed-decimal format by using the Convert-to-Decimal instruction.

Arithmetic Instructions

You may be wondering why the conversion instructions are necessary. When data is read into storage from a card, it is in the EBCDIC format. However, on System/360, arithmetic can take place only on fields that are in packed-decimal or binary format. Before the results of a calculation can be printed, they must be converted back to EBCDIC format.

In arithmetic operations on packed-decimal fields, two fields are involved and the result replaces one of the fields. Consider the following decimal ADD instruction:

	Field-1	Field-2
Before:	10 00 0C	01 0C
After:	10 01 0C	01 0C

In this example, 10 is added to 10000, and the result, 10010, replaces the contents of field-1. Similarly, decimal subtract, multiply, and divide instructions operate on two fields, with the result of the calculation being placed in field-1. In the DIVIDE instruction, both quotient and remainder are placed in the result field.

On System/360, binary arithmetic instructions typically involve one field in storage and the contents of a register. For example, a binary field can be added to a register, as follows:

	Register	Storage Field
Before:	00 00 00 10	00 00 00 0A
After:	00 00 00 1A	00 00 00 0A

Similarly, a field in storage can be subtracted from, multiplied by, or divided into the contents of a register, with the result being stored in the register. There are separate instruction codes for operating on half-words or fullwords in storage.

Binary arithmetic can also be performed on the contents of registers only. For example, the contents of register 4 can be subtracted from the contents of register 5, with the answer being stored in register 5. Register-to-register calculation is the fastest form of System/360 arithmetic.

Which type of arithmetic is more efficient? It depends on the number of times a field is to be arithmetically operated upon, the number of digits in the fields involved, and the amount of data conversion required. Although binary arithmetic instructions are normally executed faster than decimal arithmetic instructions, binary arithmetic usually requires more conversion. For example, if two EBCDIC fields are added using decimal arithmetic, the following sequence of instructions is required: (1) pack field-1, (2) pack field-2, and (3) add the two fields together. The result can then be unpacked or edited. However, to add two EBCDIC fields using binary arithmetic, the following sequence of instructions is required: (1) pack field-1, (2) convert packed field-1 to binary — the result is in a register, (3) pack field-2, (4) convert packed field-2 to binary — the result is in a register, and (5) add the contents of one register to the contents of the other register. If the result is then to be converted back to EBCDIC, two more instructions are required: (1) convert the contents of the register to packed decimal and (2) unpack the field. Because of the additional conversion instructions required for binary operations, packed-decimal arithmetic is used for most business programs, while binary arithmetic is used for the lengthy series of calculations common to scientific and mathematical problems.

Logical Instructions

System/360 COMPARE instructions can be executed on EBCDIC, packed-decimal, or binary fields. There are separate operation codes for each type of comparison. When packed-decimal or binary fields are compared, the evaluation is done numerically. Thus, +123 is greater than −580. When EBCDIC fields are compared, the fields are evaluated on the basis of the System/360 *collating sequence*, in which special characters come before (are less than) letters and letters come before numbers. Thus, $ is less than B, and B is less than 5. If two fields of different formats are compared, the results are unpredictable. For example, if an EBCDIC Compare instruction (called a Compare Logical) compares an EBCDIC field containing decimal 123 (hex F1F2F3) with a packed-decimal field containing decimal 58234 (hex 58234C), the EBCDIC field will be considered greater since the comparison is made bit by bit, from left to right.

System/360 BRANCH instructions are executed on the basis of the results of a comparison—field-1 is less than field-2, is equal to field-2, or is greater than field-2. A branch can also be based on the results of an arithmetic operation—the result is less than, equal to, or greater than zero, or the result is larger than the size of the result field (called arithmetic overflow). In addition, certain branch instructions take place based on the status of an I/O device: it is busy, available, or not in operation.

I/O Instructions

The System/360 I/O instructions are perhaps the most complex in the instruction set. In fact, a computer user's program never executes I/O instructions. Instead, they are executed by a *supervisor program* supplied with the computer. This program is loaded into storage at the start of the day and remains in storage while all other programs are executed. Whenever a user's program requires an I/O operation, it branches to the supervisor, which causes the appropriate instructions to be executed by *channels*, special components outside of the CPU that are designed to execute I/O instructions. (For further explanation, see chapter 13, Overlap.) A programmer need not be concerned with this complexity, however, when using a symbolic language.

DISCUSSION

Although this has been but a brief introduction to storage organization and instruction sets, I think you may realize that the study of machine language can be a detailed and complex assignment. The question, then, is: Who needs to know this amount of detail? Although storage organization and instruction sets can affect the efficiency of internal computer operations, how do data-processing personnel use this knowledge?

The primary user of machine knowledge is the assembler-language programmer. Because he is working with symbolic machine language, he must know the function of all the machine-language instructions of a computer. Since he debugs his programs using machine language, he needs to know the internal codes and storage organization of a computer.

Other than for the assembler-language programmer, though, machine knowledge is largely irrelevant. Since problem-oriented languages such as COBOL and FORTRAN are designed to be independent of the computer used, COBOL and FORTRAN programmers need little, if any, machine knowledge. Although a limited amount of knowledge—such as the data formats or types of arithmetic used—may be helpful when coding or debugging, there are many high-level language programmers who don't have the background presented in this chapter.

As for system designers, the primary purpose of machine knowledge is to enable them to compare the capabilities of two different types of computers. For example, when making a decision as to which computer to buy, a system designer might be asked to compare the storage organization and instruction sets of two different computers. In general, however, system designers make little use of CPU knowledge.

SUMMARY

1. Three of the most common internal codes used by computers are 4-bit BCD, EBCDIC, and true binary. Four-bit BCD and binary are used to represent numbers, while EBCDIC can be used to represent any characters.

2. The System/360 has eight data bits and one parity bit per storage position and uses three formats for representing data: EBCDIC, packed decimal, and binary.

3. The size of an instruction set varies by computer, but all have data-movement, arithmetic, logical, and I/O instructions.

**FOR
REVIEW**

binary components
magnetic core
core storage
binary digit
bit
4-bit BCD
EBCDIC
zone bits
digit bits
true binary
byte
parity bit
parity checking
hexadecimal notation
hex
zoned decimal

packed decimal
halfword
fullword
doubleword
boundary alignment
halfword boundary
fullword boundary
doubleword boundary
instruction set
base register
displacement factor
general-purpose register
base address
collating sequence
supervisor program
channel

When describing a computer system, a programmer or system designer often specifies the number of storage positions. For example, "We have a 16K Model 20 System/360 computer," meaning it has 16,000 storage positions. Similarly, a programmer or system designer may refer to a computer's speed: "Our system has an access-cycle time of 2 microseconds." These specifications, however, can be highly misleading. Unless all other factors are equal, it is possible that an 8K computer can store more data and instructions than a 16K machine. It is possible that a machine with an access-cycle time of 1 microsecond be slower than a machine with an access-cycle time of 2 microseconds.

COMPARING STORAGE CAPACITIES

As you have already seen, the effective storage of data depends on the storage organization of a computer. If a computer has forty-eight data bits per storage position, it can store up to six EBCDIC characters per storage position or a binary number up to a value in the trillions. In contrast, a machine such as the System/360 with an 8-bit byte can store only one EBCDIC character per storage position and requires eight storage positions to store a binary number with a value in the trillions.

When a program is being executed, though, the storage of a computer contains both data and instructions—perhaps 20 percent data and 80 percent instructions, depending on the type of program being run. As a result, the number of storage positions used for a program depends largely on how effectively the computer stores instructions. Two factors involved are (1) the average instruction length (how many positions required per instruction) and (2) the instruction set (how many instructions required per program).

To illustrate, suppose a System/360 program averages 4.5 bytes per instruction, while the same program on another computer averages 5.2 bytes per instruction. If both programs have 1000 instructions, the first program's instructions will require 4500 storage positions, while the second program's instructions will require 5200 storage positions.

In actuality, however, the same program written for different computers would require different numbers of instructions, depending on the instruction set used. If a computer has a large instruction set, its programs will likely be written with a minimum number of instructions. In contrast, a computer with a limited instruction set may require many extra instructions to accomplish the same processing.

To illustrate this with an obvious example, one fairly common computer doesn't have the multiply instruction. Thus, if this operation is to be performed, it must be accomplished with a series of add instructions. On computers with the multiply instruction, of course, this operation requires a single instruction.

If the instruction set of one computer allows its programs to be written using fewer instructions than another type of computer, there can be a considerable difference in the number of storage positions used. For example, if one computer requires only 1700 instructions for a program, another requires 2100 instructions for the same program, and both computers have an average instruction length of five bytes, the first computer will use 2000 less storage positions for its program.

In summary, the number of storage positions a computer has can be misleading. Effective use of storage depends on storage organization, instruction length, and instruction set. Only when these factors are equal can we say that a 32K machine has twice the memory capacity of a 16K machine.

COMPARING CPU SPEEDS

Access-cycle time is one measure of the speed of a CPU. To appreciate what this speed indicates, you must have a conceptual understanding of how a computer executes an instruction.

Although a CPU consists of hundreds of thousands of electronic components, these components can be divided into three sections: (1) the *control unit*, (2) the *arithmetic and logic unit*, and (3) *main storage* (core storage). (Although some people maintain that main storage isn't part of the CPU, I think you'll agree that it's a trivial distinction.) When an instruction is executed, it is moved from main storage into the control unit, and the data fields to be operated upon are moved into the arithmetic and logic unit. In some cases, the result of the operation is returned to storage from the arithmetic and logic unit.

To illustrate what takes place during the execution of an instruction, consider figure 12-8, which represents the execution of an add instruction operating upon two packed-decimal fields. First, the instruction is accessed from main storage into the control unit. Second, the two data fields are accessed into the arithmetic and logic unit and the addition is performed. Third, the result is returned from the arithmetic and logic unit to main storage.

Depending on the instruction and the computer model, there are many variations as to exactly how an instruction is executed. Some instructions, such as the branch, do not operate on data. As a result, only the instruction is accessed from storage and the arithmetic and logic unit isn't used. Other instructions involve only one data field; after the instruction is accessed, the data field is accessed from storage into the arithmetic and logic unit and the operation is performed. In all cases, however, the instruction is first accessed into the control unit; then the data fields, if any, are accessed to and from the arithmetic and logic unit.

When instructions or data are accessed to and from storage, *access cycles* are required. The exact number of cycles required depends on

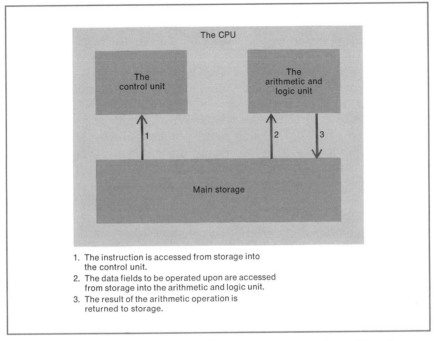

1. The instruction is accessed from storage into the control unit.
2. The data fields to be operated upon are accessed from storage into the arithmetic and logic unit.
3. The result of the arithmetic operation is returned to storage.

FIGURE 12-8   Data movement within the CPU (execution of an arithmetic operation involving two packed-decimal fields)

the *access width* of the computer being used. On the System/360 Model 40, for example, the access width is two storage positions (two bytes). This means that two bytes are moved to or from storage during each access cycle. If a six-byte instruction is to be executed, then, three access cycles are required to move the instruction to the control unit. Similarly, if two four-byte fields are going to be operated upon, two access cycles will be needed to move each field into the arithmetic and logic unit—a total of four access cycles.

Other machines, of course, have different access widths. Smaller machines such as the HIS H200/115 have access widths of one byte, so only one byte is accessed during each cycle. The Burroughs B6500 accesses one 48-bit storage position during each access cycle, the equivalent of six bytes. And a machine such as the System/370 Model 155 accesses eight bytes during each access cycle.

Each computer requires a fixed amount of time for an access cycle. This is called *access-cycle time*, or just *cycle time*. For example, the HIS H200/115 has a cycle time of 2.75 microseconds (2.75 millionths of a second); the B6500, 600 nanoseconds (600 billionths of a second); and the System/370 Model 155, 345 nanoseconds.

Once you know the cycle time and access width of a computer, you have some idea of a computer's speed. If you divide the cycle time by the access width, you derive a rough measure that is called the *access speed*. Thus, the H200/115 has an access speed of 2.75 microseconds per byte; the B6500 has an access speed of 600 nanoseconds per storage position, or about 83 nanoseconds per byte; and the System/370 Model 155 has an access speed of about 43 nanoseconds per byte.

Because access cycles account for the major portion of a CPU's processing time, access speed is a good indication of a computer's internal speed. Although the arithmetic and logic unit may require a certain amount of time to actually perform an operation—such as an addition or a comparison—this time is normally insignificant compared to the time required for accessing instructions and data to and from storage.

On the other hand, access speed can be misleading because different computers require different numbers of access cycles to perform the same processing functions. Just as effective use of storage capacity depends on storage organization, instruction length, and instruction set, so does the number of access cycles required by a program. If a computer stores data efficiently, if its instructions are short, if its instruction set is comprehensive so the resulting program is short— then program execution is likely to require a reasonable number of access cycles. If these conditions are not true, the computer is likely inefficient and may require many more access cycles to run a program than the efficient computer. Thus, it's possible that a computer with an access speed of 1.5 microseconds per byte will take longer to run a program than a computer with an access speed of 2.0 microseconds per byte.

The message? Although access speed is a good indication of CPU speed, it is not an exact measure and should be used only when all other factors are equal.

COMPUTER GENERATIONS

To give you an idea of how internal computer speeds have developed, consider what is referred to as the first three generations of computers. The *first generation* is usually considered to have begun with Univac I, the first commercially sold computer. In general, the machines in this generation used a type of drum storage (see chapter 6) for main storage and had access speeds that were measured in milliseconds (thousandths of a second). One of the major components of the CPU was the vacuum tube, which took up space, gave off heat, and was relatively unreliable.

The *second generation* of computers began in the late 1950s with the development of the IBM 1401 and the IBM 1620. These machines used transistors instead of vacuum tubes, core instead of drum storage, and consequently were smaller in size, gave off less heat, and were more reliable than first-generation machines. Their access speeds were measured in microseconds—for example, 11.5 microseconds per storage position on the 1401.

The *third generation*, starting in the mid-1960s with machines such as the System/360, continued the trend toward greater speed, greater reliability, and less heat. Instead of transistors and conventional wiring, these machines used microminiature components and solid logic components. Access speeds were now often measured in nanoseconds.

As these developments took place, the computer user got more and more processing capability for his dollar. In 1965, for example, if a computer user replaced his IBM 1401 with a System/360 or a Honeywell 200, he could run his 1401 object programs without reprogramming, run the programs in shorter amounts of time (often cutting run times by 50 percent or more), and pay less monthly rental for the new system. Technological development lowered computing costs, and thus, computers became practical for more users.

Because technological improvements—however marked—are often implemented somewhat gradually, there are no clear-cut definitions as to what is a second- and what is a third-generation computer. Some computers have components common to both generations and are therefore difficult to classify. In addition, many people classify generations based on more than just hardware technology. These people consider such factors as the I/O devices, the programming support provided by the manufacturer, and the data-communication capabilities —thus complicating the job of classifying a system.

In any event, we now seem to be on the verge of, and in fact may have entered, the fourth generation of computers. Some people, for instance, classify the IBM System/370 as a fourth-generation machine, although others disagree. The problem is in determining what should make up a fourth-generation machine. Although the System/370 uses primarily third-generation technology, it is used in a more sophisticated way. For example, through a technique called *interleaving*, four access cycles from four different areas of main storage can take place at one time. Are developments such as this enough to mark fourth-generation equipment?

The question, of course, can't be settled until enough time has passed to gain some perspective. Perhaps a major technological development that clearly marks the fourth generation will take place. Or perhaps, unlike the industry's first twenty years, future developments will be gradual and distinctions between generations will be hazy.

DISCUSSION

As I have tried to point out in this topic, comparing storage capabilities and internal speeds requires a complicated analysis of storage organization, instruction lengths, and instruction sets. To further complicate the process, what may be true for one type of program—say a certain program on system A requires less storage and runs faster than it does on system B—may not be true for another type of program.

Depending on design, one computer may be adapted for one type of program—for example, one involving extensive calculations—and another computer may be adapted for another type of program—for example, one involving high volumes of printed output.

In addition, program execution speed depends on many factors other than internal speeds. The I/O devices, the programming languages, the degree of overlap (see chapter 13), and the operating system (see chapter 14)—these all have an effect on the time it takes to execute a program. As a result, it is almost impossible to determine which of two computers will execute programs faster based on technical specifications only. Instead, it has become common to try a series of *benchmark runs* (or just *benchmarks*) on the two computers to be compared.

A benchmark is a timed test run that approximates actual conditions as closely as possible. To make sure that the test doesn't favor one particular type of computer design, benchmarks are normally run using three or more different types of programs. After the benchmark runs, the system analyst has some actual data on which to base his choice of computer. Because of the effectiveness of the benchmark procedure and because of the increasing complexity of hardware, there seems to be a trend away from the detailed hardware analysis that was once quite common when making a buying decision.

SUMMARY

1. The common measure of a computer's storage capacity is the number of storage positions it has. However, the efficiency of a computer in using its storage depends on its storage organization, instruction lengths, and instruction set.

2. Access cycles take up the major portion of CPU time during the execution of a program. Thus, access width, cycle time, and the resulting access speed are good measures of a computer's internal speed. Here again, however, storage organization, instruction lengths, and instruction set must be considered when comparing two computers.

3. The computer industry has already seen three generations of computers. These generations are distinguished by different types of electronic components, with resulting improvements in speed, reliability, size, and heat.

4. Because of the difficulty of hardware analysis based on technical specifications alone, benchmarks are commonly used.

control unit
arithmetic and logic unit
main storage
access cycle
access width
access-cycle time
cycle time

access speed
first generation
second generation
third generation
interleaving
benchmark run
benchmark

CHAPTER THIRTEEN

Until the mid-1960s, most computer systems could perform only one operation at a time. For instance, a typical card system read a card, processed it, and printed an output line on the printer. This sequence was then repeated for the next card record. Similarly, a typical tape system read input, processed it, and gave output—but only one operation at a time. The problem with this method of processing is that the components of the computer system are often idle, even though the system is running.

To illustrate, suppose a tape system executes a program that reads a tape record, processes it, and writes a tape record. Figure 13-1 might then represent the relative amounts of time that the CPU and the tape drives would be busy during execution of the program. (These percentages, of course, would vary depending on the speed of the components.) In this example, the CPU is busy 44 percent of the time that the system is running, while each tape drive is busy only 28 percent of the time.

To overcome this problem of idle components, systems were developed to overlap I/O operations with CPU processing. The difference between nonoverlapped and overlapped processing is illustrated in figure 13-2. On system A, the nonoverlapped system, nine time intervals are required to read, process, and write three records. On system B, the overlapped system, nine records have been read, eight have been processed, and seven have been written at the end of nine time intervals. Although this example is based on the unlikely assumption that reading, processing, and writing each take equal amounts of time, the message is clear: overlap can significantly increase the amount of work that a computer system can do.

One reason earlier computers weren't able to overlap operations is

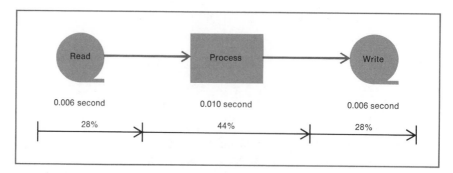

FIGURE 13-1   The problem of idle computer components

that the CPU executed all of the instructions of a program, one after the other. In contrast, the CPU of an overlapped system doesn't execute I/O instructions. Instead, *channels* are used to execute the I/O instructions, while the CPU executes the arithmetic, logic, and data-movement instructions. The I/O instructions executed by the channels are called *channel commands*. Figure 13-3, then, illustrates the components of an overlapped system: one channel executes an input command, a second channel executes an output command, and the CPU executes other instructions of the program—all at the same time. (Although the CPU is generally considered to consist of storage and control circuitry,

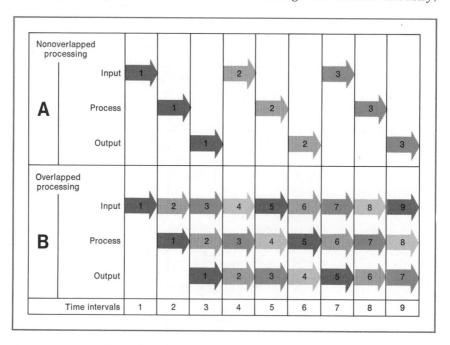

FIGURE 13-2   Overlapped and nonoverlapped processing

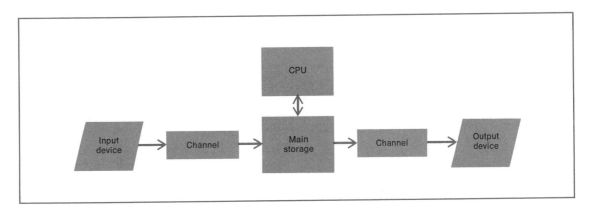

FIGURE 13-3   Computer system components with overlap capabilities

the CPU and storage are shown separately in the illustration to indicate that both CPU and channels access data from storage.)

Whenever data is transferred from a channel to storage or from storage to a channel, CPU processing is interrupted for one *storage access cycle* (or just *access cycle*). Because of the tremendous difference between access-cycle speeds and I/O speeds, however, this is a minor interruption. To illustrate, suppose cards read by a 600-card-per-minute card reader are being processed by a computer that transfers one byte of data during each access cycle. If an access cycle takes 2 microseconds (millionths of a second), which is a typical access speed of a medium-sized computer, CPU processing will be interrupted for a total of 160 microseconds to read all eighty card columns. In contrast, the card reader takes 1/10 second, or 100,000 microseconds to read all eighty card columns. This means that while each card is read, the CPU can spend over 99 percent of its time, 99,840 out of 100,000 microseconds to be exact, executing other instructions of the program.

Although tape and disk devices are many times faster than card readers and printers, this same type of inequality is likely to exist between the speeds of these I/O devices and access-cycle speeds. For example, a tape drive with a 50,000-byte-per-second transfer rate reads or writes one byte of data every 20 microseconds. If the CPU requires 2 microseconds to transfer the byte to or from storage, 18 microseconds per byte are available for other processing. In other words, with overlap capability, the CPU can spend 90 percent of its time executing other instructions.

Since a channel, like a CPU, can execute only one operation at a time, the number of overlapped operations that a system can have is limited by the number of channels on the system. For instance, a one-channel system can overlap one I/O operation with CPU processing, and a three-channel system can overlap three I/O operations with CPU processing.

The one exception to this is the *multiplexor channel*, which can read
or write on two or more slow-speed I/O devices at one time.

The multiplexor channel has the ability to alternate between several
I/O devices. For example, if a card reader, a card punch, and a printer are
attached to a multiplexor channel, the channel can accept one byte of
data from the card reader, send one byte to the card punch, send one
byte to the printer, and then accept another byte from the card reader.
By switching from one device to another, this single channel can overlap several different devices. Here again, the extreme difference in
speeds between I/O devices and access cycles makes this possible.

Figure 13-4 shows a typical configuration of a tape system with four
tape drives. All of its slow-speed devices—the card reader, card punch,
printer, and console typewriter—are attached to a multiplexor channel,
while the tape drives are attached to the other type of channel, a *selector
channel*. This system, then, can overlap card reading, printing, punching, console-typewriter operations, and reading or writing on one tape
drive. Because a selector channel can do only one operation at a time,
however, reading from tape drive 1 and writing on tape drive 2 cannot
be overlapped. Since tape drives are considerably faster than the slow-
speed devices, it is more important that slow-speed operations be overlapped than tape operations. In general, a computer system consists of
one multiplexor channel and one or more selector channels.

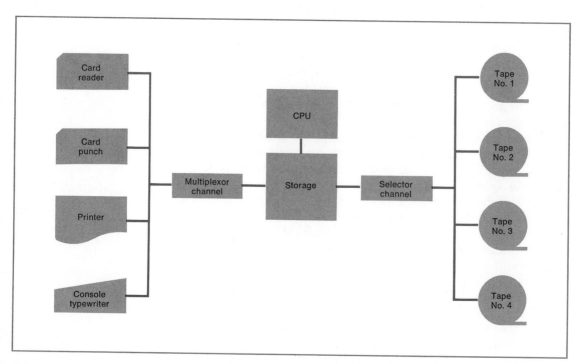

FIGURE 13-4   Configuration of a typical tape system

A programming complexity resulting from overlap is that two I/O areas in storage must be used for each I/O operation. If only one input area was used for a card-reading operation, for example, the second card would be moved into the input area while the first card was being processed — thus destroying the data from the first card. Instead, the second card is read into a second input area of storage while the first card is being processed in the first input area. Then, the third card is read into the first input area, while the second card is processed in the second input area. This switching from one input area to the other is continued throughout the program. Similarly, all other I/O operations that are overlapped must use dual I/O areas in storage.

So the programmer doesn't have to worry about the switching of I/O areas and the other complexities associated with overlap such as writing channel commands, a *supervisor program* and I/O modules are supplied with an overlapped system. The supervisor is loaded into storage at the start of a day's operations and remains in storage while all programs are executed. It is responsible for issuing all I/O commands. The I/O modules, which are loaded into storage along with a user's program, are responsible for handling the switching from one I/O area to the other. The programmer, then, writes his program as if no overlap were taking place. Whenever his source program issues an I/O statement, object code is compiled that causes a branch to the supervisor, which in turn, sends the appropriate channel command to the selected channel.

I/O-BOUND AND PROCESS-BOUND PROGRAMS

The illustration in figure 13-2 is, of course, unrealistic. Input, output, and processing times would never be equal; different input records would likely require different amounts of processing time; and few programs have such simple logic — read a record, process it, and write a record. Nevertheless, the illustration does demonstrate the idea of overlapped processing. With these same shortcomings, similar illustrations are used in figures 13-5 and 13-6 to represent two types of overlapped programs: *I/O-bound* and *process-bound* programs.

When an I/O-bound program is executed, the execution speed is limited by one or more I/O devices. For example, if figure 13-5 represents a program that reads a tape record, processes it, and writes a line on the printer, the printer is the limiting device. If the printer were replaced by a faster I/O device, the program could be speeded up. Thus, the program is said to be printer-bound, or I/O-bound. In general, most business programs are I/O-bound by one device or another.

In contrast, process-bound (sometimes called *CPU-bound*) refers to a program that is limited by internal processing speeds, as illustrated in figure 13-6. Here, the speed of the CPU would have to be increased in order to reduce the execution time of the program. Because they often

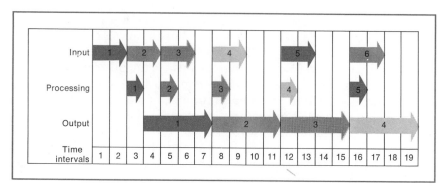

FIGURE 13-5   An I/O-bound program

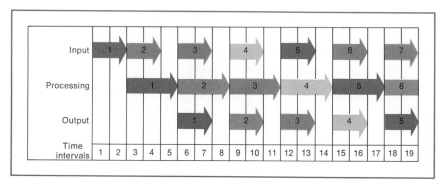

FIGURE 13-6   A process-bound program

require extensive calculations, scientific and engineering programs are commonly process-bound.

MULTIPROGRAMMING

To make better use of the components of a computer system when running I/O-bound and process-bound programs, a technique called *multiprogramming* was developed. When multiprogramming is used, two or more programs plus a supervisor program are loaded into storage at one time. Then, whenever the CPU is idle because it is waiting for an I/O operation to be completed, it branches to the supervisor, which branches to the next instruction to be executed in one of the other programs in storage. Because the supervisor must handle the switching between programs, a multiprogramming supervisor is more extensive than a supervisor for single-program processing.

Figure 13-7 illustrates how two I/O-bound programs might be executed using multiprogramming. If only program A were being executed, at the end of the third interval, the CPU would be idle until the next

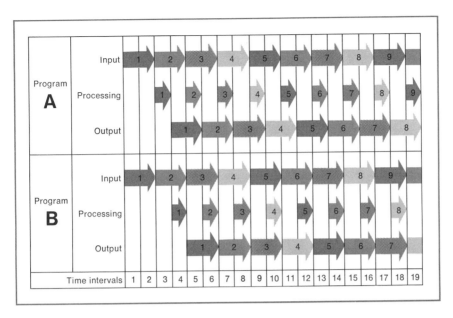

FIGURE 13-7   Multiprogramming two I/O-bound programs

I/O operation was completed. With multiprogramming, however, the program branches to the supervisor, which then branches to program B. By switching back and forth throughout program execution, the amount of processing done in nineteen intervals of time is increased considerably. In addition, the CPU is used for a much greater portion of the total execution time.

Depending on the size of the computer system, two, three, or more programs can be executed using multiprogramming. These programs can be either I/O- or process-bound. As each program is loaded into storage, it is given a priority number so that the supervisor can branch to the program with the highest priority whenever a program switch occurs. In this way, top priority programs receive the most attention from the CPU, while the lowest priority program is given use of the CPU only when all other programs are waiting for an I/O operation to end. If enough programs are loaded into storage and if enough I/O operations are overlapped, utilization of the CPU can approach 100 percent.

Some of the costs of multiprogramming include extra channels, relatively large amounts of main storage, and a relatively large supervisor program. Multiprogramming users, however, consider these costs to be well-justified. By reducing the idle time for the CPU and the I/O components, a multiprogramming system is capable of more processing per dollar spent than a system that uses single-program processing. In fact, multiprogramming is fast becoming the normal mode of operation for medium- and large-sized computers.

DISCUSSION

Depending on the computer manufacturer, overlap and channels may be referred to by other names. For example, some manufacturers refer to overlap as *simultaneity* and speak of eight simultaneous I/O operations in addition to CPU processing. Similarly, channels are sometimes referred to as *I/O trunks*. Regardless of the terminology, though, all major computer manufacturers provide systems with overlap capabilities.

The number of operations that can be overlapped by a system is another question. This, as I have said, depends on the channels available to the system. Some systems can overlap only a few operations; some can overlap dozens of operations. The overlap capability, in fact, can be one of the most critical factors in determining a system's speed. If two systems have comparable I/O devices, the one that has a higher degree of overlap is likely to be the faster machine. Because most business programs are I/O-bound, the internal processing speeds lose their significance.

SUMMARY

1. By use of channels and a supervisor program, I/O operations can be overlapped with CPU operations, thus increasing program execution speed. As a point of interest for programmers, two I/O areas must be available for each I/O device being overlapped.

2. In an I/O-bound program, speed is limited by the speed of one or more I/O operations. A process-bound program is limited by CPU speeds.

3. Multiprogramming attempts to better utilize the CPU by executing two or more programs at once. This requires extra channels, additional main storage, and an expanded supervisor program.

4. Because most business programs are I/O-bound, the degree of overlap achieved by a system is critical to the system's speed.

FOR
REVIEW

overlap	supervisor program
channel	I/O-bound
channel command	process-bound
storage access cycle	CPU-bound
access cycle	multiprogramming
multiplexor channel	simultaneity
selector channel	I/O trunk

CHAPTER FOURTEEN

This chapter is divided into two topics. In the first, the programming support commonly supplied with a computer system is described. Then, the language, called job-control language, that is required to make use of the programming support is explained in topic 2.

At one time, computer manufacturers first designed a computer and then decided what programming support, such as assemblers or compilers, should be supplied with it. About the mid-1960s, however, the manufacturers realized that the programming support, or "software," was almost as important as the equipment, or "hardware." They then began to design software in conjunction with hardware. One result was the development of *operating systems*, which are available with most of today's tape or direct-access computer systems.

An operating system is a collection of programs designed to improve the efficiency of a computer installation. It does this in two ways. First, an operating system decreases the amount of time a computer system is idle by using *stacked-job processing*. Second, an operating system increases programming efficiency by providing various processing and service programs that eliminate or reduce the programming efforts required of a computer user.

TOPIC ONE
OPERATING SYSTEMS

OPERATING SYSTEMS AND JOB-CONTROL LANGUAGE

STACKED-JOB PROCESSING

Before stacked-job processing was developed, a computer system stopped when it finished executing a program. The operator removed the program output, such as card decks or magnetic tapes, and made ready the I/O units for the next program. He then loaded the next program — usually in the form of an object deck — and placed any cards to be processed in the card reader. The program was then ready to be executed.

The problem with this intervention by the operator between programs is that it wastes computer time. If a company runs 120 programs a day and the operator takes thirty seconds to set up each program, one hour of computer time is lost. On a large system where an average program may take less than five minutes to be executed, such lost time is very costly.

When stacked-job processing is used, the computer, rather than the computer operator, loads the programs. To make this possible, all of a company's programs are stored on a system residence device, which can be either a magnetic tape or a direct-access device. However, because any program on a direct-access device can be accessed without searching sequentially through the other programs, direct access is preferred for system residence.

At the start of a day's computer operations, the computer operator loads a supervisor program into storage, and control of the computer is then transferred to this program. Under control of the supervisor program, which is one of the programs of the operating system, the other programs to be executed are loaded into storage from the system residence device. The supervisor program, which may require 6000 or more storage positions, remains in storage during the execution of all other programs.

To tell the supervisor which programs are to be executed, the operator places a stack of job-control cards such as the stack in figure 14-1 in the card reader. These cards give the names of the programs to be executed, along with information such as which tape should be mounted on which tape drive. There are usually several job-control cards for each program to be executed; if a program requires card input, the data deck follows the job-control cards. In the illustration, programs 2 and 3 require card input, while programs 1, 4, and 5 do not. The stack of job cards is commonly referred to as a job deck.

When the computer finishes executing a program, loading and executing the next one actually takes place in four steps, as shown in figure 14-2. First, control of the computer passes from the completed program to one of the instructions of the supervisor program. Second, the supervisor loads the job-control program from the system residence device and passes control to it. In the third step, this job-control program, which is one of the programs of the operating system, reads and processes the

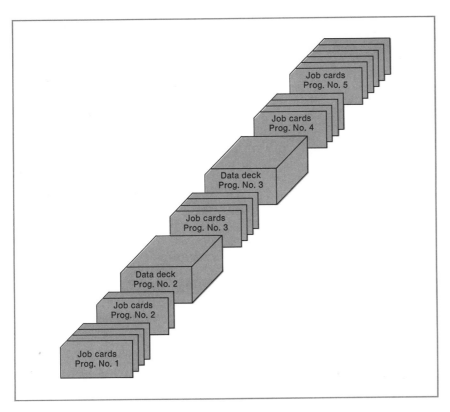

FIGURE 14-1   A job deck

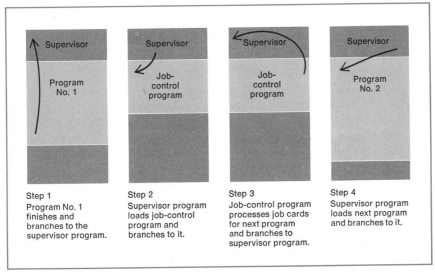

FIGURE 14-2   Job-to-job transition in stacked-job processing

job-control cards for the next program. If there are any errors in the job-control cards or if any necessary information is omitted, the job-control program prints a message on the console typewriter. When all job cards are processed, control passes back to the supervisor. Finally, the supervisor loads the next program from the system residence device and passes control to its first instruction.

To understand more completely how stacked-job processing reduces idle computer time, consider the example in figure 14-3. Here, the computer system consists of two disk drives, four tape drives, a printer, a card reader, a card punch, a console typewriter, and a CPU. The stack of jobs consists of five programs and corresponds to what might take place on a computer used for business applications. If the computer operator completes the steps indicated on the right while the program indicated on the left is running, all five programs can be executed without any idle computer time.

The first job in the stack is a card-to-tape editing run that converts inventory transaction cards into tape records. After the program is loaded from the system residence device (disk drive 1), it is executed. While this program is running, the operator mounts *scratch tapes* (tapes containing data that can now be written over) on tape drives 2, 3, and 4 in preparation for the next job.

The second job is a tape sort that uses all four tape drives. At the end of the job, the sorted tape is on tape drive 1. While this job is running, the operator mounts a disk pack that is used for compiling and testing COBOL programs on disk drive 2. This pack contains scratch areas used by the COBOL compiler and data areas containing test data for subsequent test runs. If you look ahead, you can see that the pack is used in jobs 3 and 4.

The computer and operator continue in this way until all five jobs in the job deck have been executed. Job 3 is a COBOL compilation; job 4 is a test run of the newly created object program; and job 5 is an inventory-update program using the transaction tape created in job 1 and sorted in job 2. The overall result: five programs executed with no idle time.

Of course, some operator intervention takes place even with stacked-job processing. After all, the operating system only loads the programs from the system residence device. The operator must still place the job deck in the card reader, place blank cards in the card punch, change forms on the printer, mount tapes on the tape drives, and so forth. If he can't complete the preparation for the next program in the stack while one program is being executed, idle computer time results. Nevertheless, if programs are scheduled in the proper sequence, stacked-job processing can significantly increase a computer's productive running time. In actual practice, a single job deck will keep the computer running for several hours at a time.

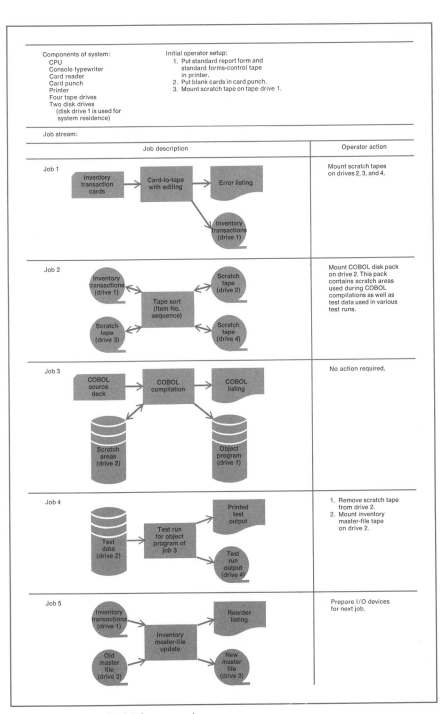

Components of system:
  CPU
  Console typewriter
  Card reader
  Card punch
  Printer
  Four tape drives
  Two disk drives
    (disk drive 1 is used for
    system residence)

Initial operator setup:
  1. Put standard report form and
     standard forms-control tape
     in printer.
  2. Put blank cards in card punch.
  3. Mount scratch tape on tape drive 1.

Job stream:

Job description	Operator action
Job 1 — Inventory transaction cards → Card-to-tape with editing → Error listing; Inventory transactions (drive 1)	Mount scratch tapes on drives 2, 3, and 4.
Job 2 — Inventory transactions (drive 1), Scratch tape (drive 2), Scratch tape (drive 3), Scratch tape (drive 4) ↔ Tape sort (Item No. sequence)	Mount COBOL disk pack on drive 2. This pack contains scratch areas used during COBOL compilations as well as test data used in various test runs.
Job 3 — COBOL source deck → COBOL compilation → COBOL listing; Scratch areas (drive 2); Object program (drive 1)	No action required.
Job 4 — Test data (drive 2) → Test run for object program of job 3 → Printed test output; Test run output (drive 4)	1. Remove scratch tape from drive 2. 2. Mount inventory master-file tape on drive 2.
Job 5 — Inventory transactions (drive 1), Old master file (drive 2) → Inventory master-file update → Reorder listing; New master file (drive 3)	Prepare I/O devices for next job.

FIGURE 14-3 Stacked-job processing

If you are familiar with multiprogramming (described in chapters 8 and 13), you will want to know that the principles of stacked-job processing also apply to multiprogramming systems. However, on a multiprogramming system, the supervisor is likely to schedule the sequence of jobs to be run. For example, a typical multiprogramming supervisor first reads the entire job deck and stores the information about each program to be run. The supervisor then determines the most efficient sequence for running the programs, taking into consideration the priority given to each program, the I/O devices used and available, and so on. In this way, the supervisor maximizes the use of the components of the system and thus maximizes the amount of work the system can do. After it determines the most efficient schedule of jobs and while the programs are being executed, the supervisor prints messages on the console typewriter indicating which actions the operator should take.

PROCESSING AND SERVICE PROGRAMS

The programs of an operating system can be divided into (1) control programs such as the supervisor and job-control programs, (2) processing programs, and (3) service programs. The processing programs include language translators, sort/merge programs, and utility programs. The service programs include library-maintenance programs and a linkage editor.

Language Translators

Language translators are the assemblers, compilers, and generators that are supplied with a computer system. For example, a typical operating system might include an assembler, COBOL, FORTRAN, and PL/I compilers, and an RPG generator. The purpose of the translator is to reduce the programming time required to prepare a working object program. As a result, the translators always print diagnostic listings to aid in correcting clerical errors in the source deck and often provide debugging statements to aid in testing the object program.

Sort/Merge Programs

In any computer installation, much of the processing requires that records be in certain sequences. As a result, two or more tape or direct-access files often have to be merged into one file, or one tape or direct-access file has to be sorted. This sorting and merging may take as much as 40 percent of the total running time of a computer system. All sort/merge programs operate much the same; they differ primarily in the number of files to be merged or sorted, the length of the records in the files, the blocking factors used, the length and location of the field on which the file is to be sequenced, and the number of I/O devices to be used.

An operating system, then, provides one or more *sort/merge programs*. These are generalized programs that can be used for many different jobs. The user simply supplies coded specifications and the sort/merge program adjusts accordingly, thus eliminating the need for sort programs to be written by the computer user.

Utility Programs

Many of the programs of a typical computer installation are relatively simple ones that convert data from one I/O form to another; for example, printing the contents of a tape file or converting a disk file to a tape file. To eliminate the need for a computer user to write such programs, an operating system provides *utility programs*, in which the user need only specify in coded form the characteristics of the files involved. The utility programs then adjust accordingly and do the desired processing. Thus, routine programs such as card-to-printer, card-to-tape, card-to-disk, tape-to-printer, tape-to-tape, and many others are supplied with an operating system.

Library-Maintenance Programs

To reduce duplication of programming effort within a company, an operating system allows for segments of both source and object code to be stored in *libraries* on the system residence device. Thus, if a programmer writes a routine for calculating the square root of a number, the operating system can store the routine in one of the libraries as either source code or object code. Any other program that involves square roots can then retrieve this routine from the appropriate library. If the routine is stored as source code, the statements can be placed in the program and compiled along with the rest of the source code. If the routine is stored as object code, the object code of the main program and the object code of the square-root routine can be combined before execution of the complete program.

To add new routines to a library and to delete old routines, *library-maintenance programs* are required. These, of course, are supplied as part of the operating system. Library-maintenance programs also provide for printing the names of segments stored within a library or for printing the segments themselves.

The Linkage Editor

Combining two or more segments of object code, called *object modules*, can be a very complex procedure. To illustrate, suppose that the object module for the square-root routine takes the 200 storage positions from locations 4001 through 4200. When the main program is compiled, however, its object module takes the 8000 storage positions from 4001 through 12,000. Before the object modules can be combined, one of the modules must be relocated. But when a module is relocated, the addresses of the data fields upon which it operates also change. Since two object modules such as this operate on common data fields—for example, the square-root module determines the square root of one of the fields in the main program and returns the answer—changes must be made to both modules when one is relocated. If more than two object modules are linked, the problem becomes even more involved.

The *linkage editor* handles the relocation of the object modules and the eventual linking of them into a complete program. Besides making it possible for commonly used routines to be stored in an object library and combined before execution, the linkage editor also makes it possible to divide a large program into several segments, each of which can be assigned to a different programmer. Each segment can then be written in the most appropriate language, translated into an object module, and tested. When all object modules are ready, the linkage editor performs the necessary relocating and linking; the complete program can then be tested. By dividing a programming task into segments, the total time for completing a program can be reduced and each segment can be assigned to the programmer best qualified for the job—the most difficult segment to the most experienced programmer, and so on.

DISCUSSION

To a certain extent, the terminology used for the components of an operating system varies depending on the computer manufacturer. For example, some manufacturers refer to supervisor programs as monitors, some as executives, and some as MCPs (Master Control Programs). Regardless of the terminology, however, most operating systems provide the capabilities described in this chapter.

Because the supervisor program is mentioned in several different contexts in this book (chapters 8, 12, 13, and 14), it might be good to summarize the major functions of the supervisor. First, the supervisor issues all I/O commands for all programs run by a system. Second, the supervisor handles the switching from one program to another during multiprogramming. And third, the supervisor loads the programs of a system and handles the transition from one job to another during stacked-job processing.

SUMMARY

1. An operating system increases productivity in two ways: (1) by reducing idle time between programs and (2) by eliminating the duplication of programming effort.

2. When stacked-job processing is used, a job deck containing job-control cards for each job to be run is placed in the card reader. When one program finishes, the supervisor program loads the next program to be executed from the system residence device.

3. In addition to control programs, an operating system contains language translators, sort/merge programs, utility programs, library-maintenance programs, and a linkage editor.

FOR REVIEW

operating system
stacked-job processing
system residence device
supervisor program
job-control card
job deck
job-control program
scratch tape
processing program

service program
language translator
sort/merge program
utility program
library
library-maintenance program
object module
linkage editor

TOPIC TWO

JOB-CONTROL LANGUAGE

Each computer manufacturer supplies one or more operating systems with each of its tape and direct-access systems. For example, IBM supplies three operating systems that can be used with System/360 direct-access systems; they are the Basic Operating System (BOS), the Disk Operating System (DOS), and the full Operating System (OS). These vary in the features they provide and the amount of storage they require. For example, BOS requires a computer with at least 8000 storage positions and provides translators for assembler language and RPG, whereas DOS requires at least 16,000 storage positions and provides translators for assembler language, COBOL, FORTRAN, PL/I, and RPG. OS, the most advanced of the IBM operating systems, requires a computer with at least 64,000 storage positions and supplies translators for an advanced version of FORTRAN in addition to assembler language, PL/I, RPG, COBOL, and ALGOL.

Operating systems also vary as to the job-control cards required. The job-control cards used for executing a program under DOS, for example, cannot be used for BOS or OS. Thus, each operating system is said to have its own *job-control language*. Although a programmer should have a basic understanding of job-control language, it isn't practical for each programmer in a company to be familiar with all of the details. Usually, only one person in each installation is responsible for handling the complexities of job-control language.

Job-control language is introduced in this topic by looking specifically at the job-control language for the Disk Operating System, which is probably the most widely used operating system. My theory is that it is better for you to know some specific details about one job-control language than to know general characteristics about all job-control languages. Then, when you encounter a different job-control language, you will have a basis for understanding and comparison.

Because different functions of the operating system require different forms of job-control cards, the remainder of this topic is broken down by function. Depending on what you have covered up to now, only selected functions may be of interest to you. Instead of including detailed descriptions of the formats of the job-control cards, only the basic patterns are given. After you become familiar with several of these patterns, I think you will have a good idea of how a job-control language works.

For all of the job-control card setups that follow, assume that the system described in figure 14-4 is being used. This system consists of a System/360 Model 40 CPU, with a three-spindle 2314, four 2400 tape drives, a 2540 card reader and punch, a 1403 printer, and a 1052 console typewriter. The symbols '00C', '00D', '00E', and so forth are used to refer to the devices. These symbols are hardware addresses assigned to each I/O device at the time that the computer is installed. The list of standard options and standard I/O assignments relates to the Disk Operating System and will be explained later.

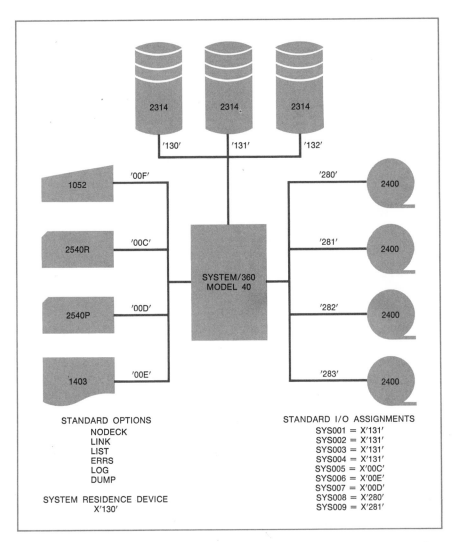

FIGURE 14-4   System configuration

BASIC JOB-CONTROL CARDS

Compiling a Program

Figure 14-5 illustrates the job-control cards needed to compile an object deck from a COBOL source deck. It begins with a JOB card, which gives a *jobname* to the *job* (or operation) that is about to be performed. Its format, which is typical of many job-control cards, begins with two slashes (columns 1 and 2) followed by one or more blanks and the operation—in this case, JOB. This is followed by one or more blanks and the operand or operands—in this case, the jobname COMPILE. After one or more blanks, the operands of a job card can be followed by comments

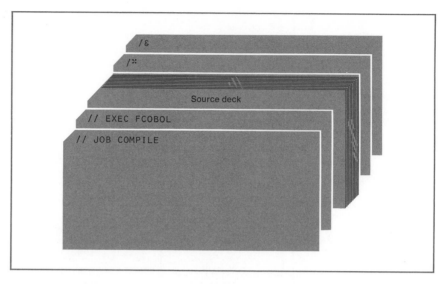

FIGURE 14-5   Job-control cards for a COBOL compilation

(any data), which are ignored by the operating system. The jobname can be up to eight alphabetic or numeric characters long but must start with a letter. Although the jobname is used in certain error messages printed by the job-control program, it has little significance for the student programmer. In this example, it is used to indicate the type of job being run.

The second card, // EXEC FCOBOL causes the COBOL compiler to be loaded into storage and executed. FCOBOL is the name given to the compiler stored in the libraries of the system residence device. When the compiler is executed, it reads the source deck and uses four work areas on the disks that are symbolically designated SYS001, SYS002, SYS003, and SYS004. If you check the list of standard I/O assignments used by this operating system, you can see that SYS001, SYS002, SYS003, and SYS004 are all assigned to the same disk drive, X'131'.

The /* card (slash in column 1, asterisk in column 2) indicates to the compiler that there are no more source cards. The /& card (slash in column 1, ampersand in column 2) indicates that the job is completed. In DOS, a job may consist of one or more *job steps.* For each job step, there is one EXEC card between the JOB card, which is always the first card for a job, and the /& card, which is always the last card. The job in the example consists of one job step since there is only one EXEC card.

Because of the standard options specified for the operating system (see figure 14-4), the COBOL compiler will not punch the object deck (NODECK). Instead, because of the LINK option, it will store the object program on a work area of one of the disk drives so that it is ready to be processed by the linkage editor. In addition, the standard options will cause the source statements to be printed on the printer (LIST) along with

a diagnostic listing (ERRS). The options called LOG and DUMP mean
that the contents of the job-control cards will be printed (logged) on the
printer, and, if the computer is unable to execute a program because of
error, the program will be cancelled and a storage dump will be printed.

The standard options can be overruled by using the OPTION card. For
example, if a programmer wants the object deck to be punched, he can
use the following cards for compilation:

```
// JOB COMPILE
// OPTION NOLINK,DECK
// EXEC FCOBOL
    (SOURCE DECK)
/*
/&
```

Because of the difficulty in handling object decks, however, the DECK
option is rarely used.

The following is a partial list of valid operands that can be specified
in an OPTION card:

```
LINK
NOLINK
DECK
NODECK
LIST
NOLIST
ERRS
NOERRS
DUMP
NODUMP
LOG
NOLOG
```

If two or more operands are used, they must be separated by commas,
as follows:

```
// OPTION DECK,NOLINK,LIST,ERRS,NODUMP,NOLOG
```

When an option is specified, it stays in effect until the next /& card, at
which time the standard options are put back into effect.

The same principles apply to compiling a program written in some
other language. For example, a Basic FORTRAN program can be compiled using these job-control cards:

```
// JOB COMPILE
// EXEC FORTRAN
    (SOURCE DECK)
/*
/&
```

Here, the name for the Basic FORTRAN compiler is FORTRAN (// EXEC

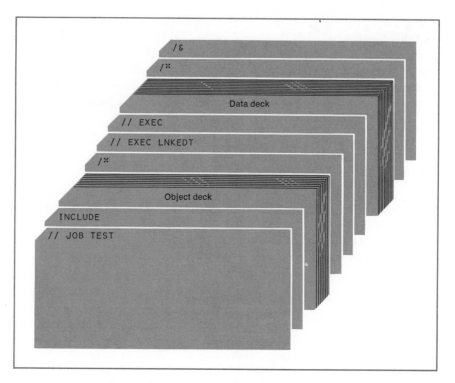

FIGURE 14-6   Loading and executing an object deck

FORTRAN). If the full version of FORTRAN is used, the compiler name is FFORTRAN (// EXEC FFORTRAN).

Loading and Executing an Object Deck

Before an object program can be executed using the Disk Operating System, it must be processed by the linkage-editor program. The linkage editor stores the object program in one of the libraries of the system residence device so that the program can be loaded by the supervisor. Loading and executing an object deck is actually done in two job steps: first, the object program is transferred from cards to a work area on a disk device and the linkage editor then stores the program in a library of the system residence device; second, the object program is loaded and executed.

Figure 14-6 shows the job cards required for loading and executing the program in figure 17-3. The cards for the first job step are as follows:

```
// JOB TEST
      INCLUDE
      (OBJECT DECK)
/*
// EXEC LNKEDT
```

The INCLUDE card simply indicates that an object deck will follow. The /* card indicates the end of the object deck.

The word INCLUDE in the INCLUDE card can start anywhere after column 1 of the card. Incidentally, in a strict sense, this card is not a job-control card but rather a linkage-editor control card; it is processed by the linkage editor. All job-control cards begin with at least one slash.

The first job step ends with this job card:

```
// EXEC LNKEDT
```

In other words, LNKEDT is the name used for the linkage-editor program. It is loaded from the system residence device and executed. When it is finished, the object program to be executed is stored in one of the libraries of the system residence device, ready for execution.

The second job step is loading and executing the user's program. The job-control cards for this step are as follows:

```
// EXEC
   (DATA DECK)
/*
```

Because the EXEC card doesn't specify a program or phase name (as in // EXEC COBOL), it indicates that the program can be found in a temporary area on the system residence device.

Depending on how the program is written or what the standard I/O assignments of a system are, one or more ASSGN cards may be needed before the // EXEC card. To illustrate, suppose the standard I/O devices assigned to SYS005 and SYS006 are tape drives as follows:

```
SYS005 = X'280'
SYS006 = X'281'
```

Then, ASSGN cards would be needed before the COBOL program in figure 17-3 could be run. Because the SELECT statements specify that SYS005 should be the 2540 card reader and SYS006 should be the 1403 printer, ASSGN cards would be used as follows:

```
// JOB TEST
   INCLUDE
   (OBJECT DECK)
/*
// EXEC LNKEDT
// ASSGN SYS005,X'00C'
// ASSGN SYS006,X'00E'
// EXEC
   (DATA DECK)
/*
/&
```

Because of the ASSGN cards, the standard I/O assignments would be changed as required by the program. When the /& card is read at the end of the job, the standard I/O assignments are again in effect. By writing your program to conform to standard I/O assignments, though, you eliminate the need for ASSGN cards.

Because a FORTRAN program doesn't use SYS numbers, you may wonder how ASSGN cards apply to FORTRAN object programs. Each device number in a READ or WRITE statement has an implied SYS number. For example, 4 corresponds to SYS001, 5 to SYS002, 6 to SYS003, and so on. As a result, if a FORTRAN statement refers to device 5, as in

```
READ (5,100) A,B,C,D,E
```

SYS002 can be used in an ASSGN card as follows:

```
// ASSGN SYS002,X'00C'
```

Thus, the READ statement would read from a card reader. (As a general rule, if device numbers 1, 2, and 3 are used for the card reader, the card punch, and the printer, respectively, ASSGN cards aren't needed for FORTRAN programs.)

Compiling, Loading, and Executing

The following job-control cards can be used to compile, load, and execute the FORTRAN source program that is given in figure 20-3:

```
// JOB COMPILE AND TEST
// EXEC FORTRAN
    (SOURCE DECK)
/*
// EXEC LNKEDT
// EXEC
    (DATA DECK)
/*
/&
```

Because of the standard LINK option, the object program is written on a work area of a disk after compilation, ready to be processed by the linkage editor. When the linkage editor is finished, the object program is loaded into storage and executed.

This job-control setup, which can be used repeatedly for card and printer programs, is the one normally used by programmers when preparing programs. As a result, the DECK option is rarely used. If ASSGN cards are needed, they come between the // EXEC LNKEDT and // EXEC cards. Note that the jobname specified in the JOB card in this example is actually COMPILE—the words after COMPILE are treated as comments.

JOB-CONTROL CARDS FOR TAPE FILES

When a program involves tape input or output, label information must be supplied at the time the program is executed. For this purpose, a

TLBL card is required. To specify that extra storage is required for label information, a LBLTYP card is used just prior to the linkage-editor run. The following cards, then, could be used to load and execute an object deck for the program given in figure 19-1:

```
// JOB TAPE EXAMPLE
    INCLUDE
    (OBJECT DECK)
// LBLTYP TAPE
// EXEC LNKEDT
// ASSGN SYS006,X'282'
// TLBL SYS006,'SAMPLE LABEL',73/031,24893
// EXEC
    (DATA DECK)
/*
/&
```

Here, the LBLTYP card specifies TAPE, indicating that the linkage editor must provide for an eighty-byte tape label.

The TLBL card has the format given in figure 14-7. The brackets indicate that all operands other than filename are optional. At the top of figure 14-7, the format of the file label used on the tape is given. As you can see, the TLBL card corresponds closely to the fields of the file label. In the example, only the filename, file identifier, date, and file serial number are given. For an input file, the date in the TLBL card will be checked against the creation date in the header label. For an output file, the TLBL date will be stored as the expiration date in the label.

As you can see from this example, the job-control cards are basically the same as before, with LBLTYP and TLBL cards added. As a result, compiling, link editing, and testing the program in figure 19-1 could be done as follows:

```
// JOB COMPILE AND TEXT
// EXEC FCOBOL
    (SOURCE DECK)
/*
// LBLTYP TAPE
// EXEC LNKEDT
// ASSGN SYS006,X'282'
// TLBL SYS006,'SAMPLE FILE',73/031,24893
// EXEC
    (DATA DECK)
/*
/&
```

If tape files are used in FORTRAN programs, there is no SYS number or filename that can be used in the TLBL card. Instead, each device number is associated with a standard filename that is used in the TLBL card. For instance, device number 4 has the filename IJSYS01, device number 5 has the filename IJSYS02, device number 6 has the filename IJSYS03, and so on. Thus, a tape-to-printer program using device number 8 for

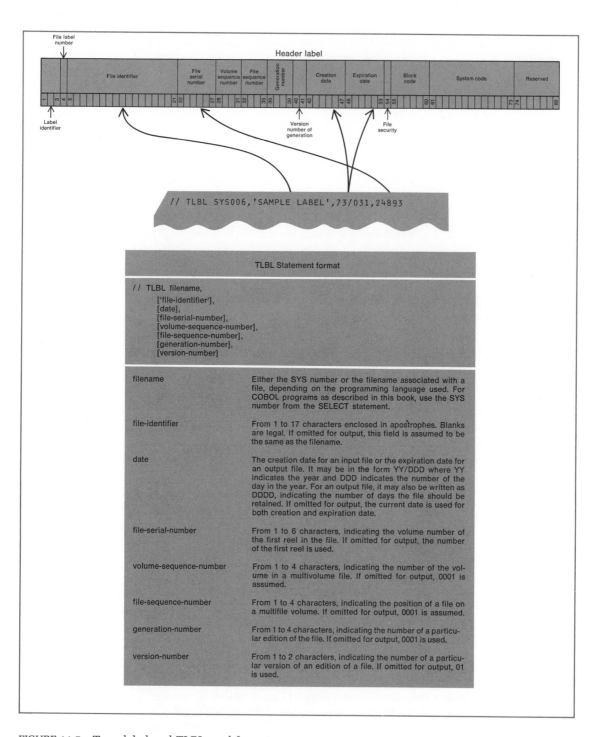

FIGURE 14-7 Tape label and TLBL card formats

the tape input file could be compiled and executed with the following job-control cards:

```
// JOB TAPE TO PRINTER
// EXEC FORTRAN
   (SOURCE DECK)
/*
// LBLTYP TAPE
// EXEC LNKEDT
// ASSGN SYS005,X'281'
// TLBL IJSYS05,'FORTRAN FILE'
// EXEC
/&
```

Here, only the file-identification field of the input label will be checked. Because the program doesn't use card input, the job deck doesn't include a data deck.

JOB-CONTROL CARDS FOR SEQUENTIAL DISK FILES

To supply the information used in label-checking routines for sequential disk files, the DLBL and EXTENT cards are used. The formats for these cards and the format of the basic disk file label are given in figure 14-8. Because a file may consist of several different areas of a disk, several EXTENT cards may be required for one file. The DLBL card must always come first, however. In both cards, all fields other than filename are optional. If fields are omitted for an input file, those fields aren't checked. If fields are omitted for output files, the fields in the file labels are usually given assumed values.

The following cards could be used to compile, load, and execute the disk program given in figure 19-3:

```
// JOB DISK EXAMPLE
// EXEC FCOBOL
   (SOURCE DECK)
/*
// EXEC LNKEDT
// ASSGN SYS006,X'132'
// DLBL SYS006,'DISK EXAMPLE FILE',14,SD
// EXTENT SYS006,1,0,200,220
// EXEC
   (DATA DECK)
/*
/&
```

Here, the updated master file will be retained for at least fourteen days before being destroyed. The file is located in cylinders 11 through 21 (220 tracks beginning with the two-hundredth track). Because the serial number is omitted from the DLBL card, this field won't be checked in the label-checking routine.

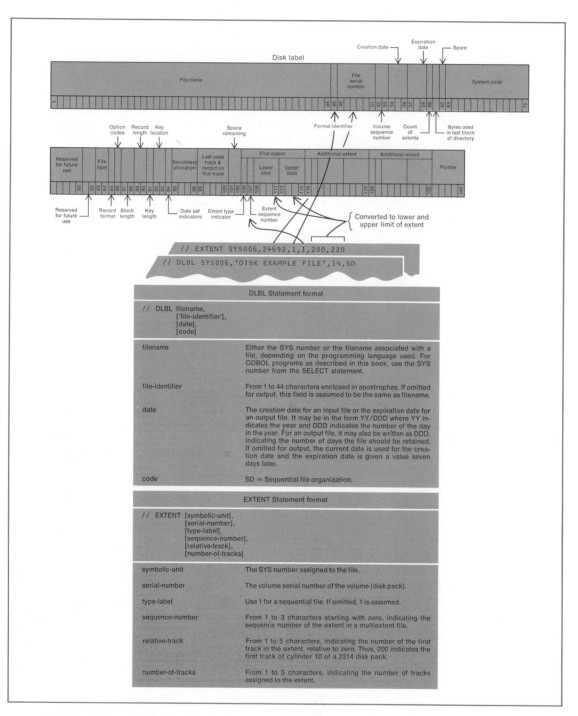

FIGURE 14-8   Disk label and DLBL and extent card formats

USING THE DOS LIBRARIES

There are usually three libraries that are stored on the system residence device for the Disk Operating System: the core-image library, the source-statement library, and the relocatable library. For example, the core-image library may be stored in cylinders 1–50, the relocatable library in cylinders 51–60, and the source-statement library in cylinders 61–70. To find programs or segments of source or object code in these libraries, a *directory* is kept for each library. These directories maintain the names and locations of each library's contents. In this topic, only the use of the core-image library is explained, although the principles are the same for all three libraries.

Before object code can be executed, it must be stored in the *core-image library*. This library has two sections: a permanent section in which the commonly used programs are kept and a temporary section in which programs are stored for one-time use. If a program is stored in the permanent section, it is given a *phase name* that is used to call the program into storage. Thus, the phase name FCOBOL is used to call the COBOL compiler into storage. The EXEC card for this purpose, then, would be // EXEC FCOBOL. Similarly, LNKEDT is the phase name for the linkage-editor program. When a program is stored in the temporary section of the core-image library, a phase name is not put in the library's directory; thus, the EXEC card does not require a phase name.

In the examples given so far, all of the user programs have been executed from the temporary core-image library. To catalog a program into the permanent core-image library, the OPTION card must specify CATAL, and a PHASE card must follow the OPTION card. Thus, the object deck for the program in figure 17-3 can be stored in the permanent core-image library by using the following cards:

```
// JOB CATALOG EXAMPLE
// OPTION CATAL
   PHASE REORDER,*
   INCLUDE
   (OBJECT DECK)
/*
// EXEC LNKEDT
/&
```

The PHASE card gives the phase name REORDER to the program, followed by a comma and an asterisk. The asterisk indicates that whenever the program is executed, it is to be loaded into storage immediately following the supervisor. There are a number of other operands that can be used in place of the asterisk, indicating other locations in storage. The phase name is formed according to the rules for forming job names — up to eight letters or numbers and starting with a letter. The word PHASE can start anywhere after column 1 in the control card.

After the inventory-control program is cataloged, it can be executed by using the phase name as follows:

```
// JOB EXECUTE
// EXEC REORDER
      (DATA DECK)
/*
/&
```

If ASSGN cards are needed, they come between the JOB and the EXEC cards. As you might guess, most programs that a company uses are cataloged in the core-image library using a similar job-control card setup.

SUMMARY

1. There are many different operating systems and, as a result, many different job-control languages. In general, however, all job-control languages supply the same types of information.

2. All jobs in DOS job-control language begin with a JOB card and end with a /& card. Each job may consist of one or more job steps, each of which is indicated by a // EXEC card. Some of the most commonly used cards in the DOS job-control language are the JOB, EXEC, /*, /&, OPTION, INCLUDE, and ASSGN cards. For tape and direct-access files, LBLTYP, TLBL, DLBL, and EXTENT cards are used.

FOR REVIEW

job-control language
jobname
job
job step
directory
core-image library
phase name

CHAPTER FIFTEEN

In the first topic of this chapter, program flowcharting techniques are explained. Then, the second topic presents some programming routines likely to be found in a typical business program. Because the two topics are unrelated, either can be read first, and either can be read without reading the other.

In chapter 4, you were introduced to the basic flowcharting symbols and concepts; the intent of this topic is to broaden that base.

A flowcharting form such as the one illustrated in figure 15-1 is often used when drawing flowcharts. This form consists of fifty boxes that are numbered so each block can be identified. For example, box C2 refers to the I/O symbol containing the words READ RECORD; G5 refers to the terminal symbol containing the word STOP. By using these letter/number combinations in connector symbols, it becomes easy to follow connections within a flowchart. For instance, the connector symbol exiting from box H3 indicates a branch to connector symbol A4, thus connecting with the symbol to the left of box A4.

If the connector symbol is used to connect a flowline on one page to a flowline on another page, the number of the page to be branched to

PROGRAM FLOWCHARTING AND PROGRAM CONTROLS

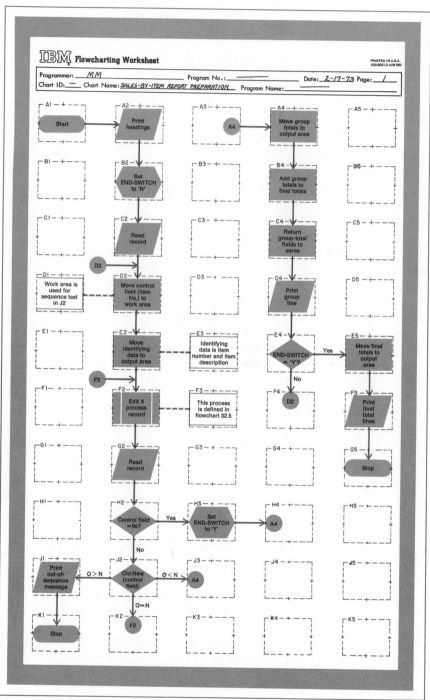

FIGURE 15-1   Flowchart for summary-report preparation

should be written to the upper left of the connector symbol. Thus,

indicates that the program continues at box A4 on page 4. Similarly,

indicates a return to box J2 on page 1.

The flowchart in figure 15-1 introduces the following flowcharting symbols:

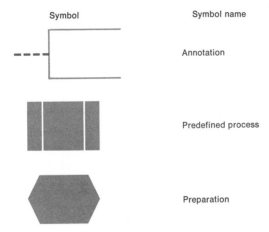

As with the other symbols used in this book, these symbols conform to standards set by the American National Standards Institute. The first symbol, the annotation symbol, is used in figure 15-1 in boxes D1, E3, and F3. As you can see, it can open either to the left or the right, and the dotted line, which can be vertical, horizontal, or diagonal, connects the annotation symbol to the symbol it explains.

The predefined process symbol is used in box F2 of figure 15-1. A predefined process consists of one or more program steps that are defined in another set of flowcharts. Often, the predefined process, which may have been programmed by another programmer, is used in two or more different programs. For example, the editing and processing routine of figure 15-1 might be used in an update program as well as a sales-report program.

The preparation symbol represents the modification of an instruction or a constant that in some way affects the flow of a program. In figure 15-1, for example, the preparation symbol is used in box B2 to set the field named END-SWITCH to N and in box H3 to set END-SWITCH to Y. Then, in box E4 the flow of the program depends on the contents of END-SWITCH: if N, the program continues with box D2; if Y, the program continues with box E5. By using the preparation symbol, the programmer can more easily locate the points in the program at which the contents of the END-SWITCH data field are changed. Incidentally, modifying the contents of a field in this way to determine which of two paths a program should take is often referred to as *setting a switch*.

Two other flowcharting conventions you should be familiar with concern flowlines. First, if flowlines connect as in the following examples,

arrowheads should be used on every flowline entering and leaving the junction to indicate the direction of flow. If flowlines cross without arrowheads, as in the following examples,

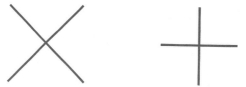

the lines have no logical relationship. In other words, the direction of flow is not changed at the junction of lines.

Second, several different paths from a single decision symbol may be shown as in this example:

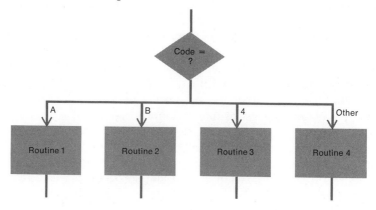

Here, if the code is A, B, or 4, routine 1, 2, or 3 is performed. If the code is not A, B, or 4, routine 4 is performed. Similarly, multiple exits from a decision can be shown by using flowline variations such as these:

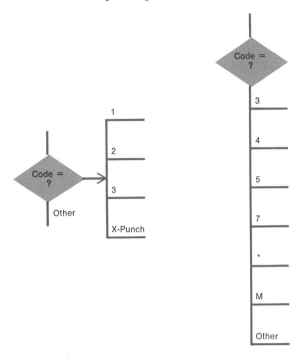

Program Design

One aspect of flowcharting that is being emphasized more and more is that of program design—in particular, the concept of *modularity*. The idea is to break a program into a number of separate *modules*—one *mainline module* and one or more *subroutine modules*. As much as possible, each module should be independent of the other modules. The advantage of modularity is that the logic of the total program becomes more manageable. Instead of one extensive program, it becomes a group of small, understandable programming segments. Thus, it is easier to code the program, and, if a problem occurs during testing, it is easier to locate the routine (module) that is causing the error. Similarly, if the program needs to be modified later because of a change in processing requirements, locating, modifying, and testing the routine that needs to be changed can be done more efficiently.

To achieve modularity, the mainline module should indicate all of the major processing routines as well as the logical decisions required to direct the program to these routines. For instance, figure 15-2 illustrates the mainline module of a typical tape master-file update program.

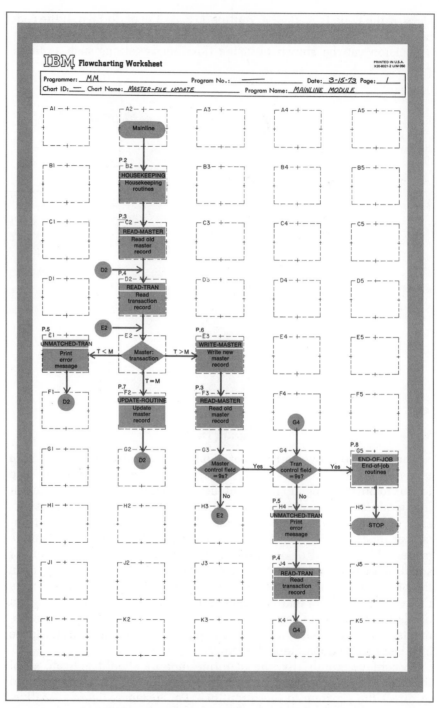

FIGURE 15-2   The mainline module—master-file update program

Each symbol that represents a subroutine module uses *striping* at the top of the symbol to indicate the name of the module. As a result, the update program consists of the mainline module plus seven other modules, named HOUSEKEEPING, READ-MASTER, READ-TRAN, UNMATCHED-TRAN, WRITE-MASTER, UPDATE-ROUTINE, and END-OF-JOB.

Although this mainline module consists of only sixteen blocks, it could well be the mainline for a program requiring many hundreds of instructions; it depends upon the complexity of the subroutine modules. As a general rule, even in complex programs, the mainline module should not require more than two dozen flowcharting blocks. Because the primary purpose of the mainline module is to direct the flow of processing to the other modules, it could well be the shortest module of the program.

After the mainline module is flowcharted, each of the subroutines can be flowcharted at a semidetailed level. To continue the concept of modularity, each subroutine module can be broken into additional, more specific modules, depending of course on the length and complexity of the module. Since the idea is to make each programming segment manageable, each module should be kept to between 50 and 200 statements in length.

To easily relate subroutine flowcharts to a higher level flowchart such as the mainline flowchart, cross references are used as shown in the mainline flowchart of figure 15-2 and the subroutine flowchart of figure 15-3. In block E1 of the mainline flowchart, for example, the stripe gives the name UNMATCHED-TRAN to a subroutine. Page 5 (P. 5), which is written to the upper left of the flowcharting symbol, indicates that the flowchart for the UNMATCHED-TRAN module can be found on page 5 of this set of flowcharts. (Page 5 is shown in figure 15-3.) To complete the cross referencing, UNMATCHED-TRAN is written in the terminal symbol at the start of the subroutine flowchart on page 5, and page 1 (P. 1), which is a reference back to the mainline flowchart, is written to the upper left of this terminal symbol. Similarly, flowchart page numbers and module names are used to cross-reference the other module flowcharts and the mainline flowchart.

One of the critical points in developing a modular program is to keep each module independent of the other modules. In other words, each subroutine module should branch back to only the next block in the mainline module, not to other subroutine modules. Furthermore, no subroutine module should contain any processing that affects the flow of any other subroutine module. For example, no subroutine module should set a switch that will be tested in another subroutine module.

Although it may be difficult to appreciate the value of flowcharting and modularity since you have probably worked primarily on short programs (if any), the flowchart becomes absolutely essential when a program reaches a certain level of complexity. If a programmer attempts

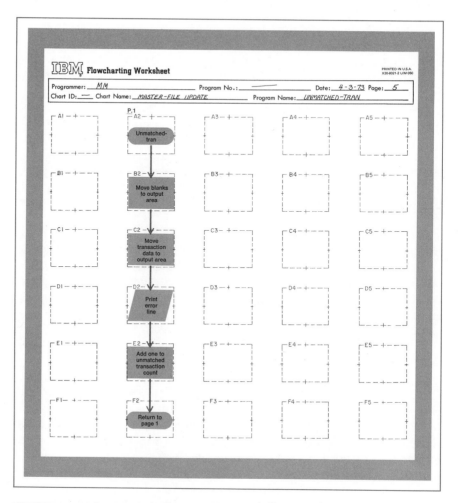

FIGURE 15-3   The unmatched transaction module—
master-file update program

to write a program without using a flowchart (except on the simplest of programs), coding will likely take longer, and testing will almost certainly take longer than if a flowchart were used. As a result, many companies require that flowcharts be completed before any coding is started. Modularity may also be required so that even simple programs are divided into at least five modules: (1) the mainline module, (2) a housekeeping module that does the processing required at the start of the program, (3) at least one input module, (4) at least one output module, and (5) an end-of-job module that does the processing required at the end of the program.

FLOWCHART EXPLANATIONS

The flowcharts in figures 15-1 and 15-2 represent some typical business programs. In the first flowchart, for example, a sales-by-item report is prepared from a file of transaction records. For each group of input records that have the same control field—in this case, item number—one output line is printed, giving the total sales for that item. The input file must be in sequence by control field, and a final total is printed when all of the cards in the input deck have been read. The flowchart in figure 15-1 assumes that a record containing all 9s in the control field indicates there are no more records to be processed.

In box D2, the item number of the first record in each item-number group is stored in a work area. In box J2, the number in this work area is compared to the item numbers of records that follow to determine whether the group number has changed. (OLD:NEW in box J2 means that the old control field in the work area is compared with the control field of the record just read.) If the old value equals the new value (O = N), the totals for the record just read should be added to the group totals (block F2). If the old value is greater than the new (O > N), the last input record is out of sequence. If the old number is less than the new (O < N), it indicates the start of the next group, so the summary line for the present group must be printed (starting in box A4).

As mentioned earlier, the END-SWITCH field is used to indicate when the last record has been read. If it contains an N, the last record hasn't been read. If it contains a Y, it has been read, in which case a summary line for the last item-number group is printed, the switch is tested and found to be Y, the final totals are printed, and the program stops.

Figure 15-2 represents the updating of a sequential master file. This normally takes place as represented by the system flowchart in figure 15-4. The program reads one tape master file, called the old master, and one or more tape transaction files. The output is an updated tape master file, called the new master, plus a printed listing of invalid or unmatched transactions. If a master record has no matching transactions, the record is written unchanged on the new master tape. In this example, the program assumes that a master or transaction record containing all 9s in the control field indicates that there are no more records in the file.

Perhaps the key to the mainline flowchart in figure 15-2 is the decision in box E2. When the control field of the master record is compared with the control field of the transaction record, there are three conditions that can occur. If the control fields are equal (T = M), the transaction is used to update the old master record. If the transaction is greater than the master (T > M), the master record is written in the new file and another master record is read. If the transaction is less than the master (T < M), an unmatched transaction is indicated.

When the end of the old master file is detected (box G3), the program

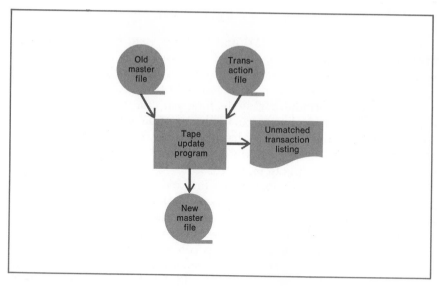

FIGURE 15-4   System flowchart for a master file update

tests to make sure that the last transaction has also been read and processed. If it hasn't been read (the control field isn't equal to 9s), one or
more unmatched transactions are indicated. As a result, the program
lists the unmatched transactions, reads another transaction record, and
tests again to see if a control field containing 9s has been read. If not,
the program loops again. If so, the program ends.

SUMMARY

1. Although from company to company there are variations in the use
of flowcharting rules and symbols, the trend is toward using standards
set by the American National Standards Institute. These standards
give specifications concerning the use of symbols, flowlines, and
methods of cross-referencing between flowcharts within a set of flowcharts.

2. Modular program design refers to dividing a program into independent modules, each consisting of 50 to 200 statements. By keeping
each module independent of the others and by designing a mainline
module to direct the flow to the subroutine modules, coding and testing
a large program becomes more manageable.

FOR REVIEW

setting a switch
modularity
module

mainline module
subroutine module
striping

In chapter 3, you were introduced to the concept of control balancing. In this technique, control totals accumulated manually are compared with totals accumulated by the computer. If they agree, it is assurance that processing has taken place correctly.

In addition to this very basic control over input and output data, many other control methods are used. In this topic, program controls— control routines that are performed within a program—are described. Although all programs do not use all of these routines, a business program will typically include two or more of them.

Sequence Checking

When sequential files are processed, it is usually critical that the input records be in the proper sequence. Thus, all programs processing sequential files will check the control field of each record to make sure that the proper sequence is maintained. This is referred to as sequence checking.

A flowchart for sequence checking is given in figure 15-5. The basic idea is to store the control number of the first card in a work area and to compare subsequent control numbers to this work-area number. If a new control number is greater than the work-area number, the new control number is then stored in the work area and another card is read. If a new control number is less than the work-area number, an out-of-sequence record is indicated and an error message is printed. Needless to say, a sequence-checking routine such as this is normally incorporated into a processing program, rather than being a program in itself as in this illustration.

Field Checking

When a computer performs an arithmetic operation, it is important that the fields being operated upon contain valid numeric data. If they don't, the computer will be unable to execute the instruction, and, in most cases, the program will end prematurely. If, for example, a computer tries to add +123 to ABC12, it will cancel the program because of a programming error. As a result, numeric input fields are commonly checked to make sure they contain valid data. This normally means no blanks within the field and a valid plus or minus sign.

Similarly, alphabetic and alphanumeric fields are often checked for valid characters. For example, an alphanumeric item-number field may require alphabetic characters in the first two positions and unsigned digits in the last three positions.

Code Checking

Codes are commonly used in all computerized input. For example, one character may indicate the type of transaction being processed,

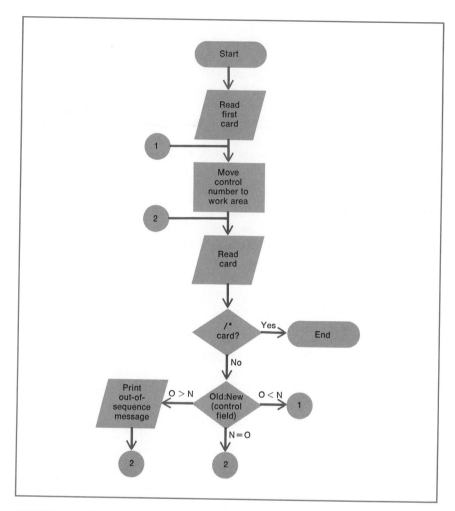

FIGURE 15-5   Sequence checking a card deck

another character may indicate the customer classification. When input records are initially read, these codes are checked to make sure that they are valid. For instance, 2, 3, 5, P, and T may be valid transaction codes, while L, 2, 3, 4, and 5 are valid customer classification codes.

Self-Checking Numbers

A *self-checking number* is a number that has one additional digit—a *check digit*— attached to it as a check on its own accuracy. For example, the account number 34219 might have the check digit 6 attached to it,

Modulus 10 method for determining check digit	
Base number	374229

Step 1 Multiply alternate digits by 2, starting with the units position.	3 7 4 2 2 9
	   2 2 2
	  14 4 18

Step 2 Add digits resulting from step 1 and digits not multiplied in step 1.	3 + 1 + 4 + 4 + 4 + 2 + 1 + 8 = 27
Step 3 Subtract answer from next highest number ending in zero. The result is the check digit.	30 − 27 = 3
Check digit	3
Self-checking number	3742293

FIGURE 15-6   Self-checking numbers

thus making the self-checking number 342196. The digit 6 is derived by a series of calculations performed on the base number 34219. When a self-checking number is read as input to the computer, the computer performs the same series of calculations on the base number and derives what should be the same check digit. If it is the same, it is assurance — usually over 90 percent sure — that the self-checking number has been recorded correctly.

To illustrate, consider one common method of determining check digits, as shown in figure 15-6. This method, called the Modulus 10 method, can be used on numbers consisting of any number of digits. To derive the check digit, these calculations are performed:

1. Alternate digits in the base number are multiplied by 2, starting with the rightmost (units) digit.

2. The digits created in step 1 and those digits not multiplied in step 1 are added together.

3. The total is subtracted from the next highest number ending in zero, thus arriving at the check digit, which becomes the rightmost digit of the self-checking number.

Since the Modulus 10 method will detect over 95 percent of transposition errors — the most common type of keypunching error — the use of self-checking numbers can improve accuracy considerably. Note, for example, that the transposed number 3742239 leads to the incorrect check digit 6; the transposed number 3472293 leads to the incorrect check digit 7. (Remember that the calculations are performed on only the first six digits since the seventh one is the check digit.) Because of the effectiveness of self-checking numbers, they are often used in control fields such as customer, item, or employee number.

Limit Checking

In many input records, certain fields have limits that they should not exceed. For example, the characters for the month in a date field shouldn't exceed 12; the characters for the day shouldn't exceed 31. By checking for known limits, unexpected processing results can be avoided.

Logical Checking

In most programs, there are any number of conditions that logically should never occur. For example, it is illogical that an hourly employee will work over 100 hours in one week or that an appliance store will order 2000 electric stoves. By setting limits based on logic, some of the disastrous computer errors that are so loudly publicized can be eliminated.

If historical data is available when a program is run, it can be used to help set logical limits. When preparing electric bills, for instance, it is unlikely that a customer's usage for one month to the next would double. By comparing the present data with past data, it is possible to question unlikely input values. If the data proves to be correct, even though it is illogical, it can be processed in subsequent runs, but the program must then have some means of getting around the logical check.

Label Checking

When magnetic files such as tape or disk files are used, it is possible for an operator to mount the wrong tape or disk on a device. To guard against this type of error, a tape or disk file commonly contains one or more records identifying its contents. These records, called *labels*, are read and checked at the start of a program to make sure that the right files have been mounted on the proper devices. This process of *label checking* is described in detail in chapters 6 and 7.

At the end of a tape file, there is usually a *trailer label*, which contains a count of the total number of records in the file. By comparing this count with a count accumulated during program execution, a program can be sure that all input records have been read.

CONCLUSION

This has been a brief introduction to some of the common program controls likely to be found in a business program. A good program, which is part of a good system, will include as many of these routines as are applicable to the problem being programmed, thus increasing the accuracy of the data-processing system. On the other hand, a program should not unnecessarily duplicate control routines done in previous processing runs. For example, if an editing program has performed sequence, field, code, self-checking number, and limit checks while creating a transaction file on tape, some of these checks need not be done again when the tape is read as input. However, if input characteristics are critical to a program—for instance, proper file sequence or valid numeric fields—these characteristics should be rechecked regardless of duplication.

SUMMARY

Program controls are designed to detect some of the human errors that can occur within a system. As a result, several different control routines are likely to be found in a typical business program.

FOR REVIEW

program control
sequence checking
self-checking number
check digit
label
label checking
trailer label

The term *computer installation* refers to the EDP department within a company. Although a large percentage of the budget of a computer installation is spent on equipment, the largest portion is spent on personnel. A 1971 survey of the nation's largest computer users, for example, showed that 44.6 percent of the average installation's budget was for personnel, while only 34.2 percent was spent on equipment. Some of the personnel requirements of a computer user are thus described in this chapter.

In general, there are three major types of activities within a computer installation: system analysis, programming, and operations. As a result, a computer user requires one or more employees skilled in each of these disciplines.

System Analysis

The term *system analysis* covers a lot of ground. From the time that a company decides that some particular operation might be a profitable computer application until the time that the application is actually running on the computer, there are many tasks required by the system-analysis function. These tasks include: (1) studying an application or group of applications to determine if computer processing is justifiable; (2) designing a generalized system that will meet the requirements of the applications; (3) making recommendations as to the hardware to be purchased or leased; (4) designing a detailed system flow that makes

PERSONNEL WITHIN
THE COMPUTER
INSTALLATION

use of the available or planned hardware; and (5) planning the installation schedule for the applications.

Three job titles commonly found on the system-analysis staff are system-analysis manager, senior system analyst, and system analyst. The system-analysis manager is in charge of a company's system-analysis activities. The senior system analyst, usually one of the more experienced members of the staff, directs various system-analysis projects. He normally works with one or more system analysts in meeting the objectives of the projects.

Because system analysis has such a major effect on the success of a system, good system analysts are a must for an EDP department. In general, the system analyst must be able to communicate with and get information from employees at all levels within a company—from a clerk to the top executive; he must be familiar with a wide range of equipment and programming support; he must have some background in programming (often, he has worked one or two years as a programmer before becoming an analyst); he must be able to develop plans, solutions, and systems from the available data; and if he has any background in accounting, statistics, or industrial engineering, that helps too. In short, the system analyst should have a broad range of abilities and still be strong enough technically to research hardware or software developments pertinent to the project on which he is working. Because it is difficult to find people with these capabilities, there is a lack of competent system analysts; this has been one of the major limitations to progress within the computer industry.

Programming

If you have read the section on COBOL or FORTRAN, you should be familiar with the duties of a programmer. Within a typical computer installation, however, there are likely to be three different types of programmers. The programmer who writes programs for business applications—such as inventory or payroll programs—is commonly referred to as an *applications programmer*. The other two types of programmers are maintenance and systems programmers.

The *maintenance programmer* is responsible for making changes to programs that are already in use. For example, if a payroll program needs to be modified because of a change in tax laws, a maintenance programmer will be assigned to the job. By using maintenance programmers, applications programmers are free to develop new programs without being interrupted.

The *systems programmer* (also known as a software programmer) writes *systems programs* such as compilers, assemblers, sort programs, and other programs of an operating system. Because these are likely to be written in assembler language and require advanced programming techniques, the job of a systems programmer is considerably more technical than that of an applications programmer. Although systems programs have traditionally been supplied by computer manufacturers and other software suppliers, the majority of large computer users now employ one or more systems programmers of their own. If these programmers don't write complete systems programs, they at least modify the system software supplied to them in order to make it more applicable to the requirements of their company.

Within a programming department, there are also job titles that indicate rank or tenure. For instance, senior programmer, programmer, junior programmer, and programmer trainee are commonly used titles that indicate the amount of experience a programmer has. After a person has done programming for a few years, he can advance in either of two directions: he can advance within the programming department—from junior programmer to programmer to senior programmer to programming manager—or he can switch to the system-analysis department. In some companies, the term programmer/analyst is used to indicate that a person has both system-analysis and programming responsibilities.

Operations

Operations refers to the daily production activities of an EDP department. This includes preparing data (usually, keypunching and verifying), scheduling and controlling the jobs to be run, operating the computer and associated equipment, and keeping a library of system and programming documentation, magnetic tapes, disk packs, and other records essential to the system. The various job titles within the operations department include manager or supervisor of operations, computer operator, punched-card equipment operator, keypunch supervisor, keypunch operator, scheduler, control clerk, and librarian. As you might guess, one of the responsibilities of the control clerk is to record and balance control totals that are kept within the EDP department.

While many of the jobs in operations are narrowly defined and thus routine, that of a computer operator can be quite demanding—particularly, with large computer systems. In addition to loading cards, mounting tapes and disk packs, and operating the computer console, the computer operator must be able to use job-control language and to locate and correct error conditions that occur during processing. Since this often requires knowledge of programming and operating systems, a good computer operator is likely to be promoted to a position as a programmer.

THE ORGANIZATION OF AN EDP DEPARTMENT

An EDP department can be organized in several ways, depending on the size and goals of the department. For example, the EDP department

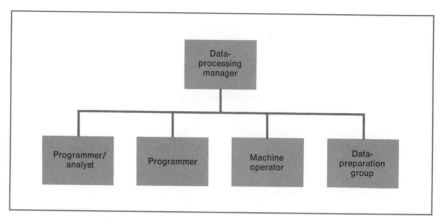

FIGURE 16-1   Organization of a small EDP staff

of a small company may be organized as shown in figure 16-1. This department consists of one programmer/analyst, one programmer, one machine operator, and a data-preparation group—all reporting directly to the data-processing manager.

In contrast, a large computer installation might be organized as shown in figure 16-2. Here, the department manager will likely be referred to as the director of information systems rather than the data-processing manager. Reporting to him are the system-analysis, programming, and operations managers who direct the activities of the department.

Needless to say, there are many other ways in which a department can be organized. It is common, for example, for system analysis and programming to be managed by a systems and programming manager. It is also common for maintenance programmers to report to the operations manager rather than the programming manager. Regardless of the variations, however, figures 16-1 and 16-2 are typical of small and large EDP departments.

DISCUSSION

In addition to the normal computer user such as a bank or wholesale distributor, there are many other types of companies that require people trained in system analysis, programming, and operations. Computer manufacturers, for example, employ thousands of people trained in system analysis as marketing representatives. Software houses employ systems programmers to develop system software that can be marketed to computer users. When one company operates another company's computer system on a fee basis, it is referred to as *facilities management*. Facilities-management companies, therefore, require operations managers and other operations personnel. The advantage of working

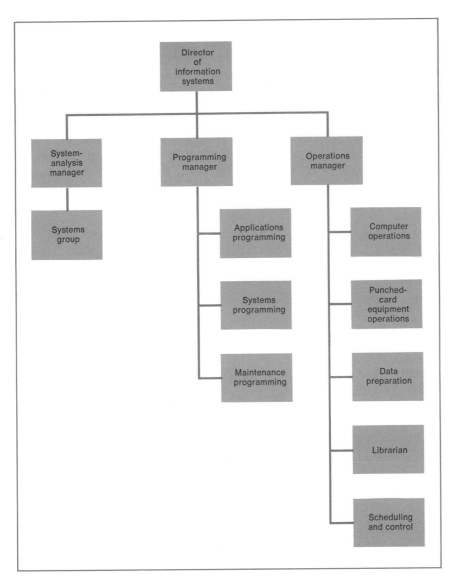

FIGURE 16-2   Organization of a large EDP staff

for companies such as these is that in a relatively short period of time, you are exposed to the data-processing problems of many companies.

Regardless of the type of company, pay levels vary considerably for each kind of job. For example, the range of salaries for programmers in 1971 was from below $6,000 per year to over $16,000 per year, with the largest group being in the $8,000 to $10,000-per-year classification. In general, the pay level for a job depends on two factors: (1) the sophistication of the computer system used and (2) the type of problem or application being worked on. For instance, a programmer writing a real-time production-control program for a large direct-access system will be paid considerably more than a programmer working on a payroll application for a tape system. Similarly, an operator of a large, multiprogrammed disk system will be paid more than an operator of a card system.

SUMMARY

In general, the jobs within an EDP department center around three types of activity: system analysis, programming, and operations. Within any given company, there can be several levels of jobs and pay for each type of activity.

FOR
REVIEW

computer installation
applications programmer
maintenance programmer
systems programmer
systems program
operations
facilities management

IV

COBOL

COMPUTER DATING... IN SEARCH OF THE AMERICAN DREAM

RALPH MASON

CHAPTER SEVENTEEN

In chapter 4, you were introduced to programming concepts that applied to all programming languages. In this chapter, you will be introduced to the COBOL language. Topic 1 presents a COBOL program that includes many of the basic COBOL elements. Then, in topic 2, the remaining basic elements are explained. When you have finished this chapter, you will have covered everything you need to know in order to write complete COBOL programs of considerable complexity.

TOPIC ONE
AN INTRODUCTION TO COBOL PROGRAMMING

As mentioned in chapter 4, COBOL is one of the oldest programming languages, first introduced in 1959. It is also one of the most widely used languages—probably second to FORTRAN in total number of users, but first in number of users for business applications. One of the major attractions of COBOL is that a COBOL compiler is available for nearly all medium- and large-sized business computers. As a result, the COBOL language can be used on most business computers.

Although all COBOL compilers are based on a single set of language specifications, each computer manufacturer's version of COBOL traditionally has had its own peculiarities. Thus, you could not take a COBOL program for one type of computer—say an IBM System/360— and compile it on another manufacturer's system—say a Honeywell 200. Instead, a series of changes would first have to be made to the source program.

In an attempt to standardize COBOL—to make it easier to transfer from one computer to another—the American National Standards Institute studied the problem and in 1968 approved a standard COBOL

BASIC COBOL PROGRAMMING

language. This standard language has specifications at three levels — low, middle, and high — so that standard COBOL can be implemented on computers of varying sizes. For example, the low-level COBOL might be implemented on a computer system with 16,000 storage positions, and the high level on a system with 64,000 storage positions. The low-level American National Standard (ANS) COBOL consists of selected elements from the middle level (so the low level is called a *subset* of the middle level); the middle level is a subset of the high level. Thus, low ANS COBOL can be compiled on a high-level compiler, but high ANS COBOL cannot be compiled on a low- or middle-level compiler.

Regardless of the attempts at standardization, variations from one manufacturer's COBOL to another's still exist. Sometimes these deviations are designed to take advantage of some feature of the manufacturer's equipment that is not provided for by the ANS specifications. Sometimes these deviations are intended to improve upon the standard COBOL at the expense of standardization. The trend, however, is toward more strict application of the ANS specifications.

A SAMPLE ANS COBOL PROGRAM

Figure 17-1 gives the characteristics of an inventory-control program that is to be written in COBOL. The input consists of a deck of balance-forward cards, one card per inventory item. The output of the program is a listing of those items in inventory that need to be reordered. The illustration indicates the card columns of each input field and the print positions for each item to be printed on the output listing. It also gives some sample input and output data. As you can see from the processing specifications, a line is printed whenever the available stock for an item (on hand plus on order) is less than the reorder point. This is basically the same program described in chapter 4, and a partial flowchart for its solution is given in figure 4-4.

After defining the problem and flowcharting a solution for it, the programmer codes this program using a coding form such as the one in figure 17-2. The form in the illustration, in fact, is the first page of the reorder listing program. To distinguish the number zero from the letter O, the programmer adds a slash to the number 0 (∅) wherever it appears. When the program is completed, one source-deck card is keypunched for each line of coding.

If you study the form, you will see that a total of eighty card columns are indicated. The first three columns (1–3) are used for the page number of the coding form; the next three columns are used for the line number of the coding line. Thus, 001020 in the first six columns of a source card represents the line numbered 020 on page 001, and 005010 represents the line numbered 010 on page 005. Although lines can be numbered consecutively such as 001, 002, 003, it is more common to number

Sample input

Field name	Item code	Item description	Unit cost	Unit price	Reorder point	On hand	On order
Card columns	1—5	6—25	26—30	31—35	36—40	41—45	46—50
Card 1	00101	GENERATOR	04000	04000	00100	00070	00050
	00103	HEATER SOLENOID	00330	00440	00050	00034	00000
	03244	GEAR HOUSING	06500	07900	00010	00012	00000
	03981	PLUMB LINE	00210	00240	00015	00035	00000
Card 5	04638	STARTER SWITCH	00900	00980	00030	00016	00000

Sample output

	Item code	Item description	Unit price	Available	Reorder point
Print positions	6—10	16—35	41—46	52—56	62—66
Line 1	103	HEATER SOLENOID	4.40	34	50
	4638	STARTER SWITCH	9.80	16	30
	7846	MANIFOLD GASKET	1.98	52	60
	11946	TRANSFORMER	112.50	10	12
Line 5	16438	CLUTCH BEARING	13.20	5	6

Processing specifications

1. Add on hand to on order to derive available.
2. Print a line on the reorder listing only when available is less than the reorder point.

FIGURE 17-1   The inventory-control program

by tens such as 010, 020, 030. Then, if a line of coding has to be added to a program, it can be done by using a number of appropriate numerical value. For example, line number 165 would fall between 160 and 170.

The last eight columns of the source-deck cards are used to identify the cards. For example, in this program, ORDERLST is punched in columns 73–80 of each card in the source deck. Although the identification columns should indicate the type of program, the punches in these columns do not affect compilation or the resulting object program in any way.

Column 7 of the coding form is used to indicate that certain types of coding lines are continued from the preceding line. This will be explained in topic 2 of this chapter, so you can ignore this column for now.

The actual program is coded in columns 8–72. Within these columns, only column 8, called the A margin, and column 12, called the B margin, require special mention. In general, each line of COBOL coding starts at one of these two margins, depending on the function of the coding. In figure 17-2, the first eight lines of coding start at the A margin and the coding on lines 100, 110, 160, and 170 begins at the B margin. Although it is customary to start lines of coding specified for the A

IBM **COBOL Coding Form**

SYSTEM	PUNCHING INSTRUCTIONS	PAGE 1 OF 5
PROGRAM REØRDER LISTING	GRAPHIC / PUNCH / CARD FORM # *	IDENTIFICATION ORDERLST (73–80)
PROGRAMMER MRM — DATE 3-10-73		

SEQUENCE (PAGE) (SERIAL) | CONT. | A | B | COBOL STATEMENT

```
ØØ1010  IDENTIFICATION DIVISION.
   020  PROGRAM-ID.  INVENTORY-REORDER-LISTING.
   03
   040  ENVIRONMENT DIVISION.
   050  CONFIGURATION SECTION.
   060  SOURCE-COMPUTER.  IBM-360.
   070  OBJECT-COMPUTER.  IBM-360.
   080  INPUT-OUTPUT SECTION.
   090  FILE-CONTROL.
   100      SELECT BAL-FWD-FILE ASSIGN TO SYS005-UR-2540R-S.
   110      SELECT REORDER-LISTING ASSIGN TO SYS006-UR-1403-S.
   12
   130  DATA DIVISION.
   140  FILE SECTION.
   150  FD  BAL-FWD-FILE
   160      LABEL RECORDS ARE OMITTED
   170      DATA RECORD IS BAL-FWD-CARD.
   18
   19
   20
```

*A standard card form, IBM Electro C61897, is available for punching source statements from this form.
Instructions for using this form are given in any IBM COBOL reference manual.
Address comments concerning this form to IBM Corporation, Programming Publications, 1271 Avenue of the Americas, New York, New York 10020.

Form No. X28-1464-4 U/M 025
Printed in U.S.A.

FIGURE 17-2 A COBOL coding form

margin in column 8, most compilers provide leeway for starting any-where between column 8 and column 11. Similarly, most compilers allow B margin coding lines to begin anywhere between column 12 and column 72.

Since columns 1–7 and columns 73–80 of a source deck can be dis-regarded without affecting the program, a COBOL program can be illustrated as shown in figure 17–3. Here, the coding form has been discarded and the A and B margins are indicated by two vertical lines four characters apart. For the remainder of this section, programs will be illustrated in this way. Remember, however, that when you actually code COBOL programs, you use COBOL coding forms.

Take a minute to look at the program in figure 17-3. It is the complete program for printing the reorder listing from the balance-forward cards. It is written for a System/360 computer, but as you will see, only four lines of coding need be changed in order to compile the program on any computer system with a standard COBOL compiler. The spacing be-tween the lines is used simply to set off the various divisions of the program and is at the option of the programmer in any program. If you scan the program, you will see that it is made up of four divisions: the Identification, Environment, Data, and Procedure Divisions. Although the Identification and Environment Divisions are first, the Data and Procedure Divisions are the essence of the program.

THE IDENTIFICATION DIVISION

The Identification Division is used to identify the program. It does not cause any object code to be compiled and requires only two coding lines. In figure 17-3, the programmer has written:

```
IDENTIFICATION DIVISION.
PROGRAM-ID.   INVENTORY-REORDER-LISTING.
```

Except for INVENTORY-REORDER-LISTING, which is the *program name* made up by the programmer, these two coding lines will be the same for all COBOL programs.

The rules for forming a program name in ANS COBOL are as follows:

1. The name must be thirty characters or less and must consist of letters, numbers, and hyphens (-) only.

2. The name cannot begin or end with a hyphen or contain blanks.

Thus, X123, ORDLST, and ORDER-LISTING are valid program names, but LIST-, X$YZ, and ORDER LIST are not. Although X123 is a valid name, program names are usually chosen so that they indicate the nature of the program; for example, INVENTORY-REORDER-LISTING indicates that the program involves a listing of inventory items to be reordered.

```
IDENTIFICATION DIVISION.
PROGRAM-ID.  INVENTORY-REORDER-LISTING.

ENVIRONMENT DIVISION.
CONFIGURATION SECTION.
SOURCE-COMPUTER.  IBM-360.
OBJECT-COMPUTER.  IBM-360.
INPUT-OUTPUT SECTION.
FILE-CONTROL.
    SELECT BAL-FWD-FILE ASSIGN TO SYS005-UR-2540R-S.
    SELECT REORDER-LISTING ASSIGN TO SYS006-UR-1403-S.

DATA DIVISION.
FILE SECTION.
FD  BAL-FWD-FILE
    LABEL RECORDS ARE OMITTED
    DATA RECORD IS BAL-FWD-CARD.
01  BAL-FWD-CARD.
    02  BF-ITEM-CODE      PICTURE IS 9(5).
    02  BF-ITEM-DESC      PICTURE IS A(20).
    02  FILLER            PICTURE IS X(5).
    02  BF-UNIT-PRICE     PICTURE IS 999V99.
    02  BF-REORDER-POINT  PICTURE IS 9(5).
    02  BF-ON-HAND        PICTURE IS 9(5).
    02  BF-ON-ORDER       PICTURE IS 9(5).
    02  FILLER            PICTURE IS X(30).
FD  REORDER-LISTING
    LABEL RECORDS ARE OMITTED
    DATA RECORD IS REORDER-LINE.
01  REORDER-LINE.
    02  FILLER            PICTURE IS X(5).
    02  RL-ITEM-CODE      PICTURE IS Z(5).
    02  FILLER            PICTURE IS X(5).
    02  RL-ITEM-DESC      PICTURE IS A(20).
    02  FILLER            PICTURE IS X(5).
    02  RL-UNIT-PRICE     PICTURE IS ZZZ.99.
    02  FILLER            PICTURE IS X(5).
    02  RL-AVAILABLE      PICTURE IS Z(5).
    02  FILLER            PICTURE IS X(5).
    02  RL-REORDER-POINT  PICTURE IS Z(5).
    02  FILLER            PICTURE IS X(66).
WORKING-STORAGE SECTION.
77  WS-AVAILABLE          PICTURE IS 9(5).
```

FIGURE 17-3 The reorder-listing program in COBOL (Part 1 of 2)

THE ENVIRONMENT DIVISION

The Environment Division of a COBOL program specifies the hardware components that are to be used for the compilation and for the execution of the object program. As a result, this division shows the

```
PROCEDURE DIVISION.
SET-UP.
    OPEN INPUT BAL-FWD-FILE.
    OPEN OUTPUT REORDER-LISTING.
BEGIN.
    READ BAL-FWD-FILE RECORD AT END GO TO END-OF-JOB.
    MOVE BF-ON-HAND TO WS-AVAILABLE.
    ADD BF-ON-ORDER TO WS-AVAILABLE.
    IF WS-AVAILABLE IS LESS THAN BF-REORDER-POINT
        GO TO PRINT-LINE.
    GO TO BEGIN.
PRINT-LINE.
    MOVE SPACES TO REORDER-LINE.
    MOVE BF-ITEM-CODE TO RL-ITEM-CODE.
    MOVE BF-ITEM-DESC TO RL-ITEM-DESC.
    MOVE BF-UNIT-PRICE TO RL-UNIT-PRICE.
    MOVE WS-AVAILABLE TO RL-AVAILABLE.
    MOVE BF-REORDER-POINT TO RL-REORDER-POINT.
    WRITE REORDER-LINE.
    GO TO BEGIN.
END-OF-JOB.
    CLOSE BAL-FWD-FILE.
    CLOSE REORDER-LISTING.
    STOP RUN.
```

FIGURE 17-3   (Part 2 of 2)

greatest variance from one computer manufacturer to another. When converting a COBOL program from one computer system to another, this division must always be changed.

The Environment Division for the reorder-listing program is as follows:

```
ENVIRONMENT DIVISION.
CONFIGURATION SECTION.
SOURCE-COMPUTER.   IBM-360.
OBJECT-COMPUTER.   IBM-360.
INPUT-OUTPUT SECTION.
FILE-CONTROL.
    SELECT BAL-FWD-FILE ASSIGN TO SYS005-UR-2540R-S.
    SELECT REORDER-LISTING ASSIGN TO SYS006-UR-1403-S.
```

This format will be the same for all programs that use card input and printer output. As a result, though it may look confusing, this division is quite routine.

In the CONFIGURATION SECTION, SOURCE-COMPUTER specifies the computer that will be used for the compilation. In most cases, this will be the same as the computer used for executing the object program, known as the OBJECT-COMPUTER. In the example, the computer used is the System/360, always indicated as IBM-360. If you are writing a program for the NCR Century 200, this section would read:

```
CONFIGURATION SECTION.
SOURCE-COMPUTER.   CENTURY-200.
OBJECT-COMPUTER.   CENTURY-200.
```

Since you will generally be writing all of your programs for the same computer, once you learn how to code these statements, they will be the same for each program.

In the INPUT-OUTPUT SECTION, the programmer gives symbolic *file names* to the I/O devices that will be used by the program. For example, the first SELECT statement assigns the name BAL-FWD-FILE to the IBM 2540 Card Reader, which will read the file of input cards. The format for the SELECT statement is as follows:

SELECT file-name ASSIGN TO system-name.

Here, the capitalized words are always the same (they are part of the COBOL language), while the lower-case words represent names that are assigned by the programmer.

When a programmer makes up a file name, it must conform to these rules:

1. It must be thirty characters or less and must consist entirely of letters, numbers, and hyphens.

2. It must not end or begin with a hyphen and cannot contain blanks.

3. It must contain at least one letter, and in low-level ANS COBOL must start with a letter.

These same rules apply when forming several other kinds of names in COBOL and, except for the requirement of at least one letter, are the same rules used in forming program names.

The *system name* given in the SELECT statement specifies the I/O device that is to be used for a file. Since this name must meet the specifications of the computer manufacturer, system names must be changed as you move from one type of computer to another. Before writing a COBOL program, then, you will need to find out the system names for the I/O devices that your program will use.

The system names used in SELECT statements for the System/360 vary depending on the type of operating system used. (See chapter 14, Operating Systems and Job-Control Language.) For the IBM Disk Operating System (described in chapter 14), the system name has this format when using card or printer devices:

SYSnnn-UR-device-S

(Here again, the capital letters are always the same, the small letters are replaced by specifications supplied by the programmer.) For device, the programmer inserts the number of the I/O device that is to be used — such as 2540R for the IBM 2540 Card Reader, 2540P for the IBM 2540 Card Punch, 1403 for the IBM 1403 Printer, or 2501 for the IBM 2501 Card Reader. The SYS number is simply a number between SYS000 and SYS221 — a number used by the Disk Operating System. For now, code SELECT statements by using consecutive SYS numbers for each I/O device. Because SYS000 through SYS004 often have special assignments, begin with SYS005 for the first device, SYS006 for the second device, and so on. In this book, whenever coding examples for the System/360 are given, the system name will have the format used by the Disk Operating System.

The second SELECT statement gives a file name to the listing that will be printed on the IBM 1403 Printer. The system name in this statement is

SYS006-UR-1403-S

where 1403 represents the number of the device used. If a different model printer is to be used, the number in the system name would be changed accordingly. Although a printer listing isn't commonly thought of as a file, in COBOL it is, and each line on the listing is considered to be a record in the file. The file name in this statement is REORDER-LISTING.

For other computers, the Environment Division will use different computer and system names. For example, the Environment Division for the same program on a Burroughs B2500 might read as follows:

```
ENVIRONMENT DIVISION.
CONFIGURATION SECTION.
SOURCE-COMPUTER.  B-2500.
OBJECT-COMPUTER.  B-2500.
INPUT-OUTPUT SECTION.
FILE-CONTROL.
      SELECT BAL-FWD-FILE ASSIGN TO READER.
      SELECT REORDER-LISTING ASSIGN TO PRINTER.
```

For any computer, you must use the exact computer and system name formats specified for the compiler that is used.

THE DATA DIVISION

The DATA DIVISION can consist of two sections. The first, called the FILE SECTION, gives the characteristics of the input and output files and records. The WORKING-STORAGE SECTION describes the other fields of storage required by the program.

The file and record descriptions for the balance-forward cards are as follows:

```
FD  BAL-FWD-FILE
    LABEL RECORDS ARE OMITTED
    DATA RECORD IS BAL-FWD-CARD.
01  BAL-FWD-CARD.
    02  BF-ITEM-CODE      PICTURE IS 9(5).
    02  BF-ITEM-DESC      PICTURE IS A(20).
    02  FILLER            PICTURE IS X(5).
    02  BF-UNIT-PRICE     PICTURE IS 999V99.
    02  BF-REORDER-POINT  PICTURE IS 9(5).
    02  BF-ON-HAND        PICTURE IS 9(5).
    02  BF-ON-ORDER       PICTURE IS 9(5).
    02  FILLER            PICTURE IS X(30).
```

FD stands for file description and is followed by the file name that was originally created in the SELECT statement of the Environment Division. The next two lines provide information about the file.

LABEL RECORDS ARE OMITTED is required for every card and printer file. It means that the file has neither beginning or ending labels. In contrast, tape and direct-access files usually do have labels.

The DATA RECORD IS statement assigns a symbolic *record name*, BAL-FWD-CARD, to the card input record. The rules for forming a record name are the same as those for forming a file name—up to thirty letters, numbers, or hyphens and containing at least one letter. In low-level COBOL, the letter must be at the start of the record name.

The line starting with 01 begins the description of the card record. The 01 level number indicates that the name following is the name for an entire record—namely, BAL-FWD-CARD, originally created by the programmer in the DATA RECORD IS statement.

The 02 level numbers indicate that the lines describe fields within the 01 record. Following the 02 numbers are *data names*, which are made up using the rules for file or record names, or the word FILLER, which is used for those fields or card columns that are not used by the program. For example, the first two 02 lines give the data names BF-ITEM-CODE and BF-ITEM-DESC to the item-code and item-description fields of the input cards. The third 02 line, which is FILLER, indicates that the third field in the input card will not be used by the program. If you refer to figure 17-1, you will see that the third field is the unit-cost field, which is not required on the output report.

Although the programmer could have used names such as S241 and B11 for item code and item description, he made up names that imply their use. In this program, BF in a name refers to the input file—Balance Forward—and the remainder of the name refers to the field. Thus, BF-ITEM-DESC indicates the item-description field in the balance-forward file. This is a common naming technique.

One point to remember when creating names such as file names, record names, or data names is that you must avoid duplicating COBOL *reserved words.* For example, the words SELECT, LABEL, RECORDS, ARE, and OMITTED are reserved words—words that are a part of the COBOL language. As a result, you cannot use any of these for a name that you make up. If LABEL is used as a file name, for instance, the COBOL compiler will diagnose an error. Appendix C contains a complete list of reserved words.

The PICTURE IS clauses that follow the data names give the characteristics of the fields. For example, 9(5) means that the field is numeric and consists of five columns. A(20) means that the field is alphabetic and consists of twenty columns. The X(5) in the third 02 line means that the next five columns could be either alphabetic or numeric.

Do you understand so far? The data names give each of the fields in the card a symbolic name that can be used later in the Procedure Division. The PICTURE IS clauses, which may start one or more spaces after the data names, indicate the nature of the data and the size of the field.

Now, look a little further. The picture for the field named BF-UNIT-PRICE is 999V99. This means that the field is five columns long (there are five 9s) and contains numeric data with a decimal point two places from the right. In other words, a 9 indicates one numeric column and the V indicates the position of the assumed decimal point. (Remember that the decimal point usually isn't punched in an input card.)

If you add up the number of columns indicated in the PICTURE clauses for the fields of the card record, you will find that there are eighty. This is reasonable since the input card contains eighty columns of data.

The next file description is for the report that is to be printed on the printer. Its coding lines are as follows:

```
FD   REORDER-LISTING
     LABEL RECORDS ARE OMITTED
     DATA RECORD IS REORDER-LINE.
```

Except for the file name, REORDER-LISTING, and the record name, REORDER-LINE, the three lines of coding are exactly like those for the card input file.

These lines of coding follow the FD for the reorder listing:

```
01   REORDER-LINE.
     02   FILLER             PICTURE IS X(5).
     02   RL-ITEM-CODE       PICTURE IS Z(5).
     02   FILLER             PICTURE IS X(5).
     02   RL-ITEM-DESC       PICTURE IS A(20).
     02   FILLER             PICTURE IS X(5).
     02   RL-UNIT-PRICE      PICTURE IS ZZZ.99.
     02   FILLER             PICTURE IS X(5).
     02   RL-AVAILABLE       PICTURE IS Z(5).
     02   FILLER             PICTURE IS X(5).
     02   RL-REORDER-POINT   PICTURE IS Z(5).
     02   FILLER             PICTURE IS X(66).
```

As you can see, the 02 levels and the PICTURE clauses define the fields of the printed line just as they did the fields of the input cards. The only new symbols used are the Z as in Z(5) and the decimal point as in ZZZ.99. Z(5) means that a five-digit numeric field is to be printed and the high-order zeros should be zero-suppressed. ZZZ.99 means that a five-digit numeric field is going to be printed with two decimal places and a decimal point. The high-order zeros to the left of the decimal point are to be zero-suppressed. Thus, the number 00718 will print as 7.18. The data names in these descriptions begin with RL, which refers to the file name, REORDER-LISTING.

The total number of characters in the PICTURE clauses for the fields in the printer area add up to the number of print positions on the printer —in this case, 132. The number of print positions, of course, depends on the model of the printer used. Notice that the FILLER lines in the printer description determine the spacing of the output report.

The WORKING-STORAGE SECTION of the Data Division defines all other data fields that are to be used by the program. For this program, the only field required is the "available" field. It is described as follows:

```
WORKING-STORAGE SECTION.
77   WS-AVAILABLE              PICTURE IS 9(5).
```

Once again, the 9(5) indicates that the field is a five-position numeric field. WS in the data name refers to Working Storage. The level number 77 is used because this is an independent storage field. Unlike a field such as BF-ITEM-CODE, WS-AVAILABLE is not a part of a record and bears no relationship to any other fields in the program. Nevertheless, it is required by the program in order to store the sum of the on-hand and on-order fields. The level number 77 cannot be used in the file section.

THE PROCEDURE DIVISION

By the time the programmer is ready to code the PROCEDURE DIVISION, he has made up the names that are to be used in his symbolic instructions. The only names he needs to create are *procedure names* that serve as paragraph names for certain sequences of instructions. A procedure name always starts in the A margin of the coding form. Thus, in figure 17-3, SET-UP, BEGIN, PRINT-LINE, and END-OF-JOB are procedure names. These names are formed using the same rules as for file names with one exception: they need not contain any letters.

The lines of coding that start at the B margin of the Procedure Division are COBOL statements that specify operations that are to take place on the fields, records, and files previously defined. These symbolic statements follow consistent formats, some of which are given in figure 17-4. To use any of these statements, the programmer substitutes the names of the files, records, and fields that are to be operated upon.

```
                    PROCEDURE DIVISION FORMATS

  I/O Statements:
        OPEN INPUT file-name.
        OPEN OUTPUT file-name.
        READ file-name RECORD AT END any-statement.
        WRITE record-name.
        CLOSE file-name.

  Data-Movement Statements:
        MOVE data-name-1 TO data-name-2.
        MOVE SPACES TO data-name.
        MOVE ZEROS TO data-name.

  Arithmetic Statements:
        ADD data-name-1 TO data-name-2.
        ADD data-name-1 TO data-name-2 GIVING data-name-3.
        SUBTRACT data-name-1 FROM data-name-2.
        SUBTRACT data-name-1 FROM data-name-2 GIVING data-name-3.
        MULTIPLY data-name-1 BY data-name-2.
        MULTIPLY data-name-1 BY data-name-2 GIVING data-name-3.
        DIVIDE data-name-1 INTO data-name-2.
        DIVIDE data-name-1 INTO data-name-2 GIVING data-name-3.

  Logic or Sequence-Control Statements:
        IF data-name-1 IS GREATER THAN data-name-2 any-statement.
        IF data-name-1 IS LESS THAN data-name-2 any-statement.
        IF data-name-1 IS EQUAL TO data-name-2 any-statement.
        GO TO procedure-name.

  Miscellaneous Statements:
        STOP RUN.
```

FIGURE 17-4   Statement formats

As you can see, all of the statements end with a period, which must be followed by at least one space. The problem for the beginning programmer, then, is to learn the function of each of these instructions.

The first procedure or paragraph in the program is named SET-UP and consists of these coding lines:

```
SET-UP
    OPEN INPUT BAL-FWD-FILE.
    OPEN OUTPUT REORDER-LISTING.
```

OPEN statements are required for each file that is to be read or written by a program. Therefore, the OPEN statements usually are written at the start of the program. If you look at the formats for the OPEN statement in figure 17-4, you will see how the actual statements above relate to the format. The programmer simply substitutes in the OPEN statements the file names that are defined in the Environment Division. The word INPUT is used for an input file; the word OUTPUT for an output file.

Although the OPEN statements are required, they actually don't cause any processing to be done for card or printer files. They do, however, become important for tape and direct-access files.

The next procedure of the program is named BEGIN and consists of the following:

```
BEGIN.
    READ BAL-FWD-FILE RECORD AT END GO TO END-OF-JOB.
    MOVE BF-ON-HAND TO WS-AVAILABLE.
    ADD BF-ON-ORDER TO WS-AVAILABLE.
    IF WS-AVAILABLE IS LESS THAN BF-REORDER-POINT
        GO TO PRINT-LINE.
    GO TO BEGIN.
```

The first statement reads one record (one punched card), but if there are no more cards to be processed (AT END), the program branches to the procedure named END-OF-JOB. (The last card in an input deck on System/360 must contain a slash in column 1 and an asterisk in column 2 for the AT END clause to function properly. Other systems have other rules for the last card in the input deck.)

The MOVE statement that follows the READ statement causes the data from the field named BF-ON-HAND to be moved to the field named WS-AVAILABLE. After the instruction is executed, both fields will contain the data originally contained in BF-ON-HAND.

The ADD instruction of this procedure causes the contents of BF-ON-ORDER to be added to the contents of WS-AVAILABLE. The result replaces the data originally contained in WS-AVAILABLE. The following is an example, using the data for the first card in figure 17-1:

Field Name:	BF-ON-ORDER	WS-AVAILABLE
Contents Before:	00050	00070
Contents After:	00050	00120

In general, there are two formats for each type of arithmetic statement (see figure 17-4). In the first format, the result of the arithmetic operation replaces the contents of the second field named (data-name-2), while the contents of the first field named is unchanged. In the second format, which uses GIVING and a third data name, neither data-name-1 or data-name-2 is changed, and the result of the arithmetic operation is placed in data-name-3. Thus, the statement

ADD BF-ON-HAND BF-ON-ORDER GIVING WS-AVAILABLE

would execute this way:

Field Name:	BF-ON-HAND	BF-ON-ORDER	WS-AVAILABLE
Before:	00070	00050	?
After:	00070	00050	00120

By using GIVING, the instruction has the effect of a move and an add instruction.

This same idea applies when using SUBTRACT, MULTIPLY, and DIVIDE statements. However, it should be noted that the remainder in a DIVIDE statement is lost. Thus,

DIVIDE MONTHS INTO TOTAL

executes in this way:

Field Name:	MONTHS	TOTAL
Before:	10	23
After:	10	02

and

DIVIDE MONTHS INTO TOTAL GIVING AVERAGE

executes in this way:

Field Name:	MONTHS	TOTAL	AVERAGE
Before:	10	23	?
After:	10	23	02

In this second case, if you needed the remainder, you could multiply AVERAGE by MONTHS and subtract it from TOTAL.

The IF statement is the logic statement of the COBOL program. It compares two fields, and then continues based on the results of the comparison. It is comparable to the combination of a compare and a branch instruction in machine language. In the inventory program, if WS-AVAILABLE is less than BF-REORDER-POINT, the program branches to the procedure named PRINT-LINE. If it is not less, the program continues with the next instruction in sequence. For the first card in figure 17-1, the program would not branch to the procedure named PRINT-LINE because WS-AVAILABLE is not less than BF-REORDER-POINT. (Since this IF statement will not fit on one coding line, two coding lines are used.)

The GO TO statement unconditionally branches to the paragraph named BEGIN. In other words, if available isn't less than the reorder point, the program goes back and reads another input card. You have already seen the GO TO statement in the READ and IF statement of this program.

The procedure named PRINT-LINE, which moves the necessary data to the printer record and then prints a line on the printer, is as follows:

```
PRINT-LINE.
    MOVE SPACES TO REORDER-LINE.
    MOVE BF-ITEM-CODE TO RL-ITEM-CODE.
    MOVE BF-ITEM-DESC TO RL-ITEM-DESC.
    MOVE BF-UNIT-PRICE TO RL-UNIT-PRICE.
    MOVE WS-AVAILABLE TO RL-AVAILABLE.
    MOVE BF-REORDER-POINT TO RL-REORDER-POINT.
    WRITE REORDER-LINE.
    GO TO BEGIN.
```

The first statement of this paragraph

```
MOVE SPACES TO REORDER-LINE
```

simply does what it says: it puts spaces or blanks in all 132 positions of the printer output area. As a result, it clears the area of any data remaining from a previous program or from a previous line of printing. A statement such as this is commonly required prior to statements that move data to an output record area. As you can see from the formats in figure 17-4, you can move ZEROS to a field by using a similar format. (In low-level COBOL, the words SPACE and ZERO—not SPACES and ZEROS—must be used, even though as many spaces or zeros are moved as the receiving field requires.)

After the output record is cleared, a series of MOVE statements move the data to the output record. These statements indicate the power of the MOVE statement in COBOL. If zero suppression or the insertion of a decimal point is necessary when a field is moved, it is accomplished with the MOVE statement. For example, when BF-ITEM-CODE is moved to RL-ITEM-CODE, leading zeros are suppressed as follows:

Field:	BF-ITEM-CODE	RL-ITEM-CODE
PICTURE:	9(5)	Z(5)
Before:	00103	?????
After:	00103	103

When BF-UNIT-PRICE is moved to RL-UNIT-PRICE, a decimal point is inserted and the leading zeros before the decimal point are suppressed, as shown in this example:

Field:	BF-UNIT-PRICE	RL-UNIT-PRICE
PICTURE:	999V99	ZZZ.99
Before:	00449	??????
After:	00449	4.49

If 00005 were moved instead of 00449, RL-UNIT-PRICE would print as: .05. As you can see, the results of a COBOL move depend on the PICTUREs given for each of the fields involved in the instruction.

When using the MOVE statement, be sure that the fields being moved are consistent. Both fields should be the same size and contain the same type of data—alphabetic, alphanumeric, or numeric. (Later, you can find out what happens when fields of different sizes are involved in a MOVE statement and you may want to use them.)

Many COBOL manuals classify the data items described in the Data Division into these groups:

1. Alphabetic items   PICTURE consists of As only.
2. Alphanumeric items   PICTURE consists of Xs only.
3. Numeric items   PICTURE consists of 9s and Vs.
4. Numeric edited items   PICTURE consists of 9s, Zs, and decimal points.

SENDING ITEM	RECEIVING ITEM			
	Alphabetic	Alphanumeric	Numeric	Numeric Edited
Alphabetic	OK	OK	Illegal	Illegal
Alphanumeric	OK	OK	Illegal	Illegal
Numeric	Illegal	Whole numbers only	OK	OK
Numeric Edited	Illegal	OK	Illegal	Illegal

The above table uses this terminology to indicate which type of field can be moved to which type of field. As you can see, it is always an error to move an alphabetic field to a numeric field and vice versa. When moving a numeric field to a numeric edited field, the number of digits (9s) in the sending field should be the same as the number of digits (9s or Zs) in the receiving field.

The WRITE statement causes one line to be printed and the form to be moved up one space. In other words, after all the fields are moved to the printer output record, the output line is printed. Then, the GO TO statement returns the program to the procedure named BEGIN.

The END-OF-JOB procedure, which is branched to when there are no more cards to be processed, consists of these statements:

```
END-OF-JOB
        CLOSE BAL-FWD-FILE.
        CLOSE REORDER-LISTING.
        STOP RUN.
```

Just as files must be OPENed at the start of the program, they must be CLOSEd at the end. The real significance of the CLOSE statement, like the OPEN, pertains to tape and direct-access files. STOP RUN means that the program has finished, and the computer system should go on to the next program.

CONCLUSION

Because the System/360 program illustrated in this topic is written in ANS COBOL, it could be compiled on any computer that has an ANS compiler. In order to do so, only the shaded words in the Environment Division that follows would have to be changed.

```
ENVIRONMENT DIVISION.
CONFIGURATION SECTION.
SOURCE-COMPUTER.    IBM-360.
OBJECT-COMPUTER.    IBM-360.
INPUT-OUTPUT SECTION.
FILE-CONTROL.
        SELECT BAL-FWD-FILE ASSIGN TO SYS005-UR-2540R-S.
        SELECT REORDER-LISTING ASSIGN TO SYS006-UR-1403-S.
```

The computer name in the source and object computer lines would have to be changed. In addition, the system names in the SELECT statements for the card and printer files would have to be changed.

As you can see from this program, the Identification and Environment Divisions are routine parts of the COBOL program. The difficulties are encountered in defining the data fields in the Data Division and in writing the processing and logic statements of the Procedure Division.

Although this inventory-control program is quite simplified, it does present many of the basic COBOL elements. With just a few additions, you will know all of the elements required for writing a program of great complexity.

One thing I haven't done is give all the rules that apply to COBOL programs or describe all the ways that each COBOL statement can be written. However, if you use this sample program as a guideline for the programs you write, I doubt that you'll violate any of the rules that haven't been mentioned.

After a program is coded, the programmer usually *desk-checks* it by studying either the interpreted source cards or an 80-80 listing of the cards as illustrated in figure 4-14. After all the errors discovered during desk checking are corrected, the program is ready for compilation. During compilation, the COBOL compiler prints a program listing, much like an 80-80 listing, followed by a list of errors detected during compilation. This error listing, called a *diagnostic listing*, is used by the programmer to make additional corrections to the source deck. Then the program is recompiled, and, if diagnostic messages appear again, the correction procedure is repeated. Depending on the compiler used, the diagnostic messages vary from being quite brief and confusing to quite understandable. In either case, it is the programmer's job to decode the error messages and make the necessary corrections.

After an error-free compilation is completed, the object program is ready to be tested by executing the program using *test data*. If the output of the test run and the expected output do not agree, one or more errors (bugs) are indicated, and the programmer must *debug* the program. During this stage, the programmer must determine what type of error in the source deck could have led to the output error. The better his deductive powers, the faster he will debug his program. When the results of the test run agree with the expected results, the program is considered to be finished.

1. One purpose of standard COBOL (ANS COBOL) is to allow a computer user to easily switch from one computer to another. If only standard COBOL elements are used, a source program for one manufacturer's computer can be compiled on another manufacturer's computer, provided the necessary changes are made to the Environment Division. The second computer, however, must have an ANS COBOL compiler at the same level or at a higher level than the first computer.

2. When coding, it is important to start each line at the correct margin of the coding form. Some types of lines must start at the A margin (column 8); and some must start at the B margin (column 12).

3. All COBOL programs consist of four divisions: Identification, Environment, Data, and Procedure. The first three are relatively routine—identifying the program, specifying the hardware to be used, and describing the input and output files and records—while the fourth, the Procedure Division, specifies the required operations and logic.

subset
A margin
B margin
program name
file name
system name
record name
data name
reserved word

procedure name
alphabetic item
alphanumeric item
numeric item
numeric edited item
desk checking
diagnostic listing
test data
debug

TOPIC TWO

BASIC COBOL ELEMENTS

In topic 1 you were introduced to the basic structure of the COBOL program. In this topic, you will build on that base with some additional COBOL elements. This topic describes how COBOL is used for punching card output, for varying the spacing on a printed form, and so on.

PUNCHING CARDS

In COBOL, the READ and WRITE statements are used for almost all input and output operations. The READ is used for an input operation; the WRITE for an output operation. The only way you can tell which device is actually being used is by referring to the corresponding SELECT statement in the Environment Division. For example,

WRITE PAYROLL-RECORD

could refer to a printed line, a punched card, a magnetic tape, or a magnetic disk. However, the following SELECT statement and file description would indicate that it is a card-punching operation using the IBM 2540 Card Punch:

```
ENVIRONMENT DIVISION.
. . .
. . .
      SELECT PAYROLL-FILE ASSIGN TO SYS005-UR-2540P-S.
DATA DIVISION.
FILE SECTION.
      . . .

FD PAYROLL-FILE
      LABEL RECORDS ARE OMITTED
      DATA RECORD IS PAYROLL-RECORD.
```

On the System/360, 2540P indicates the card punch. On other systems, the system name for the card punch could be PUNCH, NCR686-301, and so on.

To code punched-card output, then, you write the statements just as you would if coding for printer output. The differences are (1) the device number used in the SELECT statement and (2) the number of positions allotted to the output record (80 characters for a punched card instead of 132 as for the 1403 printer).

SPACING THE PRINTED FORM

In many applications, the vertical spacing of a printed form must be varied. For example, when printing an invoice, the customer name and address is printed, several lines are skipped to the body of the form where one or more body lines are printed, several more lines are skipped and the total line is printed, and then the form is skipped to the heading of the next invoice. In COBOL, this skipping is done by using the following formats of the WRITE statement:

1. WRITE record-name AFTER ADVANCING integer LINES.
2. WRITE record-name AFTER ADVANCING data-name LINES.

If the ADVANCING option isn't used, the COBOL compiler automatically provides for single spacing.

In the first format, the integer must be a positive number. (An integer is simply a whole number.) When the statement is executed, the form in the printer moves up as many lines as indicated before the output record is printed.

In the second format, the WRITE statement uses a data name described in the Working Storage section of the Data Division. Spacing of the form, then, depends on the value of the field at the time that the WRITE statement is executed. For example,

```
WRITE PAYROLL-RECORD AFTER ADVANCING
      CONTROL-FIELD LINES
```

causes triple spacing if CONTROL-FIELD contains a 3 at the time of execution. The field must always contain a positive integer.

When using the ADVANCING option of the WRITE statement, the programmer must remember two other requirements. First, if AFTER ADVANCING appears in one WRITE statement for a file, it must be used in all of the WRITE statements for the file. Second, on the System/360, one extra position must be described in the record description for the printed line. This extra storage position must be the first position of the record description and must not be used by the program since it is used for controlling the spacing of the form. When the line is printed, the contents of this storage position will not be printed. For example, the record for the 1403 printer must be 133 instead of 132 positions long. The first position should be described as FILLER with a PICTURE of X. Note that this second requirement is an IBM specification, not a specification of ANS COBOL. Thus, an extra position is not required for many other versions of standard COBOL.

DATA DIVISION ELEMENTS

Level Numbers

In topic 1, 01 and 02 level numbers were used in the Data Division to describe the fields within a record. Additional level numbers are used to describe fields within fields—such as month, day, and year fields within the larger date field. Consider, then, the following description of an accounts receivable record:

```
01  CUSTOMER-RECORD.
    02  CUSTOMER-NUMBER        PICTURE IS 9(5).
    02  CUSTOMER-NAME          PICTURE IS X(20).
    02  SALESMAN-CODE.
        03  BRANCH-OFFICE      PICTURE IS 999.
        03  SALESMAN-NUMBER    PICTURE IS 9(4).
    02  INVOICE-DATA.
        03  INVOICE-NUMBER     PICTURE IS 9(5).
        03  INVOICE-DATE.
            04  MONTH          PICTURE IS 99.
            04  DAY            PICTURE IS 99.
            04  YEAR           PICTURE IS 99.
        03  INVOICE-AMOUNT     PICTURE IS 9999V99.
    02  FILLER                 PICTURE IS X(31).
```

If these are the descriptions for the fields of an input card, the SALESMAN-CODE field is in card columns 26–32, with columns 26–28 representing the number of the branch office and columns 29–32 representing the salesman's number. Similarly, the INVOICE-DATE field is six columns long, two for month, two for day, and two for year. Notice that PICTUREs are used only for *elementary items*—data fields that are not broken down any further. *Group items*—fields that have fields within them—cannot have PICTURE clauses.

Depending on the compiler, you can use level numbers from 01 to 10 (low ANS COBOL) or from 01 to 49 (middle and high ANS COBOL) group items. As long as one level number is larger than a preceding level number, it is considered to be part of the larger field. As a result, instead of consecutive level numbers, you can use numbers such as 02, 04, 06, and 08 to show fields within fields. By using a group item such as INVOICE-DATA as well as elementary items such as INVOICE-NUMBER and INVOICE-AMOUNT, you can operate on the entire field or any of its parts when writing statements in the Procedure Division.

VALUE Clauses

Many programs require fields that have a certain starting or constant value. In COBOL, these initial values are given in the Data Division using VALUE clauses. For example, the following description in the Working Storage Section of a program gives the field named INTEREST-RATE a value of .005:

```
77  INTEREST-RATE PICTURE IS V999 VALUE IS .005.
```

In this form of the VALUE clause, any numeric value up to eighteen digits long can be used. The value can have a leading plus or minus sign, as in +.005 or −32, and it can contain a decimal point. If the value is a whole number, a decimal point should not be used. While it isn't necessary to use the same number of decimal positions and digits in the VALUE clause as in the PICTURE clause, it is a good programming habit and may lead to a more efficient object program. (Needless to say, a VALUE clause must be consistent with the PICTURE clause as to the type of data. It would be an error if a PICTURE of A(4) was given a VALUE of 1225.)

In the example above, .005 is called a *numeric literal*. The only characters that can be used in a numeric literal are the digits 0 through 9, the decimal point, and a leading plus or minus sign.

A VALUE clause can also be used to give non-numeric values to a field in storage. In this case, a *non-numeric literal* is used as in the following:

```
02   TITLE PICTURE IS X(16)
              VALUE IS 'INVENTORY REPORT'.
```

The non-numeric literal is 'INVENTORY REPORT' and all characters between the quotation marks (') are stored in the field named TITLE. In other words, TITLE is given an initial value of INVENTORY REPORT. Because the quotation mark is used to mark the beginning and end of a non-numeric literal, it cannot be used within the literal. All other characters, however, can be used.

When writing non-numeric literals that are too long for one coding line, column 7 of the coding form is used. For example, the following is a continued literal:

```
A    B
     02   TITLE PICTURE IS X(34) VALUE IS 'LISTING OF RECORDS IN A
-    |'MASTER FILE'.
```

Notice that a hyphen is used in column 7 of the continuation line and the quotation mark is repeated on the second line of coding. The literal expressed in these coding lines is:

```
LISTING OF RECORDS IN A MASTER FILE.
```

A VALUE clause can also be used with the COBOL words SPACES or ZEROS. Thus,

```
77   WS-AMOUNT PICTURE IS 9(4) VALUE IS ZEROS.
```

gives a starting value of zero to the amount field. (Remember in low-level COBOL, the words SPACE and ZERO must be used instead of SPACES and ZEROS.)

Incidentally, in strict ANS COBOL, the double quotation mark ("), rather than the single quotation mark ('), is used for non-numeric literals. However, the single mark is a common substitute since some printers are not equipped to print the double mark. Although either the double or single mark can be used on System/360, the single quotation mark is the more common and thus is used throughout this section.

One of the important uses of VALUE clauses is to store data that is to be printed as the heading of a report. For example, the COBOL statements in figure 17-5 would print this heading before processing any data:

```
                          INVESTMENT  REPORT

      ITEM  NUMBER              ITEM  NAME              INVESTMENT
```

Notice that 133 positions are allotted for the record named INVENTORY-LINE because the ADVANCING option is used.

As you can see from this example, level numbers can be used in the Working Storage Section as well as in the File Section of the Data Division. However, these group descriptions must always come after the 77 level numbers if 77 levels are used. VALUE clauses are not allowed in the File Section of the Data Division.

USAGE Clauses

USAGE clauses are not absolutely necessary in a COBOL program. However, they can significantly affect the efficiency of the object program that is compiled. The USAGE clause allows the programmer to specify the form in which a field of data should be stored.

Although it usually isn't necessary for a COBOL programmer to know how data is actually stored, you should know that most computers store data in more than one form. Normally, a computer stores data in one way when it is not involved in arithmetic operations and in another way when it is. COBOL refers to these forms as DISPLAY and COMPUTATIONAL.

The DISPLAY form of storage means that there is one character of data in each storage position. This is how storage was described in chapter 4.

In the COMPUTATIONAL form, which applies to numeric fields only, more than one digit of a number is stored in a single storage position. On the System/360, for example, a COMPUTATIONAL field in storage is made up of two, four, or eight storage positions. If the number being stored is from one through four digits, two storage positions are required; if from five through nine digits, four storage positions are required; if from ten through eighteen digits, eight storage positions are required. Other computers have different COMPUTATIONAL forms, so the actual number of storage positions required to store a number depends on the computer used.

The two forms of the USAGE clause are as follows:

```
USAGE  IS  DISPLAY
USAGE  IS  COMPUTATIONAL
```

```
ENVIRONMENT DIVISION.
CONFIGURATION SECTION.
SOURCE-COMPUTER.  IBM-360.
OBJECT-COMPUTER.  IBM-360.
...
    ...
    ...


DATA DIVISION.
FILE SECTION.
    ...
    ...
FD  INVENTORY-LISTING
    LABEL RECORDS ARE OMITTED
    DATA RECORD IS INVENTORY-LINE.
01  INVENTORY-LINE.
    02  FILLER         PICTURE IS X(7).
    02  ITEM-NUMBER    PICTURE IS Z(5).
    02  FILLER         PICTURE IS X(6).
    02  ITEM-NAME      PICTURE IS X(20).
    02  FILLER         PICTURE IS X(4).
    02  INVESTMENT     PICTURE IS Z(6).99.
    02  FILLER         PICTURE IS X(82).
WORKING-STORAGE SECTION.
01  HEDDER.
    02  FILLER PICTURE IS X(1).
    02  FILLER PICTURE IS X(15)   VALUE IS SPACES.
    02  FILLER PICTURE IS X(17)   VALUE IS 'INVESTMENT REPORT'
    02  FILLER PICTURE IS X(100) VALUE IS SPACES.
01  COLUMN-HEADINGS.
    02  FILLER PICTURE IS X(1).
    02  FILLER PICTURE IS X(11)   VALUE IS 'ITEM NUMBER'.
    02  FILLER PICTURE IS X(8)    VALUE IS SPACES.
    02  FILLER PICTURE IS X(9)    VALUE IS 'ITEM NAME'.
    02  FILLER PICTURE IS X(11)   VALUE IS SPACES.
    02  FILLER PICTURE IS X(10)   VALUE IS 'INVESTMENT'.
    02  FILLER PICTURE IS X(83)   VALUE IS SPACES.

PROCEDURE DIVISION.
SET-UP.
    OPEN INPUT BALANCE-FORWARD-FILE.
    OPEN OUTPUT INVENTORY-LISTING.
    MOVE HEDDER TO INVENTORY-LINE.
    WRITE INVENTORY-LINE AFTER ADVANCING 1 LINES.
    MOVE COLUMN-HEADINGS TO INVENTORY-LINE.
    WRITE INVENTORY-LINE AFTER ADVANCING 2 LINES.
BEGIN-PROCESSING.
```

FIGURE 17-5   Printing a report heading

The USAGE clause is one of the clauses that can come after a data name, as in the following examples:

```
1.  77   FIELDA USAGE IS COMPUTATIONAL PICTURE IS 9(3)V99.

2.  77   FIELDB PICTURE IS 9(4) VALUE IS 1244
                USAGE IS COMPUTATIONAL.

3.       02  FIELDC PICTURE IS 9(5) USAGE IS DISPLAY.
```

In these examples for the System/360, FIELDA would require four storage positions (five digits), FIELDB would require two storage positions (four digits), and FIELDC would require five storage positions. Notice that the sequence of PICTURE, VALUE, and USAGE clauses is not significant.

Since all arithmetic takes place in the computational form of storage—whether it is specified in a USAGE clause or not—the object program is more efficient if USAGE clauses are used. When arithmetic operations are performed on DISPLAY fields, the data in the fields must be converted to a computational form before the arithmetic can take place. After the arithmetic operation is performed, the result is converted back to the DISPLAY form. It is this double conversion that is inefficient. When USAGE clauses are omitted, all data is stored in the DISPLAY form.

When should you use each of the USAGE forms? For card and printer programs, the rules are simple. Use COMPUTATIONAL for all numeric fields in Working Storage that are going to be involved in arithmetic operations. Use DISPLAY for all other fields. (There are some exceptions to this when using tape and direct-access devices.) Since USAGE IS DISPLAY is assumed by the compiler when the USAGE clause is omitted, most programmers do not bother writing the DISPLAY form of the USAGE clause. Therefore, USAGE IS DISPLAY is not used in this book. The following table summarizes the use of the DISPLAY and COMPUTATIONAL forms:

USAGE	Used For
DISPLAY	1. Card input field 2. Card output field 3. Printer output field 4. Non-numeric field in Working Storage 5. Numeric field in Working Storage not involved in arithmetic or compare operations
COMPUTATIONAL	Numeric field in Working Storage that is involved in an arithmetic or compare operation

When the data from a field of one USAGE is moved to a field of another USAGE, the data is converted to the form of the receiving field. As a result, the data in a field can be converted from one form to another by using the MOVE statement.

Signed Numbers

In many applications, input data may be either plus or minus. A card input field is considered negative, for instance, when the right-most column of the field contains an X-punch in addition to a digit punch. If an amount field in columns 41–45 of a card contains the digits 12366 along with an X-punch in column 45, the data is read into storage as −12366. In many programs, it is also possible that the result of a calculation will be negative − if 5 is subtracted from 4, the answer is −1.

In COBOL, an S must be used in the PICTURE of any input or working storage field that may be either plus or minus. The following are examples:

```
02  AMOUNT        PICTURE IS S9(4)V99.

77  NET-PAY      PICTURE IS S999V99.
```

The S doesn't require an extra card column in an input field, and it does not require an extra storage position.

If S is not specified for a field and the field becomes minus as the result of a calculation, the minus sign will be removed. Thus, −200 is converted to an unsigned 200, which is treated as +200. Of course, if the programmer didn't intend for the sign to be removed, errors are sure to occur. As a result, it is good practice to use an S on all numeric input fields and on all numeric fields in Working Storage unless deliberately intending to remove plus or minus signs that may occur during the execution of a program.

The PICTURE Clause and Editing

When data is moved to a numeric edited item, the data is normally converted to a more readable form. In group 1 of figure 17-6, for example, the numbers 12345 and 00123 are converted to 123.45 and 1.23 by using PICTURE clauses consisting of Zs, 9s, and decimal points. If a minus 00123 is moved to a field described as ZZZ.99, the minus sign is removed and the data is converted to its positive form. (A negative 00123 is represented as 0012$\overline{3}$ in figure 17-6). This conversion of a numeric item to a more readable form is often referred to as *editing*.

To further refine numeric data, editing characters such as the comma, dollar sign, and CR symbol are used. For example, commas are normally used when printing a field that has four or more digits to the left of the decimal point. This is shown in group 2 in figure 17-6. Since the num-

434
COBOL

Group	Sending field		Receiving field	
	Picture	Data	Picture	Edited result
1 Editing	S999V99	12345	ZZZ.99	123.45
	S999V99	00123	ZZZ.99	1.23
	S999V99	0012̄3̄	ZZZ.99	1.23
2 Comma	S9(4)V99	142090	Z,ZZZ.99	1,420.90
	S9(4)V99	001242	Z,ZZZ.99	12.42
	S9(4)V99	000009	Z,ZZZ.99	.09
3 Floating dollar sign	S9(4)V99	142090	$$,$$$.99	$1,420.90
	S9(4)V99	001242	$$,$$$.99	$12.42
	S9(4)V99	000009	$$,$$$.99	$.09
	S99V99	1234	$$$.99	$12.34
	S99V99	0012	$$$.99	$.12
4 Credit symbol	S9(6)	001234	ZZZ,ZZZCR	1,234
	S9(6)	00123̄4̄	ZZZ,ZZZCR	1,234CR
	S9(4)V99	00123̄4̄	Z,ZZZ.99CR	12.34CR
	S9(4)V99	142090	$$,$$$.99CR	$1,420.90
	S9(4)V99	14209̄0̄	$$,$$$.99CR	$1,420.90CR
5 Floating plus sign	S9(4)V99	142090	++,+++.99	+1,420.90
	S9(4)V99	14209̄0̄	++,+++.99	-1,420.90
	S9(4)V99	001242	++,+++.99	+12.42
	S9(4)V99	00124̄2̄	++,+++.99	-12.42
	S9(4)V99	000009	++,+++.99	+.09
	S9(4)V99	00000̄9̄	++,+++.99	-.09
6 Floating minus sign	S9(4)V99	001242	--,---.99	12.42
	S9(4)V99	00124̄2̄	--,---.99	-12.42
	S99V99	1234	---.99	12.34
	S99V99	123̄4̄	---.99	-12.34
7 Insertion character B	S9(4)	123̄4̄	ZZZZBCR	1234 CR
	S9(6)	040339	99B99B99	04 03 39
	S9(6)	001234	ZZZB999	1 234

FIGURE 17-6   Editing

bers 001242 and 000009 do not have four or more significant digits to the left of the decimal point, the comma is suppressed along with the insignificant zeros. Otherwise, the comma prints as desired. If a field can have a value in the millions or billions, additional commas may be used; for example, ZZ,ZZZ,ZZZ,ZZZ.99.

Group 3 represents the use of the floating dollar sign. Here, the dollar signs replace the Zs that would otherwise be used and one additional dollar sign is placed to the left of the field. Since there are four digit positions (9s) to the left of the decimal point in the first three examples, five dollar signs and one comma are used. When numeric data is moved to a field described with a floating dollar sign, the dollar sign will print just to the left of the first printed digit.

In the examples so far, a negative field moved to a numeric edited item would be stripped of its sign and printed as if it were positive. In group 4, the credit symbol (CR) is used to indicate that a field is negative. CR is printed to the right of the field if the number being edited is negative; if the number is positive, nothing is printed.

A floating plus (+) or minus (−) may also be used to indicate whether a field is positive or negative. Groups 5 and 6 give some examples. In either case, the number of signs used in the numeric edited item is one more than the number of digit positions to the left of the decimal point in the sending item. Since there are four digit positions to the left of the decimal point in the first eight examples, five plus or minus signs appear in the PICTURE for each receiving field. When the plus sign is used, it is printed to the left of the result if the value is positive; a minus sign is printed if the value is negative. When the minus sign is used, nothing is printed if the value is positive; the minus sign is printed if the value is negative.

To insert a blank into a field, the insertion character B may be used as shown in group 7. Wherever the B appears in the PICTURE, a blank is inserted when the field is printed. Bs may also be used in combination with any of the other editing characters.

Although there are other ways in which fields may be edited, the ones illustrated here satisfy the requirements of most business programs. When coding these PICTUREs, always try to have the same number of decimal places in the sending and receiving fields—that is, align decimal points. Otherwise, inefficient object code is likely to result. By the same token, you should try to have as many Zs and 9s in the receiving field as there are 9s in the sending field. When using floating characters, there should be one more $, +, or − than would be used if coding Zs. Incidentally, the USAGE of the sending field doesn't affect the editing that is performed when a numeric item is moved to a numeric edited field.

PROCEDURE DIVISION ELEMENTS

Literals

Literals can be used in many of the statements of the Procedure Division. The following are some examples:

1. ADD 1.57 TO RESULT-FIELD.
2. IF AMOUNT IS GREATER THAN 10000 GO TO PRINT-LINE.
3. IF CODE IS EQUAL TO 'B' GO TO PROCESS-TRANSACTION.

A literal cannot, however, be used as the receiving field in an arithmetic instruction. Therefore,

$$\text{ADD RESULT-FIELD TO 1.57}$$

would cause a diagnostic.

Series Statements

Compilers for many systems allow a series of operations to be coded in one COBOL statement, such as in the following examples:

1. OPEN INPUT BAL-FWD-FILE OUTPUT REORDER-LISTING.
   (Both input and output files are opened with one statement.)
2. ADD FIELD-A FIELD-B FIELD-C GIVING FIELD-D.
   (Three fields are added together and the result is placed in the fourth field.)
3. MOVE FIELD-1 TO FIELD-X FIELD-Y FIELD-Z.
   (The contents of one field are moved to three fields.)
4. CLOSE BAL-FWD-FILE REORDER-LISTING NEW-BAL-FILE.
   (Three files are closed with one statement.)

By using a string of three periods, the format for a statement indicates that a series of data names can be used. For example, the expanded formats of the OPEN and CLOSE statements are:

OPEN INPUT file-name . . . OUTPUT file-name . . .

CLOSE file-name . . .

While low-level compilers allow the use of series items in many types of statements, series items cannot be used in low-level OPEN and CLOSE statements.

ROUNDED and ON SIZE ERROR Options

For all arithmetic statements, there are two optional clauses that may be used. The first is the ROUNDED clause, which is used as follows:

MULTIPLY HOURS-WORKED BY HOURLY-RATE
GIVING NET-PAY ROUNDED.

If HOURS-WORKED is 40.5, HOURLY-RATE is 2.25, and NET-PAY is to have two decimal places, 91.13 (the rounded answer) will be placed in the NET-PAY field. Without the ROUNDED option, the third decimal place in the answer (91.125) would be dropped and 91.12 would be placed in the NET-PAY field. The ROUNDED option should be considered whenever the result of a calculation will have more decimal places than is specified in the PICTURE of the receiving field.

The second arithmetic option is the ON SIZE ERROR option, which is used as follows:

MULTIPLY HOURS-WORKED BY HOURLY-RATE GIVING NET-PAY
    ON SIZE ERROR GO TO ERROR-ROUTINE.

This means that the program should branch to the procedure named ERROR-ROUTINE if the result of the calculation has more digits than is specified in the PICTURE of the receiving field. If NET-PAY has a PICTURE of 999V99 and the result of the multiplication is 2125.90, a SIZE ERROR has occurred, and the program will branch to the ERROR-ROUTINE procedure. Without the ON SIZE ERROR clause, the computer would continue to execute the program, but the value in the result field would be unpredictable.

The REMAINDER Clause

High-level ANS COBOL provides for saving the remainder in a DIVIDE statement by using the REMAINDER clause. For example,

DIVIDE FIELD-A INTO FIELD-B GIVING FIELD-C
    REMAINDER FIELD-D.

When this statement is executed, FIELD C will receive the quotient and FIELD-D will receive the remainder. FIELD-A and FIELD-B will remain unchanged. If the ROUNDED and ON SIZE ERROR clauses are needed, they are used as in this example:

DIVIDE FIELD-A INTO FIELD-B
    GIVING FIELD-C ROUNDED
    REMAINDER FIELD-D
    ON SIZE ERROR GO TO ERROR-RT.

The ACCEPT and DISPLAY Statements

The ACCEPT and DISPLAY statements can be used for getting card input and printer output in a form that is used infrequently within a program. For example, if one punched card is to be read at the start of a program, the ACCEPT statement, rather than the READ statement, is likely to be used. Similarly, if an END OF JOB message is to be printed at the end of a program, the DISPLAY statement, rather than the WRITE statement, is likely to be used. The advantage of using the ACCEPT and DISPLAY statements is that the data they receive or give is never considered to be part of a file. As a result, the card reader or printer does not have to be specified in the SELECT statement in the Environment Division, and an FD description isn't required in the Data Division. This can save considerable coding.

The format of the DISPLAY statement is as follows:

$$DISPLAY \begin{Bmatrix} \text{data-name} \\ \text{literal} \end{Bmatrix} \dots$$

Therefore, the following are examples of valid DISPLAY statements:

1. DISPLAY OUTPUT-DATA.
2. DISPLAY 'END OF JOB'.
3. DISPLAY 'RECORD NUMBER ' ITEM-NUMBER ' IS IN ERROR.'.

In example 1, the contents of the field named OUTPUT-DATA would be printed on the printer. In example 2, END OF JOB (a literal) would be printed. In example 3 — which uses a series of a literal, a data name, and another literal — if the field named ITEM-NUMBER contains 7904, this line will print:

RECORD NUMBER 7904 IS IN ERROR.

When a numeric field is displayed, it is first converted to DISPLAY usage. If the field has a sign, the rightmost digit of the number will print as a letter — the equivalent of a digit plus a zone punch in Hollerith code. Thus, +184 prints as 18D, where D is the combination of the digit 4 and the zone for the 12-punch. A —184 prints as 18M, where M is the combination of the digit 4 and the zone for an 11-punch. Of course, if Ss aren't used in the PICTURES of the fields that are displayed, the fields will not carry signs.

When the DISPLAY statement is executed, the printed form is moved up one space before printing. This contrasts the WRITE statement without the AFTER ADVANCING option, which spaces one line after printing. As a result, the AFTER ADVANCING option should be used on printer WRITE statements when both WRITE and DISPLAY statements are used in the same program. Otherwise, a WRITE statement following a DISPLAY statement will print on the same line as the DISPLAY statement. You should make it a rule, then, to use the AFTER ADVANCING option on the WRITE statement if you use the DISPLAY statement.

The format of the ACCEPT statement is:

ACCEPT data-name.

When the ACCEPT statement is executed, one card is read by the card reader and the contents of as many columns as are needed are stored in the field specified. This receiving field must be of DISPLAY usage. In the statement

ACCEPT INPUT-DATA

assuming INPUT-DATA is a ten-digit numeric field in DISPLAY usage, the first ten columns of the input card are stored.

The PERFORM Statement

The PERFORM statement provides a convenient way of branching to and from a routine that is written elsewhere in a program. In figure 17-7, for example, the statement

PERFORM GROSS-CALC

causes a branch to the procedure named GROSS-CALC. After the statement in GROSS-CALC is executed, the program returns to the statement

```
PROCEDURE DIVISION.
SET-UP.
    OPEN INPUT PAYROLL-FILE OUTPUT PAYROLL-REGISTER.
    ...
    ...

BEGIN-PROCESSING.
    READ PAYROLL-FILE RECORD AT END GO TO FINISH.
    PERFORM GROSS-CALC.
    MOVE GROSS TO PR-GROSS.
    PERFORM FICA-CALC THRU FICA-EXIT.
    ADD FICA TO TOT-FICA.
    PERFORM FIT-CALC.
    ...
    ...
    GO TO BEGIN-PROCESSING.

GROSS-CALC.
    MULTIPLY HOURS BY RATE GIVING GROSS.
FICA-CALC.
    IF YTD-GROSS IS GREATER THAN 7800 GO TO FICA-CALC-A.
    ADD GROSS YTD-GROSS GIVING TEST-GROSS.
    IF TEST-GROSS IS GREATER THAN 7800 GO TO FICA-CALC-B.
    MULTIPLY GROSS BY FICA-PERCENT GIVING FICA ROUNDED.
    GO TO FICA-EXIT.
FICA-CALC-A.
    MOVE ZEROS TO FICA-EXIT.
    GO TO FICA-EXIT.
FICA-CALC-B.
    SUBTRACT YTD-FICA FROM MAX-FICA GIVING FICA ROUNDED.
FICA-EXIT.
    EXIT.
    ...
    ...
```

FIGURE 17-7   Using the PERFORM statement

immediately following the PERFORM—in this case, MOVE GROSS TO PR-GROSS.

The format of the simple PERFORM is as follows:

PERFORM procedure-name-1 [THRU procedure-name-2].

If only one procedure name is given (as in PERFORM GROSS-CALC), the entire paragraph is executed. If the THRU clause is used, execution begins with the first statement in the first procedure named and ends with the last statement in the second procedure named. Any procedures that are encountered between the two procedures are also executed. In figure 17-7, the statement

PERFORM FICA-CALC THRU FICA-EXIT

causes the program to branch to the procedure named FICA-CALC, execute FICA-CALC through FICA-EXIT, and then branch to the next statement in sequence in the BEGIN-PROCESSING paragraph (ADD FICA TO TOT-FICA).

When using PERFORM statements, you must be sure that no statement branches out of the procedures being executed without also returning. Otherwise, the procedure would never be completed and the normal return to the statement following the PERFORM would be impossible. If this happens, the results during the execution of the object program are unpredictable.

To make possible a branch to the end of the procedures named in a PERFORM, the EXIT statement is used. This is a one word statement that does not cause any processing to take place. It has this format:

procedure-name. EXIT.

To illustrate its use, consider again the PERFORM statement in figure 17-7 that reads

PERFORM FICA-CALC THRU FICA-EXIT.

The procedure named FICA-CALC is designed to calculate the amount of social security tax an employee should pay based on his gross pay and to place the result in a field named FICA. Since no payment is required after the first $7800 of yearly income, the first statement in this paragraph tests the value of the year-to-date income (YTD-GROSS). If it is greater than 7800, the routine branches to FICA-CALC-A, which moves zeros to FICA, and then branches to FICA-EXIT. Since FICA-EXIT consists of the EXIT statement (which does nothing), the procedures named in the PERFORM are completed and the program continues with the statement following the PERFORM statement. Similarly, if TEST-GROSS is greater than 7800, the routine branches to FICA-CALC-B, which calculates a value for FICA and branches to FICA-EXIT. In short, the EXIT statement simply provides an end paragraph that can be branched to.

PUNCTUATION AND SPACING

With few exceptions, the only marks of punctuation used in the examples so far have been the period, quotation marks, and parentheses. For low-level ANS COBOL, this is all that is allowed. High-level COBOL, however, allows the use of the comma and semicolon in much the way they would be used in English. When a high-level compiler encounters a comma or a semicolon, it simply ignores it. As a result, a comma or semicolon must always be followed by a space to indicate the end of one word and the start of another. For example,

ADD FIELD-A, FIELD-B, FIELD-C, GIVING FIELD-D.

is acceptable COBOL, but

ADD FIELD-A,FIELD-B,FIELD-C,GIVING FIELD-D

would cause a diagnostic because the data names aren't separated by one or more spaces.

As for spacing, the only requirement is that COBOL words, names supplied by the programmer, and literals be separated by one or more spaces. As a result, statements can be written on more than one line, as in these examples:

```
1.  MULTIPLY HOURS BY HOURLY-RATE GIVING GROSS-PAY
        ROUNDED ON SIZE ERROR GO TO ERROR-ROUTINE.


2.  02  INTEREST-RATE      PICTURE IS 9V99,
                           VALUE IS 4.50,
                           USAGE IS COMPUTATIONAL.
```

Statements can also be written one after the other as shown here:

```
OPEN-ROUTINE.  MOVE HEADER-LINE TO OUTPUT-LINE. WRITE
    OUTPUT-LINE AFTER ADVANCING TOP-PAGE.  MOVE
    COLUMN-HEADING TO OUTPUT-LINE.  WRITE OUTPUT-LINE
    AFTER ADVANCING 2 LINES.
```

Coding in this way makes it more difficult to change the source deck, and thus is not a recommended programming practice. (Note that words, names, and numeric literals should not be split between two coding lines as this makes it difficult to read and program; it also requires the use of a hyphen in column 7 of the coding form.)

One other matter of form is that it is not necessary to end every statement with a period. A series of statements may be written without periods, thus making up one *sentence*. For example, the following are valid COBOL sentences:

1. CLOSE INPUT-FILE, OUTPUT-FILE, STOP RUN.

2. READ CARD-FILE RECORD AT END MOVE 'E' TO X-CODE,
   GO TO FINISH.

3. IF FIELD-1 IS EQUAL TO 14.5, MOVE I-FIELD-A
   TO O-FIELD-A, MOVE I-FIELD-B TO O-FIELD-B.

In each case, the sentence doesn't end until a period followed by one or more spaces is reached.

COBOL FORMATS

So far, this book has used somewhat simplified formats when presenting a new COBOL element. Not all of the variations of a statement or clause have been given, and, as much as possible, the common technical notation has been avoided. In contrast, a COBOL technical manual normally expresses COBOL formats as shown in the sample in figure 17-8. Here, the following notation is used:

1. All words printed entirely in capital letters (such as DATA DIVISION) are COBOL reserved words.

2. Words that are printed in lower-case letters (such as file-name) represent names or words supplied by the programmer.

3. Braces ({ }) enclosing a stack of items indicate that the programmer must use one of the items. In the PICTURE clause, for example, the programmer can use either PICTURE or the shortened form, PIC.

4. Brackets ([ ]) are used to indicate that the enclosed item may be either used or omitted, depending on the requirements of the program. For example, the ROUNDED clause in the ADD statement is optional.

5. The ellipsis (. . .) indicates that an element may appear once or any number of times in succession. Thus, a series of fields may be added together in the ADD statement.

6. Underlined reserved words are required unless the element itself is optional, but reserved words that are not underlined are optional. Thus, the LABEL RECORDS clause can be written

LABEL RECORDS OMITTED.

Since this notation is common to all COBOL manuals, it is used in the COBOL chapters that follow.

```
DATA DIVISION.
FILE SECTION.
FD     file-name.
       LABEL RECORDS ARE OMITTED
       DATA RECORD IS record-name.
01—49  {data-name}
       {FILLER   }

       {PICTURE}  IS character-string.
       {PIC    }

WORKING-STORAGE SECTION.
77     data-name

01—49  {data-name}
       {FILLER   }

       {PICTURE}  IS character-string.
       {PIC    }

                   {DISPLAY          }
                   {COMPUTATIONAL    }
       USAGE IS    {COMP             }
                   {COMPUTATIONAL-3  }
                   {COMP-3           }

       VALUE IS literal.


PROCEDURE DIVISION.
       ADD  {data-name-1}  [data-name-2]  . . .
            {literal-1   }  [literal-2   ]
            TO data-name-n  [ROUNDED]
            [ON SIZE ERROR any-statement] .
       CLOSE file-name-1  [file-name-2]  . . .
            {data-name-1}      {GREATER THAN}  {data-name-2}
       IF   {literal-1   }  IS {LESS THAN   }  {literal-2   }  any-statement.
                               {EQUAL TO    }
       READ file-name RECORD AT END any-statement.
       WRITE record-name  [AFTER ADVANCING  {literal LINES     }] .
                                            {data-name LINES   }
```

FIGURE 17-8   A sample of COBOL formats

By studying the formats in figure 17-8, you can see that a large amount of coding can be eliminated by using shortened forms of words and omitting optional words. For example, a COMPUTATIONAL field can be described as follows:

```
77  DATA-FIELD  PIC S999V99, VALUE 3.40, COMP.
```

Similarly, an IF statement can be written as:

```
IF FIELD-A GREATER FIELD-B GO TO NEXT-ROUTINE.
```

Although it reduces coding to eliminate all optional words, it is good practice to use the optional words if they add to the sense of a Procedure Division statement. It is then easier to read the program. As a result, a

WRITE statement is usually written as

WRITE record-name AFTER ADVANCING 2 LINES

rather than

WRITE record-name AFTER 2.

Both are acceptable COBOL, however. In the Data Division, it is common to omit all optional words in PICTURE, VALUE, and USAGE clauses and

```
IDENTIFICATION DIVISION.
PROGRAM-ID.  MANHATTAN-PROBLEM.

ENVIRONMENT DIVISION.
CONFIGURATION SECTION.
SOURCE-COMPUTER.  IBM-360.
OBJECT-COMPUTER.  IBM-360.

DATA DIVISION.
WORKING-STORAGE SECTION.
77   YEAR              PIC S9(4).
77   INTEREST-RATE     PIC SV999      VALUE .045    COMP.
77   PRINCIPAL         PIC S9(9)V99   VALUE 24.00   COMP.
77   YEARLY-INTEREST   PIC S9(7)V99   VALUE ZEROS   COMP.
77   STARTING-YEAR     PIC S9(4)      VALUE 1627    COMP.
01   ANSWER-LINE.
     02   FILLER             PIC X(14), VALUE 'THE ANSWER IS '.
     02   EDITED-PRINCIPAL   PIC $$$$,$$$,$$$.99.
     02   FILLER             PIC X,     VALUE '.'.

PROCEDURE DIVISION.
BEGIN.
     ACCEPT YEAR.
MAINLINE-ROUTINE.
     PERFORM CALCULATE-NEW-PRINCIPAL.
     IF STARTING-YEAR IS EQUAL TO YEAR, GO TO PRINT-ANSWER.
     GO TO MAINLINE-ROUTINE.
CALCULATE-NEW-PRINCIPAL.
     MULTIPLY INTEREST-RATE BY PRINCIPAL GIVING YEARLY-INTEREST
          ROUNDED ON SIZE ERROR GO TO PROGRAM-ERROR-1.
     ADD YEARLY-INTEREST TO PRINCIPAL ON SIZE ERROR
          GO TO PROGRAM-ERROR-2.
     ADD 1 TO STARTING-YEAR.
PRINT-ANSWER.
     MOVE PRINCIPAL TO EDITED-PRINCIPAL.
     DISPLAY ANSWER-LINE.
     STOP RUN.
PROGRAM-ERROR-1.
     DISPLAY 'YEARLY-INTEREST FIELD IS TOO SMALL--JOB ENDED.'.
     STOP RUN.
PROGRAM-ERROR-2.
     DISPLAY 'PRINCIPAL FIELD IS TOO SMALL--JOB ENDED.'.
     STOP RUN.
```

FIGURE 17-9   The Manhattan problem

to use the shortened forms of the words PICTURE (PIC) and COM-
PUTATIONAL (COMP).

AN EXAMPLE

To appreciate how some of the COBOL elements presented in this
topic are used in a complete program, consider the program listing in
figure 17-9. This program solves the Manhattan problem described in
chapter 4. The purpose of the program is to determine how much the
$24.00 paid for Manhattan Island would be worth today if it had been
left to accumulate in a savings account at 4½% simple interest per
year. Many of the COBOL elements described in this topic are used.

Because the ACCEPT and DISPLAY statements are used for all input
and output in this program, there is no INPUT-OUTPUT section in the
Environment Division. Because there are no input or output files, there
is no File Section in the Data Division and no OPEN or CLOSE statements in the Procedure Division.

In the first paragraph, named BEGIN-PROCESSING, one punched card
is read and the data from columns 1–4, which is the present year, is
stored in YEAR. In the MAINLINE-ROUTINE, the PERFORM statement is
used to branch to and return from the interest and principal calculations, CALCULATE-NEW-PRINCIPAL. When control returns to the
MAINLINE-ROUTINE, the program tests to determine if the value in
STARTING-YEAR is equal to the value in YEAR. If so, the program
branches to PRINT-ANSWER, the answer is printed, and the program
ends. Although the ON SIZE ERROR clause branches out of the CALCU-
LATE-NEW-PRINCIPAL paragraph without returning, no problem will
arise because the program stops after two more statements.

SUMMARY

**This topic has presented a series of commonly used COBOL elements
and principles. By applying these along with the elements presented
in topic 1, you should be able to write programs of considerable complexity. Then, when you learn the elements required for using tape
and disk files, you will be able to program most of the functions that
a computer is capable of executing.**

**FOR
REVIEW**

**elementary item
group item
numeric literal
non-numeric literal
editing**

ACCELERATION & COASTING

Time to distance
Time to speed
Coasting

Elapsed time in sec

CHAPTER EIGHTEEN

Tables are used in many data-processing applications. For example, a tax table may be used to look up the amount of income tax to be withheld from paychecks. To find the premium to be charged for an insurance policy, rating tables are often used. And in many statistical analyses, tables are printed to show how data breaks down into categories.

Tables in COBOL can be classified as one-, two-, and three-level tables. The low-level COBOL compilers have elements for storing and processing one-level tables. The middle- and high-level compilers have elements for two- and three-level tables as well. Topic 1 of this chapter covers one-level tables, while topic 2 covers two- and three-level tables.

A *one-level table* is a table that tabulates data for one variable factor. For instance, the rate table in figure 18-1 is a one-level table in which the pay class is the variable. As the pay class increases, so does the rate of pay.

To illustrate the coding for one-level tables, suppose that you wanted to store the rate table shown in figure 18-1 and use it to look up employees' pay rates. You would start by describing the table in the Working Storage Section of the Data Division. In this section, you would use the OCCURS and the REDEFINES clauses.

TOPIC ONE
ONE-LEVEL TABLES

The OCCURS Clause

The format of the OCCURS clause is this:

OCCURS integer TIMES.

TABLE HANDLING IN COBOL

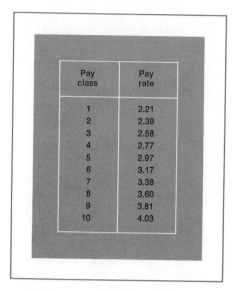

FIGURE 18-1   A one-level table

This clause can be used to describe any data name as long as it is not on the 01 level. The integer in the clause refers to the number of times a field or group of fields is repeated. To set up the fields for the table in figure 18-1, the OCCURS clause is used as follows:

```
WORKING-STORAGE SECTION.
01   RATE-TABLE-1.
     02   RATE   PIC S9V99, OCCURS 10 TIMES.
```

By using this clause, ten fields are set up in storage, each with a PICTURE of S9V99.

If necessary, an OCCURS clause can be used on a group item as well as an elementary item. For example, the rates in the table could be broken into dollars and cents using the OCCURS clause as follows:

```
01   RATE-TABLE-2.
     02   RATE   OCCURS 10 TIMES.
          03   DOLLARS   PIC S9.
          03   CENTS     PIC S99.
```

In this case, there would be ten sets of the two fields—DOLLARS and CENTS—assigned in storage.

Whether group or elementary, a USAGE clause may be given to the fields in a table. If the rates in the example are going to be used in calculations, for instance, the following coding could be used:

```
01   RATE-TABLE-3.
     02   RATE       PIC S9V99,   COMP,
                     OCCURS 10 TIMES.
```

Here, the number of storage positions required by the table in System/360 storage is reduced from thirty to twenty by using the computational form of storage.

The REDEFINES Clause

Because VALUE clauses can't be used on items that have OCCURS clauses, the REDEFINES clause is necessary. This clause does not cause fields to be assigned to storage, but is used to redefine or give additional information about fields that are already defined. Suppose, for example, that the following record description is used to store the table in figure 18-1:

```
01  RATE-TABLE-VALUES.
    02  FILLER  PIC S9V99, VALUE 2.21.
    02  FILLER  PIC S9V99, VALUE 2.39.
    02  FILLER  PIC S9V99, VALUE 2.58.
    02  FILLER  PIC S9V99, VALUE 2.77.
    02  FILLER  PIC S9V99, VALUE 2.97.
    02  FILLER  PIC S9V99, VALUE 3.17.
    02  FILLER  PIC S9V99, VALUE 3.38.
    02  FILLER  PIC S9V99, VALUE 3.60.
    02  FILLER  PIC S9V99, VALUE 3.81.
    02  FILLER  PIC S9V99, VALUE 4.03.
```

Then, REDEFINES can be used with the OCCURS clause as follows:

```
01  RATE-TABLE  REDEFINES RATE-TABLE-VALUES.
    02  RATE  PIC S9V99,  OCCURS 10 TIMES.
```

Thus, the ten fields defined in the OCCURS clause are made to correspond to the ten values defined earlier. When the REDEFINES clause is used this way, its PICTUREs and USAGEs should correspond to the fields it is redefining.

Subscripts

To process the fields defined with an OCCURS clause, *subscripts* must be used. For example, the first rate in the table in figure 18-1 can be referred to as RATE (1), the second rate as RATE (2), and so on. In each case, the number in the parentheses is called the subscript. When coding COBOL subscripts, there must be a space between the data name and the parentheses following it.

If an OCCURS clause is used on a group item, all of the elementary items within it must be referred to using subscripts. In the dollar and cents example, the dollars in the third rate would be referred to as DOLLARS (3), the cents in the fourth rate as CENTS (4).

A data name can be used as a subscript in the same way as an integer. Then, the table item that is referred to depends on the value of the subscript field at the time the instruction is executed. For example, CLASS is a subscript in the following statement:

```
MULTIPLY RATE (CLASS) BY HOURS-WORKED
        GIVING GROSS-PAY ROUNDED.
```

If CLASS contains a 1 at the time of execution, 2.21 is referred to; if CLASS contains a 2, 2.39 is referred to; and so forth. Although a data name used as a subscript can be DISPLAY or COMPUTATIONAL, USAGE IS COMPUTATIONAL generally leads to a more efficient object program.

Now can you follow the program in figure 18-2? (The Identification and Environment Divisions are omitted since they don't affect the processing of tables.) This program reads an input card containing employee data that includes the number of the employee's pay class and the number of hours he worked. It then looks up the appropriate pay rate in the rate table, calculates gross pay, and punches a card containing employee data and gross pay. When IC-PAY-CLASS is moved to CLASS for use as a subscript, the data is converted from DISPLAY to COMPUTATIONAL form. Although this program could be written without using OCCURS, REDEFINES, and subscripts, the total amount of coding required is reduced by using these table-handling COBOL elements.

PROCESSING TABLES

In some applications, the tables themselves are processed instead of being used to look up values. For this purpose, COBOL provides a variation of the PERFORM statement. To illustrate its use, assume that the contents of the table in figure 18-3 are stored in eleven fields defined this way:

```
01  EMPLOYEE-TABLE.
    02  NO-IN-DEPT        PIC S9(4), OCCURS 11 TIMES.
```

Then, NO-IN-DEPT (1) has a value of 912, NO-IN-DEPT (2) has a value of 1023, and so on. This table shows the number of employees that work in any one of the company's eleven departments.

The PERFORM Statement

Suppose that you want to find the average number of employees in a department. To make it easy, the PERFORM statement with the following format can be used:

```
PERFORM procedure-name VARYING subscript
    FROM integer BY integer UNTIL condition.
```

This format of the PERFORM statement is available with middle- and high-level compilers. Figure 18-4 shows how this PERFORM is used to

```
DATA DIVISION.
FILE SECTION.
FD  INPUT-FILE
    LABEL RECORDS ARE OMITTED
    DATA RECORD IS INPUT-CARD.
01  INPUT-CARD.
    02  IC-CARD-INFO.
        03  FILLER            PIC X(25).
        03  IC-PAY-CLASS       PIC S99.
        03  IC-HOURS-WORKED    PIC S99V9.
    02  FILLER                PIC X(50).
FD  OUTPUT-FILE
    LABEL RECORDS ARE OMITTED
    DATA RECORD IS OUTPUT-CARD.
01  OUTPUT-CARD.
    02  OC-CARD-INFO          PIC X(30).
    02  OC-GROSS-PAY          PIC S999V99.
    02  FILLER                PIC X(45).

WORKING-STORAGE SECTION.
77  CLASS                     PIC S99, COMP.
01  RATE-TABLE-VALUES.
    02  FILLER  PIC S9V99, VALUE 2.12.
    02  FILLER  PIC S9V99, VALUE 2.39.
    02  FILLER  PIC S9V99, VALUE 2.58.
    02  FILLER  PIC S9V99, VALUE 2.77.
    02  FILLER  PIC S9V99, VALUE 2.97.
    02  FILLER  PIC S9V99, VALUE 3.17.
    02  FILLER  PIC S9V99, VALUE 3.38.
    02  FILLER  PIC S9V99, VALUE 3.60.
    02  FILLER  PIC S9V99, VALUE 3.81.
    02  FILLER  PIC S9V99, VALUE 4.03.
01  RATE-TABLE  REDEFINES  RATE-TABLE-VALUES.
    02  RATE    PIC S9V99, OCCURS 10 TIMES.


PROCEDURE DIVISION.
BEGIN.
    OPEN INPUT INPUT-FILE, OUTPUT OUTPUT-FILE.
READ-AND-PROCESS.
    READ INPUT-FILE AT END GO TO FINISH.
    MOVE SPACES TO OUTPUT-CARD.
    MOVE IC-PAY-CLASS TO CLASS.
    MULTIPLY RATE (CLASS) BY IC-HOURS-WORKED GIVING
        OC-GROSS-PAY ROUNDED.
    MOVE IC-CARD-INFO TO OC-CARD-INFO.
    WRITE OUTPUT-CARD.
    GO TO READ-AND-PROCESS.
FINISH.
    CLOSE OUTPUT-FILE, INPUT-FILE.
    STOP RUN.
```

FIGURE 18-2   Finding a value in a one-level table

Department number	Number of employees
1	912
2	1023
3	411
4	23
5	530
6	4987
7	221
8	231
9	720
10	984
11	1349

FIGURE 18-3   An employees-by-department table

accumulate the total number of employees in the field named WS-TOTAL.

When the PERFORM statement in the procedure named FIND-AVERAGE is executed, it causes the procedure named ADDITION to be executed eleven times—once for each of the values of the subscript named DEPT-NO. After the eleven values of NO-IN-DEPT are added together, the processing continues with the statement following the PERFORM—namely, the DIVIDE statement. In other words, besides varying the subscript from 1 to 11, the PERFORM statement causes a branch to and from the procedure named ADDITION. Without this format of the PERFORM statement—when using low-level COBOL, for example—the programmer would have to vary the subscript by adding one to it each time the ADDITION procedure was executed; he would also have to test by using an IF statement to see when the procedure has been executed eleven times. GO TO statements would have to be used to branch to and from the ADDITION procedure.

One point worth noting is that the condition in the PERFORM is stated UNTIL DEPT-NO IS GREATER THAN 11—not UNTIL DEPT-NO IS EQUAL TO 11, as you might think. This is necessary because the test to determine whether the condition has been met is made before the procedure named ADDITION is executed. If the PERFORM were stated UNTIL DEPT-NO IS EQUAL TO 11, the ADDITION procedure would be executed only ten times, and the eleventh value in the table would not be added to WS-TOTAL.

```
DATA DIVISION.
FILE SECTION.
    . . .
    . . .
    . . .

WORKING-STORAGE SECTION.
77  DEPT-NO        PIC S99      COMP.
77  WS-TOTAL       PIC S9(6)    COMP       VALUE ZEROS.
77  WS-AVERAGE     PIC S9(4)    COMP.

01  TABLE-OF-VALUES.
    02  FILLER     PIC S9(4)    COMP       VALUE 912.
    02  FILLER     PIC S9(4)    COMP       VALUE 1023.
    02  FILLER     PIC S9(4)    COMP       VALUE 411.
    . . .
    . . .
    . . .
    02  FILLER     PIC S9(4)    COMP       VALUE 1349.
01  EMPLOYEE-TABLE  REDEFINES TABLE-OF-VALUES.
    02  NO-IN-DEPT PIC S9(4)    COMP
                   OCCURS 11 TIMES.


PROCEDURE DIVISION.
    . . .
    . . .
    . . .
FIND-AVERAGE.
    PERFORM ADDITION VARYING DEPT-NO FROM 1 BY 1
        UNTIL DEPT-NO IS GREATER THAN 11.
    DIVIDE 11 INTO WS-TOTAL GIVING WS-AVERAGE-ROUNDED.
    . . .
    . . .
    . . .

ADDITION.
    ADD NO-IN-DEPT (DEPT-NO) TO WS-TOTAL.
    . . .
```

FIGURE 18-4   Processing values in a one-level table

The PERFORM statement can also be written in this format:

```
PERFORM procedure-name-1 THRU procedure-name-2
    VARYING subscript FROM integer BY integer
    UNTIL condition.
```

In this case, the PERFORM will branch to and execute more than one
procedure. It begins with the first statement of the first procedure named
and continues until the last statement of the second procedure named

is executed. (One or many procedures can come between the two procedures named.) These procedures will continue to be executed with varying subscript values until the condition stated in the PERFORM is met.

```
DATA DIVISION.
FILE SECTION.
    ...
    ...
    ...

WORKING-STORAGE SECTION.
77  DEPT-NO              PIC S99     COMP.
77  LARGEST-DEPT-NO      PIC S99     COMP.
77  LARGEST-DEPT-VALUE   PIC S9(4)   COMP.

01  TABLE-OF-VALUES.
    02  FILLER           PIC S9(4)   COMP     VALUE 912.
    02  FILLER           PIC S9(4)   COMP     VALUE 1023.
    02  FILLER           PIC S9(4)   COMP     VALUE 411.
    ...
    ...
    ...
    02  FILLER           PIC S9(4)   COMP     VALUE 1349.
01  EMPLOYEE-TABLE  REDEFINES TABLE-OF-VALUES.
    02  NO-IN-DEPT       PIC S9(4)   COMP
                         OCCURS 11 TIMES.


PROCEDURE DIVISION.
    ...
    ...
    ...


FIND-LARGEST-DEPT.
    MOVE 1 TO LARGEST-DEPT-NO.
    MOVE NO-IN-DEPT (1) TO LARGEST-DEPT-VALUE.
    PERFORM SEARCH-DEPARTMENTS THRU SEARCH-EXIT
        VARYING DEPT-NO FROM 2 BY 1
        UNTIL DEPT-NO IS GREATER THAN 11.
    ...
    ...
    ...
SEARCH-DEPARTMENTS.
    IF LARGEST-DEPT-VALUE IS GREATER THAN NO-IN-DEPT (DEPT-NO),
        GO TO SEARCH-EXIT.
    MOVE NO-IN-DEPT (DEPT-NO) TO LARGEST-DEPT-VALUE.
    MOVE DEPT-NO TO LARGEST-DEPT-NO.
SEARCH-EXIT.  EXIT.
```

FIGURE 18-5   Finding the largest department

The EXIT Statement

When GO TO and IF statements are used in the procedures named in a PERFORM, the programmer must be sure that they do not branch out of the procedure without also returning. If they do, the normal functioning of the PERFORM (including the return to the statement following it) is destroyed, and a program error results. If branching is necessary within the procedures, you must make sure that all paths lead to the last statement in the second procedure named. To make this possible, COBOL provides the EXIT statement as described in chapter 17. This statement does no processing, but it can be used as the only statement in the second procedure named in the PERFORM.

To illustrate the use of the EXIT statement during table processing, suppose you wanted to search the employee table in figure 18-3 to find which department has the most employees. Figure 18-5 shows how this can be done. Here, the procedures named, SEARCH-DEPARTMENTS and SEARCH-EXIT, are executed ten times. (The subscripts vary from 2 through 11.) The IF statement used in the SEARCH-DEPARTMENTS procedure branches to the procedure named SEARCH-EXIT, which consists of one statement: EXIT. The SEARCH-EXIT procedure does nothing but provide a paragraph that can be branched to so that the MOVE statements following the IF statement aren't executed. The EXIT statement must be used since a procedure must always consist of at least one statement.

SUMMARY

Everything that can be accomplished using the table-handling elements of COBOL can be done using the basic COBOL elements described in chapter 17. For some tables, it may even be preferable to use basic COBOL elements. However, for most table-handling routines, the use of OCCURS, REDEFINES, subscripts, PERFORM, and EXIT can significantly reduce the coding time.

FOR
REVIEW

one-level table
subscripts

Many tables used in data-processing applications involve two or three variables. The insurance rates in the rating table in figure 18-6, for example, vary based on an applicant's age and job classification. Because two variables are involved, this table is called a two-level table. Similarly, the table in figure 18-7 can be called a three-level table since its rates vary by sex (male or female), age group, and job classification.

In COBOL, two- and three-level tables are handled in much the same way as one-level tables. The OCCURS and REDEFINES clauses are used in the Data Division; subscripts, a variation of the PERFORM statement, and the EXIT statement are used in the Procedure Division.

To illustrate, suppose the table in figure 18-6 was to be used in a program. Its values could be described in the Data Division in this way:

```
WORKING-STORAGE SECTION.
01   TABLE-VALUES.
     02   FILLER   PIC S99V99   VALUE 23.50.
     02   FILLER   PIC S99V99   VALUE 27.05.
     02   FILLER   PIC S99V99   VALUE 35.25.
     02   FILLER   PIC S99V99   VALUE 52.90.
     02   FILLER   PIC S99V99   VALUE 24.00.
     02   FILLER   PIC S99V99   VALUE 27.55.
     . . .
     . . .
     . . .
     02   FILLER   PIC S99V99   VALUE 57.40.
```

Then, the REDEFINES and OCCURS clauses could be used as follows:

```
01   RATE-TABLE REDEFINES TABLE-VALUES.
     02   AGE-GROUP OCCURS 6 TIMES.
          03   RATE-BY-CLASS       PIC S99V99,
                                   OCCURS 4 TIMES.
```

This coding would cause twenty-four fields to be set up in storage. The first field would correspond to the rate in class 1, age-group 1 (18–34); the second field would correspond to class 2, age-group 1; the third

Age	Class 1	Class 2	Class 3	Class 4
18–34	$23.50	$27.05	$35.25	$52.90
35–39	24.00	27.55	35.75	53.40
40–44	24.60	28.15	36.35	54.00
45–49	25.30	28.85	37.05	54.70
50–54	26.30	29.85	38.05	55.70
55–59	28.00	31.55	39.75	57.40

FIGURE 18-6   A two-level rating table

field to class 3, age-group 1; the fourth field to class 4, age-group 1; the fifth field to class 1, age-group 2 (35-39); and so on. In other words, the field named RATE-BY-CLASS occurs four times in each field named AGE-GROUP. Of course, the PICTUREs and USAGEs given in the table that assigns values must correspond to the table that redefines it.

If the original table has fields with DISPLAY usage, non-numeric literals can be used to give the table values. For example, the following coding would have the same effect as the previous coding:

```
01   TABLE-VALUES.
     02   FILLER   PIC X(16)   VALUE '2350270535255290'.
     02   FILLER   PIC X(16)   VALUE '2400275535755340'.
     02   FILLER   PIC X(16)   VALUE '2460281536355400'.
     02   FILLER   PIC X(16)   VALUE '2530288537055470'.
     02   FILLER   PIC X(16)   VALUE '2630298538055570'.
     02   FILLER   PIC X(16)   VALUE '2800315539755740'.
01   RATE-TABLE REDEFINES TABLE-VALUES.
     02   AGE-GROUP OCCURS 6 TIMES.
          03   RATE-BY-CLASS        PIC S99V99,
                                    OCCURS 4 TIMES.
```

In either case, the rates in the table can be referred to using a two-level subscript. For example, RATE-BY-CLASS (1, 4) refers to the first age group (18–34), fourth class—a value of 52.90. Similarly, RATE-BY-CLASS (3, 1) refers to the third age group, first class, or a value of 24.60. Notice that the data name used is RATE-BY-CLASS, the lowest-level data name in the table, and the subscripts are used in the order in which the table is described. The subscripts themselves are separated by a comma followed by a space. When data names are used as subscripts—for instance, RATE-BY-CLASS (AGE-GROUP-SUB, CLASS-SUB)—the rate referred to depends on the values of the data names at the time the instruction is executed.

This same type of thinking is used to define and reference three-level

Age	Men		Women	
	Class 1	Class 2	Class 1	Class 2
18—34	$23.50	$27.05	$24.75	$28.45
35—39	24.00	27.55	25.80	29.50
40—44	24.60	28.15	27.10	30.80
45—49	25.30	28.85	29.10	32.80
50—54	26.30	29.85	31.55	35.25
55—59	28.00	31.55	35.00	38.70

FIGURE 18-7   A three-level rating table

tables. For example, the following coding defines and gives values to the table in figure 18-7:

```
WORKING-STORAGE SECTION.
01  TABLE-VALUES.
    02  FILLER  PIC X(16)  VALUE '2350270524752845'.
    02  FILLER  PIC X(16)  VALUE '2400275525802950'.
    02  FILLER  PIC X(16)  VALUE '2460281527103080'.
    02  FILLER  PIC X(16)  VALUE '2530288529103280'.
    02  FILLER  PIC X(16)  VALUE '2630298531553525'.
    02  FILLER  PIC X(16)  VALUE '2800315535003870'.
01  RATE-TABLE REDEFINES TABLE-VALUES.
    02  AGE-GROUP OCCURS 6 TIMES.
        03  SEX OCCURS 2 TIMES.
            04  RATE-BY-CLASS    OCCURS 2 TIMES,
                                 PIC S99V99.
```

In this case, the rate for a 51-year-old woman in job class 1 is referred to as RATE-BY-CLASS (5, 2, 1)—the subscripts are specified in the order in which the table is defined.

Suppose the table were described this way instead:

```
01  RATE-TABLE REDEFINES TABLE-VALUES.
    02  SEX OCCURS 2 TIMES.
        03  CLASS OCCURS 2 TIMES.
            04  RATE-BY-AGE-GROUP  PIC S99V99,
                                   OCCURS 6 TIMES.
```

Then, the rate for a 51-year-old woman in job class 1 would be referred to as RATE-BY-AGE-GROUP (2, 1, 5). And the rates assigned to the table would have to be in this order:

```
01  TABLE-VALUES.
    02  FILLER  PIC X(24)  VALUE '235024002460253026302800'.
    02  FILLER  PIC X(24)  VALUE '270527552815288529853155'.
    02  FILLER  PIC X(24)  VALUE '247525802710291031553500'.
    02  FILLER  PIC X(24)  VALUE '284529503080328035253870'.
```

The PERFORM Statement

The PERFORM statements for processing two- and three-level tables allow a procedure to be executed for each of the possible subscript values. For a two-level table, the basic format is this:

```
PERFORM procedure-name-1 [THRU procedure-name-2]
    VARYING subscript-1 FROM integer BY integer
    UNTIL condition-1
    AFTER subscript-2 FROM integer BY integer
    UNTIL condition-2.
```

Since THRU procedure-name-2 is enclosed in brackets, it is optional; it is needed only when more than one procedure is to be executed.

To illustrate the use of the PERFORM, suppose the rates in the table in figure 18-6 were to be printed, one rate per printed line. The relevant

```
DATA DIVISION.
FILE SECTION.
    ...
    ...


FD  RATE-LISTING
    LABEL RECORDS ARE OMITTED
    DATA RECORD IS RATE-LINE.
01  RATE-LINE.
    02  O-RATE          PIC ZZ.99.
    02  FILLER          PIC X(127).

WORKING-STORAGE SECTION.
77  AGE-GROUP-SUB       PIC S9, COMP.
77  CLASS-SUB           PIC S9, COMP.

01  RATE-TABLE.
    02  AGE-GROUP                   OCCURS 6 TIMES.
        03  RATE-BY-CLASS           PIC S99V99,
                                    OCCURS 4 TIMES.


PROCEDURE DIVISION.
    ...
    ...
    ...

    PERFORM PRINT-TABLE
        VARYING AGE GROUP-SUB FROM 1 BY 1
        UNTIL AGE-GROUP-SUB IS GREATER THAN 6,
        AFTER CLASS-SUB FROM 1 BY 1
        UNTIL CLASS-SUB IS GREATER THAN 4.
    ...
    ...
    ...

PRINT-TABLE.
    MOVE RATE-BY CLASS (AGE-GROUP-SUB, CLASS-SUB)
        TO O-RATE.
    WRITE RATE-LINE.
```

FIGURE 18-8   Processing a two-level table

coding is shown in figure 18-8. In this example, the rates would print
as follows:

$$23.50$$
$$27.05$$
$$35.25$$
$$52.90$$
$$24.00$$
$$27.55$$

and so on.

In other words, the procedure named PRINT-TABLE is executed twenty-four times, once for each of the possible combinations of subscripts.

In stating a two-level PERFORM, the order in which the subscripts are named can have an important effect on the resulting processing. To illustrate, suppose the PERFORM in figure 18-8 were stated in this way:

```
PERFORM PRINT-TABLE VARYING CLASS-SUB FROM 1 BY 1
        UNTIL CLASS-SUB IS GREATER THAN 4
        AFTER AGE-GROUP-SUB FROM 1 BY 1
        UNTIL AGE-GROUP-SUB IS GREATER THAN 6.
```

Then, the rates would print in this order:

$$
\begin{array}{c}
23.50 \\
24.00 \\
24.60 \\
25.30 \\
26.30 \\
28.00 \\
27.05 \\
27.55 \\
\end{array}
$$

and so on.

In either case, the procedure named in the PERFORM is executed until both conditions are met. First, subscript-2 is varied for its values while subscript-1 is held constant at its first value; then subscript-2 is varied for its values while subscript-1 is held constant at its second value; and so on, until both condition-1 and condition-2 are satisfied.

The three-level PERFORM statement extends this idea to vary the value of a third subscript. Its format is as follows:

```
PERFORM procedure-name-1 [THRU procedure-name-2]
        VARYING subscript-1 FROM integer BY integer
        UNTIL condition-1
        AFTER subscript-2 FROM integer BY integer
        UNTIL condition-2
        AFTER subscript-3 FROM integer BY integer
        UNTIL condition-3.
```

In this PERFORM, the last subscript named is varied first, followed by the second subscript named, followed by the first subscript named. A flowchart indicating the sequence of operations in a three-level PERFORM statement is given in figure 18-9.

When a two- or three-level PERFORM statement involves branching in the procedures it names, the EXIT statement may be needed. Remember that all paths through the procedures must end on the last statement of the second procedure named. The EXIT statement for a two- or three-level PERFORM is used in exactly the same way as for any other PERFORM: it does nothing but provide a statement for a dummy procedure.

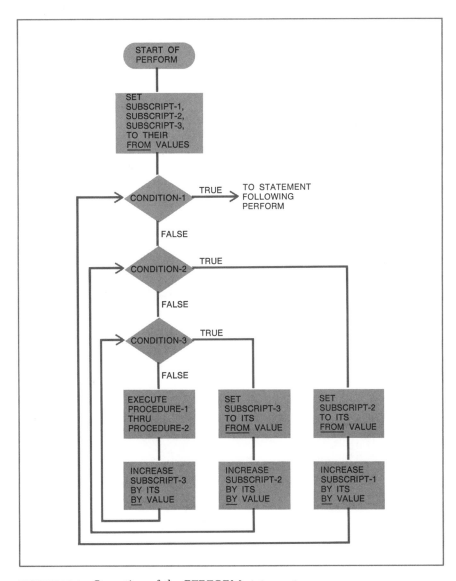

FIGURE 18-9   Operation of the PERFORM statement

SUMMARY

The COBOL elements used for handling one-level tables apply also to two- and three-level-tables. To set-up the tables in storage, multiple levels of the OCCURS clause are used. To process the tables, two- and three-level subscripts are varied by the PERFORM statement.

FOR REVIEW

two-level table
three-level table

CHAPTER NINETEEN

Before reading this chapter, you should be familiar with the nature of sequential tape and disk files (chapters 6 and 7). The basic COBOL coding for tape files is explained in topic 1, while the basic coding for sequential disk files is presented in topic 2. This second topic is applicable to all sequential files on direct-access devices, regardless of the device used.

Most tape files consist of blocks of fixed-length records—for example, ten records to a block, each record 120 bytes long. When coding COBOL programs, these tape files are handled very much like card or printer files. Only minor adjustments are required in the Environment, Data, and Procedure Divisions.

TOPIC ONE
TAPE FILES

THE ENVIRONMENT DIVISION

The following is an example of a SELECT statement for a tape file using an IBM 2400 Tape Unit:

```
SELECT TAPE-FILE ASSIGN TO SYS005-UT-2400-S.
```

The only way this differs from the SELECT statement for a card or printer file is in the system name given to the I/O device. Instead of the initials UR following the SYS number, the initials UT are used for a tape file. Instead of device numbers such as 2540R and 1403, 2400 for the IBM 2400 tape drive is used.

COBOL FOR SEQUENTIAL FILES

The SELECT statement for other manufacturers' tape files varies from card and printer files in much the same way. For example, a card file on a B3500 may be specified as

SELECT CARD-FILE ASSIGN TO READER.

while a tape file may be specified as

SELECT TAPE-FILE ASSIGN TO TAPE.

For any compiler, you need to find out the exact formats of the acceptable system names.

THE DATA DIVISION

In the file description (FD) in the Data Division, the programmer gives the characteristics of the tape file. The following is a typical FD for a fixed-length tape file:

```
FD  TAPE-OUTPUT-FILE
    BLOCK CONTAINS 5 RECORDS
    LABEL RECORDS ARE STANDARD
    DATA RECORD IS TAPE-OUTPUT-RECORD.
```

The BLOCK CONTAINS clause states the number of records in each block (the blocking factor), and the DATA RECORD IS clause gives a record name to the individual records of the file.

The LABEL RECORDS clause specifies the type of labels used on the tape file. STANDARD means that the labels follow the label specification given by the computer manufacturer. Although tape labels can be omitted or designed according to a computer user's specifications, STANDARD is recommended and used in a large majority of cases. When labels aren't STANDARD, the label-checking routines are usually written by the most experienced programmer of a company. Once written, these routines are inserted into each program using tape files. As a result, the average COBOL programmer need never worry about labels that aren't STANDARD.

After the FD statement, the tape record and its fields are described just as they are for a card or printer record. For example, a tape record consisting of 120 bytes might be described as follows:

```
01  TAPE-OUTPUT-RECORD.
    02  TO-CUST-NO           PIC S9(5).
    02  TO-CUST-NAME         PIC X(20).
    02  TO-CUST-ADDRESS      PIC X(20).
    02  TO-CUST-CITY-STATE   PIC X(20).
    02  FILLER               PIC X(55).
```

Regardless of the blocking factor, only one record is described since all of the records in the file are the same.

Unlike card and printer files, the fields in tape records can have

COMPUTATIONAL usage. For example, a 50-byte record on a System/360 might be described like this:

```
01   TAPE-RECORD.
     02   TP-CODE          PIC  X(7).
     02   TP-DESCRIPTION   PIC  X(25).
     02   TP-NUM-FLD-1     PIC  S9(3)        COMP.
     02   TP-NUM-FLD-2     PIC  S9(7)V9(4)   COMP.
     02   TP-NUM-FLD-3     PIC  S9(3)V99     COMP.
     02   TP-NUM-FLD-4     PIC  S9(5)V99     COMP.
```

Because the number of storage positions required for COMPUTATIONAL fields varies depending on the type of computer used, this same description might require more or less storage positions on another computer. The advantage of using COMPUTATIONAL fields is in (1) reducing the size of tape records and (2) reducing the amount of data conversion required during the execution of a COBOL program.

THE PROCEDURE DIVISION

In the Procedure Division, OPEN, CLOSE, READ, and WRITE are used in the same way as for a card or printer file. The common formats are as follows:

```
OPEN INPUT file-name.
OPEN OUTPUT file-name.
READ file-name RECORD AT END any-statement.
WRITE record-name.
CLOSE file-name.
```

But, what about blocking and deblocking, error-recovery, and label-checking routines? They are all taken care of by the OPEN, CLOSE, READ, and WRITE statements. For example, when an OPEN is given for an input file, the volume and header labels are checked to make sure that the correct tape has been mounted. Similarly, the CLOSE statement takes care of checking and creating trailer labels and rewinding files, while the READ and WRITE statements handle error-recovery, blocking, and deblocking routines. If an input or output file requires more than one volume, the READ and WRITE statements also process the trailer labels at the end of one file and the volume and header labels at the start of the next. In short, although many more machine-language instructions are executed for tape I/O routines than for card or printer routines, the COBOL programmer codes them both in approximately the same way.

Where is the information needed for label checking derived from? For example, if a label on an input tape is being checked to make sure that it is the right file, how does the program know what information the label should contain? This information can be given in two ways.

On System/360, the label information is given in *job-control cards* at the time the object program is executed (see chapter 14). The information in the job-control cards is compared with the information in the volume and header labels; if equal, the program assumes that the correct tape has been mounted and the tape is processed.

On other systems, some label information may be given in the FD for a file so that it is actually a part of the COBOL program. For instance, the following file description for an output file on a B3500 using ANS COBOL gives some label information:

```
FD  CUSTOMER-FILE
    BLOCK CONTAINS 10 RECORDS
    LABEL RECORDS ARE STANDARD
    VALUE OF ID IS "C23456"
    SAVE-FACTOR IS 014
    DATA RECORD IS CUSTOMER-RECORD.
```

In this case, the header label of the output tape will be given an expiration date that is fourteen days from the date the file is created (SAVE-FACTOR IS 014), and C23456 will be placed in the identification field (ID). (Remember that in strict ANS COBOL the double quotation mark is used to set off non-numeric literals, although the single mark is an acceptable substitute.)

The actual format of the VALUE clause in an FD statement is given in ANS specifications as:

<u>VALUE OF</u> data-name-1 IS literal-1

[data-name-2 IS literal-2] . . .

The data names to be used for fields in a tape label are assigned by the computer manufacturer. Thus, ID and SAVE-FACTOR are names assigned by Burroughs. When coding the VALUE clause, then, you will have to find out the correct data names and literals for the tape files your program is processing.

EXAMPLE OF TAPE CODING

To illustrate the use of COBOL for tape files, consider the program in figure 19-1. It is a card-to-tape program that simply converts the first twenty-five columns of a deck of input cards into tape records. Although a card-to-tape program would normally check individual card fields to make sure that they contain valid data, the purpose of this program is to illustrate tape coding.

By studying the Data Division, you can determine that each tape block contains 1250 bytes of data. When the OPEN and CLOSE statements are executed, the appropriate label-checking routines are performed. When the WRITE statement is executed, the appropriate error-recovery and blocking routines are performed.

```
IDENTIFICATION DIVISION.
PROGRAM-ID.  CARD-TO-TAPE.

ENVIRONMENT DIVISION.
CONFIGURATION SECTION.
SOURCE-COMPUTER.  IBM-360.
OBJECT-COMPUTER.  IBM-360.

INPUT-OUTPUT SECTION.
FILE-CONTROL.
    SELECT CARD-FILE ASSIGN TO SYS005-UR-2540R-S.
    SELECT TAPE-FILE ASSIGN TO SYS006-UT-2400-S.

DATA DIVISION.
FILE SECTION.
FD  CARD-FILE
    LABEL RECORDS ARE OMITTED
    DATA RECORD IS CARD-RECORD.
01  CARD-RECORD.
    02  CARD-DATA        PIC X(25).
    02  FILLER           PIC X(55).
FD  TAPE-FILE
    BLOCK CONTAINS 50 RECORDS
    LABEL RECORDS ARE STANDARD
    DATA RECORD IS TAPE-RECORD.
01  TAPE-RECORD          PIC X(25).

PROCEDURE DIVISION.
BEGIN.
    OPEN INPUT CARD-FILE, OUTPUT TAPE-FILE.
READ-AND-PROCESS.
    READ CARD-FILE AT END GO TO FINISH.
    MOVE CARD-DATA TO TAPE-RECORD.
    WRITE TAPE-RECORD.
    GO TO READ-AND-PROCESS.
FINISH.
    CLOSE CARD-FILE, TAPE-FILE.
    STOP RUN.
```

FIGURE 19-1 A card-to-tape program

SUMMARY

With few exceptions, a tape file is coded just like a card file. The exceptions are the system name in the SELECT statement, the BLOCK CONTAINS, LABEL RECORDS, and VALUE clauses in the FD statement, and the fact that COMPUTATIONAL fields can be used in tape records.

job-control card

**FOR
REVIEW**

TOPIC TWO
DISK FILES

Sequential files on direct-access devices are handled much like card or tape files. The only significant difference is in writing update programs. On a direct-access device, the updated master record can be written in the same location from which it was read. In contrast, an update program for tape usually reads the old master records from one tape and writes the updated master records on another tape.

Figure 19-2 summarizes the COBOL elements used for describing and operating upon sequential files on direct-access devices. Figure 19-3 shows how these elements are used in an update program.

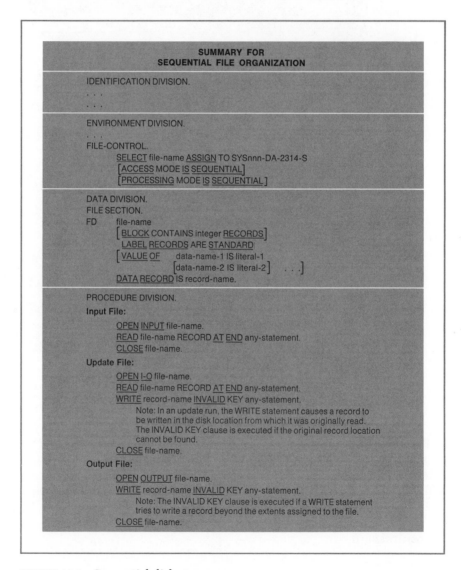

FIGURE 19-2 Sequential-disk summary

THE ENVIRONMENT DIVISION

In the SELECT statement in the Environment Division, the system name has this general format:

SYSnnn-DA-device-S

DA indicates direct access and S refers to sequential file organization. The SYS numbers are used as they are for any other IBM file. Although acceptable device numbers for IBM ANS COBOL include 2311 for the 2311 Disk Unit, 2314 for the 2314 Disk Unit, and 2321 for the 2321 Data Cell, the program in figure 19-3 uses 2314.

The system names for devices on other computer systems vary widely. For example, the B2500 uses the name DISK, while the Century 100 uses a code such as NCR655-101. In any case, you will need to find out the correct system names for the direct-access devices you are going to use.

Following the ASSIGN clause of the SELECT statement, two other clauses can be used for a sequential disk file as shown in this Burroughs statement:

```
SELECT DISK-FILE ASSIGN TO DISK
    ACCESS IS SEQUENTIAL
    PROCESSING IS SEQUENTIAL.
```

The ACCESS and PROCESSING clauses indicate the order in which the records of the file are going to be accessed and processed. Although most systems assume sequential access and processing if these clauses are omitted, some companies insist that they be used because they make a program easier to understand. In System/360 ANS COBOL, these clauses can be omitted for sequential files.

THE DATA DIVISION

The FD description in the Data Division gives the characteristics of the direct-access file. In the program in figure 19-3, the FD for the disk master file is as follows:

```
FD  DISK-FILE
    BLOCK CONTAINS 10 RECORDS
    LABEL RECORDS ARE STANDARD
    DATA RECORD IS DISK-RECORD.
```

LABEL RECORDS ARE STANDARD means that the volume and file labels conform to the manufacturer's specifications. Although labels can also conform to user's specifications, STANDARD is used for most files. When labels aren't STANDARD, the label-checking routines are normally written by a company's most experienced programmer. Since these routines are inserted into each program using the files, the average COBOL programmer need never worry about nonstandard labels.

```
IDENTIFICATION DIVISION.
PROGRAM-ID.  UPDATE.

ENVIRONMENT DIVISION.
CONFIGURATION SECTION.
SOURCE-COMPUTER.  IBM-360.
OBJECT-COMPUTER.  IBM-360.
INPUT-OUTPUT SECTION.
FILE-CONTROL.
    SELECT RECEIPT-FILE ASSIGN TO SYS005-UR-2540R-S.
    SELECT DISK-FILE ASSIGN TO SYS006-DA-2314-S,
        ACCESS IS SEQUENTIAL,
        PROCESSING IS SEQUENTIAL.

DATA DIVISION.
FILE SECTION.
FD  RECEIPT-FILE
    LABEL RECORDS ARE OMITTED
    DATA RECORD IS RC-RECORD.
01  RC-RECORD.
    02  RC-ITEM-NO        PIC S9(7).
    02  RC-QTY-RECEIVED   PIC S9(5).
    02  FILLER            PIC X(68).
FD  DISK-FILE
    BLOCK CONTAINS 10 RECORDS
    LABEL RECORDS ARE STANDARD
    DATA RECORD IS DK-RECORD.
01  DK-RECORD.
    02  DK-ITEM-NO        PIC S9(7).
    02  FILLER            PIC X(21).
    02  DK-ON-HAND        PIC S9(5)    COMP.
    02  FILLER            PIC X(23).

WORKING-STORAGE SECTION.
77  UPDATE-CODE           PIC X        VALUE 'I'.
```

FIGURE 19-3   A sequential-disk update program (Part 1 of 2)

The BLOCK CONTAINS clause indicates the number of records in each block of the file. If the records aren't blocked, this clause can be omitted. The DATA RECORD IS clause is used as it is for any other input or output file.

Following the file description, the direct-access record and its fields are described in the same way as for a card or printer record. In the example, the fields of the master record are described as follows:

```
01  DK-RECORD.
    02  DK-ITEM-NO        PIC S9(7).
    02  FILLER            PIC X(21).
    02  DK-ON-HAND        PIC S9(5), COMP.
    02  FILLER            PIC X(23).
```

```
PROCEDURE DIVISION.
SET-UP.
    OPEN INPUT RECEIPT-FILE, I-O DISK-FILE.
    READ DISK-FILE AT END GO TO ERROR-HALT.
READ-TRAN.
    READ RECEIPT-FILE AT END GO TO WRITE-LAST-RECORD.
TEST-TRAN.
    IF RC-ITEM-NO IS EQUAL TO DK-ITEM-NO,
        GO TO UPDATE-MASTER.
    IF RC-ITEM-NO IS GREATER THAN DK-ITEM-NO,
        GO TO WRITE-MASTER.
    DISPLAY 'INPUT CARD FOR ITEM NUMBER ', RC-ITEM-NO,
        ' IS UNMATCHED.  CARD IGNORED.'.
    GO TO READ-TRAN.
UPDATE-MASTER.
    ADD RC-QTY-RECEIVED TO DK-ON-HAND.
    MOVE 'A' TO UPDATE-CODE.
    GO TO READ-TRAN.
WRITE-MASTER.
    IF UPDATE-CODE IS EQUAL TO 'A',
        MOVE 'I' TO UPDATE-CODE,
        WRITE DK-RECORD INVALID KEY GO TO PUZZLED.
    READ DISK-FILE AT END GO TO ERROR-HALT.
    GO TO TEST-TRAN.
WRITE-LAST-RECORD.
    IF UPDATE-CODE IS EQUAL TO 'A',
        WRITE DK-RECORD INVALID KEY GO TO PUZZLED.
    GO TO STOP-PROGRAM.
PUZZLED.
    DISPLAY 'INVALID KEY ON ', RC-ITEM-NO, ', JOB STOPPED.'.
    GO TO STOP-PROGRAM.
ERROR-HALT.
    DISPLAY 'END OF DISK FILE BUT CARDS REMAIN.  FIND OUT WHY.'
STOP-PROGRAM.
    CLOSE RECEIPT-FILE, DISK-FILE.
    STOP RUN.
```

FIGURE 19-3   (Part 2 of 2)

Since all ten records in each block have the same format, only one record need be described.

Unlike card or printer records, fields in a direct-access record may be described as COMPUTATIONAL. In fact, since more than one digit can be stored per byte by using COMPUTATIONAL, storage space can be saved on the disk. For example, on the System/360, a field of five digits can be stored in four bytes by using COMPUTATIONAL, thus saving one byte of storage.

Although the System/360 program in figure 19-3 doesn't use the VALUE clause in the FD statement, this clause is used by some manufacturers to specify the contents of the fields in the disk labels. The manufacturer specifies the data names to be used for the fields in the file label, and it is the responsibility of the programmer to find out the literal values to be used for the files his program uses. On System/360, file-label information is given in job-control cards at the time a program is executed.

PROCEDURE DIVISION ELEMENTS

As you can see from the summary in figure 19-2, reading an input file is handled exactly as it would be for reading a card or tape file. The records in the file are read in sequence starting with the first record on the first track of the file. The AT END clause is executed when the program reads the last record in the area assigned to the file. This area can be defined in several ways, depending on the system used. On System/360, the area is defined by job-control cards that are read just before the program is executed.

To update a master file, the OPEN and WRITE statements are used somewhat differently than for tape files. OPEN I-O means that the file specified will be both an input and an output file. In other words, the updated record will be written back on the disk in the same location from which it was read. When the WRITE statement is executed for an I-O file, it writes the record in the location that was read from in the preceding READ statement.

Notice in figure 19-2 that the WRITE statement for an update file requires an INVALID KEY clause. The statements in this clause are executed if the original record location can't be found when the WRITE statement is executed. Since the WRITE statement must logically be preceded by a READ statement in an update program, the INVALID KEY clause would be executed if a WRITE statement was issued before any READ statement was issued.

For an output file, the WRITE statement also has an INVALID KEY clause. The statements specified in this clause are executed when a WRITE statement tries to write a record beyond the disk area assigned to the file. For example, if cylinders 21 through 30 were assigned to a file, the INVALID KEY clause would be executed when the WRITE statement tried to write a record in the first record location of the first track of cylinder 31. Similarly, if disk segments numbered 1000 through 1999 were assigned to a file, the INVALID KEY clause would be executed when the WRITE statement attempted to write in segment 2000.

What about blocking, deblocking, error-recovery, and label-checking routines? As with tape files, they are taken care of by OPEN, CLOSE, READ, and WRITE. In figure 19-3, for example, the appropriate label-checking routines are executed when OPEN I-O DISK-FILE is given: the volume and file labels are checked to make sure that the right disk pack containing the right file is mounted on the right disk drive. The OPEN can also check the extents given in the job-control cards to make sure that they correspond to the extents given in the file label.

Similarly, the READ and WRITE statements handle error-recovery, blocking, and deblocking routines. If an input or output file requires more than one disk pack, the READ and WRITE statements also process the labels for additional packs. And if an input or output file is stored on more than one area of the disk—say cylinders 31–50, 81–100, and 121–140—the READ and WRITE statements switch from one area to the next. In short, though hundreds of machine-language instructions may be executed in disk I/O routines, the COBOL programmer need only concern himself with OPEN, CLOSE, READ, and WRITE.

THE UPDATE PROGRAM

The update program illustrated in figure 19-3 may seem unnecessarily complicated at first. If you study the program, however, you will see that all of the procedures are necessary to handle the error conditions that might occur and to make sure that (1) a disk master record is written only when it is affected by one or more transactions, and (2) a master record is written only after all transactions for the master record have been processed. If the INVALID KEY clause is executed when attempting to write a master record, the DISPLAY statement is used to print an error message and the program is stopped (see the PUZZLED paragraph). Because of the nature of a sequential update program, the execution of the INVALID KEY clause indicates a serious programming error.

SUMMARY

Coding for sequential disk files is much the same as coding for tape files. The main conceptual difference is that updated records can be written back onto the same disk location from which they were read. The main coding differences are found in the SELECT statement and in the use of the INVALID KEY clause on WRITE statements.

V

FORTRAN

CHAPTER TWENTY

In chapter 4 you were introduced to programming concepts that apply to all programming languages. In this chapter, you will be introduced to the FORTRAN language. In topic 1, many of the basic FORTRAN elements are presented along with a description of three relatively simple programs. Then in topic 2, the remaining basic elements are presented. When you finish this chapter, you will have covered everything you need to know in order to write complete FORTRAN programs of great complexity.

FORTRAN is the most widely used of all programming languages. It is also one of the oldest programming languages, first introduced in 1956. Because the language is essentially mathematical, FORTRAN, which stands for FORmula TRANslator, can be easily learned by scientists, engineers, and mathematicians. One of the attractions of FORTRAN is that a FORTRAN compiler is available for nearly all major computer systems.

Although all FORTRAN compilers are based on similar specifications, each computer manufacturer's version of FORTRAN traditionally has had its own peculiarities. In an attempt to standardize FORTRAN—to make it easier to switch from one computer to another—the American National Standards Institute developed specifications for a standard FORTRAN in 1966. This standard gives specifications for a Basic FORTRAN and a full FORTRAN, so standard FORTRAN can be used on relatively small computers as well as on medium- and large-sized computers. Because Basic FORTRAN consists of selected elements of

TOPIC ONE
AN INTRODUCTION TO FORTRAN

BASIC FORTRAN PROGRAMMING

the full FORTRAN, it is said to be a *subset* of full FORTRAN. Thus, a Basic FORTRAN program can be compiled by a full FORTRAN compiler, but a full FORTRAN program using some of the advanced FORTRAN elements cannot be compiled by a Basic compiler. Some computers have both Basic and full compilers, in which case the Basic compiler (because it allows fewer elements) compiles at higher speeds than the full compiler.

For the most part, this book presents standard Basic FORTRAN. Whenever an element from full FORTRAN is presented, it is identified as such. If the computer you are using has only a Basic compiler, you must avoid the full FORTRAN elements.

FORTRAN ARITHMETIC STATEMENTS

The stated objective of the original FORTRAN language is this: "The FORTRAN language is intended to be capable of expressing any problem of numerical computation." As a result, the FORTRAN arithmetic statement is basic to any FORTRAN program. Once you have learned how to write arithmetic statements, writing I/O and control statements should be easy.

Because FORTRAN statements correspond closely to arithmetic statements, it shouldn't take you long to learn how to write them. For example, the FORTRAN statement

$$PAY = HOURS * RATE - TAXES$$

can be used to indicate that the contents of a field named HOURS should be multiplied (*) by the contents of a field named RATE and the contents of a field named TAXES should be subtracted from the product. After the calculation has been completed, the result should be placed in a field named PAY. Similarly, the FORTRAN statement

$$Y = 4.0*A + 7.5*B - .045*C$$

is equivalent to the arithmetic statement

$$y = 4a + 7.5b - .045c$$

Before learning the rules for writing FORTRAN arithmetic statements, you must know how to form names for unknown quantities such as HOURS, RATE, A, B, and C in the examples above. In FORTRAN, these unknowns are called *variables*, and the names given them are called *variable names*. Quite simply, a variable name in full FORTRAN consists of six or less letters or numbers, starting with a letter. Thus, H24, SLSRTE, and N0045L are valid variable names, but 3X24, N#35, and DEDUCTION are not. In general, a variable name is chosen to be indicative of the data it represents, so UCOST is a better name than H24 for a unit-cost field. (Although Basic FORTRAN standards limit variable names to five characters, six-character names are used in this book.)

When variables are placed in storage as the result of FORTRAN statements, they take one of two forms, depending on which letters the variable name begins with. If the variable name begins with the letters I, J, K, L, M, or N, the name represents an *integer variable*, which means that the variable is a whole number. If the variable name begins with any of the other letters, the name represents a *real variable*, which means the variable has one or more decimal positions. As a result, the names I, JRATE, and NET represent integer variables such as 12, −44, and +807; the names A, X, and WAGES represent real variables such as 3.1416, +817.0, and −.0045. As you will see, it is important to be able to distinguish between integer and real names and numbers when writing FORTRAN arithmetic statements. (You might note that integer variable names start with the letters I through N, the first letters of the word INteger.)

Constants are used in arithmetic statements to represent values that do not change. Like variables, there are both integer and real constants. An *integer constant* is a number that does not contain a decimal point and that may or may not have a leading plus or minus sign. In contrast, a *real constant* must always be written with a decimal point, whether or not any decimal digits follow the point. Thus,

$$12077$$
$$-302$$
$$+428967$$

are integer constants, and

$$12077.$$
$$-3.02$$
$$+0.0428967$$

are real constants. Please note that commas are not allowed in either an integer or a real constant.

To form a FORTRAN *arithmetic expression*, variables and constants are connected with the following operators:

Operator	Meaning
+	Addition
−	Subtraction
*	Multiplication
/	Division
**	Exponentiation

Since exponentiation means "raising to a power of," the FORTRAN expression

$$X**2$$

is equivalent to the arithmetic expression x^2. And the FORTRAN expression X**.5 is equivalent to the arithmetic expression $x^{\frac{1}{2}}$, or $\sqrt{x}$ (the square root of x).

To show you the relationship between arithmetic and FORTRAN expressions, consider the following pairs of expressions:

Arithmetic	FORTRAN
$x + y - z$	X + Y − Z
$3i + 2kl$	3*I + 2*K*L
$7x + \dfrac{y}{z}$	7.*X + Y/Z
$x^3 + x^5$	X**3 + X**5

As you can see, constants and variables in a FORTRAN expression must be separated by arithmetic operators. Thus, the arithmetic $3ax$ must be written in FORTRAN as 3.*A*X, not as 3.AX.

You should note that all of the above FORTRAN expressions are consistent as to mode. This means that each expression is made up of either real constants and variables, in which case it is said to be in the *real mode*, or of integer constants and variables, in which case it is said to be in the *integer mode*. This is a requirement of standard FORTRAN, which prohibits *mixed-mode* expressions. Since standard FORTRAN allows an exponent in a real expression to be in either the real or integer mode, both

X**3 + X**5 and X**3. + X**5.

are in the real mode. Similarly,

X**I + X**J

is in the real mode. (Incidentally, integer exponents should be used whenever possible since they lead to faster object-program execution.)

One question you might be asking is when to use real and when to use integer expressions. Generally, use a real expression if one of the variables or constants in the expression requires decimal positions or if the calculated value of the expression might require decimal positions. An integer expression should be used only in a relatively simple expression involving whole numbers, and even then, a real expression will normally lead to the same results.

When a series of arithmetic operations is expressed in a single FORTRAN expression, it is important to know in which order the operations will be performed. The expression H − R * D, for example, can have different values depending on whether the multiplication or the subtraction is done first. If H = 12.0, R = 2.0, and D = 5.0, the value of the expression is 50.0 if the subtraction is done first; if the multiplication is done first, the value is 2.

In FORTRAN, the order in which arithmetic operations are performed is as follows:

FIRST — Exponentiation
SECOND — Multiplication and division
THIRD — Addition and subtraction

If the same level operation is used more than once in an expression, the sequence is from left to right for each level. As a result, multiplication takes place first in the expression $H - R * D$. In the expression

$$A * B + C * D - E ** 2$$

first E is squared, then A and B are multiplied together, C and D are multiplied together, the products of A times B and C times D are added, and finally, the square of E is subtracted from the sum.

If an expression is so complex that it is difficult to keep track of the order of operations, parentheses can be used to indicate which operations should be done first. In the expression

$$A + B ** 2 / C - D * E * F$$

parentheses can be used as follows to specify the order of operations:

$$((A + B ** 2) / C) - (D * E * F)$$

Here, as in any arithmetic statement, operations within parentheses are performed before operations outside of parentheses. When there are parentheses within parentheses, the operations in the innermost set of parentheses are performed first. To begin then, the expression $A + B ** 2$ is evaluated; then $(A + B ** 2)$ is divided by C and $(D * E * F)$ is evaluated; in the final operation, the value of $(D * E * F)$ is subtracted from the value of $((A + B ** 2) / C)$. Because parentheses help to clarify the order of operations, they should be used whenever there is a possiblity of confusion. The following shows some other examples of expressions using parentheses and the corresponding arithmetic statement:

FORTRAN	Arithmetic
$(A + B)/(C - D)$	$\dfrac{a + b}{c - d}$
$X ** (N + 1)$	x^{n+1}
$3.*(X/(2.*Y + 1.)$	$3\left(\dfrac{x}{2y + 1}\right)$

To form an arithmetic statement in FORTRAN, a variable name is written followed by an equals sign and an arithmetic expression, as illustrated in these examples:

```
AREA = 3.00                 NEWVAL = IVAL1 − IVAL2
VALUE = −.045 * VARX        J = J + 1
Y = X**2 + 2.*X + 7.533
```

When an arithmetic statement is executed, it is done so in two stages: first, the value of the arithmetic expression on the right of the equals sign is calculated; second, this value is placed in the variable named to the left of the equals sign. Note that the FORTRAN use of the equals sign is different than the use of the equals sign in an arithmetic statement. That's why a statement such as

$$J = J + 1$$

is legal FORTRAN, but illegal arithmetic. If the starting value of J is 5, J + 1 is calculated to be equal to 6 and 6 replaces the initial value of J. As a result, J will have a value of 6 after the statement is executed.

Although the variable to the left of the equals sign and the expression to the right are usually in the same mode, this is not a requirement of FORTRAN. If they are of oppositie modes, however, the execution of the statement takes place in three stages: first, the value of the arithmetic expression is calculated; second, the value is converted to the mode of the variable; third, the converted value is placed in the variable to the left of the equals sign. Since the conversion from one mode to another can significantly change the value of an expression, it is important to know what takes place during conversion. For example, when the statement

$$K = 9.88799$$

is executed, the value 9 is placed in the variable K. In other words, the decimal positions in the real constant 9.88799 are dropped when converting to integer mode. On the other hand, if the statement

$$X = M/N$$

is executed at a time when M has a value of 5 and N has a value of 2, X will receive the value of 2.0. Here, 5 is divided by 2 giving 2.5, but since the expression is in the integer mode, the .5 is dropped. Then when 2 is converted to the real mode, it becomes 2.0.

You can see that converting from one mode to another can lead to lost decimal positions. If the value of the expression does not involve decimal fractions, however, converting to another mode changes only the form of a variable, not its value; thus,

$$X = -2$$

causes X to receive a value of −2.0, and

$$I = 5.00$$

gives I a value of 5.

One final point about writing arithmetic statements: blanks can be used anywhere within a statement or they can be omitted entirely. Thus,

$$X = (A + B)/(C * D - E)$$

can be written like this:

$$X = (A+B)/(C*D-E)$$

or like this:

$$X = (A + B) / (C * D - E)$$

You may very well have several questions at this point. What is the significance of having two forms for variables—real and integer? When should the mode of the variable differ from the mode of the arithmetic expression in an arithmetic statement? How do the arithmetic statements fit into the rest of a FORTRAN program? For now, though, concentrate on writing valid arithmetic statements and understanding the sequence in which the operations are performed. The other questions will be answered before you complete this chapter.

THE REORDER LISTING PROGRAM

Figure 20-1 gives the characteristics of a reorder-listing program that is to be written in FORTRAN. The input is a deck of balance-forward cards, one card per inventory item. The output of the program is a listing

Sample input

Field name:	Item No.	Item description	Unit cost	Unit price	Reorder point	On hand	On order
Card columns:	1—5	6—27	28—32	33—37	38—42	43—47	48—52
Card 1:	00101	GENERATOR	04000	04000	00100	00070	00050
	00103	HEATER SOLENOID	00330	00449	00050	00034	00000
	03244	GEAR HOUSING	06500	07900	00010	00012	00000
	03981	PLUMB LINE	00210	00240	00015	00035	00000
Card 5:	04638	STARTER SWITCH	00900	00980	00030	00016	00000

Sample output

Field name:	Item No.	Unit price	Available	Reorder point
Print positions:	1—5	11—16	22—26	32—36
Line 1:	103	4.49	34	50
	4638	9.80	16	30
	7846	1.98	52	60
	11946	112.50	10	12
Line 5:	16438	13.20	5	6

Processing specifications

1. Add on hand to on order to derive available.
2. Print a line on the reorder listing only when available is less than the reorder point.

FIGURE 20-1 The reorder-listing problem

of those items in inventory that need to be reordered. The illustration indicates the card columns of each input field and the print positions for each item printed on the output listing. It also gives some sample input and output data. As you can see from the processing specifications, a line is printed whenever the available stock for an item (on hand plus on order) is less than the reorder point. This is basically the same program that is discussed in chapter 4, and a flowchart for its solution is given in figure 20-2. In this and all other FORTRAN problems discussed in this book, the last card in the input deck is indicated by all 9s in the control field (in this case, the item-number field).

When a FORTRAN programmer codes this program, he uses coding forms such as those in figure 20-3. The form in the illustration, in fact, contains the complete reorder-listing program. If you study the coding form, you will find eighty columns are indicated from left to right. When

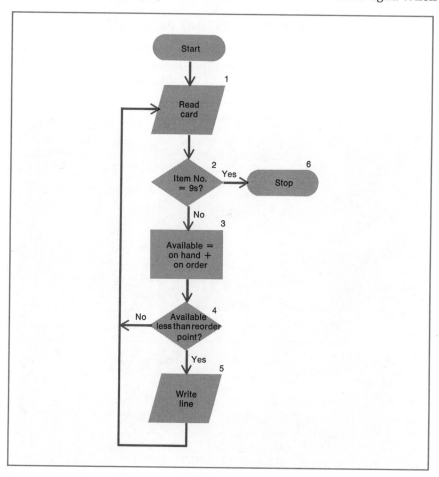

FIGURE 20-2   Flowchart for the reorder-listing program

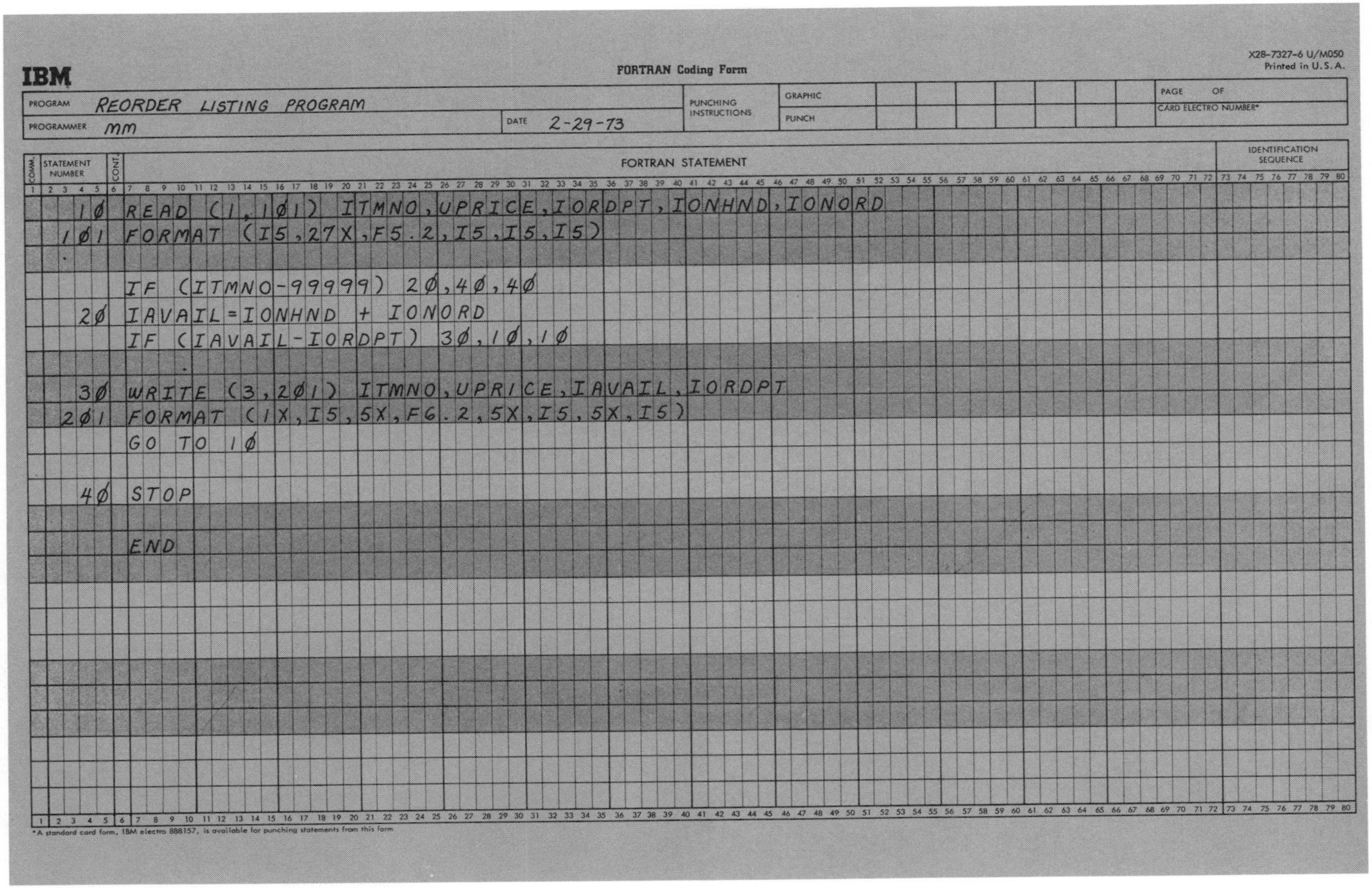

IBM FORTRAN Coding Form X28-7327-6 U/M050 Printed in U.S.A.

PROGRAM: REORDER LISTING PROGRAM
PROGRAMMER: mm
DATE: 2-29-73

```
   1Ø READ (1,1Ø1) ITMNO,UPRICE,IORDPT,IONHND,IONORD
  1Ø1 FORMAT (I5,27X,F5.2,I5,I5,I5)
    .
      IF (ITMNO-99999) 2Ø,4Ø,4Ø
   2Ø IAVAIL=IONHND + IONORD
      IF (IAVAIL-IORDPT) 3Ø,1Ø,1Ø
      .
   3Ø WRITE (3,2Ø1) ITMNO,UPRICE,IAVAIL,IORDPT
  2Ø1 FORMAT (1X,I5,5X,F6.2,5X,I5,5X,I5)
      GO TO 1Ø

   4Ø STOP

      END
```

*A standard card form, IBM electro 888157, is available for punching statements from this form

FIGURE 20-3 The reorder-listing program

the program is completed, one source-deck card is keypunched for each coding line.

Because it is difficult to distinguish between some handwritten letters and numerals, programmers usually write certain characters in a distinctive way. In figure 20-3, for example, zeros have a slash through them (Ø) while the letter O does not. It is also common for programmers to write the letter Z with a bar through it (Ƶ) to distinguish it from the numeral 2 and to write the numeral 1 as a simple vertical (I) but the letter I with top and bottom cross members (I).

As far as the FORTRAN compiler is concerned, only columns 1–72 of the coding form are significant. Columns 73–80 can be used to identify the source-deck cards or to give them sequence numbers, but they are not processed by the compiler. Their use is at the option of the programmer; in this book, columns 73–80 aren't used.

If you look at the program in figure 20-3, you can see that FORTRAN statements are written in columns 7–72, while columns 1–5 are used to give statement numbers to some of the statements. For example, statement number 20 is given to the arithmetic statement

IAVAIL = IONHND + IONORD

A statement number can be written anywhere in columns 1–5, with leading or trailing blanks. In Basic FORTRAN, statement numbers must be four digits or less; in full FORTRAN, they can be up to five digits long. Although any number can be used for any line, the same number cannot be used for two different lines. As the reorder-listing program is explained, you will see when statements require statement numbers.

The READ and FORMAT Statements

The first two statements of the program in figure 20-3 correspond to block 1 of the flowchart in figure 20-2. They are called the READ statement and the FORMAT statement; together they cause one card record to be read each time the READ statement is executed. The READ statement gives variable names to the fields that are to be read; the FORMAT statement tells the location and form of the fields in the input card.

The READ statement in figure 20-3 is as follows:

READ (1,101) ITMNO,UPRICE,IORDPT,IONHND,IONORD

Within the parentheses following the word READ, two numbers are given, separated by a comma. The first of these numbers indicates the I/O device to be used. The numbers used for various devices depend on the system being used; a common convention is to use 1 for the card reader, 2 for the card punch, and 3 for the printer. Since this convention is used in this book, the device referred to by the READ statement above is the card reader.

The second number in the parentheses is the statement number associated with the FORMAT statement. Since the number 101 is given, the FORMAT statement on line 2 of the coding form is indicated. The statement number used can be any number provided it is not used for any other statement in the program.

Following the parentheses in the READ statement is a list of variable names. These names refer in sequence to the fields of the input card that are to be used. Thus, ITMNO is an integer variable name for the first field in the input card to be used by the program, the item-number field; UPRICE is a real variable name for the second input field to be used, the unit-price field; IORDPT is an integer variable name for the third field to be used, the reorder-point field; and so on. Since the item-description and unit-cost fields aren't going to be used by this program, they are not given names in this list. The programmer selects integer or real names for the fields based on (1) whether or not the input field contains decimal positions and (2) the extent to which the field will be involved in arithmetic statements. Since this program involves only simple arithmetic — the addition of two whole numbers — and since only unit price has decimal positions, all fields except unit price are given integer names.

In the parentheses of the FORMAT statement, codes are given so the compiler knows in which card columns each of the variables named in the READ statement can be found. The first specification given is I5, indicating a five-column integer (I) field. In other words, the first variable named in the READ statement list (ITMNO) is located in card columns 1–5. The FORMAT statement indicates next that twenty-seven card columns are to be skipped (27X); item description and unit price are in these card columns. The third code given is F5.2. This indicates that the next variable named in the READ list is a real number that is five-card columns long and has two decimal positions. Thus, the location and the nature of the UPRICE field are given. In a similar manner, the FORMAT statement specifies that the next three variables named in the READ list are five-position integer fields (I5,I5,I5).

Do you see the relationship between the READ and FORMAT statements? The codes in the FORMAT statement are given in the same sequence as that for the variables listed in the READ statement. For each variable named, the FORMAT statement must have one I or F specification, and the codes and names should be of the same mode — integer (I) or real (F). To show that input columns are to be skipped, the X code is used. In both the READ and the FORMAT statements, the use of parentheses and commas is significant. If they are omitted or misplaced, the statement will not perform as intended.

The First IF Statement

The third coding line in figure 20-3

IF (ITMNO-99999) 20,40,40

corresponds to block 2 of the flowchart. This is the IF statement, one of the FORTRAN logic statements. In the parentheses following the word IF, an arithmetic expression is written. This expression, which can be either real or integer mode, can be as simple as (X) or as complex as you wish it. Following the parentheses, three statement numbers are given, separated by commas. When the IF statement is executed, it is done in two stages: first, the arithmetic expression is evaluated; second, the program branches to one of the statement numbers listed. If the value of the arithmetic expression is negative, the program branches to the first statement number in the list; if the value is zero, it branches to the second statement number; if the value is positive, it branches to the third statement number.

In the IF statement, the arithmetic expression is

ITMNO-99999

This is an integer expression that subtracts the constant 99999 from the value of the item-number field. If the item number is less than 99999, the value of the expression is negative and the program branches to statement number 20. If the item number is 99999, as it will be when the last input card is read, the value of the expression is zero and the program will branch to statement number 40, the second to the last coding line of the program. Since a five-digit field can't be greater than 99999, the expression will never be positive; thus, any statement number can be used as the third number in the list.

The Arithmetic Statement

The fourth coding line, corresponding to block 3 of the flowchart, is as follows:

IAVAIL=IONHND + IONORD

This arithmetic statement causes on hand and on order to be added together and the sum to be placed in the field named IAVAIL. Note here that IAVAIL is a variable name that has not appeared previously in the program. Thus, it is said to be *defined* by the arithmetic statement. Once defined, by placing it as the variable to the left of the equals sign, the name can be used in other statements later in the program.

The Second IF Statement

The fourth flowchart block determines whether an output line should be printed. It is coded by this IF statement:

IF (IAVAIL—IORDPT) 30,10,10

Since the arithmetic expression is IAVAIL—IORDPT, its value will be negative when the available stock is less than the reorder point. For example, if available is 34 and the reorder point is 50, the value of IAVAIL—IORDPT is −16, and the program branches to statement number 30, which causes a line to be printed. If the value of the expression is zero or positive, meaning available is not less than the reorder point, the program branches to statement number 10, which is the start of the program, and another input card is read.

The WRITE and FORMAT Statements

The WRITE and FORMAT statements, statement numbers 30 and 201, are as follows:

```
30 WRITE (3,201) ITMNO,UPRICE,IAVAIL,IORDPT
201 FORMAT (1X,I5,5X,F6.2,5X,I5,5X,I5)
```

The WRITE statement, which corresponds closely to the READ statement, indicates that device number 3 is going to be used and that FORMAT statement number 201 gives the layout of the output record. Since device number 3 is used for the printer in this book, this WRITE statement will cause one line to be printed each time it is executed. The fields to be printed are given in sequence in the list following the parentheses. In order, they are ITMNO, UPRICE, IAVAIL, and IORDPT.

The FORMAT statement gives the print layout for each output line. Because the first character in each output line is never printed, the first specification in the FORMAT statement is 1X. Since X in an output format indicates a blank, 1X means one blank is placed at the start of the output line.

The next specifications in the parentheses of the FORMAT statement represent the actual printed output data. I5 means a five-position integer field will be printed in print positions 1–5. Since the first variable named in the WRITE list is ITMNO, item number is printed in positions 1–5. Then, 5X indicates that five blanks are to be printed in positions 6–10, while F6.2 indicates that the next variable to be printed is six print positions with two decimal positions. Since the decimal point is printed for a real variable, this variable—UPRICE in the WRITE list, consisting of five digits—will take up six print positions (11–16). For example, if the input card contains 11250 in the unit-price field, 112.50 will be printed. In a similar manner, the next specifications—5X,I5,5X,I5—give the spacing for the last two variables in the WRITE list: IAVAIL and IORDPT are integers and will print in positions 22–26 and 32–36.

In FORTRAN, when a field is printed, lead zeros are automatically zero-suppressed. Thus, 00125 with a format of I5 will print as 125, and 01145 with a format of F6.3 will print as 1.145. If a negative value is printed, FORTRAN automatically prints a leading minus sign, as in −33.3. When programming, you must be careful to use a format for the output field that is large enough to accommodate the full number plus the decimal point and minus sign (if any).

The GO TO Statement

After block 5 of the flowchart, the WRITE block, the program branches to the READ block. In the FORTRAN program, this is accomplished by the following GO TO statement:

GO TO 10

After the words GO TO, a statement number is given. When the GO TO statement is executed, a branch takes place to the statement number specified — in this case, statement number 10, the READ statement.

The STOP Statement

The first IF statement of this program branches to statement number 40 when a card with an item number of 99999 is read. When statement number 40 — the STOP statement — is executed, the program stops.

The END Statement

The last statement of every FORTRAN program must be the END statement consisting simply of the word END. It is used to tell the compiler that there are no more statements in the source deck. Unlike the STOP statement, the END statement does not cause object code to be compiled.

SOME REFINEMENTS

Because it is the first FORTRAN program presented, the reorder-listing program in figure 20-3 is simplified. In actual practice, a program such as this would print headings at the top of the report and would likely print a message at the end of the program to indicate that it has run to completion. This additional printing is shown on the print chart in figure 20-4.

The coding required for the reorder listing with headings and an end-of-job message is shown in figure 20-5. This coding also illustrates some refinements used in most FORTRAN programs. For example, there are six lines in this program that have a C in column 1. These lines, called *comment lines*, are used to identify or explain various routines within a program and thus make the program easier to follow. Any characters may be coded in columns 2–80 of a comment line since the compiler ignores the comments — they are for the convenience of the programmer only.

Unlike the program in figure 20-3, all of the FORMAT statements in figure 20-5 are grouped at the start of the program. Although FORMAT statements can be placed anywhere in a program, many programmers group them at the beginning. By studying card layouts and print charts, the FORMAT statements can usually be coded independent of the remainder of the program.

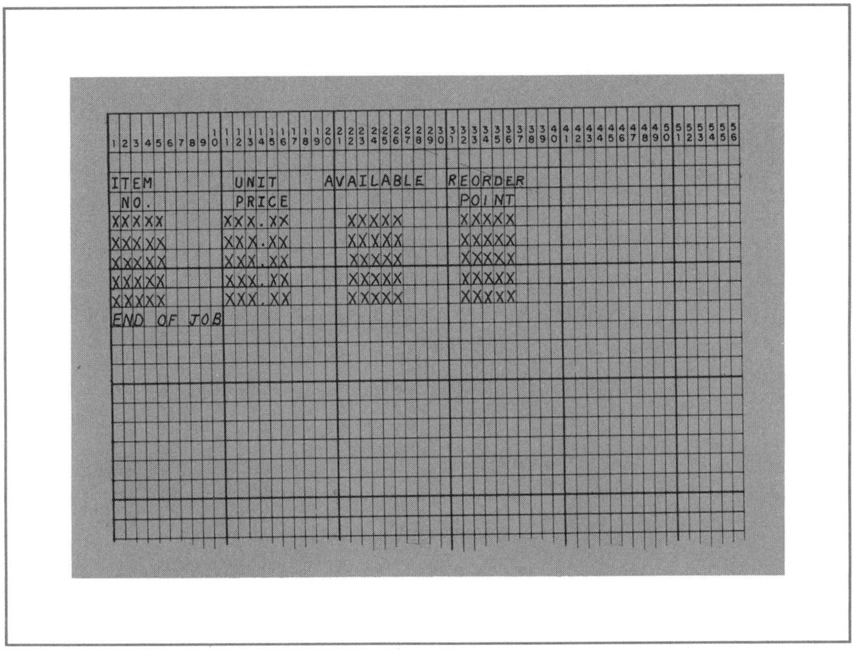

FIGURE 20-4   Print chart for the refined reorder-listing program

The first FORMAT statement, statement number 501, gives specifications for the input cards. This is the same as in figure 20-3 with one exception: 3I5 is used to mean I5,I5,I5. They are, of course, equivalent. When a number is placed before the I or F in a format specification, it means the specification is repeated that number of times. Thus, 5F15.5 is the equivalent of F15.5,F15.5,F15.5,F15.5,F15.5; and 4I2 is the equivalent of I2,I2,I2,I2.

The second FORMAT statement, statement number 502, gives the specifications for the two heading lines and introduces the H format. H, which stands for Hollerith, indicates that the characters that follow are to be printed when the corresponding WRITE statement is executed. Thus, 4HITEM means the four Hollerith characters ITEM should be printed. If you look at the specifications through column 61 of FORMAT statement 502, you can see how they correspond to the first heading line. 1X is the first specification because the first character in a FORMAT statement for the printer is never printed; 4HITEM means ITEM will be printed in print positions 1–4; 7X means the next seven print positions will be blank; 4HUNIT means UNIT will print in the next four print positions; 4X means the next four print positions will be blank; and so forth.

The slash (/) in column 62 indicates the end of the first heading line and the start of the second. Then, 2X is used—one of the Xs is required as for all print lines and the other means print position 1 of this line will

IBM FORTRAN Coding Form

X28-7327-6 U/M050
Printed in U.S.A.

PROGRAM: THE REFINED REORDER LISTING PROGRAM
PROGRAMMER: MM
DATE: 2-29-73

```
C THE REORDER LISTING PROGRAM
C FORMAT STATEMENTS--INPUT
  5Ø1 FORMAT (I5,27X,F5.2,3I5)
C FORMAT STATEMENTS--OUTPUT
  5Ø2 FORMAT (1X,4HITEM,7X,4HUNIT,4X,9HAVAILABLE,2X,7HREORDER/2X,3HNO.,
     1       7X,5HPRICE,15X,5HPOINT)
  5Ø3 FORMAT (1H ,I5,F11.2,2I1Ø)
  5Ø4 FORMAT (11H END OF JOB)

C PRINTING REPORT HEADINGS
      WRITE (3,5Ø2)

C BODY OF PROGRAM
   1Ø READ (1,5Ø1) ITMNO,UPRICE,IORDPT,IONHND,IONORD
      IF (ITMNO-99999) 2Ø,4Ø,4Ø
   2Ø IAVAIL=IONHND+IONORD
      IF (IAVAIL-IORDPT) 3Ø,1Ø,1Ø
   3Ø WRITE (3,5Ø3) ITMNO,UPRICE,IAVAIL,IORDPT
      GO TO 1Ø

C END OF JOB ROUTINE
   4Ø WRITE (3,5Ø4)
      STOP
      END
```

*A standard card form, IBM electro 888157, is available for punching statements from this form

FIGURE 20-5 The refined reorder-listing program

be blank. Then, 3HNO. means NO. will print in print positions 2–4. At this point, there is no more room on that coding line, so the FORMAT statement is continued on the next line. 7X indicates that the next seven print positions are blank; 5HPRICE means PRICE is printed in the next five print positions; and so on.

Notice that when a *continuation line* is used, 1 is coded in column 6. The actual requirement of FORTRAN is that any character other than zero or blank be used in column 6 of a continuation line. If additional continuation lines are used, they too must have some character other than zero or blank in column 6. Continuation lines may be used for any FORTRAN statement with a maximum of five continuation lines in Basic FORTRAN and nineteen in full FORTRAN.

FORMAT statement 503, which gives the specifications for the printed columns of data, illustrates some other common coding techniques. First, 1Hb (where b is a blank) is used instead of 1X for the first character of the printed line. This, of course, is equivalent. Second, instead of using the X format code for spacing, enlarged I and F codes are used. Thus, F11.2 will cause five extra blanks to be printed to the left of the number because the field actually has the format F6.2. Similarly, 2I10 will print two I5 fields with five blanks before each field. In other words, the effects of

$$\text{FORMAT (1X,I5,5X,F6.2,5X,I5,5X,I5)}$$

and

$$\text{FORMAT (1H,I5,F11.2,2I10)}$$

are identical.

The last FORMAT statement, statement number 504, gives the specifications for the end-of-job message. Notice that the first character following the H is blank because this first character isn't printed.

Once you understand the FORMAT statements, the rest of the program should be easy to follow since it is basically the same as in figure 20-3. The first WRITE statement of the program

$$\text{WRITE (3,502)}$$

causes both heading lines to be printed. By using slashes in the FORMAT statement, then, a single WRITE statement can be used to print multiple lines. If the slash wasn't used, both heading lines could be printed using this coding:

```
511 FORMAT (1X,4HITEM,7X,4HUNIT,4X,9HAVAILABLE,3X,7HREORDER)
512 FORMAT (1X,4H NO.,7X,5HPRICE,16X,5HPOINT)
    WRITE (3,511)
    WRITE (3,512)
```

Here, the WRITE statement has to be written twice.

The body of the program is the same as in figure 20-3, but the end-of-job routine differs. Here, the words END OF JOB are printed before the program is ended. Note again that the END statement must always be the last statement of a FORTRAN program.

THE MANHATTAN PROBLEM

To illustrate the use of FORTRAN in another type of problem, consider again the Manhattan problem originally described in chapter 4. To refresh your memory, the problem is to determine how much the $24.00 supposedly paid for Manhattan Island in 1627 would be worth today if it had been placed in a savings account at 4½ percent annual interest. Assume that the present year is punched into columns 1–4 of a card that is read at the start of the program.

A flowchart for the solution of the problem is given in figure 20-6. After the card containing the present year is read and initial values are given to I (the starting-year field) and PRINC (the principal field), the program goes into a loop (blocks 3, 4, and 5). Each time through the loop, PRINC is recalculated and I is increased by 1. When I equals IYEAR (the value read from the input card), the program leaves the loop and the answer is printed.

The FORTRAN solution for this problem is given in figure 20-7. Except for the second coding line,

DOUBLE PRECISION PRINC

the coding should be self-explanatory since nothing new is included. One point worth noting is that the principal calculation is done in the real mode while the year counting (I=I+1) is done in the integer mode. When an integer variable is used to count in this manner, it is often referred to as a counter. Thus, I in this program is the counter.

To understand why the DOUBLE PRECISION statement is needed, you must first learn the form in which FORTRAN variables are stored. Integer variables, for example, are stored as whole numbers, but have a *range* that they must not go beyond. This range varies from computer to computer but typically is from seven to eighteen digits. On the System/360, the range is up to ten digits—more specifically, a maximum value of $+2,147,483,647$ and a minimum of $-2,147,483,647$.

When real numbers are stored, they are generally stored using *floating-point representation*. This means that they take the form of a decimal number and an exponent. For example, the number 361.399 might be stored in this form

.361399E+3

which means

$$.361339 \times 10^3$$

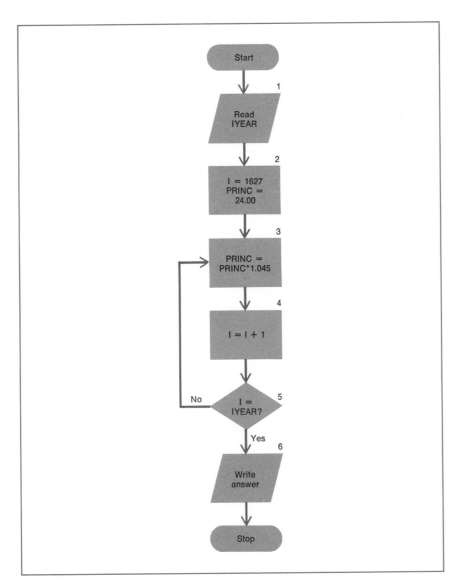

FIGURE 20-6 Flowchart for the Manhattan problem

Similarly, 10,000,000 would be stored as .1E+8 and .00000117 would be stored as .117E−5 (that is, $.117 \times 10^{-5}$, or $.117 \times 1/10^5$, or $.117 \times .00001$). The advantage of using floating-point representation is that very large and very small numbers can be stored in a limited amount of storage space. Thus, the maximum value of a real number on the System/360 is around 10^{75}, or a value of 1 followed by seventy-five zeros. Even though this is considerably larger than the range of an integer number, both real and integer numbers require the same number of storage positions (four) on the System/360.

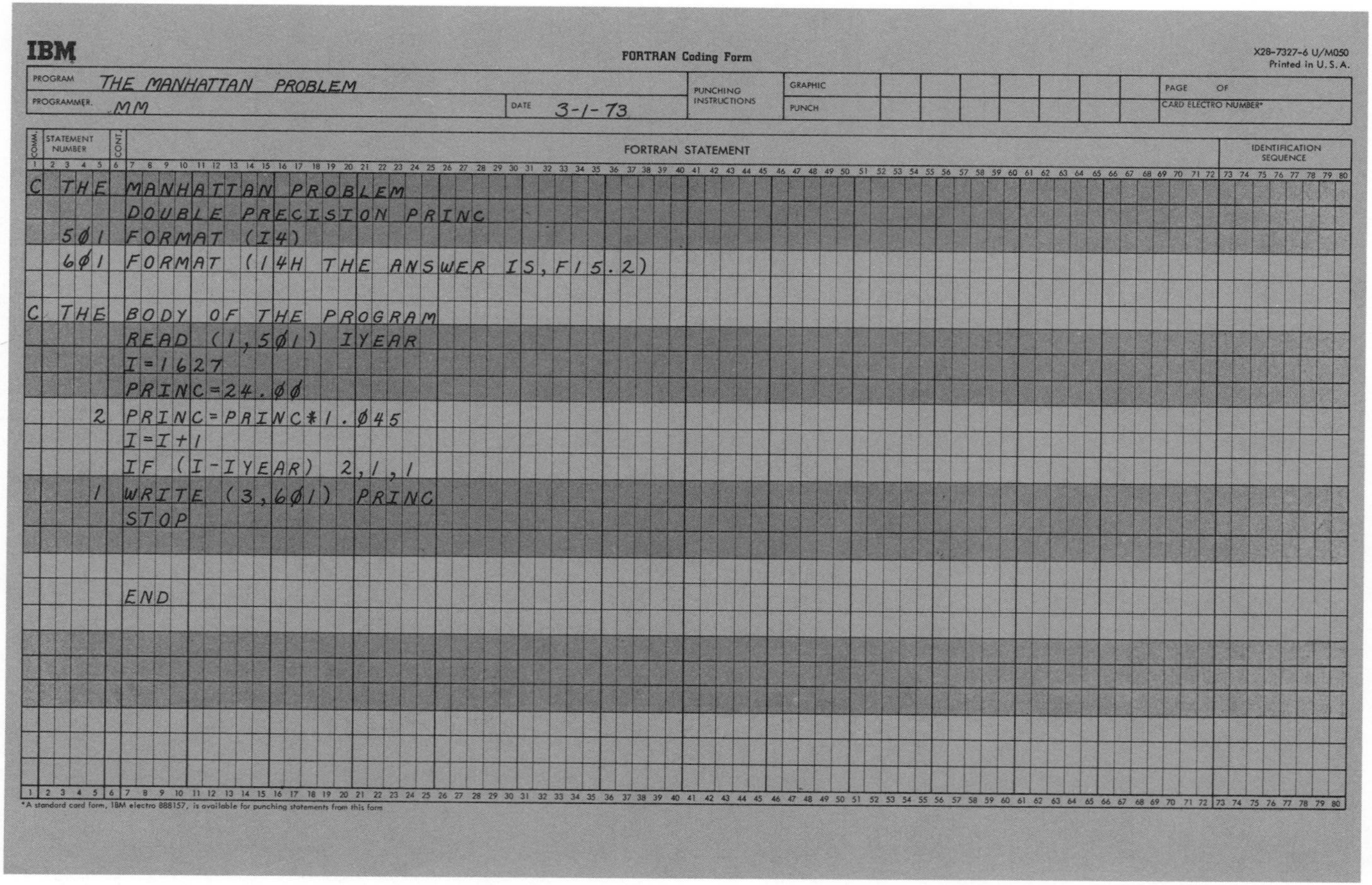

FORTRAN Coding Form

IBM

X28-7327-6 U/M050
Printed in U.S.A.

PROGRAM THE MANHATTAN PROBLEM
PROGRAMMER MM
DATE 3-1-73

PUNCHING INSTRUCTIONS — GRAPHIC / PUNCH
PAGE   OF
CARD ELECTRO NUMBER

FORTRAN STATEMENT

```
C THE MANHATTAN PROBLEM
      DOUBLE PRECISION PRINC
  501 FORMAT (I4)
  601 FORMAT (14H THE ANSWER IS,F15.2)
C THE BODY OF THE PROGRAM
      READ (1,501) IYEAR
      I=1627
      PRINC=24.00
    2 PRINC=PRINC*1.045
      I=I+1
      IF (I-IYEAR) 2,1,1
    1 WRITE (3,601) PRINC
      STOP
      END
```

FIGURE 20-7   The Manhattan problem

The diasdvantage of using floating-point representation is that only a limited number of actual digits are stored. This is referred to as a number's *precision*. On a System/360, for example, a real variable is normally stored with only seven significant digits plus the exponent. Thus, the number

79,812,533,101

is stored as

.7981253E+11

When operated upon, it is treated as a value of

79,812,530,000

In other words, a computer's precision limits the degree to which an exact answer can be computed. If the precision of a computer is seven digits, the results of calculations can have only seven significant digits.

This brings us back to the Manhattan problem. Since the calculation is done in the real mode and the answer is ten or more significant digits — for example, the answer is 98,701,004.67 in 1973 — the precision of many computers will be exceeded. Thus, the answer will not be exact. On System/360, for instance, the answer line in 1973 would print as

THE ANSWER IS 98695744.00

(In actuality, the precision of System/360 is slightly more than seven digits; that's why eight are printed here.)

Admittedly, this is a small degree of inexactness in relationship to the size of the answer, and for that reason, the lack of precision can often be ignored. However, if a more precise answer is required, the DOUBLE PRECISION statement can be used. This statement consists of the words DOUBLE PRECISION followed by a list of variable names separated by commas, as in this example:

DOUBLE PRECISION X,Y,XINT,PAYMNT

By placing this statement at the start of a program, the variables named are stored in *double-precision* format, which means they have at least twice as many significant digits as they would otherwise. On System/360, a double-precision number has sixteen significant digits in contrast to the seven of single precision, and it takes up eight storage positions in contrast to the four for single precision. Since the variable named PRINC is specified as double precision in the Manhattan program, enough significant digits will be stored to give an exact answer to the problem. However, since the DOUBLE PRECISION statement is not included in the standards for Basic FORTRAN but only for full FORTRAN, it is not possible to obtain an exact answer to the Manhattan problem using standard Basic FORTRAN as implemented on most computer systems.

DISCUSSION

Although I haven't given you all the rules for using the FORTRAN statements presented so far, you should be able to write acceptable FORTRAN programs by following the examples shown in figures 20-3, 20-5, and 20-7. Remember that the placement of commas and parentheses is critical to the correctness of a FORTRAN statement, while blanks do not affect a statement in any way. Statement numbers are given to all FORMAT statements and to all statements that the program branches to. These statement numbers can be assigned in any order although it is common to keep all statements other than the FORMAT statements in numerical sequence, usually in increments of ten such as 10, 20, 30, and so on. Although FORMAT statements and comment lines can be placed anywhere in the source deck, the DOUBLE PRECISION statement, if used, must come at the start of the program, and the END statement must be the last statement in the deck. You might note that of the statements discussed so far, the DOUBLE PRECISION, FORMAT, and END statements do not cause object code to be compiled. They only give information that allows the other statements to be compiled into object code.

After a program is coded, the programmer usually *desk-checks* it by studying an 80-80 listing of the source deck. Figure 20-8, for example, is an 80-80 listing of the source deck for the Manhattan problem. After all errors discovered during desk checking are corrected, the program is ready for compilation. Since the 80-80 listing is the common form in which a program is studied, these listings will be used for all other FORTRAN examples presented in this book.

During compilation, the FORTRAN compiler normally prints a program listing, much like an 80-80 listing, along with *diagnostic messages* that indicate errors discovered during compilation. These diagnostic messages are used by the programmer to make additional corrections to the source deck. Then the program is recompiled, and, if diagnostic messages appear again, the correction procedure is repeated. Depending on the compiler used, the diagnostic messages vary from being quite brief and confusing to quite understandable. In either case, it is the programmer's job to decode the error messages and to make the necessary corrections.

After an error-free compilation is completed, the object program is ready to be tested by executing the program using test data. If the output of the test run and the expected output do not agree, one or more errors (bugs) are indicated, and the programmer must *debug* the program. During this stage, the programmer must determine what type of error in the source deck could have led to the output error derived. The better his deductive powers, the faster he will debug his program. When the results of the test run agree with the expected results, the program is considered to be finished.

```
C THE MANHATTAN PROBLEM
        DOUBLE PRECISION PRINC
  501 FORMAT (I4)
  601 FORMAT (14H THE ANSWER IS,F15.2)
C THE BODY OF THE PROGRAM
        READ (1,501) IYEAR
        I=1627
        PRINC=24.00
    2 PRINC=PRINC*1.045
        I=I+1
        IF (I-IYEAR) 2,1,1
    1 WRITE (3,601) PRINC
        STOP
        END
```

FIGURE 20-8   An 80-80 listing of the Manhattan problem

Although this has been a somewhat brief introduction to FORTRAN, enough elements have been presented to allow you to write programs of great complexity. On the other hand, you have not been shown some elements that allow you to do some very basic functions. For instance, you still can't read or write alphanumeric fields or double-space a printed report. The elements to do these and other basic functions are described in topic 2.

SUMMARY

1. In 1966 the American National Standards Institute published standards for Basic and full FORTRAN. These standards are intended to reduce the variations in FORTRAN as you go from one manufacturer's equipment to another's. If the standards are rigidly followed, a FORTRAN program can be compiled and run on many different computers without modifying the source program.

2. FORTRAN arithmetic statements correspond in several ways to arithmetic notation. Three of the operators (+, −, and /) are the same, and parentheses in FORTRAN are used just as they are in arithmetic notation. However, FORTRAN variables and constants must be written in a rigidly prescribed way, an expression must be of only one mode, and the equals sign (=) in FORTRAN means "replace the present value of the variable with the computed value of the expression."

3. A complete program consists of I/O statements (READ, WRITE), FORMAT statements, arithmetic statements, control statements (IF, GO TO, STOP), and the END statement.

4. On most systems, integer and real numbers are stored in two different forms. Integer variables and constants are stored as whole numbers and have a range that is considerably less than that of real numbers. Real variables and constants are stored — in coded form, of course — as the combination of a decimal fraction and an exponent. Thus, real variables are likely to have less significant digits than integer variables, but a much greater range. A double-precision real variable is one with the same exponent range as a single-precision variable but with at least twice the precision (twice as many significant digits).

5. After a programmer has defined the problem and flowcharted a solution to it, he codes the solution. After the code is keypunched, the programmer desk-checks an 80-80 listing of the source deck, corrects errors (diagnostics) detected during compilation, and tests or debugs the program.

FOR REVIEW

subset	statement number
variable	defining a variable
variable name	comment line
integer variable	continuation line
real variable	counter
constant	range of a number
integer constant	floating-point representation
real constant	precision
arithmetic expression	double precision
mode	desk checking
integer mode	diagnostic message
real mode	debugging
mixed mode	

This topic consists of seven unrelated subjects. When you have completed the topic, you will have covered FORTRAN elements that allow you to use most of a computer's capabilities. With few exceptions, the elements that are not covered in this chapter do not give you additional processing capabilities, but only allow you to code in a more efficient manner.

Alphanumeric Input and Output Data

When fields containing letters or special characters are stored using FORTRAN, each variable named can hold only a limited number of characters, depending on the computer used. For example, each variable on a System/360 can hold up to four alphanumeric characters, while each variable of the Burroughs B5500 and the Univac 1108 can hold up to six characters. As a result, several different variable names must be used for a twenty-character field such as item description or employee name.

To illustrate, suppose a card with the following format is to be read:

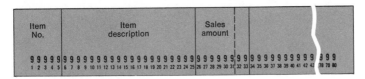

Then, READ and FORMAT statements such as the following are needed in System/360 FORTRAN:

```
      READ (1,101) ITMNO,DES1,DES2,DES3,DES4,DES5,SLSAMT
  101 FORMAT (I5,5A4,F8.2)
```

If the three input fields are to be printed, statements such as these are needed:

```
      WRITE (3,201) ITMNO,DES1,DES2,DES3,DES4,DES5,SLSAMT
  201 FORMAT (1H ,I5,5X,5A4,5X,F9.2)
```

Here, the format code A is used for each alphanumeric variable. In general, this code is followed by a number that is not larger than the maximum number of characters each variable can hold. The number preceding code A indicates how many times the specification is to be repeated, so 5A4 is the same as A4,A4,A4,A4,A4. Unlike the variable names for numeric fields, the first letter of a variable name for an alphabetic field is insignificant: it can be any of the letters A-Z.

If an input field is smaller than the number of characters each variable can hold, the format specification is made accordingly. For example, a three-column input field is specified as A3. Similarly, a twenty-two-character field can be treated as six variables with these format specifications: 5A4,A2. In figure 20-9, which is a modification of the reorder-listing program from topic 1, the twenty-two-character item-description field is read and printed. Statement 501 is the FORMAT statement for the input

```
C THE MODIFIED REORDER LISTING PROGRAM
  501 FORMAT (I5,5A4,A2,5X,F5.2,3I5)
  601 FORMAT (1H1,23X,15HREORDER LISTING//1X,4HITEM,12X,4HITEM,17X,
     14HUNIT,5X,9HAVAILABLE,2X,7HREORDER/2X,3HNO.,9X,11HDESCRIPTION,13X,
     25HPRICE,16X,5HPOINT/)
  602 FORMAT (1X,I5,5X,5A4,A2,F11.2,2I10)
  603 FORMAT (11HOEND OF JOB)
  701 FORMAT (I5,5A4,A2,2I5)

C PRINT HEADINGS
      WRITE (3,601)

C BODY OF PROGRAM
   10 READ (1,501) ITMNO,D1,D2,D3,D4,D5,D6,UPRICE,IORDPT,IONHND,IONORD
      IF (ITMNO+99999) 20,40,40
   20 IAVAIL=IONHND-IONORD
      IF (IAVAIL-IORDPT) 30,10,10
   30 WRITE (3,602) ITMNO,D1,D2,D3,D4,D5,D6,UPRICE,IAVAIL,IORDPT

C PUNCHED CARD OUTPUT
      WRITE (2,701) ITMNO,D1,D2,D3,D4,D5,D6,IAVAIL,IORDPT
      GO TO 10

C END OF JOB ROUTINE
   40 WRITE (3,603)
      STOP
      END
```

FIGURE 20-9   The modified reorder-listing program

card read by statement number 10; statement number 602 is the FORMAT statement for the output line printed by statement number 30.

It is interesting to note that the A format is not included in the standards for Basic FORTRAN. As a result, alphanumeric input and output fields cannot be processed using Basic FORTRAN. This gives you an idea of how inadequate some versions of FORTRAN are when used for business applications.

Carriage Control

Carriage control refers to the spacing or skipping of the continuous form in the printer. Thus far, single spacing has been used exclusively because the first character defined by the FORMAT statement for the printer has always been a blank. If this first character, the carriage-control character, is not blank, however, some variations in carriage control can be achieved.

In the standards for full FORTRAN, the following carriage-control characters can be used:

Character	Meaning
blank	Advance one line before printing
0 (zero)	Advance two lines before printing
1	Skip to the first line of the next page before printing
+	No advance before printing

In figure 20-9, then, the continuous form is skipped to the top of the next page before printing the first heading line (FORMAT statement 601). The body of the report is single-spaced (FORMAT statement 602), but two lines are advanced before printing the end-of-job message (FORMAT statement 603). In the standards for Basic FORTRAN, only single spacing is allowed.

Within a FORMAT statement, the slash (/) can also be used for spacing a printed form. For example,

603 FORMAT (///11H END OF JOB)

will cause three lines to be skipped before printing. If slashes are used at the beginning or end of the FORMAT specifications, they cause as many lines to be skipped as there are slashes. If they are used in the middle of the specifications, they cause one less line to be skipped than there are slashes. In FORMAT statement 601 in figure 20-9, which causes three heading lines to print, one line is skipped between the first and second heading lines, no lines are skipped between the second and third heading lines, and one line is skipped after the third heading line. Thus, the report printed for the five cards indicated in figure 20-1 would be as shown in figure 20-10.

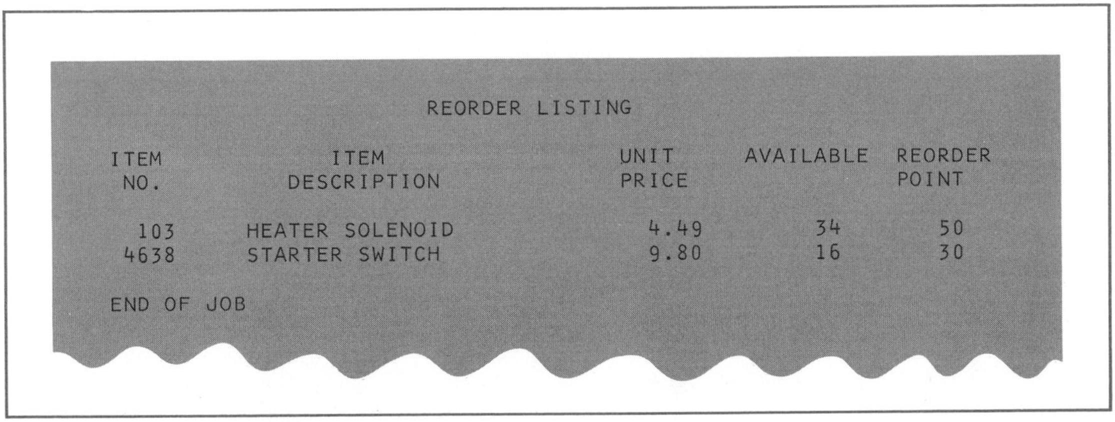

```
                          REORDER LISTING

      ITEM              ITEM                 UNIT    AVAILABLE   REORDER
      NO.           DESCRIPTION              PRICE               POINT

      103         HEATER SOLENOID            4.49       34         50
     4638         STARTER SWITCH             9.80       16         30

   END OF JOB
```

FIGURE 20-10   Output of the modified reorder-listing program

Other I/O Media

Thus far, the READ and WRITE statements have been used for reading input cards and printing output lines. These same statements, however, can be used for getting input or giving output on any sequential I/O device. Therefore, the READ statement can be used for reading magnetic-tape records or records from a sequential file stored on a direct-access device. The WRITE statement can be used for punching cards, writing magnetic-tape records, or writing sequential records onto a direct-access device.

There is nothing new to learn about the READ, WRITE, and FORMAT statements because they are used just as they are for card input and printer output. The only differences are (1) the device numbers used and (2) the fact that carriage-control characters are only used in the FORMAT statement for the printer. Thus, the following statements can be used for magnetic-tape output:

```
1000 FORMAT (F8.2,3F6.2,I4,F7.4)
     WRITE (5,1000) FLDA,FLDB,FLDC,FLDD,IFLDE,FLDF
```

Here, device number 5 refers to a magnetic tape drive.

Similarly, one output card is punched by the program in figure 20-9 for each item to be reordered. Device number 2 is used for the card punch, and the format of the output card, corresponding to FORMAT statement 701, is as follows:

The device numbers used for the various devices depend on the system used. On some systems, any device number can be used for any device as long as each device is given a different number. Just before the object program is executed, then, an actual device is assigned to each device number by using job-control cards (see chapter 14). On other systems, device numbers are rigidly defined as in this example:

Device Number	Device
1	Card reader
2	Card punch
3	Printer
4	Tape drive 1
5	Tape drive 2
6	Tape drive 3
7	Tape drive 4

In either case, you must find out which device numbers to use for the I/O units of the system you are using.

When planning FORTRAN programs, you must keep in mind the maximum record lengths allowed by the system you are using. On a System/360 using the Disk Operating System, for example, magnetic-tape and disk records cannot exceed 260 characters. For planning purposes, remember that the decimal point in a real variable takes up one position in an output record just as it does in an output line. Similarly, you must be careful that card input and output formats do not exceed eighty positions and that printer formats do not exceed the maximum length of the print line (usually, 100, 120, or 132 characters, depending on the printer used), plus one character for carriage control.

Two other Basic FORTRAN statements that can be used for tape files are as follows:

REWIND device-number

ENDFILE device-number

When the REWIND statement is executed for an input or output tape file, the tape indicated by the device number is rewound to the start of the tape. When the ENDFILE statement is executed for an output tape, an end-of-file record is written, and, if tape labels are used (see chapter 6), a trailer label is written. Thus, the end-of-job routine for a tape output file on device number 6 might be as follows:

```
C END OF JOB ROUTINE
      ENDFILE 6
      REWIND 6
      WRITE (3,101)
  101 FORMAT (///11H END OF JOB)
      STOP
```

I and F Formats

Unlike an assembler language or COBOL, FORTRAN allows considerable flexibility when keypunching input data. In an integer field, for example, blanks are automatically converted to zeros. Thus, bb12bbb (where b is a blank) in an I7 field is treated as 12000. When using other languages, a blank in a numeric field is often considered to be an invalid character that cannot be processed. If an integer field is signed, the sign is punched preceding the digits, so −bb47 or bb−47 in an I5 field is treated as −47. This contrasts languages that require an X-punch in the rightmost position of a numeric field to indicate that it is negative.

Similarly, blanks in an F format input field are treated as zeros, and a leading plus or minus sign can be used to indicate the sign of the field. In addition, a decimal point can be punched in a real input field, in which case it overrides the specifications used in the associated FORMAT statement. To illustrate, suppose a real variable named FLD1 is punched in columns 1–10 of a card and the format statement is

FORMAT (F10.3)

Then, the following table indicates the data punched in the card and the value given to the stored variable (b = blank):

Punched Data	Value of FLD1 (F10.3)
bbb1234567	+1234.567
bbbbb382.9	+382.9
−112.5678b	−112.5678
bb201147bb	+20114.700
+1.2bbbbbb	+1.2

Because it is easier to left-justify than to right-justify when keypunching, it is common to left-justify all real fields and to actually punch the decimal point. This tends to reduce the number of input errors.

For an I or F output field, leading zeros are suppressed, the decimal point is automatically placed, and a leading minus sign is given if the field is negative. In addition, the output field is automatically rounded if less decimal positions are specified for the output field than are stored in the variable. Thus, a variable with a value of −12.1176 printed with the format F8.2 would print as bb−12.12. Of course, if the output format specification is too small to accomodate all of the digits and the sign (if any) of a variable, this causes problems. Thus, a variable with a value of 12345.67 printed with the format F7.2 would print as asterisks — ******* — on System/360.

Library Functions

When writing programs, there are many routines that are used repeatedly. For example, in certain statistical problems, it is common to convert an arithmetic expression to its absolute value before operating upon it. Similarly, in certain civil engineering problems, finding the sine or cosine of an angle is common. To eliminate the duplication of programming effort, many of these often used programming routines are stored in object code in a *function library* that is available to the FORTRAN compiler. Then, if the *function name* is used in a FORTRAN arithmetic expression, the compiler retrieves the appropriate routine from the library and inserts the object code into the program.

Figure 20-11 lists the *library functions* that are available with standard Basic FORTRAN. To use these functions in an arithmetic statement, you give the function name followed by a variable name or an arithmetic expression enclosed in parentheses, as in these examples:

1. ABSVAL=ABS(VAR1)
2. SIDEA=HYP*COS(RADA)
3. HYP=SQRT(A**2+B**2)

Function	Function name	Example	Definition	No. of arguments	Argument type	Function type	Comments
Absolute value	IABS ABS	IABS(J) ABS(X)	Take absolute value of argument: |arg|	1 1	Integer Real	Integer Real	
Float	FLOAT	FLOAT(J)	Convert from integer to real mode	1	Integer	Real	
Fix	IFIX	IFIX(X)	Convert from real to integer mode	1	Real	Integer	
Transfer of sign	SIGN ISIGN	SIGN(X,Y) ISIGN(J, K)	Take sign of argument-2 and apply it to the absolute value of argument-1	2	Real Integer	Real Integer	
Exponential	EXP	EXP(X)	e^{arg}	1	Real	Real	
Natural logarithm	ALOG	ALOG(X)	$\log_e(arg)$	1	Real	Real	Argument > 0
Trigonometric sine	SIN	SIN(X)	sin(arg)	1	Real	Real	Argument in radians
Trigonometric cosine	COS	COS(X)	cos(arg)	1	Real	Real	Argument in radians
Hyperbolic tangent	TANH	TANH(X)	tanh(arg)	1	Real	Real	Argument in radians
Square root	SQRT	SQRT(X)	$\sqrt{arg}$ or $arg^{1/2}$	1	Real	Real	Argument > 0
Arc tangent	ATAN	ATAN(X)	arctan(arg)	1	Real	Real	

FIGURE 20-11 The basic FORTRAN functions

In statement 1, the absolute value (ABS) of the variable named VAR1 is taken; in statement 2, the cosine (COS) of RADA is taken and multiplied by the variable named HYP; in statement 3, the square root (SQRT) of the expression A**2+B**2 is taken. Because the square-root function leads to more efficient object code than exponentiation (for example, X**(1/2) or X**5), SQRT is recommended whenever a square root is required.

When a function is used, the variable or expression in the parentheses following the function name is called the *argument*. Thus, VAR1 is the argument in statement 1 above; RADA is the argument in statement 2; and A**2+B**2 is the argument in statement 3. In order for a function to work correctly, the argument or arguments must be of the proper type—real or variable—as indicated in figure 20-11. Similarly, the function itself is of a certain type, as indicated by the first letter of the function name, and must be used in statements of the same mode. For example, IABS is in the integer mode and gives an integer result, so it should be used in an integer expression. Because of these requirements of standard FORTRAN, the following statements contain programming errors:

JVAL=IABS(A)	(Wrong type argument)
Z=3.*FLOAT(X+Y+2.)	(Wrong mode argument)
IANS=I+COS(X)	(Mixed-mode expression)
X=SIGN(FLD1,IFLD2)	(Argument 2 is the wrong type)

Functions can be used in a variety of ways within expressions. Multiple functions can be used in one statement as in

$$Y=A*SIN(X1) + B*COS(X2)$$

Functions can be nested within functions as in

$$Y=SIN(SQRT(X+3.))$$

Extensive expressions can be used as the argument of a function as in

$$EOQ=SQRT((2.*YRSLSQ*ORDEXP)/(CARRY*COST))$$

And expressions containing functions can be used in IF statements as in

$$IF\ (IABS(I-IAVE)-10)\ 90,100,100$$

When an expression containing functions is evaluated, the functions are evaluated first, as in this hierarchy:

FIRST — Functions
SECOND — Exponentiation
THIRD — Multiplication and division
FOURTH — Addition and subtraction

If parentheses are used, the expressions in the innermost parentheses are evaluated first, then the expressions in the next set of parentheses are evaluated, and so on. The expression

$$FACT1 * SQRT(ABS(SUM-100.))$$

is therefore evaluated as follows: first, 100 is subtracted from SUM; then the absolute value of this result is taken; then the square root of this result is taken; and finally, this result is multiplied by FACT1.

When full FORTRAN is used, some fifty-five functions are available in the standard function library. For example, a function in the real mode named AMAX1 is available to determine the largest variable in a list of arguments, as in this statement:

$$Y=AMAX1(A,B,C,D,E,F,G,H,O,P,Q,R)$$

If P has a value of 312.77, which is larger than any of the other arguments, Y will receive the value of 312.77. Because the use of functions can save considerable coding, a professional programmer familiarizes himself with all of the functions available in the library of the system he is using.

To illustrate the use of functions within a program, consider the program listing in figure 20-12. This program reads in the length of the hypotenuse of a right triangle (HYP) and the measure of one of the acute angles in degrees (A), and then calculates the lengths of the two legs of the triangle (SIDEA and SIDEB) using the SIN and COS functions. Because these functions require the argument to be in radians rather than degrees, the program divides A by 57.29578 (one radian=57.29578 degrees) before calculating the side lengths.

```
C FINDING THE LENGTHS OF THE SIDES OF A RIGHT TRIANGLE
   1 FORMAT (F7.2,F6.3)
   2 FORMAT (5H HYP=,F7.2,4H  A=,F6.3,8H  SIDEA=,F7.2,8H  SIDEB=,F7.2)
C START
  10 READ (1,1) HYP,A
     IF (HYP-99999.99) 20,30,30
  20 RADA=A/57.29578
     SIDEA=HYP*COS(RADA)
     SIDEB=HYP*SIN(RADA)
     WRITE (3,2) HYP,A,SIDEA,SIDEB
     GO TO 10
  30 STOP
     END
```

FIGURE 20-12   A program using functions

The Logical IF Statement

The logical IF statement is not in the Basic FORTRAN subset; it can be used only with full FORTRAN. Its format is as follows:

IF (logical-expression) any-statement

For example, the following are valid logical IF statements:

IF (X.LT.Y) GO TO 105
IF (A+B+7.5.GE.10.−X) GO TO 10
IF (M.EQ.N) X=20.5

The first example is read: if X is less than (LT) Y, go to statement number 105. The second statement is read: if A + B + 7.5 is greater than or equal to (GE) 10. − X, go to statement number 10. The third is read as: if M is equal (EQ) to N, then X equals 20.5.

To form a *logical expression*, the following *logical operators* can be used:

Operator	Means
.LT.	Less than
.LE.	Less than or equal to
.EQ.	Equal to
.NE.	Not equal to
.GT.	Greater than
.GE.	Greater than or equal to

These operators separate two real or two integer arithmetic expressions (both expressions must be of the same mode). Either expression can be as simple as a single variable name or constant or it can be as complex as is required by the logic of the program.

When the logical IF statement is executed, first the logical expression is evaluated. If it is true, the statement following the expression is executed. If it is not true, the statement following the expression is skipped, and the program continues with the statement following the logical IF statement.

In the program in figure 20-9, the body of the program could be rewritten using logical IF statements as follows:

```
C BODY OF PROGRAM
   10 READ (1,501) ITMNO,D1,D2,D3,D4,D5,D6,UPRICE,IORDPT,IONHND,IONORD
      IF (ITMNO.EQ.99999) GO TO 40
      IAVAIL=IONHND+IONORD
      IF (IAVAIL.LT.IORDPT) GO TO 20
      GO TO 10
   20 WRITE (3,602) ITMNO,D1,D2,D3,D4,D5,D6,UPRICE,IAVAIL,IORDPT
```

Because the logical IF statement can make a program easier to follow, it is often preferred over the arithmetic IF statement described in topic 1.

Program Cancellations

When a program is being executed, there are two possibilities: (1) it can run to completion, or (2) it can be cancelled before reaching the program end. If cancelled, it is usually because the computer has come to an instruction that it cannot execute because of a programming or input error. If this happens, an error message is usually printed on the console typewriter indicating the type of error, the program is cancelled, and the computer goes on to the next program to be executed. On small systems that do not have console typewriters, the computer usually stops altogether, and the type of error is indicated by the lights displayed on the console.

Three of the most common causes of FORTRAN program cancellations are *exponent overflow*, *exponent underflow*, and division by zero. Exponent overflow refers to the fact that the result of an arithmetic operation in real mode has exceeded the maximum size allowed on the system being used. Thus, a real mode operation on System/360 that leads to a result with an exponent of $+76$ will cause program cancellation due to exponent overflow. Similarly, exponent underflow refers to an arithmetic operation in which the result has an exponent smaller than the minimum allowed on the system being used. Because operations in which exponent underflow, overflow, or division by zero are involved cannot be completed correctly, the program has to be cancelled.

One other common cause of program cancellation is the misuse of a library function. For example, if the argument of the SQRT function has a negative value, the square-root operation cannot be performed. Similarly, arguments for other functions must be within ranges proper to the function being performed. If not, an error message is printed on the console typewriter and the program is cancelled.

This topic presents elements that complete a subset of FORTRAN that allows a programmer to use most of a computer's capabilities. Alphanumeric I/O fields, carriage control, I/O on sequential devices, I and F formats, library functions, the logical IF statement, and program cancellations are covered.

SUMMARY

carriage control
function library
function name
library function
argument

logical expression
logical operator
exponent overflow
exponent underflow

FOR
REVIEW

CHAPTER
TWENTY-ONE

Tables are used in many data-processing applications. For example, a tax table may be used to look up the amount of income tax to be withheld from paychecks. Rating tables are often used to find the premium to be charged for an insurance policy. And in many statistical analyses, tables are printed to show how data breaks down into categories. Topic 1 of this chapter covers the FORTRAN elements used for handling one-level tables, while topic 2 covers the elements for two- and three-level tables.

Figure 21-1 gives an example of a one-level table. To find the pay rate for any given pay class, you search the table in only one direction. For example, you find the rate for pay class 6 by searching down the pay-class column. The proper pay rate is then adjacent to the 6 in the pay-rate column.

When a column from a one-level table is operated upon using FOR-TRAN, it is called an *array*. Thus, the pay-rate column might be referred to as the pay-rate array. When the column is stored in the computer, one FORTRAN variable name—such as RATE—is used to refer to the entire array. The variable name can be either integer or real, depending on the type of variable to be stored in the array.

Subscripts

To refer to the *array elements* within an array, subscripts are used. For example, if the pay-rate array is given the *array name* RATE, the first rate

FORTRAN
FOR TABLES
AND ARRAYS

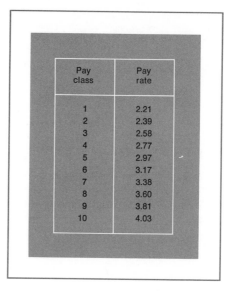

FIGURE 21-1 A pay-rate table

can be referred to as RATE (1), the second as RATE (2), and so on, as shown in the following table:

Array Name = RATE	
Variable Name	Value
RATE(1)	2.21
RATE(2)	2.39
RATE(3)	2.58
RATE(4)	2.77
RATE(5)	2.97
RATE(6)	3.17
RATE(7)	3.38
RATE(8)	3.60
RATE(9)	3.81
RATE(10)	4.03

In each case, the integer constant in parentheses following the array name is called the *subscript*. The subscript must always be greater than zero and less than or equal to the total number of elements in the array.

An integer variable name can be used as a subscript in the same way that an integer constant is. Then, the array element that is referred to depends on the value of the subscript field at the time the statement is executed. For example, ICLASS is the subscript in the following arithmetic statement:

GROSS = RATE(ICLASS)*HRSWKD

If ICLASS contains a 1 when the statement is executed, 2.21 is referred to; if ICLASS contains a 2, then 2.39 is referred to; and so on.

Certain arithmetic expressions can also be used as subscripts. If IVALUE is the name of an array, IVALUE(K+1) is a legal subscripted variable. Then, if K equals 5, the sixth element in the array is referred to. Note, however, that the expression must be in the integer mode, and it must be in one of the following forms.

Constant * Variable + Constant

Constant * Variable − Constant

Constant * Variable

Variable + Constant

Variable − Constant

Thus, IVALUE(4*NUM−2) and IVALUE(2*N) are valid subscripted variables, but IVALUE(NUM/4+3) is not.

The DIMENSION Statement

The DIMENSION statement is required near the start of any FORTRAN program that uses arrays. It tells the compiler the number of locations in storage to set aside for each array used. For example, the statement

DIMENSION ARRAY1(120),ARRAY2(50),IARRAY(12)

specifies that the program is going to use three arrays: the first, named ARRAY1, consists of 120 real elements; the second, named ARRAY2, consists of 50 real elements; and the third, named IARRAY, consists of 12 integer elements. The DIMENSION statement does not cause any object code to be compiled, and one DIMENSION statement can be used for all arrays used by a program. This statement is usually found at the start of the source deck and must always be ahead of any of the executable FORTRAN statements.

The DO Statement

The DO statement is used to cause one or more statements to be executed a specified number of times. It is particularly helpful when processing arrays because it automatically increases the value of a variable that can be used as a subscript. To illustrate, suppose the rate array in figure 21-1 is punched into cards, one rate per card in columns 1-3. Fol-

lowing the ten rate cards in the data deck are employee payroll cards
with this format:

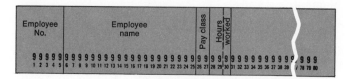

The program to be written is supposed to read an employee card, look
up the correct pay rate in the rate table, calculate the gross pay for an
employee (hours worked times rate of pay), and print a listing of the
results.

Figure 21-2 shows a FORTRAN program that accomplishes the processing described using the DO statement, the DIMENSION statement,
and subscripts. The first statement of the program, the DIMENSION
statement, gives the name RATE to the rate array and indicates that it
consists of ten elements. The DO statement is then used to read the rates
from rate cards into the RATE array, as follows:

```
         DO 10 I=1,10
      10 READ (1,1) RATE (I)
       1 FORMAT (F3.2)
```

The effect of the DO statement is to repeatedly execute all statements
that follow it, up to and including statement number 10 (DO 10), the
READ statement. Since the *index definition* within the DO statement
(I=1,10) specifies a counter or *index* named I with a starting value of 1
and an ending value of 10, the READ statement is executed ten times.
During the first execution, I has a value of 1; during the second execution,
I has a value of 2; and so forth. As a result, the rate from the first card is
stored in RATE(1), the rate from the second card is stored in RATE(2), and
so on, until the rate from the tenth card is stored in RATE(10). Because
the DO statement causes repeated execution of one or more statements
(looping), the statements under control of the DO statement are often
referred to as the *DO-loop*. After the DO-loop has been executed as many
times as indicated in the index definition of the DO statement, the program continues with the next statement following the DO-loop.

The exact form of the DO statement is as follows:

$$\text{DO } n \; i = m_1, m_2, m_3$$

where

   $n =$ the statement number of a statement
       physically following the DO statement
       in the source deck.

   $i =$ an integer variable used as an index.

```
C USING A PAY RATE TABLE
      DIMENSION RATE(10)
C READ ARRAY NAMED RATE
      DO 10 I=1,10
  10 READ (1,1) RATE(I)
   1 FORMAT (F3.2)
C PRINT REPORT HEADING
      WRITE (3,2)
   2 FORMAT (1X,16HEMP. NO.    CLASS,3X,5HHOURS,3X,4HRATE,5X,5HGROSS/)
C PROCESS DATA CARDS
  20 READ (1,3) IEMPNO,ICLASS,HRSWKD
   3 FORMAT (I5,20X,I2,F3.1)
      IF (IEMPNO-99999) 30,40,40
  30 GROSS=RATE(ICLASS)*HRSWKD
C PRINT OUTPUT LINE
      WRITE (3,4) IEMPNO,ICLASS,HRSWKD,RATE(ICLASS),GROSS
   4 FORMAT (2X,I5,I9,F9.1,F7.2,F11.2)
      GO TO 20
C END OF JOB ROUTINE
  40 WRITE (3,5)
   5 FORMAT (11HOEND OF JOB)
      STOP
      END
```

FIGURE 21-2 A program using a pay-rate table

m_1 = an unsigned integer constant or an integer variable that gives the starting value of i.

m_2 = an unsigned integer constant or an integer variable that gives the test value that determines the number of times the DO-loop is executed.

m_3 = an unsigned integer constant or an integer variable that tells the number by which i should be increased each time the DO-loop is executed; if m_3 is omitted, it is assumed to have a value of 1.

When the DO statement is executed, i is given the value represented by m_1. Then, all of the statements following the DO statement, up to and including the statement with the number given in the DO statement, are executed. At this point, a test is made to determine whether the value of i is equal to or greater than m_2. If not, i is increased by the value of m_3 (normally, m_3 is omitted, so its value is 1), and the DO-loop is repeated.

The effect of the DO statement, then, is to set up a counter to determine how many times a DO-loop is executed. Thus, the following groups of code lead to the same results:

```
      I=0
   5  I=I+1                          DO 10 I=1,10
      READ (1,1) RATE(I)            READ (1,1) RATE(I)
   1  FORMAT (F3.2)               1 FORMAT (F3.2)
      IF (I-10) 5,6,6
   6  CONTINUE
```

The advantage of the DO statement, of course, is that less coding is required, so programming speed is increased.

One point to remember when using DO-loops is that a program cannot branch into the middle of a loop from outside the loop. If it did, the counter would not be set up properly and the results would be unpredictable. On the other hand, it is perfectly legal to branch out of a DO-loop before the test value (m_2) is reached. In this case, the value of the integer variable used as the index is available to subsequent statements of the program. This technique of branching out of a DO-loop is illustrated later in this topic.

Incidentally, the DO statement can also be used for controlling DO-loops that do not make use of subscripts. For example, the new principal at 5 percent interest compounded annually for twenty years can be calculated as follows:

```
      DO 50 M=1,20
   50 PRINC=PRINC*1.05
```

In general, however, DO-loops are most useful when arrays are being processed and subscripts are used.

The CONTINUE Statement

Although unlimited branching can take place within a DO-loop, all paths through the DO-loop must end with the last statement in the loop. As a result, a DO-loop cannot end with a branch statement such as the IF or the GO TO. Instead, FORTRAN provides the CONTINUE statement. This statement, which is used as the last statement in a DO-loop, does nothing as far as processing is concerned. It simply provides a dummy statement that an IF or GO TO statement can branch to and thus complete the DO-loop.

To illustrate the use of the CONTINUE statement, consider a program that uses a table such as the one in figure 21-3 for calculating the premium to be charged for an insurance policy. After the rate is found by searching for the appropriate age bracket, the total premium is derived by multiplying this base rate by the number of hundreds of dollars of

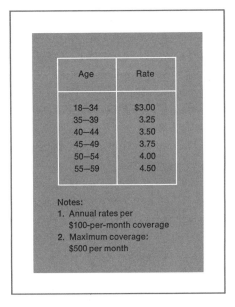

FIGURE 21-3   Rating table for a wife's
in-hospital disability
income insurance

coverage applied for. Thus, $300-per-month coverage for a 41-year-old wife costs $3.50 times 3, or $10.50.

Using FORTRAN, the insurance table would be treated as two separate arrays. In the first array, the elements would be the maximum ages from each age bracket, as follows:

Array Name = MAXAGE	
Variable Name	Value
MAXAGE(1)	34
MAXAGE(2)	39
MAXAGE(3)	44
MAXAGE(4)	49
MAXAGE(5)	54
MAXAGE(6)	59

In the second array, the elements would be the rates.

These two arrays could be punched into input cards in several different formats. One way would be to punch two numbers, one value from each array, into each input card, as follows:

Here, the maximum age for each bracket is punched in columns 1 and 2, and the rate in columns 3–5.

After the arrays are read into storage, application cards containing the applicant's account number, amount of insurance applied for, and age are read and processed. If the applicant is between the ages of 18 and 59 and does not apply for over $500-per-month coverage, the program prints out the premium to be charged. Otherwise, the program prints the account number, age, and amount of insurance applied for, along with the message UNINSURABLE.

The program to accomplish this processing is listed in figure 21-4. To make it easier to follow the listing, the program flowchart is given in figure 21-5. After the table cards are read into storage and the report headings are printed, the program reads one card and determines if the applicant's age is less than 18 or if the coverage applied for is over $500 per month. If not, the program enters the following lookup routine:

```
C TABLE LOOKUP
  50 DO 60 I=1,6
     IF (MAXAGE(I)-IAGE) 60,70,70
  60 CONTINUE
```

This DO-loop will be executed up to six times, depending on the value of the applicant's age (IAGE). Each time through the loop, IAGE is subtracted from one of the values in the MAXAGE array. If the result is zero or positive—meaning IAGE is equal to or less than MAXAGE(I)—the program branches to statement number 70, thus leaving the DO-loop. Because a DO-loop can't end with an IF statement, the CONTINUE statement is the last statement in the DO-loop.

To show more explicitly how the DO-loop operates, suppose IAGE has a value of 48. The following table then shows the values for the variables involved each time the DO-loop is executed:

```
C ONE LEVEL INSURANCE RATE TABLE LOOKUP
      DIMENSION MAXAGE(6),RATE(6)
C READ ARRAYS NAMED MAXAGE AND RATE
      DO 10 I=1,6
   10 READ (1,1) MAXAGE(I),RATE(I)
    1 FORMAT (I2,F3.2)
C PRINT REPORT HEADINGS
      WRITE (3,2)
    2 FORMAT (10H ACCT. NO.,3X,3HAGE,3X,9HPOL. AMT.,3X,8HRATE/100,4X,
      14HRATE/)
C READ APPLICANT CARD AND DETERMINE IF AGE IS UNDER 18 OR
C      COVERAGE APPLIED FOR IS OVER $500
   20 READ (1,3) IACCT,AMOUNT,IAGE
    3 FORMAT (I5,F3.0,I2)
      IF (IACCT-99999) 30,99,99
   30 IF (IAGE-18) 98,40,40
   40 IF (AMOUNT-500.) 50,50,98
C TABLE LOOKUP
   50 DO 60 I=1,6
      IF (MAXAGE(I)-IAGE) 60,70,70
   60 CONTINUE
C APPLICANT IS UNINSURABLE--AGE IS UNDER 18, OVER 59, OR AMOUNT
C      APPLIED FOR IS OVER $500
   98 WRITE (3,4) IACCT,IAGE,AMOUNT
    4 FORMAT (1H0,I7,I8,F10.2,4X,11HUNINSURABLE/)
      GO TO 20
C CALCULATE AND PRINT APPLICANT'S RATE
   70 PLRATE=RATE(I)*(AMOUNT/100.)
      WRITE (3,5) IACCT,IAGE,AMOUNT,RATE(I),PLRATE
    5 FORMAT (1X,I7,I8,F10.2,F11.2,F11.2)
      GO TO 20
C END OF JOB ROUTINE
   99 WRITE (3,6)
    6 FORMAT (11HOEND OF JOB)
      STOP
      END
```

FIGURE 21-4   A one-level insurance-rating program

I	IAGE	MAXAGE(I)
1	48	34
2	48	39
3	48	44
4	48	49

Since IAGE is less than MAXAGE(I) when I is equal to 4, the program
leaves the DO-loop at this time. On the other hand, if IAGE has a value

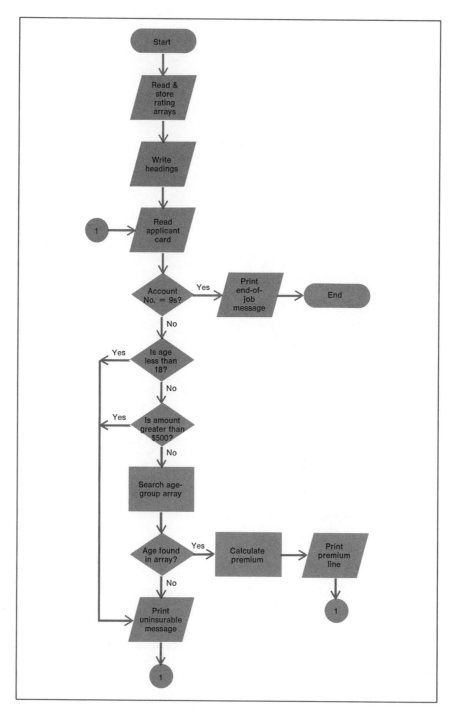

FIGURE 21-5   Program flowchart for the insurance-rating program

of 68, the DO-loop is executed the maximum of six times, and the program then continues with statement number 98.

When an IF or GO TO statement branches out of a DO-loop before it has been executed the maximum number of times, the value of the integer variable used as the counter is available to subsequent program statements. When IAGE is 48, for instance, the program branches to statement number 70 when I equals 4. Statement number 70 then uses this value as a subscript:

```
PLRATE=RATE(I)*(AMOUNT/100.)
```

In other words, the fourth element in the RATE array is used as the base rate for calculating the total rate to be paid for the policy.

DO-Implied READ and WRITE Statements

In the program in figure 21-2, the pay rates are punched one per input card and read using this code:

```
     DO 10 I=1,10
10   READ (1,1) RATE(I)
1    FORMAT (F3.2)
```

By using a DO-implied READ statement, the same results can be accomplished using less coding, as follows:

```
     READ (1,1) (RATE(I),I=1,10)
1    FORMAT (F3.2)
```

Here, the READ statement itself specifies a DO-loop. Following the variable named RATE(I), the index definition I=1,10 is given just as in a DO statement. This means that the READ statement should be repeated until ten values are placed into the array named RATE. Since the associated FORMAT statement specifies only one value per card (F3.2), ten cards are read as a result of the *DO-implied statement*. When coding a DO-implied loop, the index definition and the variable or variables to which it applies must be enclosed in parentheses.

Now suppose that the ten pay rates are punched five per card. Then, the same READ statement with a modified FORMAT statement would read two cards and store all ten values:

```
     READ (1,1) (RATE(I),I=1,10)
1    FORMAT (5F3.2)
```

The advantage of the READ statement is that it gives the programmer increased flexibility since it will read as few or as many records as is necessary to fill the array elements specified.

If elements from two or more arrays are punched in one input card, this too can be specified in a DO-implied statement. For example, this statement would read the arrays used in the program in figure 21-4:

```
     READ (1,1) (MAXAGE(I),RATE(I),I=1,6)
1    FORMAT (I2,F3.2)
```

If all six values of each array are punched into one card, as shown here:

the same READ statement could be used with this FORMAT statement.

```
1 FORMAT (6(I2,F3.2))
```

By using parentheses within the FORMAT statement, the compiler is told that the two-column integer field and the three-column real field are repeated six times in one card. As a result, this statement is equivalent to

```
1 FORMAT (I2,F3.2,I2,F3.2,I2,F3.2,I2,F3.2,I2,F3.2,I2,F3.2)
```

Like an index definition in a DO statement, a DO-implied index definition can be given an increment value as follows:

```
READ (1,1) (A(J),J=1,100,2)
```

This statement would read values into the odd-numbered elements of the array named A. Thus, positions 1, 3, 5, and so on would be filled.

In some cases, the number of elements in an array is not known at the time a program is coded. Then, an integer variable must be used as the test value in an index definition. For example, if 200 or less values are to be read and stored in an array, a lead card can be used as follows to give the test value for the index definition:

```
DIMENSION X(200)
...
...
  READ (1,1) LIMIT
1 FORMAT (I3)
  READ (1,2) (X(K),K=1,LIMIT)
2 FORMAT (10F8.2)
```

If the lead card contains 177 in columns 1–3, the program will read eighteen cards. It will take ten values from the first seventeen cards and seven from the eighteenth card. Note that the DIMENSION statement must give a range for the X array that is larger than the value of LIMIT.

In certain cases, other variables can be recorded in the same card as the elements of one or more arrays. For example, an alphanumeric field in a typical card record can be treated as an array in the following manner:

```
  READ (1,1) IEMPNO,(NAME(I),I=1,5),ICLASS,HRSWKD
1 FORMAT (I5,5A4,F3.2)
```

Here, the DO-loop within the READ statement is used to read the five parts of a name field into a five-element array. Note again that the variable or variables in the DO-loop, as well as the index definition, must be enclosed in parentheses.

The principles of the DO-implied READ statement can also be used in a WRITE statement. For example, if the table used in the program in figure 21-4 is to be printed with one pair of values per output line, this WRITE statement could be used:

```
    WRITE (3,5) (MAXAGE(I),RATE(I),I=1,6)
  5 FORMAT (1X,I5,F9.2)
```

And, if the six rates are to be printed, three per line, this coding could be used:

```
    WRITE (3,5) (RATE(I),I=1,6)
  5 FORMAT (1X,3F10.2)
```

DISCUSSION

To show the use of the FORTRAN array processing elements in a more sophisticated program, consider the program listing in figure 21-6. This program reads a deck of student registration cards containing name and height as follows:

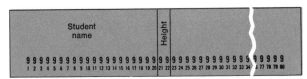

The output of the program is a listing of students in order of height — the tallest, the second tallest, and so forth. Since the input deck is not in order by height, the program must store all input data in arrays, sort by heights, and print the listing. The number of student cards in the input deck, which must be 100 or less, is indicated by a lead card that has the exact number of students punched in columns 1–3.

To read and store the data from the student cards, the following DO-implied READ statement is used:

```
  READ (1,2) (N1(I),N2(I),N3(I),N4(I),N5(I),IHGT1(I),I=1,NUMBER)
2 FORMAT (5A4,I2)
```

This means that one element is stored in each of six different arrays each time a card is read. Because NUMBER is used as the test value in the index definition, as many elements will be stored in each array as the number read from columns 1–3 of the first input card.

After a heading is printed for the listings, the elements in the array named IHGT1 are copied into the IHGT2 array as follows:

```
       DO 10 I=1,NUMBER
    10 IHGT2(I)=IHGT1(I)
```

```
C SORTING CLASS LIST BY HEIGHT
      DIMENSION N1(100),N2(100),N3(100),N4(100),N5(100),
     1    IHGT1(100),IHGT2(100),IORDER(100)
C READ AND STORE ARRAYS
      READ (1,1) NUMBER
    1 FORMAT (I3)
      READ (1,2) (N1(I),N2(I),N3(I),N4(I),N5(I),IHGT1(I),I=1,NUMBER)
    2 FORMAT (5A4,I2)
C PRINT LIST HEADINGS
      WRITE (3,3)
    3 FORMAT (1X,30H          NAME              HEIGHT/)
C SET ELEMENTS OF ARRAY NAMED IHGT2 EQUAL TO ELEMENTS OF
C     ARRAY NAMED IHGT1
      DO 10 I=1,NUMBER
   10 IHGT2(I)=IHGT1(I)
C THE TWO DO LOOPS THAT FOLLOW GIVE VALUES TO THE ELEMENTS
C     OF THE ARRAY NAMED IORDER--AT THEIR COMPLETION, THE
C     FIRST ELEMENT OF THE IORDER ARRAY WILL HAVE THE
C     SUBSCRIPT OF THE LARGEST HEIGHT IN THE IHGT1 ARRAY,
C     THE SECOND ELEMENT WILL HAVE THE SUBSCRIPT OF THE
C     NEXT LARGEST HEIGHT, ETC.
      DO 40 I=1,NUMBER
      LRGHGT=IHGT1(1)
      LRGSUB=1
      DO 30 J=2,NUMBER
      IF (LRGHGT-IHGT1(J)) 20,30,30
   20 LRGHGT=IHGT1(J)
      LRGSUB=J
   30 CONTINUE
      IORDER(I)=LRGSUB
   40 IHGT1(LRGSUB)=0
C PRINT CLASS LIST IN ORDER OF HEIGHT
      DO 50 I=1,NUMBER
      J=IORDER(I)
   50 WRITE (3,4) N1(J),N2(J),N3(J),N4(J),N5(J),IHGT2(J)
    4 FORMAT (1X,5A4,I8)
C END OF JOB ROUTINE
      WRITE (3,5)
    5 FORMAT (11HOEND OF JOB)
      STOP
      END
```

FIGURE 21-6   Sorting by height

IHGT2 is needed because the values in the IHGT1 array are set to zero later in the program. Then, IHGT2 is used to print the height field in the output listing.

Although the output of this program is in order by height, the program does not actually rearrange the values in the arrays. Instead, it uses another array named IORDER to store the subscripts required to retrieve the N1,N2,N3,N4,N5, and IHGT2 arrays in the correct order. Suppose, for example, that the IORDER array has these values for its first ten elements at the end of processing:

Array Name = IORDER	
Variable Name	Value
IORDER(1)	22
IORDER(2)	58
IORDER(3)	11
IORDER(4)	10
IORDER(5)	74
IORDER(6)	67
IORDER(7)	59
IORDER(8)	46
IORDER(9)	45
IORDER(10)	23

Then, the ten tallest heights in the IHGT2 array are stored in IHGT2(22), IHGT2(58), IHGT2(11), IHGT(10), IHGT2(74), IHGT2(67), IHGT2(59), IHGT2(46), IHGT2(45), and IHGT2(23). By using the values of IORDER as subscripts, then, the N1, N2, N3, N4, N5, and IHGT2 arrays can be printed in the proper order.

To place the appropriate values in the IORDER array, the following code is used:

```
    DO 40 I=1,NUMBER
    LRGHGT=IHGT1(I)
    LRGSUB=1
    DO 30 J=2,NUMBER
    IF (LRGHGT-IHGT1(J)) 20,30,30
 20 LRGHGT=IHGT1(J)
    LRGSUB=J
 30 CONTINUE
    IORDER (I)=LRGSUB
 40 IHGT1(LRGSUB)=0
```

Here, one DO-loop is within another DO-loop. This condition, referred to as *nested DO-loops*, is legal as long as the inner DO-loop does not extend beyond the outer DO-loop. In fact, there can be loops within loops within loops. In this example, the inner loop is executed as many times as indicated by the index definition each time the output loop is executed once. In other words, if NUMBER has a value of 51, the inner loop will be executed 50 times for each execution of the outer loop. Since the outer loop is executed 51 times, the total number of executions of the inner loop is 51 multiplied by 50, or 2550 times.

As you might guess, the technique illustrated in this program is by no means the most efficient technique that could be used. However, it is rather straightforward. The first time the outer loop is executed, the subscript of the greatest height in the IHGT1 array is placed in IORDER(1), after which the greatest height is set to zero. The second time through the outer loop, the subscript of the second greatest height in the IHGT1 array is placed in IORDER(2), after which the second greatest height is set to zero. The loops continue until the IORDER array is filled, and all the elements in the IHGT1 array are zero. The program is then ready to print the student list in order.

To print the list, the values in the IORDER array are converted to the subscript J:

$$J = IORDER(I)$$

This is necessary since you can't have subscripted subscripts such as N1(IORDER(I)). For each of the subscript values taken from the IORDER array, one output line is printed.

This explanation may leave you with some unanswered questions. If so, you should go through the program, assuming some input values and keeping track of the array elements as you do. This is a good technique when trying to understand another person's program or when desk-checking your own program.

SUMMARY

In order to store and process arrays, FORTRAN provides subscripts, the DIMENSION statement, the DO statement, the CONTINUE statement, and DO-implied READ and WRITE statements. These FORTRAN elements give the capability of looking up values in an array, as well as the capability of changing or rearranging values in an array.

FOR REVIEW

array
array element
array name
subscript
index definition

index
DO-loop
DO-implied statement
nested DO-loops

Many tables used in data-processing applications involve two or three variables. The insurance rates in the rating table in part A of figure 21-7, for example, vary based on an applicant's age and his job classification. Because two variables are involved, this is called a two-level table. Similarly, the table in part A of figure 21-8 can be called a three-level table since its rates vary by age group, sex (male or female), and job classification.

In FORTRAN, two- and three-level tables are stored as two- and three-dimensional arrays. Basic FORTRAN allows two-dimensional arrays; full FORTRAN allows two- and three-dimensional arrays. To process these arrays, nested DO-loops are commonly used.

To illustrate the subscripts used for a two-dimensional array, consider part B of figure 21-7. This indicates the normal way in which the array elements are referenced using subscripts. Thus, the rate for a 42-year-old man in class 2 can be referred to as RATE(3,2), and the rate for a 32-year-old man in class 4 can be referred to as RATE(1,4).

Part B of figure 21-8 indicates the way in which subscripts are used to refer to elements in a three-dimensional array. Thus, the rate for a 53-year-old woman in class 2 can be referred to as RATE(5,2,2). And RATE(6,1,1) indicates a man in class 1 between the ages of 55 and 59.

In a FORTRAN program the subscript used can be an integer, an integer variable, or any of several limited arithmetic expressions in the integer mode. As a result, RATE(I,J+1) and ARRAY1(2,IVAL1,2*IVAL2−3) are valid two- and three-dimensional subscripted variables. The array element that is referenced depends on the value of the variables used in the

Age	Class 1	Class 2	Class 3	Class 4
18—34	$23.50	$27.05	$35.25	$52.90
35—39	24.00	27.55	35.75	53.40
40—44	24.60	28.15	36.35	54.00
45—49	25.30	28.85	37.05	54.70
50—54	26.30	29.85	38.05	55.70
55—59	28.00	31.55	39.75	57.40

Part A — Rating table

Age	Class 1	Class 2	Class 3	Class 4
18—34	RATE (1,1)	RATE (1,2)	RATE (1,3)	RATE (1,4)
35—39	RATE (2,1)	RATE (2,2)	RATE (2,3)	RATE (2,4)
40—44	RATE (3,1)	RATE (3,2)	RATE (3,3)	RATE (3,4)
45—49	RATE (4,1)	RATE (4,2)	RATE (4,3)	RATE (4,4)
50—54	RATE (5,1)	RATE (5,2)	RATE (5,3)	RATE (5,4)
55—59	RATE (6,1)	RATE (6,2)	RATE (6,3)	RATE (6,4)

Part B — Subscript notation

FIGURE 21-7   A two-level rating table and subscript notation

Age	Men		Women	
	Class 1	Class 2	Class 1	Class 2
18—34	$23.50	$27.05	$24.75	$28.45
35—39	24.00	27.55	25.80	29.50
40—44	24.60	28.15	27.10	30.80
45—49	25.30	28.85	29.10	32.80
50—54	26.30	29.85	31.55	35.25
55—59	28.00	31.55	35.00	38.70

Part A — Rating table

Age	Men		Women	
	Class 1	Class 2	Class 1	Class 2
18—34	RATE (1,1,1)	RATE (1,1,2)	RATE (1,2,1)	RATE (1,2,2)
35—39	RATE (2,1,1)	RATE (2,1,2)	RATE (2,2,1)	RATE (2,2,2)
40—44	RATE (3,1,1)	RATE (3,1,2)	RATE (3,2,1)	RATE (3,2,2)
45—49	RATE (4,1,1)	RATE (4,1,2)	RATE (4,2,1)	RATE (4,2,2)
50—54	RATE (5,1,1)	RATE (5,1,2)	RATE (5,2,1)	RATE (5,2,2)
55—59	RATE (6,1,1)	RATE (6,1,2)	RATE (6,2,1)	RATE (6,2,2)

Part B — Subscript notation

FIGURE 21-8   A three-level rating table and subscript notation

subscript at the time a statement is executed. The forms of the arithmetic expressions that can be used for two- and three-dimensional subscripts are the same as those acceptable for one-dimensional subscripts.

PROCESSING A TWO-LEVEL TABLE

Figure 21-9 is a program listing that illustrates how FORTRAN is used to process the two-level table in figure 21-7. This program treats the table as two arrays: a one-dimensional array called MAXAGE that contains the maximum age for each age group, and a two-dimensional array that contains the rates for six age groups and four job classifications. At the start of the program, the table is read into storage; then application cards are read, and the table is used to print the appropriate rate for each applicant. At the end of the program, the average rate in the table is calculated and printed, and the values in the RATE array are printed.

In the DIMENSION statement, the dimensions for the arrays used are given as follows:

DIMENSION MAXAGE(6),RATE(6,4),NAME(5)

This indicates that the MAXAGE array consists of six elements and that the RATE array is a two-dimensional array consisting of six rows of four elements each. A third array called NAME is used to store the name field from the application cards.

```
C TWO LEVEL INSURANCE RATING (AGE,CLASS)
      DIMENSION MAXAGE(6),RATE(6,4),NAME(5)
C READ AND STORE INPUT TABLE
      DO 10 I=1,6
   10 READ (1,1) MAXAGE(I),(RATE(I,J),J=1,4)
    1 FORMAT (I2,4F4.2)
C PRINT REPORT HEADINGS
      WRITE (3,2)
    2 FORMAT (8X,4HNAME,14X,4HRATE/)
C READ AND PROCESS APPLICATION CARDS
   20 READ (1,3) (NAME(I),I=1,5),IAGE,ICLASS
    3 FORMAT (5A4,I2,I1)
      IF (IAGE-99) 30,99,99
   30 IF (IAGE-18) 98,40,40
C SEARCH MAXAGE TABLE FOR PROPER AGE GROUP
   40 DO 50 I=1,6
      IF (MAXAGE(I)-IAGE) 50,60,60
   50 CONTINUE
C PRINT UNINSURABLE MESSAGE FOR APPLICANTS UNDER 18 OR OVER 59
   98 WRITE (3,4) (NAME(I),I=1,5)
    4 FORMAT (1X,5A4,15H IS UNINSURABLE)
      GO TO 20
C PRINT APPROPRIATE RATE FOR APPLICANTS BETWEEN 18 AND 59
   60 IAGEGR=I
      WRITE (3,5) (NAME(I),I=1,5),RATE(IAGEGR,ICLASS)
    5 FORMAT (1X,5A4,F10.2)
      GO TO 20
C CALCULATE AVERAGE RATE
   99 RTESUM=0.
      DO 70 I=1,6
      DO 70 J=1,4
   70 RTESUM=RTESUM+RATE(I,J)
      RTEAVE=RTESUM/24.
C PRINT AVERAGE RATE
      WRITE (3,6) RTEAVE
    6 FORMAT (///1X,16AVERAGE RATE IS ,F5.2)
C PRINT RATE ARRAY
      WRITE (3,7) ((RATE)I,J),J=1,4),I=1,6)
    7 FORMAT (1X,4F10.2)
C END OF JOB ROUTINE
      WRITE (3,8)
    8 FORMAT (11HOEND OF JOB)
      STOP
      END
```

FIGURE 21-9 A two-level rating program

The table for this program is punched into six cards as follows:

59	2800	3155	3975	5740	
54	2630	2985	3805	5570	
49	2530	2885	3705	5470	
44	2460	2815	3635	5400	
39	2400	2755	3575	5340	
34	2350	2705	3525	5290	

This means that one value from the MAXAGE array and four values from the RATE array are punched into each table card. Thus, the following code is required to read the table:

```
      DO 10 I=1,6
10    READ (1,1) MAXAGE(I),(RATE(I,J),J=1,4)
 1    FORMAT (I2,4F4.2)
```

Here, the variable J is moved from 1 through 4 each time the READ statement is executed. Because the READ statement is in a DO-loop, it is executed six times, once for each value of I. Note that RATE in the READ statement has a two-value subscript, one value varied by the DO-implied loop of the READ statement, and the other value varied by the DO-loop itself.

This, of course, is only one of the forms that the input table could be in. Another typical form, for example, would be to punch the age-group maximums into one card, followed by cards with the rates punched four to a card as follows:

2800	3155	3975	5740		
2630	2985	3805	5570		
2530	2885	3705	5470		
2460	2815	3635	5400		
2400	2755	3575	5340		
2350	2705	3525	5290		
34	39	44	49	54	59

The following code could then be used to store the arrays:

```
      READ (1,1) (MAXAGE(I),I=1,6)
 1    FORMAT (6I2)
      READ (1,2) ((RATE(I,J),J=1,4),I=1,6)
 2    FORMAT (4F4.2)
```

After the MAXAGE array is stored using a one-dimensional DO-implied READ statement, the RATE array is stored using a two-dimensional DO-implied READ statement. In the two-dimensional statement, J is varied from 1 through 4 for each value of I, as I is varied from 1 through 6. In other words, the effect is that of nested DO-loops. The index definition specified in the inner parentheses represents the inner loop; the index definition within the outer parentheses represents the outer loop. As with all FORTRAN statements, note the placement of the parentheses and commas since they are critical to the operation of the statement.

After the report heading is printed, the program reads the first application card, which has this format:

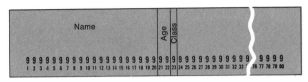

The NAME array is used for the name field, and four columns of the field are read into each of the five elements of the array. After a card is read, two IF statements test to determine whether the last input card has been read (9s in the age field) and whether the applicant is less than 18 years old. If neither condition is true, the program searches the MAXAGE array to find the applicant's age group by using this coding:

```
      DO 50 I=1,6
      IF (MAXAGE(I)-IAGE) 50,60,60
   50 CONTINUE
```

If the age is equal to or less than the maximum age for a group, the program branches out of the loop to statement number 60. If the program finishes the loop, a message indicating that the applicant is uninsurable is printed, and the program reads another application card.

Beginning with statement 60, the program sets the value of IAGEGR to I, the value of the index at the time the program left the previous DO-loop. RATE(IAGEGR,ICLASS) then indicates the appropriate rate for the application being processed. After the applicant's name and rate are printed, the program reads the next application card.

When the last application card is read, the program branches to statement 99. Here, the average rate in the rate table is calculated as follows:

```
   99 RTESUM=0.
      DO 70 I=1,6
      DO 70 J=1,4
   70 RTESUM=RTESUM+RATE(I,J)
      RTEAVE=RTESUM/24.
```

Using nested DO-loops, the twenty-four values of the RATE array are added to RTESUM in this order:

RATE(1,1)
RATE(1,2)
RATE(1,3)
RATE(1,4)
RATE(2,1)
and so on.

In other words, J is varied from 1 through 4 for each value of I. After the DO-loops have been completed, RTESUM is divided by 24 to give the average rate, RTEAVE.

The final statements in the program print the average rate, print the values in the RATE array using nested DO-implied loops in a WRITE statement, print an end-of-job message, and stop the program. In the DO-implied WRITE statement, the important thing to note is the order in which the index definitions are given. Because the index J is in the inner parentheses, the values are printed as follows:

RATE(1,1)   RATE(1,2)   RATE(1,3)   RATE(1,4)
RATE(2,1)   RATE(2,2)   RATE(2,3)   RATE(2,4)
and so on.

However, if the index definitions were reversed as in

WRITE (3,6) ((RATE(I,J),I=1,6),J=1,4)

the table would print like this:

RATE(1,1)   RATE(2,1)   RATE(3,1)   RATE(4,1)
RATE(5,1)   RATE(6,1)   RATE(1,2)   RATE(2,2)
RATE(3,2)   RATE(4,2)   and so on.

This, of course, would not be the intent of the programmer.

PROCESSING A THREE-LEVEL TABLE

Figure 21-10 is a program listing that processes the three-level table given in figure 21-8. The processing is similar to that of the previous program: the table is read into storage, a listing of applicants and rates is printed, the average rate is calculated and printed, the RATE array is printed, an end-of-job message is printed, and the program ends. The main difference between this and the previous program is that the rates are treated as a three-dimensional array. Thus, three-dimensional subscripts are used and three levels of nested DO-loops and nested DO-implied loops are used.

As the comment line at the start of the program indicates, the subscript values for the RATE array represent in order the age group, the sex code, and the job classification. Thus, the DIMENSION statement gives the RATE dimension as (6,2,2). Because the MAXAGE elements are punched into one card and the RATE elements are punched four per card into the next six cards, the following code is used to read the rating table:

```
    READ (1,1) (MAXAGE(I),I=1,6)
  1 FORMAT (6I2)
    READ (1,2) (((RATE(I,J,K),K=1,2),J=1,2),I=1,6)
  2 FORMAT (4F4.2)
```

Here, the second READ statement has three DO-implied loops that vary

```
C THREE DIMENSIONAL INSURANCE RATING (AGE,SEX,CLASS)
      DIMENSION MAXAGE(6),RATE(6,2,2),NAME(5)
C READ AND STORE INPUT TABLE
      READ (1,1) (MAXAGE(I),I=1,6)
   1 FORMAT (6I2)
      READ (1,2) (((RATE(I,J,K),K=1,2),J=1,2),I=1,6)
   2 FORMAT (4F4.2)
C PRINT REPORT HEADINGS
      WRITE (3,3)
   3 FORMAT (8X,4HNAME,14X,4HRATE/)
C READ AND PROCESS APPLICATION CARDS
  10 READ (1,4) (NAME(I),I=1,5),IAGE,ICLASS,ISEX
   4 FORMAT (5A4,I2,2I1)
      IF (IAGE-99) 20,99,99
  20 IF (IAGE-18) 98,30,30
C SEARCH MAXAGE TABLE FOR PROPER AGE GROUP
  30 DO 40 I=1,6
      IF (MAXAGE(I)-IAGE) 40,50,50
  40 CONTINUE
C PRINT UNINSURABLE MESSAGE FOR APPLICANTS UNDER 18 OR OVER 59
  98 WRITE (3,5) (NAME(I),I=1,5)
   5 FORMAT (1X,5A4,15H IS UNINSURABLE)
      GO TO 10
C PRINT APPROPRIATE RATE FOR APPLICANTS BETWEEN 18 AND 59
  50 IAGEGR=I
      WRITE (3,6) (NAME(I),I=1,5),RATE(IAGEGR,ISEX,ICLASS)
   6 FORMAT (1X,5A4,F10.2)
      GO TO 10
C CALCULATE AVERAGE RATE
  99 RTESUM=0.
      DO 60 I=1,6
      DO 60 J=1,2
      DO 60 K=1,2
  60 RTESUM=RTESUM+RATE(I,J,K)
      RTEAVE=RTESUM/24.
C PRINT AVERAGE RATE
      WRITE (3,7) RTEAVE
   7 FORMAT (///1X,16AVERAGE RATE IS ,F5.2)
C PRINT RATE ARRAY
      WRITE (3,8) (((RATE(I,J,K),I=1,6),J=1,2),K=1,2)
   8 FORMAT (1X,6F10.2)
C END OF JOB ROUTINE
      WRITE (3,9)
   9 FORMAT (11HOEND OF JOB)
      STOP
      END
```

FIGURE 21-10 A three-level rating program

the subscript values in this order: class, sex, and age group. Thus, the RATE elements are filled in this order:

RATE(1,1,1)
RATE(1,1,2)
RATE(1,2,1)
RATE(1,2,2)
RATE(2,1,1)
RATE(2,1,2)
RATE(2,2,1)
RATE(2,2,2)
RATE(3,1,1)
and so on.

Note again the use of the commas and the parentheses in the DO-implied portion of the READ statement.

The remainder of the program should be self-explanatory. Three levels of nested DO-loops are used to total the rates in the table before the average-rate calculation; three levels of DO-implied loops are used in printing the RATE array near the end of the program. Because the WRITE statement varies the subscript values in reverse order from the way the input array is read and because the FORMAT statement specifies 6F10.2 for the output line, the table will print as follows:

23.50	24.00	24.60	25.30	26.30	28.00
27.05	27.55	28.15	28.85	29.85	31.55
24.75	25.80	27.10	29.10	31.55	35.00
28.45	29.50	30.80	32.80	35.25	38.70

One of the most difficult aspects of handling three-dimensional arrays is maintaining consistency in the use of subscripts. In other words, if you read an array into storage with the subscript values in order representing age group, sex, and job classification, you must be careful to keep this order throughout the program. If you reference an array element thinking that the subscript values in order are age group, job classification, and sex code, a programming error will result.

Basically, two- and three-dimensional arrays are processed using the same FORTRAN elements that are used for one-dimensional arrays. However, nested DO-loops and DO-implied loops are more prominent, and two- and three-value subscripts must be used.

VI

APPENDIXES

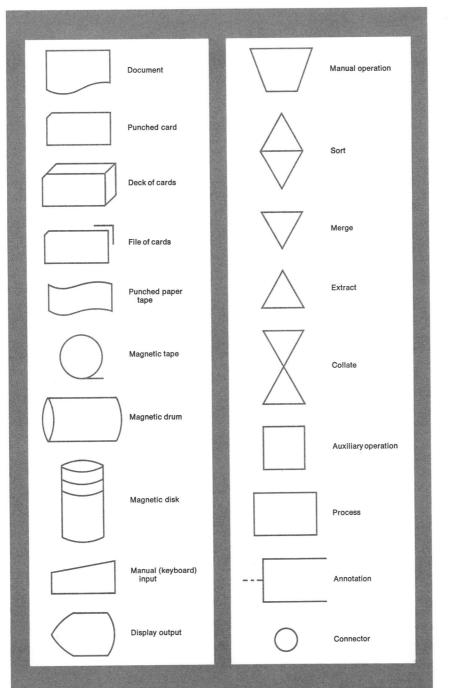

Document	Manual operation
Punched card	Sort
Deck of cards	Merge
File of cards	Extract
Punched paper tape	Collate
Magnetic tape	Auxiliary operation
Magnetic drum	Process
Magnetic disk	Annotation
Manual (keyboard) input	Connector
Display output	

**APPENDIX A
STANDARD
SYSTEM
FLOWCHART
SYMBOLS**

APPENDIX B
STANDARD
PROGRAM
FLOWCHART
SYMBOLS

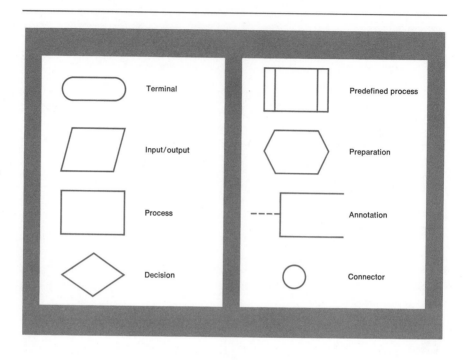

The American National Standards Institute (ANSI) provides COBOL specifications consisting of a nucleus and seven functional modules: sequential access, table handling, random access, sort, report writer, segmentation, and library. Within the nucleus and the seven modules are specifications for low, middle, and high levels of the COBOL elements as indicated in the following chart:

Nucleus	Table Handling	Sequential Access	Random Access	Sort	Report Writer	Segmen- tation	Library
High	High	High	High	High	High	High	High
	Mid		Mid	Mid	Mid	Mid	Mid
Low	Low	Low	Null	Null	Null	Null	Null

In other words, there are low and high levels in the nucleus and sequential-access modules, there are low, middle, and high levels in the table-handling module, and there are middle and high levels in the random-access, sort, report-writer, segmentation, and library modules. Null means that a module does not contain any elements at that level.

A compiler conforming to minimum ANS standards must contain the low-level elements of the nucleus and the table handling and sequential-access modules. On the other hand, a full ANS compiler must contain the high elements of the nucleus and each functional module. Between the two extremes, an ANS COBOL compiler can be composed of varying levels of the modules. For example, ANS COBOL for the IBM 1130 consists of low nucleus and sequential-access elements and middle random-access, table-handling, and library elements.

This book covers selected COBOL elements from the following modules:

Nucleus
Table handling
Sequential access

The summary that follows is divided into these sections:

COBOL Reserved Words
General COBOL Information
Basic COBOL Elements
Table-Handling Elements
Sequential-Access Elements — Tape
Sequential-Access Elements — Disk

To the left of each COBOL element described is a column that indicates the ANS level for the element—L, M, or H for low, middle, or high. If the element is peculiar to IBM COBOL, IBM is specified in this column.

This summary includes only elements or variations of elements covered in this book. To find complete coverage of the available COBOL elements for a specific compiler, you must refer to the applicable reference manual.

COBOL RESERVED WORDS

The following list of reserved words includes all the words required by full ANS COBOL (highest level), plus all the words required by IBM compilers.

ACCEPT	CHANGED	CYL-INDEX
ACCESS	CHARACTERS	CYL-OVERFLOW
ACTUAL	CLOCK-UNITS	C01
ADD	CLOSE	C02
ADDRESS	COBOL	C03
ADVANCING	CODE	C04
AFTER	COLUMN	C05
ALL	COM-REG	C06
ALPHABETIC	COMMA	C07
ALTER	COMP	C08
ALTERNATE	COMP-1	C09
AND	COMP-2	C10
APPLY	COMP-3	C11
ARE	COMPUTATIONAL	C12
AREA	COMPUTATIONAL-1	
AREAS	COMPUTATIONAL-2	DATA
ASCENDING	COMPUTATIONAL-3	DATE-COMPILED
ASSIGN	COMPUTE	DATE-WRITTEN
AT	CONFIGURATION	DE
AUTHOR	CONSOLE	DEBUG
	CONTAINS	DECIMAL-POINT
BASIS	CONTROL	DECLARATIVES
BEFORE	CONTROLS	DELETE
BEGINNING	COPY	DEPENDING
BLANK	CORE-INDEX	DESCENDING
BLOCK	CORR	DETAIL
BY	CORRESPONDING	DISP
	CSP	DISPLAY
CALL	CURRENCY	DISPLAY-ST
CF	CURRENT-DATE	DIVIDE
CH		

DIVISION
DOWN

EJECT
ELSE
END-OF-PAGE
ENDING
ENTER
ENTRY
ENVIRONMENT
EOP
EQUAL
ERROR
EVERY
EXAMINE
EXHIBIT
EXIT
EXTENDED-
   SEARCH

FILE
FILE-CONTROL
FILE-LIMIT
FILE-LIMITS
FILLER
FIRST
FOOTING
FOR
FROM

GENERATE
GIVING
GOBACK
GREATER
GROUP

HEADING
HIGH-VALUE
HIGH-VALUES

I-O
I-O-CONTROL

IDENTIFICATION
INDEX
INDEXED
INDICATE
INITIATE
INPUT
INPUT-OUTPUT
INSERT
INSTALLATION
INTO
INVALID

JUST
JUSTIFIED

KEY

LABEL
LABEL-RETURN
LAST
LEADING
LEAVE
LEFT
LESS
LIMIT
LIMITS
LINE
LINE-COUNTER
LINES
LINKAGE
LOCK
LOW-VALUE
LOW-VALUES

MASTER-INDEX
MEMORY
MODE
MODULES
MORE-LABELS
MOVE
MULTIPLE
MULTIPLY

NAMED
NEGATIVE
NEXT
NOMINAL
NOT
NOTE
NSTD-REELS
NUMBER
NUMERIC

OBJECT-
   COMPUTER
OCCURS
OMITTED
OPEN
OPTIONAL
OTHERWISE

PAGE
PAGE-COUNTER
PERFORM
PF
PH
PIC
PICTURE
PLUS
POSITION
POSITIONING
POSITIVE
PRINT-SWITCH
PROCEDURE
PROCEED
PROCESSING
PROGRAM
PROGRAM-ID

QUOTE
QUOTES

RANDOM

RD	SET	TIMES
READ	SIGN	TO
READY	SIZE	TOTALED
RECORD	SKIP1	TOTALING
RECORD-	SKIP2	TRACE
OVERFLOW	SKIP3	TRACK
RECORDING	SORT	TRACK-AREA
RECORDS	SORT-CORE-SIZE	TRACK-LIMIT
REDEFINES	SORT-FILE-SIZE	TRACKS
REEL	SORT-MODE-SIZE	TRANSFORM
RELEASE	SORT-RETURN	TYPE
REMAINDER	SOURCE	
REMARKS	SOURCE-	UNIT
RENAMES	COMPUTER	UNTIL
REORG-CRITERIA	SPACE	UP
REPLACING	SPACES	UPON
REPORT	SPECIAL-NAMES	UPSI-0
REPORTING	STANDARD	UPSI-1
REPORTS	START	UPSI-2
REREAD	STATUS	UPSI-3
RERUN	STOP	UPSI-4
RESERVE	SUBTRACT	UPSI-5
RESET	SUM	UPSI-6
RETURN	SUPPRESS	UPSI-7
RETURN-CODE	SYNC	USAGE
REVERSED	SYNCHRONIZED	USE
REWIND	SYSIN	USING
REWRITE	SYSIPT	
RF	SYSLST	VALUE
RH	SYSOUT	VALUES
RIGHT	SYSPCH	VARYING
ROUNDED	SYSPUNCH	
RUN	S01	WHEN
	S02	WITH
SAME		WORDS
SD	TALLY	WORKING-
SEARCH	TALLYING	STORAGE
SECTION	TAPE	WRITE
SECURITY	TERMINATE	WRITE-ONLY
SEEK	THAN	WRITE-VERIFY
SEGMENT-LIMIT	THEN	
SELECT	THROUGH	ZERO
SENTENCE	THRU	ZEROES
SEQUENTIAL	TIME-OF-DAY	ZEROS

GENERAL COBOL INFORMATION

<u>ANS
Level</u>

Character Set

Characters used for words and names:

L   A–Z

L   0–9

L   - (hyphen)

Characters used for punctuation:

L   . ()   space or blank

H   , ; (The semicolon is not discussed in this book, but it is
used like a comma.)

L   " or '

IBM   Note: On an IBM system, you have the option of using
" or ' for the quotation mark. This is determined by a control
card at the time of compilation.

Characters used in editing:

L   B + − CR Z $, .

Name Formation

Program name:

L   1. Maximum of 30 characters.
L   2. Letters, numbers, or hyphens only.
L   3. Can be all numeric.

Data name:

L   1. Maximum of 30 characters.
L   2. Letters, numbers, and hyphens only.
L   3. Must contain at least one letter.
L   4. Must start with a letter (Low ANS).
H   5. Need not start with a letter (High ANS).

Procedure name:

L   1. Maximum of 30 characters.
L   2. Letters, numbers, and hyphens only.
L   3. Can be all numeric.

File name and record name:

L   Same as for data name.

ANS Level	Figurative Constants
L	ZERO
H	ZEROS, ZEROES
L	SPACE
H	SPACES

Rules for Forming Literals

Numeric literals:

L	1. From 1 through 18 digits.
L	2. Consisting of 0–9, + or −, and the decimal point.
L	3. Only one sign character (if unsigned, assumed positive).
L	4. Only one decimal point.

Non-numeric literals:

L	1. From 1 through 120 characters.
L	2. Enclosed in quotation marks.

Use of A and B Margins

L   A margin:

Division headers	FD
Section names	01 level numbers
Procedure names	77 level numbers

L   B margin:

All other entries.

Use of Coding Form

L	1. Use of sequence numbers is optional.
L	2. Use of program identification (columns 73–80) is optional.
L	3. If sequence numbers are used, they should be in ascending sequence. If not, an error message (diagnostic) will print, but the compilation will still take place.

Use of Blank Lines

L	1. A blank line is any card that is blank in columns 7–72.
L	2. Can be used anywhere in the program other than between continuation lines.

BASIC COBOL ELEMENTS

ANS
Level

Identification Division

L	IDENTIFICATION DIVISION.
L	PROGRAM-ID. program-name.
L	[AUTHOR. sentence . . .]
L	[INSTALLATION. sentence . . .]
L	[DATE-WRITTEN. sentence . . .]
H	[DATE-COMPILED.] (Current date inserted by compiler.)

Environment Division

L	ENVIRONMENT DIVISION.
L	CONFIGURATION SECTION.
L	SOURCE-COMPUTER. computer-name.
L	OBJECT-COMPUTER. computer-name.
L	INPUT-OUTPUT SECTION.
L	FILE-CONTROL.
L	SELECT file-name ASSIGN TO system-name.

System name format for card and printer devices on the System/360 using DOS:

IBM

$$\text{SYSnnn-UR-}\begin{Bmatrix} \text{device} \\ \text{number} \end{Bmatrix}\text{-S}$$

where nnn is a number from 000 through 221.

Data Division

L	DATA DIVISION.
L	FILE SECTION.
L	FD file-name
L	LABEL RECORDS ARE OMITTED
L	DATA RECORD IS record-name.
L	01–10 $\begin{Bmatrix} \text{data-name} \\ \text{FILLER} \end{Bmatrix}$

ANS
Level

H   01–49 $\begin{Bmatrix} \text{data-name} \\ \text{FILLER} \end{Bmatrix}$

L $\begin{Bmatrix} \underline{\text{PICTURE}} \\ \underline{\text{PIC}} \end{Bmatrix}$ IS character-string

L   USAGE IS <u>DISPLAY</u>.

L   <u>WORKING-STORAGE</u> <u>SECTION</u>.

L   77   data-name

L   01–10 $\begin{Bmatrix} \text{data-name} \\ \text{FILLER} \end{Bmatrix}$

H   01–49 $\begin{Bmatrix} \text{data-name} \\ \text{FILLER} \end{Bmatrix}$

L $\begin{Bmatrix} \underline{\text{PICTURE}} \\ \underline{\text{PIC}} \end{Bmatrix}$ IS character-string

L   USAGE IS $\begin{Bmatrix} \underline{\text{DISPLAY}} \\ \underline{\text{COMPUTATIONAL}} \\ \underline{\text{COMP}} \end{Bmatrix}$

L   <u>VALUE</u> IS literal.

Procedure Division

L   <u>PROCEDURE</u> <u>DIVISION</u>.

ACCEPT Statement:

L   <u>ACCEPT</u> data-name.

ADD Statement:

Format 1:

L   <u>ADD</u> $\begin{Bmatrix} \text{data-name-1} \\ \text{literal-1} \end{Bmatrix}$ $\begin{bmatrix} \text{data-name-2} \\ \text{literal-2} \end{bmatrix}$ . . . TO data-name-n

          [<u>ROUNDED</u>] [ON <u>SIZE</u> <u>ERROR</u> any-statement . . .].

ANS
Level   Format 2:

L   <u>ADD</u> $\begin{Bmatrix} \text{date-name-1} \\ \text{literal-1} \end{Bmatrix}$ $\begin{bmatrix} \text{date-name-2} \\ \text{literal-2} \end{bmatrix}$ . . .

           <u>GIVING</u> data-name-n

           [<u>ROUNDED</u>]   [ON <u>SIZE</u> <u>ERROR</u> any-statement . . .].

           Format 3:

H   <u>ADD</u> $\begin{Bmatrix} \text{data-name-1} \\ \text{literal-1} \end{Bmatrix}$ $\begin{bmatrix} \text{data-name-2} \\ \text{literal-2} \end{bmatrix}$ . . .

           <u>TO</u> data-name-m [<u>ROUNDED</u>] $\begin{bmatrix} \text{data-name-n} \ [\underline{\text{ROUNDED}}] \end{bmatrix}$ . . .

           [ON <u>SIZE</u> <u>ERROR</u> any-statement . . .].

CLOSE Statement:

Format 1:

L   <u>CLOSE</u> file-name.

Format 2:

H   <u>CLOSE</u> file-name-1 [file-name-2]   . . .

DISPLAY Statement:

L   <u>DISPLAY</u> $\begin{Bmatrix} \text{data-name-1} \\ \text{literal-1} \end{Bmatrix}$ $\begin{bmatrix} \text{data-name-2} \\ \text{literal-2} \end{bmatrix}$ . . .

DIVIDE Statement:

Format 1:

L   <u>DIVIDE</u> $\begin{Bmatrix} \text{data-name-1} \\ \text{literal} \end{Bmatrix}$ <u>INTO</u> data-name-2

           [<u>ROUNDED</u>]   [ON <u>SIZE</u> <u>ERROR</u> any-statement . . .].

Format 2:

L   <u>DIVIDE</u> $\begin{Bmatrix} \text{data-name-1} \\ \text{literal-1} \end{Bmatrix}$ $\begin{Bmatrix} \underline{\text{INTO}} \\ \underline{\text{BY}} \end{Bmatrix}$ $\begin{Bmatrix} \text{data-name-2} \\ \text{literal-2} \end{Bmatrix}$

           <u>GIVING</u> data-name-3   [<u>ROUNDED</u>]

           [ON <u>SIZE</u> <u>ERROR</u> any-statement . . .].

ANS
Level

Format 3:

H

DIVIDE $\left\{\begin{array}{l}\text{data-name-1}\\ \text{literal-1}\end{array}\right\}$ <u>INTO</u> $\left\{\begin{array}{l}\text{data-name-2}\\ \text{literal-2}\end{array}\right\}$

<u>GIVING</u> data-name-3 [<u>ROUNDED</u>]

<u>REMAINDER</u> data-name-4

[ON <u>SIZE</u> <u>ERROR</u> any-statement . . .].

EXIT Statement:

L

procedure-name. <u>EXIT</u>.

GO TO Statement:

L

<u>GO</u> <u>TO</u> procedure-name.

IF Statement:

L

IF $\left\{\begin{array}{l}\text{data-name-1}\\ \text{literal-1}\end{array}\right\}$ $\left\{\begin{array}{l}\text{IS }\underline{\text{GREATER}}\text{ THAN}\\ \text{IS }\underline{\text{LESS}}\text{ THAN}\\ \text{IS }\underline{\text{EQUAL}}\ \underline{\text{TO}}\end{array}\right\}$ $\left\{\begin{array}{l}\text{data-name-2}\\ \text{literal-2}\end{array}\right\}$ statement . . .

MOVE Statement:

L

<u>MOVE</u> $\left\{\begin{array}{l}\text{data-name-1}\\ \text{literal}\end{array}\right\}$ <u>TO</u> data-name-2 [data-name-3] . . .

MULTIPLY Statement:

Format 1:

L

<u>MULTIPLY</u> $\left\{\begin{array}{l}\text{data-name-1}\\ \text{literal-1}\end{array}\right\}$ <u>BY</u> data-name-2

[<u>ROUNDED</u>] [ON <u>SIZE</u> <u>ERROR</u> any-statement . . .].

Format 2:

L

<u>MULTIPLY</u> $\left\{\begin{array}{l}\text{data-name-1}\\ \text{literal-1}\end{array}\right\}$ <u>BY</u> $\left\{\begin{array}{l}\text{data-name-2}\\ \text{literal-2}\end{array}\right\}$

<u>GIVING</u> data-name-3 [<u>ROUNDED</u>]

[ON <u>SIZE</u> <u>ERROR</u> any-statement . . .].

ANS
Level   OPEN Statement:

Format 1:

L

$$\text{\underline{OPEN}} \quad \begin{Bmatrix} \underline{\text{INPUT}} \\ \underline{\text{OUTPUT}} \end{Bmatrix} \quad \text{file-name.}$$

Format 2:

H   OPEN INPUT file-name-1 [file-name-2] ...

               OUTPUT file-name-m [file-name-n] ...

PERFORM Statement:

L   PERFORM procedure-name-1 [THRU procedure-name-2].

READ Statement:

L   READ file-name RECORD AT END any-statement ...

STOP Statement:

L   STOP RUN.

SUBTRACT Statement:

Format 1:

L

$$\text{\underline{SUBTRACT}} \quad \begin{Bmatrix} \text{data-name-1} \\ \text{literal-1} \end{Bmatrix} \quad \begin{bmatrix} \text{data-name-2} \\ \text{literal-2} \end{bmatrix} \quad ...$$

              FROM data-name-n [ROUNDED]

              [ON SIZE ERROR any-statement ...].

Format 2:

L

$$\text{\underline{SUBTRACT}} \quad \begin{Bmatrix} \text{data-name-1} \\ \text{literal-1} \end{Bmatrix} \quad \begin{bmatrix} \text{data-name-2} \\ \text{literal-2} \end{bmatrix} \quad ...$$

              FROM data-name-m GIVING data-name-n

              [ROUNDED] [ON SIZE ERROR any-statement ...].

ANS
Level

Format 3:

H

$$\underline{SUBTRACT} \quad \begin{Bmatrix} \text{data-name-1} \\ \text{literal-1} \end{Bmatrix} \quad \begin{bmatrix} \text{data-name-2} \\ \text{literal-2} \end{bmatrix} \quad \dots$$

$$\underline{FROM} \text{ data-name-m } [\underline{ROUNDED}]$$
$$\left[\text{data-name-n } [\underline{ROUNDED}] \right] \dots$$
$$[\text{ON } \underline{SIZE} \text{ } \underline{ERROR} \text{ any-statement } \dots].$$

WRITE Statement:

Format 1:

L

$$\underline{WRITE} \text{ record-name } \left[\begin{Bmatrix} \underline{BEFORE} \\ \underline{AFTER} \end{Bmatrix} \text{ ADVANCING integer LINES} \right].$$

Format 2:

H

$$\underline{WRITE} \text{ record-name } \left[\begin{Bmatrix} \underline{BEFORE} \\ \underline{AFTER} \end{Bmatrix} \text{ ADVANCING} \right.$$

$$\left. \begin{Bmatrix} \text{integer} \\ \text{data-name} \end{Bmatrix} \text{ LINES} \right].$$

TABLE-HANDLING ELEMENTS

General

L   One-level subscripting

H   Two- and three-level subscripting

Data Division

REDEFINES Clause:

L   data-name-1 $\underline{REDEFINES}$ data-name-2

OCCURS Clause:

L $\underline{OCCURS}$ integer TIMES

ANS Level	Procedure Division

PERFORM Statement:

H PERFORM procedure-name-1 [THRU procedure-name-2]

VARYING data-name-1 FROM $\begin{Bmatrix} \text{literal-1} \\ \text{data-name-2} \end{Bmatrix}$

BY $\begin{Bmatrix} \text{literal-2} \\ \text{data-name-3} \end{Bmatrix}$ UNTIL condition-1

$\Bigg[$ AFTER data-name-4 FROM $\begin{Bmatrix} \text{literal-3} \\ \text{data-name-5} \end{Bmatrix}$

BY $\begin{Bmatrix} \text{literal-4} \\ \text{data-name-6} \end{Bmatrix}$ UNTIL condition-2

$\Bigg[$ AFTER data-name-7 FROM $\begin{Bmatrix} \text{literal-5} \\ \text{data-name-8} \end{Bmatrix}$

BY $\begin{Bmatrix} \text{literal-6} \\ \text{data-name-9} \end{Bmatrix}$ UNTIL condition-3 $\Bigg]\Bigg]$.

SEQUENTIAL-ACCESS ELEMENTS — TAPE

Environment Division

L INPUT-OUTPUT SECTION.

L FILE-CONTROL.

L SELECT file-name ASSIGN TO system-name.

System/360 DOS system name format:

IBM   SYSnnn-UT-2400-S

Data Division

L FD file-name

L [BLOCK CONTAINS integer RECORDS]

L LABEL RECORDS ARE STANDARD

L [VALUE OF data-name-1 IS literal-1

    [data-name-2 IS literal-2] ...]

L DATA RECORD IS record-name.

ANS Level	Procedure Division

Open Statement:

Format 1:

L   OPEN $\left\{ \begin{matrix} \underline{INPUT} \\ \underline{OUTPUT} \end{matrix} \right\}$ file-name.

Format 2:

H   OPEN $\left[\underline{INPUT}\ \text{file-name-1}\ \ [\text{file-name-2}]\ \ldots \right]$
$\left[\underline{OUTPUT}\ \text{file-name-m}\ \ [\text{file-name-n}]\ \ldots \right]$.

READ Statement:

L   READ file-name RECORD AT END any-statement . . .

WRITE Statement:

L   WRITE record-name.

CLOSE Statement:

Format 1:

L   CLOSE file-name.

Format 2:

H   CLOSE file-name . . .

SEQUENTIAL-ACCESS ELEMENTS—DISK

Environment Division

L   INPUT-OUTPUT SECTION.

L   FILE-CONTROL.

L   SELECT file-name ASSIGN TO system-name

L   [ACCESS MODE IS SEQUENTIAL]

L   [PROCESSING MODE IS SEQUENTIAL].

ANS
Level

IBM

System name format for System/360 DOS:

$$\text{SYSnnn-DA-}\begin{Bmatrix}\text{device}\\\text{number}\end{Bmatrix}\text{-S}$$

where nnn is a number from 000–221, and the device
number is 2311, 2314, or 2321.

Data Division

L   FILE SECTION.

L   FD   file-name

L   [BLOCK CONTAINS integer RECORDS]

L   LABEL RECORDS ARE STANDARD

L   [VALUE OF data-name-1 IS literal-1

[data-name-2 IS literal-2] . . .]

L   DATA RECORD IS record-name.

Procedure Division

OPEN Statement:

Format 1:

L   OPEN $\begin{Bmatrix}\text{INPUT}\\\text{OUTPUT}\\\text{I-O}\end{Bmatrix}$ file-name.

Format 2:

H   OPEN [INPUT file-name-1 [file-name-2] . . .]

[OUTPUT file-name-m [file-name-n] . . .]

[I-O file-name-x [file-name-y] . . .].

READ Statement:

L   READ file-name RECORD AT END any-statement . . .

ANS
Level

WRITE Statement:

L   WRITE record-name INVALID KEY any-statement . . .

CLOSE Statement:

Format 1:

L   CLOSE file-name.

Format 2:

H   CLOSE file-name . . .

The American National Standards Institute (ANSI) provides two sets of FORTRAN specifications. One is referred to as Basic FORTRAN; the other as FORTRAN, or full FORTRAN. Because Basic FORTRAN is a subset of full FORTRAN, a Basic FORTRAN program can be compiled by a full FORTRAN compiler. The reverse, however, is not true.

The summary that follows is divided into these sections:

General FORTRAN Information
FORTRAN Statements

To the left of each FORTRAN specification is a column that indicates whether the specification applies to a Basic or a full FORTRAN compiler: B indicates Basic, while F indicates full. This summary includes only those elements or variations of elements covered in this book

GENERAL FORTRAN INFORMATION

ANS Level	
	Character set:
B	A–Z
B	0–9
B	Blank = + − * / ( ) , .
F	$
B	Arithmetic operators:
	+ − * / **
F	Relational operators:

    .LT. Less than
    .LE. Less than or equal to
    .EQ. Equal to
    .NE. Not equal to
    .GT. Greater than
    .GE. Greater than or equal to

Rules for forming variable names:

B	1. Five or less letters or numbers, starting with a letter.
F	2. Six or less letters or numbers, starting with a letter.
B	3. Names starting with the letters I–N are integer variables; names beginning with other letters are real variables.

ANS
Level

F Double precision variables:

Specifying a variable as double precision by using the DOUBLE PRECISION statement doubles the number of significant digits in a real variable, but does not change the range of the variable. Only real variables can be double precision.

B Rules for forming integer constants:

1. Can have a leading + or − sign; if omitted, constant is assumed to be positive.
2. Other than a lead sign, it must consist entirely of decimal digits.

B Rules for forming real constants:

1. Can have a leading + or − sign; if omitted, constant is assumed to be positive.
2. Must have one and only one decimal point within a decimal number.

Rules for statement numbers:

B From 1 to 4 decimal digits located anywhere in columns 1–5 of the coding form. Leading zeros are not significant.

F From 1 to 5 decimal digits located anywhere in columns 1–5 of the coding form. Leading zeros are not significant.

Subscripting and arrays:

B One- or two-dimensional arrays only.
F One-, two-, or three-dimensional arrays.
B All subscripts must be integers or integer expressions.

B Allowable subscript expressions:

Constant * Variable ± Constant
Constant * Variable
Variable ± Constant

ANS
Level

B   Order of source deck:

        DOUBLE PRECISION and DIMENSION Statements
        FORMAT Statements
        Executable Statements
        END Statement

        (Note: FORMAT statements may also be placed anywhere within the executable statements.)

B   Use of coding form:

        1. Use of program identification (columns 73–80) is optional.
        2. Blanks are ignored by the compiler.

B   Comment lines:

        1. The letter C is required in column 1.
        2. Any other characters can be punched in columns 2–80 since they are ignored by the compiler.

      Continuation lines:

B   1. If a FORTRAN statement requires more than one coding line, column 7 of the continuation line must receive a character other than zero or blank.
B   2. Up to five continuation lines are allowed.
F   3. Up to nineteen continuation lines are allowed.

FORTRAN STATEMENTS

I/O and FORMAT Statements

      READ statement:

B   READ (device-number, format-statement-number) list

      WRITE statement:

B   WRITE (device-number, format-statement-number) list

ANS
Level

FORMAT statement:

B   FORMAT $(qf_1,f_2,f_3, \ldots .f_n qf_{n+1},f_{n+2}, \ldots .)$

q = slashes or empty
f = field descriptor

Field descriptors:

ANS Level		
B	rFw.d	(Real variable, no exponent)
B	rIw	(Integer variable)
B	nHcharacter-string	(Alphanumeric constant data)
B	nX	(Skipped data or blanks)
F	rAw	(Alphanumeric variable)

r = repeat count
n = number of characters in string
w = field width
d = number of decimal positions

Carriage-control characters:

ANS Level		
B	blank	One line spaced before printing
F	0	Two lines spaced before printing
F	1	Skip to first line of next page before printing
F	+	No advance

DO-implied lists in READ and WRITE statements:

B   1. One-dimensional:

(variable-list,index-definition)

where index-definition is in the form

$$i=m_1,m_2,m_3$$

B   2. Two-dimensional:

((variable-list,index-definition-1),index-definition-2)

F   3. Three-dimensional:

(((variable-list,index-definition-1),index-definition-2)
index-definition-3)

ANS
Level

B   REWIND statement:

    REWIND device-number

B   ENDFILE statement:

    ENDFILE device-number

Arithmetic Statements

B   Arithmetic assignment statement:

    variable-name = arithmetic-expression

Control Statements

B   Unconditional GO TO statement:

    GO TO statement-number

B   Arithmetic IF statement:

    IF (arithmetic-expression) statement-no.-1,statement-no.-2, statement-no.-3

F   Logical IF statement:

    IF (logical-expression) statement

B   DO statement:

    DO statement-number $i = m_1, m_2, m_3$

    where i = integer variable

          m_1 = starting parameter

          m_2 = ending parameter

          m_3 = incrementation parameter

B   STOP statement:

    STOP

ANS Level	Nonexecutable Statements

B   CONTINUE statement:

   CONTINUE

B   DIMENSION statement:

   DIMENSION array-name(array-declarator). . .

F   DOUBLE PRECISION statement:

   DOUBLE PRECISION variable-list

B   END statement:

   END

As you read through these procedures, use figures E-1 and E-2 to locate parts of the 029 keypunch.

MANUAL OPERATION OF THE 029 KEYPUNCH

Setup

1. Turn on the power switch located beneath the desklike surface of the keypunch.
2. Place blank cards in the input hopper.
3. Depress the FEED key twice to move a card to the punching station.
4. Push the program-control lever to the right so that program control is off.
5. Set the switches located above the keyboard so that AUTO FEED and PRINT are on and AUTO SKIP DUP and LZ PRINT are off. (The positions of the other switches don't matter.)

Operating Procedures

1. Key the data. The keyboard is normally in alphabetic shift. If numbers or other upper-shift characters are to be punched, the NUMERIC key

**APPENDIX E
PROCEDURES
FOR
KEYPUNCHING
SOURCE
DECKS**

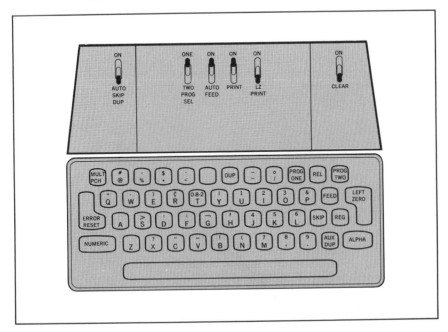

FIGURE E-1 The keyboard of the 029 keypunch

must be used. The column indicator shows the next column to be punched. When all columns that are to be punched have been keyed, push the REL (release) key.

2. The backspace key can be used to move a card back one column at a time.

3. To duplicate data from one card to the next, press the DUP key for those columns.

4. When you are finished keypunching, flip the CLEAR switch to the ON position to clear the reading and punching stations of cards.

PROGRAM-CONTROL OPERATION OF THE 029 KEYPUNCH

Simple Program Card for COBOL Source Deck

This card assumes that sequence numbers (columns 1–6) and identification codes (columns 73–80) are not used.

Columns	Punches	Meaning
1–7	-&&&&&&	Columns 1–7 are skipped.
8–11	1AAA	Columns 8–11 are in alphabetic shift.
12–80	1 followed by 68 As	Columns 12–80 are in alphabetic shift.

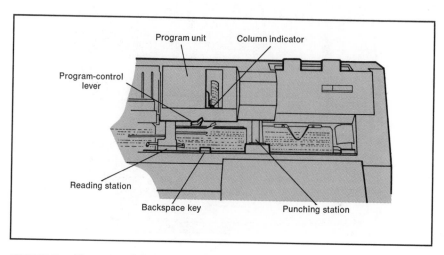

FIGURE E-2 Features of the 029 keypunch

Simple Program Card for FORTRAN Source Deck

This card assumes columns 73–80 of the source cards are not used for identification or sequence codes.

Columns	Punches	Meaning
1–6	b&&&&& (b=blank)	Columns 1–6 are in numeric shift.
7–80	1 followed by 73 As	Columns 7–80 are in alphabetic shift.

Setup

1. Raise the starwheels in the program unit by pushing the program-control lever to the right.
2. Pull the cover of the program unit forward.
3. Lift the program drum from its spindle.
4. Remove the old program card (if any) and mount the new program card on the program drum, as demonstrated in class.
5. Put the drum back on its spindle in the program unit, making sure that the alignment pin on the bottom of the drum is in the alignment hole in the program unit.
6. Close the cover of the program unit and lower the starwheels by pushing the program-control level to the left. Then, press the REL key. This causes the program drum to rotate once, thus engaging the starwheels in the holes of the program card.
7. Place blank cards in the input hopper.
8. Depress the FEED key twice to move a card to the punching station.
9. Set the switches located above the keyboard so that AUTO FEED, PRINT, and AUTO SKIP DUP are on and LZ PRINT is off.

Operating Procedures

1. Skipping and shifting of the keyboard are now under program control as dictated by the program card. To punch alphabetic data in a numeric field, use the ALPHA key. To punch numeric data in an alphabetic field, use the NUMERIC key. To skip to the end of a field, press the REL (release) key.
2. If you make an error, it can be corrected in this way. First, push the REL key, thus releasing the error card to the reading station. Second, turn off the AUTO SKIP DUP switch. Third, press the DUP key until

the keypunch reaches the column that contains the error. This duplicates all data that was punched correctly before the error was made. Now, corrrct the error, turn AUTO SKIP DUP back on, and continue punching as usual. Be sure, however, that you remove the error card from the source deck.

VARIATIONS WHEN USING THE 026 KEYPUNCH

1. The 026 requires a warmup period of about half a minute after the mainline switch is turned on. As a result, it is customary to press the REL key after turning the machine on. When the warmup period is over, the program drum rotates once (since the REL key was depressed), thus indicating that the machine is ready for operation.

2. There is no CLEAR switch on the 026 keypunch. To move cards to the output stacker, the AUTO FEED switch must be turned off. Then the release and register (REG) keys are pressed alternately—REL, REG, REL, REG, REL, REG—until all cards are moved to the stacker.

3. The 026 keyboard, illustrated in figure E-3, does not have all of the special characters that the 029 has. For example, it does not have the semicolon (;), the single quotation mark ('), and the equals sign (=). To punch these characters on the 026 keypunch, the MULT PCH key must be used. When it is depressed, the keyboard is in numeric shift, and the card does not advance until the MULT PCH key is released. To punch a quotation mark, which consists of a 5- and an 8-punch, the MULT PCH key is pressed and the 5 and 8 keys are struck. When the MULT PCH key is released, the card moves to the next card col-

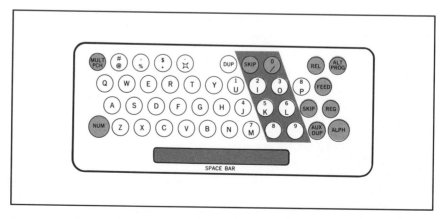

FIGURE E-3 The keyboard of the 026 keypunch

umn. The following are the special characters for which MULT PCH must be used:

Character	Card Code
<	12,4,8
(	12,5,8
+	12,6,8
)	11,5,8
;	11,6,8
—	0,5,8
>	0,6,8
?	0,7,8
'	5,8
=	6,8

SPECIAL PROCEDURES

Resetting a Locked Keyboard

In some cases, the keyboard will lock because of an error; for example, keying a non-numeric character such as the letter A in a numeric field. On the 026 keypunch, the keyboard can be unlocked by pressing either the REL or the backspace key; on the 029 keypunch, the ERROR RESET key must be pressed.

Duplicating a Damaged Card

1. Turn off AUTO FEED and AUTO SKIP DUP, and clear the machine of cards. (Cards can be left in the stacker, however.)
2. Smooth the card and insert it through the plastic guides at the reading station. Slide the card forward as far as it will go, and then pull it back about one-quarter inch.
3. Place a blank card through the guides at the punching station. Again, slide the card forward until it stops, and then pull it back about one-quarter inch.
4. Press the REG key to register the cards at the reading and punching stations.
5. Press the DUP key until all of the data in the damaged card is punched into the new card. Then, press the REL key to release both cards.
6. Clear the cards from the machine.

Correcting a Few Columns of an Error Card

1. Follow steps 1–4 above for duplicating a damaged card.
2. Push the DUP key for all correct card columns; rekey the error columns.

Adding Data to a Card

1. Insert the card through the guides at the punching station. Slide the card forward as far as it will go; then pull it back about one-quarter inch.
2. Press the REG key to register the card at the punching station.
3. Using the space bar, space over the punched columns to the columns that need to be punched.
4. Key the additional data in the indicated columns.

The text of this book was set in 10 point Melior by Applied Typographic Systems of Mountain View, California. Display type is Melior Semibold Outline, also by ATS.

House of Graphics of Palo Alto, California prepared the illustrations. The art for the chapter openers is by Ralph Mapson, San Francisco.

The book was printed on 50# Warren Opaque paper at the Kingsport Press, Kingsport, Tennessee.

Sponsoring Editor
Stephen Mitchell

Project Editor
Betty Drury

Cover and Book Design
Naomi Takigawa